A SHORT HISTORY
OF THE
JEWISH PEOPLE

MOSES ON SINAI
Miniature from the Sarajevo Haggadah

A SHORT HISTORY
OF THE JEWISH PEOPLE

BY

CECIL ROTH

REVISED AND ENLARGED
ILLUSTRATED EDITION

HARTMORE HOUSE · HARTFORD

EAST AND WEST LIBRARY · LONDON

THE FIRST EDITION WAS PUBLISHED BY MACMILLAN & CO. LTD. IN 1936
THE SECOND EDITION BY THE EAST AND WEST LIBRARY IN 1943
THIS ILLUSTRATED EDITION WAS FIRST PUBLISHED IN 1948
REVISED AND ENLARGED IN 1953 AND IN 1959
NEWLY REVISED AND ENLARGED IN 1969

LIBRARY OF CONGRESS CATALOG CARD NUMBER 70 107212
SBN 87677 004 9 *1-17-73*

THE EAST AND WEST LIBRARY
PUBLISHED BY
THE HOROVITZ PUBLISHING CO. LTD.
5 CROMWELL PLACE · LONDON SW 7
PRINTED IN GREAT BRITAIN
BY ROBERT MACLEHOSE AND CO. LTD THE UNIVERSITY PRESS GLASGOW W.3

IN MEMORY
OF MY FATHER
JOSEPH ROTH
1866-1924

PREFACE TO THE SIXTH
(FOURTH ILLUSTRATED) EDITION

Thank God that I have been privileged to witness and to record the crowning mercies inadequately described in the new pages now appended to this work.

NEW YORK/JERUSALEM
June 1967

CECIL ROTH

PREFACE TO THE FIFTH
(THIRD ILLUSTRATED) EDITION

The publication of a new edition of a book is inevitably a cause of gratification to the author, but in the present case there is a special reason. The first edition of this work (1936) appeared when the Nazi persecution had already begun its deadly work and the noble fruits of Jewish Emancipation were being destroyed in Germany. The second (1943) was distributed to the fighting forces when the reaction had already engulfed, in a manner too ghastly for belief, almost all of the continent of Europe, and the note of optimism at the end of the new material was justified only by faith. The third (1948) had to chronicle in its additional pages the virtual annihilation of European Jewry. But the fourth (1953) was privileged to tell the amazing story of national resurrection and the establishment of the State of Israel, whose first ten years of heroic achievement are briefly summarised in the final section that has now been added (1958).

The author is fortunate whose subject can rise thus above disaster and demonstrate the eternal validity—valuable to mankind at large in such troubled hours as these—of the fundamental Jewish principle of optimism.

OXFORD, 1958

CECIL ROTH

PREFACE TO THE ILLUSTRATED EDITION

This work was originally published only ten years ago, but in a world entirely different from the world of today. At that time, it was possible to regard the rise of the Nazis to power in Germany merely as an exceptionally unpleasant episode. It was impossible to foretell that the result was to be the utter overwhelming, and almost extermination, of European Jewry. For this new edition, a further section has been written epitomising the unhappy history of the past few years. (This embodies the summary of events 1935-1939 which was appended to the second edition.) The whole text has been revised and corrected in the light of ten years' reading and research. There are some stylistic changes, a few additions, an entirely new Bibliography. But even the revision has been a bitter task. The work was written in the first instance in an optimistic spirit, reflected in an Epilogue (now omitted) which at present seems grotesquely antiquated. For the author was brought up to believe that persecution belonged to the past; that Jewish emancipation in the Occident was final; that notwithstanding local relapses the world had progressed out of barbarism; that a monument preserved from antiquity might be considered, barring accident, safe for all time; that massacres were out of the question in modern society; that the great mass of European Jewry was settled in Europe for good, unless it were slowly dissolved by emigration or assimilation.

Inevitably, this meliorist outlook was discernible throughout the text, and not only in the last chapters. It was bitter for the Author to find that he had referred to medieval massacres of the Jews as unexampled in history, when in recent years they have been exceeded a hundred- or even a thousand-fold. Centuries-old tranquillity in country after country has proved to be the prelude to unmitigated disaster in our own day. The martyrdom of the Jews in the Ghetto period was paradise as compared with the indescribable horrors of the decade of Nazi domination.

To enter into the details of the tragedy of the past ten years, on the scale devoted to analogous episodes of the past, would have demanded a volume many times greater than the whole of this work. The happenings in German-occupied territory from 1939 to 1945 are not an episode, but the most important event in all Jewish history during the past nineteen centuries at least. When I wrote of European Jewry ten years ago, I was dealing with a healthy living organism; today it is a charnel-house. Jewish history must be regarded henceforth, unhappily, in a completely different light. Perhaps nevertheless this volume benefits from its deficiencies; for the full history of the Jews in our time is too agonising to tell.

OXFORD, 1947   CECIL ROTH

PREFACE TO THE FIRST EDITION

The present *Short History of the Jewish People* differs fundamentally from most works of the sort which have preceded it. The story presented is something more than a record of persecution, suffering, and scholarship; and massacre does not alternate with literature, as has hitherto been almost always the case, on the forefront of the stage. It is rather a social history. I have tried to shew the ordinary Jew as he was—how he was embarked on his distinctive career, what he achieved, what his occupations were and why he adopted them, why his present distribution and activities were brought about, and how those characteristics generally associated with him became evolved. Literature and spiritual life have not, of course, been neglected—such an omission is even less pardonable in Jewish than in other spheres of history. But an attempt has been made to shew them, as well as the tragic record of persecution, in their proper perspective—not as the substance of national existence, but as aspects of it.

In general, it will be seen that I have put a somewhat fresh emphasis on the story. Nothing in literature is quite so conservative as Jewish historiography, which, to the present day, continues to follow with the utmost fidelity the lines laid down by its magnificent, but not always impeccable, pioneers of a century ago. I have endeavoured to break with this tradition. Numerous points and aspects and characters, over-stressed in the traditional tale of woe, have been relegated to the background. Others, which seem to me to have played more important a part in Jewish life, have been brought forward. But I have tried to prevent the wood from being obscured by the undergrowth, and to convey above all the glorious sweep and continuity which make Jewish history the most fascinating, and not the least important, of historical studies.

My heartfelt gratitude is due to my brother, Professor Leon Roth, of the Hebrew University, Jerusalem, and to my friend, Mr J. L. Cohen, of London, for the many valuable suggestions which they made while this work was in preparation: to Mr Leon Simon, C.B., without whose helpful criticism the concluding chapter would have been lamentably inadequate: and to my uncle, Mr J. M. Jacobs, who read and criticised the proofs with an assiduity worthy of a better cause.

It is my duty to add that I have plagiarised repeatedly and without acknowledgement in the course of the following pages from my own publications on kindred subjects: for I have never been able to comprehend why, when one has said a thing once as well and as forcibly as one is capable of doing, there should be any moral obligation to vary the phraseology on future occasions.

LONDON, *December* 1935   C. R.

CONTENTS

* The conventional B.C. and A.D. are used throughout this work,
notwithstanding their primary semi-theological implication.

BOOK IV. TWILIGHT: 1492-1815

BOOK V. THE NEW AGE: 1815-1918

LIST OF ILLUSTRATIONS

ACKNOWLEDGEMENTS

Most of the illustrations in the present volume are taken from material in the possession of the author or the publisher. Further material has been generously provided by the following : Sir Leonard Woolley (pl. 14, reprinted from his book *Ur of the Chaldees* by courtesy of the publishers, Messrs. Faber & Faber); Mrs. R. Wischnitzer-Bernstein, New York (pl. 106); Mr. L. Edwards, London (pl. 137); Mr. A. Rubens, London (pl. 117); Mr. J. Crowfoot (pl. 20, 21, 50); Fratelli Alinari, Florence (pl. 42-43); D. Anderson Ltd., Rome (pl. 59, 102); Mr. A. Reifenberg and the Department of Antiquities, Hebrew University, Jerusalem (pl. 12, 20, 21); the Yale University Art Gallery, New Haven, Connecticut (pl. 52-54); the British Museum (pl. 10, 16, 19, 25, 27, 28); the Matson Photo Service, Jerusalem (pl. 30); the Print Room of the Basle Museum (pl. 142); the Friends of the Hebrew University of Jerusalem (pl. 154); the Touro Synagogue, Newport, R.I. (pl. 132); the London Museum (pl. 130); the Jewish Museum, London (pl. 4); the Israeli Embassy, London (pl. 162, 169); the Bibliothèque Nationale, Paris (pl. 97); the Jewish Theological Seminary, New York (pl. 96, 101); the Museo Correr, Venice (pl. 98); the Wiener Library, London (pl. 156-160); the Jewish Chronicle Library, London (pl. 161; photo K. Meyerowitz, Jerusalem, pl. 164; photo W. Braun, Jerusalem, pl. 165); United Press International (U.K.) Ltd., London (pl. 166, 168); and Camera Press Ltd., London (pl. 167). The three maps on pp. 2, 76 and 136 are reproduced by courtesy of the Commission for Jewish Education, New York.

2. PRINTER'S MARK OF ELIAKIM HALICZ
CRACOW 1534

3. Scenes from Biblical History

First page of an illuminated Pentateuch. Franco-German School, about 1300.
Jerusalem, Schocken Library

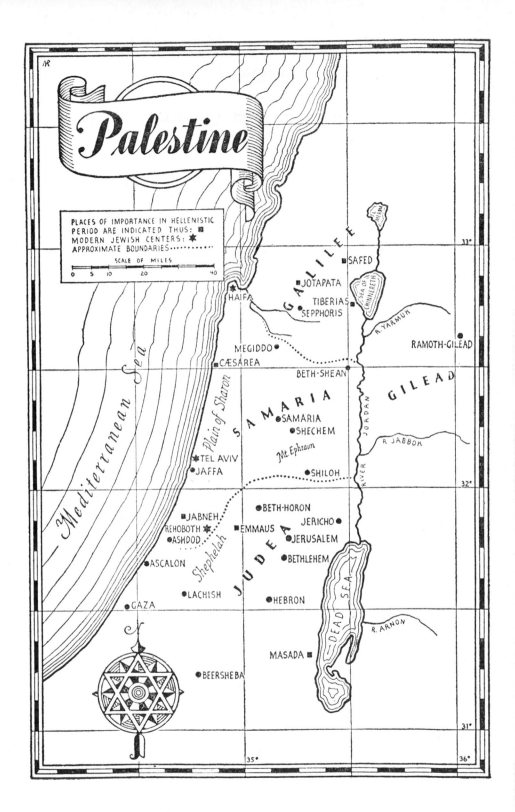

Chapter I

THE BIRTH OF THE HEBREW PEOPLE

———————— • ————————

I

Between the sands of the Arabian Peninsula and the Mediterranean shore lies a narrow strip of fertile soil. It is a land of hills and valleys, of luxuriant vegetation and austere wastes, of exuberant plains and vistas which stir the depths of human imagination. To the north, it borders upon Syria; to the south, on the Egyptian desert. The river Jordan (rising beneath the snow-capped peak of Mount Hermon and, after flowing through the Lake of Tiberias, losing itself in the bitter waters of the Dead Sea, far below the level of the Mediterranean) divides the intervening area into two portions. Towards the desert are the rolling pastures of what was formerly called Gilead and Bashan. But the essential Palestine (as we now call this country) lies between the river and the sea, from which no part is far distant.

Even this tract is by no means homogeneous. A low-lying fringe runs along the coast from the Egyptian desert as far as the promontory of Mount Carmel, with the magnificent roadstead of Haifa—strangely neglected by antiquity—nestling in its shelter. The foot-hills bordering on this, known in the south as the *Shephelah* or lowland, are covered at harvest-time by fields of waving corn. Beyond there, the southern uplands of limestone, sparsely covered with pasture in the spring and finally merging in the desert, contrast strikingly with the fertile central plateau northwards. This in turn is cut off from the tree-clad hills of Galilee by the luxuriant valley of Jezreel or Esdraelon. Through this and the coastal plain into which it leads, merchants have travelled and armies have marched, on their way between Egypt and Africa on the one hand, and Syria, further Asia, and Europe on the other, ever since the dawn of history. Ideas, too, travelled between the Nile delta and the valley of the Euphrates in the path of the caravans. From the point of view of civilisation as of strategy, the position is all-important.

(3)

At the period when the mist hitherto enveloping human affairs begins to rise, and historical record at last becomes continuous (after the beginning of the second millennium before the Christian era, that is), this land harboured a medley of races. There still appears to have been some remnant of the primitive, cave-dwelling, neolithic stock, whose gigantic stature subsequently became proverbial.[1] These had been dispossessed by the Semitic stock known as the Amorites, who had migrated not long since from the barren wastes of Arabia and, abandoning their nomadic life, had settled on the soil. In the area to the north—especially along the Phoenician coast beyond Mount Carmel—were trading Canaanites, who gave their name to the country ('the Land of Canaan', it was generally called). The mysterious Hittite had made his appearance, not only as conqueror, but also as colonist. The all-powerful Egyptian Empire was making sporadic attempts to spread its influence northward, and its garrisons and fortified posts were dotted throughout the country. Assyrian rulers marched and countermarched, in campaigns against Egypt or efforts to subdue the local chieftains. And, in their wake, there came numbers of immigrants from the crowded plains of Mesopotamia, desirous to establish themselves in this enviable land. *Ibrim*, or Hebrews, they were called—either from their legendary descent from one Eber, or else from the fact that they came from 'beyond' the Great River, the Euphrates.

One of these Aramaean immigrants stands out from the rest: a certain Abram, or Abraham, a native of Ur of the Chaldees. His home-city, as recent excavations have shewn, was already at that time the seat of an ancient and highly polished culture. Its religious life, on the other hand, was polytheistic, revolving about stately temples in which a gross ceremonial was carried on by a hierarchy of priests. It was with the glimmering of something higher, and in the hope of attaining a more complete spiritual fulfilment, that Abraham is said to have left his country. In this sense he is rightly considered the founder of the Jewish people, and it is significant that converts to Judaism even to-day are termed 'children of Abraham our Father'.[2]

We have the picture of a stately sheik-like figure moving through

---

[1] These were not by any means the earliest inhabitants of Palestine. The 'Galilee Skull,' found not long since in a cave near Tiberias, is one of the earliest extant relics of primitive man. It is significant that through this discovery the country has been linked up with the first known appearances of the human race.

[2] For the point of view here adopted see the Additional Note at the end of this chapter.

Palestine from north to south, with his flocks and his herds and his tents and his wife and his concubines. On one occasion he was driven by famine to seek refuge in Egypt. The 'land of the Canaanite' had already established its hold upon him, and he took an early opportunity to return. Yet he considered that he belonged to a higher civilisation than did the other inhabitants of the country, and it was to his own kinsfolk, in his native Mesopotamia, that he sent for a wife for his son, Isaac.

The latter is the next leader of the group. He stands out less distinctly and with less grandeur than the majestic Abraham, and in the evening of his days his children, Esau and Jacob, quarrel violently between themselves. It is only with the next generation that the family becomes a tribe. Jacob, or Israel, has twelve stalwart, prolific sons: and, by the time of his old age, his descendants number some seventy souls. His had been an adventurous, troubled career. Driven from home in youth through his brother's jealousy, he returned to his mother's kinsfolk in Mesopotamia. Many years later he came back to Palestine with his growing family, and lived the life of a wandering sheik, as his father and grandfather had done. Another famine drove the household (to be known in future as Israelites) down into Egypt. Here one of the family had preceded them. It was the period of the horse-riding Shepherd, or 'Hyksos', Kings, who were perhaps of Semitic origin; and it may have been because of this fact that Joseph had been able to make himself a position at court. In consequence, his father and brothers received a warm welcome, and were permitted to settle in the province of Goshen.

It was not long before the Hyksos monarchy fell (1583 B.C.)—an event which must have affected the position of the Israelites adversely. Under succeeding rulers, or Pharaohs, their position deteriorated more and more, until at last they were reduced to unqualified serfdom. Their individuality was preserved, not only by their common origin, but also by the fact of the survival amongst them of their ancestors' spiritual ideals. Their religion may have been corrupt, but it stood out in favourable contrast to the fantastic polytheism of their masters. It is significant that their revolt and deliverance came about under the inspiration of a leader who was at once a political and a religious reformer.

II

It was a certain Israelite named Moses, who had been brought up in the royal court, who placed himself at the head of the movement for the regeneration and deliverance of his people. After many vicissitudes (recounted with a wealth of detail in the traditional lore of his folk), he succeeded in leading his fellow-tribesmen out of the country in the direction of the land in which their fathers had been settled (perhaps about 1445 B.C.).[1] We read of a disaster which overwhelmed the pursuing Egyptian forces in the Red Sea, where they were caught by the tide. The feast of Passover, which the fugitives instituted in celebration of their deliverance, is observed by their descendants to the present day. With the Israelites, there went out also a medley of other races—mainly belonging, in all probability, to the 'Hyksos' and other depressed elements. The latter became absorbed in the twelve families, or tribes, into which the descendants of Jacob's twelve sons had by now become divided.

The entrance to Palestine, where the Egyptian power was still strong, could not be achieved immediately. For a prolonged period (traditionally reckoned at forty years) the Israelites remained in the wilderness of Sinai, between the two lands. It was a stern period of probation. Moses, a stupendous figure, welded the jealous families into a people. He inculcated a purer idea of monotheism. He laid down the basis of an advanced moral and ethical system. He promulgated a code of laws, which has formed the foundation of Jewish practice and jurisprudence to our own day, as well as of much of the humanitarian idealism of modern times. This in itself was epoch-making. Never before, so far as is known, had worship been associated with morals. Never before had rules for the government of relationships between man and man been presented or considered as divine ordinances.

It is said by some critics that not a shred of evidence for the historicity of Moses exists. That may be so, if we are to regard potsherds as more significant and more reliable than the memory of a people, or written records of immemorial antiquity. But the influence which the great law-giver had on the Hebrew mind, traceable from a very early period, is so profound that it can hardly fail to depend ultimately upon a personality which made an indelible impression on contemporaries. Even if no account of Moses were extant,

[1] An alternative date which commands influential support is *c.* 1226 B.C. But tradition, as well as archaeology, supports the earlier period.

it would be necessary to assume the activity of a person such as he is said to have been, in order to explain the existence of the Hebrew people, with its distinctive literature, its laws, its ethics, and its religious code.

III

The story of the Hebrews, as it has been told thus far, follows in its general lines the traditional record, embodied in the historical books of the Old Testament, which has become absorbed into the fibre of the Jewish being. It is proper to append a summary account of the same events as they appear from the angle of modern Biblical criticism: not, indeed, from that of radicals who question the veracity of the traditional story in almost every detail, but of the less advanced school who accept at least its outline.

According to the latter, the so-called 'Israelites' did not possess a common origin, nor did they share the same history until after their settlement in Palestine. They were composed of a number of different elements, allied only by language and possibly by descent from a common Aramaean stock. Each fraction had its own history and folk-lore, and it was only at a comparatively late date that the various traditions became fused into the familiar account which every child knows to-day.

If Abraham existed (and some would question this), he was simply an outstanding personality, to whom many of the shrines of Palestine traditionally owed their foundation; he was not in any sense the ancestor of the Hebrew people. Isaac and Jacob are regarded as semi-symbolic figures, perhaps representing tribal motifs. The latter, indeed (who is believed to perpetuate the name of some forgotten Palestinian deity), was personified in order to provide a common progenitor for the Twelve Tribes—in fact named not after their ancestors but for the most part after their respective totems. Not all of these (perhaps only the 'Joseph' clan, comprising the tribes of Menasseh and Ephraim) were once in Egypt: while if Joseph himself was an historic figure, he can have been nothing more than a prominent tribal leader.

Moses himself according to this view was a Hebrew, or Israelite, with some Egyptian affiliations; in all probability belonging to the tribe of Ephraim rather than to that of Levi, to which he is assigned by tradition. During a period of exile or of travel, he was brought into contact with a deity YHWH,[1] formerly known only amongst the Kenites, whom he induced the various Hebrew tribes to accept as the object of their worship. From now only, the Israelites (or a portion of them) became united by the bonds of a common faith. However, though the new cult was exclusive, and implied the abandonment of polytheism, and though Moses insisted upon a moral code sterner and purer than the ordinary, YHWH was, in effect, a deity of the same type as any other—sometimes indeed being represented by concrete symbols. It was only very much later, under the Hebrew monarchy, that this 'monolatry' was reformed, purified, and spiritualised, developing into a 'monotheism' in the proper sense of the term.

Palestine was entered in a number of distinct nomadic waves, the most important being that of the so-called 'Joseph' clan, who arrived from the south. Yet some of the tribes had participated neither in the Egyptian bondage nor in the Exodus—in particular that of Judah, apparently a settled Canaanite clan rather than a body of immigrant Aramaeans. This tribe entered the Israelitish polity and absorbed its national outlook at a comparatively late date. Only during the long period of warfare and of travail which succeeded the entry of the Hebrews into Palestine did these various sections, with their different origins and different traditions, acquire a rudimentary sense of unity and develop a common faith.

The new conception of early Israel thus presents the monotheistic principle, which has been at the basis of Jewish history, as a slow and gradual evolution rather than a sudden emergence. It is a theory which does credit to the national genius no less than the traditional story, though it may rob the latter of much of its personal interest and of its naïve charm. It is a record, not of the cataclysmic revelation of the Deity to man, but of the gradual discovery by humanity of the Divine.

IV

Even before Moses' death, the tribes whom he controlled had begun to establish themselves in the fertile strip on the eastern side of the Jordan, between the river and the Arabian desert. The great leader 'who had known God, face to face,' passed away before anything more could be done under his immediate direction. It was

---

[1] The exact transcription of the Tetragrammaton; current amplifications are based on conjecture.

5. THE CODE OF HAMMURABI, SHOWING THE LEGISLATOR BEFORE THE SUN-GOD SHAMASH
About 1950 B.C. Paris, Louvre

6. The Pharaoh of the Oppression? Rameses the Great, Conqueror of Palestine
(1292-1225 B.C.)
Granite Statue. Museo Egizio, Turin

7. Semitic (Israelite) Prisoner in Egypt
Stone Relief at Luxor. 13th Century B.C.

8. 'HEBR
Semitic Prisoners in Bondage. Limestone Relief from th

nb of Haremheb, about 1350 B.C. Leyden, Rijksmuseum

9. 'Israel is desolate, her Seed is not': First Mention of Israelites
in Contemporary Records

Stele of the Pharaoh Merenptah, 1223 B.C. Egyptian Museum, Cairo

10. CANAANITE EMISSARIES IN EGYPT
Wall Painting, British Museum

11. JUDAEAN CAPTIVES BEFORE PHARAOH SHISHAK
Relief from Temple of Amon at Karnak, about 931 B.C. Berlin, Museum

12. 'LION' SEAL OF SHEMA, MINISTER OF KING JEROBOAM
Found at Megiddo, later in the Museum of Antiquities, Constantinople

13. 'ASTARTE, GODDESS OF THE SIDONIANS'
Clay Figurine from a tomb near Hebron

under a certain Joshua, of the powerful tribe of Ephraim (unlike Moses, a military commander, rather than an essentially spiritual force), that the penetration of Palestine began. The Jordan was crossed at a point near the mouth of the Jabbok, some twenty-five miles north of the Dead Sea. Jericho, a strong city which appears to have continued faithful to the Egyptian suzerainty, was stormcd. A confederation of petty rulers was defeated in the historic pass of Beth Horon. The Israelites were now in control of the hill-country in the centre of Palestine. Hence they spread by slow degrees northwards, until their progress was checked by the chain of strong positions which protected the plain of Jezreel (Esdraelon). Thus began the settlement of the Israelites in the land with which they were to be associated, more closely or less, in all subsequent history.

The conquest was a slow, laborious process. The invaders were unable to reach the coast until many generations after. Several of the principal cities continued to owe allegiance to the Pharaohs, or to be occupied by Egyptian garrisons. The original inhabitants retained many a mountain fastness long after the surrounding countryside had fallen. On the borders, peoples of allied speech and race, who had established themselves at much the same time, were perpetually restive and sometimes aggressive—Edomites and Amalekites to the south, Moabites and Ammonites to the east. Often, the invaders in their turn found themselves so hard pressed that their own existence was threatened. The various sections were isolated from one another by long strips of enemy territory—Judah, Simeon, and Reuben to the extreme south; Naphtali and Zebulun to the north, cut off from the centre by the Canaanite fortresses which stretched from Beth Shean to Megiddo; the all-powerful Menasseh and Ephraim in the central hill-country, with an off-shoot on the other side of Jordan. Under such circumstances, intense local jealousies made themselves felt. Thus, foreign incursions were facilitated, and sometimes invited. Ancient records preserve the names of no fewer than six foreign powers who oppressed all or part of the Hebrew race in the course of the generations which immediately succeeded the death of Joshua. It was only on very few occasions of emergency that the Hebrews were able to sink their internal jealousies and make common cause against the foe. But, in spite of all obstacles, the work of expansion slowly continued.

By the close of the twelfth century before the Christian era, the population of Palestine, within its historic borders, was fairly homogeneous. There were numerous relics of heathenism, and sometimes barbarous lapses, but the old monotheistic ideals of Israel were remembered even when they were not obeyed. The former wandering shepherds had renounced their nomadic, pastoral life and settled down to till the soil. The countryside was dotted with small towns and villages, crowning every eminence. A system of terracing, traces of which may still be seen, rendered fertile even the rockiest hillside. Commerce, on the other hand, was undeveloped, still lying mainly in the hands of Canaanite traders. At the period with which we are dealing, the total population was probably a little more than 1,000,000.

The constitution was rudimentary. There was a certain vague national feeling, expressed in and consolidated by the common religious cult; and the tribes might come to one another's aid in time of danger. Even the section beyond the Jordan was regarded as part of the same body politic, notwithstanding its isolated position and its specific interests.

The tribal organisation itself was weak. Each town and village was, in effect, an independent unit, ruled and judged by its elders. Occasionally, some outstanding figure might attain wider recognition —generally by reason of a military achievement against the national enemies. In virtue of this, he would be in a position to 'judge' his people or a portion of it for some time to come.

We read of a number of these 'judges' in the obscure period which succeeded the death of Joshua—a woman, Deborah, who effected a temporary coalition of almost all the tribes against the Canaanite menace in the north, under the King of Hazor and his powerful general (or ally) Sisera (c. 1150); Ehud, who assassinated the marauding king of Moab and thereby secured an interlude of peace; Gideon, who, with a picked force, overwhelmed the Midianite raiders by a stratagem (c. 1100); Jephtha, a famous outlaw of Gilead, whose aid was enlisted to crush the Ammonites; and a number of other even more shadowy figures. Except in the first-mentioned case, the enemy were seldom Canaanites. Generally they were invaders from beyond the Jordan, seeking to repeat what Israel had already performed: and the struggle assisted in welding the whole population into a unity. Egypt, looming in the background, continued to maintain a nominal suzerainty over the whole country; and the land 'had rest' (in the Biblical phrase) in those rare interludes when she was powerful enough to assert her influence and put down disorder.

At times, too, there was internecine warfare among the tribes: as, on one occasion, when that of Benjamin was almost annihilated, in consequence of a lawless incident which had taken place within its boundaries. Once, at least, an attempt was made (by Abimelech, son of the Gideon mentioned above) to set up a monarchy, with its capital at Shechem. But the sentimental centre of the country was Shiloh, where the national Palladium, the 'Ark of the Lord' (constructed, according to tradition, during the forty years of wandering in the wilderness), had found its home, and where the religious worship of the whole people had its focus. Thus, under conditions which are to us to-day wrapped for the most part in obscurity, the Hebrew people passed three of the most crucial centuries of its existence.

NOTE TO CHAPTER I

In dealing with the Biblical age, the author has made what must nowadays be considered the innovation of adhering in general outline to the traditional account: though presenting it as far as possible in a coherent fashion, neglecting the miraculous element and using a vocabulary such as one would in dealing with any other sequence of events. This has not been due to any inherent obscurantism on his part, nor to ignorance of the conclusions of Higher Criticism, with which he has done his best to familiarise himself. The critical attitude, however (contrary to the popular belief), is by no means unimpeachable in every detail. Moreover, its conclusions are constantly changing from generation to generation, almost from year to year. Penetrating though its destructive criticism has been, it has thus far failed to provide any alternative account which commands universal acceptance. A majority of 'modern' histories thus resolve themselves, in point of fact, into a highly unimpressive discussion of the sources.

On the other hand, an unmistakable reaction has set in against the radical school of the last century. Weaknesses have been discovered in the critical analysis; Egyptian and allied studies have shewn that the Biblical narrative is at least consistent with contemporary conditions; and archaeological opinion on the whole favours the traditional story in at least its broad outline. It is a somewhat ironic consideration that, as usual, the popularisation of these ideas lags behind, so that the hypothetical 'man in the street' has just managed to absorb the advanced views which were abandoned in the better-informed scientific circles some time ago.

It is thus impossible to formulate an account of the origins of the Jewish people which will, first, command universal agreement even among the Higher Critics of to-day; and secondly, is likely to remain valid in ten or twenty years' time. The traditional story, on the other hand, is always likely to retain the same validity, whether it be much or little, which it now possesses.

There is one further consideration, perhaps more fundamental. There is a subjective as well as an objective historicity. A personality which a people has cherished in its heart for a score of centuries, whether he existed or no, attains an importance of his own in sentimental reality. The incidents legendarily connected with his name crystallise the national ideal of conduct. The mere fact that they were believed to have taken place may itself exercise a profound influence upon the course of events. The lives of the Patriarchs and the succeeding episodes, whether story or history, thus constitute an essential part of the background of the Jewish people, and it is out of the question to neglect them.

14. House in Ur of the Chaldees of the time of Abraham
Reconstruction, after Sir Leonard Woolley

Chapter II

THE ESTABLISHMENT OF THE
MONARCHY

━━━━━━━━━●━━━━━━━━━

I

The condition of the Hebrews in Palestine, at the close of what is known as the Age of the Judges, was very similar in every respect to that of the Anglo-Saxons in England two thousand years later. In each case the country was occupied by the descendants of invaders of some generations before. They had settled down, they had intermarried with and assimilated the original inhabitants (losing in the process something of their martial qualities), and they were now divided into a number of independent units. There was in each case a rudimentary sense of solidarity, fostered by a common blood and a common faith. The stimulus and the agonies of a universal danger were necessary to weld the scattered tribes into a people. In the one case it was provided by the incursions of the Danes. In the other, it came from a maritime people strikingly similar to them—the Philistines.

At the beginning of the twelfth century B.C., some local upheaval, or the magnet of loot, seems to have caused a wholesale migration southwards from Crete and the coast-lands of Asia Minor. The strangers—sea-raiders, constantly reinforced by their compatriots in the north, and acting in conjunction with detachments marching overland—had made an attempt to enter Egypt. In 1194 they were overwhelmingly defeated by Rameses III. They fell back accordingly upon the rich Palestinian coastal plain. Here they had little difficulty in establishing themselves. Their superior culture and their use of iron weapons (with which they superseded the bronze hitherto universal in south-western Asia) made them almost invincible. Their confederation of five city-states, each under its own *Seren* or Tyrant, commanded the high-road between Asia and Africa. Such was the impression which they made upon the ancient world that ultimately

(13)

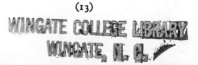

their name was given to the whole of the country, which is still known, after them, as Palestine (*Philistina*).

Once they were firmly established on the coastal plain, the restless invaders pushed inland. The Israelites of the lowlands began to live in constant fear of their raids. It was the neighbouring tribe of Dan which first felt the brunt of the attack. A single individual, Samson (a man of gigantic strength and quickness of resource, who remained long afterwards the hero of many a Hebrew saga), did something to stem the attack for a time. Ultimately he was captured and blinded; though (the story recounts) he did yet more execution at his death than in his life. The Philistine attacks redoubled in intensity. Ultimately the tribe of Dan (now reduced to no more than 600 fighting men) was forced to evacuate its territory and to look for another home in the extreme north, where they in turn displaced the earlier inhabitants. Henceforth, 'from Dan to Beersheba' was considered to comprise the full extent of the Israelitish territory.

The Philistine attacks had by now assumed the character of a systematic war of conquest. In the face of common danger, the tribes were compelled to patch up their internal differences and present a united front. Overwhelmed in an encounter near Aphek, it seemed to them in their panic that victory could be achieved against this invincible enemy only through supernatural aid. The next time they went into battle, they were given heart by the presence of the portable shrine long since established in the sanctuary at Shiloh. Even this failed to give them victory. Once more, they were crushingly defeated, while the precious relic itself was captured.

For many years to come, Israel lay under the Philistine heel. Archaeological evidence shews that Beth Shean was captured from its Egyptian garrison. An enemy governor with a strong force was installed at Gibeah, in Benjamin. The country was completely disarmed. Even the smiths were deported; and when the simplest agricultural implement became blunt, it was necessary to take it down to the coast to be sharpened, at a heavy price. By this means, the invaders hoped to maintain the initial advantage which they derived from their superior weapons.

II

One important change in the internal affairs of the nation had resulted from the disaster at Aphek. The two priests who had accompanied the Ark into the field had both fallen: their father, Eli, had died on hearing the news. This, coupled with the capture of the object about which their functions had hitherto centred, undermined the influence of the corrupt priesthood, which had been the principal unifying bond in national life for some generations past. A certain Samuel, who had been brought up in the sanctuary at Shiloh but did not belong to the priestly line, henceforth received by virtue of his commanding personality much of the consideration previously paid to them; and his home, at Ramah in the hill-country of Ephraim, became in a sense the national centre.

The new leader realised that the country required a strong unified government if it was to make headway against the enemies who were threatening its independence. Only a king could command the obedience of the whole people, and thus stem the danger. It was true that the establishment of a monarchy was contrary to immemorial tradition, and perhaps to individual interest; but there seemed to be no other solution. The choice, on the other hand, presented a difficult problem. To favour one of the more powerful tribes at the expense of the others would invite civil war. The recent campaign had broken the power of haughty Ephraim, whose supremacy had hitherto been unquestioned, while a member of any one aristocratic family would plainly be unacceptable to the rest.

At this period, as it happened, the Ammonites made one of their intermittent attacks upon the trans-Jordanic tribes, which appealed to their kinsfolk for help. The whole people was so disheartened that the summons fell on deaf ears. However, a courageous Benjaminite farmer named Saul took it upon himself to assume the leadership. There was a sudden counter-raid across the Jordan, and the enemy was repulsed. The effect on the Hebrews was magnetic. Saul seemed to be marked by heaven as the national leader. With Samuel's approval, he was proclaimed king by the people.

Not long elapsed before the War of Liberation began, the signal being given by the assassination of a Philistine official by the king's son, Jonathan. It was a guerilla campaign. Saul and his followers, familiar with every fold of the land, were able to fall upon enemy detachments when they were least expected. The fortunes of war varied. At times the patriot forces were reduced to no more than a few hundred men. But a spectacular victory at Michmash led to the expulsion of the enemy from the central range and from a portion of the south of the country, including the territory of Judah and

Benjamin. Punitive or retaliatory raids were executed against several neighbouring tribes—the Moabites, Ammonites, and Aramaeans to the east and south-east; and, on a somewhat larger scale, against the Amalekites to the south. Under the stimulus of this series of victories, following the stress of a common oppression, the Israelites gradually acquired a sense of cohesion. Eventually, the country was cleared almost entirely of the Philistine forces. The peril nevertheless remained one of the dominating factors in national affairs for a full generation to come.

As time went on, it became evident that the national choice for its monarch had been unwise. Saul was a gifted and undaunted military commander, but nothing more. He was, as it were, a Wallace—qualified only to take the lead in the war of liberation; not a Washington, who could both command in the field and mould the destinies of his people in peace. Saul's court was always a camp. He was capable of sudden, irresponsible outbreaks of barbarity, which not even the interest of the state could palliate, and to unreasoning fits of melancholy, which temporarily incapacitated him. Moreover, though the central and northern tribes (possibly because of their distance from the seat of authority) were disposed to favour, or at least to tolerate, his rule, the powerful tribe of Judah found its eclipse by that of Benjamin insufferable.

David, son of Jesse, a Judaean farmer, enjoyed great consideration in Saul's rough military household. He had come into prominence while still a boy, by defeating a gigantic Philistine champion in single combat. Since then he had been a popular darling. He had married the king's daughter; he was the bosom friend of the king's son, Jonathan; and his daring raids on the enemy were the burden of popular ballads. At length, Saul's jealousy became aroused. Finding his life in danger, David escaped to his native district, the hill-country of Judah. For the next few years he lived as an outlaw, at the head of a band of devoted followers. Saul made sporadic attempts to hunt him down, and shewed little mercy to his sympathisers. At last, the rebel chieftain was forced to take refuge amongst the Philistines, in the campaigns against whom he had made his name: and he was living at Ziklag, under the protection of the King of Gath, when Saul (together with Jonathan and two of his other sons) fell in battle on the slopes of Mount Gilboa, in an ineffectual attempt to stem a further Philistine incursion into the heart of the country (1013).

III

The dead king was succeeded (thanks to the devotion of his kinsman, Abner) by one of his surviving sons, Ishbaal. In consequence of the recent disaster, the country was once again under the Philistine heel. The royal residence, together with the seat of administration, was accordingly removed to Mahanaim, on the other side of Jordan, where the memory of Saul's courageous exploit many years previous was still strong.

David, though he had bewailed Saul's death in one of the most touching elegies in all literature, lost no time in availing himself of the opportunities it afforded him. He immediately re-entered the country with his seasoned veterans and seized Hebron—very probably by leave, and even with the aid, of the Philistines, who were not averse to seeing their enemies weakened by internal divisions. The Judean tribesmen already looked up to him as their leader. It did not need much persuasion for them to accept him as their king (1013).

David's ambition was too great for him to be satisfied by the exiguous area in the extreme south which recognised his authority. He looked with longing eyes to the north, restive under Ishbaal's weak rule. Clashes between the two factions followed as a matter of course; though they were confined to the immediate followers of the two rivals, only slightly affecting the country as a whole. In the end, David succeeded in detaching the all-powerful Abner from his allegiance to the house of Saul. This leader had a blood-feud with Joab, one of David's most trusted followers, who took advantage of his enemy's presence in Hebron to murder him. A couple of the dead man's under-officers, on hearing the news, carried out what may or may not have been their late leader's intention, and assassinated his puppet-king. Tardily, and somewhat unwillingly, the northern tribes now transferred their allegiance to David, who was thus recognised as king over all Israel (1006).

The great event of his reign, in the political sphere, was the shattering of the Philistine power. Another incursion had threatened to engulf the whole country, and David had been driven out of his capital. Unlike Saul, however, he did not rely entirely on force of arms, or on his own personal following. He countered attacks by alliances, and enlisted mercenaries to pit against the trained enemy troops. After two victories in the Vale of Rephaim, the country was freed from the invaders, and the war was carried back into their own

B

territory. The capture of the city of Gath (one of the federation of five which had overawed Israel for the past century) ended the campaign. Henceforth the Philistine menace belonged to the past. Its influence upon Hebrew history, however, had been incalculable; for it had been the hammer through the blows of which the divided fragments had been welded into a whole.

A succession of foreign campaigns followed this triumph. David took advantage of the temporary weakness of Egypt to the south, and of Assyria to the north, to build up a powerful border kingdom. His veterans swept all before them. He secured his frontiers by a succession of wars against neighbouring states. The insulting treatment of an embassy sent to the Ammonites was the pretext for a punitive expedition, which achieved a decisive victory. An Aramaean coalition, comprising a number of petty principalities stretching northwards as far as the Euphrates, was overwhelmed in an attempt to relieve Rabbah, the besieged Ammonite capital. A Hebrew garrison was placed in Damascus. Moab and Amalek were subdued (in the latter case, finally); and the land of Edom was annexed, after a brief campaign under Joab. One or two enclaves of non-Israelitish settlement, which remained from a past age to disturb the homogeneity of the country, were conquered; the last relic of the Jebusite strip which cut Judah off from the northern tribes thus becoming absorbed. Alliances were entered into with powerful neighbours such as Hamath and Tyre. The authority of David was recognised from the borders of Egypt and the Gulf of Akabah on the south, to the banks of the Euphrates on the north.

Within the historic frontiers of the country, the administration was revolutionised. The military camp, which had served Saul as the seat of government, developed into a court, with all its defects as well as its advantages. The long roll of officers of state testifies to the elaboration, if not necessarily the efficiency, of the new regime. The system of military service was revised around the nucleus of a standing force of foreign mercenaries. The civil service was remodelled and elaborated. Even the priesthood was drastically reorganised. The loose confederation of clans was becoming converted into a strongly centralised kingdom.

Yet the monarchy established by David retained certain elements of what we would to-day call the constitutional ideal. The democratic feeling of the nomadic Aramaean tribes to which the Hebrew race owed its origin was still strong. The rights of the sovereign were limited by public opinion, which was fearlessly voiced. There was the basic idea of a 'covenant' between the king and his people, executed under the auspices of a Deity who hated oppression and would not tolerate injustice. We find none of the unbridled absolutism tradition-ally associated with the Oriental ruler. The king might covet the wife of one of his subjects, but would not seize her from her husband; he had the latter put out of the way by a subterfuge, which itself demonstrates his recognition of the limitations imposed upon his rights. When a popular representative arraigned him for his conduct, he did not dare to manifest his resentment, though he could find no answer. It is obvious from this episode and others like it that he considered his prerogatives strictly limited. Under his successors, we find a similar state of affairs. This conception of a monarchy based in the last instance upon an agreement between the ruler and his subjects, the rights of the former being narrowed down by popular opinion and moral restrictions, is one of the utmost significance in the history of human ideas: for, studied, revived, and imitated in the seventeenth and eighteenth centuries, it led to the growth of the constitutional idea in modern Europe and America and thus played a part of immeasurable importance in shaping the destinies of mankind.[1]

The new-born nation still lacked its centre, for Kirjath-Jearim, where the sanctuary was now situated, never attained the status held by Shiloh before the battle of Aphek; while Hebron, far away to the south, was too closely associated with the tribe of Judah to be generally acceptable to the majority of the Hebrews. Among the cities captured by David within the natural borders of the country there was one, Jerusalem, against which no such objections could be raised. It was centrally situated. It was historically associated with no single tribe. The site was almost impregnable, by reason of the precipices (to-day almost filled up by the debris of centuries) which surrounded it on three sides. It lay close to important highways of communications and commerce. Above all, it was a conquest—almost a creation—of David's own. He lavished upon his new capital all his energies. He enlarged the fortifications to comprise the mountain of Zion, calling the part thus included within the walls 'the city of David'. He con-structed a sumptuous royal palace. He transferred thither the ancient shrine of the God of Israel: and he made preparations for the con-

[1] According to one theory, there was a popular assembly, 'The People of the Land', which on occasion exercised a dominant role in national affairs.

struction of a magnificent Temple to house it. From the reign of David, Jerusalem and Mount Zion remained the sentimental, if not always the political, centre of allegiance for the most vital portion of the Hebrew people.

The later years of the reign were troubled and disturbed. The royal harem, which the King maintained in conformity with Oriental tradition as well as with his own deeply sensuous nature, bore its usual fruit of cruelty, jealousy, and household dissension. David himself, worn out by a life of constant struggle and hardship, became prematurely aged. His sons by various wives quarrelled fiercely amongst themselves, so that the royal house itself was stained with bloodshed. Ultimately his own son, Absalom, broke into open revolt. The pace of the recent reforms had been too rapid for a large proportion of the population. The whole country accordingly flocked to his standard. The new capital was occupied. David himself was driven to seek refuge beyond the Jordan, and was saved from immediate ruin only by the devotion of his bodyguard. Absalom's death, in the campaign that followed, robbed the victory of its glory.

Not long afterwards, David died. Forty years had passed since he had returned from exile to become King of Judah, and thirty-three since his authority had been recognised by the rest of Israel. There are few characters of ancient history whom we know more intimately. We see an intrepid youth develop into a passionate manhood and a cold, calculating old age. We see the gifted lyric poet who won the name of 'the sweet singer of Israel' sinking to some of the lowest depths of depravity. But there is about it all an engaging sincerity, a faculty for admitting fault, a final recognition of moral standards, which does something to palliate even his most shameless wrong-doing. David's political ability, moreover, was exceptional. It was not simply as the founder of the royal line, nor as reputed writer of many lyrics, that his people has chosen to enshrine David in its heart with peculiar affection. If Hebrew history before his day is a labyrinth, but with him acquires consistency and cohesion, the reason lies above all in his energy and genius. He had found Israel a collection of warring tribes. He left it a strong and (as it seemed for the moment) united people.

IV

On his death-bed, David ordered his youngest son, Solomon (973-933), as yet hardly out of childhood, to be 'anointed' his successor.

The new ruler was faced at the opening of his reign by a formidable discontent, which he put down with a heavy hand. Thereafter, his rule was predominantly pacific. Legend has chosen to remember Solomon as the type of human wisdom. This is perhaps based on the appreciation of the fact that he forwarded the interests of his realm primarily by statecraft, while his father had employed force of arms. It was a period of profound peace. The position of Palestine as the highway between Africa and Asia was thus realised more acutely than ever before. David, in the course of his campaigns, had succeeded in occupying Ezion-Geber, on the Gulf of Akabah (an inlet of the Red Sea). Solomon realised to the full the value of this possession. There was, in those days, no Suez Canal to join the Mediterranean Sea and the Indian Ocean. But Ezion-Geber, or the neighbouring port of Elath, was the point of embarkation for India and the Far East; and he who possessed it and Palestine commanded the bridge which joined three continents.

The Israelitish sovereign first consolidated his position on the south by an alliance with Egypt, through whose aid he added to his territories Gezer, the last remaining Canaanite fortress and one of the great trading emporia of the Near East. Thus the Hebrew kingdom obtained at last a foothold on the Mediterranean. He fortified the positions which commanded the great trade-routes passing through his territory—from Egypt to Babylonia on the one hand, and from the Mediterranean to India on the other. Linen-yarn and trained chariot horses were imported from Egypt, to be exchanged with the precious woods of the Lebanon and the spices of Arabia. The intimate relations established by David with the Phoenicians were continued. The latter, happy to be allowed the use of the ports on the Gulf of Akabah for their expeditions to the Far East, permitted Hebrew sailors to join them, and assisted their ruler in his various enterprises. The trade from north to south, and from east to west, flowed through Palestine. In return for the security which his policy gave, Solomon exacted a tribute from the merchant caravans. He himself did not disdain to participate in various trading expeditions. His treasury became filled to overflowing, and the rare beasts and commodities of the Orient became familiar in Jerusalem as they had never been before.

The Court was resplendent, with its elaborate organisation and its numerous functionaries. The size of the royal harem became proverbial. Distant princes came to visit the wisest of monarchs. The capital was enlarged and transformed. Supplies of material and skilled artificers were obtained from Phoenicia, while labour was provided by forced native levies. Tyrian workmen assisted in constructing a series of magnificent royal palaces. For financial and administrative purposes, the country was divided into twelve districts, which neglected the old tribal boundaries; though, as events were to shew, the centrifugal tendency was too strong to be submerged. The defences of the realm were strengthened by the fortification of several border towns; while here and there forces of chariotry were established, with vast stables which recent excavations have laid bare.

As has generally been the case under similar circumstances throughout history, a literary renaissance followed this sudden enlargement of the horizons of the country and the rapid increase in its wealth. The name of the king himself was associated with vast numbers of polished epigrams, of a style similar to those found in the Biblical Book of Proverbs—itself traditionally ascribed to his authorship. The contrast with his father's spontaneous lyrical outbursts is characteristic of the change that had taken place in the condition of the nation and of the royal house.

The climax of the reign came with the erection on Mount Zion of a magnificent Temple, to house the shrine transferred thither by David. This was dedicated with immense pomp on the Feast of Tabernacles, c. 953. Jerusalem thus became the religious as well as the political capital of the country. The three pilgrim feasts (especially the Passover), when every male was supposed to appear before the common Deity, served to enrich the city and make it, in a very real sense, the centre of national life. In order to accentuate the importance of the Temple, there was an increasing tendency to prohibit animal sacrifice at any other spot.[1] In origin this may have been a political move, intended to enhance the importance of the sanctuary and of the priests who officiated in it. But, in the long run, it added to the spiritual potentialities of Hebraic monotheism, shewing its followers that religion was possible without sacrifice, and enabling them to maintain their beliefs even when the Temple was no more.

The magnificence of Solomon's reign was not achieved without recourse to heavy taxation, from which, as it seems, Judah was partially exempted. Even had this not been the case, the southern part of the

---

[1] Critical opinion post-dates this prohibition by some hundreds of years; but, even if the late dating of the documents in question is correct, the tendency must have been present long before it was formally enunciated.

country was bound to the dynasty not only by ties of blood, but more especially by the economic prosperity which resulted from the royal policy and from the presence of the new capital. It found ample compensation in these facts. In the north, however, discontent was general. Even before the death of the Jewish *roi soleil*, the empire which his father had founded shewed signs of breaking up. The Aramaeans to the north-east had recovered their independence, setting up a new state with its centre in Damascus. The Edomites had revolted. Unrest had made its appearance among the northern tribes. On the accession of Solomon's untried young son, Rehoboam, in 933, a petition was presented for the revision of taxation; and on its rejection, a general revolt broke out. The North rose in rebellion, and a certain Jeroboam ben Nebat, who had been at the head of a similar conspiracy during the previous reign, was acclaimed King.

It spoke well for the statesmanlike qualities of David and his son that the tribe of Benjamin, formerly the most unrelenting opponent of the dynasty, now threw in its lot with Judah, alone, except for the remnant of Simeon which, isolated in the extreme south, had almost lost its identity. David's Empire, with all its magnificent potentialities, fell to pieces. The outlying dependencies broke away. Henceforth, for a period of two centuries, Hebrew history has to divide its attention between two neighbouring states, akin in blood, but generally in opposition, and sometimes at war. There was the kingdom of Judah, with its capital Jerusalem; and that of Israel, centring about Shechem.

It is noteworthy that the ties of a common origin, language, and tradition were frequently able to nullify political separation. The literature of the period consistently represents the people as one, notwithstanding the political fissure. Intercourse between the northern kingdom and the southern remained intimate down to the end. Prisoners of war, captured in the not infrequent campaigns, could expect more humane treatment than would have been the lot of a stranger. Yet the strength of the country was wasted in internecine warfare, and the development of Palestine into the centre of a great empire, such as its geographical position justified and David's work might have led contemporaries to expect, was henceforth impossible. Palestine's might was not to be in the political sphere.

Chapter III

THE KINGDOM OF SAMARIA

———————•———————

I

It was in the southern kingdom—that of Judah—that the Hebraic tradition perpetuated itself, and thereby has been transmitted to our own day. By reason of the inclusion in the Hebrew Bible of a more detailed history of the northern tribes (thus setting a model which has been imitated in subsequent historiography), this fact tends to be obscured. For the sake of clarity, it is better to pursue the record of the so-called 'Kingdom of Israel' to its end before returning to follow the main stream on its majestic course.

In contrast to the comparative tranquility of the kingdom of Judah, where the Davidic dynasty had already established a strong hold on popular imagination, that of Israel was in a state of continual unrest. There was perpetual jealousy of tribe against tribe. Any successful military leader was a menace to the stability of the throne. The northern monarchy had precisely the same number of rulers in its two centuries of existence (nineteen in all) as its neighbour had in a period more than half as long again. Many reigned for only a couple of years; some, for no more than a few months; at least half died violent deaths—in most instances, at the hands of their successors. It was in a minority of cases that a ruler was succeeded by his own son, and only two dynasties lasted for more than as many generations.[1]

Jeroboam had noted, with foreboding, the dominant role which Jerusalem had come to play during the past two reigns—a consequence not only of its dignity as capital, but also of the fact that it was the seat of the national shrine. With considerable insight, he set about undermining the esteem which it enjoyed by reason of this. At the two extremes of his realm, at Dan and at Bethel, he erected rival sanctuaries, which would deflect the pilgrims who had formerly gone up to Jerusalem, and attract something of that allegiance which the

[1] The dynastic history of the two kingdoms may be traced in the table given on p. 48.

(24)

15. THE MOABITE STONE
About 847 B.C. Paris, Louvre

16. 'Black Obelisk' of Shalmaneser III, King of Assyria
Found at Qual'a, now in the British Museum. 841 B.C.

17-19. JEHU, KING OF ISRAEL, DOES HOMAGE TO SHALMANESER III
(Details from the Black Obelisk)

20-21. RELICS OF AHAB'S 'HOUSE OF IVORY'
Decorative tablets found in the ruins of the Royal Palace, Samaria. 9th Century B.C.

national capital had previously enjoyed. The schism was accentuated by the introduction of a revised religious calendar, which resulted in the observance of the outstanding feasts by the two sections of the Hebrew people at different dates. At the same time, Jeroboam made, or perpetuated, a concession to popular weakness. He set up in these shrines images of bulls, overlaid with gold, intended to represent in a concrete form the God of Israel—'These are your Gods, O Israel, who brought you forth from the Land of Egypt'. The inevitable effect was to lessen the sternness of the monotheistic conception, and to modify the national distinctiveness. The consequences were to become increasingly manifest in later years.

II

After Jeroboam (who died in 912, after a reign of twenty-one years), one or two outstanding rulers only are encountered. Omri (887-876), who mounted the throne in 887 after a civil war, proved himself a vigorous and far-seeing monarch. So greatly did his personality impress itself upon contemporaries that, until its independence was finally destroyed nearly two centuries later, the country over which he ruled continued to be known in foreign records as 'The House of Omri'. For some years he was at the head of a powerful nucleus of tributary and allied states. The former suzerainty over Moab was renewed. The material culture of the kingdom increased, as well as its wealth, and a foreign trading quarter came into existence in the capital. This Omri transferred from the ancient Shechem, which had been ill-fated for three of his predecessors, to a new site six miles to the north-west called Samaria. Henceforth, the kingdom as a whole is often known by this name. In order to develop the commerce of his realm, as well as to safeguard himself from the advancing power of the kingdom of Damascus, he entered into an alliance with the Phoenicians, cemented by a marriage between Jezebel, daughter of the King of Tyre, and his son Ahab.

It was in the latter's reign (876-853) that the policy of Omri bore its fruit. The extraneous influences resulting from the king's foreign connections culminated in the importation from Tyre of the *Baal* (Melkart) worship in its grossest forms, with its accompaniment of human sacrifice. Queen Jezebel introduced ideas of absolutism completely alien to the traditional Hebraic conception of monarchy. Justice was corrupted; and the story of how the king's ill-fated neighbour, Naboth, was deprived simultaneously of his vineyard and his life, made an indelible impression upon the popular mind.

From the political and military points of view, Ahab's reign was predominantly successful until its close. Notwithstanding the advance of the Assyrian power (which forced a temporary coalition only in 853, when Ahab contributed the largest number of chariots, and the third largest army, to the allied forces pitted against it at the indecisive battle of Karkar), bickering with the kingdom of Damascus continued, with varying fortune. There was a continual succession of border-raids; and at intervals the Syrian bands penetrated far into the country. At length open war broke out. After two serious defeats, King Benhadad sued for peace. But hostilities were eventually renewed. In the year 853, Ahab fell in an attempt to recover Ramoth-Gilead. He was succeeded in turn by his two sons, Ahaziah (853-852) and Jehoram (852-843). Meanwhile the queen-mother, Jezebel, remained all-powerful in Samaria, and the better elements continued to be antagonised by the all-pervasive foreign influence, as well as the palpable injustice of the court. In the end they instigated Jehu, the most dashing of Jehoram's generals, to make a bid for the throne (843). It was a religious as well as a political revolution. The dynasty of Omri was entirely wiped out, and the followers of Baal-worship were relentlessly exterminated in a massacre long remembered with horror by the people at large.

III

The dynasty of Jehu lasted for precisely one century (843-744), son succeeding father for five generations—a record unprecedented in the history of the northern monarchy. The new royal house (necessarily deprived through the recent revolution of the Phoenician alliance, and faced with the enmity of its closest neighbours) abandoned the idea of maintaining a *bloc* of the Syrian border-states against the advancing power of Assyria, and entered instead into friendly relations with the Great King. This was feasible only at the expense of the new dynasty which had risen to power simultaneously in Syria, whose hostility was thus a foregone conclusion. Profiting by the momentary diversion of Assyrian interests in a different direction, Hazael of Damascus turned his fury against his southern neighbour. Defeat followed defeat. The trans-Jordanic territory was invaded, and much of it wrenched away. The country was disarmed, its military forces being limited in a very modern spirit. The border states began to make incursions on Israelitish territory. Eventually, during the reign of Jehu's son, Jehoahaz (816-800), Samaria was itself blockaded, and saved from capture only by a sudden panic in the enemy camp. Respite was gained only when the Assyrian advance, under Adad Nariri III, reduced Damascus to temporary impotence (805). Israel, with the other Palestinian states, henceforth recognised the Assyrian suzerainty; but in dealing with the neighbouring powers she now had a free hand.

Under Jeroboam II (785-745), Jehu's great-grandson, there was a brief return of the halcyon days of a former age. By reason of internal weakness the Assyrian advance was momentarily halted. Damascus was no longer a serious rival. Israel was the most powerful of the minor Syrian states; and, as under David and Solomon, her authority extended over the neighbouring territories, from the Orontes down to the Red Sea. Once more the great caravan routes on either side of Jordan were under Israelitish control. Trade and industry revived. There was a considerable influx of wealth into the country, and a corresponding growth of luxury. We read of summer and winter residences; of houses of ebony and houses of ivory—relics of which, indeed, have been found in the course of recent excavations; and the rude hovels of Samaria gave place to magnificent 'palaces'. Yet it was a fictitious tranquility, based on nothing more solid than the temporary quiescence of the Great King, and not long passed before the storm broke.

IV

The dynasty of Jehu ended, as it had begun, in blood. When Jeroboam's son Zechariah was assassinated in 744, the country lapsed into semi-anarchy. During the course of the next ten years, five rulers succeeded one another on the throne, only one of whom died a natural death. Egypt to the south, and Assyria to the north, maintained their parties in the state and fostered palace intrigues. In 738, in the course of a foray to the Mediterranean coast, Tiglath Pileser III, greatest of Assyrian sovereigns, exacted a tribute from Menahem of Israel. This was raised by a poll-tax of fifty shekels on every well-to-do householder—a striking testimony of the wealth accumulated during the past generation.

Under Pekah ben Remaliah (who mounted the throne 735, in as

the result of an insurrection fostered by the Egyptian interest),
Damascus and Israel, with some Philistine and Phoenician cities,
formed a coalition against Assyria. They were overwhelmed, in a
lightning campaign. Israel was stripped of Gilead and its northern
provinces, the population of which was deported. Pekah himself was
deposed and murdered by the opposition party (730), his assassin,
Hoshea, being raised to the throne in his place as a tributary. It was
no comfort that the great rival of the past century was finally laid low,
Damascus being captured by the invader after a two years' siege (732);
for nothing now stood between Israel and the northern fury.

V

A change of ruler in Assyria, and the momentary diversion of her
attention northwards, were enough to embolden Hoshea (still hope-
ful, like all petty sovereigns, of establishing complete independence)
to listen to the tempting suggestions put forward by Egypt. An understanding was reached with the reigning Pharaoh, and the heavy
tribute annually exacted by Assyria was provocatively withheld.
Punishment was prompt and terrible. Shalmaneser V thundered
south with his army. As so often, the promised Egyptian aid failed
to materialise. Hoshea was captured and imprisoned, and no doubt
in the end was put to death. Samaria itself was besieged. Month after
month the city managed to hold out—a tribute to the strength of its
position and the massiveness of its fortifications. After a three years'
siege, it was captured—not by Shalmaneser, but by Sargon, his
successor—and razed to the ground (721). In accordance with the
ruthless but invariable Assyrian policy, the more valuable elements
in the population, including the nobility and the wealthier citizens,
were deported to distant parts of the empire. Here, divorced from
their ancestral soil and intermingled with other races, their fidelity
could be assumed.

A few years later (715), in consequence of a further local revolt,
the process was repeated on perhaps a larger scale. The former
kingdom of Samaria was re-organised in Assyrian provinces, each
under its own governor. The military garrison now installed was
reinforced by settlers from distant lands, who performed the same
function in Palestine as the Palestinian exiles were expected to fulfil
elsewhere. Ultimately, these intermarried with the native population
and partially absorbed its traditions. Thus a new race arose (later to

be known after their capital as the Samaritans). They were akin to their Judaean neighbours in blood and in culture, but cut off from them by political interests, and not quite to be identified either spiritually or ethnically with the Hebrews whose place they had taken. Those deported—the fabled 'Lost Ten Tribes'—ultimately lost their identity, becoming merged either in the races amongst whom they were settled, or else in those of their Judaean kinsmen with whom they came into contact. For generations to come, indeed, some individuals were able to trace their descent from one or the other of the old Israelitish tribes. But the political independence, and the spiritual identity, of the northern principality belonged to the past. It was in the kingdom of Judah that all that was truly characteristic and vital in the national consciousness was henceforth concentrated.

22. LAVER FROM SOLOMON'S TEMPLE
Reconstruction after H. Gressmann

Chapter IV

THE KINGDOM OF JUDAH

———— • ————

I

The record of the sister kingdom of Judah was very different from that of Israel. It was, on the whole, quiet and unadventurous, generally remaining undisturbed by internal dissension. The house of David never lacked an heir to occupy the throne of their great ancestor: and, until its last days, a disputed succession (so common in the northern kingdom) was exceptional. Thus, the royal dynasty acquired a hold upon the sentiment of the people which could never be wholly eradicated, even when independence had become a remote dream.

On the other hand, the history of the southern kingdom was politically undistinguished. Its magnitude was barely one-fifth that of its rival, whether from the point of view of population or of territory. Unlike Samaria, it stood athwart none of the great caravan routes; it commanded no great military highway; and so long as it remained quiet, it could be neglected by the powerful empires, to the north and south respectively, which contended for the mastery of the ancient world.

The part which Judah played in international affairs was therefore negligible. It was completely overshadowed by, and over a considerable period even subject to, the northern kingdom. Yet this political insignificance is more than outweighed by its crucial importance in the history of the human race. The whole of Palestine is only about the size of Wales; Judah comprised an area not much greater than a few of its counties, with a population which in historical times never probably exceeded 500,000 (as against perhaps three times that figure in the neighbouring state). But from that tiny territory—the nursery of the Jewish people and the Jewish religion—there issued conceptions which, together with those of Athens and Rome, have been all-powerful in moulding human civilisation. Even if some of the literature in which they are enshrined owed its origin to the kingdom of Samaria, it was by that of Judah that they were preserved and developed, to become the common heritage of mankind.

II

The reigns of Rehoboam of Judah (933 917) and his immediate successors were largely taken up by a contest against the secessionists —a contest which alternated, according to the fortunes of the campaign, between a war of conquest and a struggle for independence. At the outset, it seemed as though the revolt of the North might collapse. Jeroboam, compelled to move his capital beyond the Jordan, now appealed for help to Egypt, where he was well known in consequence of his residence there as an exile. Shishak (Sheshonk), the first Pharaoh of the Twenty-Second, or Lybian, dynasty, appeared before the gates of Jerusalem, and had to be bought off by a heavy bribe. We have a pathetic account of the removal from the Temple of the targets of gold deposited in it by Solomon to adorn the walls. They were replaced by similar objects in brass, with which the royal body-guard continued to perform the same stately ceremonial. It was symbolic of the change which had come about in the monarchy.

Under Rehoboam's successors the struggle continued. To secure his country's military position, his son Abijam (917-915) concluded an alliance with the kingdom of Damascus, thus initiating that power's encroachments on Palestine. It was the old story of a foreign invasion, which in the end was to prove all but fatal, invited in the first instance by domestic dissension. For the moment, the policy was successful; and in the long reign of Abijam's son and successor, Asa, (915-875), the independence of Judah at last became assured.

Under Asa's son, Jehoshaphat (875-851), relations between the two neighbouring states became more cordial, though the subordination of the southern power to the northern was very marked. The heir-apparent, Jehoram (851-844), married Athaliah, daughter of Ahab and Jezebel. It was in alliance with his son-in-law that the former began the campaign against Damascus, which was to cost him his life: and an abortive expedition against Moab, commemorated by the king of that country in the famous Moabite Stone (almost the oldest archaeological monument with a direct Biblical bearing which has thus far been found), was similarly undertaken in collaboration a few years later. The failure of this enterprise led to the revolt of the

Edomites and some of the Philistine cities. The kingdom was so far weakened in consequence that it seems to have become tributary to Samaria.

It was not surprising, under the circumstances, that the political and religious revolution led by Jehu implicated Judah as well. At the time, Ahaziah, (844-843), Jehoram's son and successor, had led his forces to assist in a further attack on Ramoth. He fled for his life, but was overtaken on the road by the rebel general and mortally wounded. This was the first king of the line of David who is recorded to have met a violent death. It is a significant contrast that, in the same period, no fewer than five of the Israelitish rulers perished by the sword.

When the news reached Jerusalem, the reins of government were seized by Athaliah, the Queen-mother. She proved a true daughter of Jezebel—energetic, unscrupulous, and devoted to the interests of her foreign kinsfolk. To secure her personal position, she made away with all the members of the seed royal, including even her own grand-children—an extraordinary procedure, explicable only on the assumption that she planned the establishment of a new Tyrian dynasty in Jerusalem. After six years of rule, however, a reaction took place. The chief priest, Jehoiada, who was allied by marriage to the royal house, planned the revolt. Athaliah was put to death, and the youthful Jehoash (Joash), a seven-year-old son of Ahaziah who had escaped the butchery, was placed on the throne.

It was a foregone conclusion that the long reign of the new king (837-798), should have witnessed (in its early stages at least) the triumph of priestly influence, and a revival of traditional religious values. The Baal-worship introduced by Athaliah was suppressed. The Temple buildings were restored by public subscription (one reads in this connection of a primitive money-box, devised by the High Priest to receive the oblations of the faithful). In foreign affairs the country suffered in consequence of the temporary decline of the northern kingdom, to which it continued subservient. On one expedition, Hazael of Damascus, who had become all-powerful in Palestinian politics, captured Gath, and prepared to march on Jerusalem; and he consented to withdraw only on the payment of a heavy indemnity. This misfortune was perhaps responsible for Jehoash's assassination, which took place not long after. His son, Amaziah (798-780), attempted to initiate a more vigorous policy. A successful expedition against Edom emboldened him to throw off his allegiance to Samaria.

However, he was heavily defeated, and his capital captured and despoiled. The political subordination of Judah to Samaria, hitherto a matter of surmise, is from now on an indubitable fact. It is no wonder that Amaziah's reign was ended by a palace revolution, which cost him his life.

The reign of Amaziah's successor, Uzziah, or Azariah (780-740) coincided over a number of years with that of Jeroboam II of Israel. The dependence upon the neighbouring power continued throughout this period—a last interlude of peace and prosperity before the final storm broke. The army was reorganised, we read, with a special expeditionary force of 'raiders'; fresh provision was made for armaments; and extensive additions were made to the fortifications of Jerusalem. The countryside was tranquil and prosperous; and the king's devotion to agriculture earned him the name of 'a lover of husbandry'. While the Israelitish border stretched as far as the Orontes, that of Judah again extended, thanks to a successful war with Edom, down to the Gulf of Akabah. Towards the close of the reign, there was a violent quarrel with the priesthood, occasioned by an attempt of the King, in his restless passion for reform, to usurp the sacerdotal functions. Except in this respect, Uzziah's policy was faithfully followed by his energetic son and successor Jotham (740-735), who had acted as regent during his father's last years.

On Jeroboam's death in 745, and the violent end of the dynasty of Jehu in the following year, Judah seems to have broken away from its allegiance to its neighbour. The country did not adhere to the anti-Assyrian *bloc* formed by Samaria and Damascus, with such fatal results. To punish the new ruler, Ahaz (735-720), an expedition was undertaken by the two northern monarchs against Jerusalem, where they intended to set up their own puppet king. In the south, Edom was able to recover the port of Elath. Ahaz, terrified in spite of the calm confidence of some of the wisest among his advisers, appealed to Assyria for help. The pretext was barely necessary to provoke intervention. The invaders were drawn off by an onslaught from the north. Damascus, as we have seen, was attacked and ultimately captured, and Samaria was stripped of her northern provinces. Judah itself (one of the few local states which preserved nominal independence) was henceforth considered a tributary. In captured Damascus, Ahaz paid homage to Tiglath-Pileser. He took the opportunity to send back to Jerusalem, for erection in the Temple (to the consternation of religious purists), a copy of the altar he saw there.

c

At the same time, he introduced into the Temple precincts figures of sacred horses in honour of the sun-god—a tangible expression of loyalty to Assyria's all-powerful Deities, as well as to the King of Kings himself.

III

Ahaz lived long enough to see the fall of Samaria (721), dying two years later. Any feeling of exultation which might normally have been occasioned by the downfall of the rival kingdom was qualified by the fact that Judah herself was now face to face with the Assyrian power, being the solitary buffer-state which henceforth divided the latter from Egypt, on which its eyes were turned longingly. The road between the two lay through Palestine, which thus became the cock-pit for the ensuing conflict.

Year after year, the great armies of the Assyrian war-lords devastated the country. It was in the troubled but not inglorious reign of the Judaean ruler Hezekiah, Ahaz' son (720-692), that the principal features of the struggle were staged. At the outset he managed to maintain a precarious neutrality, while at the same time preparing his capital for all emergencies by provision of a new water supply (the so-called 'Siloam Inscription' which commemorates this, discovered in 1890, is the oldest Hebrew monument of its kind). For a long time he steadily resisted the temptation to join a coalition formed by the southern states with Egyptian support. But the general revolt which broke out on the accession of Sennacherib in 705 throughout the Assyrian Empire, from Babylon almost to the Nile, ultimately emboldened him to alter his policy, and he became one of the principal members of a new combination of the Palestinian princes.[1]

The reaction was not long delayed. This was the famous occasion when the Assyrian swept down 'like a wolf on the fold'. He subdued the Phoenician cities of the coast one by one, defeated an Egyptian army at Eltekeh, received the submission of some of the minor rulers and penetrated into Judah. One fortress after another opened its gates. Lachish, twenty-five miles south-west of Jerusalem, was besieged and sacked (701): 2,600 years later, there were found the

---

[1] The only western vassal who remained faithful to Assyria was Padi, king of Ekron, who (as we are told in a famous inscription of Sennacherib) was deposed by his subjects and sent to Jerusalem for safe custody.

remains of 1,500 human bodies which were thrown at this time through a hole in the roof of a tomb-chamber. A force under the king's principal lieutenant, Rabshakeh, was sent to invest the capital in which, Sennacherib boasted, Hezekiah was shut up 'like a caged bird'. The whole population was in a panic, heightened by the persistence of the Assyrian envoys, sent to demand surrender, in browbeating the king's representatives publicly in the Hebrew tongue. Preparations for siege were begun. It appeared that Jerusalem was about to share the fate of Samaria. But some unexplained cause led to a change of Assyrian policy. Peace was hastily concluded with Egypt, and the army entrenched before Jerusalem was withdrawn. The capital, and the state, were saved; and though in a subsequent campaign Sennacherib subjugated southern Palestine, and even stripped Hezekiah of some of his territory, Jerusalem was never again threatened. Later generations could ascribe this deliverance to nothing less than supernatural intervention, second only to that which had delivered the Israelites from the Egyptian captivity.

The Assyrian suzerainty continued throughout the long reign of Hezekiah's son, Menasseh (692-638), which at last witnessed the occupation of Egypt by Esarhaddon. Tribute was regularly and un-questioningly paid, and Hebrew contingents fought in the ranks of the northern armies in their various campaigns. When a new suburb was constructed at Nineveh, the King of Judah was among the petty monarchs summoned to assist in the work, and to add to the impressiveness of the scene by paying homage. For some years (though he was afterwards suffered to return) he was treated as a prisoner of state. Political dependence was reflected in the intellectual sphere. Foreign social and religious influences, profoundly distasteful to the conservative body of the people, acquired an ever-tightening hold. Old local sanctuaries were restored. Human sacrifice was practised; and fashionable alien cults were introduced into the Temple of Jerusalem itself.

The conflict of parties and policies within the country now became more intense. Menasseh's successor, Amon (638-637), was assassi-nated in the second year of his reign by his own servants. The revolu-tionaries were soon suppressed by the 'people of the land', who placed on the throne the dead king's young son, Josiah (637-608)—then only eight years of age. During the regency, the *status quo* was maintained. When he reached manhood, however, a patriotic reaction took place. The Temple was repaired and purged of the foreign influences which had trespassed upon its ritual during past reigns. The Mosaic code, which had fallen into desuetude, was repromulgated on the basis of a manuscript stated to have been found during the work.[1] In the rest of the kingdom, the local shrines in the 'high places' were suppressed. The royal authority seems to have been extended over part at least of the provinces formerly subject to the kingdom of Samaria, for an attempt was made to secure a similar revival there, and the sanctuary at Bethel—the great rival of Jerusalem ever since the days of Jeroboam I.—was destroyed. The feast of Passover, commemorating the deliverance from Egypt, was celebrated with a patriotic fervour never before equalled.

Following this, a determined attempt was made to reassert the independence of the country, which had been in eclipse during the past four reigns. Political conditions were propitious. The Assyrian Empire had received a fatal blow at the hands of the raiding Scythian and Cimmerian hordes from the north. A Babylonian prince, Nabopolassar, making common cause with the Medes, had raised the standard of revolt. Ashur fell before them in 614 and Nineveh itself, amid the frenzied exultation of the Hebrew prophets, in 612. It was upon the new distribution of power that Josiah's hopes were pinned, and when in 608 the Egyptians under Necho sent an expeditionary force to assist Assyria against the rebels (who had long since opened up diplomatic relations with Judah), he attempted to interrupt their march. In a battle at Megiddo, he was defeated and mortally wounded. The clouds were henceforth to gather ever more thickly.

IV

Josiah's family were made to pay dearly for their father's policy. The popular voice had placed upon the throne his second son, Jehoahaz (a striking illustration of the essentially democratic character of the Hebrew monarchy). The latter, who attempted to continue the same line of conduct, was deposed after a few months by the Assyrio-Egyptian alliance and sent in chains to Egypt, where he died. In his place, his unscrupulous brother Jehoiakim, upon whose sympathies full reliance could be placed, was raised to the throne (608-598). Once again, an anti-national policy was followed: and patriotic spokesmen, who denounced corruption in the state, were in peril of their lives.

[1] See below, p. 46.

Necho's assistance proved powerless to save his allies. The Egyptian military power was finally overthrown by the insurgents at Carchemish in an attempt to cross the Euphrates (605). Within a few months Assyria collapsed; and Nebuchadnezzar, heir-apparent and before long King of the new Babylonian Empire, came to the fore as the military colossus who bestrode the Middle East.

Under the stress of circumstance, Jehoiakim recognised the suzerainty of the power to oppose which he had been installed. Three years later he threw off his allegiance. During the disorders which followed the approach of Nebuchadnezzar's armies, preceded by undisciplined bands of auxiliaries, the king perished: put to death, in all probability, by the pro-Babylonian party, who by this means hoped to secure the city from aggression. His son, Jehoiachin (598-597), a youth of eighteen, was made ruler in his place. Seeing that resistance was useless, he decided to throw himself on the enemy's mercy. With the Queen Mother and the whole of the royal household, he came out of the beleaguered city and made his way to Nebuchadnezzar's headquarters: surrendering, according to tradition, on condition that his capital remained unharmed. He was despatched in triumph to Babylon,[1] together with thousands of the nobility, the priesthood, and the middle-class population, as well as the treasures both of the Temple and of the royal palace.

The Babylonian ruler tempered justice with moderation. For some years he did his best to maintain Judah in existence as a semi-independent but subordinate monarchy. Jehoiachin's throne was filled by his uncle Zedekiah or Mattaniah (596-586), a younger son of Josiah—a well-meaning weakling, whose treachery did not have even the palliation of success. He too, like so many of his predecessors, began to toy with the idea of an Egyptian alliance, and ultimately threw in his lot with a fresh southern coalition formed to oppose the Babylonian domination.

In the winter of 588-587, Nebuchadnezzar appeared once more before the walls of Jerusalem. The advance of an Egyptian force led to the suspension of the siege; and the hopes of the war party were raised to dizzy heights. But the trained Babylonian veterans had little difficulty in defeating this new enemy, and in the winter of 587-586, on 10th Tebeth, the blockade recommenced. Six months later, a breach was made in the walls on 17th Tammuz (a date henceforth to be observed, like the former, as a public fast). Zedekiah, seeing that

[1] Official documents relating to his prison-allowance have recently come to light.

there was no further hope in resistance, attempted to flee. He was captured at Jericho, and forced to witness the butchery of all his family and courtiers; after which his eyes were put out, and he was sent in chains to Babylon. In the following month a Babylonian general, Nebuzaradan, was sent to complete the work of destroying Jerusalem. The city was looted, the principal buildings destroyed by fire, and the fortifications completely dismantled. A large proportion of the population was led captive to Babylonia, in pursuance of the deliberate policy which the new Empire had inherited from its Assyrian precursor. Only the rural population (or some of it) was allowed to remain. It was plainly the Chaldean intention to make Judah and its capital impotent, so that it should never serve again as a focus of rebellion.[1]

V

Even now (contrary to the general view) the existence of the state was not at an end. The seat of government was transferred to Mizpah, some five miles from Jerusalem, and the administration entrusted to a certain Gedaliah—a nobleman belonging to the conservative family of Shaphon and grandson of Josiah's chancellor, who was permitted to exercise authority as a Babylonian official. For a short period he did what was possible to nurse the country back into a healthy state and to repair the ravages of war. But, even at this stage, the old factions were not stilled. One Ishmael ben Nethaniah, a member of the former royal house, enlisting Ammonite support, murdered the governor and butchered the garrison. No attempt was made to set up an alternative government. The surviving leaders and gentry, fearing fresh Babylonian reprisals, fled to Egypt, taking with them all who cared to follow. The land of Judah was left without any settled government, deserted by all its former children, save for a handful of refugees lurking in the ruined towns and the hillside caverns. It was not without reason that Jewish tradition prescribed in perpetual remembrance of this an annual fast, which still commemorates the death of Gedaliah as a major national disaster.

[1] Recent excavations at Tel Duweir (the Biblical Lachish) have brought to light a series of Hebrew letters, of exceptional interest, which vividly illustrate the last days of the Kingdom of Judah.

Chapter V

THE PROPHETS OF ISRAEL

———————— • ————————

I

The story of the Hebrew kingdoms, as recorded down to this point, is not materially different from that of half a dozen neighbouring countries. There is a succession of wars of offence and defence. Monarch succeeds monarch on the throne—some more able and some less; some remembered with gratitude and some with horror. We have occasional glimpses of deeds of passion and bloodshed, of palace revolutions and of popular insurrections. In the end, the advance of a mightier power puts an end to the welter. Nothing in all this to deserve study after an interval of three thousand years, or to secure national perpetuity long after great empires had been forgotten.

If this has been the lot of the kingdoms of Judah and Samaria, alone among all the lesser states of the Asiatic world of that far-off age, the reason is to be sought in one factor only: the Hebrew prophets. For, whether we follow the traditional view and regard the Hebrew religion as having sprung up full-fledged in the wilderness of Sinai, to be renewed and reinforced during this epoch; or whether we adopt the critical attitude and think of the Mosaic code with its ethical ideals as a gradual evolution which now reached its culminating point; the fact must remain that the Prophets constituted the characteristic feature of the period of the monarchy, their utterances being the trumpet-calls through which the national conscience was shaped and expressed, and, in subsequent generations, intermittently revived.

The Biblical account, of prosperity invariably following obedience to the Divine will, and disaster coming in consequence of the crowning sin of idol-worship, appears to the modern mind excessively naïve. Yet the association of ideas is not so untoward. The religious state of Palestine, in the seventh and eighth centuries before the Christian era, necessarily reflected its political condition. The worship of foreign deities was the inexorable consequence of the infiltration of foreign influence. A diplomatic match between the ruling monarch and the daughter of a neighbouring potentate would automatically lead to the establishment in his capital of a new shrine, at which she and her entourage might worship. The political ascendancy of a foreign power was often accompanied by the introduction of its deities into the national pantheon—in part out of compliment, in part out of fashionable imitativeness, in part out of the conviction that the god who had raised his protégés to such pinnacles of glory was, of necessity, all-powerful. At the time when Babylon and Egypt were competing for the support of Judaea, the adherents of either party in Jerusalem had their own shrines, at which they practised the rites of one or the other state religion.

A truly patriotic ruler—a Josiah or a Hezekiah, who attempted to shake himself free from foreign ascendancy—made a clean sweep also of extraneous religious accretions, thus leading a return to the purer method of worship followed by his ancestors. A weak sovereign, who aped strange fashions, and was amenable to every outside influence, permitted or even encouraged the introduction of any aberration. The recurrent record of the monarch who 'did that which was good in the eyes of the Lord', broke down the heathen shrines, and was generally successful in his rule, is therefore on the whole a true one; for it was precisely the ruler who acted in this manner who was capable of governing his country in the spirit and interest of his people. The fact that the national fibre (exemplified in the tenacity of the ancestral monotheism) was stronger in Judah than in Israel was indeed the principal factor which enabled the former state to weather the storm which overwhelmed the latter. Looking a little further, one may suspect that one reason for Judah's greater fidelity was, precisely, her political unimportance. Isolated among her hills she could watch unmoved the tides of empire as they swept past. Foreign powers did not trouble to establish relations with her; foreign merchants turned contemptuously aside; and foreign influences, whether in politics or in religion, only occasionally had the opportunity to penetrate within her border.

II

Throughout this period it was the prophets (*nebi'im*) who were the watchdogs of the national conscience. A *nabi* signifies a delegate,

23-24. *Above:* THE SIEGE OF A CITY. *Below:* JUDAEAN DRIVEN INTO CAPTIVITY
Reliefs from the Palace of Ashurbanipal of Assyria (883-859 B.C.) at Nimrod

25. THE CAPTOR OF SAMARIA: SARGON, KING OF ASSYRIA (722-705 B.C.)
Paris, Louvre

26. An Assyrian King (Sargon) in conference with a Commander
Relief in British Museum

27-28. Siege of Lachish by Sennacherib, King of Assyria (701 b.c.)
Above: Assyrian Soldier with Judaean Captive.
Below: Sennacherib on his Throne by the City Wall.
Relief from the Royal Palace, Nineveh, now in the British Museum

or mouthpiece, or announcer. The conception of seer, or foreteller of the future, is secondary. For the Hebrew prophet was not, essentially, one who foretold coming events. He was one, rather, who examined the present. If he suggested that the deliverer of his people would be lowly, and riding on an ass, he did not purpose an exact forecast of the method of locomotion. He indicated simply that the person whom he had in mind might well be of the humblest condition or state of mind.

The *nabi*, as the mouthpiece of the moral consciousness of the people, is encountered at an early date. Moses himself was considered the prototype. There was no limitation as to sex, for, in the age of the Judges, Deborah the Prophetess was recognised to be the foremost national figure. By virtue of sheer moral force, he or she might receive local or (as in the case of Samuel) general recognition. From the beginning of the period of the monarchy, gilds of 'children of the prophets' became a familiar feature in national life: younger men, who followed as closely as possible the example of better-known leaders, and like them endeavoured to stir the feelings of their neighbours at times of emergency. Some, at least, stimulated the power of 'prophecy' by falling into ecstatic frenzies (fostered in some cases by music), when the Deity might best express himself through their mouths. It seems that Saul himself, the first King of Israel, had at one time belonged to a group of this kind.

At every hour of crisis, a 'prophet' was likely to come forward to chide the people for its backsliding, to stir it up against an enemy, to rebuke the king himself for some misdeed, or to advise how to counteract an imminent danger. Not all were necessarily genuine or sincere. Many were demonstrably self-seeking hypocrites. But there was a considerable proportion whose character and sincerity were above suspicion. There was always among the prophets a residuum which refused to bow the knee to Baal, whether literally or metaphorically. They represented the cause of the Lord against His rivals. But at the same time they represented the cause of the Hebrew against his enemies, of the poor man against his oppressor. Their function was indeed religious, but only in the sense in which religion embraces the whole of life, and is not confined to questions of theology.

These teachers and preachers might be drawn from all ranks of society, from the highest to the lowest. There were courtiers, priests, shepherds, and ploughmen. It was a prophet who, in the name of his

God, fostered the revolt of the northern tribes at the outset of the reign of Rehoboam; and it was a prophet who foretold (and, by fore-telling, instigated) many of the succeeding dynastic changes in the northern kingdom. When, in the reign of Ahab, Samaria reached the apex of its luxury, its corruption, its idolatry and its vice, Elijah the Tishbite led the spirit of protest: a rough countryman, clad only in skins, who could appear out of nowhere to upbraid the sovereign or his consort, and disappear into nowhere afterwards. His personality made an indelible impression on the popular imagination. Marvellous stories were recounted about his achievements, and, to the present day, Hebrew fantasy regards him as alive and active among the people to which he dedicated his life. He was succeeded by Elisha—a more spectacular figure, at home in the court as well as in the fields, and in constant intercourse with members of the upper classes. His influence was hardly less in Damascus than it was in Samaria, and he looms vaguely behind the scenes as instigator of the revolution which replaced the house of Omri by that of Jehu.

Neither of these towering characters left any written record which could remind succeeding generations of the exact purport of his teaching. It was from the reign of Jeroboam II that the messages of the prophets began to be preserved in written form. The names of many of these early God-intoxicated reformers are no doubt lost, and it is probable that, of the 'prophecies' of those whose names are remembered, only a very small proportion survives. They are suffi-cient, nevertheless, to have had a lasting influence on the life of mankind, and of the Hebrew people in particular. They embody the ideals of righteousness which dreamers and reformers, of all races and in all countries, have continually had before them from that day to this. (English history and American, in particular, would have been very different but for the influence of the handful of Hebrew writers fragments of whose rhapsodies are preserved in the so-called 'Prophetical' books of the Bible.) Not a small degree of the effective-ness of these utterances is due, not merely to the moral indignation which burns within them, but also to the inimitable style in which they are composed—alternating between prose and poetry, vivified by graphic similes, and turning aside at intervals to include lyrics, dirges, satires, and parables which are still reckoned among the masterpieces of world literature.

III

Thanks to these writings, and the parallel historical works, we have a strikingly clear picture of the social background of the canonical prophets. Hand in hand with the political development of Palestine, a revolution had come about in its social structure. The stern morality of the nomad (as expressed in the earliest Hebrew records) is always likely to become modified when he settles down as a tiller of the soil, in an organised community. This change had begun to take place amongst the Hebrews in the twelfth century; but it was only with the increasing 'civilisation' of the period of the monarchy, four or five hundred years later, that the climax was reached.

The settled rule of the House of Omri fostered the growth of a capitalist class, with luxurious standards of personal comfort, and little regard for the basic rights of others. While during the period of the monarchy the total population (never probably exceeding 1,800,000 for the whole country) seems to have dwindled, that of the cities increased both proportionately and absolutely. The small-holders and peasant farmers, formerly the backbone of the country, were slowly eliminated. A bad season would place them in the hands of their wealthy neighbours, to whom they had recourse for assistance; and the process of dispossession was hastened, in defiance of the Hebraic tradition, by the pitiless administration of the laws of debt. Large estates were accumulating, worked by slave labour. Official religion tended to be more and more formalised, concentrating its attention upon the execution of ceremonial, to the exclusion of all that was spiritual. Justice was frequently corrupt, and at its best, rigid. This was the state of affairs which evoked the prophetic protest, setting Israel and mankind a new standard of moral ideals and social justice.

IV

About the year 765, a simple Judaean shepherd named Amos made his appearance at a feast at the shrine of Bethel, in the kingdom of Samaria, then at the height of its power. His denunciation of the assembled people—of their greed, their dishonesty, their exploitation of the poor—was unsparing. He disturbed their complacency by the unprecedented theory that the Divine choice, on which they prided themselves, indicated a greater responsibility, not freedom from it.

He warned them that their superficial religiosity could not save them on the day of punishment which was impending. The essential quality of true religion was clean living, justice, and righteousness, not the mechanical observance of an external pietism. The whole tirade has been described as one of the marvels of literature for its comprehensiveness, variety, compactness, methodical argument, eloquence, and force of expression.

A little later than Amos was Hosea, a rustic, slow of speech, who found difficulty (to judge from the involved style of his writings) in expressing the message which he felt surging within. Like his precursor, he was preoccupied with the imminence of an Assyrian invasion and the problems to which it gave rise. The temporary triumph of the aggressor appeared to him inevitable. Though God had dearly cherished His people in the past, they had proved unfaithful to Him, like a pampered woman careless of her marriage vows. In consequence, their downfall was a foregone conclusion. If their God nurtured a special regard for them, He would express it, not by undue favour, but by the sharpness of the punishment which He would mete out. Yet His infinite love would purify His people and bring them back to Him, in the end, in perfect repentance.

Almost contemporaneously, Micah, essentially a man of the people, was foretelling disaster upon the whole community—Judah as well as Israel—in consequence of their manifold sins, particularly their systematic exploitation of the poor. 'What doth the Lord require of thee', he cried, in a famous verse which embodies the quintessence of the prophetical teaching, 'but to do justly, and to love mercy, and to walk humbly with thy God?' To the fundamental point of social justice, the Hebrew prophet never fails to recur.

V

The northern kingdom was tottering to its fall, and the pivot of Hebraic life, with the centre of interest, had been transferred to Judah. Isaiah ben Amoz, a statesman and an aristocrat (according to tradition, he was a member of the royal house), was a commanding figure in the court of Hezekiah and his immediate predecessors. In periods of unrivalled eloquence he denounced the luxury and the frivolity which pervaded the whole land and foretold speedy retribution. Assyria was, he thundered, the instrument through which the iniquities of the people were to be purged.

Yet his prophecies had their more comforting side. The triumph of the foreign power was not to be final, nor was the Hebrew state to be utterly overthrown. At the moment, the country was profaning itself by its secular interests, and it was about to receive a sharp lesson. Nevertheless, the people might look forward to their ultimate destiny with optimism, so long as they clung to the religious ideals of their fathers, reverted to a purer and simpler manner of life, and did not entangle themselves in foreign alliances. Isaiah, in his denunciation of moral shortcomings, coupled with shrewd political insight and confidence in a brighter future, represents the Hebrew prophet at his highest and most characteristic. If Judah weathered the storm which was about to break over her, it was due largely to his statesmanlike advice, and the Golden Age for which mankind has intermittently been striving, from that day to this, has always been coloured, if not inspired, by the graphic picture which he drew.

Lesser figures now begin to appear on the scene in comparative profusion. The Scythian invasion, which menaced the existence of the whole country about 626 B.C., evoked the stirring addresses of Zephaniah, who saw in these ruthless invaders, too, an instrument in the Lord's hand to punish the crass injustice of the social order. The fall of Nineveh, and of the Assyrian power with it, was greeted in exultant rhapsodies by Nahum. Habakkuk grappled with the moral problems raised by God's use of the idolatrous Babylonian Empire, newly arisen to pre-eminence, and its apparent triumph over all the neighbouring nations. Without a doubt there were many others (such as Huldah, the prophetess, of whom we obtain a fleeting glimpse during the reign of Josiah), equally polished and equally forceful, all record of whose allocutions has perished.[1]

Throughout the alternations of hope and despair which preceded the final debacle, the background is filled by the sombre utterances of Jeremiah, a priest from Anathoth, near Jerusalem. His writings reveal the man: a powerful orator, fearless and intrepid, refusing to admit that loyalty to his country could justify him in outraging his conscience, foretelling disaster because disaster was merited, and suffering continual persecution because he refused to be silent when silence was acceptable at court. Like Isaiah, he stood for neutrality in external politics. He was opposed to intrigues with Egypt or any other power. He anticipated the inevitable triumph of the all-

[1] One may instance also the martyred Urijah ben Shemaiah, who figures in Jeremiah xxvi, 20-23, and also in the newly discovered Lachish correspondence.

powerful Babylonian, and lived to know his anticipations realised. But he saw no reason why exile should put an end to the national existence, or to the distinctive national conceptions. It was in this that his supreme historical importance resides. Even beyond the Euphrates, the Hebrew could still remain a Hebrew. Even beyond the Euphrates, he could maintain his own ideals, and refrain from contaminating himself by the worship of idols. Not that this implied disloyalty to the state; and, when asked for advice by the exiles who had been deported with Zedekiah, the grim priest counselled them to plant vineyards, and to build houses, and to seek the peace of the cities in which they were settled. They did so, and it was as a result of his influence that the Judaean exiles, alone of all the peoples deported at this ruthless age, were able to maintain both their identity and their ideals until the dawn of a brighter day.

VI

In the eighteenth year of the reign of Josiah (621 B.C.), there had taken place in Jerusalem an episode which stands in close connection with the prophetic utterances. During the restoration works in the Temple, there was found a copy of the long-forgotten 'Law of Moses'. According to the modern, critical view, what was actually in question was a revised code of the earlier laws, corresponding in the main to what we now call the Book of Deuteronomy. This had been compiled by the Priests, and was now presented under the guise of an ancient composition of immemorial antiquity. The traditional view, on the other hand, envisages the Pentateuch as we now have it, which, in that case, must have fallen into entire oblivion during past generations.

The publication and diffusion of this codex, whatever its nature, its origin, and its authorship, was of cardinal importance in the spiritual history of the Hebrew people. We have already seen[1] something of the immediate spiritual revival which resulted. The repercussions did not by any means end with this. From now onwards the 'Law of Moses' no longer signified a half-forgotten body of regulations, known only through oral tradition, but an ascertainable written corpus, accessible to every man who could read. (The proportion of illiterates in ancient Israel, it may be observed, seems to have been low: and it was nothing unusual for an ordinary village boy to be able to read and write.)

[1] Above, pp. 35-6.

It was a code which, however much it may breathe the spirit of the age in which it was composed, is immeasurably superior to anything else of its day. It shews close analogies, indeed, to the code of Hammurabi (itself based upon an older Sumerian code), promulgated in the heyday of the first Babylonian Empire, many centuries before. The differences between the two, however, are even more significant than their similarities. In many respects the Mosaic code provides an ideal which even our modern age has failed to realise. It prescribes not so much right believing as right living. It is a social code of unique importance, inculcating humanity to animals as well as to human beings. It breathes throughout, besides its stern monotheism, that ideal of 'righteousness', of charity towards one's neighbour, and of justice to the poor, which was at the basis of the teaching of the Prophets. In subsequent years, when the latter referred (as they so often did) to the neglect of the 'Law of Moses', it was this code that they had in mind. And it was this which constituted the nucleus of the body of literature which the exiles took with them into Babylonia to preserve their distinctive consciousness and conceptions, when all else in the traditional scheme of life had toppled in ruins about their heads.

29. ARRIVAL OF THE MESSIAH, WITH THE PROPHET ELIJAH
Woodcut from the Venice Haggadah, 1609

THE HEBREW MONARCHIES

*Saul (1033-1013)

David (1013-973)   *Ishbaal, son of Saul, in
                                     Transjordan, etc. (1013-1006)
Solomon (973-933)

Kings of Judah   *Kings of Israel*
Rehoboam (933-917)   Jeroboam (933-912)

Abijam (917-915)   *Nadab (912-911)
                          Baasha (911-888)
Asa (915-875)
                          *Elah (888-887)
                          *Zimri (887)
                          Omri (887-876)

Jehoshaphat (875-851)   Jezebel = *Ahab (876-853)

Prophets

Elijah   Jehoram (851-844) = *Athaliah*   Ahaziah (853)

Elisha   *Ahaziah (844-843)   *Jehoram [*Brother*] (853-843)
                                       Jehu (843-816)
            Athaliah | (843-837)
                                       Jehoahaz (816-800)
            *Joash (837-798)
                                       Jehoash (800-785)

                                       Jeroboam II. (785-745)

            *Amaziah (798-780)

Amos   Azariah (Uzziah) (780-740)
Hosea
Isaiah   *Zechariah (744)
i-xxxix   Jotham (Regent)   *Shallum (743)
            Jotham (740-735)   Menahem (743-736)

Micah   Ahaz (735-720)   *Pekahia (736-735)
                                       *Pekah (735-730)
            Hezekiah (720-692)   *Hoshea (730-721)

            Menasseh (692-638)

            *Amon (638-637)

Jeremiah
Finding of   *Josiah (637-608)
Law-Book, 621

Zephaniah   Jehoahaz (608)   *Jehoiakim (608-598)
Nahum
Habakkuk   Jehoiachin (598-597)
                                  (First Babylonian
                                  Deportation, 597)

                                             Zedekiah (597-586)
                                             (Second Babylonian
                                             Deportation, 586)

*Met a violent end.

30. TRADITIONAL BURIAL PLACE OF THE SANHEDRIN ('TOMBS OF THE JUDGES') OUTSIDE
JERUSALEM
Copyright, Matson Photo Service, Jerusalem

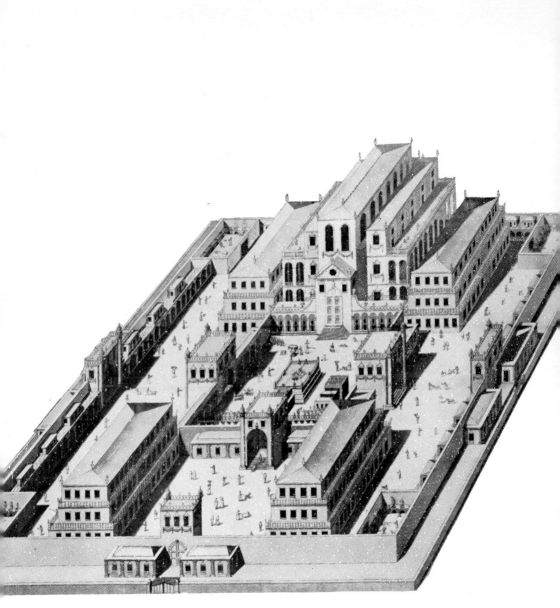

31. THE TEMPLE IN JERUSALEM
Conjectural Reconstruction by S. Bennett

BOOK II

THE JEW: 586 B.C.–A.D. 425

———————●———————

32. RETURN FROM EXILE
Woodcut after Hans Holbein

Chapter VI

THE RETURN FROM EXILE

——————•——————

I

In the course of the year 538 B.C. a succession of convoys plodded their way along the ancient caravan routes which cross the vast expanse of desert to the west of Mesopotamia. It was no ordinary movement of wayfarers or of merchants: it was a people returning to take up its destiny anew.

The population deported from Palestine by the Babylonians in their successive campaigns, from 597 to 586, had found no difficulty in accommodating themselves to their new conditions. They retained their freedom, and were permitted to live where they pleased. The ordinary folk became peasant-cultivators in their new land, as they had been in the old. The craftsmen settled in the cities, where they continued their former professions. There was, no doubt, a sprinkling of merchants in addition. A considerable colony (the name of which was subsequently to be revived in a new Palestine) was to be found at Tel-Aviv, near the Great Canal, and there were many minor centres in the same neighbourhood. On the accession to the throne in 561 of Emul-Marduk (the Biblical Evil-Merodach), the ex-king Jehoiachin had been released from prison and accorded royal honours: a token that the ancient hostility might be considered at an end.

Yet, contrary to historical precedent and actual expectation, the Judaean exiles had not lost their distinctiveness. Long before the catastrophe, men of foresight (like Amos the shepherd and Jeremiah the priest and the aristocratic Isaiah) had predicted their vicissitudes, which hence appeared in retrospect in the light of a punishment rather than a disaster. Their devotion to the one God whom their forefathers had discovered thus became strengthened, and not extinguished, through the apparent triumph of an alien deity. In their exile, too, eloquent teachers like Ezekiel, one of the group settled at Tel-Aviv, had arisen among them to perpetuate the prophetic tradition, exhorting them in passionate orations to preserve their confidence and their faith.

The unwilling emigrants had accordingly retained their ethnic, their linguistic, and their religious identity. They had borne with them into captivity, whether orally or in writing, a large body of literature—laws ascribed to Moses, the first organiser of their race; religious poetry which was linked up with the name of David, the best-loved of their kings; chronicles of the old royal dynasty; appeals for justice and denunciations of wrong-doing, whether in individuals or in peoples, from the inspired teachers whom they called 'prophets'. To comfort themselves for the loss of their country, they began to study this rich literature with increased affection, sifting it, arranging it, copying it, and perhaps reading it aloud when they came together. The Temple in Jerusalem, formerly the centre of their religious life, lay in ruins, and it was out of the question for them to construct a substitute in the land of their captivity. Worship, therefore, took the place of sacrifice, and prayer-meetings, at which the ancient literature was read and discussed, now became in all probability a regular institution.

The Babylonian Empire had fallen as suddenly as it had appeared. Under Nabu-Nahid (Nabonidus), a petty Elamite chieftain named Cyrus rose in rebellion and, advancing from success to success, established a new Persian Empire. Marching south, he overwhelmed the Babylonian forces under Besharuzur (Belshazzar, in the Biblical account), the heir-apparent. Then, aided by treachery within the gates, he seized the capital during the course of a state banquet (538).

He purported to come in the guise, not of a conqueror, but of a deliverer. Enthusiastically welcomed as he entered into Babylon, he testified to his good faith by reversing the political and religious policy of the preceding dynasty. Among the most unpopular actions of Nabu-Nahid (an antiquary who had missed his vocation) had been the concentration in the capital of the images of various gods whose worship had previously been associated with outlying temples. Cyrus ordered these to be sent back, together with those elements of the population who had been dragged with them into exile. But the Persian religion, with its high idealism and its cult of the Sky-God, Ahura-Mazda, had little in common with the gross Babylonian polytheism, and could not fail to instil in its adherents a certain degree of sympathy towards a monotheistic creed. It is not extraordinary, therefore, that the conqueror extended his favour to the people which Babylonian ruthlessness had uprooted from the land of Judah. Within a few months of his victory (538), he issued an edict authorising any persons who so desired to return to Jerusalem and there rebuild a Temple for the worship of the Most High God. Thus the enthusiastic hopes which had been centred about his advance by certain sections of the exiles, whose sentiments are expressed in the lyrical outbursts of the second half of the book of Isaiah, became fulfilled.

II

It was of these returning exiles that the convoys which crossed the desert in 538 were composed. According to contemporary records, they numbered in all something over 40,000 souls: those who preferred to remain in Mesopotamia supporting the expedition with monetary contributions. With few exceptions, those who returned could trace their ancestry for several generations, and in many cases knew in what part of the country their family property had been situated. The priests, who had formerly been associated with the Temple worship, were naturally prominent, comprising something like one-tenth of the whole party. The convoys were accompanied by some 7,000 slaves of either sex—eloquent testimony to the degree of well-being which some at least of the exiles had attained.

The expedition was under the leadership of a member of the late royal house—Sheshbazzar, probably a son of King Jehoiachin. Before he left, the High Treasurer entrusted to his care the sacred vessels carried away half a century before among the loot from Jerusalem, and since stored in the temple of the god Bel. The other outstanding figure was Jeshua ben Jehozadak, a member of a distinguished priestly family.

As the caravans successively entered the country, one may imagine that they dispersed, each family going to reassert its claim on the plot of land which it previously owned. That autumn, however, they came together in Jerusalem in order to re-institute Divine worship at the Temple. On the occasion of the solemnity at the beginning of the seventh month (subsequently known as the New Year), the debris was cleared away from the middle of the ruined courts, and a rough altar set up. From that date, for a period of three and a half centuries, the regular sequence of sacrifice, morning and evening, was uninterrupted.

From this point, preparations for the complete restoration of the sanctuary were pressed on. Two years after the Return, the foundation stones were laid. The old pomp seemed to be revived in the stately ceremonial and in the bursts of psalmody, led by the Levites of the clan of B'ne Asaph. A shout of jubilation from the assembled people re-echoed across the hills. But many of the older men, who could remember the splendour of the former building upon this site, wept at the recollection of the glory that had been, and of its tragic end.

The sentiments, in either case, proved premature, as, owing to political intrigues on the part of the neighbouring peoples in Palestine, the work was soon suspended. Meanwhile the returned exiles settled down in their new homes. Gradually the streets of Jerusalem began to be cleared of ruins, and its houses to be repaired. Some sort of spiritual life slowly manifested itself, and teachers like Haggai and Zechariah ben Iddo arose, to fill the place of Jeremiah and Hosea. Sheshbazzar, who had led the Return, apparently died very shortly after. He was succeeded in the office of governor (*Tirshata*: 'magnifico') by his nephew(?) Zerubbabel ben Shealtiel (unless, as has been suggested, the two names indicate the same person).

On the death of Cyrus (529), the peace of the state which he had built up was disturbed by a succession of rebellions and civil wars, from the effects of which Palestine cannot have escaped. It was only in 521, when power fell into the capable hands of Darius I—the real creator of the Persian Empire—that order was restored. The interregnum led to a revival of nationalist feeling. The fiery Haggai, aghast at the rebuilding of private houses while the national shrine still lay in ruins, had meanwhile been pleading for the task of reconstruction to be taken in hand once more, and he foretold that the glory of this second House would be greater than that of its precursor. Accordingly, in the winter of 520, after a cessation of sixteen years, the work was recommenced, the revival of activity being so marked as to make modern critics date the real beginning of the national rebirth from this point. Notwithstanding the interference of an over-zealous Persian official, in the spring of 515, after five years' further labour, the building was completed and dedicated.

Of internal history in the following years we know very little. The country undoubtedly suffered from the disturbances resulting from the various Persian campaigns in Egypt. Zerubbabel, as a descendant of the royal house of David, appears to have had dreams of seeing the

monarchy restored in his favour. In this hope he found encouragement from some of the more enthusiastic elements in the population,
led by Haggai. The priestly faction ranged themselves in opposition
to him. Feeling between the two parties ran high, notwithstanding
the attempts of the prophet Zechariah to effect a compromise. Then,
suddenly, Zerubbabel disappears from the scene. It is highly probable
that he was recalled, or perhaps even may have met a violent end as
a punishment for his ambition.[1]

III

The political condition of the restored community was very different from that of their fathers of a century before. The territory on
which they settled was restricted to a very small area round Jerusalem. It included no more than thirty rural settlements, scattered
over a radius of a few square miles. During the captivity, the
surrounding tribes had pushed forward and occupied many outlying
tracts which had previously belonged to Judah. The Edomites,
pressed by the Nabataean Arabs, had been permitted to take possession of the south. The Philistinian cities, such as Ashdod, had made
similar advances on the west, while towards the desert there were
encroachments by Moabites and Ammonites—old enemies of the
kingdom of Judah—and some of the local Arab tribes.

Most important was the half-idolatrous residue of the Israelitish
kingdom to the north, with its heterogeneous admixture of foreign
military settlers. They felt a distinct sense of kinship with the
returned émigrés, and had a sincere, if not exclusive, veneration for
the incorporeal deity worshipped in Jerusalem. At the outset, they
had shewn a cordial enough feeling, and had desired to collaborate in
the work of restoring the national shrine. The others would not hear
of it. Their attitude was not altogether one of unreasoning intolerance.
Their revival was both national and religious. From the former point
of view, they did not welcome the intrusion of aliens; from the
latter, they were unwilling to endanger their newly purified monotheism by association with elements whose motives and whose
principles were by no means above suspicion. Long residence in
Babylonia, the centre of the civilisation of the age, possibly rendered
them somewhat contemptuous of uncouth provincials. On the other

[1] There is ground for believing that Zerubbabel's ambitions led to a further national
disaster on a large scale, thus explaining the desolate state of the country in the following
century.

hand, the Governor of Samaria no doubt looked with jealousy on the establishment to the south of a centre of authority which might rival his own, and did his utmost to frustrate it.

One may assume yet a further cause of dissension. Those who remained in Palestine during the Captivity would obviously have seized the most fertile vacant estates. The returned exiles, armed with letters-patent from the Persian king authorising them to occupy the country, and actually descended from the former owners, naturally disputed the claims of these 'squatters'. To admit them to participation in the national life would have been tantamount to confirming their claims. It is thus easy to understand the ill-feeling which arose between the two sections, which may well have been agrarian rather than theological in origin.[1]

Whatever the cause, the rival elements systematically obstructed, by fair means and foul, the work of reconstruction. It was due to their intrigues that the rebuilding of the Temple was suspended between 536 and 528: and the recurrent dispute between the neighbours was to remain during the whole of the following century the key-note of Palestinian politics.

It is hardly likely that the country reoccupied by those who returned had been entirely depopulated during the past few generations. There must have been many who had eluded capture and deportation, and who continued to live near their old homes, seeking refuge among the ruins or in the mountain fastnesses whenever an armed force approached. These, presumably, now came into the open, though a differentiation long continued to be drawn between the returned 'children of the captivity' and other elements in the population, whom the former considered their inferiors.[2]

---

[1] Modern critical opinion, indeed, completely discredits the Biblical story of a 'Return' from Babylon, with its corollary of a complete exile: suggesting that the rebuilding of the national centre was due to the population which had remained in the country. The references in contemporary literature to the activities of the 'exiles' returned to Judaea are, however, too numerous, too ingenuous, and too explicit to make this hypothesis at all probable. That a considerable element in the population escaped deportation is by no means unlikely: but they would naturally have gravitated to the northern centre governed from Samaria, to which perhaps they gave something of its importance in Judaean affairs.

[2] With regard to the history of this period, one important consideration, generally overlooked, should be taken into account. It is not seriously disputed that our main sources —the books of Ezra and Nehemiah—do not long post-date the events which they describe. In an Oriental country of retentive memory such as Palestine, it hardly seems likely that, in the brief intervening period, a major falsification or misconception of outstanding events in recent history could have taken place.

Palestine at this time formed part of the Fifth of the twenty Satrapies of the Empire of the Achaemenids—that of Transpotamia, or of the Western Provinces, with its administrative centre at Damascus. This extended from the Orontes to the borders of Egypt, comprising also Syria, Phoenicia, and Cyprus. The colony itself was under the direct rule of a governor, who was subordinate to the sub-satrap of Samaria. The seat of administration was Jerusalem, where he resided in a fortress called the Birah, overlooking the Temple. Those carried into captivity by the Babylonians had belonged to all of the various 'tribes' which had formed the former kingdom. In exile, they had become consolidated around that of Judah, as had indeed been the tendency for some little time before the final tragedy.[1] After the return, they settled down promiscuously. The old territorial distinctions were thus abandoned. Gradually, therefore, the entire population became known as men of Judah (*Yehudim*), or Jews.[2]

The members of the colony were, almost without exception, agriculturists. None were now landless, even the poorest, whose fathers had nothing, receiving allotments. It would appear that the majority of the craftsmen and artisans deported from Jerusalem in 597 had prospered in their new homes. The urban element was thus sparsely represented amongst the immigrants, and Jerusalem was slower than the rest of the territory in becoming resettled. Nevertheless the population of the city gradually increased and it became a centre of trade for the surrounding countryside. Tyrian traders went there regularly, with fish from the Mediterranean and less perishable merchandise. Craftsmen began to ply their trades in the bazaars, especially the goldsmiths and apothecaries (or perfumers), who became organised in rudimentary gilds.

In spite of its manifold difficulties, the colony made gradual progress. The area of settlement gradually increased, extending within

---

[1] The 'language of Judah' (*Yehudit*) is mentioned as early as the reign of Hezekiah (II Kings xviii, 26). After the Return, whereas the people spoke of themselves as 'the children of Judah and Benjamin', their enemies referred to them as 'Jews'. The name thus appears, like so many others, to have been applied contemptuously in the first instance. In the following century we find it used with a somewhat self-conscious pride.

[2] Individual families (quite apart from those of the 'tribe' of Levi, which for special reasons has retained its individuality to the present day) continued to trace their tribal origin as late as the beginning of the Christian era, or even after. Some of them belonged to those tribes formerly included in the northern kingdom. We may deduce from this that the Jews were recruited during the exile by some of those deported previously to the same regions by the Assyrians, or after it by those who remained in the country.

the next generation as far as Bethlehem. It is not improbable that the country contributed its quota to the contingent of 'Syrians from Palestine' who accompanied Xerxes on the disastrous campaign of Salamis in 480. After Zerubbabel's death or deposition, the office of governor was occupied by a succession of Persian officials. Of their policy, we know almost nothing, but it may be assumed that little or nothing was done under their auspices to foster the National Home.

IV

It is fortunate that the Jewish people was not restricted to Palestine. Those who had remained in Babylon probably exceeded in number those who had returned: and they were watching affairs with pathetic eagerness. Political emissaries, casual visitors, returning pilgrims, kept them in touch with local conditions, and the national feeling still alive amongst them resulted every now and again in the migration westwards of some further band of enthusiasts. One of the most memorable of these expeditions took place in the reign of Artaxerxes Longimanus. There was about his court a certain devoted Jew named Nehemiah, who had attained high office as royal cup-bearer. Greatly perturbed by the news brought from Palestine by his brother, Hanani, he obtained permission from the king in 445 to visit Jerusalem, 'the city of his fathers' sepulchres'. Like Sheshbazzar and Zerubbabel before him, he was given full civil authority as *Tirshata*— an office filled during the intervening period by strangers.

Three days after his arrival, the new governor rode round the walls of the city by moonlight, followed by a few retainers. The account which had reached him was accurate in all its details. In consequence of the siege of a century and a half before, or possibly of more recent disturbances, the fortifications were in a state of ruin, the walls being half broken down and the gates lying in ashes. Jerusalem was, in fact, all but an open city, exposed to any onslaught. On the following day, Nehemiah summoned together the principal citizens and informed them of the authority which he had received, and of the measures he proposed to take. His news was greeted enthusiastically; and, led by the priests and craft gilds, the people set themselves energetically to the task of reconstruction, labourers streaming in also from the surrounding countryside and subordinate townships.

The sub-satrap of Samaria, Sanballat, jealously watched while this was going on. Unable to prohibit it, he embarked upon a campaign of obstruction, the devices to which he resorted ranging from accusations of treason, levelled against Nehemiah, to an attempt at his assassination. At one time the devoted band at Jerusalem had to go about their work armed, so as to be prepared against a surprise attack. Nevertheless, despite interruptions, the work of reconstruction was completed in little more than two months, and the walls were dedicated with great solemnity. The area enclosed in the fortifications was sparsely inhabited, the population being insufficient to defend it in case of emergency. It was accordingly agreed that one family out of every ten from the countryside should be selected by lot to live in the capital, though most of them probably continued to cultivate their holdings outside the walls. The inhabitants were organised into watches, and the gates strictly closed each night. The Jewish settlement in Palestine, instead of being an agglomeration of rural colonies, was now the nucleus of a state, with at least one stronghold which might hold an invader at bay.

The security of the capital once assured, Nehemiah threw himself, with the same zeal and organising ability, into the work of moral regeneration. In the long night of the Babylonian Exile, the conception of the 'Law of Moses' had gained a stronger, more intimate hold upon the consciousness of the Jewish people, but it was not yet observed in all its details by the masses. Ezra, a royal scribe of priestly descent, who had led a large party from Mesopotamia thirteen years previous, in 458, had been authorised to make an enquiry into the general state of the country, and to enforce such reforms as he thought fit.[1] In fact he had done little beyond securing the appointment of a commission to enquire into the mixed marriages which had been made,[2] and to enforce the severance of all extraneous family ties.

[1] According to the critical view, the mission of Ezra came (if at all—for his existence has been called into question) either after, or at least during, that of Nehemiah, his work being said to presuppose the other's. History does not always work, however, on so symmetrical a pattern.

For a Jewish colony in Egypt at this time, see below, pp. 87-8.

[2] This phenomenon was perhaps due in part to the fact that the returning settlers comprised, as was inevitable under the circumstances, a disproportionate number of adult males. It is significant that a contemporary puts down as an almost Utopian ideal a Jerusalem in which old men and old women would be seen in the streets, with boys and girls playing at their feet. The dissolution of foreign matrimonial alliances was a drastic step, but perhaps the perpetuation of the individuality of the Jewish people over the intervening two and a half millennia provides its justification. It is curious that, almost contemporaneously, the problem of extramarriage was confronted, in much the same spirit, both in Athens and in Rome.

He had subsequently remained in Jerusalem—burning with enthusiasm for the 'Law' though unable to give effect to his ideals. His zeal was now reinforced by Nehemiah's executive genius.

On the anniversary of the rededication of the altar two generations before, Ezra recited the Law before the assembled people from a pulpit of wood, while a number of Levites (whose function it was to assist the Priests in the Temple worship) collaborated with him in expounding it. The function had an immediate effect. The Feast of Tabernacles, which was only a few days off, was observed with unprecedented zeal. On its conclusion, a special fast was ordained to express the general contrition. Immediately afterwards, the whole of the assembled people entered into a solemn League and Covenant. A formal contract was drawn up, binding all who subscribed to observe certain fundamental prescriptions. To this, the chiefs of all the clans, from the governor himself downwards, affixed their seals. It was a memorable gathering, marking the beginning of the implicit reign of Law over the Jewish people, and it seems to have lived in the popular recollection as the Great Assembly, to which the last of the prophets were supposed to have handed on the torch of tradition.

As ever, religious and social problems were closely interwoven. The period was one of great economic stress. In order to discharge their obligations, many of the proletariat had been compelled to mortgage their holdings to their wealthier brethren. Some insolvent debtors had been made to forfeit their liberty, while impecunious parents sometimes sold their children outright as slaves. The Governor, to whom these complaints were loudly voiced, was quick to sympathise. He summoned a meeting of the notables, whom he upbraided for their rapacity. In consequence, they agreed (not altogether with a good grace) to restore the holdings on which they had foreclosed and to remit henceforth, in accordance with the prescriptions of the Mosaic code, the interest hitherto charged on loans. As a further means of ameliorating the condition of the country, Nehemiah waived his right to the tribute which former governors had exacted, notwithstanding his numerous household and the lavish hospitality which he maintained. Simultaneously, in accordance with the terms of the recent agreement, he rigorously enforced the observance of the Sabbath. From the previous sunset, he kept the gates of Jerusalem closed, setting some of his own retainers in charge; and he took drastic steps to prevent buying and selling from being continued outside the walls.

Nehemiah had been unable to carry all the patrician houses with him in his reforms. When in 433 he was recalled to Susa, after twelve years of unremitting activity, a reaction set in. Close relations were re-established with the rival centre of government at Samaria, with which the Judaean notables were in close and constant communication. Intermarriage had begun again on such a scale that, to patriotic eyes, the existence of the Hebrew language seemed endangered. The High Priest, Eliashib, had permitted one of his grandsons, a certain Menasseh, to marry a daughter of Sanballat, the Governor of Samaria; while the latter's secretary, Tobiah, was permitted to occupy a chamber in the Temple on the occasion of his visits to Jerusalem. Reports regarding this state of affairs brought Nehemiah back to Palestine, after a lengthy absence. He must, by now, have been advanced in years; but he had lost none of his vigour. Tobiah's property was thrown out of the Temple, and the chamber which he had occupied restored to its former use. Menasseh, the arch-offender, was expelled from the community outright. The errant priest, followed by others who shared his views, sought refuge with his wife's kinsfolk in Samaria. Here, under his auspices, the usages of the Temple of Jerusalem were imitated in a rival sanctuary which was now erected on Mount Gerizim. The breach between the Jews and Samaritans thus became complete.

Ezra had died, apparently, in the interval between Nehemiah's first and second visit: according to legend, while on his way to Susa for the purpose of conferring with the Great King. Of Nehemiah's last years nothing more is known, but the memoirs of his activity, incorporated in the Bible, preserve an immortal picture of his pious, forthright character.

V

Jewish tradition has tended to subordinate the name of Nehemiah to that of his colleague, notwithstanding the fact that the latter appears in the original sources as a personality less active, less authoritative, and less distinct. Later literature speaks of Ezra the Scribe almost as a second Moses, and numerous religious institutions of hoary antiquity are traced back to his initiative. There is in this something more than pure fancy. For the essential part of the work of resettlement in Palestine lay not so much in the political as in the literary and spiritual sphere.

The modern critical school ascribes to Ezra, not merely the enforcement, but the redaction and even the authorship of a substantial portion of what subsequently became known as the *Torah*—the Law of Moses. Whether or no this is the case, it remains an indisputable fact that, with Ezra, the reign of the *Torah* over the Jewish people began—enforced, in the first instance, with the aid of the civil authority. It is significant that the institution of the public reading and interpretation of the scriptures is associated traditionally with this period. Houses of prayer were now set up perhaps for the first time in localities distant from the Temple: a practice encouraged by the exigencies of the Babylonian exile.

This was the origin of what was afterwards to be known as the Synagogue, the prototype of the Church on the one hand and of the Mosque on the other—one of Israel's most important contributions to civilisation. Here the *Torah* was not only read, but also expounded. The teacher thus acquired an increasing importance, at first rivalling and then surpassing that of the Priests and Levites who ministered in the Temple. The diffusion of this fundamental literature was aided by the new 'Assyrian' alphabet which had become familiar during the Exile and is still current—an advance upon the angular old Phoenician forms, hitherto universally employed.

The *Torah* was far from being a dry code. It served as the basis of human life and conduct in every branch, and it was constantly scrutinised and rescrutinised for fuller implications. The system, with all its extensions and rigours, came to be adopted with an ungrudging zeal. The Jews had returned from the Exile a rough, half-educated band, carelessly tolerant, indifferent even to the creed of their women-folk. Their religious ideals were concentrated in the Temple worship, and they were ignorant of what were subsequently considered fundamental practices of their faith. The succeeding period is obscure in the extreme. But, when the curtain rises again to its full height, four centuries after the Return, the scene is very different. We find a people fanatically monotheistic, with a faith and a standard of life which mark them off from all other peoples. Each action of their daily existence is governed by their *Torah*, whose every letter and every implication they endeavour to carry into effect. They are distinguished from other men by the rigorous observance of certain religious practices, such as the Sabbath, which are to remain henceforth quintessentially characteristic of them. They came back into Palestine, as it were, still Israelites, at one in essence with their ancestors of the period of the Exodus or of the Monarchy. The work of Ezra and his colleagues converted them into Jews, hardly distinguishable from their descendants of the Middle Ages.

In the traditional view, the memoirs of Nehemiah constituted the last of the canonical books of the Hebrew Bible. The subsequent period was, from the literary standpoint, an utter blank. The modern critical school has endeavoured to amend this impression. What was hitherto considered a period of intellectual quiescence now appears as one of unparalleled literary activity. It is regarded as the period of the final redaction of the Pentateuch: of the composition of literary masterpieces such as the books of Job or Joel, of idylls like Ruth, of poems like the Song of Songs, of narratives such as the book of Jonah, of many of the immortal songs of worship included among the Psalms, of philosophical meditations like Ecclesiastes, and of maxims like those contained in the Book of Proverbs. The question cannot be said, even now, to be finally settled. The account is corrected periodically in points of detail: and serious arguments may be advanced against the thesis as a whole. Nevertheless, the problem must be approached from the standpoint of scientific enquiry, and not of prejudice. The modern view indeed robs many parts of the Old Testament of something of their immemorial antiquity. It compensates, however, by establishing, in the course of the Dark Age which succeeded the return from Babylon, a period of literary activity which makes it comparable, in the annals of human culture, only with the Golden Age of Athens or the Renaissance in Italy.

33. LIGHTING OF THE CANDELABRUM

Chapter VII

THE STRUGGLE AGAINST HELLENISM

———————— • ————————

I

From the close of the period of Nehemiah's activity, an almost
complete darkness falls upon Palestinian affairs. Within the
country, it was a period of consolidation. In political affairs, we
read of the succession of High Priests. We are informed of a persecution throughout the Persian Empire which was foiled through the
influence at court, of a Jewish woman, named Esther. On the death
of Cambyses (the successor of Darius the Great) in 485, Assyria and
Egypt rose against the Persian yoke; and, whether Palestine was
involved in the rebellion or not, there can be no doubt that the
country must temporarily have been thrown into turmoil. Any hopes
of independence which Nehemiah's successive nominations may have
aroused were nullified by the appointment as his successor of a
Persian official named Bagohi.[1] About this time, a dispute for the
High Priesthood resulted in the perpetration of a murder in the
Temple itself, and the consequent intervention of the civil power.
In 365 there took place a revolt of the Phoenician cities, which was
put down only some fifteen years later, but we have no inkling as to
whether the Jews were implicated in this or no. Thirty years later,
Alexander of Macedon descended like a whirlwind on Asia, and the
Persian Empire collapsed before his onslaught.

An old legend, which tells how the conqueror was appeased by a
visit from the High Priest while preparing to march on Jerusalem, is
indicative of the pacific acceptance of the new regime by the Jews of
Palestine. On the death of the great conqueror, his empire fell to
pieces. His principal generals (known to history as the *Diadochi*, or
'successors') quarrelled fiercely amongst themselves for control,
either of the whole or of some fragment. In 320, three years after

---

[1] It appears probable that Bagohi was the governor of Samaria, Judaea being now
subordinated completely to that province.

34. PERSIAN SOLDIERS
Enamelled Brick Panels from Susa, now in the Louvre, Paris

35. Entrance to the Fortress of Hyrcanus, son of Joseph, in Arak-el-Emir, Transjordan (Reconstruction.) About 180 B.C.

Alexander's death, Ptolemy, who had taken possession of Egypt, invaded Palestine and appeared before Jerusalem. It happened to be the Sabbath. The children of those who barely a century before had been compelled by a display of force to observe the day of rest were now so far altered that they would do nothing even to defend themselves on that occasion, and the city was occupied without resistance. After five years of rule, Ptolemy was compelled to evacuate the country to Antigonus, ruler of Asia Minor, the fortifications of Jerusalem and other strongholds being razed to the ground before his departure. The battle of Gaza in 312 restored the control of Palestine to the southern power. At this period, many of the inhabitants were deported to Egypt—the beginning of the intensive Jewish settlement in that country.

The war of the Diadochi was ended by the Battle of the Kings (fought near Ipsus in 301), which cost Antigonus his life and established Ptolemy definitely in Palestine. The latter's ally, Seleucus, was henceforth master of Syria, which he ruled from Antioch. Once more, Judaea lay between rival powers to the north and south, constantly struggling for supremacy.

Of the internal history of the Jewish people at this period we still know very little. The Ptolemies who succeeded one another on the Egyptian throne shewed themselves kindly and tolerant rulers, content to allow Judaea almost complete autonomy, subject only to the payment of a moderate annual tribute. It was, according to an ancient legend, under the auspices of the second of the dynasty, Ptolemy Philadelphus (285-247), that the Bible was translated into Greek by seventy elders sent from Palestine—the so-called 'Septuagint' version.[1] The son of this monarch, Ptolemy Euergetes I (247-222), is said to have visited Jerusalem and offered sacrifice in the Temple. The absence of any other authority in the political sphere crystallised national sentiment increasingly around the person of the High Priest. We read at this period of one, Simon, called the Just, who represented to later ages the ideal leader and teacher, and was considered the prototype of the Rabbi of subsequent generations.

After his death, the sacerdotal office became more and more political in character. In the course of the following generation, two parties rose in the state: one led by the High Priest, and the other (which apparently comprised the wealthy patricians) by the family of a certain Tobias, who farmed the taxes and enjoyed the favour of the

[1] See below, p. 89.

E

Egyptian court. There were occasional clashes between the two, and even outbursts of violence. Palestine seemed to be developing on the lines of a Greek city-state of the period, a prey to opposing factions, and lorded over by a 'tyrant' of one or another predominant clan.

Meanwhile war had been carried on intermittently between the Ptolemies and the house of Seleucus. For brief periods (295, 219-217, 202) the latter managed to occupy Palestine. The Ptolemies always succeeded in resuming control until 198, when Antiochus the Great secured an overwhelming victory over the Egyptian forces at Paneas, near the sources of the Jordan, and the country passed definitely under Seleucid rule.

II

Not long after, in 175, Antiochus IV ascended the throne of Seleucus. He had been born in Athens and was intensely proud of the fact that he had once been elected chief magistrate of that famous city. This strengthened to an inordinate degree his naturally keen admiration for Greek culture, which represented to his mind the acme of human progress and perfection. It became the object of his life to 'civilise' his dominions, as he considered it, by the introduction of Hellenic standards of life; and the shallow, unbalanced nature, which caused him to assume the name of *Epiphanes* ('the illustrious' or 'god manifest'), converted this ambition into something little less than a mania.

Conditions throughout his empire, under these circumstances, became very similar to those in the more backward colonies of the European powers in the nineteenth and twentieth centuries. The native population avidly adopted all the superficial characteristics of its conquerors, their language, their costume, their architecture, their diversions, their social and domestic habits—under the impression that this constituted the essential part of a civilisation greater, because materially more powerful, than their own. The tendency had been present ever since the days of Alexander the Great: henceforth, under royal direction, the process penetrated into every corner of the state, and made feverish progress.

Jerusalem, of course, was not immune. Here, the section headed by the High Priest Onias III, a descendant of Simon the Just, was nationalistic: scrupulously orthodox in matters of traditional practice and strenuously opposed to assimilation. His opponents, therefore, put themselves at the head of those who favoured the policy of the house of Seleucus. They looked sympathetically towards Greek culture; slavishly followed the usages of their masters in their mode of life, clothing, nomenclature, language, and customs; and were prepared to temporise even in matters of religion. The High Priest's brother, Jason, hoping to profit from the suspicion with which the former was now regarded at court, joined the party of assimilation, and by promising a larger tribute (a fatal precedent) he succeeded in having himself installed in the supreme dignity in his brother's place.

Under Jason's rule, the process of Hellenisation made further strides. Nothing was left undone to convert Jerusalem into a Greek city. Buildings were constructed in the Hellenic style. A gymnasium was established in the shadow of the citadel, in which—an abomination in Jewish eyes—young men exercised naked. Priests neglected their duties in the Temple to join in the fashionable craze. Greek names became common, or the old Hebraic ones were transmuted. When, in 170, Antiochus was hovering about the Egyptian border with his army, he shewed his approval by visiting Jerusalem, where a torchlight procession was organised in his honour. As a special sign of favour, the citizens were authorised to call themselves, after their sovereign, by the name of 'Antiochites'.

Yet the infiltration was not going rapidly or deeply enough for the king, who, after his visit, resented all the more the fact that religious separatism continued. The opportunity soon came for him to take a further step. A dispute broke out in the dominant party at Jerusalem between Jason and a certain Menelaus, a member of the tribe of Benjamin and hitherto his closest associate. The latter's insatiable ambition would not be satisfied with any but the highest place. The Priesthood was confined by old prescriptive right to the *Cohen*, traditionally descended from Aaron, Moses' brother. Nevertheless, by means of a court intrigue, backed up by the promise of a yet higher tribute, Menelaus secured the deposition of Jason, and his own nomination to office. To support his authority, a Greek garrison, with its heathen rites and its open contempt of local customs, was installed in the citadel at Jerusalem.

Hellenisation now went on with redoubled energy and comprehensiveness. Under the new High Priest, not even religious matters were immune; and discontent, aggravated by the merciless demands of the royal treasury, seethed more and more deeply. When a couple of years later Antiochus invaded Egypt, Jason, the deposed High Priest, raised a force in Transjordania and made a raid on Jerusalem. Aided by the government troops, Menelaus beat off the attack. The episode was enough to convince Antiochus that the Jewish people favoured his enemies. On his homeward march he passed through Jerusalem. More blood flowed in the streets. Worse still, the High Priest himself conducted the tyrant into the Temple, which was systematically despoiled of its remaining treasures.

The following winter saw a second campaign against Egypt. The Syrian forces appeared to be on the point of victory, when news arrived of the defeat of the King of Macedon by the Romans at the battle of Pydna. This plainly signified that another state, which would not allow the balance of power to be disturbed, had risen to a position of supremacy in the Near East. There followed the famous scene outside Alexandria, when the Roman envoy demanded from the reluctant Antiochus, before he stirred from a circle drawn round him in the ground, an undertaking to evacuate Egypt. There was no sane alternative but to consent. His heart filled with bitterness, Antiochus withdrew his army ingloriously northward (168).

It was natural for his mind to turn, at this juncture, to Palestine. If Egypt was to be maintained in perpetuity as a rival power, it became all the more important that the southern outpost of the Syrian Empire should be thoroughly organised as a Seleucid province. As he marched northward, Antiochus detached his general, Apollonius, to occupy Jerusalem. He was admitted without difficulty. On the following Sabbath (when, as he had heard, the Jews would not resist) he turned his forces on the population. Large numbers of inoffensive persons who belonged to the faction opposed to Menelaus were butchered, while others were sold into slavery. The city walls were razed to the ground. On the site of the citadel of David, a new fortress, known as the Acra, was constructed, to hold the city in check. It was garrisoned with a large force, and a Phrygian named Philip was installed as governor, to carry out the new policy.

After these preliminaries, a systematic attempt was begun to Hellenise the country by force. No form of separatism was henceforth to be permitted. A proclamation was issued which ordered the fusion of all the nationalities of the empire, without exception, into one people, and the general acceptance of the Greek deities. An elderly Athenian philosopher was despatched to Jerusalem to supervise the enforcement of the new order. It pleased his fancy to identify the God of the Jews with the Olympian Jove. A bearded image of this pagan deity, perhaps in the likeness of Antiochus himself, was set up upon the altar: and the Jews were informed that this was the God of Heaven whom they were henceforth to revere. Amongst themselves, they referred to it with a shudder of horror as the Abomination of Desolation.

The courts of the Temple were thronged with Greek soldiers and their paramours, performing the licentious heathen rites. To increase the horror of pious Jews, swine were sacrificed on the altar. In various provincial centres, shrines to lesser deities were set up. Every month, in celebration of the king's birth, a pagan festivity was held in which the Jews had perforce to participate. On the feast of Bacchus, they were compelled to take part, crowned with ivy leaves, in a drunken procession. On the other hand, the observance of any of the practices of the Jewish religion was made a capital offence. The sacred scrolls in which the Law of Moses was written were destroyed or defiled whenever they were found. Special watch was kept for such as observed the Sabbath and festivals, or practised the rite of circumcision.

All this was enforced with the utmost harshness. Two mothers, who had circumcised their new-born children, were driven through the city with their babes hanging at their breasts, and were then cast headlong from the wall. An aged scribe named Eleazar, who refused to eat swine's flesh, was flogged to death. On one occasion a mother and her seven children were successively butchered, in the presence of the governor, for refusing to pay homage to an image. Similar scenes were to be witnessed throughout the Seleucid dominions, wherever Jews were to be found. Even in Samaria the temple on Mount Gerizim was converted into a shrine to Jupiter Xenius, the Defender of Strangers. The usurper Menelaus meanwhile continued in office at Jerusalem, serving Jupiter (with whatever qualms or reservations) as he had formerly administered to the invisible God of his fathers.

The Jews were, as yet, an obscure people, insignificant as far as numbers were concerned. They had shewn themselves, during the course of the past four centuries, unusually submissive. Antiochus, however, had attacked the thing they had held most sacred. His attempt to Hellenise the country, successful up to a certain point, broke against this obstacle. There was a minority only of complete assimilationists who were willing to accede. But those who had been unwilling to adopt Hellenic customs and habits even in non-essential matters stood out defiantly against this attempt to interfere with what they regarded as their holy of holies, and even amongst former Hellenisers there were many who refused to go to this extreme. The lead was taken by an old priest of the house of Hasmon, named Mattathias, whose family possessions lay at Modein, between Jerusalem and the sea-coast. The occasion was the setting up at this place of a pagan altar, on which the assembled populace was expected to sacrifice. As one of the local notables went up to set the example, Mattathias cut him down. Then, with his five sons, he turned against the royal commissioner, who shared the same fate. After destroying the altar, they escaped into the hills followed by the more intransigent element in the population, and raised the standard of revolt.

III

Around the old priest, in the mountain fastnesses of Judaea, there gradually gathered a considerable band of malcontents—*Hassidim*, as they called themselves; the 'pious', who refused to contaminate themselves by the worship of idols. At intervals, sweeping down by night into the valleys, they made raids on the country towns and villages, where they killed the royal officers and the Hellenising Jews who supported them. The Greeks had mastered one simple piece of strategy for use in this campaign against the Jews: to fight against them on that day when they would not defend themselves. One Sabbath, one of the insurgent bands found itself surrounded, and was cut down to a man rather than lift a finger in self-defence. It was obvious that, were this precedent always followed, the suppression of the revolt would be only a matter of time. Mattathias was strong enough to override the accepted religious standard, and gave his followers instructions that fighting in self-defence was to be regarded as permissible even upon the divinely ordained day of rest. This rule of practice henceforth prevailed.

The Hasmonaean revolt followed the lines of so many other successful movements of the sort in the world's history. The rebels would probably have been unable to hold out had their oppressors put forward their full strength. At the beginning, however, the government refused to take the menace seriously. Hence, the patriots were able to score some notable successes (the importance of which was exaggerated in subsequent legend) against minor detachments which were marching light-heartedly against them. Once or twice they even managed to ambush more important bodies, the defeat of which supplied them not only with training and confidence, but also with weapons. When the government at last realised the importance of the movement and put an adequate army into the field, the country was reoccupied without difficulty. But it was impossible to follow the insurgents into their native hill-fastnesses, where they knew the ground minutely and could count upon the sympathy of the entire population, and each successive attempt to do so ended in disaster. And so the Syrians were driven to adopt the policy which many another government has done under similar circumstances. A truce was concluded which conceded a great part of the demands of the rebels and satisfied the more moderate elements. From now, the patriotic leaders consolidated their positon: sometimes by force of arms and sometimes by shrewd bargaining, in which they took advantage of every temporary weakness or embarrassment of their former tyrants. Belated attempts to suppress them would meet with much the same result as at the outset: until, from weariness rather than compulsion, and as the result of negotiation rather than of military force, the Syrians were at last forced to concede complete independence.

The movement was peculiarly fortunate in its leaders. It is not often that history can shew in one family such examples of perfect devotion and self-sacrifice as that of the Hasmonaean brothers, who followed Mattathias as leaders of the revolt. Three in succession were at the head of the Jewish state. Two fell valiantly in the field, under circumstances of exceptional gallantry; another was ambushed at a dark period in his people's fortunes; another put to death in cold blood by the national enemy; the survivor murdered for dynastic reasons. Of the five, not one died a natural death.

Mattathias had passed away not long after he raised the standard of revolt. On his death-bed, he advised his followers to choose as their military leader his third son, Judah, known as the Maccabee.[1] The insurgents were never overwhelmed, and on more than one occasion, by surprise attack, they cut to pieces the forces sent

---

[1] The generally accepted derivation of this word is from *Makkabah*, a hammer, the name being thus a close parallel to that of Charles Martel in European history. A recent hypothesis suggests that it is an allusion to Isaiah lxii, 2, meaning thus 'He who is named by the Lord'. The other Hasmonaean brothers (not, properly speaking, 'Maccabees') had similar titles. The name 'Judah' is used here instead of the usual, but in the case of this patriotic leader unjustifiable, Greek form 'Judas'.

against them. Such an engagement, brilliant though not decisive, took place in the pass of Emmaus in 165, when an army led by Gorgias was almost annihilated while endeavouring to penetrate to Jerusalem. Larger and better-equipped forces were proof against such checks, but were unable to follow Judah into the hill-country and so finally suppress the revolt. While Antiochus was absent on his last campaign in Parthia in 164 B.C., Lysias, who had been left behind as Regent, suffered a severe check in an attempt to reach Jerusalem from the south. He accordingly attempted to pacify the country by adopting a more moderate policy. An edict was issued restoring liberty of worship. Judah was permitted to reoccupy Jerusalem. The Temple was cleansed, the pagan altars were destroyed, and on 25th Kislev— the same date on which pagan worship had been instituted three years before—the sacred edifice was rededicated to its original usage. It was the date of the winter solstice, and, with the annual feast of dedication, or *Hanukah*, there has ever since been associated the kindling of lights characteristic of the primitive celebration of this day.[1]

IV

Victory on the main issue had been won. The practice of Judaism in its traditional form was once more legalised. However, the revolt had altered and extended in scope. From one purely religious in inspiration it had become in some measure political. The persecution had brought about a revival of national spirit. For the first time since the Exile, a movement for complete independence developed. Emboldened by success, Judah embarked on wider activities. Taking advantage of the disorders which succeeded the death of Antiochus Epiphanes in 163, he made a number of raids in all directions in retaliation for the maltreatment of his co-religionists during the recent persecutions. Finally he made preparations for assaulting the citadel of Jerusalem, still held by its Greek garrison. Lysias, who maintained a precarious tenure as Regent of the realm, had no choice but to intervene. It was in vain that Judah flung himself upon the Syrian forces at Beth Zechariah, to the south of Jerusalem, where one of the Hasmonaean brothers was left on the field of battle. Disaster

---

[1] The traditional view, that Judah occupied Jerusalem by force after a signal victory over Lysias, hardly seems to be borne out by the actual circumstances. The fact that Menelaus appears to have continued to function as High Priest even after the reoccupation of the capital adds to the improbability of the story.

appeared imminent; but domestic difficulties summoned Lysias back to Syria and so saved the situation. A compromise was arranged. The High Priest Menelaus was sent back to Antioch, where he was tried and put to death; and a certain Eliakim, or Alcimus, who at least had the qualification of Aaronic descent, was appointed his successor.

Alcimus, a Helleniser who was accused of having polluted himself with pagan practices, proved unacceptable to the mass of the people. Judah was the popular idol: and, immediately the Syrian forces had withdrawn, the new High Priest found himself unable to exercise his functions. He appealed to Demetrius Soter, who had seized the throne of Syria in 162. A strong force was despatched south under his general, Bacchides, who had no difficulty in reinstating the Syrian nominee. Immediately he left the country, discontent flared up again: and Judah scored, near Beth Horon, a signal success over Nicanor, commander of the elephant corps, which was long commemorated amongst the Jews as a public holiday.

This check was too great for Syrian pride to overlook. A month later, Bacchides was back again in Judaea with an overwhelming force. Judah, followed by a handful of barely eight hundred men, threw himself in the path of the invaders at Elasa, north of Beth Horon, but unsuccessfully. His little band was overwhelmed, and he himself died fighting. He had been leader of the insurgents for about five years. Under his guidance, the Jewish people had gained sufficient confidence to be able to envisage an encounter with the Syrian troops in the field. Above all, the resistance which he had inspired had shewn the danger of interference with the practice of Judaism. After his death, therefore, though the overthrow of the Jewish people was actually more complete than ever before, the Seleucid government did not venture to repeat the disastrous experiment of Antiochus, though all vestiges of political independence were again suppressed. The surviving Hasmonaean brothers withdrew to the expanses beyond the Jordan with their few remaining followers. The eldest, John, was waylaid and killed by some unfriendly tribesmen, while attempting to convey the baggage to the Nabataean Arabs for custody. There remained only Simon, the second brother, and Jonathan, the youngest, who took over the military command.

A year later, Alcimus died. For the moment, the office which he had occupied was left vacant. Not long after, Bacchides, having apparently succeeded in pacifying Palestine, returned to Syria. As soon as his back was turned, the country relapsed into disorder, and he came again. After a futile attempt to follow the insurgents beyond the Jordan, he arrived at the conclusion (as Lysias had done before him) that the best course was to conclude a pacific arrangement with them. A truce was therefore arranged, the rebel leaders being permitted to return unmolested on condition that they disbanded their forces and did not approach Jerusalem. Jonathan therefore established himself at Michmash, where his camp became once more the centre of the patriotic sentiment. In the absence of any superior authority, he developed from a proscribed rebel into an independent ruler, dominating all Judaea outside the capital.

V

It was a dynastic dispute which gave the opportunity for the final step. As the reign of Demetrius Soter had progressed, his difficulties increased. A youth named Alexander Balas, who bore a remarkable physical resemblance to the dead Antiochus Epiphanes, gave himself out to be that monarch's son. With powerful foreign support, he made a bid for the throne, and civil disturbances continued to rack the country over a long period. Both factions now endeavoured to obtain the assistance of the Judaean military chieftain and his veterans. Gifts, titles, honours, privileges, bribes, were showered upon him by both sides. By careful fishing in the ever-troubled waters, he received constant accretions of territory until he became the master of nearly the whole of Palestine. Good fortune constantly smiled upon his arms. He captured Jaffa, Ascalon, and Ashdod, where he burned the Temple of Dagon over the heads of the fugitives who had crowded into it. But his successes in diplomacy were even more remarkable than his victories in the field. Whatever party was in the ascendant, he managed to retain its friendship, and to have yet further gifts and privileges laid at his feet. Almost at the outset he was authorised by Demetrius to enter Jerusalem, and invested with the vacant office of High Priest, with all the religious and political authority which it implied. He was thus officially recognised as the head of the Jewish state, and on the Feast of Tabernacles in 152 he officiated in the Temple for the first time. After a few years, nothing but a tribute of 300 talents yearly, and the continued presence of the Greek garrison in the Acra, remained to recall the nominal suzerainty of a foreign power. The friendly relations which continued with the Syrian Court were exemplified by the loan of a detachment of Hasmonaean veterans to reinforce the royal guards at Antioch.

In the end this triumphant progress aroused the jealousy of Tryphon, the unscrupulous military leader who, for the moment, dominated Syrian affairs. The latter attempted to secure by treachery what his more capable predecessors had been unable to do by force of arms. He lured Jonathan to meet him for a friendly conference at Ptolemais, where he had him seized, ultimately putting him to death. But, owing to the unique devotion and ability of the Hasmonaean brothers, this act failed of its effect. Simon, the last survivor of Mattathias' five sons, automatically took over the command. In retaliation for his brother's treatment, he seized the city of Jaffa, and (thanks to a providential snow-fall) was able to prevent Tryphon from marching on Jerusalem. When the latter declared himself sovereign, in 142, Simon had ample excuse for withdrawing the titular allegiance which had hitherto been continued to the successive Syrian rulers. Accordingly he offered his support to Demetrius, the rival claimant to the throne, in return for a general amnesty and immunity from all future tribute. The latter was happy to comply. Even the Acra was at last evacuated by the Greek troops; and it was entered by the national forces, amid delirious scenes of rejoicing, in the summer of 141. In the autumn of the following year, Simon's title was approved by an assembly at Jerusalem, which confirmed him in the offices of High Priest, Prince, and military commander, henceforth to be hereditary in his house.

The Syrians did not abandon all hope of regaining their lost influence. In 138 Antiochus VII (Sidetes), the last strong representative of the house of Seleucus, endeavoured to reimpose the tribute and to obtain the evacuation of the recent territorial acquisitions. His forces were heavily defeated by John Hyrcanus, the old High Priest's son. Two years later, Simon was assassinated by his son-in-law, Ptolemy, whom he had appointed governor of Jericho, and the reins of government were assumed by his warlike heir. Antiochus, considering the moment ripe for another attempt, again marched upon Jerusalem, and, after a lengthy siege, reduced the city. Thanks to the intervention of the Romans (the advancing power with which successive members of the Hasmonaean house had been careful to maintain friendly relations), he did not push his victory to an extreme. Though he insisted on the reassertion of his suzerain rights and the payment of an indemnity, he allowed John Hyrcanus to continue in office as a feudatory prince, and even permitted the retention of recent conquests. It seemed as though the interlude of independence of the past ten years had been no more than a passing phase. But not long after, in 129, Antiochus was killed in battle against the Parthians. The Seleucid Empire fell to pieces in a final maze of civil war, and John Hyrcanus was able to resume the independent status which his father had won and enjoyed. It was the beginning of a brief golden age of political freedom which was to last for some two-thirds of a century.

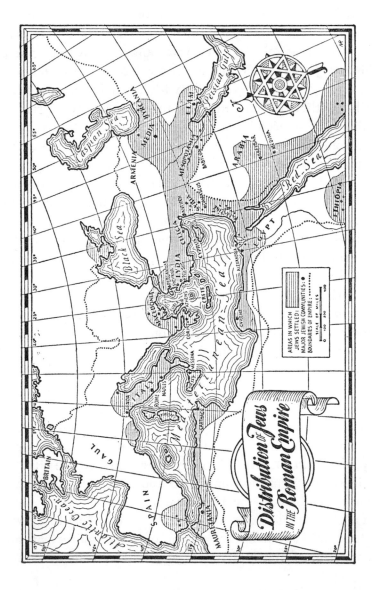

Distribution of Jews in the Roman Empire

Chapter VIII

THE HASMONAEAN STATE

———————————— • ————————————

I

With the long hegemony of John Hyrcanus (135-104) a period of national expansion, of unique importance in the growth of the Jewish people, reached its climax. So strongly localised geographically had they still been at the beginning of the second century B.C. that the Greek historian Polybius could speak of them as 'those who lie round about the sanctuary called Jerusalem'. During the course of the generations that had elapsed since the Return, the population of Judaea had indeed become consolidated, and even pushed out colonies into some of the surrounding areas— particularly, as will be seen later,[1] into Egypt. But, with this solitary exception, these offshoots were of no great importance. After his occupation of Jerusalem, Judah the Maccabee had made it his business to succour these national outposts, which had suffered at the hands of their Gentile neighbours during the recent period of stress. So exiguous were they in point of number that he was able to remove the entire Jewish population from Galilee and Transjordania *en masse* and bring it back into Judaea with him. His policy was therefore essentially one of concentration.

His brothers were more aggressive and more ambitious, and they set themselves deliberately to extend the territories under their rule. They followed the harsh standards of warfare which prevailed universally at that period. Conquered peoples could expect little consideration from their hands. In many cases, they were expelled; in others, they were forcibly converted to Judaism. However, the facility with which they accepted their new religion, and the fidelity with which they afterwards retained it, seem to indicate that the ground was already well prepared. Jonathan, by his skilful bargaining, had succeeded in annexing to his dominions Ekron and other places

[1] Below, p. 88 *sqq.*

(77)

on the coast, as well as three districts of Samaria. To these acquisitions Simon added the important seaport of Jaffa (from which he expelled the Gentile inhabitants), and Gezer, which guards the approaches into Judaea from the south-west.[1]

Under John Hyrcanus expansion became the key-note of national policy. He pushed forward the frontiers of the state on every side. East of the Jordan he occupied Medeba and the adjacent territory. A sharp campaign subjected the Samaritans, whose sanctuary on Mount Gerizim was destroyed. The city of Samaria, now among the greatest Hellenic centres in Palestine, was captured and obliterated, notwithstanding Syrian efforts to create a diversion; and legend recounts how the High Priest, while officiating at the altar, suddenly became aware that victory had been achieved by his sons. Another wealthy Greek centre, Beth Shean (Scythopolis), the most important member of the league known as the Ten Cities, or Decapolis, was occupied without opposition. To the south the policy followed was more energetic still. The age-long enmity between the Jews and Idumaeans (Edomites), which had found its expression in the raids of Judah the Maccabee, culminated in the final subjection of the country, the inhabitants of which were compelled to accept the Jewish religion.

The death of John Hyrcanus, in 104, was followed by a dynastic struggle between his children. His eldest son, Judah, or Aristobulus, succeeded him, assuming the title of King. In his short reign, of only one year, he extended the boundaries of the state even further to the north, conquering the rest of Galilee and part of the territory about Mount Lebanon, which he forcibly Judaised. He was followed on the throne by his able but unscrupulous brother, Alexander Jannaeus, or Jannai (103-76). The campaigns of this sovereign were not uniformly successful. Nevertheless he was able to extend his frontiers along the Philistine coast, towards the frontiers of Egypt, and above all, on the other side of Jordan.

The Jewish state now rivalled or exceeded in size what had hitherto been its greatest extension, in the glorious days of David or of Solomon. It comprised the whole of Palestine proper and the adjacent territories, from the Lake of Merom down to the borders of Egypt. On the east it embraced wide areas in Transjordania, known as Perea: on the west it included, with the exception of Ascalon, almost the whole of the coastal plain, over which the old Israelitish kingdoms

---

[1] On a potsherd found in the ruins of this city there is scratched a rude inscription calling down a curse upon the conqueror's newly built palace.

had never been able to establish control. Ships sculptured on the family tomb of the Hasmonaeans near Modein, and depicted on the coins minted by successive rulers, indicated the maritime ambitions of the dynasty. The kingdom was not by any means homogeneous. Here and there were Greek cities, such as Apollonia or Scythopolis, with only a small Jewish element amongst their population. The Samaritans, in spite of their complete overthrow, continued to resist assimilation. But other parts of the country became completely Judaised, their inhabitants being counted henceforth an integral part of the Jewish people. The Edomites, hereditary enemies for untold generations, came to exercise an important, and at times preponderant, influence upon internal affairs. Fertile Galilee was reckoned from this time one of the principal centres of Judaism, whether from the point of view of numbers, of sentiment, or of devotion: though here old Israelitish elements, with lingering recollections of their ancestral faith, may perhaps have been reincorporated into the population. Within a century of the Hasmonaean revolt, the area of the Jewish state was increased perhaps tenfold, and its population in proportion. It is from the ethnic group formed in these years that the Jewish people of to-day is predominantly descended.

II

In the course of this period there had been an increasing rift between the ruling house and certain elements of their subjects. The Hasmonaean brothers had risen to power as the leaders of a popular revolt. The hereditary principality had been conferred upon the house by 'the great congregation of the priests and people and rulers of the nation and elders of the country'—perhaps identical with the body afterwards known as the Sanhedrin—while the early coinage bore, in addition to the name of the ruler, an allusion to the council, or commonwealth (*Heber*), of the Jews. The elements at least of democratic theory were thus alive.

After the return from Exile, the highest authority in the Jewish state had been the High Priest, whose influence had been exercised solely by virtue of his spiritual office. The assumption of the title of King by Judah Aristobulus and his successors introduced a completely fresh element into the constitution. By immemorial tradition, royalty was restricted to the house of David. This conception was not yet perhaps so widely spread as was afterwards to be the case. Nevertheless, by the amalgamation of the royal rank with that of High Priest, the rulers of the new dynasty became invested with a power which, even in the heroic days of the Israelitish kingdom, had been unknown.

A powerful section of the people objected to this overwhelming concentration of authority in the hands of one person. They had been willing to fight for their religious identity. Political independence, on the other hand, had been a remote memory for so long that they attached no great importance to it—indeed, a representative gathering of *Hassidim*, the 'pious' who had been the backbone of the Hasmonaean revolt, had formally confirmed the appointment of the temporising Alcimus as High Priest. When the monarchy was established, and the abuses inherent in the institution shewed themselves, some of these elements began to recall almost with regret the passing of the conditions which had previously prevailed and to look forward with resignation, or sometimes with eagerness, to foreign intervention and the re-establishment of Gentile hegemony in the political sphere.

The Hasmonaean dynasty could of course count upon the support of the priestly element—powerful, wealthy, and cultured. On the other hand, opposition to the priesthood had grown in recent years. In the period of the First Temple, and even after the return from Exile, its members had been regarded as the official depositories of learning and tradition. It was their task to interpret the *Torah* and to formulate decisions in any difficult point of law and practice. But, since the days of Ezra, the *Torah* had been the property of the whole people. It had been publicly read and expounded at frequent intervals in every town and village, and the deference previously centred about the Priests had come to be given to any person who shewed himself a skilful exponent of Holy Writ ('*Rabbi*', or 'My Master', such a person would be called, deferentially, by his disciples). Tradition had gradually broadened, from precedent to precedent; the decisions or practices of one Rabbi served as guidance for successive generations; a considerable body of oral tradition grew up to reinforce or supplement or clarify the Biblical text; fresh ideas were assimilated and given a Jewish tinge.

Thus there had come into existence a body of teaching more modern, more pliable, more living, than that which the Temple priesthood could provide. The interpretation of the Bible, as the Rabbis conceived it, was less stereotyped; their legal decisions tended to be milder; and they did not scruple even to circumvent the strict letter of the *Torah* by transparent legal fictions. Comfort for the vicissitudes of this world was found in the doctrine of the immortality of the soul and the resurrection of the dead, which the priests (not finding any specific Biblical authority for it) strenuously denied. In points of practice, their respective legal decisions reflected the divergent interests of the two classes—the land-owning aristocracy on the one hand, and the artisans and yeomen on the other.

Two parties had thus developed in the state—one of them looking to the Temple as the centre of instruction as well as of sacrificial worship, while the other sought enlightenment wherever it might be found. The one was essentially conservative, and the other eclectic, in point of doctrine and practice. The one was recruited especially from the priesthood, backed up by the aristocracy and landowners, and the other amongst the lower and middle classes. The former supported the absolute monarchy, vested in the hereditary High Priests, whereas the latter tended to be democratic. Gradually the one party came to be known after the priestly house of Zadok, ancestors of the Hasmonaeans, as *Zadukim*, or Sadducees, while the others were given the name of *Perushim* (Pharisees), or Seceders.[1]

III

While the Hasmonaean dynasty retained its primitive simplicity, and the danger from without remained threatening, national unity continued to be maintained. Towards the close of the reign of John Hyrcanus, the character of the ruling house began to deteriorate. Rabbinical tradition speaks wistfully of the change in this ruler, who 'served in the High Priesthood for seventy years, but in the end became a Sadducee.' His successor, King Aristobulus, aped Greek customs, and plunged into an unnatural palace feud which resulted in the imprisonment of his mother and the murder of his brother. Alexander Jannai himself acted in the manner of an Oriental despot— unscrupulous, bloodthirsty, and passionate: and he maintained his

---

[1] These are the most probable, though by no means the only, derivations suggested for the two terms. But the precise etymology is unimportant, as in all history the names of parties tend to be derived from incidental details of little or no significance. (Cf., in English and American history, the titles of Whigs and Tories.) That the difference between the sects was essentially political in origin rather than theological, turning about the method of interpreting the Law, is probable from the bitterness of the feeling between them, and the part which they played in the affairs of state. Rabbis of a later generation naturally viewed the dispute from their more specific angle.

The semi-monastic sect of this period, the Essenes, played no part in political affairs; and too little is known about them with certainty to justify a detailed account here.

F

authority by the swords of foreign mercenaries. It was in his reign that the final rift occurred.

At a banquet given on the return of the king from a triumphant military expedition, a Pharisee leader openly bade him dissociate the civil and religious functions which he enjoyed, giving up either the one or the other; and a legal justification, of an unflattering nature, was found for questioning his actual right to the priesthood. On a succeeding feast of Tabernacles, while he was officiating in the Temple, the King-Priest retaliated by publicly expressing his contempt of Pharisaic teaching, pouring out the libation of water at his feet instead of on the altar: a trivial point, but one which indicated his attitude towards new ceremonial not prescribed in the Pentateuch. The people, enraged, pelted him with the citrons which they were carrying in honour of the feast, and order was restored only after much bloodshed. Several of the Pharisee leaders fled from the country.[1]

The discontent smouldered until, in 94, Alexander returned, discredited, after an unsuccessful campaign. Popular feeling again flared up. Jerusalem rose in rebellion. For six years civil war raged ferociously. The Pharisee insurgents were no match for the king's hardened mercenaries. In spite of this, they refused to come to terms; and, preferring alien rule to the arbitrary oppression of one of their own people, they appealed for help to Demetrius III, ruler of Syria for the time being. Alexander was overwhelmingly defeated. But as so often happens in such cases, his misfortunes caused a revulsion of feeling in his favour, and in the end the invaders were forced to withdraw. The king profited from the change in popular sentiment by hounding down his domestic enemies, on whom (notwithstanding a protracted and tenacious resistance) he avenged himself ferociously. During the last few years of his reign opposition was crushed. Realising, however, that it would not be easy for a ruler less vigorous than himself to maintain his position without the support of all elements, on his death-bed he advised, as a cardinal point of policy, that reconciliation should be attempted.

Alexander Jannai was succeeded by his wife, Salome Alexandra (76-67), who had formerly been married to his brother, Judah Aristobulus. Her brother, Simeon ben Shetah, was one of the leaders of the Pharisee party, and she was accordingly all the more inclined to follow her husband's advice. The fact of her accession illustrates

---

[1] Another account places this episode in the reign of John Hyrcanus, Jannai's father.

the high status of woman in Jewish life of the period,[1] for neither of her two sons was so young as to justify a regency. The elder, Hyrcanus, who was of an inactive and accommodating temperament, was invested with the office of High Priest; the younger, Aristobulus, received the military command. Salome's seven years of rule were peaceful by comparison with the constant warfare of the previous reigns. Aristobulus led an expedition against Damascus, but without result. On the other hand, an invasion menaced by Tigranes, King of Armenia, was averted by a judicious admixture of bribes and diplomacy.

The elderly queen (she was nearly seventy years of age at the time of her accession) managed to maintain the equilibrium between the two warring elements in the state. But the sympathies of the monarchical party became centred in the dashing Aristobulus, who appeared to have inherited the charm and the warlike instincts of his house. While his mother was on her death-bed, he made a bid for the throne, with Sadducaean support; and, almost as soon as the breath was out of her body, he turned his arms against his brother, who had been recognised as the legitimate heir. A short campaign decided the issue in favour of the younger man, who assumed the supreme dignity. After a brief interlude of peace, Hyrcanus fled to Aretas, king of the Nabataean Arabs, who (like the Jews) had formed a state on the ruins of the Syrian Empire. The latter invaded Palestine and laid siege to Jerusalem. The fall of the city appeared imminent, when an intervention took place which was to change the face of Palestinian affairs permanently and to put an end to these futile dynastic disputes for good.

IV

Rome, blindly following her Imperial destinies, had been blundering on, in these last few years, from conquest to conquest. Her influence had long been felt in Asia. Nearly a century before (accord-

---

[1] It must be added that this does not appear to have been exceptional. On the death of John Hyrcanus, his widow was charged with the government, though control was subsequently seized by her son, Aristobulus; and on the latter's death Salome herself had enjoyed a brief period of authority.

Simeon ben Shetah is presumably to be regarded as a political rather than an intellectual leader, as later generations imagined him. He is traditionally associated with the institution of a comprehensive system of elementary education, which certainly dates back to about this period.

ing to report) Judah the Maccabee had thought it desirable to send an embassy to Italy, to conclude a treaty of peace and amity. His example had been followed by his brothers Jonathan and Simon. It had been Roman influence which had saved John Hyrcanus in 136, and Roman pressure which had been responsible, in part, for the withdrawal of Tigranes of Armenia in 70. The latter, with his father-in-law Mithradates VI of Pontus, had become embroiled with the new world-power, and the popular idol, Pompey, had been sent into Asia against them. His lieutenant, Scaurus, was now in Syria, and both of the Hasmonaean brothers appealed to him for justice. Scaurus ordered the Arabs to withdraw, and Aretas, fearing the might of Rome, unquestioningly obeyed. Aristobulus was thus left in possession (64).

A short while later, when Pompey himself arrived in Damascus, deputations from the rival claimants to the throne waited upon him soliciting his support. More remarkable than this, some of the Pharisees, who regarded this deadly dynastic dispute as an internal affair of the Sadducaean or monarchical elements, requested the Romans to assume the political control of Palestine themselves and to restore the old constitution, under a High Priesthood which did not trespass upon secular politics.

Pompey was so long pondering over his decision that Aristobulus anticipated the worst, and fled to Jerusalem. When he found himself pursued, he realised that resistance was useless and, making his way to the Roman camp, offered to surrender the city. His followers within the walls refused to obey his instructions, and established themselves on the almost impregnable Temple mount. Here, they held out for three months, until one Sabbath (or, according to another account, on the Day of Atonement), in the year 63 B.C., their fortifications were stormed, and the defenders massacred. The victorious Pompey entered into the Holy of Holies, whence even the High Priest was excluded excepting on one solemn occasion in the year. With the pomp of the Roman temples in his mind, he could not understand the impressive emptiness which he found there. In after years the malicious slander was spread about that he had discovered, as the central object of Jewish adoration, an ass's head.

The capture of Jerusalem by Pompey marked the end of the exceptional period of complete independence which the Hasmonaean kingdom had enjoyed since the days of John Hyrcanus. The remarkable recent expansion of the national boundaries was partially cancelled by the conqueror. The coastal plain with its chain of Greek cities, together with Samaria and Scythopolis, was annexed to the new Roman province of Syria. However, the work of Judaisation in the north of the country had been so thorough and so successful that it was out of the question to treat that region in a similar fashion. Henceforth, therefore, the centre of Jewish life lay in two distinct areas, Judaea and Galilee, cut off from the coast by the Greek cities and from one another by the Samaritan belt. Judaea retained also both the land of Edom (Idumaea) to the south, and the Perea on the eastern side of Jordan.

These territories were left under the rule of the High Priest, Hyrcanus, who lost the title of King and governed the country as a Roman tributary, in much the same manner as his predecessors had done in the period of the Persian and Greek domination. A few years later (57), after an unsuccessful revolt headed by his nephew, Alexander, son of Aristobulus, the High Priest was deprived of all political authority, the country being divided into five districts, each with its own council immediately subject to the Proconsul of Syria. Henceforth, so long as the Roman Empire retained its might, Palestine remained in fact (if not always in name) a Roman province.

V

The recent national reawakening had been accompanied, as is almost invariably the case in history, by a cultural revival. It found an outlet in an outburst of building, in the monumental tomb constructed for the Hasmonaeans near Modein, in Simon's palace at Gezer, in the earliest Jewish coinage, struck by his descendants and bearing unmistakable Jewish symbols. But, above all, it expressed itself in literature. While the 'abomination of desolation' still stood in the Temple, a zealous believer is believed to have composed the Book of Daniel—the last to enter into the canon of the Scriptures. Here, in words ascribed to a figure purporting to have flourished in Babylon nearly four centuries before, an effort was made to shew that this was the final attempt to suppress the Jewish people and their holy city. The Babylonians, Medes, and Persians had done their worst. Now it was the turn of the Greek—the 'little horn', as the author contemptuously designated Antiochus. But this, too, would end in failure, and it would be followed by the final triumph of the Saints of the Most High.

This mystical composition served to strengthen the conviction of the *Hassidim*, as they strove for victory. And, when they achieved it, they expressed their exultation in a burst of song. The so-called *Hallel* (or 'Praise': Psalms cxiii-cxviii), which the Jewish people has ever since associated with any occasion of public thanksgiving, is thought to have been composed to celebrate the Hasmonaean triumph; allusions to contemporary events have been traced in several others; and in any case there can be little doubt that the collection was edited and received its final form at this time.

The national vicissitudes and triumph are reflected, too, in various anecdotal or liturgical additions to the books of Esther and of Daniel. Joshua, son of Sirach, a contemporary of Mattathias the Hasmonaean, composed *Ecclesiasticus*—a wisdom book containing counsels for daily life, and culminating in a panegyric of the High Priest Simon, son of Onias.[1] A highly coloured account of a hypothetical deliverance of the Jewish people from the Assyrians through the devotion of a woman named Judith was presumably written to encourage the national morale during the struggle, while the beginning of the reign of Alexander Jannai witnessed the composition of the First Book of Maccabees—a semi-official history of the recent war. The original Hebrew text of all these works is lost; they are extant only in ancient Greek renderings included in the supplement to the Bible known as the Apocrypha,[2] and for a long time were almost entirely unknown in Jewish circles. They remain, notwithstanding the shackles of a foreign tongue, clear testimony of the literary activity which was fostered by the Hasmonaean triumphs—the swan-song of Biblical literature.

VI

The Jewish people, during this period, was not confined wholly to Palestine and the immediately adjacent territories; and its extension outside the country was fully as noteworthy as its consolidation within it. Descendants of the exiles from the sister kingdoms of Israel and Judah had been found throughout the legendary 'one hundred and twenty-seven' provinces of the Persian Empire, where they remained and whence they spread even after the conquests of Alexander the

---

[1] Probably identical with Simon the Just (above, p. 65).

[2] A great part of the Hebrew Book of Ecclesiasticus has, however, been brought to light in the lumber-room (*Genizah*) of a Cairo synagogue—one of the most remarkable literary discoveries of modern times.

Great brought them into closer connection with the Hellenic world. There was still a solid nucleus, though we know little of its history, living in Mesopotamia. Hence, as well as from Palestine itself, mercantile intercourse or the vicissitudes of war spread them throughout the neighbouring lands, whether as freemen or as slaves who might ultimately win their freedom. The later Biblical writers apparently knew of Hebrews settled in the Greek islands.[1] Aristotle, the father of mediaeval philosophy, is recorded to have met a learned Jew in Asia Minor, in the fourth century B.C. Antiochus III removed a large body of loyal Jews from Mesopotamia to secure the fidelity of Phrygia. On the island of Cos, Mithradates VI of Pontus confiscated a vast sum of money which the Jews of those parts had collected for transmission to the Temple; and so great were the throngs of pilgrims who went up thither that, in 49, the Roman consul ordered the islanders to give them facilities to pass.

The advance of the Romans brought all these areas within the orbit of the new world-power centred in Italy, and so fostered further expansion; while every campaign resulted in the removal as slaves of large numbers of the population, who must have included some Jews. Already in the first century B.C., the geographer Strabo spoke of the Jews as having penetrated into all states, so that it was difficult to find a single place which had not received them, and in which (he sarcastically added) they had not become ruler. Flaccus, Roman Proconsul in Asia Minor in 62-61, confiscated the offerings collected for the Jerusalem Temple at Apamea, Laodicea, Adramyttium, and Pergamum; and when, two or three years later, he was set on trial at Rome, this figured amongst the charges against him. All this serves to indicate the vast, and growing, significance of the Diaspora, as it was called,[2] during this period. Palestine was of importance, not only intrinsically, as a minor Asiatic power, but also as the sentimental centre of a vast number of persons scattered throughout the Empire and beyond—4,000,000 at least, it has been computed—only half of whom were resident in Syria. The Jews were a small people, but Judaism was already a world religion.

Nowhere was the Jewish settlement more important than in Egypt. Individuals had migrated thither, probably, even in the days of the first Temple: a considerable body had transferred themselves *en masse*

---

[1] See below, p. 139.

[2] The word is a Greek one meaning 'scattering'. The Hebrew equivalent was *Golah* or *Galuth* ('exile').

after the national debacle. Subsequently Jews figured among the
mercenaries recruited by the last Pharaohs for the defence of their
southern frontier, retaining their importance under the Persian rule;
and a miniature sanctuary which was established by the Aramaic-
speaking military colony settled at Elephantine (the modern Assouan)
continued to exist till the fourth century.[1]

After the Greek conquest the migration was intensified. Jews
followed the expedition of Alexander the Great, and were included
amongst those settled by him in his new city of Alexandria. For many
years after, Palestine was an appanage of Egypt, and the greater
country exercised a powerful attraction, as always, on the inhabitants
of the smaller. In the course of their various campaigns, successive
Ptolemies brought large numbers of Jews back with them to Egypt,
and particularly to their flourishing capital. Their numbers increased
apace. In the whole of the country, they are said to have numbered
as many as one million—more, perhaps, than there were in Palestine
itself. There was an important offshoot, from an early date, in
Cyrene. In Alexandria, there were some hundred thousand, occupying
two out of the five divisions into which the city was divided. They
were permitted to live according to their traditional law, under their
own Ethnarch,[2] with his council of seventy elders, while they were
represented on the municipality by their communal leaders. At
Leontopolis there was actually a Temple (founded during the persecutions in Palestine by Onias, son of the dispossessed High Priest,
Onias III), which, modelled on that of Jerusalem, continued to exist
for nearly two and a half centuries.

The Egyptian Jews entered into every branch of life. They were
merchants, artisans, farmers, labourers. Many were settled in military
allotments in various parts of the country. Some rose to high rank in
the administration. The army sent into Palestine by Cleopatra III in
the reign of Alexander Jannai was commanded by the two sons of the
High Priest of Leontopolis, Onias IV, whose influence prevented the
country from being reabsorbed into the Ptolemaic dominions. In
every respect, excepting religiously, the Egyptian Jews were
thoroughly assimilated to their environment.

Egypt was, at this time, the greatest centre of Hellenic culture.
Through Alexandria, in large measure, the treasures of ancient

[1] Aramaic records and documents relating to this colony, discovered at Elephantine
early in the present century, throw a striking sidelight upon the age of Ezra.

[2] 'Ruler of a race' (Greek).

Greece became known to the Roman world. It was in the famous academies on the banks of the Nile that the lore of Athens and of Corinth was most sedulously studied, attracting as teachers the greatest scholars of the age. The Jews could not fail to be influenced by this welter of activity. They speedily relinquished the language of their fathers in favour of Greek; they universally adopted Hellenic names (a process, indeed, which made great progress even in Palestine); and they produced a whole literature in the vernacular to satisfy their cultural requirements. As early as the third century B.C. there had been begun, under royal patronage, that Greek translation of the Hebrew Scriptures which goes by the name of the Septuagint, and which enjoyed unquestioned authority in Alexandrian Jewry. Imitations of, and supplements to, the Bible (mostly comprised in the Apocrypha or the looser collection known as the Pseudepigrapha) were composed in Alexandria in Greek, heavily tinged with local philosophical conceptions. The First Book of Esdras thus paralleled the canonical Ezra; while Jason of Cyrene provided Greek-speaking Jewry with a history of the Hasmonaean revolt, now known as the Second Book of Maccabees. Even the patriotic grandson of the author of the Book of Ecclesiasticus thought it necessary to secure the work a wider public by translating it into the universal language of thought and letters.

As was natural, many writers abandoned the traditional models: with the result that there grew up in Alexandria an entirely independent literature, intended to familiarise Hellenised Jews with their own national culture, and to demonstrate to Gentile critics and observers the superiority, or at least rationality, of Judaism. There were historians who wrote accounts of the kings of Judah; archaeologists who studied Hebrew antiquities; poets who composed dramas or epics on Biblical subjects; apologists who defended their people against the anti-Semites of the day; and philosophers who analysed the Mosaic laws and proved that they did not conflict with, or perhaps even anticipated, the fashionable Greek culture. This tendency, already present in the third century before the Christian era, and active in the second, continued after the Roman occupation of Egypt, in the middle of the first. It culminated in the noble figure of Philo of Alexandria (20 B.C.-A.D. 45), through whose philosophical works Hellenic Jewish culture is best known to the modern world. The Egyptian scene was vital, crowded, and conspicuously modern in tone. It was nevertheless in Palestine that the heart of the Jewish nation, and the main tradition of Jewish civilisation, were still to be.

Chapter IX

THE ROMAN HEGEMONY

———————•———————

I

Ever since the beginning of the petty dynastic dispute which had lost Judaea her independence, the blundering Hyrcanus had been under the influence of a certain Antipater. The latter was an Idumaean, a member of the race whose forcible conversion to Judaism had been one of the outstanding episodes of recent Palestinian history. His father, Antipas, had been appointed governor of his native province by Alexander Jannai. The son succeeded him in this rank, his fear of dismissal by Aristobulus being responsible for his unwavering devotion to the elder brother. It had been on his advice and at his instigation that Hyrcanus had consistently acted during the prolonged struggle for the throne, which in all probability he would otherwise have abandoned long before. After the Roman occupation, Antipas continued to serve in a similar capacity. The reorganisation of Palestine which followed the abortive revolt of 57 gave him an opportunity to exercise a more direct authority. He was recognised as the principal personality in Jerusalem, and probably became farmer of taxes for the whole country.

Roman rapacity was responsible, meanwhile, for a whole succession of rebellions—in 56, under Aristobulus and his son Antigonus (in Hebrew, Mattathias), who had escaped from Rome; in 55 in favour of his second son Alexander; and again, in 53-51, under a certain Pitholaus, in consequence of the pillaging of the Temple by the pro-consul Crassus. Notwithstanding all temptations, the High Priest was persuaded by his wily adviser to remain loyal. With consummate skill, Antipater managed to retain the favour of whatever faction was uppermost in Rome during the civil wars which now began. The conflict which broke out in 49 between Julius Caesar and Pompey called for all his finesse, but in the end he managed to range himself on the side of the victor. A Jewish force assisted Caesar in Egypt, and the influence of the High Priest was exerted to make the communities of the Nile delta rally to his eagles. He in turn shewed his gratitude by restoring to Hyrcanus part of his political power, with the title of Ethnarch, and reuniting with Palestine some of the territory taken away by Pompey. His assassination, on the Ides of March 44, was mourned by the Jews as their own loss.

The High Priest's influence was by now purely nominal. The Romans were the overlords of the country; Antipater was the force behind the throne; and the latter's two sons, Phezahel and Herod, were appointed governors of Jerusalem and Galilee respectively. The latter, though younger in years, was the abler and the more strenuous, and gradually began to occupy the forefront of the stage. When, in 43, Antipater was poisoned by a rival, it was to this son that he transmitted his authority in the state.

Herod shewed himself no less adroit than his father had been. When the triumph of Philippi made Mark Antony the master of Asia, there was a skilful change of front; and Herod's honeyed words and lavish promises outweighed the impression caused by the Jewish deputations who appeared before the victor to complain at the harshness of the regime. The result was a further promotion. Hyrcanus was deprived of the remnant of the political authority which he had nominally enjoyed during the past few years; this was divided between Herod and his brother, each now given the title of 'tetrarch'.[1]

There was a brief period when the house of Antipater seemed to be in eclipse. Antigonus, son of Aristobulus (who had already attempted to regain his throne with the help of the King of Chalcis), now had recourse for help to the Parthians, the only important power of the Middle East which held out against Rome. He was unexpectedly successful. Jerusalem was occupied; Phezahel committed suicide in prison; the unfortunate old Hyrcanus was mutilated, so as to disqualify him for ever from carrying out the sacerdotal functions; and for four years (40-37) Antigonus reigned as King and High Priest. Even after the Roman legions had driven the Parthians out of Syria again, he managed to maintain his position for a short while, thanks to skilful diplomacy and the payment of a high tribute. Herod, on the other hand, who had been left by his brother's death the sole representative of his house, realised that the fate of Palestine had to be decided, not in the East, but in Rome. Thither he made his way,

[1] Literally, 'ruler of a fourth part', but loosely applied to any subordinate prince.

and his personal suppleness and lavish gifts secured the support both of Antony and of Octavian, the two rulers of the Roman Empire. His new patrons had no difficulty in securing his nomination by the Senate as tributary King of Judaea. With the aid of a couple of Roman legions and his wild Idumaean kinsmen, the country was reconquered despite a dogged resistance. Jerusalem was captured again after five months' siege, and Antigonus, the last Hasmonaean sovereign, was put to death. During the course of the campaign, Herod married Miriam (Mariamne)[1] a grand-daughter of Hyrcanus II. Thus the usurper was able to attract some of the popular sympathy which still lingered about the name of the Maccabees, and to begin his long reign, which was to last a third of a century, with a semblance of legitimate right.

II

'I had sooner be Herod's swine than his son' was the commentary upon his creature's family record of the Emperor Augustus, Herod's friend (who knew, like all Romans, that Jews abstained from pork). This is the aspect of the reign which impressed popular recollection. The new ruler was supremely able and energetic. He lacked entirely, on the other hand, the qualities which appeal to the imagination. He was cold, calculating, and cruel. He was aware that his rule was profoundly distasteful to his people, and that their sympathies inclined to the remnant of the old royal house, which had delivered them from foreign oppression and ushered in a brief period of glorious freedom. But, in consequence of his marriage, he himself was closely allied with the Hasmonaeans. His own children, descended from them on their mother's side, were therefore his most dangerous rivals. As his reign continued, and other possible claimants disappeared from the scene, his mind became more and more suspicious, even of his nearest of kin; until his life closed under the shadow of the darkest tragedy of all.

Almost the first act of the reign was the arrest and execution of forty-five members of the leading aristocratic families of the realm. He was persuaded against his will to appoint his wife's handsome young brother, another Aristobulus, to the High Priesthood (an

---

[1] Mariamne was doubly of Hasmonaean blood, being the daughter of Hyrcanus' daughter Alexandra and her cousin Alexander, son of the ill-fated Aristobulus: see the table at the end of this chapter.

office to which he could not aspire himself); but the popularity which the latter achieved aroused his enmity, and he had him drowned. His own uncle was executed for failing to act with due energy during one of his absences from the country. The aged and mutilated Hyrcanus, his wife's grandfather, formerly King and High Priest, was murdered lest he might again become a competitor for the throne. The climax came in 29 when his own wife, Mariamne, was put to death on suspicion of conspiracy and infidelity—an outrage which he soon repented, and from the effects of which he never recovered. Her mother Alexandra, whose proud and independent spirit shewed her a true member of the old royal house, was the next victim. A less sanguinary period followed, if only for lack of victims. Herod's children by Mariamne, Alexander and Aristobulus, were however growing to manhood; and the King could see that, by virtue of their mother's birth, they appealed to the popular sentiment as he had never been able to do. Gradually his mind became filled with gnawing suspicion even against them. In the end, the two young princes were formally arraigned on a charge of treachery, and, after a travesty of trial, were strangled in prison (7 B.C.).

It is entirely wrong to regard this succession of palace tragedies as constituting the essential feature of the reign, any more than the marital vicissitudes of Henry VIII form the substance of English history in the second quarter of the sixteenth century. Cold and cruel as Herod was, he counted nevertheless amongst the most competent rulers of his day. For sheer ability he ranks perhaps second to none in all Jewish history, and his reign was memorable, for more reasons than one, in the annals of his people. The ultimate Roman overlordship was at all times plain. The tribute paid to them was heavy. Roman legionaries were never absent from Jerusalem, and Roman institutions prevailed in the country more and more. Yet within these limitations there was a considerable element of success, and even glory, in the reign. In spite of all turns in the wheel of political fortune, the Jewish king managed to maintain his position. So long as he did nothing which conflicted with the wishes of his suzerain, his power was absolute. The old constitution of the country was overruled. The Sanhedrin[1] was deprived of all executive or deliberative

---

[1] Greek συνέδριον (= 'sitting together'). The fact that a Greek name was applied to the supreme Jewish council is a remarkable testimony to the inroads of Hellenic influence. The precise constitutional position of the Sanhedrin before the reign of Herod is uncertain: see, however, above, p. 79.

power, so that it became to an increasing degree an academic and religious council. Everything was done to prevent national sentiment from crystallising again around the High Priesthood, as had been the case in former days. The incumbent of the office (formerly regarded as a life-appointment) was changed with indecorous frequency, and even the sacred robes which constituted his insignia were kept in the royal custody.

In compensation, there was a long period of peace, broken only by local revolts or border raids. In consequence of successive Imperial grants, the boundaries of the kingdom were enlarged almost to the extent of the old Hasmonaean state, excepting that the Greek cities of the Decapolis were not reabsorbed. A period of intensive development followed. The wealth and population of the country rapidly increased. Though taxation was heavy, the proceeds were largely devoted to public works. It could be supplemented, moreover, and sometimes remitted, as a result of the king's successful private ventures—working the state-owned copper-mines in Cyprus, or lending money at interest to neighbouring rulers. The frontiers were fortified. Recent acquisitions were colonised. The seaports along the Mediterranean coast were developed, and communications opened up through them with the western world. An ambitious building programme was followed. Samaria was rebuilt and called Sebaste, in honour of the Emperor:[1] Straton's Tower, an unimportant coast town, was developed into the city of Caesarea, modern down to its drainage, which ultimately became one of the most important seaports of the Levant. Magnificent royal palaces were constructed in Jerusalem and elsewhere. On the other hand, the king attempted to conciliate his subjects, adorn his capital, and perpetuate his name, by reconstructing in magnificent style the Temple at Jerusalem, which had stood without substantial alteration since the return from the Exile. The work occupied many years, and the building, when it was finished, was one of the wonders of the Mediterranean world; though a golden eagle surmounting the gateway served as a perpetual reminder of the Roman overlordship.

Herod ruled, it may be said, in a dual capacity. On the one hand, he was King of Palestine, with its conflicting elements and creeds. Between these he endeavoured to maintain an even balance, lavishing his favours impartially upon Jew and Gentile, the cult of the Most High on the one hand and the pagan sanctuaries on the other. In

---

[1] *Sebastos* is the Greek equivalent of the Roman *Augustus*.

religious matters he was nominally a follower of the Law of Moses: in an incomplete and somewhat furtive fashion indeed, which did not unduly hamper his conduct if he went abroad or visited a Greek city. Outside the country, on the other hand, he was regarded as King of the Jews, and all sections of the Diaspora looked to him for assistance at time of stress. Thus, the same person who was thought of only with execration by his Jewish subjects at home was the centre of the national sentiment of their co-religionists abroad, whom he was always ready to help and to protect.

Little, perhaps, earned Herod so much domestic unpopularity as the devotion which he shewed, at every possible opportunity, to the fashionable Hellenic culture, to the complete neglect of everything Jewish. In all his building operations (except possibly the Temple at Jerusalem) the classical style of architecture was employed. The urban centres throughout Palestine, and especially the new cities which he developed, became centres of Greek and Roman influence. In Sebaste he actually established a temple for the cult of the Emperor. In Jerusalem itself he constructed a Hippodrome, where public games were performed such as had so scandalised a former generation. He sent his sons to complete their education at Rome; was himself initiated in middle age into the mysteries of Greek philosophy; and surrounded himself with Greek savants, poets, and historians. He maintained an obviously self-conscious pose, as an enlightened exponent and supporter of all that was highest in contemporary culture. From the borders of Egypt to the Greek archipelago, and even in Athens and Sparta, he was known as a munificent patron of the arts and a sumptuous builder, prepared to construct temples, colonnades, and public halls on the slightest provocation. One has the impression of an Indian prince of the past generation, sloughing the better characteristics of his own national tradition, and endeavouring to erect on the banks of the Ganges a miniature Paris or London. In the process Palestine itself became a medley of languages, cultures, and creeds. The Hellenisation against which the Hasmonaeans had fought became deeply implanted in a period of profound peace. When the king died, in a welter of blood, in 4 B.C., vast strides had already been made, under his inspiration, in the process which was to end with the final extrusion of Judaism from the country.

III

Herod's death was succeeded by a general flare-up of insurrection, which was put down with needless ruthlessness by the Roman legionaries. Meanwhile the future of the kingdom was decided in Italy. By other wives than the unfortunate Mariamne, Herod had left several children. In accordance with the terms of his will, Palestine was divided up between them. One, Archelaus, son of the Samaritan Malthace, was invested with the rule of the southern part of the country, including Judaea, Samaria, and the contiguous territories; his brother, Antipas (whose step-daughter was the notorious Salome), was nominated 'tetrarch' of Galilee and Perea; Philip, son of Cleopatra of Jerusalem, was given the north-eastern province about the upper reaches of the Jordan. Only in one important respect were Herod's final dispositions neglected. Archelaus was deprived of the title of King, which his father enjoyed, and had to content himself with that of 'ethnarch', which accentuated his subordination to the power of Rome. After such a beginning, his reign was not likely to be successful. After no more than ten years (4 B.C.-A.D. 6), the Emperor Augustus took advantage of the complaints voiced by his subjects to depose him and annex his territories.

The kernel of the Jewish homeland was henceforth a Roman possession, nakedly and without disguise. Its constitution and administration were much the same as those of any other province of the empire. It was ruled over by a Procurator, who was himself subordinate to the Legate of Syria. Jerusalem, notoriously recalcitrant and troublesome, was deprived even of the titular dignity of capital, the seat of administration being removed to upstart Caesarea. Ample garrisons were stationed throughout the country. The taxation, more crushing than ever before, was farmed out to private contractors, or 'publicans'. The High Priesthood was rigorously subordinated and prevented from attaining independent authority, the succession being controlled by the Roman authorities, who kept the robes of office in their custody. Within these limitations there was a certain degree of local autonomy; but the ever-present Roman legionaries, and the relentless activities of the publicans, served as constant reminders of the overlordship of an alien power. The country was in a continuous state of discontent, which flared out from time to time into actual rebellion. Judaea had the name of being the most inflammable and difficult of all Roman provinces. On the occasion of the

36. PALESTINIAN COIN WITH INSCRIPTION 'YAHUD'
Persian period

37. JEWISH COIN OF THE FIRST REVOLT, A.D. 66-70

38-39. JEWISH COINS OF THE SECOND REVOLT, A.D. 132-5

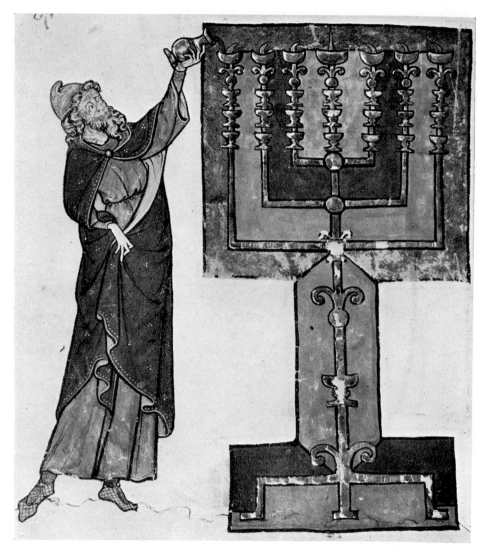

40. THE HIGH PRIEST
Miniature from a 13th-century Hebrew manuscript. British Museum

great festivals, when pilgrims flowed into Jerusalem in vast numbers from every quarter of Palestine and the Diaspora, and the whole people was tense with memories of past triumphs and deliverances, an outbreak was constantly feared. The Procurator would transfer himself from Caesarea to Jerusalem, and every precaution would be taken to maintain the peace.

In spite of this, outbreaks were frequent. The upper classes, including a great proportion both of the Sadducaean priesthood and of the Pharisaic scholars, were opposed to any display of violence, believing that deliverance would come from Heaven in God's own time. Yet the ordinary people were not always amenable to their influence. Groaning under the weight of the foreign oppression, they looked forward to salvation with increasing eagerness. Assuredly, God would have mercy upon their affliction and redeem them, as He had done their fathers in days of similar distress. The Hasmonaeans had failed them. Then it would be a descendant of the royal house of David who would be sent to deliver them and prove to be the Lord's Anointed—the Messiah. Large numbers were determined to chase out the oppressor by force of arms, just as Judah the Maccabee had done two hundred years before, and to avenge themselves on those who favoured alien rule.

In the mountains of Galilee (still nominally under the tetrarch Antipas, though in fact little other than a Roman province), a state of revolt became endemic. A certain Judah, whose father Hezekiah had been executed by Herod, and who had himself risen in arms at the time of the tyrant's death, placed himself at the head of the insurgents. He was defeated and put to death. Nevertheless his spirit continued to inspire his sympathisers, who for long years after looked up to his sons as their leaders. They became known as the *Kannaim* or Zealots; and, in the remoter parts of the country, they cut down without scruple any person who appeared too friendly towards the Roman oppressor. At the Pilgrim Festivals especially, Jerusalem continued to be a hotbed of excitement; and in the year 33, a religious revivalist and social reformer from Galilee named Joshua (Jesus), who laid claim to Davidic descent, was crucified on Passover eve, after a summary trial, by the nervous administration.[1] Further acts of

[1] For a somewhat fuller account of Jesus and the rise of Christianity so far as our subject is affected, see below, p. 142 *sqq.*

Another contemporary Jewish preacher and reformer who suffered for his criticism of the ruling house was Johanan ben Zechariah the Priest, better known to-day as John the Baptist.

G

violence were perpetrated in subsequent years under the same Procurator, Pontius Pilate, who was ultimately cashiered in consequence of the complaints levelled at him from all quarters.

In the period which followed the state of affairs became even more delicate. Peace had been maintained in Palestine only by treating the religious susceptibilities of the Jews with the utmost regard. The current interpretation of the Ten Commandments precluded any 'graven image' whatsoever. Accordingly, taught by bitter experience, the Roman legions went so far as to discard their Eagles and the effigies of the Emperor before entering Jerusalem; the tactless Pilate had been forced to remove the shields with the Imperial insignia which he had exhibited in the governor's palace; and the Legate of Syria, passing through Judaea immediately afterwards, refrained from marching his army to Jerusalem with their standards displayed. The crazy Emperor, Caius Caligula, failed to appreciate this. It had become customary throughout the Roman dominions for the ruler to be adored as Divine, and for his effigy to be set up in all the temples. That the Jews refrained from following this example appeared to him a deliberate affront. Shortly after his accession to the throne, in 37, he made an attempt to enforce the erection of his statue in the synagogues of Alexandria, and even in the central shrine at Jerusalem. There was consternation throughout the Jewish world. The Egyptian communities sent a deputation to Rome headed by the philosopher Philo, who has left a vivid record of his impressions of the court of the mad Emperor. The governor of Syria, who was entrusted with the execution of the order, was wise enough to temporise: and Caius was assassinated before his resolution could be enforced. A repetition of a general revolt like that against Antiochus Epiphanes was—providentially, as it seemed—averted.

IV

There followed a brief glimmer of brighter things—the last that Jewish Palestine was destined to know. Aristobulus, the murdered son of Herod and Mariamne, had left behind him one child—a boy, named Agrippa after Augustus' friend. He had been brought up at the Roman court with Caius Caligula, with whom he was on most intimate terms. One day he was overheard to speak with longing of the day when his boon companion would ascend the throne of the Caesars, and was in consequence thrown into prison by the Emperor

Tiberius. On the latter's death in 37, the wish he had expressed was realised; and one of Caligula's first actions was to order his friend's release and to nominate him successor to the tetrarch Philip, who had just died. In addition he was given the title of King. To his principality was added, shortly after, Galilee and the Perea, formerly under the rule of his other uncle Antipas (who had fallen into disgrace, notwithstanding his sycophantic naming of the city which he had built on the shores of the Sea of Galilee, Tiberias, after the reigning Emperor). It was the jubilant reception which Agrippa received from the Jews of Alexandria, while he was on his way to take over the reins of government, which set into motion the wave of anti-Jewish feeling that had prompted Caligula's recent mad order. When the first news of the opposition to this measure arrived he was in Rome, and exerted his influence to the utmost to obtain its repeal.

Caligula's successor, the affable Claudius (41-54), shewed himself no less friendly towards Agrippa, and made over to him those parts of the country formerly directly subject to the Romans—including Samaria, Idumaea, and Judaea itself (41). Thus the unity of Palestine was restored, and the kingdom of Herod was revived in the hands of his grandson, whose dominions were nearly co-extensive with the empire of David or of Alexander Jannai.

Agrippa united in his veins the blood of Herod and of the Hasmonaeans. His vigour and his adroitness testified to the first; his personal charm, his popularity, and his intense Jewish feeling to the second. Long years after his death, men continued to speak of his piety and of his scrupulous observance of the Mosaic code—how no day passed without an offering being made at the altar at his expense; how he took the first-fruits to the Temple Mount on his shoulder, like the simplest farmer; how, on the Feast of Tabernacles, he read the Book of Deuteronomy before the assembled people, in accordance with custom. But, in spite of the royal state which he enjoyed and the show of independence, the shadow of Rome remained only too apparent; and when, after a brief reign, the popular Jewish monarch died suddenly at Caesarea in 44, it was thought safest to bring the dynasty to an end. His young son, Agrippa II, was ultimately invested with the rule of the northern territories formerly subject to his great-uncle Philip, in Transjordania. In Judaea he retained a sentimental hold. He was, after all, the Jewish king, if not King of the Jews. He ultimately received from the Emperor the right to supervise the Temple and to appoint the High Priest; and he was not slow in speaking out, whether in Rome or elsewhere, at any time when the interests of the Jewish people were involved. His actual political authority was however confined to an unimportant area with a mixed population far to the north. The rest of the country was once more annexed to the province of Syria, being governed by a succession of tyrannical Procurators as it had been before the recent interlude.

V

The period which followed was one of misgovernment, accentuated by an utter absence of appreciation of Jewish standards of life and religious ideals. One Procurator after another trampled on the susceptibilities of the people. The earliest, Fadus (44-45), reasserted the prerogative of keeping the robes of the High Priest in his custody —a measure which appeared sacrilegious to the mass of the people. The next was Tiberius Alexander (45-48), a renegade nephew of Philo of Alexandria, and for that reason the object of universal abhorrence. Cumanus, his successor (48-52), shewed such severity in suppressing disorder that he was removed from office. He was outdone by Felix (52-60), who moreover outraged Jewish sentiment by taking as his wife Drusilla, sister of Agrippa II, and a married woman. Disorders broke out intermittently up and down the country. A prophet named Theudas, who had promised to imitate the miracles of Moses, was surrounded and put to death, with many of his followers. A little later, the insulting behaviour of a Roman soldier, while on guard at the Temple during the Passover celebrations, brought about a riot in Jerusalem, which was put down only after great loss of life. There was a clash between the Jews and Samaritans, which assumed almost the proportions of an armed revolt (52).

Their exploitation at the hands of the Roman tax-gatherers, and of the wealthy landowners who flourished under the regime, drove the common people to sullen hatred of the existing state of affairs. Everywhere the malcontents, inspired by the family of Judah the Galilaean, became increasingly active; and an extremist party, who became known as Sicarii, sprung up amongst them. At intervals the latter would come down from their mountain fastnesses and raid the villages and townships, looting the houses of Roman sympathisers and putting their occupants to death without remorse.[1] Marriage

---

[1] The similarity to conditions in Ireland from 1916 onwards (or, for that matter, in America in the early stages of the War of Independence) is obvious. It must be pointed out

with a Gentile was sometimes sufficient to cost a man his life. An attempt of the Procurator Felix to suppress the rebels ended in failure. Their leader, Eleazar, was treacherously seized and sent to Rome, where he perished; but his fate stimulated his followers to greater efforts. From Galilee their activities extended into Judaea. Roman partisans were unsafe even in Jerusalem, where they ran the risk of falling under the dagger of some enthusiast who mingled with the crowd and escaped before his crime was discovered. One day the High Priest himself, who was adjudged to have shewn himself too accommodating, was assassinated by members of the patriot party. In Caesarea a state of semi-overt warfare existed perpetually between the Jewish and the Gentile population.

After an interregnum which allowed the forces of disorder to gain a stronger hold, a new Procurator named Florus arrived in 64, to find Judaea seething with discontent. Nevertheless, he followed the example of his precursors. His maladministration became more and more glaring, culminating in the seizure of seventeen talents of gold from the Temple treasury. A riot ensued; and a basket was passed round by a sarcastic citizen into which the charitably inclined might drop coins for the relief of the indigent Procurator. Furious at this insult, the latter turned his troops loose on the city, part of which was sacked; and the disorder was put down in blood. Two cohorts were summoned from Caesarea to reinforce the garrison. After much trouble, the High Priest persuaded the citizens to give them a friendly reception. Their overtures were treated with contempt; and the anti-Roman demonstration flared up again. There was fighting up and down the steep streets, where a hail of missiles from the housetops greeted every Roman helmet. The insurgents seized the Temple Mount, and all efforts to dislodge them proved unavailing. The city was now untenable, and the legionaries withdrew to the citadel, the colonnade between which place and the Temple had been broken down. King Agrippa, who was in Alexandria when the news reached him, set out post-haste for Jerusalem. Here he exerted all his influence to persuade the citizens to resume their allegiance. He was told that the revolutionary movement had been, not against the Emperor, but against

that all we know of the activity of the so-called 'Zealots' comes from the writings of their adversaries, who represent as mere brigands a section whose motives were essentially patriotic. Without taking up a partisan attitude it may be said that the Irish 'gunmen' of the twentieth century, and the patriotic 'Assassins' of the first, are exactly parallel. The comparison can be carried down to the Revolution of the year 66 and its aftermath, when the former outlaws became national leaders. See note on page 108.

Florus. His efforts to re-establish the authority of the hated Procurator were powerless; and, in the end, his exasperated co-religionists drove him from the city.

Meanwhile the spirit of revolt was spreading. A patriotic contingent seized the fortress of Masada, on the banks of the Dead Sea, putting the garrison to death—an overt act of warfare. Eleazar, son of the High Priest Hananiah (Ananias), and captain of the Temple, persuaded his fellow-priests to refuse all offerings for or on behalf of Gentiles. In consequence, the daily sacrifice hitherto presented in the name of the Emperor was discontinued. This was equivalent to the repudiation of Roman overlordship. Some of the more moderate elements, having failed to avert this drastic step, sent to the Roman authorities and to Agrippa, protesting that the mass of the people was loyal, and asking for assistance to assert their authority. With the reinforcements which Agrippa sent, they took possession of the upper city. After sharp fighting, they were driven out, and the palaces of the old royal house were fired. This success was followed up by the occupation of the citadel. The surviving Roman troops took refuge, with some of their sympathisers, in Herod's palace. Here they were submitted to a regular siege. After some time, the Jews among them, with Agrippa's troops, were allowed to leave unmolested. The Romans held out in the towers for a little while longer. Ultimately they agreed to lay down their arms; but, as they left their stronghold, they were attacked and butchered to a man.

Judaea and Galilee were now in full revolt. The events at Jerusalem exacerbated feelings in Caesarea, always a hotbed of religious animosity; and here, on the day of the slaughter of the garrison at Jerusalem, the Jews were set upon by their Gentile neighbours and massacred. Racial riots swept through the whole of Syria. Every place where Jews were in the majority rose in revolt. Marauding parties raided the neighbouring Gentile townships, some of which were reduced to ashes. Scythopolis, Samaria, and many other places were sacked. Elsewhere reprisals were carried out against the Jews.

At length, Gallus, the Imperial Legate in Syria, determined to strike, and led a strong force to suppress the revolt. He met with no opposition on his way to Jerusalem, where he camped outside the walls and defeated a sortie with ease. The insurgents remained unintimidated by this display of vigour, and the troops at his disposal were inadequate to carry out a formal siege. There was no alternative but to withdraw. As it passed through the historic gorge of Beth

Horon, the Roman force was surrounded and attacked. The retreat developed into a rout. The invaders were able to extricate themselves only after the loss of six thousand men and the whole of their baggage (autumn, 66). It was one of the most signal defeats inflicted upon the Roman arms since the establishment of the Empire. A victory so unexpected and so overwhelming encouraged the insurgents to dream of complete triumph, and made the war party supreme; while the Romans could not lay down their arms until they had wiped out the affront. Henceforth all possibility of conciliation was at an end.

VI

Meanwhile the revolutionary government had continued in control at Jerusalem, the ultimate authority being exercised by a general assembly of the citizens which met in the courts of the Temple. Steps were immediately taken to prepare for the inevitable Roman onslaught, and commissioners were sent to the provincial centres to take over the administration and to make ready the defence. For a brief period Jewish Palestine enjoyed a last glimpse of independence. The country was filled with warlike preparations. Jerusalem and the other principal cities were put into a state of defence. Men of military age were given desultory training, in vague imitation of the Roman methods. Coins were again struck, in token of the restored independence. A determined attempt was made to break through the hostile strip which shut off Judaea from the sea by a succession of unsuccessful attacks on Ascalon. Yet, even in this grave hour, there was no unity in the country. The patriots who had seized Masada, led by Menahem, the son of Judah the Galilaean, attempted to control the capital, though they lost their leader in the fighting which ensued. The Assassins continued active. The extremists intrigued continually against the more moderate elements, and energy which should have been turned against the common enemy was wasted in operations against internal opponents.

Preparatory measures on the other side were meanwhile being pressed on. Vespasian, one of the ablest living Roman generals, who had achieved high reputation as the conqueror of Britain, was despatched to Syria to direct operations. During the winter of 66-67 he was at Antioch, recruiting his forces. Early in the following year he advanced to Ptolemais, on the edge of the revolted area. Here he was joined by his son Titus, who had brought up a legion from Egypt.

In addition to his seasoned Roman troops, he had at his disposal a strong force of auxiliaries sent by friendly local rulers, including, to his shame, King Agrippa. Galilee was in no condition to put up a defence. The governor who had been appointed to the command of this province in the patriotic interest on the outbreak of the revolt was a certain Joseph ben Mattathias, the Priest, better known to posterity as Josephus. His principal recommendation was a recent visit to Rome, where, it was presumed, he had learned something of Roman methods. But his sincerity was suspect. It was noticed that he treated Roman partisans in too kindly a fashion, and his sympathies were obviously with the aristocratic party. The more earnest patriots, grouped about the fervent John of Gish-halab (Gischala), opposed him tooth and nail. At one time they even managed to procure his recall from the revolutionary junta in Jerusalem, but the supple governor circumvented them.

The past year had thus been wasted in internal squabbles and intrigues, sometimes accompanied by bloodshed. In spite of a few spectacular measures carried out by Josephus, no serious steps had been taken to put the country in a state of defence. Accordingly the Jewish resistance crumbled before the Roman advance (spring, 67). The wealthy city of Sepphoris, one of the most important in Galilee, had already anticipated attack by a spontaneous surrender. The Jewish levies could not face the Roman army in the field, and dispersed almost without striking a blow. Josephus retired to Jotapata, occupying an immensely strong position among the mountains. After a defence of two months, the city was captured; and Josephus, saving his life by a stratagem, went over brazenly to the Romans—an act of treachery to which the Jewish people is indebted for the fact that its knowledge of this period, if one-sided, is at least minute. Gish-halab and Mount Tabor, together with Taricheae and Gamala on the further shore of the Sea of Galilee, continued to hold out for a while, The full force of the Roman armies was brought to bear upon them, one by one; and, before the autumn rains halted the campaign, the whole of Galilee and of northern Palestine was once more in Roman hands. Simultaneously, Jaffa, which had been occupied by the insurgents and had served as the centre of attacks upon the Roman shipping, was recaptured after the only maritime engagement of any importance in the whole of Jewish history.

The effect in Jerusalem was the reverse of what might have been expected. The Patriots who managed to escape from the disaster in

41. SPOILS FROM THE TEMPLE OF JERUSALEM
Relief from the Arch of Titus, Rome

42. THE TRIUMPH OF TITUS
Relief from the Arch of Titus, Rome

43. THE SEVEN-BRANCHED CANDELABRUM FROM THE TEMPLE OF JERUSALEM
Detail from the Arch of Titus, Rome

44. THE DESTROYER OF THE TEMPLE: TITUS (40-81)
Naples, Museo Nazionale

45. JEWISH CATACOMB AT BETH-SHEARIM, GALILEE, Entrance

46. JEWISH CATACOMB AT BETH-SHEARIM, GALILEE, Interior

Galilee made their way to the capital, where they reinforced the extremists. The moderate elements were overridden by force of numbers, and the revolution entered upon a second, more violent phase. It was a Jacobin sequel to the orderly change of government which had taken place in the first instance. Suspected Roman sympathisers were thrown into prison or put to death. The High Priesthood, hitherto regarded as the preserve of a few privileged families, was thrown open to all those qualified by descent, and filled by lot —the usual democratic device of classical times; and the aristocrats of Jerusalem were scandalised to see a simple stone-mason elevated to the supreme rank. This was the last straw. The moderates, headed by the ex-High Priest Hanan (Ananus), took up arms and drove the Zealots from the city, though they were unable to dislodge them from the Temple. A rumour circulated that they intended to come to terms with the Romans. The Zealot leaders countered this menace by sending for reinforcements to their friends in Idumaea—recent converts to Judaism, but none the less devoted to the Jewish cause. On the latter's arrival in the city, during a heavy downpour of rain, they effected a juncture with their allies and a combined attack was delivered upon the common enemy. A veritable reign of terror set in. Hanan and the other moderate leaders were butchered. The prisons were filled with suspects. A revolutionary tribunal was set up, which condemned its opponents to death without compunction. The original leaders of the revolt were thus swept out of the way. The administration was now in the hands of the extremists, headed by John of Gischala (Josephus' former opponent), who had managed to escape from his native city after holding out bravely for some months.

Vespasian had determined to isolate the capital before striking his final blow. During the winter of 67-68 he reduced the majority of the territories beyond the Jordan to obedience. In the spring he marched southwards. The towns in the Judaean lowlands were captured one by one. A strong force was left in Idumaea to overawe the country. Then, wheeling northwards, he occupied Jericho. With the exception of a small strip around Jerusalem, the whole of the country was now in Roman hands. The commander-in-chief returned to Caesarea to make final preparations for besieging the capital. While he was here, news arrived of the death of the Emperor Nero. The political outlook became so uncertain (all the more so when Nero's successor, Galba, was assassinated in the following January) that, for the moment, it seemed inadvisable to recommence the campaign.

In Jerusalem, meanwhile, John of Gischala was supreme. He shewed in his administration many of the qualities of a real statesman. He strengthened the fortifications of the city, where the Lower City, the Upper, and the Temple constituted three almost self-sufficient strongholds. He made provision to withstand a blockade. Above all, he entered into relations with the Jews living under Parthian rule in Mesopotamia, whom he incited to attack the Romans in the flank. Yet satisfaction with his rule was by no means universal. The aristocrats, whose devotion to the cause of independence was suspect, had indeed been driven from power. But there were other elements whose democratic and revolutionary principles carried them even further than the dominant regime. At their head was a certain Simon bar Giora ('son of the Proselyte'), a young man whose mixed blood did not lessen his devotion to the Jewish cause. In contradistinction to John of Gischala, who had come to the fore as the champion of the middle class against the aristocrats, he was a democrat, or rather demagogue, in the more modern sense of the word. He championed the cause of the lowest elements, shewed himself a determined enemy of the wealthy, and endeavoured to extend the scope of the revolution from the purely political to the social and economic spheres. On the outbreak of the revolt, he had made himself master of Acrabatene in Idumaea, though his conduct here was such that he was expelled by a force sent against him from Jerusalem. He had then joined the political extremists, who had seized upon the fortress of Masada.

When news arrived of the recent change of government at Jerusalem and the overthrow of the moderates, he came forward openly a champion of extreme revolutionary principles, proclaiming the equality of all and (in pursuance of this) liberating the slaves. He soon had a force of some 15,000 at his disposal, mastered the south of the country, captured Hebron, and swept up to the gates of Jerusalem. Here the remaining Idumaeans (whose main body had left the city some time before) had quarrelled with John of Gischala and come to an understanding with what was left of the moderates. In the hopes of ridding themselves of the Zealot domination, they now invited Bar Giora and his followers into the city (April, 69). Civil warfare broke out once more, and the streets again flowed with blood. It proved impossible to dislodge the 8,400 Zealots from the Temple Mount, even though they too were hopelessly divided amongst themselves. The dispute was nevertheless not allowed to interfere with the regular sequence of public worship, and the faithful continued to be admitted, after scrutiny, to sacrifice at the Altar. Both sides supported themselves upon the civil population, with the result that the food supplies rapidly diminished. Simon's followers in the end fired the granaries, whether to keep them from their rivals or to shew their implicit confidence in Divine succour. Thus utter famine was hastened, followed by horrors which are depicted for all time in the graphic pages of Josephus.

Internal dissension was stayed by the advance of the Romans (summer, 69). Hebron, Bethel, and all the Judaean uplands were occupied. The only places which now held out, besides Jerusalem, were the mountain-fastnesses of Herodium, Masada, and Machaerus. While Vespasian was at Caesarea making ready for further operations, news arrived of the elevation of Vitellius to the throne of the Caesars by the army of the Rhine. His own legionaries, indignant, proclaimed their own general Emperor. The latter abandoned the campaign and hastened Romewards to assert his claim. At Alexandria, he learned that Vitellius had been assassinated, so that his own title was now virtually unopposed. Before embarking, therefore, he sent his son Titus back to complete the conquest of Judaea.

In the spring of the year 70, the new commander arrived beneath the walls of Jerusalem. The ranks of the besieged closed in the face of danger. But, for the past three years, they had been frittering away their energies in internal discord, and they were in no condition to withstand a siege. The Lower City was stormed without much difficulty, after a breach had been made in the walls; but the Upper City and the Temple Mount continued to hold out. The defenders, encouraged by 'prophets' who lacked nothing of the old fire and confidence, fought with unbelievable valour. God Himself, they thought, was on their side; and, when all seemed blackest, He would assuredly intervene to deliver them in miraculous fashion, as He had so often done in the days of their fathers.

At midsummer, conditions had become so desperate that the regular sequence of morning and evening sacrifice had to be discontinued at the Altar, for the first time since the triumph of Judah the Maccabee. On the ninth of Ab—almost the exact anniversary of the destruction of Jerusalem by Nebuchadnezzar—the Temple was stormed, and (whether by accident or by design) committed to the flames. The Upper City held out for a month longer; but, before the autumn, all was in Roman hands. The few fastnesses still held were reduced without much difficulty, with the exception of Masada, which continued to resist under the Zealot leader Eleazar, a descendant of Judah the Galilaean.[1] In the spring of 73, this, too, fell; and the last vestige of Jewish independence was crushed. The Imperial City had meanwhile witnessed yet another triumph, graced by the presence and slaughter of the surviving patriot-heroes: a commemorative arch, with reliefs depicting the Jewish captives and the Temple spoils, was erected in the Forum; and the classical world gave a sigh of relief at the thought that this bulwark of obscurantism, which had withstood the tide of progress for so many centuries, had at last been swept away.

[1] The 'Dead Sea Scrolls' discovered in and after 1948 near the ruins of the ancient communal buildings at Qumran apparently comprise part of the basic literature of the Zealot sect, illustrating its organisation and its politico-religious programme, and throwing new light on conditions in Judaea at the time of the capture of Jerusalem in the year 70. Much of the literature found here is however obviously much older, providing Biblical manuscripts nearly one thousand years earlier than any previously known, and illustrating a feverish literary activity in Judaea, hitherto unsuspected, in the period of the birth of Christianity.

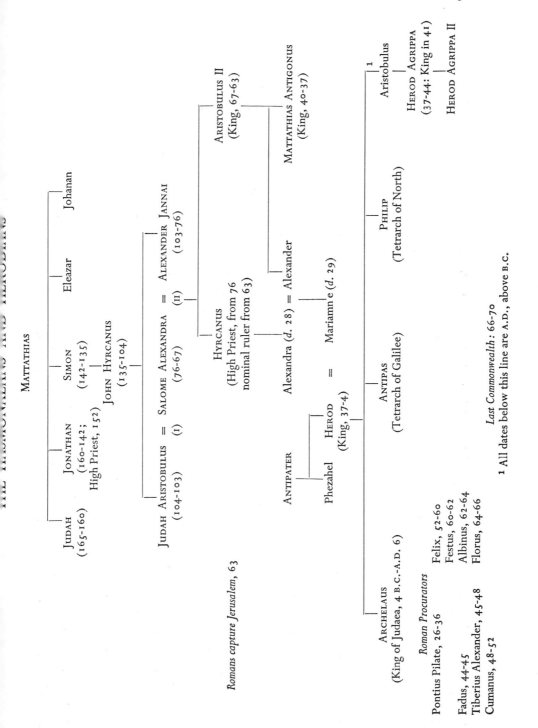

THE HASMONEANS AND HERODIANS

MATTATHIAS

JUDAH
(165-160)

JONATHAN
(160-142;
High Priest, 152)

SIMON
(142-135)

JOHN HYRCANUS
(135-104)

ELEAZAR

JOHANAN

JUDAH ARISTOBULUS = SALOME ALEXANDRA = ALEXANDER JANNAI
(104-103) (I) (76-67) (II) (103-76)

HYRCANUS
(High Priest, from 76
nominal ruler from 63)

ARISTOBULUS II
(King, 67-63)

Alexandra (d. 28) = Alexander

Alexandra (d. 28) = Mariamne (d. 29)

MATTATHIAS ANTIGONUS
(King, 40-37)

ANTIPATER

Phezahel HEROD
(King, 37-4)

ANTIPAS
(Tetrarch of Galilee)

PHILIP
(Tetrarch of North)

Aristobulus[1]

HEROD AGRIPPA
(37-44: King in 41)

HEROD AGRIPPA II

ARCHELAUS
(King of Judaea, 4 B.C.-A.D. 6)

Romans capture Jerusalem, 63

Roman Procurators
Pontius Pilate, 26-36

Felix, 52-60
Festus, 60-62
Albinus, 62-64
Florus, 64-66

Fadus, 44-45
Tiberius Alexander, 45-48
Cumanus, 48-52

Last Commonwealth: 66-70
[1] All dates below this line are A.D., above B.C.

Chapter X

THE RULE OF THE WISEST

———————•———————

I

Contrary to what is generally imagined, the fall of Jerusalem was an episode in the history of the Jewish people, rather than the close of an epoch. Some contemporaries, indeed, regarded the last struggle in the light of a civil war instead of a national rebellion. There had been important Jewish settlements outside Palestine, and one or two within its traditional borders, which had remained 'loyal'. The Roman camp was continually thronged by influential Jews who were bitterly opposed to the revolution which had taken place at Jerusalem, and encouraged intervention. King Agrippa, the lay representative of the Jewish people, actually sent his troops to participate in the operations; Tiberius Alexander, the apostate nephew of Philo of Alexandria, acted as Titus' chief of staff; the renegade Josephus became a court favourite and official historian. Though the Romans were fiercely vindictive to all who were captured under arms, they took care that those who had not been implicated in the revolt, whether in Palestine or elsewhere, were unmolested.

It is true that Jerusalem, and the Temple, lay in ruins, and their rebuilding was forbidden; while, in consequence of disorders which the fugitives from Palestine stirred up subsequently in Egypt and Cyrene, even the imitative sanctuary at Leontopolis, founded by the High Priest Onias nearly two and a half centuries before, was closed. It is true that the voluntary tax of half a shekel, which had hitherto been collected annually throughout the Diaspora on behalf of the Temple at Jerusalem, was made compulsory, and assigned to a department of the Imperial treasury at Rome, the *Fiscus Judaicus*. It is true that the people as a whole sat in mourning for those who had fallen in the war, and for the glory that was gone from Israel. Yet, in spite of all this, the state of Palestine, when order was restored, did not materially differ from before. The population of Judaea and Galilee, at least, remained preponderantly Jewish. The country continued to be administered by a Roman governor resident at Caesarea. The Jewish state had fallen a century and a half earlier, when Pompey captured Jerusalem. The constitutional position of the Jewish people, after the great revolt was suppressed, remained substantially the same as before it began.

In the sphere of religion, the recent upheaval resulted in one new development of extraordinary importance. The stately ceremonial which had hitherto been carried on in the Temple on Mount Moriah now became impossible; for, as we have seen,[1] the Pentateuchal code forbade animal sacrifice anywhere but in the central sanctuary. The consideration formerly enjoyed by the Temple was henceforth inherited by the Synagogue, which during the six centuries since the return from Exile had become a feature of every town and village. Their importance, as 'lesser sanctuaries', prayer in which was no less dear to God than a heart poured out by the side of the Altar, was deliberately emphasised by the teachers of the period, no matter how eagerly they looked forward to restoration of the conditions which prevailed before. The profoundest outcome of the apparent disaster was that it forced Judaism to exist—the first of the world's great religions to do so—without sacrificial worship.

The spokesmen of the Jewish people had hitherto been the rulers of the house of Herod; but the last male representative of that family Herod Agrippa II, was estranged from his people, and had not much longer to live. The High Priest had been hardly less prominent: but, with the destruction of the Temple, the High Priesthood itself had come to an end. But, even before the fall of Jerusalem, there had been a category which enjoyed almost equal, if not superior consideration. The Rabbis—the scholars who expounded the Holy Writ —had always been looked up to by the people with reverence. Now, there was no one else to revere. It happened that, before Jerusalem fell, one of the outstanding scholars of his generation, Johanan ben Zakkai, had managed to escape from the city—according to legend, in a coffin borne by his disciples. Titus had permitted him to settle in the township of Jabneh (Jamnia), on the coast near Jaffa, used as a concentration camp, where he opened a school for the study and exposition of the traditional lore. The most eminent of contemporary scholars gathered round him there. The Sanhedrin, formerly the highest Council of State, became reconstituted from members chosen

[1] See above, p. 22

for their erudition rather than for political influence or wealth. As its head was subsequently elected Gamaliel, a descendant of the great Hillel, one of the best beloved figures of the Herodian era,[1] whose teachings and whose personality were still cherished more than those of any other scholar of his generation.

This body ultimately acquired semi-official status. Its president, or *Nasi* ('Patriarch', as he was called in the outside world), became recognised in due course as the representative of the Jewish people in its relations with the Roman authorities. Over a period of three and a half centuries, for some ten generations in all, the dignity was transmitted from father to son. The Patriarch would sometimes be on terms of real intimacy with his suzerain, and if the occasion arose, he was prepared to go to Rome itself on a mission on behalf of his people. Thus the political leadership of the Jewish people, which after the return from the Babylonian Exile had resided in the High Priest, and was afterwards usurped by the King, now devolved upon the Scholar. It was a phenomenon uniquely Jewish—a family raised to the dominant position in national affairs by virtue, not of physical prowess, or material wealth, or some mysterious supernatural force, but simply intellectual pre-eminence. Learning, however, did not always descend by hereditary right. It happened more than once that the titular president of the Sanhedrin was overshadowed by some more profound scholar of humble origin, and bitter dissension occasionally ensued.

With the fall of the Temple, the Sadducees, whose whole existence had been bound up with its worship, lost their separate individuality. The Pharisee scholars were left masters of the field. The internecine academic strife (the expression, it almost seems, of two opposing philosophies of life), which had so long prevailed between the disciples of the mild and lovable Hillel and those of his more stringent rival, Shammai,[2] was amicably settled. Under these auspices, life in Palestine was reorganised. There was a double system of government —that of the Romans, with their subordinate officials and tax-gatherers, centring upon the Procurator at Caesarea; and that of the scholars, revolving about the Sanhedrin and the Patriarch in Jabneh or elsewhere. The people voluntarily set aside tithes for the priest, and gave offerings to the charity collector sent round by the schools, with better grace than they paid their imposts to the Roman publican. Courts, for deciding legal cases in accordance with Jewish law, con-

---

[1] See below, pp. 125, 131.   [2] *Ibid.*

47. GAMALIEL AND HIS PUPILS
Miniature from the Sarajevo Haggadah

48. Ruins of the Synagogue at Tel-Hum (Capernaum?), Galilee
Second Century

tinued to be maintained in every town, with the Great Academy as co-ordinating authority. The Synagogue and the house of study became, more than ever before, the centres of local life. The educational system was developed, until it attained a perfection unrealised in Europe until the nineteenth century was far advanced; and the population continued to lead a full, and on the whole a tranquil, Jewish existence.

II

The work of reconstruction was interrupted by one outstanding triumph, followed by a terrible catastrophe. A people confident of Divine succour could not accept defeat as a final solution. For nearly a generation Palestine was kept in cowed subjection. But, forty-five years after the fall of Jerusalem, the eastern frontier of the Roman Empire was again in a blaze, and the Jews of the Levant and Africa, inspired with a vague Messianic hope, rose simultaneously, with a spontaneity and cohesion which make one suspect a master mind behind the movement. In Mesopotamia, Egypt, Cyrene, and Cyprus, the revolt assumed menacing proportions. It was put down, with an excess of cruelty, only after much blood had been shed on either side (115).

For the moment, thanks to a formidable display of severity, peace was apparently maintained in Palestine. However, shortly after the accession of the Emperor Hadrian, an insurrection on an imposing scale took place here also (132). At its head was a leader of gigantic strength and rare fascination of character, named Simon bar Kozeba, or (as his admirers called him) Bar Kocheba—the Son of a Star. Amongst those who rallied round him was the outstanding scholar of his generation, Rabbi Akiba ben Joseph,[1] whose whole-hearted adhesion gave the movement exceptional significance. It spread with lightning rapidity. No Josephus was present to write an account of the revolt, which apparently met at the outset with almost complete success. The Roman garrisons were driven out of the southern part of the country, at least. Jerusalem was captured. An attempt seems to have been made to restore the Temple. Coinage was struck of a perfection hitherto unparalleled, and bearing an inscription, in the old Hebrew characters, commemorating the liberation of the Holy City.

[1] Below, pp. 125, 127.

For three years the insurgents maintained themselves. At last, Julius Severus was recalled from Britain to take charge of operations, though command was ultimately assumed by Hadrian himself. The Roman military machine, once its full weight was exerted, was invincible. The country was methodically reduced, and Jerusalem recaptured. The last place to resist was the mountain fastness of Bether (Beth-ther), between Jerusalem and the sea-coast. In 135, after a long and stubborn defence, it fell—men said on the ninth of Ab, the anniversary of the double national disaster. The rebels were systematically hunted down. Those leaders of the revolt who had not fallen in battle, like Bar Kocheba himself, were cruelly put to death, as was Akiba ben Joseph. A harrow was drawn over the site of Jerusalem, and a new city erected, under the name Aelia Capitolina, into which no Jew was allowed to set foot save once a year, when they were suffered to 'buy their tears' (in the words of a Church Father) at the Temple site. The rest of Judaea lay desolate, its population almost annihilated by the war and the wholesale enslavement which followed. No longer was the stretch of territory about the ancient capital to remain the heart of the Jewish people. The centre of national life was transferred to the north of the country, to Galilee. From this time onwards, the Jews were in a minority in the land of their fathers; and, even there, their most populous settlements were in that area least closely associated with bygone glories.

III

The suppression of the Revolt was followed by religious persecution. Like Antiochus Epiphanes before him, Hadrian seems to have hoped to suppress the existence of the Jews as a people by forbidding the exercise of their religion. Until his reign was at an end, the fundamental practices of Judaism, from circumcision downwards, remained proscribed.[1] Even the teaching of the Law was forbidden; and tradition recalled ten outstanding scholars who suffered martyrdom rather than comply. Ultimately Hadrian's successor, Antoninus Pius, came to the conclusion that the new policy was unwise, and freedom of conscience was restored (c. 138). The intolerant laws were rescinded, with the significant reservation that circumcision might be practised henceforth only on persons of the Jewish race.

[1] Below, pp. 140-1.

Conversionism, as it had hitherto been carried out widely through the entire empire,[1] thus became a capital offence. From this enactment may be dated the close of the missionary activities of Judaism on a large scale.

The survivors of the school of Jabneh managed to re-establish themselves at Usha, in Galilee. Here a great Synod was held which decided upon a series of measures for the reorganisation of national life, shattered by the recent disaster. Simon, son of the late patriarch Gamaliel, became *Nasi*, that office now apparently receiving official recognition. He was a man of no great scholarship—a fact which demonstrates the commanding position which the family had by now established in the affections of the nation. His general policy was broad-minded and statesmanlike: and he made an energetic attempt to restore good relations between the Jews on the one hand and their Samaritan or Pagan neighbours on the other. The quiet of the country was, however, disturbed by a Parthian invasion of Syria, which found its sympathisers amongst the Jews; and subsequently there seems to have been a recurrence of repressive legislation, accompanied by the temporary withdrawal of juridical autonomy.

Simon ben Gamaliel was succeeded in his office by his son Judah (170-217), under whom the Patriarchate reached its fullest development. The family had by now attained economic affluence. Judah himself was a close friend of the Roman representative in Palestine, if not (as legend would have it) of the Emperor Marcus Aurelius himself. The state which he maintained was little less than royal. His strong personality dominated the Sanhedrin. He made a point of seeing that Hebrew was spoken in his household, considering it to be, with Greek, the only tongue fitted for civilised intercourse. When the condition of his health forced him to take up his residence in the high altitude of Sepphoris, that place became one of the centres of national sentiment. It was under his auspices that there took place the great codification of the traditional jurisprudence, known as the *Mishnah*, which was to constitute the basis of the national culture and literature in succeeding generations.[2]

Judah, who died in 217, was the last commanding figure in the Patriarchate. He was followed by a monotonous succession of Gamaliels, Judahs, and Hillels.[3] Scholarship was by now a superfluous qualification for the office, which had definitely become hereditary. The duty of presiding over the Sanhedrin was little more than a form.

[1] Below, p. 141.   [2] pp 127-130.   [3] See the table, below, p. 133.

There were many scholars in the country who overshadowed the Patriarch from the point of view of learning, though the latter appears to have regarded the supervision of elementary education as one of his main cares. Politically, indeed, the lustre of the office was undiminished. The authority of the Patriarch (now established permanently at Tiberias) was recognised to the utmost ends of the Diaspora, from which a voluntary tribute flowed in for the upkeep of his state, as had previously been the case for the maintenance of the Temple. The Emperor himself deigned to address him official communications; and high ecclesiastical dignitaries wrote to him with deference, if not affection.

Under this organisation the Jews of Palestine continued a compact group, nursing their traditional culture and maintaining at least juridical autonomy. But they were a dwindling community. Christianity was slowly extruding Judaism from the land of its birth. Economically, the country was in decline. The devastation effected by the Romans in suppressing the two great revolts of 66-70 and 132-135 left a permanent mark, from which it never recovered. There is evidence of a progressive desiccation, or diminution of rainfall, which was robbing the whole of the Arabian Peninsula and the adjacent lands of their fertility. Taxation, too, became crushingly heavy as Roman misgovernment increased. Every civil and military disturbance tended to affect the Jews more than any other section of the population—except, perhaps, their unhappy kinsmen, the Samaritans, who were no less unruly and whose history was in consequence even more chequered. For a few years previous to 272, the country was under the rule of the famous Zenobia, Queen of Palmyra (herself reputed to be of Jewish blood), and the seat of repeated campaigns. Under the Emperor Constantius II there was a local outbreak, put down by his general Ursicinus with barbarous severity (351). Tiberias, Sepphoris, and Lydda—all famous seats of learning —were stormed and destroyed, and the schools established in them never recovered from the blow.

There was a last fitful ray of light before the darkness finally gathered. The Emperor Julian the Apostate, in his reaction against Christianity,[1] shewed distinct favour to Judaism, and, in a letter to his 'brother, the venerable Patriarch Hillel' (II, 330-365), he announced his intention to rebuild the Temple at Jerusalem, on his return from a projected campaign against the Persians. But he never

[1] Below, p. 145.

returned, and exultant Christian writers regarded the disappointment of the Jewish hopes as a final proof that the Divine favour had departed from the former people of God.

Henceforth conditions deteriorated with increasing momentum. After the Christianisation of the Roman Empire, while the status of the Jew declined[1], Palestine became more and more a place of Nazarene pilgrimage and a centre of monastic life, which engendered a growing fanaticism; and the burning of synagogues by zealous ecclesiastics became a matter of regular occurrence. When in the course of the fourth century the Empire was severed into two separate states, this region naturally fell to the Eastern, or Byzantine division. In 399 Honorius, Emperor of the West, jealous at the transmission of bullion from his dominions to those of his rival, temporarily prohibited the collection in Italy of the voluntary tax, which every Jew had hitherto sent each year for the maintenance of the Patriarchate. It was a severe blow, which must have been keenly felt at the miniature court in Sepphoris. In the following year the Patriarch Judah IV (380-400) was succeeded by his son, Gamaliel VI. Twenty-five years later the latter died without leaving male issue; and Theodosius II, who had already suspended his functions on a flimsy pretext, seized the opportunity to abolish the office entirely and divert its emoluments to his own treasury (425).

Thus the last vestige of Jewish independence, the lingering shadow of the glories of the past age, was swept away. It was true that Jews were still to be found in Palestine in some numbers. Synagogues of considerable magnificence (like that recently excavated at Beth Alpha) continued to be constructed; schools and scholars managed to maintain themselves at Tiberias and elsewhere. *Archipherekites*, or Masters of Courses, attempted to revive on a smaller scale the dignity of the Patriarchate. The Biblical text was scanned and finally settled by the so-called Massorites,[2] and a quantity of literature (much of which, long lost, has been recovered in the course of the past few years) was compiled. At the time of the great struggle between the Persians and Byzantines for the mastery of Palestine in the reign of Heraclius, the Jews of the country, led by a certain Benjamin of Tiberias, took the part of the former, and had to pay a terrible price when their previous masters returned (628). It was not until the time of the Crusades that the dwindling Jewish settlement in Palestine finally decayed; and it is said that even down to our own days there

---

[1] See below, pp. 144-6.   [2] *Massorah* = 'tradition.'

remains a little village community in a remote corner of Galilee which was never uprooted throughout the millennia from the ancestral soil. With the abolition of the Patriarchate, however, the last relic of the Jewish autonomy, which had existed since the return from Exile nearly one thousand years before, passed away; and the last feeble succession to the political authority of the House of David, of the High Priests, and of the Hasmonaeans, belonged to the past. The Jew was divorced in the fullest sense of the word from his land. The most characteristic, and most amazing, chapter in his history was now to begin.

49. 'JUDAEA CAPTA'
Coin struck by Vespasian to commemorate the defeat of the Jews, A.D. 70

Chapter XI

THE MESOPOTAMIAN CENTRE

———————— • ————————

I

The period of the decline of the Patriarchate in Palestine co-incided with the heyday of a new centre of Jewish life in Mesopotamia. It is possible that only a fraction of the Jewish exiles deported by the Babylonians had seized the opportunity to return to Palestine with Sheshbazzar and Ezra. Throughout the six centuries when the Second Temple had stood in Jerusalem, a second important centre of population had remained, under Persian and then under Parthian rule, in the Land of the Twin Rivers—still calling themselves and known in the Jewish world as 'The Captivity' (Golah).[1] Occasionally their numbers were recruited by prisoners of war captured by their overlords in various campaigns. Of their general condition and history we know little. They appear to have been engaged for the most part in agriculture, cultivating every inch of ground by intensive methods, and even encroaching upon the statutory width of the tow-paths along the rivers and canals. There were especially important settlements at Nisibis and Nehardea, on the Euphrates. At the frontier city of Dura-Europos, there was in the third century a highly cultured community, the archaeological relics of which provide a remarkable parallel to early Christian art, and suggest that it may have had Jewish antecedents.

The population seems to have been punctilious in its allegiance to Jewish law. An old legend recounts how his devout Jewish troops refused to assist Alexander the Great in rebuilding the temple of Bel at Babylon. Each year the half-shekels and other gifts contributed by every Jew for the upkeep of the Temple were assembled in the chief cities, being taken thence to Jerusalem by a very numerous escort.

---

[1] There are extant a number of clay tablets of the fifth century B.C. containing the names of Jewish farmers and craftsmen who were parties or witnesses to the transactions of a certain Babylonian banking-house.

Relations between the two sections of the Jewish people were thus both close and cordial. There was a Babylonian colony, and probably a Babylonian synagogue, at Jerusalem. Babylonian priests, who called attention upon themselves by their uncouth manners, sometimes made the long journey to exercise their sacerdotal privileges at the national shrine, one of them being raised to the High Priesthood. Occasionally an outstanding character detaches himself from the general obscurity of the background. Thus a Babylonian Jew named Zamaris was permitted by Herod to establish a semi-autonomous settlement near Antioch, from which he was able to safeguard the pilgrim convoys of his co-religionists on their road to Palestine. Similarly, about A.D. 20 two brothers, named Asinai and Anilai, set up a bandit-state at Nehardea, which they managed to maintain for fifteen years. In the end it was suppressed by force; the consequent ill-feeling against the Jews of the whole region leading to a series of sanguinary outbreaks against them.

At approximately the same period, the entire royal house of the vassal principality of Adiabene, on the Tigris, embraced Judaism. The Rabbis told fantastic stories regarding the religious punctilious-ness of Queen Helena and her household. She herself, with some of her family, was buried outside the walls of Jerusalem in what has since been known as the Tombs of the Kings; and at the time of the great war against Rome, the King of Adiabene and his brother fought gallantly on the Jewish side. As we have seen, one of the more statesmanlike actions of John of Gischala, the patriot leader, was to enter into relations with his co-religionists in Babylonia, in the hope of persuading them to stir up their Parthian overlords against Rome. At this juncture the Jews of the 'Exile' appear to have remained somewhat apathetic. Not so, however, later on, when after many attempts Rome had temporarily established her rule in Mesopotamia: and the disastrous movement which is associated with the name of Bar Kocheba was preceded in 115 by a similar rising against their new masters on the part of the Babylonian Jews.

The recognised head of Babylonian Jewry, in its dealings with the state, was the Prince, or Head, of the Captivity (*Resh Galutha*: generally known as 'Exilarch')—legendarily, a descendant of David. The state which he maintained was almost royal. Even the Palestinian Patriarch, Judah I, treated the contemporary incumbent of the office with real deference. He maintained a lavish hospitality at his table; and it was through his medium that the government exacted the

50. ANIMALS LEAVE THE ARK
Mosaic from the Synagogue at Gerasa (Jerash), Transjordan. Sixth Century

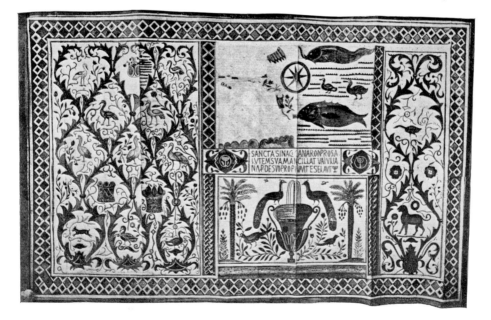

51. THE GARDEN OF EDEN
Mosaic from the Synagogue at Hammam-Lif, Tunisia. Fifth Century

52. FINDING OF THE INFANT MOSES
Fresco from the Synagogue of Dura-Europos, 245. Now in Damascus

53. THE ARK OF THE COVENANT RESTORED BY THE PHILISTINES
Fresco from the Synagogue of Dura-Europos

54. THE TEACHER (MOSES OR JEREMIAH?) EXPOUNDS THE LAW
Fresco from the Synagogue of Dura-Europos

55. THE SIGNS OF THE ZODIAC
Mosaic from the Synagogue of Beth-Alpha, Galilee. Sixth Century

taxation, usually of crushing weight, imposed on the Jewish community. The vernacular of Mesopotamian Jewry was Aramaic—a language closely akin to Hebrew, which by now had lost currency even in Palestine. Juridically at least, the community was completely autonomous. Internal disputes were settled according to Jewish law; and if only for that reason it was natural that the traditional learning continued to be eagerly cultivated. Throughout the period of the Patriarchate, therefore, relations with Palestine remained close and constant. Babylonian scholars went to perfect themselves at the feet of the great masters of Tiberias or Sepphoris. On the other hand, with the deterioration of conditions in Syria, many families transferred themselves eastwards in order to enjoy the more favourable circumstances of their Mesopotamian co-religionists. On the failure of Bar Kocheba's revolt emigration increased, and the revival in Babylonian Jewry which soon followed was stimulated by the new arrivals.

II

Excepting as regards spiritual and intellectual life, about which we are singularly well informed, our knowledge of affairs in Mesopotamia remains scanty in the period of resurgent nationalism, from 226, when the province was under the rule of the Persian sovereigns of the Sassanid line. Notwithstanding the intense literary activity, which was the distinguishing feature of the period, conditions do not appear to have been ideal. Under their new rulers, the Jews lost the right of inflicting capital punishment, and were excluded from certain governmental appointments previously open to them. The influence of the Magi (as the priests of the Zoroastrian religion were called) sometimes resulted in a persecution of other creeds, the followers of which were compelled to observe the ceremonial regulations of their new masters. Throughout the country synagogues were destroyed and burial-places desecrated. At the best, the Jews were prevented by force from doing anything which appeared in fanatical eyes derogatory to the practices of the established faith. On the other hand, some rulers, like King Sapor I (241-272), were remembered lovingly for the favour which they shewed to their Jewish subjects.

About 261, a major disaster occurred. The city of Nehardea, hitherto the centre of Jewish life in Mesopotamia, was captured and destroyed by Odenath, Prince of Palmyra, Zenobia's consort; and activities centred henceforth at Sura, some distance nearer the Persian Gulf. General conditions were unaffected by this blow. For another two centuries, life under the Exilarchs continued its even tenor; and it is in this period that Mesopotamian Jewry attained its greatest importance, and made its imperishable contributions to Jewish literature and thought.

III

In the middle of the fifth century, the conditions of the 'Exile' in Mesopotamia took a definite turn for the worse. The ever-present religious prejudice found its outlet in a long succession of persecution. King Yezdegerd II (438-457) instituted a repressive policy which outdid anything hitherto experienced, even the observance of the Sabbath being prohibited. Under his successor, Firuz (459-486), the community which had established itself at Ispahan, the Persian capital, was accused of having flayed two Magi alive. In punishment for this, one-half of the Jewish population was slaughtered, and the children seized to be brought up in the dominant faith. The wave of brutality soon spread to Babylonia. The Exilarch, Mari Huna V, was put to death; synagogues were destroyed; children were kidnapped; assemblies for the study of the Law were prohibited; teachers lost their lives; and the Rabbis regarded this year, 468, as that of the destruction of their world. It is probable that the foundation of the very ancient Jewish communities which still survive on the Malabar coast in India is due to refugees who fled eastwards from Mesopotamia at this period of crisis.[1]

For a couple of decades there was some respite. However, at the beginning of the sixth century, the Persian ruler Kobad adopted a new faith, Zendicism, which (according to its enemies, at least) taught the community, not only of property, but also of wives. The Exilarch, Mar[2] Zutra II, at length rose in armed revolt. For seven years he managed to maintain his independence, in the region about Mahuza, with the support of some of the non-Jewish as well as the Jewish population. Ultimately he was borne down by weight of numbers, and after his defeat he was crucified upon the bridge of his native place (520). His little son, Mar Zutra III (born on the day of his death), was carried off to Palestine, where an unsuccessful attempt was made to revive the dignity of Patriarch in his favour.

[1] The so-called Bene Israel of Bombay have a different and perhaps remoter origin.
[2] 'Master'.

The Jews of Mesopotamia never wholly recovered the prosperity and influence which they had enjoyed previous to these tragic events, though under the last Persian rulers conditions to some extent improved, except at the time of Hormuz IV (578-590), when there was a recrudescence of persecution. The details of these vicissitudes are of minor significance from our point of view. These fleeting glimpses are sufficient to illustrate the background of the thriving, well-organised life of the Jews in Babylonia in the first few centuries of the Christian era. The total population was to be reckoned by hundreds of thousands. By the time of the decay of the Patriarchate, it had numerically equalled, or perhaps even outstripped, that of Palestine. Above all, it had become the seat of a unique intellectual life which was to have a permanent influence upon the being and the mentality of the Jewish people at large.

56. RABBI AKIBA
Woodcut from the Mantua Haggadah of 1568

Chapter XII

THE TALMUD AND ITS DEVELOPMENT

————————•————————

I

The distinctive feature of Hebrew history in the period of the
First Temple had been the Prophet, and its distinctive product
had been the Bible. In the period of the Second Temple, with
its sequel down to the divorce of the Jews from the lands with which
they had hitherto been exclusively associated, the distinctive feature
was the Rabbi and its literary monument the Talmud.

The one was a logical, and natural, outcome of the other. Once the
Jew was provided with a written text containing the history of his
people, the moral teachings which should govern his life, and the
national code of jurisprudence and religious practice, the next stage
was the rise of a class of teachers. These on the one hand expounded
the sacred text; they decided on the other on legal cases brought to
them for solution. At the beginning (as has been suggested above),[1]
these functions were regarded as the prerogative of the Priesthood
or of the Levites. However, as the Temple came to occupy a less
important place in the national life, and houses of prayer became a
recognised institution in every town, the function of teacher was
assumed by any person whose tastes led him in this direction, and
whose intellect gave him pre-eminence. Ultimately the priesthood
tended to be merged in the Sadducaean party, with its narrower outlook and its absorption in the details of the Temple service. With the
destruction of Jerusalem, their importance as an independent force
was ended.

Long before that event the teachers of the Law, or Rabbis, had
begun to occupy a prominent position in national life. The legendary
chain of tradition associates them with the last of the prophets, and
regards Simon the Just, High Priest[2] in the Greek period, as first of
the new line. Even in the age of Herod, the Rabbi (as the New

---

[1] Above, pp. 62, 80. [2] Above, p. 65.

Testament amply reminds us) was important, even if not all-important; and towering figures such as Hillel and Shammai, whose memory is still alive in the consciousness of the Jewish people, had come to the fore.

The fall of Jerusalem swept away aristocracy and priesthood. Nothing was left but the scholar; and, thanks to the far-sighted policy of Rabbi Johanan ben Zakkai, the scholar became the dominating influence in the affairs of the Jewish nation for centuries to come. We have seen how the Sanhedrin was reorganised, and how its president was recognised as the representative of the Jewish people of Palestine. But the important work was done in the synagogues and schools, which the Roman legionaries passed by with such supreme contempt. The national ideal was henceforth not the priest, the warrior, or the landowner, but the student; and aristocracy was reckoned in terms of the learning, rather than the wealth, of a man's family. Not that scholarship was to serve as a career, in the material sense. A man was indeed advised to regard study as a fixed obligation, and earning a livelihood as incidental. But, at the same time, the Torah was not to be considered as a 'spade wherewith to dig'. The Rabbi, therefore, was expected to have another occupation, and the more lowly it was, the more he was esteemed. Thus the democratic Rabbi Joshua ben Hananiah, a disciple of Johanan ben Zakkai, who had served as a singer in the Temple in his youth and was the most strenuous opponent of the overweening Patriarch Gamaliel II, was a blacksmith by trade. His younger contemporary, Akiba ben Joseph, began life as an illiterate shepherd-boy. It goes far to shew the position which these two scholars enjoyed in national life that they were associated with the Patriarch himself in a mission sent to Rome, in 95, to procure the withdrawal of an anticipated anti-Jewish edict.

II

The tragedy of the Bar Kocheba rising and its relentless suppression proved all but fatal to the intellectual life of Palestine. So important had been the part played in it by outstanding scholars like Rabbi Akiba, that an attempt was made by the Roman authorities to suppress the schools entirely. Judah ben Baba secured the chain of tradition, at the cost of his life, by secretly ordaining some of Akiba's leading disciples after their master's martyrdom. Slowly, the old life re-established itself in Galilee, under the leadership of outstanding scholars such as the kindly, tolerant Rabbi Meir, who earned his living as a scribe; or Simeon ben Jochai, later to be regarded as the founder of Jewish mysticism.

Hitherto the teachings of the Rabbis had centred upon no written text other than the Bible. But there had already grown up about this a vast amount of oral lore. There were ancient legends elaborating the information contained in Scriptural history—some of them, perhaps, based upon fact, some on mere fantasy. There were tales connected with more recent events. There were ethical and moral teachings. There was Palestinian folk-lore, pure and simple, possibly in some instances antedating the coming of the Hebrews. But, above all, there was the elaboration and exposition of Biblical precept.

No written code can cover all possible emergencies. From the very beginning there had been questions and difficulties concerning one point or another on which there was no direct guidance in the Torah. Legal disputes on business or matrimonial matters, upon which the Scriptures were silent, were brought before the courts daily for settlement. The Rabbis scanned the Holy Writ for analogous cases, and decided accordingly. Similarly, with regard to religious practice. The prophets had insisted (Jeremiah xvii. 22) that a man should not carry a burden upon the Sabbath day. What, however, constituted a 'burden'? and what precisely is 'carrying'? It is facile to say that every Israelite must 'afflict himself', or his soul (Leviticus xvi. 31; xxiii. 27), on the Day of Atonement; but it is not easy to decide in what such affliction should consist. The dimensions, and construction, and materials, and use, of the Tabernacle in which every Israelite was to 'dwell' (ibid. xxiii. 42) at the feast of Ingathering each autumn; the time and method of the slaughter of the Paschal Lamb (Exodus xii.); the nature of the 'blessing' prescribed after eating and being satisfied (Deuteronomy viii. 10): all such points required amplification. Gradually there came into being various hermeneutic rules, or canons of interpretation, according to which the Scriptures should be understood, the most important system being one formulated by Rabbi Ishmael, a contemporary of Akiba.

Moreover, it was logical to enlarge the scope of the Biblical precepts in certain cases a little further: to 'make a fence round the Law', as it was expressed, so as to prevent a person from infringing it unawares. The Sabbath was made to begin a little before sunset, and to end a little after, in order to forestall inadvertent desecration. If an animal which died of itself was forbidden for food (Leviticus

xxii. 8), it was natural enough to extend the prohibition (in an extremely modern spirit) to one suffering from some disease likely to be fatal. The next thing to decide was precisely what constitutes a disease of this nature. The general issue was not what a man must do and what a man must not. It was, rather, what a man should do and should not, if he desired to carry out the *Torah* in its every detail. It was a code of life rather than one of law.

In this way there had grown up, in addition to the written code, a vast amount of 'case law', which was handed down in the schools from generation to generation by word of mouth. Much of it, indeed, was of such antiquity that it was regarded as tradition received by Moses himself at Sinai. It was Rabbi Akiba ben Joseph who began to reduce this heterogeneous mass to order. In the first place, he attempted to find justification for every item of the traditional extension in the Biblical text. Thus an unusual spelling, or the duplication of some word, served to correlate a recent development of legal practice with the ancient written code (just as it had given Philo of Alexandria a century before the opportunity of justifying his neo-Platonic allegories). Secondly, he was the first scholar to arrange the accumulated traditions according to subject matter. His pupil, Rabbi Meir, revised and elaborated the body of teaching which his master had assembled. It is possible that these scholars continued to rely on oral instruction without committing anything to writing. The prodigious Oriental memory might have made it feasible for this method of transmission to continue indefinitely, granted tranquil conditions. But conditions in Palestine were far from tranquil, and, by the end of the second century, the living tradition appeared to be dwindling with startling rapidity.

In these circumstances, a final redaction was undertaken under the auspices of the Patriarch Judah I, with whose name the enterprise is associated. Traditions handed down in the names of no fewer than 148 scholars were collected and scrutinised. The material co-ordinated by Akiba and Meir was revised, supplemented, and, where necessary, rearranged. Traditions of doubtful validity were excluded. The division according to subjects was perfected. In cases of dispute, the majority ruling and the accepted view were indicated. The whole was arranged in six 'Orders', each divided into tractates, chapters, and clauses. The language employed was pure, vigorous Hebrew, for which the Patriarch had a predilection. This new code was called the *Mishnah*, or Teaching; those Rabbis who had collaborated in its production, from Hillel and his predecessors down to the editor himself, being subsequently known (after an Aramaic word derived from the same root) as *Tannaim*.

III

No sooner was the work completed than fresh discussions began to centre round it. It was no more possible for it than for the Pentateuch to be so comprehensive as to meet all conceivable cases. Fresh problems of a religious or legal nature were always arising, and were brought to the schools for decision. In addition, eager students raised theoretical points (sometimes more remarkable for ingenuity than plausibility) which were taken into consideration no less seriously than the practical issues. They would be examined carefully from all sides, in the light of the *Mishnah* or of less authoritative independent compilations—such as the *Tosephta* ('supplement') or *Baraita* ('outside statements'), which stood in much the same relation to the former as the Apocrypha does to the Bible. Moreover, there was a vast amount of traditional lore—history, legend, ethical teaching—which had not found its way into the severely practical code drawn up by the Patriarch. All this formed the subject matter of the lectures and discussions in the schools.

Notwithstanding the political and economic decadence of the country, there were scholars in the generation succeeding the compilation of the *Mishnah* qualified to take their place by the side of the most illustrious of the former age—men like the tolerant Johanan bar Nappaha (*d.* 279), the son of a blacksmith, or his brother-in-law, Simon ben Lakish, who had been a gladiator before the other's influence turned him into a student.

The overwhelming passion for study was not confined to Palestine. For generations already, young students had come in considerable numbers from Mesopotamia to frequent its schools: it is sufficient to instance Hillel himself, or Nathan, son of the Prince of the Captivity, in whose favour it was at one time intended to depose the Patriarch Simon (*c.* 150). The national calamity in Palestine in 135 and the consequent emigration stimulated this tendency. One of the most brilliant students who sat at the feet of Judah I was Abba the Tall (Rab, or Master *par excellence*, as he was subsequently called: *d.* 247), a Babylonian by birth, who, on his return to his native land, founded a school of his own at Sura. A rival institution (originally established after the Bar Kocheba war by a certain Hananiah, a nephew of Rabbi Joshua, who had escaped to Babylonia) was situated at Nehardea, the principal Jewish settlement on the Euphrates. This was brought to a high pitch of excellence by a certain Samuel (*d.* 254), Abba the Tall's contemporary, and the exponent of a rival system of jurisprudence, who was at the same time a physician, anatomist, and astronomer. On the sack of Nehardea by the Palmyran forces (*c.* 261), this academy was transferred, after many vicissitudes, to Mahoza on the Tigris, the wealthy Jewish suburb of the Persian capital Ctesiphon, near the site of Bagdad. In the meantime, a more important centre of study had come into existence at Pumbeditha, a few miles from Sura.

For the next eight centuries, with slight interruptions, the schools of Sura and Pumbeditha continued to dominate Jewish intellectual life. They constituted, as it were, the Oxford and Cambridge of Mesopotamian Jewry. We must endeavour to picture, however, a state of affairs in which scholarship received all the deference which the Middle Ages paid to religion; in which the heads of the two seats of learning were no less powerful than the Archbishops of Canterbury and of York in medieval England; and in which the Masters of the Law did not hesitate to pit themselves against the civil power— sometimes with conspicuous success.

The organisation of intellectual life, too, differed radically from the European conception. There was no professional class, who studied in order to qualify for some appointment. To absorb himself in the law of God was regarded as the privilege and the duty of every man, from the highest to the lowest. The Exilarch himself was some- times a capable scholar. An artisan or peasant would attend the school each day after the morning and evening services, working in his shop or fields in the interval. During the day, eager students would be unflagging in their attendance on some famous Rabbi, listening to his verdict in cases which were brought him for decision and mentally noting not only his arguments and precedents but also his small-talk, his conduct, his most trivial habits. In the spring and autumn, when agricultural work was suspended, students would flock to the aca- demies from every part of the country, and for a whole month instruction was continuous. This (the *Kallah* as it was termed) corresponded in its way to the modern University extension system, though carried on with an intensity and generality unparalleled in our more sophisticated age.

I

IV

As the years passed, the mass of the material which was treated of in the schools of Palestine and of Mesopotamia became immense. The groundwork was the *Mishnah* itself, with the case-law, hypothetical or actual, which had accumulated since its redaction. This was known as the *Halakhah* (way of walking, manner of life). But, in addition, there was the *Haggadah* (or 'Telling') comprising everything that was not *Halakhah*: the Humanities of Rabbinical teaching, as it were. Everything was in it: history, folk-lore, medicine, biology, biography, ethical teaching, astronomy, science, logic, personal reminiscence of the great teachers of the past, and above all, a vast amount of down-right legend, sometimes very beautiful, sometimes a little puerile. All this heterogeneous mass—*Halakhah* and *Haggadah* together—was currently known as the Teaching, or *Talmud;* the Rabbis of the generation taking their name after the *Amoraim*, or Interpreters, who acted as the mouthpiece of prominent scholars when they lectured. The *Talmud* was repeated, by word of mouth, in the course of discussions in the schools, or of public discourses in the synagogues. Eager students made occasional notes, while mnemonics were some-times devised to ensure that no detail should be forgotten.

By slow degrees these discussions, too (though they remained always subject to additions and modifications), became stereotyped and crystallised. In Palestine the foundations at least of the definitive form were laid by Rabbi Johanan bar Nappaha before his death in 279. About the middle of the fourth century, the parts relating to civil law were apparently edited in Caesarea: the following generation saw the redaction of the remaining tractates by the scholars of Tiberias. However, the disturbed state of the country and the dwindling of the schools prevented this, the so-called Palestinian (or, less accurately, Jerusalem) Talmud, from becoming fully developed; and it is extant only in a fragmentary state. The parallel body of lore which came into existence in Mesopotamia is considerably greater both in bulk and in importance. Its redaction was due to Ashi, principal of the school of Sura. During the fifty-two years that he presided over this institution (375-427) he was able to go twice over the whole *Mishnah*, tractate by tractate, with all the supplementary material and traditional lore associated with each portion, which he sifted, rearranged, and stabilised. Subsequent generations continued to make additions and alterations. However, by the close of the fifth century, the Zoroastrian persecutions made it appear likely that the Mesopotamian schools would soon go the same way as those of Palestine, and Rabina II, (474-499) a successor of Ashi, took what was regarded as the momentous step of committing the whole vast agglomeration to writing. The final redaction was due to the industry and logical analysis of the *Saboraim*, or 'Reasoners', who lived in the following obscure generations. Thus the so-called Babylonian Talmud came into being.

In form the Talmud—whether that of Babylon or that of Palestine —is a running commentary on the *Mishnah*, written in racy Aramaic, alternating with Hebrew. That code, indeed, serves simply as a point of departure. The reader is transplanted bodily into the schools. He witnesses the thrust and parry of the Masters of the Law as they endeavour to find analogous cases. There is a pertinent, or sometimes an impertinent, interruption. An anecdote is told about some Rabbi of the past, whose name has been brought up in the course of the argument. Is the discussion centred about an astronomical detail? Then it is assuredly not beside the point to recall the great Samuel, director of the school of Nehardea, who boasted that he was as familiar with the paths of heaven as with those of his native city. The rules for saying 'Amen' after a benediction lead to an account of the fabulous synagogue of Alexandria, where the reader's voice was lost in the vastness, and a signal had to be made with flags to indicate when the proper moment had arrived. Rabbi Akiba is mentioned. Do you not know the story of his romantic youth, and of his martyrdom, and of the great revolt under Bar Kocheba? One of the many closely argued disputes between Abaye (last principal of the Academy of Pumbeditha) and Raba (his contemporary at Mahoza and adviser to the Exilarchs Mar Huna III and Mar Abba), leads to an enumeration of the six exceptional cases in which the former carried the day. Apropos of one solemnity or the other of the religious year, prayers are cited which embody some of the finest specimens of post-Biblical Hebrew prose, and are still integral portions of the traditional liturgy. Both fancy and legalism delighted to linger about the contrasting personalities of Hillel and of Shammai, the rival intellectual giants of the age of Herod—the former proverbial for his sweetness of character, the latter so stern and unbending as to withstand the tyrant himself. This Rabbi had a special formula, which he used to recite before entering the house of study: that one would never decide on a case after he had drunk wine; Rabba, the grandson of Hanna, had a store of improbable travellers' tales, strangely anticipatory of Baron Munchausen. . . . And so the reader is drawn on, through sharp dialectic, richly embroidered legend, strange scraps of scientific knowledge or fantastic folk-lore, until he is abruptly stirred by some immortal aphorism: 'The world is poised on the breath of the school-children'; 'The altar itself weeps when a man is reft of the wife of his youth'; 'Even a voice from Heaven cannot override logic'; 'If thou hast wisdom thou hast all: if thou hast no wisdom thou hast nothing'; ' "And thou shalt love God with *all* thy heart"—even with thy baser impulses.'

V

The importance in Jewish life of the Talmud (with which we may associate the contemporary Palestinian compilation, the *Midrash*, containing the homiletic and legendary embellishment of the Biblical story) is not by any means purely academic. It comprises the accumulated wisdom of the Jewish people over many generations. No aspect of Hebrew thought, and no subject of human interest, is unrepresented in it. The period of its redaction coincided with the growth of independent centres of life in far-distant regions, cut off politically and linguistically from the former nuclei. The Jewish people was about to enter on an entirely different phase of its being, in countries of which their fathers had never heard, in callings with which they had previously been unfamiliar, in the face of difficulties hitherto unimaginable. But they possessed, to bring with them into their new existence, a code, not merely of religion or of law, but of civilisation. The way of life which the Talmud so minutely illustrated and prescribed made the whole people of Israel one, wheresoever they might be found and into however many political fractions they might be divided. It gave them the characteristic imprint which distinguished them from others, as well as their remarkable power of resistance and cohesion. Its dialectic sharpened their wits, and conferred upon them a preternatural mental acuteness.

But, though it may seem an exaggeration, there was more in it even than this. For the Talmud gave the persecuted Jew of the Middle Ages another world into which he could escape, when the vicissitudes of that in which he lived had become too great to bear. It gave him a fatherland, which he could carry about with him when his own land was lost. And, if he was able to maintain his identity in the course of the long centuries to come, under conditions such as no other people has ever been able to surmount, it is with the Talmud, above all, that the credit lies.

THE PATRIARCHS

Contemporary Scholars (Palestine)		*Contemporary Scholars* (Babylonia)
Simeon b. Shetah (*c.* 100 B.C.) Shammai	HILLEL (active 30 B.C.-A.D. 9)	
	| *Simeon I*	
	| *Gamaliel I*	
	| *Simeon II* (*d.* 70)	
R. Johanan b. Zakkai R. Joshua ⎱ R. Akiba ⎰ R. Judah b. Baba	| Gamaliel II (80-110) | Simeon III (*c.* 135-165)	
	| Judah I (165-217)	
R. Meir R. Simeon b. Jochai R. Johanan ⎱ R. Simeon b. Lakish ⎰	| Gamaliel III (217-*c.* 235) | Judah II (*c.* 235-250)	⎰Rab (Abba Arikha) ⎱Samuel Huna
	| Gamaliel IV (*c.* 250-265)	
	| Judah III (265-330)	
	| Hillel II (330-365)	
	| Gamaliel V (365-380)	Ashi (375-427)
	| Judah IV (380-400)	
	| Gamaliel VI (succeeded 400, suspended 415, *d.* 425)	
		Rabina (474-499)
		Geonim Natronai (853-856) Amram (856-874) Zemah (882-887) Saadiah (928-942) Sherira (968-998) | Hai (988-1038)

The dates in the right-hand column indicate years of activity at the head of the respective Academies.

57. Page of a Fourteenth-Century Talmud Codex
Formerly in the Staatsbibliothek, Munich (the only surviving ancient MS. of the Talmud)

BOOK III

DIASPORA: 425-1492

———●———

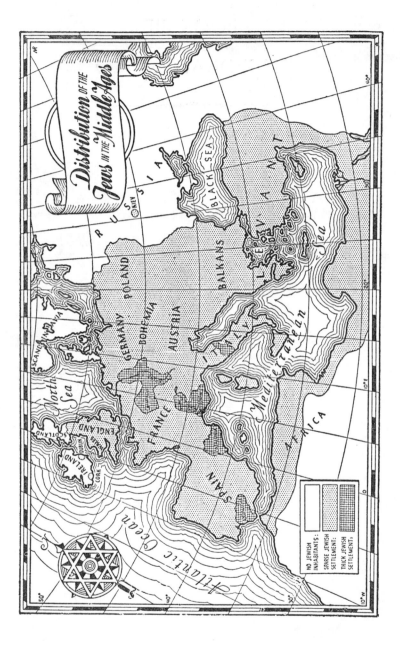

Distribution of the Jews in the Middle Ages

NO JEWISH
INHABITANTS:

SPARSE JEWISH
SETTLEMENT:

THICK JEWISH
SETTLEMENT:

Chapter XIII

THE DIASPORA IN EUROPE

———— • ————

I

As early as the period of the Assyrian and Babylonian campaigns in Palestine, the forefathers of the Jewish people first came into touch with Europe and the Europeans. Even before the close of the Biblical Age, Hebrews were settled within the periphery of the Hellenic world. The prophets Isaiah and Jeremiah seem to envisage distant limbs of the captivity as far afield as the 'isles of the sea' (Isaiah xi, 11, etc.), by which the Aegean archipelago and the adjacent coast-lands are probably indicated. The conquest of the Babylonian Empire by Persia brought the mass of Jewry under the rule of a power which had continual contact with Europe. In the later books of the Bible, such as Ecclesiastes, some critics have traced distinct Hellenic influence. The constant succession of wars, the international traffic in slaves, and the inevitable process of commerce, all tended to bring settlers to Greece and her colonies. After the battle of Issus (333 B.C.), when the Persian Empire was overthrown by Alexander, the Near East became Hellenised, and the Jews of Palestine and the neighbouring centres came definitely into the European orbit.

The revolt of the Hasmonaeans—essentially a reaction against Hellenism—actually resulted in bringing the Jews into touch, for the first time, with their ultimate enemy—Rome. The embassies sent to Italy by Judah the Maccabee and his brothers provide us with the earliest actual record of the presence of Jews so far to the west, as well as that of the first European Jews known to us by name. Permanent settlers followed those hardy pioneers. There is a vague report of the expulsion from Rome in 139 B.C. (the same year as Simon's mission) of Jews who had attempted to infect Roman *mores* with their religious cult. After Pompey's capture of Jerusalem (63 B.C.), Palestine was virtually a Roman province, and belonged to that vast nexus of subject territories which looked to Rome as their capital.

In celebration of his success, Pompey had sent to grace his triumph the Golden Vine from the Temple, together with many of his prisoners. According to the practice of the times, the latter were sold as slaves—generally through the medium of the contractors who followed the armies. Similarly, from 190 B.C. onwards, in all the Roman campaigns in Asia Minor (already, from its propinquity to Mesopotamia, a centre of Jewish settlement), numerous Jews had been captured and enslaved. The same was the case in the innumerable Judaean revolts, culminating in the insurrection of 66-70, and in the Bar Kocheba war of 132-135, after which the captives were reckoned by hundreds of thousands. The greater proportion, probably, found their way to Italy, but others were distributed throughout the Empire, from Spain and Gaul on the one side to Phrygia on the other. But the Jew was a bad servant. This was due in part to his independent temperament. A more important factor, perhaps, was his stubborn adherence to the practices of his ancestral faith, which would not permit him to work on the Sabbath, or to eat the food provided by his master. Hence it was natural that in the end the purchaser rid himself of what appeared an unprofitable bargain. Moreover, the intense solidarity which the Jews felt more than any other people (the 'redeeming of the captives', was regarded amongst them, indeed, as a primary religious duty) prompted them to help one another to freedom whenever the opportunity presented itself.

It must not be imagined, to be sure, that the origin of the Jewish settlement in Europe was due entirely to the slave element. Commerce is a factor more potent, though not always more prominent, than warfare. Palestinian merchants established connections as a matter of course with the capital of the empire and of the world. As we have already seen, there was from early times a very considerable Jewish colony in Alexandria—the greatest commercial centre of the Mediterranean. It is not to be doubted that the primitive settlement in Rome included a large number of traders who came thence, probably in connection with the grain trade in which Egypt played so important a part, and there were other centres along the line of communication between the two cities.

II

The Diaspora, or 'Scattering', of the Jewish people dates back, therefore, even as far as western Europe was concerned, to a very early period. Abundant testimony exists to shew how numerous they were in Greece and the adjacent islands, even before the fall of Jerusalem. In Rome their number was already so considerable that when in 59 B.C. the famous orator Cicero spoke in defence of Flaccus (former Proconsul in Asia Minor, who had confiscated large sums of money collected by the local communities for the maintenance of the Temple in Jerusalem), he tried to make out that the court was overawed by the crowd of Jews who had flocked to be present at the hearing. A petition to depose the tyrant Herod was said to have been supported by no less than 8,000 persons in the capital alone.

If this was the case even when the Jewish state maintained some vestige of independence, it can be imagined to what an extent the process was accentuated after the final tragedy, when Palestine was a mere province of the Empire, and when successive revolts had glutted the market with slaves. Early in the second century, the Jews of Cyrene were so numerous that a little before the Bar Kocheba rebellion in Palestine they rose in revolt and dominated the whole province for some time. It is almost certain that, by the third century, the process of penetration had reached even the most distant provinces. We have positive evidence of the existence of Jews in over forty places in Italy, as well as in the Crimea, Scythia, Dalmatia, France, and elsewhere. In Spain, and even in Germany, their numbers at the beginning of the fourth century were already so considerable as to justify special mention in legislation. But places with regard to which certain proof survives must necessarily be in the minority. Just as to-day a Jewish community exists in every city of the United States of America which has a population of 50,000 souls, a railway station, and a public theatre, so one was to be found in all probability in every *municipium* of the Roman Empire which was sufficiently important to have its forum and its hippodrome. By the time of the decline of the Roman Empire, the Jew was thus thoroughly acclimatised in Europe and identified with that European civilisation which, for better or for worse, was henceforth to mould the destinies of the world.

III

The condition of the Jews under the Romans was, on the whole, hardly distinguishable from that of any other of the many peoples of the Empire. Even the notorious unruliness of their co-religionists in Palestine did not materially prejudice their position. From certain points of view, they were actually privileged. To the Roman, religion was not of paramount importance in life. To sacrifice to the gods was the duty of every decent citizen. The Emperor himself was worshipped as a Deity. It was no more than patriotic to adore his *numen*, to refrain from doing so being regarded as a token of disloyalty. An exception was made only in favour of that strange people whose religion was different from all other religions; who admitted no image into their places of worship; and who had been prepared to rise in revolt rather than set up Caligula's statue in their Temple. From that date onwards, no attempt was made to repeat the experiment.

It was not that the Jews were popular. Contemporary poets jeered at their manner of life, singling out for ridicule in particular their strange habit of resting every seventh day. But in spite of this, the practices of Judaism were studied sympathetically in all classes. It was not easy for the ordinary woman, and especially for the ordinary man, to assume the heavy yoke of the *Torah*. But large numbers became demi-proselytes, refraining from idol-worship, and following Jewish tradition in such matters as the observance of the Sabbath and abstention from forbidden foods. At one period, this modified Judaism seems to have become positively fashionable, especially among women; and we read of adherents in the highest ranks of society— sometimes in the sphere of the Imperial Court itself.

Even after the Jewish war, Judaism continued to be regarded as a tolerated cult—the only cult, indeed, legally recognised in addition to the official one. Successive emperors guaranteed its privileges, protected its ceremonial, and even exempted its followers from appearing in the law courts on the Sabbath. The popular prejudices, such as they were, found no echo in legislation. The only disability from which the Jews suffered was that, alone of all the many races in the empire, they were compelled to pay a special annual tribute to the *Fiscus Judaicus*[1]—a precedent which, in the Middle Ages, was to prove susceptible of imitation to a fantastic degree.[2] Similarly, con-

[1] See above, p. 110.   [2] Below, p. 209.

versionism—or, at least, the circumcision of persons not belonging by birth to the Jewish people—remained a capital offence even after the abrogation of the legislation of Hadrian which had prohibited that rite entirely.[1] Except in these respects, the Jews enjoyed complete freedom. It is true that in the municipalities they could not be raised to the dignity of membership of the *curia*, which involved a certain religious ceremonial. This, however, was an invidious distinction, usually dreaded and avoided; for (quite apart from their other onerous duties) the *curiales* were corporately responsible, in their goods and persons, for the taxes of the whole area in which they lived, and the Jewish exemption was universally envied.

There was as yet no thought of restricting activities in any way. Jews are met in all branches of life—from blacksmiths to butchers, and from actors to mendicants. Those who were *libertini* (*i.e.* liberated slaves) enjoyed civic rights, and took part in public meetings. They could not indeed aspire to the highest dignities—to state employment, or to the rank of Senator or Knight. But the grandchildren of these freedmen became full citizens (*ingenui*), completely equal with all others. Finally, in consequence of the famous Edict of the Emperor Caracalla of 212, all free inhabitants of the Empire without distinction were created Roman citizens. This, in point of fact, was dictated by financial considerations, being intended to make all alike liable to taxation. But as a matter of course, they shared the advantages of citizenship as well as its burdens. The Jews of the Empire were henceforth Roman citizens in every respect, distinguished from the rest perhaps by one or two privileges, but not by any disability, other than the obligation to pay a special tax. It was a condition of affairs which was not to prevail again in Europe until the nineteenth century.

[1] Above, pp. 114-5.

58. 'FISCI JUDAEI CALUMNIA SUBLATA'
Coin struck by Nerva (96-8) on modification of regulations for Jewish tax

Chapter XIV

THE TRIUMPH OF CHRISTIANITY

―――――― ● ――――――

I

This was the state of the Jews of the civilised world at the period of the triumph of Christianity. Cursory reference has already been made[1] to Joshua or Jesus of Nazareth—a Galilaean religious reformer and preacher who was executed in Jerusalem during the procuratorship of Pontius Pilate. He had been one of many who were put to death in a similar fashion by the Roman authorities at this period, for daring to champion the cause of their people. In Jesus of Nazareth, there was indeed a double strain. On the one hand, he claimed to be the promised Messiah, who was to deliver his people from foreign bondage. On the other, he followed the tradition of the moral and social reformers who had been the characteristic product of Hebrew history.

In his wanderings throughout the country, he urged the people to mend their manner of life. In the spirit of the ancient prophets of Israel, he inveighed against the exploitation of the poor by the rich, and the stranglehold which formalism seemed in his eyes to be establishing on religion. He taught the fatherhood of God and human brotherhood, the infinite capacity of repentance to secure forgiveness of sin, the possibility of holiness even for the humblest and least learned, the certainty of life everlasting for those whose faith was complete and unquestioning, the equality of powerful and lowly before the Divine throne. His doctrines were not conspicuously original. He copied and elaborated the teachings of contemporary Rabbis, as he had heard them repeated from earliest youth in the synagogue of his native Nazareth. He presented them, nevertheless, in a new fashion, untrammelled by the shackles of ceremonial law and enlivened by continuous parables of haunting beauty.

In such circumstances, no man could have failed to concentrate

―――――――――
[1] See above, p. 97.

upon himself an overwhelming degree of opposition—from the Romans, whose rule was threatened by his presumed political aspirations; from the fashionable religious leaders, whose example he condemned; from the priesthood, through an attempt to reform the Temple administration by violence; and from the moneyed classes, whom he reviled with all the poor man's virulence.

When he perished upon the Cross (a Roman punishment, abhorred and execrated by the Jews), it was to be imagined that his influence would have died with him, as was the case with so many of his contemporaries. But his personal magnetism must have been extreme. The little group of disciples who had followed him continued to cherish his memory and his ideals, and to look forward to a second coming which would achieve all that had been left undone at the time of his death. Gradually new adherents gathered round them. Their opponents, in Greek-speaking Antioch, referred to them contemptuously as 'Christians'—after the *Christos* or 'anointed one' (Messiah) whose teachings they followed. The name, like so many others first applied in contempt, became generally adopted: and under it the Hebraic ideals which the new faith embodied were to become part of the common heritage of the western world.

The turning-point came when a Jewish tent-maker named Saul of Tarsus (known to the outside world as Paul), as he was nearing Damascus on his way from Jerusalem, suddenly became convinced of the Messianic claims of the dead leader, whose followers he had hitherto bitterly opposed. Henceforth he was one of the most prominent, and indubitably the most fiery, of the circle. With his burning faith, his unquenchable courage, his strong personal fascination, he was an incomparable propagandist. Few Jews have ever influenced the world to the same extent. It was due to him probably more than to any other person that Christianity assumed the form in which we now know it, and ultimately swept the world.

Paul undertook a succession of missionary journeys to win disciples for the new cause. The record of his wanderings throughout Syria, Asia Minor, Greece, and Italy indicates more graphically than any other document of the period the number and the distribution of the Jewish communities before the fall of Jerusalem. In every place in which he arrived, he found a synagogue which served as the scene, and subsequently as the centre, of his activities. But he gradually became convinced that it was impossible for Christianity to make headway while it was weighed down with the yoke of the Jewish law, its adherents having to submit to circumcision and to conform to elaborate dietary restrictions. Not without difficulty, he managed to achieve an almost complete break with the past. The ceremonial regulations of the Old Testament were abrogated. The fundamental Hebraic doctrines of Christianity became merged with the philosophical conceptions of the Greek world and the mystical currents which were at this time penetrating the entire Roman Empire.

This synthesis had a general appeal: and success was instantaneous. It was essentially a religion of comfort—one which offered boundless compensation in the next world in return for a simple faith and righteous living, unaccompanied by any severe code of practice, in this one. It attracted semi-assimilated Hellenic Jews and the demi-proselytes who were so common in the purlieus of the synagogues, as well as many who felt dissatisfied with the hollow formalities of classical polytheism. Despite occasional persecutions, its adherents were soon to be numbered by hundreds of thousands. Eventually the rising doctrine was adopted by the Emperor himself, and before long became the official faith of the Roman Empire.

The famous Edict of Toleration issued by Constantine the Great at Milan in 313—a political move intended to secure the adhesion of its followers in his civil war against Maximin—indicated the beginning of the ascendancy of Christianity.[1] It marks the end of the classical period in the realm of ideas, and in that sense is to be considered the real point of division between ancient and modern times. In the provisions of the new law, Judaism was included with other faiths. Its position was thus maintained juridically. In fact, it soon began to deteriorate. Christianity, although dominant, was not yet sufficiently sure of itself to shew real tolerance. The line of demarcation between the two faiths was still, in some respects, a little indistinct. The fathers of the Church hence engaged in a perpetual effort to make it clearer and more sharply defined, in order to prevent Christians from following Jewish rites, perhaps unwittingly, and so falling under Jewish influence. Moreover, Christianity still regarded Judaism as a dangerous rival—to be repressed if it could not be suppressed. This attitude found its expression in the Edicts of a succession of Church Councils, especially that held at Nicaea in 325, at which the calendar and the religious week were manipulated in order to prevent future confusion.

---

[1] Constantine was baptized only on his death-bed in 337: it is thus technically inaccurate to consider his Milan Edict and his formal conversion to Christianity as synchronous.

59. ROMAN JEWISH CHILD AND PET DOG
Lid of a Sarcophagus. Rome, Lateran Museum

60. JEWISH SARCOPHAGUS WITH GENII BEARING SEVEN-BRANCHED CANDELABRUM
Rome, Museo Nazionale

61. Jewish Burial Place ('Colombario') in Rome
Second Century

This clerical policy was henceforth to be adopted, almost in its entirety, by the state. In Imperial edicts, the fact soon became apparent. From 'a distinguished religion, certainly permissible' as it had been referred to previously, Judaism now became 'a sacrilegious gathering' or 'nefarious sect'. In 315 its followers were threatened with burning if they dared to persecute converts to the faith of the true God. A little later, the exemption from municipal offices, which they had hitherto enjoyed, was withdrawn. In 339 they were forbidden to have Christian slaves in their possession, or to convert to their own faith those who were pagans. Proselytes, and those who had won them over, were menaced with death. Intermarriage between Jews and Christians was prohibited under the pain of capital punishment. Apostasy was not only protected, but even encouraged.

Constantine's son, Constantius, outstripped his father, prohibiting the possession even of pagan slaves. There was, of course, nothing humanitarian in this. To the institution of slavery as such, the Church had no objection.[1] The whole of the economic organisation of the period was based however upon slave labour, and the effect of regulations such as these was to drive the Jew out of ordinary walks of life. There was a brief intermission under Julian the Apostate (361-363) due not so much to his friendly sentiments towards Judaism as to his antipathy towards Christianity. He even went so far as to destroy the records of the *Fiscus Judaicus*,[2] and (as we have seen) played with the idea of rebuilding the Temple at Jerusalem. On his death, the reaction was resumed to the full, coming to its height under the Emperor Theodosius II (408-450)—'the first Christian Inquisitor'—who in 438 rigidly excluded the Jews from all public office. His famous code, which formed the basis of later European jurisprudence, embodied all the prevailing anti-Jewish conceptions and regulations. These thus became implicit in the legal background of the medieval world which was about to come into being. Meanwhile, the unending series of massacres at Christian hands began early in the fifth century with an outbreak against the ancient community of Alexandria; and all over the Empire zealous clerics stirred up mobs to destroy the synagogues and drive those who worshipped in them into the arms of the Church. It was now that the great Jewish population which had flourished under Roman rule at the beginning of the Christian era was reduced to numerical insignificance.

---

[1] See below, pp. 166-7, note.   [2] Above, pp. 110, 140.

II

The Roman Empire in the West staggered to its fall in a welter of foreign invasion, and Rome was sacked by the hordes of Alaric in 410. Our knowledge of Jewish, as of general, history is vague in the mist of the Dark Ages which succeeded. Enfeebled Jewish communities certainly continued to exist in Spain, Northern Africa, France, and Italy. They must have suffered with the rest of the population during the long succession of warfare. A period of greater tranquillity, and less obscurity, came only when the barbarians settled down and adopted the Christian religion. The effect of this upon the Jew was on the whole unfavourable. Hitherto he had been reckoned, with the conquered Romans, as a natural enemy of the new regime, standing completely outside the ordinary body-politic. But the conquered Roman was now a fellow-Christian and a brother, and the position of inferiority was left to the Jew alone.

There was one compensation. In many cases the barbarians had felt attracted to the Arian form of Christianity with its more rigid monotheism, in sharp contrast to the Trinitarian doctrines of the so-called 'Catholics'. Accordingly they tended to treat the Jews with favour, if only to enlist their support against their own rivals. We catch glimpses of the Jews protected throughout Italy by Theodoric the Ostrogoth, and fighting bravely in defence of Naples when it was besieged by Belisarius in 555. Unhappily for them, Arianism was not destined to prevail. The triumph of Catholicism was a question only of years; and, in the sixth century, it definitely gained the upper hand.

III

Orthodox Christianity, whether in its Eastern form under the Byzantines, or in its Western under the aegis of the Popes at Rome, shewed itself less tolerant than the schismatics had been. Gregory the Great, Pope from 590 to 604, set the example which was to be followed by later generations, and which was to remain the norm in Christian Europe until the Middle Ages were at an end. In his Epistles, the ideals of the later Roman Empire are summed up and re-enunciated. Active persecution was discouraged. The Jew provided standing testimony to the truth of Scripture, and in his degradation proved conclusively that Guilt (guilt for what was considered to be the greatest crime of all time) must be punished. He was, moreover, the custodian of the original text, and of the interpretation, of part of the Holy Scriptures. His conversion was to be looked forward to and worked for, but through peaceable means. Forced baptism was deprecated. The Jews might enjoy liberty of worship and maintain their synagogues, though they were allowed neither to erect new ones nor to embellish the old. On the other hand, they were not to be encouraged to fresh 'insolence'. Proselytism on their part was to be repressed. The ownership of Christian slaves was not to be tolerated in any circumstances. The imitation of Jewish rites by Christians was prohibited. Even the employment of Jewish physicians, who might obtain physical (and, ultimately, moral) control over their patients, was not to be allowed; and secular rulers were sternly warned against appointing any Jewish officials, in however unimportant a capacity.

In a long series of letters written to places as far apart as France to the north, and Sicily to the south, the Pope enforced this policy. However, its niceties could hardly be appreciated by subordinate ecclesiastics, and even less by ignorant civil potentates. In France, where Jews had been settled in considerable numbers even in Roman times, there was a succession of attacks headed by the local bishops, and leading in some cases (notwithstanding the Papal disapproval) to mass baptism. Meanwhile, in the Byzantine Empire (which embraced Greece, southern Italy, and northern Africa, in addition to the old Roman provinces in Asia) the reaction assumed yet darker colours, under the threat of attacks by the Arab tribesmen now rallied round the standard of Islam. The Emperor Heraclius (610-641) went so far as to prohibit completely the public exercise of Judaism, and it seems that he attempted to secure the imitation of his example throughout Europe. In any case, at this period, there was a simultaneous persecution in all those countries of the West in which Roman Catholicism had recently established itself. In Gaul, King Dagobert ordered in 626 a general expulsion of all Jews save those who consented to adopt the dominant religion. A like policy was adopted by his neighbours in Burgundy and in the kingdom of Lombardy (Northern Italy). But it was in Spain that the reaction reached its climax.

Here the Jews had been settled from time immemorial: legendarily from the period of the first Temple, and certainly before the destruction of Jerusalem by Titus. Their numbers at the beginning of the fourth century were already so great that a Church Council held at

Elvira found it necessary to pass special regulations in order to check the excessive familiarity which was imagined to prevail between them and their Christian neighbours. Under the Visigothic regime, which established itself upon the ruins of the Roman colony, the Arian form of Christianity was adopted. The Jews now had small ground for complaint, and indeed seem to have been especially favoured. But after conversion, their rulers hastened to demonstrate the persecutory zeal characteristic of the neophyte. In 589, when King Recared adopted Roman Catholicism, the current clerical legislation was put into effect also in Spain. Slave-owning, inter-marriage, and conversionism on the part of Jews were prohibited under the severest penalties, and they were excluded from positions of authority or trust under the state. Later rulers were a trifle more tolerant. But from 616, when King Sisebut mounted the throne, the darkness became complete. For a period of nearly a century the open practice of Judaism was absolutely proscribed. Successive Church Councils, held at Toledo under the presidency of the King himself, formulated minute regulations by which former Jews and their descendants might be weaned away from their ancestral faith. Their children were seized and taken away to be brought up in orthodox Catholic households.

Naturally, in the majority of cases, the conversions were feigned; and in the privacy of the home, Jewish customs and rites continued to be observed as far as possible. Yet officially, save for occasional brief intermissions, the practice of Judaism in Spain was forbidden down to the last days of Visigothic rule, and those who persisted in its observance were driven into exile. A universal upheaval was required to restore freedom to the Spanish Jews and to initiate what was to be their age of greatest glory.

62. MASTER AND PUPILS

Chapter XV

THE ISLAMIC PHASE

———————•———————

I

In the spring of the year 622, a moody Arab camel-driver fled in fear of his life from his native city of Mecca: and the history of Mohammedanism began. To Mohammed himself the Jews were no strangers. Long before his time, they had been familiar in Arabia. In the fifth century, the ruler of the Yemen had been converted to Judaism, and his kingdom remained half Jewish until it fell in 525 before a combined attack of the Abyssinians and Byzantines.[1] In the north-west of the peninsula, Jews continued even after this date to be powerful and numerous. Like their neighbours, they were divided into tribes, frequently at war amongst themselves. They are said to have introduced the culture of the date-palm into the region; and, in the towns, they were famous as goldsmiths and artisans. Several oases and cities (including, at one time, Medina itself) were entirely in their hands. Their poets and their poetesses were famous, and are still remembered in the annals of Arabic literature. Their relations with their neighbours were generally cordial. Many of the latter were attracted by the principles of Judaism; and their folk-lore had become an integral part of the intellectual background of the country.

When Mohammed launched his new religion, he looked upon the Jews as the section of the community amongst which it might most easily be propagated. It was similar to Judaism in its insistence upon strict monotheism, in essential rites such as that of circumcision, in its dietary laws, in its reverence for the Holy City of Jerusalem. The prophet's own utterances, later to be included in the Koran, embodied vast amounts of the Jewish history and legend, with which he (like so many of his contemporaries) had been familiar from his youth upwards. Yet, to his supreme disappointment, the Jews held

[1] It is possible that the Falashas of Abyssinia are a relic of this interlude.

themselves aloof. At the beginning, he was forced to tolerate them. But when he gained his outstanding victory over the inhabitants of Mecca at Badr, in 624, his attitude changed. The Jews of Medina were suddenly attacked, and driven into exile. Subsequently, one after another of the independent Jewish tribes was assaulted and in most cases expelled, exterminated, or forced to embrace Islam. Those who remained were permitted to do so only on the condition of paying their conqueror a tribute of one-half of all their produce. Thus the new faith began to live up to its slogan: 'There is one God, and Mohammed is his Prophet'.

This policy continued to be followed by the Prophet up to the time of his death, in 632. The first Caliphs followed his policy to its logical extreme, expelling all Jews and Christians from most of the territories subject to them. Under the rule of Omar, however, the Arab tribes burst forth from the peninsula and initiated that astonishing career of conquest which was to subject half the known world. Within the next few years, Egypt, Palestine, Syria, Mesopotamia, Persia—all the traditional seats of Jewish population and culture in the Near East—were overrun. It was impossible for the Caliph to treat the vast mass of non-Moslems who had now submitted to his rule in the same heartless, though supremely logical, fashion which had been the lot of those of Arabia. If his new dominions were not to be depopulated, it was necessary to be more tolerant. Accordingly, the official policy of Islam towards the adherents of other faiths underwent a complete change. They were indeed subjected to a number of vexatious restrictions, in great part it seems taken over from the legislation previously in force against the Jews in those provinces hitherto under Christian rule. They were to be punished severely if they reviled the Prophet or lured his followers away from their faith. They were to wear a distinctive dress. They were to pay a heavy poll-tax. They were not to be allowed to bear arms or to ride on horse-back. They were excluded from public office, and forbidden to construct new places of worship. But they were henceforth at least suffered to exist, and permitted the exercise of their religion. In the course of time the various restrictions came to be disregarded, though tending to reappear from time to time with disconcerting abruptness. But the essential tolerance of Islam, in practice more than in theory, was to remain one of the important factors in Jewish history for many centuries to come.

II

For the moment, the most important centre of Jewish population was still Mesopotamia, where the ancient schools still flourished and the memory of the Talmudic era was still fresh. It was natural for the new Arab rulers to make use of existing institutions in their relations with subject peoples. As far as the Jews were concerned, the obvious medium was the Exilarch, or *Resh Galutha*, looked up to by his co-religionists by virtue, not only of his political position, but also of his legendary descent from David. From the new rulers, the dignity received official recognition, its incumbent being endowed with the right of internal jurisdiction, as well as privileges of the spectacular sort which appeal to the Oriental mind. Graphic accounts are extant of the pomp which surrounded the office. When he went to visit the Caliph, we are told, the Exilarch was accompanied by an escort of horsemen, Moslems as well as Jews, and heralds proclaimed his approach through the streets. He was attired in luxurious robes, of semi-regal splendour. As he appeared at court, the Caliph would rise to greet him, and would place him on a throne opposite his own, while the other princes in attendance rose to shew him honour. A multiplicity of legends has clustered in particular about the person of Bostenai (*d.* 660), the first Exilarch under the new dispensation, whose descendants continued to fill the office until its final decay.

Almost on an equal footing with the Exilarchs in the popular esteem, and superior to them in the eyes of posterity, were the heads of the two great academies of Sura and Pumbeditha, at which the scholarly traditions of the previous age were still cherished. These worthies were now known as *Geonim*, or 'Excellencies' (singular, *Gaon*): and it is as the 'Age of the Geonim' that the period is generally remembered. In their respective academies, they still continued to foster and develop the traditions of the expounders of the Oral Law who had preceded them. The seat of Judaism was no longer confined to Mesopotamia and the neighbouring lands. Jews had wandered far and wide, and were no longer in personal touch with the great centres of Jewish population in the East. But, wherever they were, they still required guidance on matters connected with the Jewish law and religion: and it was natural for them to direct enquiries (accompanied frequently by contributions for the upkeep of the Colleges) to the sages in Mesopotamia. An increasing proportion of the energies of the Geonim was thus engrossed by their correspondence, addressed to almost every corner of the known world, from Spain and Germany on the one hand to Morocco and Egypt on the other. These Gaonic *responsa* (as they are generally termed) touched upon every conceivable subject in which Judaism itself was interested: Biblical exegesis, elucidations of the Talmud, religious problems, marital regulations, business law. The earliest known formularies of the Jewish liturgy[1] and the first of Jewish literary histories[2] were composed by various Geonim in response to enquiries addressed to them by eager students in what was regarded at that time as the Far West. When, about 885, an imaginative impostor who called himself Eldad the Danite appeared in North Africa, with a detailed account of the condition and usages of the Lost Ten Tribes (to whom, he alleged, he himself belonged), it was to the Gaon Zemah (879-885) that the sages of Kairouan appealed for guidance. The overwhelming proportion of what we know of the history and literature of this age has been preserved only through the medium of these unique literary documents, in which the stored-up lore of Mesopotamian Jewry was made available to the growing colonies of Europe.

The relations between Gaon and Exilarch were not always ideal. The former regarded himself, the repository and interpreter of the law of God and the tradition of the ages, as being necessarily superior to any political functionary. The latter sometimes considered that his indubitable civil and judicial prerogatives were trespassed upon by his rival. Matters became even more acute on those occasions when, as sometimes happened, the Exilarch was himself something of a scholar, and could presume to challenge the Gaon on his own ground. Disputes sometimes centred about the offerings received from abroad, which the Geonim appropriated to the requirements of the schools and those who attended them, while their rivals considered them to be intended for the support of Mesopotamian Jewry and its established institutions generally. The details of the disputes, with their displays of force on the one side and of excommunications on the other, are strangely reminiscent of the fierce struggle between a medieval ruler like Henry II and his Archbishop of Canterbury: with the significant exception that the only external authority involved was the *Torah;* that the opposition to the temporal power

---

[1] Those of the Geonim Natronai (853-856) and his successor Amram (856-874), both composed in answer to requests from Spain.

[2] The famous Epistle of the Gaon Sherira (below, p. 156), sent about 910 in response to an enquiry from the sages of Kairouan.

came from intellectual, and not religious, leaders; and that logic took the place of dogma as the ultimate argument.

III

The most pressing problem with which the Geonim were faced was the rise of the Karaite schism. There had always been two tendencies in the Jewish people: the one of them regarding Judaism as a living, organic tradition, continually growing and developing, yet in essence always the same, and represented in every age by its Rabbis and teachers; the other thinking of it as fixed and immutable, with its final expression in a specific code of law. During the period of the Second Temple, the former point of view had been represented (as we have seen above) by the Pharisees, and the latter by the Sadducees. The fall of Jerusalem, and the consequent cessation of sacrificial worship (which was to them of paramount importance), had put an end to the existence of the latter as a distinct sect. But the tendency which they had represented continued, as was only to be expected. We hear little or nothing of it in Talmudic times; but after the Arab conquest, it again rose to the surface.

Islamic sects, who scanned intensively the text of the Koran and rejected accretions, provided a model as well as an incitement. There was throughout the Caliphate a ferment of religious conflict, of philosophical speculation, of political unrest. From time to time, there arose pseudo-Messiahs (the most famous was a certain Syrian named Severus, or Serene (c. 720), whose fame spread far and wide) who, in order to justify themselves in taking independent action, rebelled more or less openly against the authority of the Rabbis. The sects which were thus formed disappeared almost as quickly as they arose. One, however, not only perpetuated itself, but for a long time actually threatened the existence of Rabbinic Judaism.

According to a tradition emanating from the opponents of the new body (not therefore to be taken over-literally), the occasion for the schism was a disputed succession to the dignity of Exilarch in the year 767. The disappointed candidate, Anan ben David, seeing himself passed over in favour of a younger brother, found consolation by organising a rival body over which to rule. He entirely rejected the authority of the Rabbis, whose opposition had ousted him from the coveted dignity. He branded the Talmud as an imposture, and those who followed it as hypocrites or dupes. He refused to admit the weight of tradition in interpreting Jewish law and practice. He recognised the authority only of the Bible (*Mikra*), after which his followers became known as the *B'ne Mikra*, or *Karaim* (Scripturalists): their opponents receiving the title *Rabbanites*.

Under Anan's guidance, the new faith, with its apotheosis of the literal interpretation of the Scriptures, was arid and uninspiring to the last degree. The eating of almost any sort of meat was forbidden; no lights or fires could be kindled on the Sabbath day; recourse to physicians in time of sickness was considered an impiety; and a hundred other impossible restrictions were introduced, for all of which Scriptural authority was adduced. Teachers of a latter genera-tion, however—in particular Benjamin of Nehawend (*c.* 830) and Daniel al-Kumisi (*c.* 900)—shewed greater humanity and insight, borrowing some of their methodology and ideas from the hated Rabbanites. The new reading of Judaism, which was in harmony with conceptions current in Moslem circles, made immediate head-way. It was looked upon with favour in the outside world: and it gained tens of thousands of adherents amongst the less learned Jews, who had found the arguments of the Rabbis above their heads, but always had the Bible at hand to consult. The movement spread from Mesopotamia to the surrounding lands. It had a foothold in Palestine itself; it established a powerful colony in Egypt; it gained adherents as far afield as Spain. It was the greatest enemy which Judaism had known for many centuries past, threatening the existence of tradition more than even the fall of Jerusalem had done. That Rabbinic Judaism was not reduced to the position of an unimportant sect was due largely to the efforts of one man.

Saadiah ben Joseph (882-942), the greatest of the Geonim, was a native of Egypt, who was summoned to Mesopotamia in 928 as head of the decaying Academy of Sura. He realised that the Karaites must be combated with their own weapons. The Academies had contented themselves hitherto with the exposition of the Talmud and Jewish law, paying little attention to new tendencies in intellectual life. The Karaites had appealed to reason: they must be followed, and defeated, upon their own ground. They had appealed to the Bible against the Talmud: the Rabbis must turn their attention again to the Bible, and shew that Jewish tradition was implicit in it. Saadiah was soaked in the general culture of his day. He had absorbed the philosophical conceptions of ancient Greece, as they were taught by his Arab contemporaries. Judaism, to his mind, was an immutable religious system. It was not necessary therefore to adapt it to the requirements of the day, but it had to be reinterpreted in modern terms. He set about doing this with industry and method which were little short of amazing.

Even before his elevation to the supreme dignity, the new Gaon had indulged in a triumphant controversy in which he vindicated the supremacy of the Mesopotamian scholars, even above those of Palestine, in the matter of fixing the Calendar. He now set about a systematic series of works against the Karaites. One composition after the other dealt with the specific questions at issue. A translation of the Scriptures into the vernacular, which is still classical in some Arabic-speaking countries, carried the war into the enemy's territory. No longer was it possible to say that the Jews who followed the Talmud were ignorant of the Bible; and the commentary which accompanied certain of the books, together with the lexicon of words which occur once only in the Scriptures, inculcated some further idea of traditional hermeneutics. An Arabic treatise on 'Beliefs and Opinions' (*Emunoth veDeoth*, as it is known in its classical Hebrew version) provided a metaphysical basis for traditional Judaism, and laid the foundations of Jewish philosophy. Other works were landmarks in the spheres of poetry, liturgy, and jurisprudence. He was thus the great pioneer in almost every branch of Hebrew scholarship.

Saadiah's last years were disturbed by a virulent dispute with the Exilarch for the time being. But by the time that he was borne to his grave, the great battle to which he had devoted his life was all but won. There were still to be occasional outbursts of rancour, spurts of activity, and interchanges of polemics. But Karaism was henceforth a lost cause—moribund through its essential aridity. Its adherents are still to be found in Egypt, in Poland, and above all, in the Crimea. They have, however, dwindled steadily in number and in influence since the great Gaon of Sura directed his hammer blows against them.[1] The counter-Reformation which the movement had provoked had, indeed, a profound influence on Judaism. The birth of Jewish philosophy, the revival of Biblical studies, the study of the humanities, and the attempt to place tradition on a rational instead of a purely arbitrary basis, are all to be traced to this period. And if in subsequent years Jewish interest in Palestine became a little less academic, and enthusiasts again turned their steps towards the

[1] Their number in the Crimea at the beginning of the present century did not exceed 10,000, with perhaps as many more elsewhere. Few survived World War II.

ancestral soil, the example of the Karaites, who had begun to follow literally the Biblical precepts, was not perhaps the least of the factors which assisted in bringing this about.

From the period of Saadiah, the Jewish settlement in Mesopotamia underwent a rapid decline. The Arabian Peninsula, and the countries bordering upon it, were slowly becoming less fertile and less able to support their population. In consequence, the inhabitants were gradually driven to seek their livelihood elsewhere. It was this, to a large extent, which had stimulated the Arabs to burst out of their former home on their career of conquest. The same factors were operative also with the Jews. Family after family was leaving the region in which its ancestors had been settled from time immemorial, and going to seek its fortune in fresh fields of opportunity. Life continued indeed in the old channels. There were still Jewish peasants as well as merchants and artisans. We know of Court Bankers, who played a prominent role in Bagdad. Exilarch still succeeded Exilarch; Gaon followed upon Gaon. Scholars like Sherira (968-998) or his son Hai (998-1038) continued to uphold worthily the academic traditions of the old academies. However, the volume of their *responsa*, directed to the furthest limits of the Diaspora, shews that they were now concerned rather with satisfying the requirements of the new Jewish settlements than with continuing to develop the living tradition of the schools over which they presided. Hai was accordingly the last of the great Geonim (for a long time, indeed, it was thought that he was actually the last of the series). After his death, in 1038, the dignity was assumed by the scholarly Exilarch, Hezekiah. The latter perished, very shortly after, in consequence of a general persecution, and with him the importance of both offices ended. For two or three hundred years more, until the close of the thirteenth century, or even later, a succession of pretenders or imitators in Mesopotamia, Syria, Palestine, or Egypt continued to keep alive the memories of past glories, under various names, and with a deplorable display of petty jealousy among themselves. Their importance was negligible, and their influence essentially local. There was a final blaze of petty glory as late as the end of the thirteenth century, not long after the Mongol conquest, when a Jewish physician, Saud ad-Daulah, became the administrator of Bagdad and the surrounding region. His assassination in 1291, after two years of highly efficient rule, proved the signal for a general attack upon the Jews by their neighbours, as a result of which the ancient communities were completely overwhelmed. When a little later the Mongols adopted Islam, reaction in the orthodox Moslem tradition finally triumphed. Long since, however, this had been a mere backwater in Jewish life. The first half of the eleventh century had witnessed the final stages of the intellectual and political supremacy of Mesopotamian Jewry, and the interruption of the chain of tradition which dated back to the period of the First Exile. But, before the torch of learning fell from their weary hands, the Geonim had succeeded in passing it to a new, vigorous colony in the West, which was to preserve the sacred flame for later ages.

IV

It had taken the Arabs somewhat less than a century from the date of the *Hegira* to sweep the Mediterranean world from end to end. In 711 an expedition under Tarik crossed the Straits of Gibraltar, and the final conquest of Spain was a matter of only four years. Later ecclesiastical chroniclers maliciously ascribed the debacle of the Visigoths to the Jews, who, they alleged, invited as well as assisted the invasion. As we have seen, recent intolerance and bigotry had left no professing Jews in the country, and the truth of the charge is highly improbable. But the change of government ushered in a fresh age for Spanish Jewry. Mesopotamia, under Persian or Parthian rule, had hitherto been outside the orbit of the Mediterranean world, which was Græco-Roman. But, with the Arab conquests, conditions changed. The great reservoir of Jewish population in the East now came under the same rule as the new fields of opportunity in the West. A man could travel from Bagdad to the foot of the Pyrenees without being hampered by any change of government, culture, or language. By the period of the conquest of Spain, moreover, the original fanaticism of the Arabs had subsided, and in return for a lucrative poll-tax they were prepared to grant ample toleration to all unbelievers, of whatever creed.

It seems that the Jews, impelled by the same natural urge or by the same economic necessities, streamed at the heels of the Arabs, as traders, as artisans, as peasants. In consequence, the most important section of Jewry—numerically, geographically, and culturally—became Arabised. They adopted Arab names, spoke only Arabic among themselves, followed Moslem intellectual fashions and standards, used the vernacular for their literature and even, to some extent, for their liturgy, and considered Europe north of the Pyrenees as a stronghold of barbarism. The ancient communities, which had continued a somewhat degraded existence under the Byzantine rule in Egypt and the adjacent countries of north Africa, were rejuvenated. Kairouan, the military camp founded in the neighbourhood of the ancient city of Carthage (subsequently to be the centre of government for the whole province), suddenly became known as a seat of learning, its scholars exchanging learned correspondence with the Babylonian Geonim even before the days of Saadiah. Spain made headway a little more slowly, but with even more dazzling results.

From Abd-ar-Rahman I (756-788) the Peninsula was the seat of an autonomous Caliphate, free from all dependence upon Bagdad. The special conditions of the country, with its large proportion of Christian or Visigothic elements, made tolerance a cardinal point of policy, the Jews enjoying it in the same way as the other sections of the population. Indeed, it was only wise to favour them and thus foster their sympathies; for they constituted an important minority in a population a large part of which was perennially disaffected. They entered into every walk of life, urban and rural. For the purposes of diplomatic intercourse with the Christian states, both in the peninsula and outside it, the Jew, with his knowledge of languages, was the ideal intermediary; and, in consequence of this, many individuals attained great influence in affairs of state. Physicians, astronomers, and astrologers (the latter two arts were at the time all but identical), similarly obtained an *entrée* to court, and in some instances wielded a vast influence.

The outstanding figure of the period was Hasdai ibn Shabrut (c. 915-970), with whom Jewish life in Spain suddenly emerged from the comparative obscurity which had hitherto enveloped it for so long. He owed his political importance to two factors: first, to his knowledge of medicine, which had originally brought him to the notice of the Caliph Abd-ar-Rahman III, who appointed him Court Physician; and secondly, to his acquaintance with the Latin tongue— at that time the international language of letters and of the diplomatic intercourse of the Christian world. From being simply a physician, Hasdai became, in consequence of this, the Caliph's confidant and adviser. Without bearing the title of vizier, he was in reality Minister for Foreign Affairs. Negotiations of the highest delicacy, both in the country and beyond its borders, were entrusted to him. In addition, as a reward for his services, he was made Inspector-

General of the Customs for Cordova. On the death of Abd-ar-Rahman (961), his son Hakam II retained Hasdai in his service; and he appears to have continued to enjoy the royal favour until his death.

In 956, when the Holy Roman Emperor Otto I sent an embassy to Cordova, it was Hasdai who was empowered to treat with it, and whose adroit persuasion led to the satisfactory termination of the transaction. Abbot John of Görz, the Imperial Ambassador, frankly confessed that he had never encountered an equal intellect in his travels. A couple of years later, Hasdai was sent to the King of the Christian state of Leon, Sancho IV, whom he treated for his excessive corpulence. Subsequently, he actually managed to persuade him and the Queen Mother to accompany him back to Cordova: and Abd-ar-Rahman had the satisfaction of seeing his most determined enemies at his feet as suppliants. Contemporary Hebrew poets celebrated the episode in exultant verses.

This activity did not divert Hasdai's attention from scientific studies. His name is still associated with a once-popular panacea which he discovered. On one occasion, when an embassy from the court of Byzantium brought as a present to the Caliph an important Greek codex, embodying Dioscorides' work on botany, a monk was found who read off passage after passage in an extemporised Latin version, which the Jew turned into polished Arabic. It was through this polyglot channel that the work of the great Greek scientist became available to the medical schools of Moslem Spain, and ultimately to medieval Europe as a whole.

In his prosperity, Hasdai did not forget his own people. Every embassy sent to Cordova from foreign powers was interrogated by him as to the condition of the Jews in his native land. It was this which led to a famous interchange of correspondence with the kingdom of the Khazars—an independent state north of the Black Sea, the ruling classes of which had accepted Judaism in the eighth century.[1] He used his influence to ameliorate the condition of the Jews in the south of France, and made representations at the court of Constantinople to avert a persecution which seemed imminent in the Byzantine Empire. It was an anticipation of what was to be a characteristic phenomenon of the nineteenth century, but in a reverse direction —an influential Jew in a *Moslem* country exerting pressure, through diplomatic channels, on behalf of his persecuted brethren in a

[1] See below, pp. 174, 287-8.

Christian land at the other end of Europe. But, unlike the majority of his imitators in a later age, Hasdai ibn Shabrut was also a munificent patron of learning, and it was under his aegis (as we shall see) that Spanish-Jewish scholarship burst upon the world.

V

A turning point in the history of Moslem Spain came some forty years after Hasdai's death, when a swarm of Berber mercenaries from North Africa captured Cordova, and the Caliphate was broken up. The Jewish community of the capital had hitherto been by far the most numerous and the most influential of the whole country. Now its scholars, its statesmen, its men of business, were scattered throughout the peninsula. Hebrew life and culture, hitherto unduly concentrated, became diffused. On the ruins of the Caliphate, there grew up a number of independent kingdoms governed by the local aristocracy or successful military leaders. There were at one time as many as twenty-three of these, known as the kingdoms of the 'Taifas', or tribes; the principalities of Granada, Malaga, and Seville being the most powerful. The new rulers turned for help in the involved and difficult labour of administration to those whose acumen best qualified them for the task. Hence it came about that, in one after another of these petty courts, Jews rose to high rank: in some cases not merely as advisers (as in former days), but with the formal rank of vizier. This was especially the case in the states which were set up by the Berbers, who made no secret of their sympathetic feelings towards the Jews, and whose ancestors had, in some cases, professed a rudimentary Judaism before their conversion to Islam.

The most famous was Samuel ibn Nagrela (993-*c.*1056), poet, scholar, and statesman, both the Beau-Ideal and the Admirable Crichton of the Spanish Jew of the period. He personified, in his many-sided activity, all the finest characteristics of his age. A man of good education, though of humble social status, he had fled after the sack of Cordova to Malaga. Here he set up a spice booth near the palace of the vizier of King Habbus of Granada. A favourite slave of the latter's discovered the talent of the Jewish spice merchant and employed him to write her letters. Her master, struck by the elegant style which these displayed, became curious as to their authorship, and in the end Samuel ibn Nagrela was invited to Granada to become his secretary. His acumen soon became notorious at court; his counsel

63. GATEWAY OF JERUSALEM
From an illuminated Manuscript. Formerly in the Synagogue at Worms. 1272

64. Illumination from the MS. of Maimonides' Mishneh Torah, 1295

65. Miniature from a Fifteenth-Century Italian MS.
(Formerly in the Merzbacher Collection)

was asked on important state matters; and the vizier, on his death-bed in 1020, advised Habbus to appoint the learned Jew as his successor.

From this time, Samuel ibn Nagrela was the real ruler of the kingdom, filling in name as well as in fact the office of vizier. It was an extraordinary display of tolerance, to be paralleled nowhere in Europe for many centuries to come. In the disputes which followed the death of Habbus in 1027, ibn Nagrela warmly espoused the cause of his son, Badis, who shewed his gratitude by confirming him in office. Thus for a period of a quarter of a century, he was almost omnipotent, being allowed to manage all the affairs of state so long as he provided a sufficient supply of money for his master to dissipate. On occasion, he even led the armies in the field, and he once had the thrill of camping with his forces on the spot where, long before, he had slept a penniless fugitive.

Many stories were recounted of his wisdom and tact. He not only patronised letters, Arabic as well as Hebrew, but was himself one of the outstanding littérateurs of his age. Though hardly a genius of the first rank, his interests extended to every field of Jewish scholarship: and he is the most representative, if not the most gifted, figure in contemporary literary life. As a poet he was prolific and capable, though he lacked fire. Any and every action of daily existence seemed to him a proper occasion for versification. In his tent, on the eve of a battle or the morrow of a victory, he could sit down and produce polished Hebrew verses to celebrate the occasion. He wrote lengthy works in imitation of the Biblical books of Ecclesiastes, Proverbs, and Psalms. He was the author of a comprehensive dictionary of Biblical Hebrew. As Talmudist, he ranked among the most distinguished scholars of the period. He presided at Granada over an Academy of his own, and was the author of more than one work which was regarded with admiration by contemporaries, and may still be studied with profit. As a patron of learning, he excelled. His bounty extended to Africa, Sicily, Egypt, Mesopotamia, and even Palestine. Needy scholars in all these lands as well as nearer home could count upon his generous support. He built up a magnificent library, enriching it with copies of the Talmud imported from the newly-defunct academy of Sura. He kept scribes at work making transcripts, which he distributed widely at home and abroad. Scholars and poets flourished under his patronage, and commemorated him gratefully in their verses. Contemporaries, with one accord, hailed

L

him as their 'prince'; and it is as Samuel haNagid, or Samuel the Prince, that he is still remembered to-day.

Ibn Nagrela died, universally mourned, about the year 1063. He was succeeded, as a matter of course, by his son Joseph. The latter, a contemporary historian informs us, possessed every one of his father's qualities except one—that of modesty. His residence was notorious for its magnificence. He took no trouble to disguise his power, and patronised his personal connections with little regard to merit. The odium against him increased, until one Sabbath day in the winter of 1066 a mob of Berber soldiers attacked his palace. Discovered cowering in a cellar, his face covered with charcoal dust, he was put to death with every circumstance of cruelty (30th December 1066). The quarter where his co-religionists lived was then assaulted ferociously. Large numbers of persons perished, and subsequently the Jews were expelled from the whole kingdom.

The downfall of the Jews in Granada did not affect their position in the sister-states. In Saragossa, Jekutiel ibn Hassan, assassinated in 1039, had enjoyed as vizier a similar status to that of Samuel haNagdi in Granada. Later in the century, Abu-Fadhel ibn Hasdai served in the same capacity at this court, and several Jews filled less exalted office. Similarly, when under al-Mutamid the Emirate of Seville rose to supremacy in Moslem Spain, Isaac ibn Albalia (1035-1094) was the royal astronomer and confidential adviser, the Jews thus sharing in the revival which fleetingly renewed the lustre of the Caliphate of the West.

This blaze of glory was not destined to endure. The crescent was no longer supreme south of the Pyrenees. In the mountainous region of Asturias, the hunted Visigoths had managed to put up a successful resistance, and to stem the Moslem advance.[1] From the eighth century this little nucleus had begun to expand, and by now there were half a dozen Christian states, controlling some of the most fertile provinces of the Peninsula. Ferdinand I of Castile (1039-1065) had compelled all the Moslem rulers to acknowledge his supremacy. Alfonso VI (1065-1109) emulated him, his triumphs culminating in the capture of Toledo, seat of one of the greatest Spanish Jewish communities in 1085.

The Andalusians saw no prospect of being able to check unaided the triumphant advance of the Christian power. There was only one quarter to which they could look for military succour. The whole of

1 For a fuller account of this see below, pp. 194-5.

north-western Africa was now comprised in the empire of the fanatical Berber tribes known as 'al-Moravides' (whose name is preserved in the English *marabout*). An embassy asking for assistance was sent to them by the Moslem powers of Spain. Without waiting for a formal agreement, they poured into the peninsula. The Moslem and Christian armies encountered at Sagrajas (Zalaca), near Badajoz (23rd October 1086). On both sides, Jewish levies figured in considerable number. Legend tells that Alfonso sent to the opposing general suggesting that, for the convenience of the three faiths represented in their forces, the engagement should take place neither on the Friday, nor the Saturday, nor the Sunday, their respective Sabbaths. It was thus only on the Monday that battle was joined. It resulted in a decisive victory for the Crescent. Though Toledo continued in Christian hands, the unity of Moslem Spain was restored before long under Almoravidan supremacy. The new rulers brought with them a tendency to the primitive sternness and simplicity of Islam. Gone was the favoured position which Jewish statesmen had enjoyed at the various petty courts; and in 1107 an attempt was made to secure, by force, the conversion of the Jews of Lucena—the principal and the wealthiest community in Spain.

But it was not long before the conquerors, like others in the same circumstances, began to lose their original ardour. Their desert fanaticism became undermined by the soft Andalusian atmosphere. The enlightened traditions of the Caliphate were revived in their courts; and, once more, Jewish physicians or astronomers came to exercise considerable influence in affairs of state. Another wave of reforming zeal had, however, sprung up meanwhile among the Moslems of northern Africa. The tribes of the Atlas region had rallied round the banner of religious puritanism, and set up a powerful state. Their insistence upon the dogma of the Divine Unity led to their assuming the name of 'al-Mohades', or Unitarians. As was the case sixty years previous, they received an appeal for help from their co-religionists in Spain, hard pressed once more by the Christian advance. In 1146 they crossed the Straits.

From the first days of their expansion, the new sect had revived the stern policy of early Islam in relation to other religions. There could be no question of non-conformity. All who were not Moslems must be forced to don the turban: the only alternatives were extermination or expulsion. The transition was not, indeed, a drastic one. It involved for a Jew no painful ceremony, nor the acceptance of any particularly distasteful dogma. Some teachers, indeed, held that under the circumstances it was permissible, according to Jewish law, for a man to save his life by a feigned conversion; and in this respect they drew a careful distinction between Islam and Christianity, which expected so much more of its adherents. Not all, to be sure, adopted this view; when the Almohades had entered Fez, many of its Jewish inhabitants suffered martyrdom rather than change their faith.

An identical policy was pursued by the invaders in Spain. In every city they captured, the Jewish and Christian inhabitants were put to the sword. The only avenue of escape was through the formal adoption of Islam. Once more, as in the days of the Visigothic kings, the cities of southern Spain were filled with insincere converts from Judaism to the dominant faith. The high-roads leading away from the Moslem territories were crowded with fugitives, seeking asylum in a more tolerant land. The synagogues were destroyed, and the academies broken up. The disaster was keenly felt; and Spanish Jewry long continued to mourn it in a touching elegy each year on the Fast of the Ninth of Ab, thus associating the catastrophe with the national one of the fall of Jerusalem.

By 1172 the Almohades had restored unity to Moslem Spain, the last of the independent rulers having submitted to them. Not a single professing Jew was now left in the south of the country. It was fortunate that the Christian kingdoms had by now made headway in the north, providing a haven of refuge in which Jewish life could take root and flourish once again.

66. JEW AND PRIEST ENJOY THE IMPERIAL PEACE

Chapter XVI

THE NORTHERN CENTRES

———————— • ————————

I

Peace and order had been brought to Western Europe, for the first time since the Barbarian invasions, by the conquests and organising genius of Charles the Great, or Charlemagne, who was crowned Emperor at Rome on Christmas Day, 800. The so-called 'Holy' Roman Empire which he created (later, when it was neither holy, nor Roman, nor an Empire, to be restricted to nominal suzerainty in Germany) extended at the outset throughout what is now France, Germany, and North Italy, with a more shadowy authority over some remoter countries.

Owing to the intolerant policy which had characterised the Merovingians and other ruling houses after their conversion to Catholicism it is doubtful whether, at the beginning of Charlemagne's reign, Jews were to be found in his dominions in any numbers. He was, however, not only a strong ruler, able to override the theological prejudices of the time, but also a far-seeing one, who could realise in what direction lay the economic interests of his empire. The Jews, at this period, controlled the trade of western Europe. Their international connections rendered them useful instruments, and their culture valuable subjects. Accordingly, as a consistent policy, Charlemagne and his house patronised the Jews and encouraged their immigration. Charter after charter is extant in which they extend protection and privileges to some Jewish merchant. When, in 797, an embassy was sent to Haroun ar-Raschid at Bagdad, a Jew named Isaac was attached to it as interpreter. His principals died on the way home; and it was he alone who returned to Aachen, bringing with him in triumph the elephant sent by the Caliph in token of his esteem. A Jew, too, was the Imperial Purveyor, who brought back precious wares from Palestine for the use of the court.

Jewish tradition has chosen to preserve the name of Charlemagne

—the prototype of his house—in more than one ancient legend, in connection with favours bestowed upon their fathers. On the capture of Narbonne (actually carried out in 759 by his father, to whom the legend should perhaps be referred) he is said to have granted the local Jewish community many outstanding privileges in reward for their help; and the successors of the Jewish *Nasi*, or Prince, first appointed at this time, continued to lord it amongst their co-religionists down to a late date. It is similarly reported that the Emperor solicited from the Caliph of Bagdad (who in response sent him the famous Rabbi Machir of Narbonne) some Jewish scholar who might transplant the traditional Hebrew lore to his dominions. The migration from Lucca in North Italy to Mayence of the learned Rabbi Kalonymus, the first recorded German-Jewish scholar and the ancestor of a famous line of sages, is similarly ascribed to his agency. These legends are too persistent to be neglected; but, considering the fact that the Jewish Rabbi of the Middle Ages was often a physician, it may well be that the reason for the Emperor's interest in these scholars is to be sought in their medical, rather than Talmudic, attainments.

Be that as it may, the reign of Charlemagne's successors saw numerous and firmly established Jewish communities throughout their dominions. In France, one of the largest centres was Lyons, where the market-day was transferred from Saturday to the middle of the week in order to meet their convenience. Traders starting from the Mediterranean ports scoured half the known world, as far as India and China, for their wares. They pressed north and east, along all the trade routes, from Germany and beyond. From the lands of the Slavs they brought back the most profitable merchandise of all—slaves—to recruit the harem or the bodyguard of the Caliph of Cordova. The ecclesiastical authorities, indeed, looked askance at this. It was not by any means for reasons of humanity—civilisation had not progressed so far. But they strenuously objected to the sale of a true believer into slavery with an infidel, and frequently intervened to prevent it. They were no less opposed to the retention of Christian servants for personal use by Jews, who thus exercised authority over them; and recalcitrant pagan slaves could often count on freedom, and always on causing their masters a great deal of embarrassment, by requesting baptism.[1]

[1] It must be repeated that the Church at this period saw nothing wrong in the institution of slavery, but only in the subjection of Christian (or potentially Christian) slaves to non-Christian masters. The Biblical code, which in effect forbade the perpetual enslave-

Successive Church Councils meanwhile re-enacted, with monotonous regularity, the old canonical restrictions, which the state was urged to put into effect. Other prohibitions, too, were periodically revived. The Jew was not supposed to trade in produce, or to hoard bullion, or to take ecclesiastical vestments in pledge. In case he had a lawsuit with a Christian, he was required to provide a greater number of witnesses to his character than the latter, as though he belonged to an inferior grade of humanity. Everything was done to ensure that he should not attain undue influence in Christian society, and above all, that he should not secure converts to his faith. Occasional episodes shewed that the latter fear was not by any means preposterous. In 839 an incident took place which greatly scandalised clerical circles. A learned priest named Bodo, who had been brought up at court and attained the dignity of Archdeacon, received permission from the Empress to make a pilgrimage to Rome with his nephew. Thence, however, he betook himself to Saragossa and openly espoused Judaism, under the name of Eleazar, ultimately marrying a Jewish maiden and conducting incisive polemics on behalf of his new faith.

Yet the ecclesiastical regulations were generally neglected, with the completest connivance of the court. In the first half of the ninth century, Agobard and Amulo, successive archbishops of Lyons (who may be considered the fathers of medieval Anti-Semitism), wrote, laboured, and intrigued incessantly to have the petty code in all its details enforced in their diocese by the civil power, but apparently without result. Even after the fall of the Carolingian dynasty, the House of Capet continued their policy of protection. Though occasionally there were darker chapters (as, for example, at Sens in 875, when the Jews were banished on a suspicion of having made common cause with the Normans; or at Limoges in 1010, when the community had to choose between forced baptism and exile), conditions continued such as to encourage immigration. The area of settlement, originally thickest in the south of the country, gradually spread. The Fairs of Champagne, which at one time were among the greatest

ment of a co-religionist, is plainly in advance of this. In England, the completely rightless *Theow* class existed until the Norman Conquest, when they constituted some nine per cent of the population; after this, they were merged in the villeins, whose condition was not much better. The institution of slavery was finally abolished in England only by the Somerset Case of 1772, which decided (without any legal basis in the narrower sense) that any slave who landed on British soil was *ipso facto* freed. This doctrine is strikingly similar to the Jewish view enunciated a thousand years earlier, that a slave who escaped to the Holy Land regained his freedom.

factors in European commerce, must have proved a fresh stimulus. Before long, the north-eastern corner of France was filled with thriving communities, in every township; and, for the next three centuries, this constituted one of the most important centres of Jewish life and culture.

II

The German communities seem to have been in the main an off-shoot of these, the earliest being situated in the commercial emporia with which the Franco-Jewish merchants carried on their trade. In Roman times (as we know from the regulations issued in 321-331 by the Emperor Constantine) there had been a synagogue with its duly-constituted officers at Cologne, and no doubt in some neighbouring *municipia* as well. This region remained the centre of settlement down to the period of the Crusades. The boundary between France and Germany was ill-defined. From the Jewish point of view, the whole of the watershed of the Rhine was one. Boys went from Champagne to study with the famous Rabbis of Worms; and French names and linguistic influences indicate the probable origin of a great number of the Rhineland Jews. But, in addition to the immigrants who came eastward from Champagne, there were others who pressed north-wards, from one commercial centre to the other, up the valleys of the Danube and of the Elbe. In the ninth century already, mention is found of Jews at Augsburg and at Metz. In the tenth, they were settled in Worms, Mayence, Prague, Magdeburg, Merseburg, Ratisbon, and other places. By the close of the eleventh, they were as numerous all along the Rhineland as they were in the adjacent areas of France. As elsewhere, there were occasional outbursts of violence. In 1012, for example, a priest's untimely conversion to Judaism, coupled with a garbled report which had arrived from the Holy Land, resulted in the expulsion of the Jews from Mayence. But such persecutions were infrequent interludes and not (as they were afterwards to become) happenings of every day.

The last of the great countries of western Europe to receive a Jewish settlement was England. No conclusive evidence exists for the presence of Jews locally in Roman or Saxon times, though it is not out of the question that some isolated merchants may have found their way thither. With the Norman conquest of 1066, England entered, for the first time since the downfall of the Roman Empire,

67. A Jewish School

From a German manuscript Bible of the 14th Century (MS. Add. 15282) in the British Museum

68. Decoration of 'El Transito' Synagogue, Toledo, showing Royal Arms of Castile
14th Century

69. Interior of Synagogue
(subsequently Church of Sta. Maria la Blanca), Toledo. 13th Century

70. Sacrifice of Isaac

Miniature from a North-French Manuscript in the British Museum (MS. Add. 11639).
Late 13th Century

71. Celebration of the Passover

From a 14th Century Spanish Haggadah in the British Museum (MS. Or. 2884)

into the European orbit. The country was opened up to foreign enterprise: and the Jews were not slow to take advantage of the opportunities which offered themselves. At Rouen, the capital of Normandy, a settlement had in all probability existed since the beginning of the eleventh century, and it was natural for some of its members to cross the channel and settle in the new realm which their Duke had conquered. By the close of the reign, a community had established itself in London, and before long there were others in the principal provincial cities—especially York, Lincoln, Winchester, Oxford, Norwich, Canterbury, and Bristol.

III

The settlement of the Jew in England was the culminating point in the movement which brought the mass of his people from East to West, and converted them from Asiatics into Europeans. Further West, there was at that time no known territory; further North, to Denmark and the Scandinavian countries, he never penetrated in medieval times to any appreciable extent. It had been in the East, in Palestine, that the Jewish people had been formed, and in the East, in Palestine and then in Mesopotamia, that it had developed its characteristic forms of life. But (as we have seen) these ancient centres were dwindling. On the other hand, those of the occident were increasing in importance. As early as the tenth century an important rôle had been filled by the Jews of Spain. From the middle of the eleventh, France, Germany, and the adjacent countries were to share with the Iberian peninsula the hegemony—spiritual, intellectual, numerical, economic—of Jewish life.

Communities continued to exist, in numbers which were far from negligible, in the Levant—in the Byzantine Empire, in Mesopotamia, in Arabia, in Egypt, in Persia—and even further East, in India and China. Their importance in Jewish life, and in the civilisation of the world, was not crucial. That section of the Jewish people which was to count for something in the history of humanity, and for most in the history of Hebraic culture, was henceforth to be associated permanently with Europe, with European culture, with the European outlook, and (for many generations, at least) with European soil.

Except to some extent for Spain, the development is vague and indistinct, and our information scanty to a degree. Through the obscurity, however, the important fact looms clear and unmistak-

able: during those centuries which coincide with the Dark Ages in
Europe, from the fourth century to the eleventh, the immemorial
seats of settlement and civilisation in Palestine and Mesopotamia
slowly decayed, and their place was taken by fresh agglomerations in
the more vigorous lands of the West. The Jew ceases, in fact, to be
an Oriental, and becomes a European.

72. MEDIEVAL JEWISH HOUSES IN STEEP HILL, LINCOLN
The House of Belaset: 'Jews' Court' and Synagogue beyond. Drawing by Hanslip Fletcher

Chapter XVII

THE NEW LEARNING

————————— • —————————

I

That a large body of people was able to transfer itself from one end of the Mediterranean world to the other, at the period of the great national displacements which succeeded the classical age, was not an unexampled feat. What rendered the Jewish migration memorable and perhaps unique was the fact that they managed to carry with them not only their religion, but also their civilisation. To keep alive a cultural life when it is no longer rooted in the soil nor even based upon a living language, to transfer it from country to country, and to develop it homogeneously notwithstanding a succession of different environments, is a delicate task. Their triumphant achievement of this is a phenomenon which distinguishes the Jews from all other peoples of history. Conditions were far more propitious in the sixteenth and seventeenth centuries, when England and Spain established their colonies on the other side of the Atlantic; but it was not until the nineteenth that native American literature may be said to have flourished. The great displacements of Jewish population in the course of the second half of the nineteenth century were not followed by the growth of a native culture in the new centres of Jewish life, notwithstanding the facilities offered by improved communications and the invention of printing. The comparison makes the achievement of the Jewish pioneers in Europe all the more memorable.

Until the close of the Talmudic age, Hebraic learning—in its classical manifestations at least—had been confined to Palestine and the adjacent countries, with a continuous tradition of Jewish settlement which went back for untold generations. That its transference thence was feasible is to be ascribed in part to the circumstances of the Arab conquests. The occupation of Mesopotamia brought under their rule what had hitherto been, not only the great reservoir of

Jewish population, but also for some centuries past the traditional seat of Jewish learning. Their subsequent conquest of Northern Africa and Spain forged a linguistic and cultural bridge over which that tradition could be transmitted to the most distant parts of Europe, so that the revival of Arabic literature found its echo throughout the Mediterranean world, from Cairo to Cordova.

The Jewish communities could not hold themselves aloof from this intellectual stir. For the moment, indeed, Jewish scholarship was almost Arabised. The Arabic language was widely used even for semi-sacred purposes; Arab methods were closely studied; and Arab models were sedulously copied. The immediate consequence was a revival of Jewish *belles-lettres*. The example of the Gaon Saadiah had been sporadically anticipated; now, it was universally imitated. Hebrew poetry began to be written on secular models; lexicons were composed in the literary tradition of the age; and just as, many centuries before, Philo and the Hellenists of Alexandria had considered that Plato had said the final word in human thought, students now imagined that the Aristotelian philosophy, which the Arabs had taken over from the Greeks, represented the acme of intellectual achievement.

Wandering scholars brought the new fashions to Spain. Here the revival under the Ommayad Caliphs (who by the tenth century had converted Andalusia into a seat of learning, and made Cordova the centre of literary and philosophical studies for the whole Moslem world) could not in any case have failed to have repercussions in Jewish life. The Spanish revival was paralleled, though in a lesser degree, in other regions which were under Saracen influence. The importance of Moslem Spain in Jewish life is not therefore a question merely of numerical weight or of political influence. It constitutes a chapter of unexampled brilliance in the history of Jewish literature and thought.

II

Hasdai ibn Shabrut was the Maecenas under whose aegis the renaissance was initiated and European-Jewish intellectual life began. He patronised scholars of the new school like Menahem ben Saruk of Tortosa (author of the first complete dictionary of Biblical Hebrew and Aramaic), or the latter's caustic rival, Dunash ibn Labrat. Both were prolific versifiers, and Dunash was one of the first to write

Hebrew verses in regular metre, in imitation (ingenious rather than discriminating) of Arabic prosody. Subsequently, Hebrew poetry above all took root in Spain, flourishing there as it has done nowhere else outside Palestine. Samuel ibn Nagrela was himself (as we have seen) a ready, if not an inspired poet. He made himself memorable, moreover, for his patronage of Solomon ibn Gabirol of Malaga (?1021-1056), 'the nightingale of piety', whose hymns immeasurably enriched the synagogal liturgy, and whose outstanding philosophical composition, preserved in Latin under the name *Fons Vitae*, became a classic among medieval Catholic schoolmen, not dreaming that its author was a Jew. Legend tells how the gifted singer was murdered by an Arab rival and buried under an almond tree, which subsequently betrayed the crime by the unusual luxuriance of its blossom.

In the following generation, his contemporary (died *c.* 1139), Moses ibn Ezra of Granada (where his father had held office under Samuel ibn Nagrela), equalled ibn Gabirol in poetic fire, and excelled him perhaps in depth of human feeling. He was, moreover, the author of the earliest work on Hebrew prosody—incongruously written (like so much of the literature of the age) in Arabic. His distant kinsman, Abraham ibn Ezra (1092-1167), might have excelled him but for his amazing versatility. A native of Toledo, he could never find rest in any one place, and wandered about throughout the known world—from Spain to Italy, from Italy to France, from France to England, and perhaps back again to Spain. He stands in the front rank of Hebrew poets and hymnologists. He was the author of a classical commentary upon the Bible, in which he shews at least a glimmering of the principles of what is now known as Higher Criticism. He wrote grammatical, philosophical, and astronomical works. In addition, he made a point of using pure Hebrew for all his writings, abandoning the convention which had hitherto prevailed almost universally of employing Arabic for any serious dissertation: he may indeed be said to have created Hebrew prose as a medium for scientific purposes.

The humanistic tradition of Spanish Jewry reached its climax with Judah haLevi (*c.* 1075-1141). Born in Central Spain, he had the breadth of outlook which is derived from a first-hand acquaintance with three cultures—the Christian, the Arabic, and the Jewish. By profession a physician, he was by vocation a poet. Never perhaps has any other person acquired such extraordinary mastery over a language no longer ordinarily spoken. His inspiration soars above the self-imposed shackles of Arabic prosody—the artificial metrical structure, the acrostics at the beginning of each line and the monotonous jingling rhyme at the end. Nothing Jewish, and nothing human, was strange to his muse—neither the pleasures of friendship, nor the ecstasies of passion, nor the grandeurs of nature, nor the mysteries of religion. Above all, he developed a transcendental passion for the Holy Land: and his hymns to Zion compare in their heart-rending appeal to the greatest love-lyrics in world literature. These exquisite religious poems (with those of the two ibn Ezras and of Solomon ibn Gabirol) gained immediate popularity, and, in the ritual of the so-called 'Sephardi' Jews, they still occupy a privileged position.[1] Following the footsteps of Saadiah, the poet also composed a philosophical work, '*al-Khuzari*', in the form of a dialogue between a Jewish savant and the king of the Khazars,[2] in which he vindicated the rational basis of Judaism.

Judah haLevi's life was as harmonious as his literary productions. It is told how, in the end, he succumbed to the mystical charms of the mistress whom he had so often celebrated in song, and set out for the Holy Land. As he arrived in sight of Jerusalem, he flung himself in ecstasy on the ground. A passing Arab horseman spurred his steed over the recumbent body, and the poet sobbed out his life with the immortal cadences of his greatest ode to Zion.

III

Less dazzling, but more vital, than the humanistic revival with which we have been dealing hitherto was the transplantation of that unique literary monument which embodied and, over long centuries, was to mould the Jewish conception of life. The origins of Rabbinic scholarship in Europe will always be associated with a romantic story told by an ancient chronicler. It is recounted how four Rabbis, collecting

---

[1] *Sepharad* (for which see Obadiah v, 20) was the name applied by the Jews during the Middle Ages to Spain, as *Tsarephath* (ibid.) was to France, *Ashkenaz* (Jeremiah li, 27) to Germany, and *Canaan* (the land of slaves) to the Slavonic countries further East. No similar Biblical term was left for England, which was generally designated as 'the Isle of the Sea', or 'the Corner of the Earth'—a literal, if unscientific, rendering of *Angle-Terre*. Later, the terms 'Sephardim' and 'Ashkenazim' were generally used to designate the two main groups of the Jewish people, each with its distinctive rite of prayers and pronunciation of Hebrew, centred in the one case upon the Spanish, and in the other on the Franco-German (later, Germano-Polish) nucleus.

[2] Won over to Judaism not long before: above, p. 159, and below, pp. 287-8.

contributions perhaps for the upkeep of the academies, set sail about 972 from the seaport of Bari, in south Italy—at this time, a great seat of learning. The ship was captured by an Andalusian corsair, and the four captives were sold in four different ports (including Alexandria and Kairouan). In each, they implanted the lore of their native place.

One of the four, Moses ben Enoch, was taken to Cordova, where he was ransomed as a matter of course by the Jewish community. One day, he found his way to the house of study, where he intervened in the discussions. Notwithstanding his rags, his genius was immediately recognised, and he was installed at the head of a school which served henceforth as the centre of Rabbinic studies for the whole of the peninsula. He was succeeded by his son Enoch, who had been captured with him. The two, between them, managed to transfer to Andalusia the method of study which had hitherto been characteristic of the Mesopotamian schools, and which could hardly be communicated except by means of oral instruction. Samuel ibn Nagrela was the foremost of their pupils, but by no means the only one. As interest in the subject increased, letters of enquiry were addressed in increasing numbers to the Geonim in the East, whose 'responsa' cleared up many difficulties and assisted in the diffusion of the stored-up erudition of which they were the last heirs. It was thus that the tradition which Palestine had handed on to Mesopotamia was transmitted in turn to Spain.

When, in the middle of the eleventh century, Isaac al-Fasi (*i.e.* of Fez: 1013-1103) emigrated from North Africa to Spain, where he became principal of the famous school established at Lucena, the supremacy of the latter country in Rabbinic scholarship was assured: for al-Fasi was recognised to be one of the greatest luminaries of his age, and his classical compendium of the Talmud, with its elimination of irrelevancies and its clear-cut decisions, had already acquired him a considerable reputation. Italy, too, had by now begun to produce great scholars in this field. Their greatest literary monument was the dictionary (*Arukh*) of Nathan of Rome (*c.* 1050-1100), al-Fasi's contemporary. This, which is indispensable to philologists and students of ancient folklore even to-day, provided yet another instrument by which the learning of Palestine and Mesopotamia could become accessible to western Europe.

IV

It was to the north of the Alps and the Pyrenees that Talmudic scholarship was especially cherished. Here it came to its prime with startling suddenness. We know almost nothing about literary life in the Franco-German communities previous to about the year 1000. This was the meridian of a certain Gershom ben Judah, a native of Metz, who passed the majority of his life at Mayence, on the Rhine. Such were this scholar's attainments that he is still remembered as 'the Light of the Exile'. Very little of his work has survived, other than some hymns (one commemorating the Rhineland persecution in 1012), some *responsa*, and a few glosses on the Talmud (probably set down by the pupils who attended his lectures). He is, however, famous as the author of a series of regulations (*Takkanoth*) intended to adapt Jewish life to the altered conditions which it had to face in Europe.[1]

The school which Gershom of Mayence founded continued to flourish for many years. The most eminent of its pupils was Solomon ben Isaac of Troyes, in Champagne, universally known by the initials of his name (*Rabbi Shelomo ben Isaac*) as *Rashi* (1040-1105). He had studied at Worms with scholars who had themselves sat at the feet of Gershom. At the age of twenty-five he returned to his native place (famous already in Christian circles for its ecclesiastical schools and—providentially—a centre of the parchment-making industry, which assisted in diffusing its literature). Here he remained apparently for the rest of his life. He earned his livelihood by wine-making, having perhaps a vineyard of his own, but he must have spent the best part of his waking hours poring over his folios. One should not have any illusions as to the environment in which he worked. Troyes was a small place, and it cannot have comprised more than a couple of score of Jewish householders at the most. But every morning, after service, and every evening, when the activities of the day were over and their neighbours were crowding into the taverns, they repaired to the synagogue or the adjacent house of study to con the traditional literature. Their young fellow-townsman, who had already acquired a name for himself, took the lead, explaining the intricacies and the implications of the concise Rabbinic argument. His fame spread to neighbouring centres. Enquiries for elucidation upon one point or another began to reach him; and promising young students were sent to sit at his feet.

[1] Cf. below, p. 218.

Not content with verbal exposition, Rabbi Solomon set down his observations, tractate by tractate, submitting them to constant revision. This was the origin of his famous Commentary upon the Babylonian Talmud. In this is crystallised the lore of countless scholars of preceding generations. The Talmud, with its medley of languages and its peculiar vocabulary and its specific manner of reasoning, was unintelligible without a chart. That chart was provided by Rashi's commentary. Students of a later generation, removed by many centuries from the living tradition of the schools of Sura and Pumbeditha, or languishing in semi-isolation in remote townships of Central Europe, could henceforth continue to study the Talmud with full comprehension. The profound influence which that great work has had upon the spiritual history of the Jew would hardly have been conceivable but for Solomon ben Isaac's simple, lucid exposition, which rapidly attained semi-classical status. A popular commentary on the Bible, learned though hardly profound, supplemented the greater work, and for many centuries served as the text-book through which the Jewish child mastered the implications of Holy Writ and received his first introduction to Rabbinic literature.

In the generations succeeding the great teacher's death, his works became the standard of further literary activity. The Talmud was studied in the light of his commentaries: points left obscure were elucidated; apparent contradictions were painstakingly traced and reconciled. This material was embodied in a series of Additions or *Tosaphoth*, the scholars responsible for which are known generally as *Tosaphists*. They were to be found throughout eastern France and the adjacent territories, especially Lorraine and the Rhineland. There were offshoots in North Italy, and even England. But they were especially numerous in Champagne, where every township had its circle of eager students, clustered about some eminent Rabbi. (When the Jew of northern Europe turned his attention to poetry there was little of the lighter touch: it was generally harsh, highly allusive, and preoccupied by martyrology or religious problems). The leading part in this spate of intellectual activity was taken by members of Solomon ben Isaac's own family, including his two grandsons, Samuel ben Meir ('*Rashbam*') and his brother Jacob, known as 'our perfect Master' ('*Rabbenu Tam*');[1] and their nephew, Isaac the Elder, of whom

[1] *Rashbam* is the abbreviation of the name *Rabbi Shemuel Bar Meir*: *Tam* ('the Perfect' or simple) is the epithet applied in the Biblical account to the patriarch Jacob. These two were the children of Rashi's daughter: the great scholar left no son.

M

it was recounted that he had sixty pupils, all at home in the whole Talmud and each capable of repeating at least one tractate of the sixty by heart. When the cup of bitterness passed to French Jewry and to German Jewry after them, this was the heritage which they took with them into exile.

V

Medieval Jewish intellectual life reached its climax in the commanding figure who combined the humanism of Spain with the practical interests of the northern countries, and who left no branch of Jewish learning untouched and unadorned. Moses ben Maimon (or, to use the incongruous Greek form which has become usual, Moses Maimonides) was born in Cordova, of a family long distinguished for its learning, in 1135. He was only thirteen years of age when his native city was captured by the Almohadan fanatics, and its community driven into exile. The family sought refuge in Morocco, where for a short time it appears to have been compelled to pay lip-service to Islam. But, after a short interval, Maimon and his sons took up the wanderer's staff anew, and set their faces eastwards. The young men settled ultimately in Egypt. This country was the seat of a Jewish community of immemorial antiquity, which had flourished again under Arab rule. Although under the unbalanced Hakim (996-1021) the most fanatical repression of dissenting faiths had been attempted, his successors treated the Jews benignly, even using them in the public administration: from 1044 to his assassination in 1047, for example, the court banker and purveyor Abraham (Abu Said) ben Sahl, vizier to the Sultan's mother, virtually ruled the country. A contemporary satirist purported to view the scene with consternation:—

> Egyptians! Hear the words I counsel you—
> Turn Jews, for Heaven itself has turned a Jew.

The country had not been affected to any appreciable extent by the wave of intolerance which had now submerged the Maghreb and Spain. Its position on the highway between east and west, and the prestige which it had gained in consequence of Saladin's victories over the Crusaders, had established its position as one of the centres of Mediterranean civilisation; its propinquity to the Holy Land and Mesopotamia enabled it to respond to every intellectual current from those countries, to harbour the remnant of their scholars, and to preserve their writings from destruction. The literature of this period, from complete juridical treatises down to the most insignificant personal notes, was brought to light not long ago, after many centuries of total oblivion, in the *Genizah*, or Lumber-Room, of one of the old synagogues at Cairo—one of the most spectacular rediscoveries of modern times[1]—and thanks to it we are informed with peculiar minuteness of the whole of that throbbing, somewhat petty society.

It was in Fustat (Old Cairo) that Moses ben Maimon settled, ultimately becoming one of the Court physicians. Late in life, he sent one of his admirers a vivid account of his busy day, which left him no leisure: how early every morning he had to go from Fustat to Cairo to see the Viceroy and his entourage, staying almost the whole day in case of illness: how his services were at the call of all the officers of state; how when he returned home—never before noon—he found the apartments filled with persons of all creeds and callings and stations of life awaiting his advice; and how when he resumed his practice, after a hasty meal, he had to lie down on a couch from sheer exhaustion. Yet notwithstanding this he continued almost to his last day to pour out a stream of works of fundamental importance to Judaism even at the present time.

His was an encyclopaedic mind: prodigiously stored, reverent yet rational, intensely logical and intolerant of confusion. His medical writings continued to be studied, and even translated into foreign tongues, as late as the sixteenth century. But it was not upon these that his reputation rested. It may be said that he took the whole corpus of traditional Judaism, theoretical and practical, and reduced it to order. From all parts of the Jewish world men appealed to him for advice. A false Messiah appeared in the Yemen: persecution was rife in the Maghreb: a philosophical doubt perplexed the Rabbis of Marseilles—the great Egyptian scholar wrote indicating in the clearest language the proper attitude to adopt in accordance with Jewish principles. Even before his arrival in Egypt, he had begun a masterly Arabic commentary on the *Mishnah,* distinguished by clarity of thought and the lucid presentation of practical issues, as well as their theoretical basis. Knowledge of the Talmud appeared to be on the wane, and the ordinary Jew seemed in consequence to need a new handbook of practice: his *Mishneh Torah* ('Repetition of the

[1] See above, p. 86, note.

Law') presented the whole mass of traditional teaching, in the purest Hebrew, in a methodical and logical order, beginning with a statement of metaphysical, physical, and ethical principles, and going on thence to the minutiae of practice, all arranged in such a manner that a comparative ignoramus could find what he needed without difficulty.

There was a widespread impression that Judaism, as a system, was antiquated, and had no appeal to the 'modern mind', brought up on Aristotle and Avicenna; in his *Guide of the Perplexed*, Moses ben Maimon put forward a philosophy of Judaism, giving it a completely rational basis, reconciling it to the fashionable philosophy of the era, and putting some apparent crudities of the Bible in what he considered to be their correct perspective. It is his greatest work, having constituted the basis of Jewish philosophy from that time onwards, and being nearly as familiar in a Latin version to the medieval schoolmen as it was to their Jewish contemporaries. It does not perhaps retain its appeal now in every detail, but its method of approach, and the spirit in which it confronts difficulties, must always remain a model.

The author survived the composition of his masterpiece for some fourteen years. Yet he could now do nothing to add to his fame, which admirers openly compared to that of Moses the Law-Giver. No contemporary received such wide recognition. In every corner of the Jewish world he was hailed as the greatest scholar of the age; and, when he was borne to his grave in 1204, a general fast was proclaimed in Jerusalem, and a Lesson was read from the Prophets, recounting the capture of the Ark of the Lord at the hands of the Philistines.

The admiration which the great Egyptian scholar received, though unbounded, was not universal. Each age has its conservatives to whom every attempt to move with the times, every step which may possibly weaken identity with the past, every conscious adaptation to current standards, seems dangerous. There was a small circle who regarded Maimonides' works in this light. It was feared that his *Mishneh Torah*, professedly written for the sake of the ignorant, might in the end prove a fatal bait to the learned, and wean them away from the Talmud—that be-all and end-all of Jewish studies. Moreover, there were in it certain omissions—some intentional, some inadvertent—which attracted the criticism of the learned; while part of its speculative teaching seemed to be of doubtful orthodoxy. In the Commentary on the *Mishnah*, there was an examination of the doctrine of Reward and Punishment, and an attempt to formulate definite articles of creed, thirteen in number, belief in which was obligatory on any person who desired to call himself a Jew. This was an innovation to which some even of the less punctilious objected, while there was profound disagreement as to the precise nature of any such fundamental doctrines. Hasdai Crescas of Saragossa (1340-1410), a trenchant critic of Maimonides in a subsequent generation, reduced the articles of faith to eight in his closely argued 'Light of the Lord'; while his pupil Joseph Albu (d. 1444), in his *Ikkarim* ('Dogmas') would not admit more than three—belief in Monotheism, in Revelation, and in Retribution. Above all, the *Guide of the Perplexed* attracted pungent criticism for its spirited rejection of the literal interpretation of Scriptural anthropomorphisms, its intellectualisation of the faculty of prophecy, its rational explanation of every Biblical precept, its interpretation of the sacrificial cult as a concession to the idolatrous propensities rooted in those for whom it was intended.

Even before the author's death, criticisms began to make themselves heard. Immediately afterwards, a storm burst, which continued to rage intermittently for some generations. An unprecedented acrimony made itself felt in the dispute. Mild scholars, such as Abraham ben David of Posquières, used language of unusual harshness in their criticisms. Famous Rabbis hurled excommunications and counter-excommunications at one another. A ban was placed by one section on any person who should dare to waste precious time and to vitiate a God-given intellect by the study of philosophy before he was thirty years of age. The aid of the civil power was invoked; and the climax was reached when the writings of Moses ben Maimon were denounced as prejudicial to faith to the newly established Dominican Order (who had already taken steps to suppress the philosophy of Aristotle) and were condemned by them to the flames (1234). Discord continued even after this: but Jewish opinion as a whole was so shocked by the episode that a reaction set in, and the reputation of the second Moses was henceforth safe.

VI

The centre of these disputes was Provence—geographically, spiritually, and linguistically a bridge between France and Spain. It stood, indeed, outside the sphere of the cultural activities of northern France and Germany, and approximated more to the Peninsula in its general humanistic and literary interests. But the function of Provence in Jewish literary history was different from either. A very large proportion of the literature of the period, including more than one of the works of Moses ben Maimon, had been written, not in Hebrew, but in Arabic—the tongue in which philosophical studies had acclimatised themselves, the cultured medium of the Mediterranean and the language normally spoken over a large part of the Jewish world. Accordingly, any Jewish writer who desired to reach the mass of his people, to secure the widest possible circulation for his views and to achieve a reputation also in non-Jewish circles, wrote in that language (much in the same way as in the past century he might have written in German, and at present in English). They could not foresee that the Arabic domination, and even the Arab civilisation, was on the wane, and that what had previously appeared the main stream of cultural life was to become a stagnant backwater. When this took place, those of their works which they wrote in the vernacular not only lost their wider appeal, but in some cases ran the danger of becoming entirely submerged. In those cases when they survived and continued to be a living influence, it was only through the medium of translations into the always living, however much unfashionable, Hebrew. This was the case, for example, with Maimonides' *Commentary on the Mishnah* and the *Guide of the Perplexed* itself, as well as with Judah haLevi's *Khuzari* and popular ethical works, like the cherished *Duties of the Heart* of the moralist Bahye ibn Bakuda (*c.* 1070).

The most important of these translations were carried out, as has been indicated, in Provence—a land which lay between the Moslem and the Christian worlds—notably by members of the family of Ibn Tibbon, who had sought refuge there from the persecutions in Spain. In addition, they translated from the Arabic into Hebrew numerous philosophical classics by Gentile authors, ancient and modern—both original works, like those of Averroes, and translations, including many which derived from Aristotle. They frequently had to invent their own vocabulary; their style was sometimes harsh, yet the service which they rendered to Jewish learning was immense. Another Provençal family of translators was that of Kimhi. Its most important member, David (*d.* 1235), played an important rôle on the liberal side in the controversy about the writings of Maimonides. He compiled the grammar and the lexicon through which successive generations of Christian scholars acquired their knowledge of Hebrew, as well as a Biblical commentary second in renown only to that of Rashi in

Jewish circles, and more influential still among their neighbours in the subsequent age of Reform. From the Hebrew, many of these works were subsequently translated into Latin for the benefit of non-Jews. A little later (especially under the patronage of the Holy Roman Emperor Frederic II; Robert of Anjou, ruler of Naples and Provence; and Alfonso the Wise, King of Castile) a systematic series of renderings was carried out by Jewish scholars at the courts of these monarchs and elsewhere.

It was a strangely involved process: the masterpieces of the classical world becoming known to medieval Christendom (ignorant of Greek as it was of Arabic) largely through the medium of Latin translations from the Hebrew versions which the Jews had prepared for their own use from the Arabic adaptations used in the schools of Cordova! This was one of the main channels whereby the philosophic and scientific treasures of ancient Greece began to penetrate again the European world, bringing about that quickening of interest and revival of learning which was to culminate in the New Birth—the Renaissance.

73. TRADITIONAL PORTRAIT OF MAIMONIDES
From Blasio Ugolino, Thesaurus antiquitatum Sacrarum, Venice 1744,
'ex tabula antiqua': autograph from manuscript in British Museum, London

Chapter XVIII

THE SHADOW OF THE CROSS

———————— ● ————————

I

As the eleventh century was drawing to its close, Christian Europe was stirred to its depths by the reports spread by pilgrims newly returned from Palestine, of the sacrilege perpetrated by the Moslems at the Holy Places and the barbarous treatment of those who came to visit them. The general indignation grew; and Pope Urban II, at a sermon preached before the Council of Clermont on 26th November 1095, summoned Christendom to take steps for the recovery of the Holy Land and its shrines from the Infidel.

Never, perhaps (according to a famous ecclesiastical historian), did a single speech of man achieve results so extraordinary and so lasting. This was the direct occasion of the succession of Crusades which, throughout the next two centuries, attempted (with varying degrees of success) to win back Palestine for the Cross. Over a period of many generations, the idea dominated international politics. Even later it exerted a profound influence on the European mind; and to the present time, the remoter repercussions continue to have a distinct effect upon many a social and political question. The power of the Papacy was strengthened by the great international movement which began under its auspices. The Church became richer, more influential, and better consolidated than ever before. The ideals of chivalry began to permeate the upper strata of society. Merchants followed the warlike pioneers; fresh trade routes were opened; and commercial relations with the Levant received a powerful stimulus. It was at this period that the delicacies of the Far East—some of them now considered everyday necessities of life—began to be familiar in the baronial halls of England, Germany, and France. Intercourse with the Arabs, more polished and more cultured than any Christian people, was not without its humanising influence.

The study of science, geography, natural history, and botany, received a powerful impetus. A distinct influence is traceable even on literature, in its historic, poetic, and romantic manifestations.

The effects of the Crusades upon the Jew were, if anything, even more pronounced. The passions and the tendencies which they set in motion continued to dominate his history for at least four centuries, and left traces upon it which are discernible even to-day. They influenced his political position, his geographical distribution, his economic activity, his forms of literary expression, even his spiritual life. It may be added that, in almost every direction, the influence was for the bad. Take any realistic description of the position of world Jewry down to the close of the last century; take any indictment drawn up by an anti-Semite in our own times; take any contemporary analysis of the weakness of the Jewish position or the alleged shortcomings of the Jewish character; and in almost every instance it will be possible to trace the origin, if not actually to the Crusades, to the currents which they stirred. And, just as the accounts of the expeditions to the East marked the beginning of medieval historiography, so the first medieval Jewish chronicles, which throw light on the obscurity in which life in Europe is hitherto wrapped, are those which deal with the sufferings from the period of the First Crusade onward. They are martyrologies rather than histories. Tales of horror abound and happy interludes are rare. It was not without reason that subsequent Jewish writers punningly called the town at which the Crusade was first preached not *Clermont*—'the Hill of Light'—but *Har Ophel*—'the Hill of Darkness'.

II

The Jews were not wholly unprepared for the storm which was about to burst over their heads. Once religious passions are aroused, it is always difficult to restrict them to one channel. It was notorious that certain Crusading leaders had vowed that the blood of Christ should be avenged in the blood of the Jews. From their point of view, it was supremely illogical to leave older and even more bitter opponents of the Christian faith undisturbed—perhaps even profiting from their holy venture—when they went to risk their lives and their substance in battle against the Saracen.

Already in January 1096, some of the communities of northern France, threatened with the alternatives of baptism and extermination, summoned their co-religionists in Germany to join them in a day of prayer and fasting. For the moment, the latter felt secure, having managed to buy off successive divisions of the Crusaders with substantial bribes. But the real peril came, not from the well-equipped and comparatively well-disciplined main forces, but from the smaller bands under local leaders, and the wild hordes of ill-armed peasantry who accompanied or preceded the armies. It was currently believed that the killing of a Jew would secure pardon for all sins and remission of purgatory, and many actually bound themselves by oath not to leave the country until they had performed so meritorious a deed with their own swords. It was noteworthy, on the other hand, that the local authorities—the burghers, and above all, the bishops of the various places—generally did what they could to prevent the attacks and protect the victims.

A preliminary outbreak in Lorraine, which cost twenty-two members of the Metz community their lives, warned those of the Rhineland that danger was imminent. The forces under the command of Emico, Count of Leiningen, began the onslaught. On 3rd May—a Sabbath—the synagogue of Speyer was surrounded and attacked. Thanks to the resistance put up by the worshippers, and to the energetic measures taken by the Bishop, the outbreak was suppressed, though not before some persons had lost their lives. On the next occasion, the Crusaders were better prepared but their victims were not. On Sunday, 18th May, an attack was made at Worms, with the connivance of the inhabitants. A few of the weaker saved themselves by submitting to baptism. The rest, with the exception of those who had found refuge in the Bishop's palace or died at their own hands, were put to death, almost to a man. A week later the episcopal palace itself was surrounded, and those who had sought protection in it exterminated. For many generations, the local communities continued to commemorate by name upwards of 350 individuals who lost their lives here on those two awful days; and the total number of victims was reckoned at more than twice as many.

From Worms, Emico's forces made their way to Mayence, where, on 27th May, similar carnage ensued. The community was fore-warned, but could make no provision excepting to leave money in the hands of Gentile neighbours, to cover the cost of their burial. A band of refugees, who attempted to escape down the river to Rüdes-heim under the cover of darkness, were immediately pursued; and the few who were not done to death by the mob laid violent hands upon themselves. In Cologne the synagogue was surrounded on 30th May, the first day of the Feast of Pentecost, by a mob of Crusaders under the command of William the Carpenter. In anticipation of attack, most of the Jews had taken refuge in the houses of friendly Christian neighbours, and there were only one or two casualties. The rest were sent by the Bishop under escort to other places in his diocese, where disturbance was considered improbable. Most of them, however, were tracked down and perished in a massacre on 1st June. Visiting agitators brought the news from the neighbouring towns to Trèves, where the cup of suffering was drained to its dregs on that same day.

Scenes of a similar nature were enacted in those weeks at place after place along the Rhine valley, in which we know of the existence of a Jewish community so early only by reason of an exterminatory massacre at this period. Identical bloodshed stained the path of the Crusading mobs throughout their march eastwards. On the day of the riot at Cologne, the community at Prague, the capital of Bohemia (where Jews had already been settled for some time), suffered martyrdom. Many of the successive waves broke, or dispersed, or turned back before they reached the Byzantine Empire; but even here Salonica Jewry was attacked. The climax of the campaign was reached in 1099, when the main body under Godfrey de Bouillon fought their way into Jerusalem. The steep streets of the Holy City ran with blood, and all the surviving Jews, whether Rabbanite or Karaite, were driven into one of the synagogues, which was then set on fire. This marked the end of the Jewish connection with their former capital for long years to come.

III

This outbreak proved to be the beginning of a long series which not only characterised successive Crusades, but continued, almost without interruption, down to the present time. The whole colouring and *tempo* of Jewish history was henceforth different. Scholars wondered whether this gigantic struggle between the nations was to be identified with the war of Gog and Magog foretold by the prophet Ezekiel, and whether the frightful sufferings undergone by their own people, 'a generation chosen by the Lord for His portion', were the prelude to the final Deliverance. Now, more than ever before, they anticipated the speedy coming of the Messiah to comfort them and restore them to their own land. So far did martyrdom become a matter of everyday occurrence that the ritual codes drily prescribed the form of benediction to be used before being put to death 'for the sanctification of the Name'. History began in the form of martyrologies. Year by year communities solemnly commemorated the names of the slain, or the Holy Congregations which suffered, on each specific day: and hymns describing successive vicissitudes were introduced into the liturgy.

From the midsummer of 1096, there was an interlude in the train of anguish. One after the other, those who had escaped massacre returned to their homes, while the minority who had been forcibly baptised were permitted to revert to the practice of Judaism. Stolen property was restored, so far as was possible: though that of the martyred dead was, as a matter of course, confiscated to the royal treasury. Finally in 1103, a truce was proclaimed, in which the Jews were included. For almost exactly half a century in all, the land had rest. In 1146, however, the straits to which the Latin kingdom of Jerusalem had been reduced led to the organisation of a new Crusade for its relief. The movement on this occasion was more compact and better organised than had been the case in 1096. Nevertheless, under inspiration of an ignorant monk named Radulph, similar scenes of horror on a minor scale were witnessed all along the Rhine—at Cologne, Trèves, and elsewhere. Subsequently the communities of Magdeburg and Halle were expelled; and notwithstanding the friendly feelings of the Christian inhabitants, an itinerant mob fell upon the Jews of Würzburg in February 1147. From Germany the infection spread to the north of France. At Ham, Sully, and Carentan—in the latter case, after an heroic defence—the Jews were assaulted and exterminated. In Ramerupt an attack took place on the second day of Pentecost (8th May 1147), when the learned Rabbi Jacob ben Meir, grandson and spiritual successor of Rabbi Solomon ben Isaac of Troyes, narrowly escaped with his life. That the excesses were kept within comparatively moderate bounds was due to the efforts of the truly saintly Bernard of Clairvaux, whose fiery oratory was the main inspiration of the Crusade, but who insisted that the Jews, though they ought not to be allowed to profit from the Crusaders, should on no account be molested.

With the Third Crusade, the infection spread to England, which had hitherto remained immune and had thus offered itself as a welcome haven to refugees from the Continent. While Richard I was being crowned at Westminster on 3rd September 1189, a riot began which ended in the sack of the London Jewry and the murder of many of its inhabitants, the work being continued overnight and well into the next day by the light of the burning buildings. The example was followed throughout the country in the following spring, as soon as the King crossed the Channel. Norwich, Bury, Lynn, Dunstable, Stamford, all added their names in letters of blood to the record of Jewish martyrdom. The culminating point was reached in York, where, after a preliminary attack, the Jews sought refuge in the Castle and held out for some time against a regular siege. In the end, seeing that there was no possibility of deliverance, they resolved to deprive their enemies at least of the delights of massacre. Led by their Rabbi, all the heads of families killed their wives and children, and then each other. When on the next morning (it was the Great Sabbath which immediately precedes the Passover, and 17th March according to the current reckoning) the gates of the Castle were opened, barely a soul was found alive to tell the tale of that awful night. It was noteworthy that in this case the ringleaders in the riot were members of the lesser baronage who had financial transactions with the Jews, and whose religious ardour was certainly heightened, if not occasioned, by their financial indebtedness.

IV

The taste for blood, once whetted, was not easily appeased. Popular religious passion was so far aroused against the Jews that, before long, the pretext of a Crusade became superfluous. On Easter Eve, 1144, the dead body of a boy named William, apprenticed to a skinner at Norwich, was found in a wood near the city. It appears that he had died in a cataleptic fit; but the story spread that he had been put to death a day or two before by the Jews, in mockery of the Passion of Jesus, to celebrate their Passover feast. Similar accusations of child murder for ritual purposes have been brought up against unpopular religious minorities in all ages—for example, against the early Christians, at the time when they were beginning to make headway in the Roman Empire, and many centuries later, against the Jesuit missionaries in China. But it was levelled against the Jews, though in a peculiarly improbable form, at a propitious moment; and, in consequence, it made exceptionally rapid headway.

Soon another element was introduced into the story—that the object of the crime was to obtain blood for use in manufacturing the

Unleavened Bread, or in some other Paschal rite; or else to remove the *foetor judaicus*, or Jewish stench, with which (it was said) implacable Providence had endowed them. The fact that consumption of animal blood in any shape or form is forbidden to the Jew by the Mosaic code, coupled with the consideration that human flesh is technically a 'prohibited food', should have been sufficient to demonstrate the exceptional absurdity of this tale, even if the Hebrew race were considered capable of habitual homicide. Princes, Kings, and Emperors issued edicts condemning the fable; Popes anathematised it; scholars methodically disproved it; common sense decried it. But still the accusation continued to flourish, gaining rather than losing in strength. The relics of the supposititious victims of impossible crimes were universally revered; miracles were wrought at their shrines; and 'St.' William of Norwich was the first of a long line of hypothetical martyrs at Jewish hands, who (in almost every case, without any sort of official ecclesiastical sanction) began to appear in the popular hagiology of every country. In May 1171 the charge (unsubstantiated on this occasion even by the discovery of a body) led to the execution by burning of almost the whole community of Blois, including seventeen women. As they died, the bystanders heard a hymn chanted in unison from the midst of the pyre: it was the sublime monotheistic confession, *Alenu*. The communities of France, England, and the Rhineland decreed a general fast in commemoration of the martyrs. It was as if they realised that this, the first continental Ritual Murder accusation, was only a sample of what lay in store: for thereafter, similar incidents recurred in rapid succession—Paris in 1180, Erfurt in 1199, Fulda and Wolfsheim in 1235, Valréas (Provence) in 1247 . . . . By the close of the fifteenth century, half a hundred cases may be enumerated, each with its trail of blood: yet the record is manifestly incomplete.

After the recognition of the doctrine of Transubstantiation by the Fourth Lateran Council in 1215, a further pretext for persecution was made available. It was alleged that from time to time the Jews would obtain a fragment of the consecrated Host, which they would cause to suffer the agonies of the Passion once again by piercing it with knives, or inflicting other tortures upon it. The outrage was generally said to have been discovered by reason of the fact that the wafer actually shed drops of blood. The accusation is, as a matter of fact, even more ridiculous (if such a thing were possible) than that of Ritual Murder, for it postulates a degree of regard for, and belief in, the consecrated elements which must be contradictory in any non-Catholic. Yet there is no need to regard all the details as spiteful invention: for a scarlet organism (known as the *micrococcus prodigiosus*) may sometimes form on stale food kept in a dry spot, having an appearance not unlike that of blood. Whenever this took place, a miracle, clearly proving previous maltreatment, was assumed; and as a matter of course the Jews of the neighbourhood would be considered guilty. The first instance on record is that of Beelitz, near Berlin, in 1243, when a large number of Jews and Jewesses were burned at the stake, on the spot subsequently known as the Judenberg, upon this charge. Later on, cases of the sort, with their accompaniment of pillage, bloodshed, and banishment, were recurrently brought up all over Europe, culminating in *causes célèbres*, which are still commemorated locally, at Paris in 1290 and at Brussels in 1370.

Sometimes not even so specious a pretext was considered necessary. In case of a destructive conflagration, so frequent and so fatal in medieval towns, who should be responsible but the Jews? If there were an outbreak of plague, it was plainly they who had introduced it—provably, if they were infected first; and none the less obviously (for it clearly demonstrated their malicious forethought) if they remained immune. All heresy was assuredly fostered by them; and it was they who were answerable for otherwise unexplained murders. In case of an enemy invasion—especially one by the Infidel—it was taken for granted that they had invited it. During civic or dynastic disturbance, they were plundered by each side, on the plea that they were in sympathy with the other. Kings accused them of complicity with rebels, and rebels asserted that they were the instruments of the king. Sometimes, no pretext at all was necessary for an attack to be made, other than the imminence of the Easter season with its reminiscences of the Passion, or even less. And, in the ordinary vicissitudes of war and peace—siege, capture, riot—they bore at least their share of suffering.

It is proper, on the other hand, to bear in mind the fact that in the Middle Ages life was cheaper than was the case in the peaceful Victorian interlude. It is true that the Jew's was considered less valuable than his neighbour's. But the latter's existence, like his own, was precarious. The normal proportion of deaths by violence was immeasurably greater than at the present time. Religious animosities devastated whole countries. Some of the most fertile and most highly civilised tracts of the south of France were reduced almost to a desert in the course of the crusade against the Albigenses. Catholics harried Hussites with as good grace as Protestants later harried Catholics. In times of war, there was no such thing as a non-combatant. The countryside was systematically wasted by any invader, and any captured town was put to the sack, as a matter of course. Even in times of profound peace, no man's tenure of life and property was certain. A marauding baron or daring bandit would take every opportunity that offered to attack unsuspecting settlements. The highways were never safe. There were frequent civic disturbances. Wealthy burghers were always nervous of attack, whether by lawless soldiers or by the populace. Bad feeling against foreigners was ever-present, and found its expression in periodical riots. Royal exactions were never moderate, and not always justified by precedent. There were other exotic sections of the population—for example, the gypsies—whose sufferings were similar, and against whom almost identical charges were occasionally brought.

The tribulations of the Jew were not therefore so exceptional in kind as is generally supposed. But they were certainly exceptional in degree. He combined, as it were, all the necessary qualifications for massacre and maltreatment. His was at the same time a distinct ethnic group and an unpopular religious minority. He was generally an urban resident, who suffered disproportionately during domestic disturbance, as well as being considered a man of substance, whose house was worth sacking. And so, at any time of civil or political unrest; on every occasion when a town was taken by storm; at every period of pestilence or misfortune, when a scapegoat was necessary; whenever religious passions were stirred up to a more than ordinary extent—in all such cases an attack upon the Jew was a foregone conclusion. It was not until the Middle Ages were at an end, until law and order became generally established, and until in western Europe at least a fresh value had been placed on human life, regardless of race and creed, that the condition of the Jew began to ameliorate, and that his existence in normal times became reasonably secure.

V

In the south of Europe conditions were by no means as bad as in England, France, and Germany. Here religion was not as yet taken quite so seriously. The Crusading spirit never obtained so strong a hold. The intermixture of peoples and influences prevented racial prejudice from becoming paramount. In Italy, above all, the path of the Jews was comparatively smooth. The Pope, however much he may have desired to prevent the contamination of Christian orthodoxy through their influence, always adhered to the principle of formal toleration. Notwithstanding the tendency of ecclesiastical policy, he never countenanced the employment of violence against them, or such atrocities as the Blood Libel or forced conversion. Time after time his voice was raised on the side of sanity and moderation in these respects (even Innocent III, who inspired the most reactionary legislation of the Middle Ages, was no exception in this). A protective Bull of Calixtus II, *Sicut Judaeis*, which strongly condemned physical attacks upon the Jews or their baptism under duress, was confirmed at least twenty-two times from its first promulgation in 1120 down to the middle of the fifteenth century. From 1130 to 1138, one of the rival competitors to the throne of St. Peter was a person of immediate Jewish extraction—Anacletus II (Piero Pierleoni). In the Papal dominions, alone almost in all Europe, the Jews never knew the last extremes of massacre and expulsion; and Rome was the centre from which little colonies pushed out into the neighbouring areas.[1]

In the south of the country too, the settlements which had existed since classical times continued without interruption. Apulia was, by tradition, the oldest haven of Jewish scholarship in Europe, and it was from Bari that the four Rabbis who were to diffuse Rabbinic learning in the Mediterranean world had set sail. The local communities had indeed suffered from Byzantine intolerance in the ninth century, and from the Saracen forays in the tenth, but they soon recovered. Sabbatai Donnolo (913-982), the earliest European Jewish author known to us by name (with the exception of Caecilius of Calacte, a rhetorician of the first century B.C.), was famous even in Gentile circles as a physician. During the period of Moslem rule in Sicily (827-1091) the lustre of the Caliphate of Cordova was in some respects imitated, though not rivalled. Paltiel, a descendant of the poet and wonder-worker, Shephatiah of Oria, rose in the tenth century to the position of vizier here, and subsequently in Egypt. The expulsion of the Moslems did not bring about any drastic change. For some generations after, the Jews of Sicily remained numerous if not particularly prosperous, and were generally unaffected by the worst of the storms which elsewhere had become a feature of Jewish life.

[1] Below, pp. 258-9.

N

On the adjacent mainland, in the kingdom of Naples, conditions were similar until the close of the thirteenth century, when the accession of the house of Anjou introduced northern ideals of intolerance, followed by a persecution and forced conversion throughout Apulia, the traces of which remained for centuries. Gradually the local communities recovered from this blow, their members being recruited by fresh immigration. Further east, in Greece and the neighbouring territories, the earliest centre of settlement in Europe, the old Jewish life wilted under the shadow of Byzantine fanaticism, which found its outlet from time to time in bursts of oppression and attempts to enforce conformity. Here and there, however, we obtain glimpses of flourishing communities, maintaining themselves largely from the silk industry, and distinguished (as the traveller Benjamin of Tudela[1] informs us) for their learning and piety.

VI

The most important centre by far of Jewish life in southern Europe still was Spain. The intolerance of the Almohadan fanatics had indeed put an end, as we have seen, to the evanescent glory which had been attained in the Caliphate of Cordova and the kingdoms of the Taifas. By now, fortunately, the territories under Moslem rule did not constitute, or even approach, a majority of the Peninsula. The Arabs had never been able to subdue the rugged north-western corner, which had held out as an independent principality. Already in the eighth century, centres of resistance, constantly though almost imperceptibly increasing, were formed at two or three points along the northern frontier. In the end, these developed into the kernels of a number of Christian states, subsequently to become consolidated around Aragon, Navarre, and Castile (with Leon), to which may also be added Portugal on the Atlantic seaboard. All these continued to live in a state of perpetual warfare, making headway by slow and painful degrees against the infidel in the intervals of fighting among themselves. In 1085 Alfonso VI of Castile captured Toledo, and from that date the Cross again commanded the obedience of a greater part of the country.

The earliest stages of the *Reconquista* had originally involved obvious danger for the Jews. The attitude of the growing Christian states towards them had been one of intense suspicion and hostility. The

[1] See p. 216.

74. THE EMPEROR HENRY VII RECEIVES A DEPUTATION OF ROMAN JEWS, 1312
From the Codex Balduini. Town Archives, Coblenz

75. MEDIEVAL JEWISH TYPES. (ST. PAUL DISPUTING WITH THE JEWS)
Enamel on copper gilt. English, about 1150. Victoria and Albert Museum, London

76. JEWS (WEARING BADGE) TAKING THE OATH MORE JUDAICO
German woodcut from Tengler, Laienspiegel, Augsburg, 1509

latter inherited all the bitterness of their Visigothic ancestors. The Jews were closely identified in their eyes with the Moslems. They spoke the same language; they shared the same culture; they dressed in the same manner; they followed an infidel religion which was, if anything, the more hateful of the two. The very fact that they were treated by the Arabs with tolerance condemned them in Christian eyes. Accordingly, in every place which the champions of the Cross captured in the course of the initial expansion, the Jews shared the fate of their overlords, or worse. 'All the synagogues which they found were destroyed', old chroniclers repeatedly record. 'The Priests and Doctors of the Law whom they discovered they slew with the sword: and the books of their Law were burned.' The old Visigothic code, the *Fuero Juzgo*, laid down for them conditions of hopeless, impracticable inferiority—the best that Jews could hope for if, by some unlikely chance, they escaped with their lives.

As early as the tenth century, a change of attitude began to manifest itself. The initial religious zeal had begun to wane. The Christian states were continually at war one against the other, and had no scruple in applying to the nearest Moslem power for help when occasion demanded. Christian knights would sometimes be found fighting under the banner of the Crescent, and Moorish paladins under that of the Cross. The line of demarcation was determined more and more by considerations of policy and interest rather than religion; and the methodical extermination of religious dissentients belonged to the past. If the Christian hold on the country was to be secure, it was plainly advisable indeed to conciliate so important an element in the population as the Jews. At the same time, by reason of their linguistic qualifications, it was sometimes found convenient to employ them as before on important diplomatic missions. Physicians and scientists, trained in the Arab schools, became prominent at court; while inherent aptitude won many individuals high office in the financial administration.

Thus the golden age of Jewish life in Spain, though without doubt largely due throughout to the propinquity and example of the Moors, did not coincide with their hegemony. On the contrary, over a prolonged period Christian tolerance compared very favourably indeed with Almohadan fanaticism. The current impression, which restricts the glories of Spanish Jewry to the age of Arab supremacy, and considers their degradation to have gone hand in hand with the Visigothic advance, is thus erroneous. It was under Christian rule, though to some extent under Moslem intellectual influence, that some of the greatest figures in the intellectual life of Spanish Jewry flourished: Judah haLevi, the sweetest singer of Zion; or Abraham ibn Ezra, the wandering poet and exegete, who spent most of his life in lands which professed allegiance to the Cross. It is highly significant that the greatest luminary of the Spanish Jewish school, Moses Maimonides, though born in Cordova, was driven into exile by Moslem (not Christian) fanaticism, and produced his immortal works in a foreign land. Jewish levies fought bravely under the banner of the Cross as well as of the Crescent, and individuals of outstanding ability served the kings of Castile and Aragon as loyally and with as much devotion as they had those of Granada or of Seville.

On the other hand, the influence of the Moslem period upon Spanish Jewry was deep and far-reaching. Down to the end it retained strong traces of its antecedents. For a long time, even under Christian rule, Arabic rather than Spanish continued to be its language. Important works were composed in that tongue when the Moslem hegemony was a distant memory. Legal documents continued to be drawn up in it. As late as the fourteenth century, it was considered requisite for the secretary of any Spanish community of importance to be well versed in it. Names with a strong Arabic tinge continued to predominate amongst the Jews of the Peninsula; while the Jewish community or quarter went by the Arabic name *aljama* (Assembly). One or two Arabic words even penetrated, through the medium of the Jews of Spain, into the *patois* of their co-religionists in the remoter countries of northern Europe.

It was in the reign of Alfonso VI of Castile (1065-1109) that the Jews of Christian Spain reached the zenith of their prosperity. His conquest of Toledo made him master of one of the oldest and most flourishing of all Spanish communities. From this time the city was the capital of Castile, and the centre of Jewish life for the whole of Spain. Alfonso's armies contained numbers of Jews; and subsequent legend told how the black and yellow turbans which strewed the ground after the battle of Sagrajas had testified to the valour with which they fought. Notwithstanding the admonitions of Pope Gregory VII, they were left in possession by the royal *fueros*, or charters, of all the privileges which they had enjoyed under the Mohammedans, and were placed with some reservations on a position of legal equality with the general population. They were systematically utilised throughout this period (as they were elsewhere in the Peninsula too) to colonise their king's new conquests, and were for that purpose granted extensive rights in the places in which they settled. The royal body-physician Joseph ibn Ferrizuel (known as Cidello) was so influential that the Jewish communities of the country considered him a *Nasi*, or Prince. He was consulted in matters of politics, countersigned state documents, and on one occasion was employed by the nobility as their spokesman to propose a match for the heiress to the throne, Urraca, who subsequently became Queen. Other Jews were used on diplomatic errands. His nephew, Solomon ibn Ferrizuel, was assassinated while on his way back from a mission to the court of Aragon; and it is said that the maltreatment of a Jewish envoy named Ibn Chalib by the Emir of Seville resulted in the outbreak of war. Urraca's son, Alfonso VII (1126-1157), continued generally speaking the same policy. Once more, Jews fought in support of their king against both domestic and foreign enemies. Jewish scientists and financial agents were prominent at court. Judah ibn Ezra, nephew of the poet Moses, a refugee from Granada (where his family had formerly held office under the Moors), stood high in the royal favour as Treasurer (*almoxarife*). When in 1147 the fortress of Calatrava was captured, he was sent to superintend the commissariat and supplies, and his influence became paramount there.

This turned out to be highly fortunate. When at this period the Almohadan persecution began in the south of the Peninsula, in the parts still subject to Moslem rule, it was northwards, to the Christian states, that the majority of the refugees turned their steps. The highroad passed through Calatrava, where the Jewish magnate did all that he could to succour them. He gave them food and sustenance, provided transport for the sick and aged, ransomed the prisoners, staved off Christian exactions, and ensured a safe passage to Toledo, where the greatest number sought refuge. The result was that the balance of Jewish life in Spain was radically altered. In the Moslem territories of Andalusia, not a single professing Jew was to be found. On the other hand, the importance of the communities in the Christian kingdoms was enormously enhanced, both relatively and absolutely; while Gerona, Barcelona, and especially Toledo (with its reputed 10,000 Jews and numerous magnificent synagogues) took the place of Granada, Seville, and Lucena as the centres of Jewish culture.

For the next three-quarters of a century, conditions in Christian Spain generally remained favourable. Jewish diplomats, financiers, and physicians abounded; supposedly Alfonso VIII's mistress was the lovely Rachel, still remembered as *La Fermosa* ('the Beautiful') about whom many romantic legends have clustered. Yet the Crusading spirit had already crossed the Pyrenees and begun to disturb the friendly relations which had hitherto subsisted. Papal pressure led to the enactment in Castile and Aragon of the anti-Jewish measures of the various Church Councils, if not to their enforcement; and at intervals a solemn protest would be made against the appointment of Jews to positions of trust. When the news reached Toledo in 1108 of the defeat of the Castilian forces at Ucles, the rabble rushed upon the *aljama* and sacked it, on the pretext that the Jewish forces of the left wing had been the first to yield ground. The *aljamas* suffered disproportionately in the civil war in Leon in 1197. But it was not until the beginning of the thirteenth century that the full flood of Crusading enthusiasm reached the country.

A Holy War had been preached against the infidel; and large numbers of knights and adventurers streamed to Spain from all parts of Europe. The point of assembly was fixed at Toledo, where all arrangements were left in the hands of Joseph ibn Shushan, the *almoxarife mayor*. Notwithstanding this, the Crusaders imitated the example set in the Rhineland, and opened their operations by attacks on the Jews of the capital and elsewhere. The pinchbeck heroes withdrew at the outset of the campaign, with the result that the decisive battle of Las Navas de Tolosa was fought without their aid. The engagement resulted nevertheless in an overwhelming victory for the Cross. The Moslem menace was finally crushed. Before long, the territory subject to the Crescent was reduced to insignificance—the kingdom of Granada and one or two outlying districts. By virtue of this very fact, the position of the Jews deteriorated. Christianity being supreme, they no longer constituted an important minority whose sympathies it was desirable to conciliate. Diplomatic errands to the Moslem powers ceased to have the same significance as hitherto. Even Moslem science, and the importance of Jewish scientists trained in the Moslem schools, now waned. Simultaneously the fierce religious intolerance, the exclusive nationalism, and the commercial rivalries which prevailed in the rest of Europe, began to penetrate the Peninsula. Political maltreatment and popular outbreaks became more common. Successive rulers restricted more and more the privileges which the Jews were theoretically allowed to enjoy, even though they did not always put their legislation into practice. Even Alfonso the Wise (1252-1284), whose court was one of the greatest centres of Jewish scientific activity, subjected them in his famous code known as the *Siete Partidas* to the most minute and galling restrictions, though these were not enforced until some time later. Occasionally (above all, in the north of the country, where the French example was more effective) there were murderous popular outbreaks. It took a long time, indeed, for the new spirit to permeate the country, and in some respects it never did so with the same thoroughness as elsewhere. Yet, from the beginning of the thirteenth century, the tranquillity of a former age began to pass; and the cloud which lowered over all Europe extended menacingly over the *aljamas* of Spain.

77. BURNING OF JEWS AT TRENT, 1475
German woodcut. Late 15th Century

Chapter XIX

THE SOCIAL REVOLUTION

———————•———————

I

The growing insecurity of the Jews in northern Europe was accompanied, as the Middle Ages advanced, by a change in their economic position. In the earliest days of their dispersal there was little to differentiate them in this respect from the ordinary population. When the Roman said that the Jew was by nature a slave, the reference was to the exceptionally wiry physique which rendered him (but for his peculiar religious practices) invaluable for the most strenuous menial labours. The abortive canal through the Isthmus of Corinth, and the stupendous Colosseum at Rome, both undertaken after the campaigns of Vespasian, were in their way monuments to Jewish brawn, no less than to Roman skill; while half a century earlier, Jews expelled from the capital by the Emperor Tiberius worked the mines of Sardinia. The Roman magnates who purchased Palestinian slaves after successive revolts must have destined them in the main for work on their estates. Many, on gaining their freedom, certainly continued to be engaged in agriculture, like their co-religionists in Palestine, Babylonia, and Persia. Even in northern Europe, the Jew was not entirely divorced from the soil until the Middle Ages were well advanced. In the south a minority remained attached to it to the end. In most cases, however, they seem to have been interested in intensive cultivation (particularly in the production of wine and oil) rather than in the more extensive and laborious processes of tilling the soil and growing crops.

One cause which tended to divorce the Jew from the countryside is obvious. His religious practices, as they had become evolved in the course of past centuries, called for a sympathetic social environment. A quorum of ten adult males was desirable for prayer: an instructor was requisite for the youth: in a dozen different ways the constant presence, or at least propinquity, of co-religionists was considered

necessary. But such social contacts were out of the question in rural
solitude, and difficult even in a village in which there was a Gentile
majority. Moreover, with the growth of religious prejudice, life in
isolation became increasingly uncomfortable, if not dangerous. Constant contact with other Jews was thus essential for security as well
as for observance.

Finally, the organisation of rural society on a feudal basis afforded
no opening whatsoever for a non-believer. Semi-servile peasants were
the vassals of the Lord of the Manor and paid him in labour or in
kind; the Lord of the Manor was vassal of the Baron, and the Baron in
turn of a major Baron or of the King—the apex of this pyramid, to
whom all, directly or indirectly, owed service. This whole organisation, moreover, was based upon the idea of allegiance to a common
faith and cemented by a series of religious oaths. In this symmetrical
edifice there was no place for eccentricities, or even for materials
which deviated from the accepted pattern. The Jew was not a villein,
and so could not be forced to till the ground; he was not a professional
fighting-man (indeed, he was generally not allowed to bear arms),
and so could not be an overlord; he was not even a Christian, and so
could neither receive nor pay homage as other men did. As though
this were not enough, he was forbidden in many places by immemorial
usage, and in most subsequently by law, from holding freehold
property (though there were some noteworthy exceptions to this). In
rural society, no place was thus available for him—no gap left, even,
into which he might insinuate himself. Banished from the countryside, his attention was necessarily confined to the town.

A willing immigrant into a country already populated can as a
matter of fact hardly find any outlet for his energies excepting in
urban life. To settle on the land presupposes that there is land to
spare, and that there are funds with which it may be acquired (one
must remember that the free agricultural labourer was unknown in
later classical times). In a city, on the other hand, any man can
normally find some sort of outlet for his energies, whether as
labourer, craftsman, or huckster. In Imperial Rome, Jews were to be
found in almost every walk of life. They were merchants, pedlars,
painters, actors, poets, singers, butchers, tailors, and blacksmiths.
As beggars they were considered importunate; and, after Christianity
established itself, some actually sold holy images on the steps of the
churches. The mainstay of the community, however, was the merchant
class. They were perhaps responsible in part for the importation of

corn, which made possible the policy of satisfying the proletariat with 'bread and circuses'. It is noteworthy that their principal centre in the capital was near the docks, and that early settlements were situated all along the trade route which joined Rome to Egypt, the granary of the ancient world.

The Dark Ages narrowed the broad horizons of Imperial Rome within narrow national limits, sweeping away the old order of things in favour of a rude military caste. International trade was thus thrown, as far as the northern countries of Europe were concerned, more and more into the hands of a class, who possessed no country of their own, yet had international connections to help them and an international language in which to correspond. Between the fifth and the seventh centuries, trade in western Europe was largely in the hands of 'Syrian' merchants, who may have included a certain proportion of Jews; for the *lingua franca* which they used was closely allied with that in which the Rabbinical correspondence was carried on, and Jewish legal instruments drawn up, at the period. When Syria was overrun by the Arabs and the majority of the inhabitants converted to Islam, they lost their special position. This was now left to the Jews alone, who for a while had few rivals. Characteristic of their function was the share they had in the slave trade (considered in those days no more reprehensible than the cattle trade in ours). In legal documents of the ninth century, the terms 'Jew' and 'merchant' are sometimes used interchangeably. The earliest communities of France, Germany, and central Europe lay along the great trade routes, being established presumably by merchants who pushed northward up the Rhone or westward up the Danube.

Ibn Khurdadbih, Postmaster of the Caliphate of Bagdad, composed in about 847 a way-book, in which he gave a remarkable picture of the activities of the polyglot Jewish merchants of this period. Setting out from southern France, they would make their way through Egypt and the Red Sea to India and China, bringing back with them musk, aloes, camphor, cinnamon, and other products of the East. An alternative route was through Mesopotamia and down the Tigris. Others went overland, across northern Africa or central Europe. The vestiges of a once-flourishing colony of Chinese Jews, still to be traced about a ruined synagogue in Kai-Feng-Fu, remain to this day in testimony of the commercial intercourse carried on in the Dark Ages with the Far East. An imposing list has been drawn up of commodities (beginning with oranges, going on to enumerate sugar, rice, slippers, and tambours, and ending with lilac) which perhaps owe their introduction to Europe to Jewish traders. Nor was this all: for Jews too brought from the Far East, on the one hand the Arabic numerals, on the other such works as the Fables of Bidpai, the source of a vast number of European fairy-tales.

II

The commercial supremacy of the Jew in western Europe came to an end in the tenth century with the growth of the Italian trading republics (particularly Venice and Amalfi), which rapidly gained the monopoly in Mediterranean affairs. The Crusades provided the final impetus which drove him out of mercantile life. Trade may not always follow the flag with such regularity as is expected of it; but it never loses the opportunity to utilise the channels of communication opened up by military enterprise. Successive campaigns for the recovery or protection of the Holy Land brought the East and the West more closely together than they had been at any time since the Roman Empire had fallen. They developed yet further the power of the Italian maritime city-states. In the final result, they safeguarded pilgrims—and with them, as a matter of course, merchants—on their way to the Holy City.

Thus, commerce was given a powerful impetus among the western European nations. No longer was it the monopoly of a small, venturesome class, with special linguistic qualifications. The Jew's personal characteristics, which had hitherto been an advantage, now told against him; for he could enjoy the privileges neither of the Christian on the one hand nor of the Moslem on the other. The insecurity of his life made his commercial ventures more dangerous. Growing intolerance put him to increasing disadvantage whenever a non-Jewish competitor was at hand. He could not hope to emulate the grandiose co-operative enterprises, under political protection, which the Italian and other commercial cities were able to organise. Obstacles were everywhere put in his way: Venice, for example, the great *entrepôt* of Mediterranean trade, not only refused to admit Jewish merchants and allow Jewish merchandise to be carried in vessels which flew her flag, but also tried to ensure the adoption of a similar policy elsewhere, from the Rhine to the Hellespont. The experience of the Jew was in fact everywhere the same. In one branch of economic activity after the other he was a pioneer. Once the lessons taught by his example had been learned, and Gentile competition became vigorous, he was generally excluded, and not infrequently even expelled.

Indeed, the medieval organisation of commerce, like the medieval organisation of agriculture and land tenure, left no opening for the unbeliever. In every city buying and selling came to be confined to members of the Gild Merchant, no stranger being allowed to enter into competition with them. But the Gild Merchant was based entirely upon the conception of uniformity. It was a social body— and no burgher desired to have social contacts with a Jew. It had its religious activities—its corporate services, its processions, perhaps its own chapel—, in which a Jew could take no part. It was based on the idea of protecting the native against the competition of a foreigner; but the Jew, for however many generations his ancestors may have been resident, was always reckoned a stranger and an interloper. In one or two instances, exceptions were made, while subterfuge and evasion could never be entirely suppressed. Nevertheless, so far as organised commerce was concerned, the Jew as such could find scant place.

In manufactures and handicrafts the position was much the same. In the early days of his settlement in Europe, the Jew had been active in these also. But he was at a disadvantage when faced with Gentile competition, while the prejudice against the subordination of a true believer to an infidel made it difficult for him to employ assistants, and so extend the scale of his operations. Finally, the organisation of the Craft Gilds, with their complete legal monopoly of one process of manufacture or another, excluded him entirely. In the logical, symmetrical, all-embracing organisation of urban as of rural life, there was (in northern Europe, at least) no room for the arch-infidel.

III

There was one indispensable economic function, however, for which medieval society made no provision. The financier, or banker, or money-lender (the terms are in fact nearly synonymous) is equally necessary in any age in which a monetary economy prevails. From time to time, the richest man may need a loan to assist him in some fresh remunerative enterprise; the poorest, to cover his immediate requirements at time of stress; the craftsman, to buy raw material to carry on his calling; the farmer, in order to tide over the period between seed-time and harvest. But the borrower, who temporarily deprives the lender of the use of his capital and thus makes it unavailable for productive purposes, plainly owes the latter some sort of compensation. Moreover, any loan has in it an element of uncertainty, the interest charged being a species of insurance against total loss.

But, as the Middle Ages progressed, the Catholic Church began to set its face against the lending of money at interest, under whatever conditions. The Mosaic code, indeed, envisaging a purely pastoral and agricultural life centred about small village communities, had prohibited (Deuteronomy xxiii, 19, etc.) profit-making on any loan to a 'brother'. The New Testament, too, in its current mistranslation (Luke vi, 35), enjoined the faithful to 'lend, expecting nothing' (the actual meaning is 'never despairing'). Aristotle, second in authority only to the Bible in the Middle Ages, took up the same attitude. Nature itself, which did not make money breed by the ordinary processes of reproduction, implicitly condemned the practice. By slow degrees, accordingly, the Church took up an attitude of unqualified opposition to 'usury,' as it was called, whether the rate charged was great or small. In the Third Lateran Council, held at Rome in 1179, the attack reached its climax, Christian burial being refused to all who followed the heinous practice.

The policy was, as a matter of fact, based on a mistaken idealism, justifiable only had steps been taken by the Church to make loans available to the needy, free of charge. Only the omnipresence of the Jew made it feasible; for the prohibition was essentially a religious one, which could be enforced even superficially against true believers only, not infidels.[1] A merchant excluded from trade finds indeed the only outlet for his capital in this direction. (It is natural to have recourse to a merchant for help when no money-lender is available; and the Jew was presumably first introduced to his new profession by this means.) Thus the Jew, just at the period when he was excluded from ordinary walks of life, found an opening in this, the most unhonoured and least popular of all pursuits. He did not have any natural proclivity for it (we find only isolated Jewish bankers even in classical times). He was little known in it in Europe prior to the close of the eleventh century. Now, however, it became his only possible walk of life—the sole manner in which he could employ his capital, and the sole fashion in which he might hope to gain a livelihood. Rabbinical authorities disapproved of the practice: where a fellow-Jew was in question,

---

[1] It is not quite correct to say that the prohibition did not *apply* to infidels.

they flatly forbade it. Nevertheless, in the end, they had to yield to circumstances. By the thirteenth century, the majority of Jews in those countries subject to the Catholic Church, with the partial exception of southern Italy and Spain, were dependent directly or indirectly, in spite of themselves, on this degraded, and (in the circumstances under which it was exercised) degrading occupation.

The economic revolution found a powerful impetus in the growing insecurity of life. It became more and more advisable for the Jew to have his capital, as far as possible, in a form in which it could soon be liquidated, and would not be jeopardised by any sporadic outburst of violence. The house of a merchant can be gutted and pillaged from roof to cellar, and he will be left penniless. Gold, on the other hand, can be concealed more or less effectively; while outstanding debts can be gathered in, to form the basis of fresh activity. As financier, moreover, the Jew enjoyed a great advantage in his widespread literary and personal connections. 'Credit' in its technical sense may not have been invented by him, though a good case may be made out to support the hypothesis. He enjoyed it, on the other hand, as a social reality. He knew that his co-religionists were generally reliable, that they would carry out his requests, and that they would honour his signature. If a Rabbi in London, at the end of a scientific communication to a Rabbi at Marseilles, requested the latter to pay a certain sum to an English Crusader about to embark for the East, holding himself in readiness to perform a like favour anywhere in England, he could be certain that if possible his request would be fulfilled. It was an initial advantage which no other social category enjoyed.

For a period therefore, the Jew was in some countries the sole legitimate capitalist. Whenever any great scheme was on foot, his services had to be sought. He would be prepared to make the Crown an advance when required, upon the 'ferm of the shire' or income of other administrative units. For the two characteristic occupations of the Middle Ages—fighting and building—his aid was indispensable. Crusades, fatal to him as they were, might have been impossible in the form in which they were undertaken had it not been for his financial assistance. Even ecclesiastical foundations had recourse to him for any important undertaking. Aaron of Lincoln, the greatest Anglo-Jewish financier of the twelfth century, assisted in the construction of no less than nine of the Cistercian monasteries of England, as well as the Cathedrals of Lincoln and Peterborough and the great

Abbey of St. Albans. The growth of the system of scutage (or money-payment in lieu of personal military service, which undermined the feudal system and facilitated the establishment of national monarchies) rendered the capital which the Jew could provide necessary even in normal conditions: and the process would have been retarded but for his co-operation. The transition of Europe from a barter-economy to a money-economy during these centuries was certainly facilitated by his presence.

As yet, it was the upper classes with whom the Jewish activities were principally concerned; not so much the great feudatories, who were wealthy enough to dispense with his services, as the lesser baronage, or city patricians. In consequence, he earned unpopularity from all classes: from his clients, as they fell deeper and deeper into his debt, and from the opposing faction, who resented this succour of their enemies. The time inevitably came when, whatever the apparent cause, this hatred expressed itself in violence. Sometimes, documentary evidence exists to prove that the ringleader in a popular attack, ostensibly motivated by religious zeal, was deeply in the debt of his victims;[1] and the destruction of the deeds which registered their transactions was a usual sequel to massacre.

The heyday of the Jewish predominance in the world of finance was in the twelfth and thirteenth centuries, when on the one hand displacement from commerce became effective, while on the other the regulations against usury were rigidly enforced. Later, the Gentile usurer, legal and canonical restrictions notwithstanding, once more became a universal, though highly unpopular figure. Legal fictions were found to get round the impracticable regulations. The interest would be euphemistically called 'usage'; a conditional clause would be inserted in the agreement stipulating that interest should be made payable only if the loan were not reimbursed within an impossibly short time; or the bond would be made out for a greater amount than was actually lent. The hands of the Papal curia itself were not clean from this offence. Throughout Europe, Italians (generally known under the generic name of 'Lombards' or 'Cahorsins') had a bad name as usurers. In Italy itself, first the Tuscans and then the Paduans made themselves notorious, the latter being assigned in Dante's *Inferno* to exemplary punishment. Against the activities of these Christian competitors, with their august patronage and their vast co-operative resources, the Jew was utterly powerless; and before

[1] Above p. 189; below, p. 222.

long he was driven to the wall. The Italians were mainly interested, however, in operations on the grand scale—making an advance on the security of the revenues of a kingdom, or transmitting Peter's Pence to the Papal court in Rome. The Jews were now forced to restrict themselves to lending money on pledge and similar petty transactions, hardly distinguishable from what we would to-day call pawnbroking.

The rate of interest charged was always high—necessarily so, in view of the scarcity of coin and the general unruliness. Even when fixed by law, it was in northern countries rarely less than 43 per cent, unless exceptional security were forthcoming.[1] The chances of violence and expropriation were high; the taxation payable into the royal exchequer was enormous; and there was a strong probability of losing both capital and interest. All these contingencies had to be taken into account. But, if they were obviated, the profits were so great as to arouse boundless jealousy, and to add yet another incitement to violence. In the course of a couple of years, a Jew's capital (subject to the exigencies of the Exchequer) might be trebled. On the other hand, a mob-rising might rob him overnight of every penny he possessed. It was a vicious circle, pacific escape from which was impossible. Yet the Christian usurers, though they did not have to safeguard themselves to anything like the same extent against the chances of murder and pillage, were no less exacting; and their rapacity often made the general population regret the departure of the Jewish competitors, whom their rise had rendered unnecessary.

IV

An inevitable result of a special occupation, in the Middle Ages, was a special status: for a person who could not be included in the feudal scheme of things necessarily had to have his place in the organisation of society outside it. It would of course have been natural for the Jews to be reckoned together with the other inhabitants of the towns. This, however, would have presumed a degree of sympathy and solidarity between the two elements which was in fact absent. The towns, moreover, were ruled by Gilds, in which the Jew

[1] In southern countries, where conditions were more favourable, the rate was far less—in Italy from 23 to 37 per cent, in Spain as low as 20 per cent. It is worth recalling that, even to-day, the English legislation regards 48 per cent as a not unconscionable rate of interest, and that the legal rate of interest on pledges in some parts of the United States may rise to as high as 12 per cent *monthly*.

78. Süsskind of Trimberg, the Jewish Minnesinger
From the Manesse Codex in the University Library, Heidelberg. 13th Century

79. Caricature showing Medieval English Jews
Exchequer Issue Roll, 1233. Public Record Office, London

could play no part. Besides, he was so frequently a stranger in reality, and he was treated as one so invariably, that it was necessary for him to look for protection to the king—the lord of all men who had no other, and the traditional protector of the merchant and foreigner. The special taxation which the Jew, and the Jew alone, had been made to pay in the Roman Empire (revived in a slightly different form by Theodosius II when he put an end to the Jewish Patriarchate in Palestine and diverted its revenues),[1] seems to have been taken in the Middle Ages as a definite proof that the Jews were, in fact, the serfs of the Emperor—and hence, outside Germany, of other monarchs. The constant appeals to the Sovereign for protection during the course of the Crusades—more especially the Third—did something to spread this conception; and, in the fourteenth century, the old Roman poll-tax was actually revived in Germany under the title of *Opferpfennig* (Tribute-Penny), as a token that the Holy Roman Emperor had inherited, from Vespasian and Titus, supremacy over the people conquered and enslaved so many hundreds of years before.

Whatever the reason, the Jews of the Middle Ages were reckoned royal serfs (*servi camerae regis*). This special relationship to the crown explains much in their position and of their tribulations. They were the king's men. He exercised the most minute control over all their activities. He taxed them arbitrarily. For a monetary consideration, he might alienate all rights over them, collectively or individually, to a third party. He might confiscate their property outright. He might expel them from the realm without giving any reason. He regulated their internal affairs down to the least detail. Above all, he found in them a source of income. Unlike the Christian usurer, the Jew was able to sue his debtors in the royal courts—but the profits of justice accrued to the king. The wealth of the dead usurer, whether Jew or Gentile, legally escheated to the Crown, though the reality was generally not so drastic, as it was to the royal advantage to leave the heirs sufficient to carry on business. If a Jew became converted to Christianity, his property (or a large proportion of it) would be confiscated: for it was not equitable that he should be allowed to enjoy the profits which he had amassed in sin. There were frequent extraordinary amercements, levied in punishment for some offence real or alleged. In Sicily, there was even a tax on Jewish births—an inverted family allowance. All this was quite apart from ordinary taxation, derived by arbitrary 'tallage'.

[1] See above, pp. 110, 117, 140.

o

It is computed that the revenue extracted from the Jews in a normal year was seldom less than one-fifth of their total wealth, and often approached one-quarter, or even one-third. They contributed, in northern countries, about one-twelfth of the total royal income. The proportion is not vast; but it is out of all ratio to their numerical importance, which was not large. In England, for example, the Jews constituted at the most 1 per cent of the total population, contributing thus at least ten times more to the Exchequer than their numbers warranted. Above all, the levies were entirely arbitrary. It was possible for the king to raise enormous sums at short notice without any customary pretext, merely to suit his convenience. Naturally, therefore, it was to his interest to protect the Jews and their activities. So much of their profit came into his coffers that he became, in a sense, the arch-usurer of the realm. The Jews constituted as it were a sponge which sucked up the floating capital of the kingdom. When the treasury was empty, the sponge would be squeezed. It was only a short-sighted ruler (though there were many of them) who would display his authority by remitting the interest, or even the whole debt, on condition that a certain proportion was paid to the treasury. This had the automatic effect of increasing the rate of usury for the future. But, besides this, it was financially unwise: for it was obvious that the Crown stood to gain more by a few years of sleeping partnership than by the most drastic measure of confiscation.

Meanwhile the people were filled with jealousy at the Jew's rapid accumulation of wealth. They watched the money which had once been theirs pass in an unending stream through his chests into the royal treasury. They saw the king grow, through this means, independent of constitutional checks. And so their hatred mounted up, until one day, upon a trivial pretext or none, they would throw themselves on the Jewish quarter, and yet another dark page would be added to the record of martyrdom.

V

The Lateran Council of 1179 (the same which, with its prohibition of Usury, had so profound an effect upon the economic organisation of Europe) deeply influenced Jewish life in other directions as well. It marked the climax of the reaction against Albigensianism—that extraordinary heretical movement which had swept the south of France, and threatened the supremacy of the Catholic Church in surrounding countries also. The tenets of the system, with its dualistic ideas and its conception of the Old Testament as being inspired by the Evil Spirit, were as a matter of fact more essentially opposed to Judaism than any orthodox form of Christianity could possibly be. But its adherents were tolerant, and the Jews of Languedoc not only flourished, but in some cases rose to positions of trust under their auspices.

The Catholic Church, made nervous by a movement which had at one time threatened to engulf it, suspected the Jews of complicity, and included all forms of dissent in the counter-attack formulated at the Lateran. This accordingly saw the revival and re-enactment of all the old anti-Jewish legislation devised under the auspices of the early Church, but almost dormant for the past seven centuries. It rigorously prohibited Jews to have Christians in their service, or Christians to enter into the employment of Jews, even as nurses or midwives. In addition, it forbade true believers to lodge amongst the infidel, thus laying the foundation of the later Ghetto system.[1]

The Fourth Lateran Council of 1215 (under the auspices of Innocent III, the greatest Pope of the Middle Ages) went even further. As a logical sequel to the anti-usury laws enacted on the previous occasion, Christian debtors—particularly Crusaders—received special protection, the latter being relieved of the obligation to pay interest on their debts. Jews were to be rigidly excluded from all public office or any position which might give them even the semblance of authority. They were ordered for the first time to pay tithes to the Church on all property they held. Converts were to be restrained at all costs from following their ancestral rites. Above all, the regulations instituted by certain Moslem rulers, by which all unbelievers (including, of course, Christians) had to wear a distinguishing badge, were introduced for the first time into the Christian world. This was ostensibly in order to prevent the heinous offence of unwitting sexual intercourse between adherents of the two faiths, considered as little better than incest and frequently punished by death. In practice, the badge consisted of a piece of yellow or crimson cloth—in England in the form of the two tables of stone which bore the Ten Commandments; in France, Germany, and elsewhere of a wheel or O (the so-called *rotella* or *rouelle*). In some lands, where a simple badge was found inadequate, the wearing of a hat of distinctive colour was ultimately prescribed.

[1] See below, chapter xxv.

Locally, the system of repression went still further. Thus, in Crete, the houses of the Jews, as well as their persons, were made to bear a distinguishing mark. In many places it was considered the prerogative of the populace to stone the Jews at Easter-tide, while here and there the leading members of the community had to submit on that occasion to a merciless buffeting from some zealous representative of Christianity—sometimes with fatal results. The Jewish community were frequently compelled to exercise the function of public executioners, the gallows often being erected in their graveyard. They were generally excluded from the public baths, or admitted to them only on the day reserved for prostitutes. The cumulative result of all this was to stigmatise the Jews in perpetuity as a race of pariahs, to single out isolated individuals for continual insult, and the whole community for attack and massacre at any outburst of popular feeling.

It must not be imagined that all the ecclesiastical regulations were immediately and consistently enforced, even in those places which were directly subject to the Church in matters temporal. Nevertheless they remained a standard of conduct to which it was always possible to revert, with increasing severity, when the occasion seemed to demand it. At any time of crisis, when a fresh heresy had arisen to threaten the Church, or some peculiarly zealous Pope was elected to the throne of St. Peter, the whole of the repressive code would be renewed and put into effect, bringing disgrace and perhaps disaster into ten thousand homes.

VI

It was not only in the political and economic spheres that the reaction affected the Jew. The counter-attack was extended to his spiritual ideals and to his literature. The Dominican Order, established as an instrument against heresy when the Albigensian peril was dying down, soon extended its activities to the Jews, and lost few opportunities of vexing them. From time to time 'disputations' would be staged under its auspices, in which some zealous but not necessarily well-informed apostate would endeavour to demonstrate the imbecility of the Talmud on the one hand, and its testimony to the teaching of Jesus on the other. All possibility of fair debate was, however, stifled by the fact that the truth of Christianity was assumed to be beyond question. Hence the Jewish protagonists would be unable to counter-attack, while even an outspoken reply on their part would be characterised as blasphemous. In consequence, the results of these encounters were almost invariably unfortunate.

They often took place under the highest patronage. The first impetus was given by the apostate Nicholas Donin, of La Rochelle, who laid before Pope Gregory IX a formal denunciation of the Talmud as blasphemous and pernicious. In consequence, the Pope gave orders for the seizure of all copies of the much-decried work and an investigation into its contents. In France, the order was implicitly obeyed, all Hebrew literature being seized throughout the country on 3rd March 1240, while the Jews were at service in their synagogues. On 12th June an enquiry into its merits and demerits was opened at Paris, in the presence of members of the royal court, including the Queen Mother. The onslaught was directed by Donin himself: the Jewish case was presented by four Rabbis, including Jehiel of Paris, one of the greatest contemporary exponents of Jewish lore, and Moses of Coucy, a popular preacher and author of the *Major Book of Precepts*, a favourite legalistic compendium. Their readiness to speak was not heightened by the fact that they were compelled to make use of the Latin tongue, with which they cannot have been over-familiar. After a prolonged but biased investigation, Donin was adjudged to have proved his case, and the work which he had denounced was formally condemned to the flames. On Friday, 17th June 1242, twenty-four cartloads of priceless Hebrew manuscripts were publicly burned in Paris. The disaster was mourned by the Jews hardly less bitterly than the physical martyrdom of their brethren. A young German student named Meir of Rothenburg (1215-1293: afterwards, when he was famous, to be held to ransom in his native country in the hopes of extorting an enormous levy from his co-religionists, and to die in captivity) witnessed the holocaust, and commemorated it in a bitter dirge, which is still recited in the synagogue:

> Ask, is it well, O Thou consumed in fire
> With those who mourn for Thee . . .

This attack upon Hebrew literature was the prelude to many more; and the Talmud was persecuted with such ferocity that, notwithstanding Jewish zeal and devotion, only one ancient manuscript of the whole text is now extant. The disputation of Paris, similarly, was repeatedly imitated. There was an approximation to freedom of speech only in 1263, when King James I of Aragon arranged a

discussion between the apostate Pablo Christiani and Rabbi Moses
ben Nahman (Nahmanides: 1194-1270), an exegete, Talmudist, and
mystic with a reputation second to none in his day. For four days the
arguments continued, in the presence of the king and his court. The
Jewish representative easily held his own; and the king, openly
recognising this fact, dismissed him with a gift. The Churchmen were
furious nevertheless at some of the opinions which he had expressed
and, notwithstanding the royal safeguard, it was considered advisable
for him to seek safety in the Holy Land.

At times the attack was transferred from the Jewish literature to
the Jewish liturgy; and it was alleged that certain ancient prayers,
composed in an age or country where Christianity was unknown,
contained passages which could be construed as derogatory to the
daughter religion and its founder. The attack centred upon the
dignified *Alenu* prayer, composed by the *Amora* Abba the Tall,[1] which
referred to the vanity and insubstantiality of the objects of heathen
worship. In 1336, in consequence of its denunciation by the apostate
Alfonso of Valladolid (formerly Abner of Burgos, who imbued Spanish
anti-Semitism with a new spirit) its recital was prohibited even in
tolerant Castile. Towards the end of the century, a similar accusation
by a certain Peter (known before his conversion as Pesah) brought
about a persecution in Prague, in consequence of which nearly one
hundred persons lost their lives. Similarly, in 1278, Pope Nicholas
III, imagining that the conversion of the Jews would be assured if
they were made to hear the exposition of Christian doctrine, ordered
them to permit conversionist sermons to be delivered in their
synagogues, as had occasionally been done under Dominican auspices
even earlier. Like so much more of the legislation of the period, this
was not consistently carried out; but it was henceforth always possible
for any fanatical friar to march to the synagogue with a mob at his
heels, to plant his crucifix in front of the Ark which contained the
holy Scrolls, and to demand the hospitality of the pulpit.

VII

The description of the position of the medieval Jew given above
is not, of course, of universal application. Generalisation in all history
is difficult, and in Jewish history peculiarly so. The nearest approach
to the typical 'feudal' Jewry (as it may be called) was to be found

[1] Above, pp. 128 and 190.

in England, where the Jews arrived at a late date and for a specific purpose. In France and Germany there was an approximation to the same economic, and therefore constitutional, status; but, by reason of the antiquity of settlement, the gradual evolution, and the lack of political uniformity in these countries, it is less easy to generalise. Thus, in Narbonne, the Jews were always allodial proprietors in consequence (according to legend) of the grant made by 'Charlemagne'.[1] In Germany the position of the Crown in its relations with the Jews (as in so many other matters) was usurped by the nobility. Here, moreover, the Jewish financial hegemony came somewhat later; for until the twelfth century loans on a larger scale were made principally by the clergy, and thereafter by the citizens and nobles, the Jews coming to the fore only after 1300.

Even in those countries where they were utterly excluded from ordinary walks of life, the Jewish communities could not be restricted to a single occupation.[2] The principal householders, indeed, might be financiers or money-lenders. Yet dependent on them, directly or indirectly, there would necessarily be numerous subordinates: agents and clerks to help in their business; synagogal officials to conduct divine worship; scribes to draw up their business documents, as well as to copy their literary and liturgical compositions; tutors for the instruction of their children; attendants to perform the household services, forbidden by the Church to Gentiles; butchers and bakers to prepare their food in accordance with ritual requirements; even a bath-keeper to facilitate the cleanliness, which was considered an integral part of godliness. In any considerable community, however restricted in its activities by ecclesiastical and governmental prescriptions, all these occupations were necessarily represented, though more than one might be filled by a single individual. The Jewish physicians (frequently, at the same time, scholars and business men) were famous for their skill. Canon law, indeed, forbade any true believer to make use of their services, lest they might obtain undue influence over a Christian soul. But, at time of emergency (and often without that pretext), such restrictions would be overlooked. Kings and princes frequently had Jews as their body-physicians; and a long succession were in attendance on the Popes themselves.

[1] Above, pp. 165-6.
[2] This passage is adapted (by permission) from my chapter on the Jews in the Middle Ages in *The Cambridge Medieval History*, vol. vii, which has been drawn upon at a few other points in the following pages.

In a few handicrafts the Jews long retained their predominance, especially in the south and east of Europe. Down to a late period they almost monopolised the dyeing and silk-weaving industries in Apulia, Sicily and Greece, as well as further east. Benjamin of Tudela, a Jew who traversed the whole of the Mediterranean world at the close of the twelfth century and was the first medieval traveller who generally told the truth, mentions place after place where the community supported itself entirely by these branches of activity: and there was one dye, discovered by the Jews, which was known by their name. They were prominent too as tanners, glass-makers and embroiderers. They seem to have shewn some proclivity for mining, in which they engaged both in Italy and Spain; while they operated salt-works even in Germany. The first (and for a long period, the only) paper manufactory in Europe was that established and maintained by the Jews at Játiva, near Valencia. The art of goldsmith and jeweller, facilitated by foreign intercourse, and above all desirable for a persecuted nomad who preferred to have his possessions in the most easily transferable form, was universally represented. All over central and eastern Europe, they were employed as minters.

In Spain and southern Italy (especially Sicily) the economic degradation of the Jew made least progress of all. The practice of handicrafts on a large scale was never abandoned. There were Jewish craft gilds and gild-halls in the larger cities. Saragossa had for example Jewish *confradias* of weavers, dyers, goldsmiths, cutlers, tanners, saddlers, and shoe-makers. Jewish jugglers in Spain were famous, and, generation after generation, Jews acted as lion-tamers to the court of Aragon. Many were absorbed by commerce, both wholesale and retail; and though money-lending and tax-farming were practised with lucrative results by an influential minority, such callings were never universally followed.

Throughout history, religious and social solidarity, reinforced by Gentile aversion, brought about a tendency for the Jews to foregather in one street or quarter of each town. This received a powerful impetus when the Third Lateran Council forbade Christians to live in the immediate propinquity of the infidel, so as to avoid any possibility of being contaminated by his disbelief. The Jewish quarter was thus universally familiar. In England it was called the *Jewry*, in France *iuiverie*, in Italy *via dei giudei* or *giudecca*, in Germany *Judengasse*, in Spain *judería* or else (in the old Arabic term) *aljama*. In northern Europe at least the Jews were among the pioneers in domestic architecture, and, for the sake of security, were driven to make consider-able use of stone. (It is significant that they were gradually extruded from the Old Jewry in London by the barons, who cast longing eyes on their solidly built dwelling-places, and that in more than one town in England old stone houses are still associated in popular lore with hypothetical Jewish owners of seven centuries ago.) The buildings would be grouped about the synagogue (the service in which had to be conducted in a subdued tone, lest it offended the ears of passers-by). Near this would be the school and bath-house, together with a work-room, a hospital (which served at the same time as a hostelry for strangers) and, in larger communities, even a hall for weddings and similar festivities.

In spite of all restrictions, and of occasional outbursts of fanaticism, the relations between the Jewish and Christian population were often intimate; though they tended to become embittered as time went on. The vernacular was invariably spoken in western Europe, with perhaps a few dialectical differences due to inbreeding, to foreign intercourse, and especially to the inadequacy of any other language to convey certain Hebrew conceptions. In writing, on the other hand, Hebrew characters were usually employed. The glosses of the northern French exegetes thus preserve some of the earliest specimens of the *langue d'oïl* vocabulary; while the elegy composed in commemoration of the thirteen martyrs burned at Troyes in 1288 in consequence of a trumped-up ritual murder charge is one of the most touching of contemporary French ballads. The superficial simi-larity between the two elements in the population must have been considerable to justify the institution of the Jewish badge: though a characteristic pointed head-dress (the wearing of which was made compulsory in Austria in 1267) was common.

Life was of course profoundly influenced by the environment. The severe Gothic of the oldest German synagogues—those for example of Worms or Prague—contrasts strikingly with the flowing arab-esques which may still be seen in Segovia, Cordova, and Toledo, or the pagoda-like wooden structures of Poland, perhaps based on primitive pagan temples. Even synagogal melodies reflected the folk-music of the various countries, and borrowed from it with a lavish hand. Hebrew codices were illuminated in the same manner as the Church missals—sometimes by the same artists. On the other hand, a Jewish *minnesinger* such as Süsskind von Trimberg (*c.* 1200) might enter the service of a German court; and a poet like Immanuel of

Rome (1270-1330), who introduced something of the careless spirit of Italian verse into Hebrew literature, could exchange sonnets in the vernacular with his Christian contemporaries. He is indeed conjectured to have been an intimate of Dante himself, whose *Divina Commedia* he parodied.

Yet the Jew's home was in a very real sense his castle. It was not that he could keep intruders out if they desired to enter—no section of the population was less able to do so. But he could keep extraneous influences at bay, and thus preserve, and even develop, his own way of life. Every trifling elaboration of tradition which had been evolved by his ancestors in Palestine or Mesopotamia was carefully preserved; every casual dictum of the Rabbis was regarded as a positive precept; every little custom, old or new, became sacrosanct, an integral part of religious life. From the moment that he rose in the morning to the moment when he went to bed at night, each action was governed by prescriptive usage. His food, his manner of dress, his fashion of dressing his hair, were hardly less characteristic than his manner of worship. The Sabbath became an oasis of repose in every week—a veritable 'Princess,' who raised him, too, to princely status; her advent was greeted with song, and her departure solaced by fragrant spices. If he was excluded from the celebration of the Gentile carnival, he evolved his own counterpart in the *Purim* festivity, in commemoration of the deliverance of the Jews in the Persian Empire in the days of yore.[1] Contrition for hypothetical religious lapses, presumably responsible for his present vicissitudes, resulted in the elaboration of a series of minor fasts and the composition of innumerable penitential prayers. A patch of unlimed rubble, on the wall of every house, reminded him perennially of the loss of Jerusalem. And every Jew went in daily expectation of the advent of the 'Messiah'-Redeemer, who was to break the yoke of exile from the neck of his people and lead them, erect and triumphant, back to their own land.

Home life was singularly warm. Polygamy had been abandoned in practice long before—even in Talmudic times, it had been exceptional. One of the earliest utterances of Rabbinic scholarship in northern Europe had been an ordinance of Gershom of Mayence (*c.* 1000) which proscribed it entirely. It is true that this was accepted explicitly only by the northern branch of the Jewish people, the so-called *Ashkenazim*. Yet even among the *Sephardim* of Spain and the older settlements in northern Africa and the Levant, the principle

---

[1] Above, p. 64.

was generally observed. Monogamy, moreover, was taken more seriously than Christian Europe had yet learned to do. Mistresses and concubines were not unknown, but (if only by reason of the restricted circle in which the Jew moved) they were rare. The treatment of the woman was more kindly than that which prevailed in ordinary society —so much so that a medieval Rabbi angrily stigmatises wife-beating as a Gentile practice.

If the woman was excluded from public life, and relegated to a special section in the synagogue, it did not imply inferiority in a wider sense. In the home she was supreme; and the home signified more in traditional Judaism than the synagogue. Her education was not neglected. There are extant many Hebrew codices on abstruse subjects copied by medieval Jewesses; and Rabbi Solomon ben Isaac of Troyes, the great *Rashi* himself, made use of his daughter as amanuensis for the purpose of his literary correspondence. Women frequently engaged in business, sometimes on a very large scale, thus leaving their husbands more leisure for study. It is significant that the proportion of martyrs for their faith was, if anything, higher among women than among men. Child betrothals were common: not, as with royalty, for reasons of state, but (severely practical consideration!) lest the parents should lose their lives before they could make arrangements for their children's future.

However depressed he might be by adverse circumstances and jealous neighbours, it was impossible for the Jew to discard his intellectual interests. The only calling in which he is universally found, other than finance, is medicine; and this in spite of innumerable ecclesiastical ordinances and of the difficulty which he found in studying at the Universities. Many courts (especially in Spain) employed a Jewish astrologer, whose activities extended also to astronomy and cartography. A daring philosopher and exegete, Levi ben Gershon (1288-1344), perfected the quadrant; while the chronicler Abraham Zacuto (c. 1450-1515), who had lectured at Salamanca before he became Astrologer Royal at the court of Portugal, composed the astronomical tables used by Columbus on his later expeditions, and manufactured the improved astrolabe employed by Vasco da Gama when he rounded the Cape. Similarly, Majorca produced a whole school of Jewish map-makers, who were famous throughout the Mediterranean world.

At a period when the vast majority of Europeans were illiterate, the Jews insisted as a religious duty upon a system of universal education of remarkable comprehensiveness. In every land to which they penetrated, schools of Rabbinic learning sprang up, in which the shrewd financiers became transmuted into acute scholars, while their clients sat toping in their castles. The rolls of the various Exchequers bear ample witness to the wide secular activities of men whose names are immortalised in the annals of Hebrew literature. The office of Rabbi became professionalised, so far as it ever was, only at a comparatively late date. To instruct the people was regarded as a privilege; and for a long time it was considered shameful to accept any remuneration for so obvious and so meritorious a function.

So, generation after generation, the wits of the Jew were sharpened by continuous exercise, from earliest youth, upon the acute Talmudic dialectic. But the Talmud meant much more to him than this. It brought him another world, vivid, calm, and peaceful, after the continuous humiliation of ordinary existence. It provided him with a second life, so different from the sordid round of every day. After each successive outbreak was stilled, and the shouting of the mob had died down, he crept back to the ruins of his home, and put away his Jewish badge of shame, and set himself to pore again over the yellowed pages. He was transported back into the Babylonian schools of a thousand years before, and there his anguished soul found rest.

80. DISPUTATION BETWEEN JEWISH AND CHRISTIAN SCHOLARS
Woodcut from Seelenwurzgarten, 1483

Chapter XX

EXPULSION AND PERSECUTION

———————————•———————————

I

On 30th November 1215 a Papal Bull was issued to put into
effect the decisions regarding the Jews which had been
reached by the Fourth Lateran Council, with its final embodiment of medieval religious prejudice. Thereafter, the clouds
gathered thick and fast. In country after country fanaticism gained
the upper hand. For the moment the Jew was regarded as an indispensable pest, by reason of the fact that recourse might be had to him
for the financial assistance which the true believer could not now
provide. As the century advanced, however, and the Cahorsins and
Lombards extended their thinly-veiled activities, he became superfluous, and his fate was sealed.

Expulsion was not indeed unknown before, yet in past centuries it
had been confined to very limited areas. Now, the authority of the
Crown was become a reality in various European states, extending
over the whole country. Hence any hostile measure at the close of the
thirteenth century meant a great deal more than could have been the
case a hundred years earlier. The layman, moreover, was unable to
appreciate the delicate logic of the Papal policy, which protected and
tolerated the Jews even when it humiliated them, and regarded their
preservation, though in ignominy, preferable to their extermination.
A secular ruler, reminded almost daily from the pulpit or in the con-
fessional of the multitudinous offences of the Jewish people; sternly
warned against shewing them the slightest favour; commanded to put
into execution the repressive ecclesiastical policy in its last impossible
detail; could hardly fail in the end to imagine that he would be performing a task supremely acceptable to God if he rid his dominions
of them entirely.

II

The first country to drive out the Jews, as the Middle Ages were reaching their zenith, was that which had admitted them last. The wave of massacres which took place in England at the time of the accession of Richard Cœur-de-Lion to the throne had important results. Such outbreaks were from every point of view contrary to the interest of the government. Any breach of order was distasteful to it; and immediate vassals of the Crown, such as the victims were, had a special title to protection. The rioters had, moreover, been careful to destroy wherever possible the bonds which proved their indebtedness. Grave loss was thereby threatened to the Exchequer, to which the claims of those who had perished (like those of all dead usurers, especially Jews) legally reverted. Punishments were imposed on the ringleaders in the riots for their unruliness, though in no case of great severity. The financial consideration, on the other hand, was of such importance that it was considered necessary to take steps to prevent any recurrence.

Accordingly, after Richard's return from captivity in Germany (to his ransom from which the Jews of the realm had been made to contribute three times as much as the wealthy burghers of London), a reorganisation was effected. In the principal cities of the country there were established 'chests' (*archae*), in which duplicate records of all debts were to be deposited. These (which were to be in the charge of a number of 'chirographers', or notaries, half of them Jews and half Christians) were kept under safe custody. Thus, whatever regrettable incidents might occur in future, at any time of civic or political disturbance, the Crown and its rights would be safeguarded. As co-ordinating authority over these provincial centres, there came into being in London the so-called 'Exchequer of the Jews' (not unlike the greater Court of the Exchequer), which sat in judgment in cases in which the Jews and their debts were implicated, however indirectly. In close connection with this was the office of *Presbyter Judaeorum*—not so much the spiritual head of the Jews of the country as an expert appointed by the Crown, without the slightest regard for his qualifications or the general desire. On one occasion, indeed, the incumbent of the office actually sought refuge from his tribulations in baptism! Through their Exchequer, the Jews of medieval England acquired an organisation (by no means to their advantage, though greatly to the benefit of the treasury) equalled in no other country of Europe.

The English communities never fully recovered from the blow they had received at the time of the massacres of 1189-1190. John Lackland, whether from his perennial neediness or from his natural sympathy with unpopular causes, conceded them in 1201 a comprehensive charter of liberties in return for a considerable subsidy. But, later in his reign, his attitude changed; and he began to squeeze money out of them by a series of expedients, from wholesale arrest down to the torture of wealthy individuals, as typical of his short-sightedness as anything else in his reign. During the minority of his son, Henry III, under the rule of a succession of statesmanlike Regents, they were treated with greater mildness. But, from the beginning of his personal rule, their condition became worse and worse. The king's own extravagance, and the rapacity of his foreign favourites, demanded a constant supply of ready money; and it was to the Jews that he looked to supply it. Tallage succeeded tallage with fatal regularity, allowing no time for recovery. When all ordinary methods had been exhausted, extraordinary ones were tried. In 1241 a Jewish 'parliament' was convoked at Worcester, consisting of a number of representatives of the communities of the realm, who became individually responsible for a fresh levy. So far did the process go that, in 1254, the Archpresbyter Elias, in one of the most pathetic speeches recorded in English history, appealed on behalf of his co-religionists for permission to leave the realm, as they had no more left to give. Far from his plea being granted, orders were issued to the wardens of the Cinque Ports to prevent any Jew from embarking. When nothing further could be extorted immediately, the king exercised his right as suzerain by mortgaging the communities of the country to his brother, Richard of Cornwall. They were subsequently made over to Edward, the heir to the throne, and by the latter to their competitors, the Cahorsins. The rapacity of the Crown over-reached itself. The goose that laid the golden eggs was worn almost to death with over-production; and the results were seen in an enormously decreased fecundity. If the figures given are correct, the annual revenue derived from this source decreased from about £3,000 at the close of the twelfth century to less than £700 a hundred years later.

Religious intolerance meanwhile came to a head. The oppressive decrees of the Lateran Councils were put into execution in England earlier and more consistently than in any other country in Europe. The wearing of the Jewish badge, in the form of the two Tablets of Stone, was rigidly enforced. A regulation of 1253 enunciated as a cardinal principle 'that no Jew remain in England unless he do the King service: and that from the hour of his birth every Jew, whether male or female, serve Us in some way'. Further clauses prohibited the building of new synagogues; enjoined prayer in a subdued voice in those already in existence, lest Christian ears should be contaminated; forbade the Jews to have Christian servants or nurses in their employment, to eat meat during Lent, to enter a Church, or to settle in any town in which a community was not already to be found. Synagogues were periodically confiscated on the plea that the chanting in them disturbed the service in a neighbouring Christian place of worship. The Blood Libel, and similar accusations, blazed out again, coming to a head with the classical case of 'Little' Hugh of Lincoln in 1255, which cost eighteen persons their lives. From several cities the Jews were entirely excluded. With the outbreak of the Civil War in 1263, the Baronial party professed to see in the Jews the instrument of the royal exactions and of their own impoverishment; and there was a recrudescence of massacre all over the country.

This was the situation which confronted Edward I on his accession to the throne in 1272. It was a state of affairs which obviously could not be allowed to continue. The Jews were so impoverished that their importance to the treasury, the needs of which were increasing year by year, had become relatively negligible. Moreover, here as elsewhere, the foreign bankers, who enjoyed a higher patronage, had begun to render the services for which infidel aid had previously been indispensable. In 1274, at the Council of Lyons, Pope Gregory X had urged the Christian world to make a strenuous effort to suppress usury. Edward obeyed implicitly, adding to his proceedings against Christian money-lenders an attempt to effect a complete change in the Jewish economic function and mode of life. By his *Statutum de Iudaismo* (Statute concerning the Jewry) of 1275 the practice of usury was forbidden, the consequent financial loss to the Crown being made good in part by the establishment of a poll-tax payable by every adult. On the other hand, the Jews were to be empowered—amazing concession—to engage in commerce and handicrafts, and (for an experimental period of ten years) to rent farms on short leases.

This was a courageous attempt to grapple with the problem, but it did not go far enough. Restrictions could be removed, yet prejudices on either side were more obstinate; indeed, that there was no tenderness in the measure was proved by the simultaneous enforcement of all the ecclesiastical restrictions so dear to the heart of the Pope. The Jew might have been diverted from his enforced activities, but only (as modern experience has so amply shewn) by removing the causes which had driven him to them. He might have turned his attention to agriculture had he been granted security of tenure, been placed on terms of equality with other persons, and allowed to engage non-Jewish labourers in case of need. He would gladly have taken up commerce again if he had been admitted to the privileges of the Gild Merchant. But to hope to change his manner of life while he remained subject to the same insecurity, the same prejudices, and the same differentiation of treatment as before was impossible: the habits of a lifetime, and the hereditary influence of past generations, could not so easily be cancelled. A Bull directed to the English Church by Honorius IV, in 1286, insisting upon yet stricter segregation, cut off the possibility of further concessions.

As a result, Edward's scheme failed utterly. Only a few of the wealthier class were able to take up commerce, particularly the export of wool—England's staple product. Others continued to carry on in a clandestine manner the money-lending operations now forbidden by law; while it appears that a few, prevented from following their old profession and seeing no real opening in any other, attempted to eke a living out of their capital by 'clipping' the coinage. This was followed by a terrible revenge, the whole of the community (together with some non-Jews against whom there were similar suspicions) being thrown into prison, and nearly three hundred hanged (1278).

Thereafter, Edward realised that his experiment had failed. For the moment he contemplated, if he did not execute, a reversal of policy, permitting the resumption of usury for a limited period. On second thoughts he preferred to sweep away the problem which he had failed to solve. On 18th July 1290 (it happened to be, by a tragic coincidence, the ninth of Ab, when a solemn fast commemorated the anniversary of the Fall of Jerusalem) a decree was issued ordering all Jews to leave the country within a little more than three months. By the Feast of All Souls (1st November) all were supposed to have embarked, excepting for the handful who succumbed to the attractions of the House for Converted Jews (*Domus Conversorum*) established in London by Henry III.

True to his upright though narrow spirit, Edward extended to the

P

Jews in the meantime a degree of protection and security which was rare in such cases. His subjects were not always so compassionate. One master mariner, who had been hired to convey a large party overseas from London, invited them to disembark at low water upon a sandbank at the mouth of the Thames. As the tide rose, he left them to their fate, recommending them to apply for succour to their teacher Moses, who had proved himself equal to a similar emergency at the Red Sea. In all, some 16,000 persons (according to the contemporary estimate, perhaps exaggerated) remained steadfast to their faith and sought new homes overseas. The exclusion of the Jews from the country in the subsequent period was not, in fact, absolute—history shows that this can seldom be the case. Nevertheless, for many centuries to come the re-establishment of a settled community was impossible. Thus the sweep of the pendulum, which had brought the centre of Jewish life from Palestine and Mesopotamia to western Europe, began its inexorable return towards the East.

III

Closest akin to the Jews of England in culture, in condition, and in history, were those of France. Here, ever since the outbreaks which had accompanied the second Crusade, they had lived a chequered existence. From the close of the twelfth century, the ruling house of Capet had developed an anti-Jewish attitude which, for sheer unreason and brutality of execution, was perhaps unparalleled in Europe as a dynastic policy. At the outset of this period, owing to the encroachments of feudalism, the royal authority was restricted to a small area in the immediate neighbourhood of Paris, being little more than nominal elsewhere. Hence the hostility of the Crown did not affect the Jews much more than that of any major baron would have done. Life in the vast majority of the communities of the country continued its fairly even tenor; and the condition of the Jews of Languedoc, in particular, remained very similar from every point of view to that of their more fortunate brethren in Spain. The history of the Jews in France is hence to be understood only in relation to the extension of the royal authority over the whole country, which in the end spelled for them utter disaster.

At the outset of his reign, Philip Augustus (1180-1223), then a youth of fifteen, set the example. Prompted by a pious hermit of Vincennes, he issued orders for the Jews of his dominions to be arrested in their synagogues one Sabbath day, and an enormous sum of money extorted from them as ransom. In the next year, he declared all debts due to them null and void, with the exception of one-fifth payable to the royal treasury; and finally, in 1182, he banished them outright from his dominions, confiscating their houses and giving them only three months to dispose of their other property. Thus the existence of the communities of the île de France was temporarily suspended. Fortunately the powerful feudal baronage forbore to follow this example, and received the refugees on their territories. Sixteen years later, faced with an empty treasury on his return from his Crusade, Philip Augustus realised his mistake. The Jews were invited back again, their financial operations being regularised and given legal authority (1198). From this period dates the establishment of the Produit des Juifs ('Jewish Revenue') as a department of the Exchequer, and the formal assimilation of the Jews both in the royal and the baronial domains to the position of serfs, unable to move from one territory to another under the penalty of losing all their property.

With Louis IX (1226-1270: better remembered as 'Saint' Louis) religious zeal reinforced ancestral prejudice in an unusual measure. The prescriptions of the Fourth Lateran Council were enforced with the utmost severity. A personal interest was taken in securing converts. It was under the royal auspices that the famous Disputation was held at Paris between Nicholas Donin and Rabbi Jehiel, and the Talmud was condemned to the flames. On one occasion the king recommended the sword 'forced into his body so far as it will enter' as the best argument for defending Christianity against the attacks of the infidel. Not only the interest on Jewish debts, but also a third part of the capital, was remitted. Finally, before setting out on his first Crusade in 1249, the king decreed the expulsion of the Jews from his realm, though the order does not appear to have been carried out.

The sufferings of French Jewry reached their climax under Philip the Fair (1285-1314), St. Louis' grandson. The ruler who could treat with such an excess of cruelty Christian financiers, like the Cahorsins and Lombards, and even a religious order like the Templars, merely for the sake of what could be extorted from them, was not likely to be any more considerate in his dealings with unbelievers. From the moment of his accession, he shewed that he considered the Jews merely as a source of gold. Spoliation succeeded spoliation, wholesale imprisonment being resorted to periodically in order to prevent evasion.

The climax came in 1306, when, the treasury being once more empty, the policy of Edward I of England was imitated, with significant differences. On 22nd July 1306 all the Jews of the country were simultaneously arrested, in obedience to instructions secretly issued some time before. In prison they were informed that, for some unspecified wrong-doing, they had been condemned to exile, and must leave the realm within one month, the whole of their property being confiscated to the Crown. The object underlying this measure, and the entire absence of religious motive, shewed itself in the fact that the king took over, not only the property of the Jews, but also their usurious claims in full. With them, the exiles (who were said—probably with some exaggeration—to have numbered some 100,000 souls) were allowed to take only twelve *sous tournois* each, and the clothes they wore on their backs. By this time, owing to the vigorous and fortunate policy of the French Crown in recent years, its authority extended over the majority of France proper, including Languedoc and Champagne, where the schools of Rabbinic learning had especially flourished. This banishment spelled accordingly the end of the ancient and glorious traditions of French Jewry.

There were, indeed, a couple of brief, ignoble interludes before the curtain finally fell. The common people, handed over to the mercies of the Christian usurers (now freed from competition), were far from approving the policy of the Crown:

> For the Jews were debonair,
> Greatly more, in this affair,
> Than now the Christians are,

a popular writer expressed it. The Treasury, moreover, was empty. The same mercenary considerations which had prompted the expulsion of the Jews now made it advisable to attempt to encourage their resettlement. Accordingly, after less than a decade, on 28th July 1315, Philip the Fair's brother, Louis X, issued an edict permitting them to return to the country for a period of twelve years, under carefully regulated conditions and guarantees, and to re-establish themselves as money-lenders in the cities in which they had previously been settled. In return for this, they were to make a cash payment of 122,500 livres. The few who cared to avail themselves of this hazardous opportunity were naturally insufficient, whether in number or in intellectual calibre, to re-establish the great tradition of their fathers.

Almost immediately after, they had to undergo a period of tribulation barely rivalled even in the tragic record of the Jewish Middle Ages. In 1320 a Crusading movement sprang up spontaneously amongst the shepherds of southern France—the so-called *Pastoureaux*. Few of them, if any, ever embarked for the East; but all seized the opportunity of striking a blow for the religion of Jesus nearer home. A wave of massacres of almost unprecedented horror swept through the country, community after community being annihilated. Subsequently, the example was imitated south of the Pyrenees. In the following year, a similar wave of feeling, founded this time on a purely ludicrous motive, brought about a recurrence. A report became generally current that the Jews and lepers, brother outcasts, had been poisoning the wells, by arrangement with the infidel kings of Tunis and Granada! This ridiculous pretext was eagerly followed up. Massacres took place in many cities. At Chinon, one hundred and sixty Jews were burned alive in a vast pit. An enormous fine was levied on the communities of the realm. Finally, contrary to the terms of the agreement of only seven years before, the new king, Charles IV, expelled the Jews from his dominions, without notice (1322).

A period of thirty-seven years elapsed before the experiment of toleration was tried again. In 1359, after the financial crisis which followed the disastrous defeat at Poitiers, a few financiers accepted an invitation to settle in the country for a twenty-year period. This was renewed on its expiration, though their treatment did not prove by any means ideal. Popular resentment against heavy taxation manifested itself in a series of attacks upon them. In 1380 and 1382, there were riots in the capital. The Crown protected them until a charge was brought against the Jews of Paris of having persuaded one of their number to return to Judaism after accepting baptism. For abetting this crime, they were all arrested and flogged; and it was determined to banish the whole of the wretched remnant. On 17th September 1394, the mad Charles VI signed the fatal order. A few months only were granted them to sell their property and settle their debts—a process not made any more easy by a subsequent order, by which their Christian debtors were absolved from paying their dues. Ultimately, when the time limit was expired, they were escorted to the frontier by the royal provosts.

Some of the exiles sought refuge in the south—at Lyons, where they were allowed to remain by the local authorities until 1420; in the county of Provence, whence they were not finally expelled until the beginning of the sixteenth century; or in the possessions of the Holy See about Avignon and Carpentras, where the Papal policy of sufferance allowed them to remain permanently, in enjoyment of toleration if of nothing else. Others crossed into Italy, where, near Asti, they established a little group of congregations which continued until our own day to preserve the ancient French rite of prayers. But the majority, in all probability, made their way over the Pyrenees or across the Rhine, where further scenes in the age-long tragedy had meanwhile been enacted.

IV

From Germany, owing to its peculiar political conditions, there was at no time any general expulsion, as in England or in France. It figures instead in history as the classical land of Jewish martyrdom, where banishment was employed only locally and sporadically to complete the work of massacre. The famous Golden Bull of the Emperor Charles IV (1356) alienated all rights in the Jews, as in other sources of revenue, in the territories of the seven greater potentates who were members of the Electoral College. Minor rulers, bishops, and even free cities, claimed similar prerogatives, subject only to a very remote Imperial control. In consequence, when the Jews were driven out of one district, there was generally another willing to receive them, in consideration of immediate monetary advantage. Thus, though there were few parts of the country which did not embark on a policy of exclusion at one stage or another, there was no period from the year 1000 onwards (if not from Roman times) when Germany was without a Jewish population.

On the other hand, there was barely any intermission in the constant sequence of massacre. The example set in the First Crusade was followed with fatal regularity. When external occasion was wanting, the Blood Libel, or a charge of the desecration of the Host, was always at hand to serve as a pretext. So long as the central authority retained any strength, the Jews enjoyed a certain degree of protection. On its decay they were at the mercy of every wave of prejudice, superstition, dissatisfaction, or violence. Boppard in 1179, Vienna in 1181, Spires in 1195, Halle in 1205, Erfurt in 1221,

Mecklenburg in 1225, Lauda and Bischofsheim in 1235, Frankfort-on-Main in 1241, Kitzingen and Ortenburg in 1243, Pforz-heim in 1244 . . . all in succession were the scenes of massacres which, in the history of any other land, would have been memorable.

In 1298, in consequence of a charge of ritual murder at Röttingen, a whole series of exterminatory attacks, inspired by a noble named Rindfleisch, swept through Franconia, Bavaria, and Austria. At Würzburg and Nuremberg the community was butchered almost to a man—in the latter case, notwithstanding the protection of the royal castle, in which they had been allowed to take refuge. In the whole of Bavaria only two cities escaped—Ratisbon and Augsburg, where the magistrates took their duties seriously. No less than one hundred and forty-six flourishing communities are said to have been wiped out; yet the Emperor did nothing to protect his vassals beyond imposing fines on the cities where outbreaks had occurred.

In 1336 a similar wave of massacres took place in Alsace, Suabia, and Franconia at the hands of a mob frankly calling themselves *Juden-schläger* ('slayers of the Jews'), led by two nobles nicknamed *Armleder* from a strip of leather which they wore round their arms. The disorders began (once again at Röttingen) at midsummer and continued intermittently for three years. It was in vain that the Emperor committed the Jews to the protection of the Count of Nuremberg, and declared that no excesses against them were to be tolerated. The names of over one hundred places where massacres occurred at this period were subsequently remembered. Yet this was but an episode in the history of German Jewry.

In 1337 the city council of Deckendorf in Bavaria determined to wipe out their indebtedness to the Jews at one stroke. The rumour was circulated that the infidels had stolen a consecrated wafer and maltreated it, and that it had displayed its indignation by a miraculous issue of blood. A meeting was held in the fields outside the city so as to avoid suspicion, and the plan of action decided. On 30th September, at the clanging of the church bells, a local knight rode into the city with his followers. Joined by the mob, he made an attack upon the *Judengasse*, and those of the inhabitants who were not killed outright were burned alive. Hence a wave of massacres swept through Bavaria, Bohemia, Moravia, and Austria, affecting fifty-one places. Only six years later, on 19th April 1343, a similar outbreak began at

Wachenheim, which wiped out many neighbouring communities before the week was over.

It was in 1348 and the following year that the fury reached its height. The Black Death was devastating Europe, sweeping away everywhere one-third or more of the population. It was the greatest scourge of its kind in recorded history. No natural explanation could be found. Responsibility for it, as for any other mysterious visitation, was automatically, therefore, laid upon the Jews. The ridiculousness of the charge should have been apparent even to fourteenth-century credulity; for the plague raged virulently even in those places (such as England) where the Christian population was absolutely unadulterated, and elsewhere the Jews suffered with the rest, though their hygienic manner of life and their superior medical knowledge may have reduced their mortality.

It was only when the outbreak reached Savoy that the charges became formulated in all their grotesque horror. At Chillon a certain Jew named Balavingus, arrested and put to torture, 'confessed' that an elaborate plot had been concocted in the south of France by certain of his co-religionists, whom he mentioned by name. These had compounded a potion, the ingredients of which were spiders, frogs, lizards, human flesh, the hearts of Christians, and consecrated Hosts. The powder made from this infernal brew had been distributed amongst the various communities, to be deposited in the wells from which the Christians drew their water. To this the terrible contagion which was sweeping Europe was due!

This ridiculous farrago of nonsense was sufficient to seal the fate of the community of Chillon, the whole of which was put to death with a refinement of horror. Hence the tale spread like wildfire throughout Switzerland, along the Rhine, and even into Austria and Poland. There followed in its train the most terrible series of massacres that had ever been known even in the long history of Jewish martyrdom. A Bull of Clement VI, true to the noblest traditions of the medieval Papacy, which condemned the new libel and ordered the Jews to be protected, proved of absolutely no avail. The Jews of Nuremberg recorded in their *Memorbuch* the names of something like 350 places which suffered at this period. Sixty large communities, and one hundred and fifty small, were utterly exterminated. At Basle, the whole congregation was burned to death in a wooden shack hastily constructed on an island in the middle of the Rhine, a subsequent decree forbidding any Jew to settle in the city for a period of two hundred years. At Strass-

81. BERTHOLD OF REGENSBURG PREACHES AGAINST THE JEWS
From a Manuscript in the Nationalbibliothek, Vienna

82. VESTIBULE OF THE THIRTEENTH-CENTURY SYNAGOGUE OF REGENSBURG
Etching by A. Altdorfer on the expulsion of the Jews in 1519

83–84. Pope Martin V receives a Jewish Deputation at Constance. 1417

206

luden schallen des
päpstlichen Segen

From the Chronicle of Ulrich von Reichenthal. Town Hall, Constance

85. 'ALTNEU' SYNAGOGUE, PRAGUE
14th Century

burg, on St. Valentine's Day, the community was concremated almost
to a man at a gigantic pyre erected in their cemetery. At Worms they
anticipated their fate by setting fire to their houses, where they
perished in the flames. The same happened at Cologne on St. Bar-
tholomew's Day, 1349. No catastrophe so ghastly and on so vast a
scale had ever yet been experienced, even by sorely tried German
Jewry. This was the climax of disaster for the local communities, just
as the great expulsions had been for those of England and France.
Never again for many generations were they to recover their previous
prosperity or numbers.

When the storm had died down, a large number of the cities
thought better of the vows made in the heat of the moment never to
harbour Jews again in their midst, and summoned them back again to
supply the local financial requirements. The period which followed
was one of comparative quiescence, if only for lack of victims. King
Wenceslaus, however (1378-1400), initiated the short-sighted policy
of the periodical cancellation of the whole or part of the debts due to
Jews in return for some immediate monetary payment from the
debtors; and a whole series of these operations was carried into effect
between 1385 and the close of the century, keeping the remnant of
German Jewry in a condition verging upon pauperdom. It was, therefore, impossible for them to recover the position which their predecessors had held; and the hegemony of German Jewry passed, with
the refugees, to the East.

There followed an interlude when the Jews of Austria (who in
1244 had received from Duke Frederick the Quarrelsome a model
charter, which guaranteed their rights and safety) enjoyed a certain
degree of relative prosperity—succeeded, as usual, by intellectual
activity and the emergence of a few scholars of note. This was ended
by the revival of religious passions following the rise in Bohemia of
the Hussite movement—an anticipation of the Protestantism which
was to make its appearance one hundred years later. The Hussites
did not shew themselves conspicuously well disposed towards the
Jews. Nevertheless the latter were suspected of complicity in the
heresy, and, notwithstanding further protective Papal Bulls, were
made to suffer on that account. Every one of the successive expeditions sent to champion the cause of orthodoxy began its work (like
the Crusaders of two centuries before) by an attack upon the various
Judengassen, and massacre once again succeeded massacre. In 1420 a
trumped-up accusation of ritual murder and Host desecration resulted

in the extermination of the community of Vienna—a disaster long remembered as the *Wiener Geserah*.[1] Further excesses at the hands of the degenerate successors of the Crusaders took place in 1421.

The eyes of the Jewish world were turned for guidance at this uncture to Rabbi Jacob ben Moses haLevi of Mayence (known f rom the initials of his Hebrew name as *Maharil*), the most eminent Rabbi of his age, whose daily practice, noted down by an eager disciple, was long after considered the standard to which every individual endeavoured to conform. He proclaimed two successive terms of penitence, each to last for three days, to be observed with the same rigour as the Day of Atonement itself. In virtue of this, the Almighty would assuredly take pity on his children and deliver them from the peril which threatened them. From 8th to the 10th September and again from 6th to the 8th October, the whole of German Jewry observed this period of affliction, pouring out their souls in their synagogues. Further disasters were not averted. Yet the very champions who had gone on their way vowing destruction to the Jews appeared at their doors a few weeks later as penniless fugitives, begging for bread.

Nevertheless conditions continued precarious. The General Council of the Catholic Church which met at Basle from 1431 to 1433, in order to cope with the threatening state of ecclesiastical affairs, solemnly re-enacted all past anti-Jewish legislation down to its least detail. Not long after, a fiery and eloquent, but strangely fanatical Franciscan friar, named John of Capistrano—almost the embodiment of the anti-Hussite reaction—was commissioned to see that the policy of the Council was carried into effect. Everywhere, from Sicily northwards, anti-Jewish excesses followed in his train. If circumstances in Italy were serious, beyond the Alps they became almost desperate. In anticipation of his arrival, the Jews of Bavaria had been imprisoned, despoiled, and subsequently expelled (1450). At Breslau, in 1453, an alleged desecration of the Host led to a mock trial under the auspices of Capistrano himself. Forty-one martyrs were burned to death before his lodgings in the Salzring. All other Jews were stripped of their goods and banished, their children under seven years of age having previously been taken away to be brought up in the Christian faith. The example was faithfully followed in the rest of the province. On 13th August similar outrages took place at Schweidnitz and Liegnitz. Thus the Papal emissary passed on, attended by a constant procession of outrages, burnings, and massacres, to Poland.

---

[1] *Geserah* = Evil Decree, with the implication 'disaster'.

The bewildering turmoil of slaughter and banishment which followed throughout Germany, down to the close of the Middle Ages and after, defies clear analysis or portrayal. The existence of one after another of the historic communities of a past age was brought to a violent end—a process which culminated in the expulsion of the ancient community of Ratisbon in 1519. Isolated handfuls continued to live here and there throughout the country. Larger agglomerations were to be found in the semi-Slavonic territories on the eastern borders. In Germany proper, no important Jewish settlements managed to maintain their existence unbroken excepting those of Worms and of Frankfort-on-Main—the mother towns of German Jewry, from which much of vital importance for the world was ultimately to proceed.

86. BURNING OF JEWS
Woodcut from Schedel's Weltchronik. 1493

Chapter XXI

THE CROWNING TRAGEDIES

———————•———————

I

South of the Pyrenees, the social and economic degradation of the Jew was never completed—not, at least, as in other parts of Europe. Individuals continued to rise to high rank in the financial administration, and sometimes enjoyed great favour at court. Notwithstanding occasional local outbreaks, life and property were generally safe. In Castile alone there were said to be no less than three hundred communities, their contribution to the Exchequer being reckoned at three million maravedis. In the lesser kingdoms—Aragon, Portugal, Navarre—the proportion was equally high. Catalonia was probably the densest Jewish centre in Europe. Cultural activities continued undisturbed. It is true that the Jews were reckoned 'serfs of the Royal Chamber', as elsewhere, but the yoke of serfdom lay none too heavily on their necks.

Occasionally, the rising tide of anti-Jewish feeling was marked even here by outbreaks of violence. In 1281, in imitation of contemporary example in France and England, all the Jews of Castile were arrested and thrown into prison, with the object of exacting an unprecedented levy. In 1339, the powerful minister of state, Gonzalo Martinez, actually contemplated the expulsion of the Jews from the kingdom. The *Pastoureaux* of southern France, beginning the redemption of the Holy Sepulchre by massacres in their native province, continued their ravages south of the Pyrenees, one of the worst outbreaks being at Jaca (1320). Eight years later, through French influence, the communities of Navarre were almost exterminated in a series of riots. At the time of the Black Death, the attacks upon the Jews of Savoy and Germany were anticipated in Catalonia, though luckily they were localised.

The actual turning-point, which marked the beginning of decline, came a few years later. The Jews had been treated with especial favour by Pedro of Castile (surnamed by his enemies 'the Cruel'). Under his rule (1350-1369) the communities of the country reached an influence seldom equalled since the *Reconquista*. Samuel Abulafia rose to the position of Treasurer of the realm; and the lovely synagogue which he built at Toledo still stands as a monument to his position, his affluence, and his taste. It is true that in the end (1360) the royal cupidity was aroused by the vast wealth which this ambitious subject was rumoured to have accumulated, and he died under torture, but this episode made no difference to Pedro's attitude towards his co-religionists as a body. When a struggle for the throne broke out between him and his bastard half-brother, Henry of Trastamara, they (like the English under the Black Prince) warmly espoused his cause. In the course of the civil war which followed, one prosperous *judería* after the other was sacked by Henry's wild troops and their wilder French allies. When Toledo was attacked in May 1355, the spirited Jewish defence saved the inner town until Pedro came to the rescue. On the other hand, the smaller Jewry, or *alcana*, was sacked, twelve hundred of its inhabitants being killed or wounded. Ultimately, when Pedro was overthrown, the Jews suffered for their loyalty. To the fanaticism of the Church and the prejudice of the people there was now added the resentment of the sovereign. The new king made no secret of his feelings. For the first time in Spanish history, the repressive ecclesiastical policy, including even the wearing of the Jewish badge of shame, was more or less systematically enforced.

In the financial administration, individuals continued to enjoy considerable influence. The most notable was Don Joseph Pichon, who occupied the position of *almoxarife* and *contador mayor*. His magnificence won him many enemies, even among his co-religionists; and they hesitated at no means to secure his downfall. On the day of the coronation of Juan I, in 1379, representatives of the communities of the realm waited upon him asking for permission to put to death, in accordance with their ancient privilege, a certain 'informer' who had been discovered in their midst. All unsuspecting, the young king complied. Forthwith the public executioner was sent to Pichon's house, or rather palace, armed with the royal warrant, and made away with him. A storm of indignation was aroused. The king, beside himself with passion, had the ringleaders in the conspiracy beheaded, and deprived the Jewish courts of their jurisdiction in criminal cases. As years passed, it became evident that he had neither forgiven nor forgotten. Amongst the population of Pichon's native city of Seville, where he had been surprisingly popular, feeling against the Jews rose to a high pitch.

One of the most influential persons in the city at this period was the eloquent Ferrand Martinez, Archdeacon of Ecija, and confessor to Queen Leonora. The pulpit had become for him little more than a platform for fulminating against those who refused to admit the truth of Christianity. On Ash Wednesday, 1391, when the approach of Eastertide had again aroused religious passions to fever-heat, his preaching bore fruit, and a frenzied mob broke into the Jewish quarter. The arrest and punishment of a couple of the ringleaders served only to infuriate the rest. After some further disturbance, order was outwardly restored; but on 6th June rioting recommenced. An orgy of carnage raged in the city. The *judería* was pitilessly sacked. The number of killed was estimated at thousands, few escaping save those who submitted to baptism.

The example of violence spread like wildfire, that summer and the succeeding autumn, throughout the Peninsula, from the Pyrenees to the Straits of Gibraltar. In place after place the entire community was exterminated. The synagogues, which had been the pride of Spanish Jewry, were turned into churches. The opulent *aljama* of Cordova was reduced to ashes. Toledo was the scene of gruesome carnage on the fast-day of the seventeenth of Tammuz.[1] Similar outbreaks took place in seventy other towns and cities of Castile. Across the border (though not in the kingdom of Aragon itself), the process was repeated, despite the protective measures adopted by the Crown. At Barcelona the entire community was wiped out, never to be re-established. In the former kingdom of Valencia, not a single professing Jew was left alive. Like scenes were perpetrated in the Balearic Islands. Outbreaks were avoided only in Granada, the last surviving outpost of Moslem rule, and (thanks to the energetic measures taken by the sovereign) in Portugal. The total number of victims amounted, it is said, to upwards of seventy thousand souls.

II

The massacres were accompanied by a process which rendered them especially memorable. In northern countries, throughout the age of persecution, it was usual for Jews to remain steadfast to the faith of their fathers at whatever cost, and they went to their deaths gladly rather than abjure it; only a weak remnant would accept bap-

[1] Above, p. 37.

tism as an alternative to martyrdom 'for the sanctification of the Name'. But in Spain conditions were different. The fibre of the Jew had been weakened by centuries of well-being. His social assimilation, as well as his philosophical synthesising, made the final step appear less drastic. The recent sequence of disaster and expulsion throughout Europe had cut off most avenues of escape, and perhaps made him despair of the future of his people. There almost seems to have been something in the atmosphere of the country which, from Visigothic times onward, had lessened the Jewish power of resistance and rendered apostasy more easy.

Whatever the reason, for the first and only time in history the Jewish morale broke when put to the test. Throughout the Peninsula, thousands accepted baptism *en masse* in order to escape death; led, in some cases, by the wisest, wealthiest, and most prominent members of their community. In some places the denizens of the *aljama* anticipated attack and came forward spontaneously, asking to be admitted to the Church. It was a phenomenon unique in the whole course of Jewish history.

When the storm died down, therefore, Spanish Jewry found its position radically changed. By the side of those, now sadly diminished in numbers and in wealth, who had managed to escape massacre and still openly professed their Judaism, there were now a vast community of *conversos*. Some of them, perhaps, were sincere enough. It is sufficient to mention in this connection Pablo de Santa Maria (1352-1435), who, as Solomon haLevi, had at one time been famous as a Rabbinic scholar but subsequently rose to the dignity of Bishop of his native Burgos, and member of the Council of Regency of Castile. This enterprising cleric took the lead in baiting his former co-religionists; while his son, Alonso, who succeeded him in the episcopal dignity, was one of the Spanish delegates at the great Church Council of Basle in 1431-1433, the anti-Jewish enactments of which he instigated. But the vast majority of the 'New Christians' (as they were called) remained unaffected by the superficial fact of baptism, though they feared to return formally to their old faith. The ordinary citizens edged away as they passed, with muttered curses. *Marranos*, or 'swine', they called them, without much mincing of language. But the constancy shewed by them and their descendants after them has redeemed the term in some measure from its former deprecatory connotation, and endowed it with associations of romance, unique perhaps in history.

III

By painful degrees, the Spanish communities recovered in part from the catastrophe of 1391—impoverished, numerically reduced, yet still unbroken. The lead in the struggle against them was now taken by some of their former co-religionists, who, with characteristic Jewish optimism, hoped to be successful in bringing about a general conversion where the Christian world had so lamentably failed.

Under the auspices of the *converso* Bishop of Burgos, an edict was issued in Castile in 1408 renewing the repressive legislation contained in the classical code of Alfonso the Wise, which had long remained in abeyance.[1] This forbade Jews to be given positions which might entail any manner of authority over Christians, thereby excluding them from employment in the financial administration. Disappointed in his hope that this measure would wear down the resistance of the higher strata of Jewish society, the Bishop procured the promulgation, four years later, of a fresh code, intended to cut off the Jews from all intercourse with the outside world and from every honourable means of gaining a livelihood. They were to be confined to their special quarters: they were to be excluded from the professions; they were not to engage in handicrafts or to deal in alimentary products; they were forbidden to have Christians in their employment in whatever capacity, to settle disputes in their courts according to Talmudic law, or to levy their own taxes. No Jew might assume the title of *Don*, or carry arms, or go beardless, or even trim his hair in the Christian fashion. Even their costume was regulated, all having to wear long cloaks of the coarsest material.

Meanwhile, at the instigation of the same evil spirit, Fray Vincent Ferrer (a fanatical Dominican friar, subsequently canonised) was traversing Castile from end to end, preaching to the Jews, and endeavouring to procure their conversion by fair means or by foul. In one place after the other he appeared in synagogue, a scroll of the Law in one arm and a crucifix in the other, while an unruly mob at his heels added force to his arguments. The result was another wave of mass conversions in 1411, during the course of which some whole communities gave way.

Subsequently this fiery missionary turned to Aragon, where he followed a similar procedure. Here he was assisted by the apostate

[1] Above, pp. 198-9.

Mestre Geronimo de Santa Fé, formerly Joshua de Lorca (*Megadef*—
'the blasphemer'—as he was acrostically nicknamed by his former
co-religionists). The latter persistently urged the anti-Pope, Benedict
XIII, whose body-physician he was, to stage a disputation between
representatives of Judaism and of Christianity upon the merits of the
two faiths. Benedict, whose authority was recognised only in a very
restricted area, hoped that a general conversion of the Jews would
strengthen his position. The communities of Aragon and Catalonia
were accordingly compelled to send their representatives to the anti-
Papal *curia* at Tortosa to champion their faith. The ensuing debate, at
which the Pope presided in person, was among the most notable of
the Middle Ages. It lasted a year and nine months, and was spread
over sixty-nine sessions (February 1413–November 1414). The pro-
tagonist for the Church was Mestre Geronimo himself, while the
Jewish representatives included Don Vidal Benveniste, Joseph Albu,
the philosopher, and especially the keen-witted, eloquent, learned
Astruc Levi, of Alcañiz, all the more useful by reason of his familiarity
with the Latin tongue. We are told how, in recognition of the solemnity of the occasion, his colleagues consented to forgo the Jewish
privilege of interruption. However, the result of the discussion was
foregone, since, as usual, the truth of Christianity was postulated as
being beyond question, and freedom of speech on the part of those
attacked was rigorously suppressed. The only tangible result was the
publication by the Pope (soon, fortunately, to be divested of the last
shreds of his authority) of a Bull of unusual severity, forbidding the
Jews to study the Talmud, to possess more than one poorly appointed
synagogue in each town, or to fail to attend at least three times yearly
at the conversionist sermons instituted for their benefit. During the
course of the Disputation and after, the labours for the faith continued.
Entire communities submitted to baptism in order to escape their
present miseries; and thirty-five thousand additional converts were
said to have been secured during the course of a very few years.

IV

Meanwhile, there had grown up a new generation of Marranos,
born and educated within the Church, yet in many instances as little
addicted to Christianity as their fathers had been. They would go to
the priest to be married; they took their children as a matter of
course to be baptised; they would attend mass and confession with

Q

the utmost punctuality. Yet, behind this outward sham, they remained Jewish at heart. They observed the traditional ceremonies, in some instances down to the least detail. They kept the Sabbath so far as lay in their power; and from a height overlooking any city, it was possible to see how many chimneys were smokeless on that day. The more punctilious would eat meat prepared in the Jewish manner and supplied by a Jewish butcher. The story is actually told of one Marrano who ate unleavened bread throughout the year, on the pretext of ill-health, so as to ensure having it on Passover. Some went so far as to circumcise their children. In most cases they married only amongst themselves. On occasion they furtively frequented the synagogues, for the illumination of which they sent gifts of oil. Alternatively, they would form religious associations with titularly Catholic objects, and ostensibly under the patronage of some Catholic saint, using this as a cover for the observance of their ancestral rites. They were Jews in all but name, and Christians in nothing but form.

Their social progress, on the other hand, was incredibly rapid. In every rank of society, in every walk of life, New Christians were to be found occupying the most prominent positions and drawing the most lucrative revenues. The more wealthy intermarried with the highest nobility of the land. In Aragon there was barely a single aristocratic family, from that of the king himself downwards, which was free from the 'taint' of Jewish blood. Half the offices of importance at this court were occupied by recent converts of more or less dubious sincerity, or else by their immediate descendants. The judiciary, the administration, the army, the Universities, the Church itself, were all overrun by them. Fernando de Rojas, author of *Celestina*—Spain's most important contribution to European letters before Don Quixote —was a Marrano. One family long familiar in the *judería* of Saragossa (that of de la Caballeria) counted among its descendants more than one bishop, the vice-principal of a University, the High Treasurer of the kingdom of Navarre, the Vice-Chancellor of the kingdom of Aragon, a leader of the Cortes, the Comptroller-General at court, and a famous anti-Semitic writer. The case was a striking but not exceptional one.

The populace, jealous at the progress of the Marranos, could see in them only hypocritical Jews, who had lost none of their characteristics, fighting their way into the highest and most lucrative positions in the country, to the detriment of true Christians. Once more, the pulpits throughout the Peninsula resounded to impassioned sermons, calling attention to the misconduct, not this time of the Jews, but of the 'New Christians', and urging that steps should be taken to check them. Their position was almost identical with that of the Jews at the close of the previous century; and it caused a similar reaction. Already in 1449, attacks were made upon them in Toledo and Ciudad Real, where terror reigned for five days consecutively. This was a faint premonition of what was subsequently to occur.

During the course of a religious procession at Cordova, on 14th March 1473, a rumour got about to the effect that an image of the Madonna had been besprinkled with foul water flung from a window by a Marrano girl. Immediately the mob got out of hand. For three days riots continued, accompanied by wholesale murder and rape, ending only when no more victims could be found. The wave of disorder spread throughout Andalusia and beyond. Massacres took place in town after town, notwithstanding the organised attempts made by the *conversos* to defend themselves. In the following year there was a similar outbreak in the north of the country, centring about Segovia, where the bodies of the victims were piled high in the steep streets. In more than one place, the municipal council passed a resolution forbidding any person of Jewish blood to live in the city henceforth. There was no parallel to this in Spanish history, excepting at the period of the massacres of 1391. There was, indeed, one significant difference. On that occasion, it had been possible for those attacked to save their lives by accepting baptism. Now, no such avenue of escape lay open.

V

This was the state of affairs in 1474, when Isabella the Catholic ascended the throne of Castile. In the negotiations leading up to her marriage with her consort, Ferdinand (who was to become king of Aragon five years later), the Jewish financier Abraham Senior on the one side, and the *converso* statesman Alfonso de la Caballeria on the other, had played important parts, unaware of the tragic importance which this match was to have. From the moment of her accession, the Queen's spiritual advisers urged her that the only manner in which the realm could be purified religiously, and so rid of the troubles which were besetting it, was by the introduction of a special tribunal for the hunting out and punishing of heretics—the dreaded Inquisition. It was rumoured, indeed, that her former confessor, Tomás de Torquemada, a fanatical opponent of the Marranos (despite the fact that he was perhaps himself of Jewish extraction), had long since exacted a promise that, should she reach the throne, she would devote herself to the extirpation of heresy.

For a few years her attention was monopolised by more pressing problems. Immediately domestic peace was restored, negotiations were set on foot with the Pope, Sixtus IV, for a Bull authorising the establishment of the Holy Tribunal. For a time he hesitated, prompted not so much by humanity as by the desire to keep the new body under his own control. Ultimately, on 1st November 1478, a Bull was issued euphemistically empowering the Spanish sovereigns to appoint three Bishops or other suitable persons above the age of forty, with un-fettered jurisdiction over heretics and their accomplices. On 17th September 1480, after some additional negotiations and delays, com-missions were issued to two Dominican friars to proceed to Seville and begin work. On 6th February of the following year, a first *Auto da Fé*, or Act of Faith, was held, six men and women of Jewish extraction being burned alive for the crime of fidelity to the faith of their fathers.

This was the prelude to a long series of holocausts. Before long, similar tribunals had been set up at a number of other centres throughout the Peninsula. They rapidly acquired an elaborate organ-isation, Torquemada becoming the first Inquisitor-General. Lists were circulated containing minute signs (many of them grotesque) by which a Judaiser could be recognised: from changing linen on the Sabbath to washing the hands before prayer, and from calling children by Old Testament names to turning the face to the wall at the moment of death. The general population were enjoined, under the most severe temporal and spiritual penalties, to denounce any persons whom they suspected to be guilty of these or similar heinous practices. The aid of the Jews themselves was enlisted, their Rabbis being compelled to force their congregations, under pain of excommunication, to reveal incriminating information which might have come to their know-ledge. Before long, nearly thirty thousand persons are said to have been put to death by the Holy Tribunal, in addition to hundreds of thousands who were penanced or sentenced to less savage punish-ments. Even the dead did not escape, their bones being sometimes dug up to be sentenced and burned, together with their effigies—no mere theatrical formality, for this entailed the confiscation of their property and disgrace of their descendants. With every year that passed, the In-quisition and its activities struck root deeper and deeper in Spanish soil, beginning the process which was to end only with the ruin of the country.

VI

All these measures were manifestly inadequate, if the land was to be purged satisfactorily of the taint of disbelief. Professing Jews had meanwhile continued to live in Spain without disturbance. As compared with a century before, they were only a miserable remnant; decimated by massacre and conversion, and crushed by the humiliatory legislation which was being enforced against them with ever-increasing severity. The recent developments had not affected them to any great extent. So long as they did not meddle in matters of faith, the Inquisition could not touch them: for technically they were infidels outside the Church, not heretics within it. The position was, indeed, preposterous. A Marrano, Christian only in name, would be burned alive for performing occasionally in secret only a tithe of what his unconverted brethren were performing daily in public with impunity. It was hopeless to attempt to extirpate the Judaising heresy from the land while Jews were left in it to teach their kinsmen, by precept and by example, the practices of their ancestral religion.

A trumped-up story of the martyrdom at Avila for ritual purposes of an unnamed child from La Guardia, said to have been perpetrated by Jews and *conversos* acting in conjunction, was taken as proof of the complicity between the two elements. Recent research has made it appear that the alleged victim never existed outside the imagination of a few fanatics. Nevertheless the Inquisition was stimulated to fresh efforts; and the episode provided a fresh weapon against the Jews, which Torquemada did not scruple to use.

The religious problem was reinforced by other considerations. Spain was at last realising its national unity. This reached its climax in 1492 in the capture of Granada, the last stronghold of the Moors, the work of reconquest, which had lasted for seven centuries, being thus completed. The Jews had contributed to the expenses of the campaign out of all proportion to their numbers. Now, however, not the slightest reason remained for conciliating their sympathies. It was therefore possible to apply the most drastic of all solutions. On 30th March 1492, in their Council Chamber in the captured Alhambra (still scented with the exotic perfumes of its former occupants), Ferdinand and Isabella appended their signatures to a decree expelling all Jews from their dominions within a period of four months.

The news was received by the *aljamas* throughout the Peninsula with stupefaction. But the victims were not disposed to accept the inevitable without a protest. The outstanding figure among them at the time was Don Isaac Abrabanel, in whom the glorious traditions of a former age seemed to be concentrated and revived. Since the days of Samuel ibn Nagdela, perhaps, Spanish Jewry had never known a more commanding and versatile personality. A member of an ancient and illustrious family from Seville—one of the most distinguished, indeed, in all Spain—he had been born in 1437 in Lisbon, where his father or grandfather had removed after the troubles of 1391. His intellectual range was vast. He was the author of a profound, if somewhat verbose, commentary upon the Bible. He had some pretensions as a prose stylist. He was the last of the Jewish philosophers of the Middle Ages. At the same time, he was recognised almost universally as a financial genius of unusual calibre. He had first shewn this in the service of the King of Portugal. Accused of complicity in a plot against the Crown, he fled across the border to Castile, with men-at-arms thundering at his heels, leaving behind him his valuable library and the manuscripts of several works of his own composition. He began to devote his enforced leisure to his literary enterprises, but was summoned from retirement to enter the service of the Catholic sovereigns in conjunction with Abraham Senior, the principal farmer of taxes and Crown Rabbi of Castile. When the edict of expulsion was issued, the two are said to have sought an audience with their royal master and mistress, and offered a magnificent bribe if they would reverse their decision. As the latter were pondering over their reply, Torquemada burst from the arras behind the throne, and flung down a crucifix before them. 'Judas sold his Master for thirty pieces of silver', he exclaimed, his eyes burning with the glow of fanaticism. 'Now, you would sell Him again. Here He is: take Him and sell Him!'

Whether this was the cause or no, there was no wavering in the decision of the Catholic sovereigns. By the end of July, all professing Jews had to leave the kingdom. Many, overwhelmed by their misfortunes, submitted to baptism, swelling thereby the number of the Marranos. They were headed by Abraham Senior himself, who is said to have taken this step in order to avert further reprisals. But the vast majority held out to the end. They had to dispose of their property— the stateliest mansions, the most fertile vineyards—for a fraction of their value. They were compelled to pay all claims in full before they left, though they were given no special facilities for collecting their own debts. They were allowed to take with them no gold or silver, lest the realm should be drained of its bullion; and letters of credit could only be obtained at great sacrifice. As they trudged along the dusty highways in the summer heat, on the way to the frontier or to the seaports, musicians played lively airs before them, by order of the Rabbis, to keep up their spirits. The total number of the exiles is reckoned conservatively at over 150,000 souls.

The stalwarts who ventured forth were by no means at the end of their tribulations. Famine and pestilence dogged their footsteps to the end of the earth. Many were robbed and murdered at sea by unscrupulous ship-masters. Those who landed on the coast of Africa had to face the terrors of fire and famine as well as the onslaughts of brigands. More unfortunate still were those who were cast ashore in Christian Europe; and even contemporaries were shocked at the spectacle of zealous friars wandering among the famished groups on the quayside of Genoa, with a crucifix in one hand and loaves of bread in the other, offering food in return for the acceptance of the religion of love.

VII

The disaster of 1492 was not confined to Spain. The terms of the edict of expulsion extended to the remoter possessions of the House of Aragon, notwithstanding the fact that the problem of the crypto-Jew—its titular pretext—was virtually unknown in them. These included, as well as Sardinia, with its ancient and flourishing community, the island of Sicily. Here the Jews had been established since the beginning of the Christian era, as archaeological relics bear witness. Their general condition had never become so degraded as elsewhere. At one time they had even been empowered to open their own University. Their number at present did not fall short of ten thousand souls (it was indeed estimated at many times more). All this carried no weight with the Spanish rulers, although the local authorities pleaded earnestly that they should reconsider their decision. The few brief delays which were accorded were only in order to complete the collection of arrears of taxation and certain special levies, which were ruthlessly extorted. Thus the date fixed for departure was brought down to 12th January 1492/3. Contemporary chroniclers tell us how, at Palermo, the inhabitants stood on the house-tops to wave farewell to their old neighbours as the boats which bore them disappeared in the distance.

A number of the exiles, from Sicily and from Spain, sought refuge on the neighbouring mainland, in the independent kingdom of Naples. They were headed by Isaac Abrabanel, who was once more summoned from a literary retirement to enter the service of the court. But they were followed, first by the plague, and then by the French invasion of 1495, which took a terrible toll. Many, like Don Isaac Abrabanel, had to seek safety once again in flight. Ultimately the wars induced further foreign intervention, and the kingdom passed under the control of Aragon. The outcome is easily imagined. In 1510, and again (more completely), in 1541, the Jews were expelled: both the natives, whose history was continuous from remote times, and the exiles who had arrived more recently. Some economists assert that even now some parts of the country have not fully recovered from the blow.

A handful of the refugees from the dominions of Ferdinand and Isabella directed their steps northward, to the kingdom of Navarre, where a number of small and impoverished communities had maintained their existence after the disaster of 1328. In 1498, however, the joint sovereigns followed the example of their powerful neighbours, and decreed a general expulsion. But Navarre was a land-bound state, surrounded on all sides by countries from which the Jews were excluded. So completely were avenues of escape cut off that most of the victims perforce accepted baptism. The Navarrese maintained their hatred notwithstanding the ostensible change of religion. Entire districts refused to tolerate them; they were excluded from public office; and, centuries later, their descendants, still suspected of secret adherence to Judaism, remained objects of undisguised contempt. The few who remained constant crossed the Pyrenees into the south of France. Here, in those parts which were under the rule of the counts of Provence, the edict of expulsion of 1394 had not been carried into effect. Yet, within a very few years, the remnant of the ancient French communities was driven hence also; and the memories of the age of Rashi and of the Tosaphists were restricted to the tiny area subject to the Holy See, comprising Avignon and the Comtat Venaissin.

The largest single body of Spanish exiles had taken the most simple, least venturesome course, crossing the frontier into Portugal. The Jews had been settled here ever since the birth of the monarchy, a little after the period of the Norman Conquest of England. They had been generally well treated. The organisation which they enjoyed in religious matters, under their *Arrabi-Mor*, or Chief Rabbi, was un-

87. The Founder of the Spanish Inquisition: Isabella the Catholic (1451-1504)
Oil painting in the former Royal Palace, Madrid

88. St. Dominic presides over an Act of Faith

By Alonso Berruguete. Commissioned by Torquemada for the monastery of St. Tomé, Avila, now in the Prado Gallery, Madrid

89. THE DIVINE JUDGMENT ON THE CITIES OF THE PLAIN
Miniature from a Medieval Hebrew Manuscript in the British Museum, London.
(Add. MS. 11639)

SPAANSCHE INQVYSITIE.

90. AN AUTO DA FÉ
Dutch Engraving of the 17th Century

Paulus. iiij. Pont Max. grauiſſimus Chriſtianæ pietatis,
eiuſq́; sincerioris cultus aſſertor, atq́; reſtaurator.

91. THE FOUNDER OF THE GHETTO: POPE PAUL IV (1555-1559)
Contemporary Engraving

usually comprehensive; and they exerted great influence in the financial administration of the country. A revulsion of feeling had taken place at the time of the accession of the House of Aviz to the throne, at the close of the fourteenth century. Nevertheless, thanks to the strong action taken by the government, the wave of massacres of 1391 had not affected them; and, save for an isolated attack upon the community of Lisbon in 1449, the reaction which had over-whelmed the rest of the Peninsula during the fifteenth century had left the country virtually untouched. It offered itself, therefore, as a natural place of refuge, particularly for the Jews of western and central Castile. Neither their native co-religionists on the one hand, nor the State Council on the other, were anxious to receive the influx. The ruling monarch, João II, actuated by anticipation of profit rather than a sense of humanity, thought otherwise. Only a handful, who could afford to pay heavily for the privilege, were indeed authorised to remain permanently, as well as the artisans, whose expert know-ledge might prove useful in the preparations for the approaching African campaign. All others might enter the country on the pay-ment of a poll-tax of eight *cruzados* for each adult, on the understand-ing that they would not remain longer than eight months. Within this period the king bound himself to find shipping for their trans-port wherever they desired. The number of those who crossed the frontier under this agreement amounted to nearly one hundred thousand souls.

The conditions upon which they entered the country were not fulfilled. Shipping was provided only tardily; and those who ventured on board were treated with the utmost cruelty, being disembarked, willy-nilly, at the nearest point of the African coast. All who remained behind, after the prescribed period had elapsed, were declared to have forfeited their liberty, and were sold as slaves. Children were torn ruthlessly from their parents' arms, hundreds being sent to colonise the tropical island of S. Thomé, off the African coast, where the majority perished.

In the midst of this, João II died. He was succeeded by his cousin, Manoel 'the Fortunate' (1495-1521). The latter, on his accession, seemed to deserve the title which posterity bestowed upon him-Recognising that those Jews who had not left the realm in time were guiltless, he restored them their liberty; and he even went so far as to refuse the gift which was offered him by the communities of the kingdom in gratitude for this generous action. But shortly after-

wards, considerations of public policy caused the young king to shew
himself in a very different light. Ferdinand and Isabella, who had
united Castile and Aragon by marriage, had a daughter, Isabella. If she
became Manoel's wife, there was every prospect that their children
would ultimately rule over the whole of the Peninsula. The Catholic
sovereigns, who unreasoningly resented the reception of the Spanish
refugees elsewhere, would consent to the match only on condition
that their own Jewish policy was imitated. Opinions in Portugal
varied; but the Infanta herself decided matters, writing that she would
not enter the country until it had been 'cleansed' of the presence of
infidels, as her parents' dominions had been. This was decisive. On
30th November 1496 the marriage treaty was signed. Less than a
week later, on 5th December, there was issued a royal decree banish-
ing all Jews and Moslems from the country within a period of ten
months.

Hardly was the ink dry on this edict, when Manoel began to take
the other side of the question into consideration. His psychology was
in its way by no means inconsistent. He recognised the value of the
Jews as citizens, and was unwilling to lose their services, though he
could no longer tolerate them if they remained faithful to their
religion. Moreover, he appears to have been genuinely anxious to
save their souls, whether they were willing or no. The conclusion
was obvious. For his own sake, for the sake of the realm, and for the
sake of the Jews themselves, they must be driven to accept the Christian faith. If only they did this, the drawbacks of his policy would be
obviated, and they would be assured of eternal felicity into the
bargain.

The parents were first struck at through the children, notwithstanding the fact that the clerical party stoutly maintained that the
step meditated was uncanonical. In the spring of 1497, at the beginning of the Feast of Passover, orders were issued for all Jewish children
between the ages of four and fourteen years to be presented for baptism on the following Sunday. At the appointed time, those who had
not been brought forward voluntarily were seized by the officials and
forced to the font. Scenes of indescribable horror were witnessed as
they were torn away by the royal bailiffs. In many cases parents
smothered their offspring in a farewell embrace, killing themselves
afterwards. Sometimes old men were dragged to church by over-
zealous fanatics to be baptised, under the impression that a general
conversion of the Jews had been ordered. The children of the Moslems,

who were included in the edict of expulsion, were untouched. The authorities cynically confessed the reason. It was because there were lands in which the Crescent was supreme, and reprisals might be carried out!

Meanwhile the date fixed for departure from the country approached. Originally three ports of embarkation had been assigned. After some vacillation the king changed his mind, and announced that all were to pass through the capital. On their arrival they were cooped up in an unbelievably narrow area, without food or drink, in the hope that their deprivations would open their eyes to the true faith. Those who still refused were closely guarded until the time-limit set for their departure had elapsed. They were then informed that, by their disobedience, they had forfeited their liberty, and were now the king's slaves to be dealt with as he pleased. By this means the resistance of the majority was broken down, and they went in droves to the churches for baptism. Others were dragged to the font by brute force. The rest, still protesting, had holy water sprinkled over them and were declared to be Christians. Only a few, led by Simon Maimi, the last *Arrabi-Mor*, kept up open opposition. In order to induce these to set an example to the rest, they were walled up in a dungeon. After a week, Maimi succumbed to his sufferings. His companions, not more than seven or eight in all, were transported to Africa. This pathetic relic was all that was left of the ancient and once renowned Portuguese Jewry.

Those who remained behind, as titular Christians, were not much changed in essence. Though they were driven to church at intervals, fathers and sons together, in order to have the rudiments of Catholicism hammered into them, their knowledge of its principles remained slight in the extreme. Many could read and write only Hebrew. Though they were known officially by high-sounding Portuguese patronymics, they preserved in the secrecy of their homes their previous Jewish names. They were similar to the Marranos of Spain, with the reservation that they comprised, not merely the weaker brethren who had submitted to baptism in order to escape death, but all, almost without exception, of the Jewish population of the country —the poor, the wealthy, the aristocratic, the ignorant, the learned, even the Rabbis. Crypto-Judaism had therefore in Portugal a greater tenacity than it had shewn even in Spain. Moreover, for a long period, it could be practised almost with impunity. It was not until 1531 that the Inquisition was introduced into the country; it was not until 1597 that the Holy Tribunal attained the same overwhelming authority which it enjoyed in the neighbouring country.

There was thus an interlude of nearly half a century in which the 'New Christians' of Portugal could adapt themselves to their new conditions. In the meantime they remained distinct from the mass of the population and the objects of a fanatical enmity, which the superficial change of religion failed to modify. Occasional outbursts of violence against them culminated in the horrors of the 'Slaying of the New Christians' at Lisbon in April 1506, in which no less than 2,000 persons lost their lives. During the whole of this period, though they were formally forbidden to leave the country, there was a steady, furtive emigration of the *conversos*, who, once they had crossed the seas, hastened to cast off all disguise and to declare once more their allegiance to the faith of their fathers. But the vast majority remained in the country, permeating every rank of society, entering into every walk of life, and contributing largely to contemporary Portuguese culture. It was by these unwilling converts that the tradition of Iberian Jewry, going back for fifteen centuries, was henceforth represented.

Thus the curtain fell upon the centuries-long drama of Jewish life in the Iberian Peninsula. The western European stage of Jewish history, which had begun with the Middle Ages, ended with them; and now, once more, the centre of gravity was to be found in the east.

An old chronicle tells how a certain Jew was driven destitute from Spain with his family. At sea he lost the little that remained to him. His wife was outraged and carried off before his eyes. At length his children too were seized by brigands. 'Then', we are told, 'that Jew stood upon his feet, and spread his hands heavenwards and cried: "Master of the Universe! Much hast Thou done to me to make me abandon my faith. Yet know Thou of a surety that, notwithstanding those who dwell on High, a Jew I am and a Jew I will remain." ' The attitude of mind was typical of the Jewish people, crushed yet unbroken: blindly refusing to recognise the supreme argument of force; and continuing to believe, no less from obstinacy than from conviction, as this crowning tragedy of the Middle Ages descended on their heads.

BOOK IV

TWILIGHT: 1492-1815

———————•———————

92-94. Woodcut Illustrations from the Prague Haggadah. 1527

Chapter XXII

RENAISSANCE AND REFORMATION

———————— • ————————

I

In only two European countries intimately concerned with his past
did the Jew remain a familiar figure in the dark epoch which opened
for him with the close of the Middle Ages. One was Germany, with
the dependent territories on its eastern border; the other was Italy.
In either case the reason was similar. Political conditions, resulting
in minute subdivision into independent or semi-independent states,
rendered concerted action in any matter of public policy a sheer impossibility. The Jews might be massacred, exterminated, or expelled
in one state; but there was always another in the immediate neighbourhood which was momentarily prepared to receive them. There
was, however, one important difference between the two countries
in question. Whereas in Italy the continued existence of a number of
Jewish communities appears to have been due in some measure to
sympathetic feeling, in Germany the parallel phenomenon was acci-
dental, and the attitude of the mob against the Jews (frequently
receiving governmental support or sanction) clearly shews that there
was as yet no glimmer of tolerance.

Jewish settlements were now to be found in very few of the German
cities which had harboured the great medieval communities. Throughout the Empire, from Alsace in the west to the borders of Poland,
there were on the other hand scattered groups, some of them of
ancient establishment, enjoying a precarious tenure by virtue of an
invitation from the City Council or local ruler. They were always
subject to the waves of unreasoning violence so especially characteristic of Germany. War, civic disturbance, the activities of some en-
venomed apostate, the momentary disappearance of a Christian child,
continued to be regarded as ample cause for assault and massacre,
sometimes followed by expulsion. The example of Brandenburg (the
nucleus of what was subsequently to be known as Prussia) may be

taken as typical of the whole country. On 21st December 1509 the Margrave Joachim issued a concession empowering a number of Jews to settle in his dominions. In the following year, a charge of desecrating the Host was brought against the community of Bernau, near Berlin. 'With a song of praise on their lips', thirty-eight persons perished in the flames; only two of the fainter-hearted accepting baptism, and thus being accorded the alternative grace of decapitation. As an inevitable consequence, all the Jews were expelled from the Mark, barely six months after their return. Subsequently, it was found that a common thief had been responsible for the outrage, though (it is said) his confession was deliberately suppressed by the ecclesiastical authorities.

We know this last detail from the reminiscences of one of the outstanding figures of the age, Joseph (better known as Joselman) of Rosheim, near Strassburg (1480-1554). A man of the world and a ready speaker, he was appointed by the communities of Lower Alsace in 1510 as their civil representative (*Parnas uManhig*), ultimately acting in the same capacity for the whole of German Jewry. He was not a man of great means or superlative scholarship. As a writer, he was mediocre. He could not thus compare with any of the great Jewish leaders of preceding centuries. But he was the perfect type of the *shtadlan*—the person who, at no matter what cost, devotes himself to the interests of his co-religionists, untiringly watches the progress of affairs on their behalf and is quick to raise his voice when the occasion demands. We catch fugitive glimpses of him hovering in the background at Imperial Diets, anxious lest the welfare of the Jewish people should be threatened; procuring letters of protection from time to time from the Emperor Maximilian I or Charles V; obtaining a decree whereby the business transactions of the Jews of the Empire were regulated and put on a legal footing; disputing at the Imperial court against an embittered apostate, Antonius Margarita, so effectively as to procure his banishment; attempting to stave off local edicts of expulsion; securing an Imperial Bull in which the recurrent Blood Accusation was once more officially condemned; making peace between warring communities; trying to dissuade a pseudo-Messiah from his dangerous activities; on one occasion warning the Emperor himself of a plot for the invasion of the Tyrol, and thereby saving his life. If, with the advance of the sixteenth century, conditions in Germany improved, the former sequence of massacres being stemmed and the Jews being brought more effectively than hitherto under the protection of public law, it is to Joselmann of Rosheim more than to any other individual that thanks were due. It was, indeed, a miserable, poverty-stricken community of pedlars and petty usurers, only a handful of privileged 'Court' Jews rising here and there above the average and enjoying a certain measure of favour and protection.[1]

An integral portion of the Holy Roman Empire was the kingdom of Bohemia (from 1526 an appanage of the House of Hapsburg), which was always within the German orbit. Its Jewish communities were partly German in origin, and wholly so in culture and in language; and, over a period of many centuries, they shared the lot of their co-religionists in the surrounding territories. Throughout the fourteenth and fifteenth centuries, there were recurrent massacres, spoliations, and expulsions, reaching their culmination, though not their conclusion, in 1400, in the persecution instigated by the apostate Pesah-Peter.[2] Yet the Jews were never entirely uprooted from the country. The *Judenstadt* of Prague, in particular, constituting almost a city within a city, was able to develop its own vigorous life. Over many centuries it was one of the most important centres of the Jewish world; and it is noteworthy as one of the few places in Europe the Jewish association with which was virtually unbroken from the Dark Ages down to the present time.

II

In the southern part of Italy, as we have seen, the Jewish settlement had been brought to an end by Aragonese intolerance at the time of the expulsion from Spain. It was thus only in parts of northern and central Italy that the Jewish connection was continuous. As far as numbers were concerned, Italian Jewry never attained any great importance. However, its propinquity to the pivotal point of European culture, religion, and art gave it a disproportionate prominence.

[1] The town of Hildesheim may be regarded as a microcosm of German Jewry. Jews are first found here in 1347. They were exterminated at the time of the Black Death massacres in 1349, formed another community in 1351, which lasted for only a few years, readmitted (in virtue of the physical prowess of one of their number, 'der grosse Michel') in 1520, exiled with one exception in 1542, promised protection by the Elector and City Council in 1585-87, driven out notwithstanding in 1595 (in punishment for setting a bad example in the matter of marriage to deceased wives' sisters!), allowed back in 1601, chased away in 1609 on a charge of having caused the plague, recalled shortly after, expelled in 1660, and finally permitted to settle in 1662. Only from that date was the history of the community continuous, until the twentieth century.

[2] See above, p. 214.

R

The capital of the Roman Empire and of the Catholic Church has never known any interruption of its Jewish associations, from the age of the Hasmonaeans down to our own day. The policy of the Church with regard to the Jews hence centred, in fact, on the treatment of those in Italy. They influenced, and in their turn were influenced by, successive phases of the Italian Renaissance. Over a long period, the conception of the Jew, as entertained in more than one remote nation, was based upon the impressions brought home by visitors who had crossed the Alps on a religious or artistic pilgrimage. The importance of Italian Jewish history is thus out of all proportion to the numbers actually involved.

In a large part of the country, the Jew was legally restricted to the practice of money-lending. Merchants and manufacturers, indeed, as well as physicians, were not unknown. But, in the mercantile republics of the north, their commercial rivalry was feared. It was hence only in the function of financiers that they could obtain admission to most places. A Jew who maintained a loan-bank for the benefit of the poor became an institution quite as necessary, and almost as usual, as the communal physician. When it was found that facilities for borrowing money on pledge were urgently required, or that the clandestine activities of Christian usurers were fleecing the townspeople, negotiations would be entered into with one or more Jewish families, varying in number according to the size of the place. With these, a formal agreement would be contracted. They would be granted the exclusive right of opening 'banks' (as they were called) for the purpose of lending money on pledge, at a specified rate of interest. On their side they would undertake to provide a minimum capital, to observe certain regulations, and to shew their appreciation by a considerable payment to the civic treasury. This mutual arrangement (*condotta*, or 'conduct', as it was termed) was generally valid for a limited number of years—generally three, five, or ten. At the close of this period, it lapsed automatically, and both sides were open to make fresh contacts.

The centre from which these Jewish 'bankers' operated was Rome and the neighbourhood, where the Jewish settlement was of very ancient establishment. From the fourteenth century, their numbers were reinforced by refugees driven over the Alps by the persecutions and expulsions which were taking place in northern Europe. Towards the close of the Middle Ages, in fact, the native Jews in the cities of the Lombard plain and the adjacent regions were almost submerged by business men and scholars from Germany. It was under such conditions that some of the most famous Italian communities were established—that of Venice in 1366, of Padua in 1369, of Mantua in 1389, of Verona in 1408. On the heels of the loan-bankers followed petty traders, physicians, goldsmiths, dealers in second-hand commodities: but the financiers continued to constitute both the justification and the backbone of a majority of the Jewish nuclei, in the north of the country.

To see the Jewish loan-bankers flourishing through their shameless activities was too much for a zealous Catholic to bear. Accordingly, with the fifteenth century, there grew up an agitation for their replacement by public pawnbroking establishments conducted on a charitable basis— Monti di Pietà, or 'Mounts of Piety', as they were termed. The movement was inspired by various Franciscan friars, of whom the most prominent was that eloquent, emotional preacher, Bernardino da Feltre. The experiment met with only a qualified success. The rival Dominican order, as a matter of principle, questioned the canonicity of the acceptance of interest, even by a public institution. In some cases the rates were so high that the institution increased rather than lessened the burden on the common people. In others they were so low that, notwithstanding public subventions, it was unable to pay its way. The Jews were not opposed to the principle of the new foundations; indeed, it is on record that they sometimes left money to support them. However, it was a natural corollary, emphasised by Fra Bernardino, that the Jews were henceforth superfluous and might be expelled. It happened more than once that they were summoned back after a few years, to supply by their acumen what it had been found impossible to replace by mere enthusiasm. In many places, on the contrary, the movement brought to an end a Jewish connection which had perhaps existed for generations.

A milder policy was indicated by the example of the Popes, who continued to accord the Jews of their dominions a considerable measure of tolerance. In the various principalities (as distinct from the republics) their example was usually followed. The overthrow of the popular rule, and the establishment of an absolutism, was very frequently followed by the admission of the Jews; and few Italian communities could compare for general prosperity and tranquillity with that of Mantua under the Gonzagas, or that of Ferrara under the house of Este. But, where the Jew was less favoured, the prejudice against him seems to have been due in many cases more to commercial jealousy than to religious fanaticism. Italy was perhaps the only country of Europe in which persecution was never elevated into a system. Mob outbreaks, though they could not always be avoided, were rare and, in general, strictly localised. The Blood Accusation (notwithstanding the notorious case of Simon of Trent in 1475, brought about by Fra Bernardino's preaching) was never widespread, and generally failed to secure official sanction; and successive waves of refugees from France, Provence, Germany, and Spain were able to maintain a momentary foothold, at least, in various parts of the Peninsula.

III

Notwithstanding the fact that the Italian Jew was restricted to occupations hardly conducive to the cultivation of the higher qualities, he could not fail, being a Jew, to develop his own intellectual life. This assumed a tone deeply characteristic of the country. The distinctive feature of Jewish culture in Spain was its poetry and its philosophy: in France and Germany, it lay in the sphere of Talmudic studies. Neither of these branches was unrepresented in Italy: witness, for the former, Immanuel of Rome, the satirist, and for the second, Nathan ben Jehiel, the lexicographer, to mention only two names. But the outstanding local characteristic was the constant action and reaction of secular and Jewish culture. There was no country in Europe in which the Jew consistently played so important a part in cultural activities, and in which the latter in their turn so deeply influenced Jewish literature and thought. There is a tradition of Jewish participation in vernacular literature dating back at least to the thirteenth century. In the fifteenth and sixteenth, on the other hand, Jews played an important part in that amazing spate of intellectual activity which goes by the name of the Renaissance.

Of this, the principal seat was Florence. In the days of the birth and growth of Florentine greatness, Jews had been excluded jealously from the city. Now, at the very period when the Florentines were obtaining an unenviable reputation as the arch-usurers of Europe, they began to feel conscientious scruples against the breach of canon law involved in making loans to their fellow-citizens; and in 1437—just as the Medicean hegemony was beginning—Jews were summoned to the city to set up their loan banks. Among these hard-headed business men there were munificent patrons of learning (such as the Da Pisa family, friends and correspondents of Isaac Abrabanel), whose names are still respected by students of Hebrew literature. The unpopular financier with whom the needy burgher deposited his pledges was at the same time a scholarly enthusiast, who would pay heavily for the luxury of a new book to add to his library and would scour Italy for a capable tutor to give his son a good Jewish education. Eager Florentine students would not hesitate to seek the aid of these savants for the solution of any intellectual problem—not necessarily of a purely Hebraic nature—in which they were interested. They were especially regarded as experts in the Aristotelian philosophy, which had become familiar to the Christian world through the translations executed by the Jews of Moslem Spain, and (though now becoming superseded by that of Plato) was still regarded with deference.

Bearded Rabbis were hence familiar figures in the Florentine humanistic circles, when these were at the height of their fame. Elijah del Medigo, of Crete (1460-1497), equally distinguished as physician, translator, and philosopher, was regarded as the outstanding contemporary exponent of the Aristotelian system. Such was his reputation that, on one occasion, he had been summoned from Venice to Padua to act as umpire in a philosophical dispute which had broken out in the famous University of that town. Here he made the acquaintance of the knight-errant of humanism, Pico della Mirandola. Subsequently he followed the latter to Florence, where he instructed him and the learned paragon, Marsilio Ficino, not only in the method of Aristotle but also in the mysteries of the Cabbala.[1] The versatile Abraham Farrisol (1451-1525: author of a geographical work which embodies the first Hebrew account of the discoveries of Columbus) was also active here; and in his writings, as in other texts of the period, there is an unexpected glimpse of the brilliant circle which was gathered about Lorenzo the Magnificent.

Florence was by no means the only centre of such activity. Many a prelate, cardinal, or secular ruler had in his employment a versatile Jewish physician whose interests extended far beyond the bounds of medicine. Cardinal Egidio da Viterbo was the Maecenas who patronised Elias Levita (1469-1549), the foremost Hebrew grammarian of his age, and who secured the translation of the Zohar[1] into Latin. Similarly, Jewish scientists engaged in investigations, and published their results, under Gentile patronage.

In the field of Botticelli and of Donatello, indeed, the Jews did not

[1] See below, pp. 282-283.

play an important role, though Jewish painters and engravers are not by any means unknown. On the other hand, Jewish musicians, singers, and actors were common. At the close of the sixteenth century, when Mantua was the centre of Italian drama, the services of the Jewish community, as a corporate body, were always called upon when a spectacle was desired at court; and it is on record that on Friday afternoons the performance had to be held earlier, so that there should be no infringement of the sanctity of the Jewish Sabbath. One of the first scientific treatises on dancing, and the very first on the theatrical art (a memorable composition), are from the pens of Italian Jews of the age of the Renaissance. We meet Jews as engineers, scientists, and inventors. (A French visitor at Ferrara, about 1510, calls attention to the disgusting habit of a certain local Rabbi, who persisted in spitting into a handkerchief, instead of using the floor like a Christian!) In the Universities they were familiar figures as students (generally, but not invariably, of medicine), and were not unknown even as teachers. Jews manufactured playing-cards (sometimes clandestinely) and were perhaps the first persons on record who performed tricks with them.

The active participation of the Jews in the Renaissance was exemplified by Don Judah Abrabanel (generally known as Leone Ebreo: c. 1465-1535), son of the great Don Isaac. On the expulsion of the Jews from Spain, he had gone with his father to Naples, where he was at one time body-physician to Gonzalo de Cordova, 'the Great Captain'. Subsequently, on the expulsion of the Jews from the Aragonese conquests, he withdrew first to Genoa, and then to Venice and to Rome. He was in touch with all that was most cultured in Italian society of his day, and his *Dialoghi di Amore*, or 'Dialogues on Love', were amongst the most influential philosophical productions of the sixteenth century.

Conversely, the Renaissance made itself most strongly felt in Hebrew literature in the *magnum opus* of Azariah de' Rossi of Ferrara (1514-1578), *The Enlightenment of the Eyes*, which introduced the scientific method to Hebraic learning, and made the Jewish reader familiar for the first time for centuries with the Apocrypha and Philo. His example, unfortunately, was isolated, and the impending reaction delayed the rebirth of Jewish studies for many generations. History was long in making itself appreciated, but Italian-Jewish chroniclers of the sixteenth century like Joseph haCohen of Genoa (1496-1576), author of *The Valley of Tears*, and his contemporary, Gedaliah ibn Jahia of Imola (1515-1587), in his *Chain of Tradition* (called by his detractors a Chain of Lies), collected the material in a newer and more comprehensive fashion than had been known in past ages.

No Italian rulers shewed themselves better disposed towards the Jews than the Popes of the Renaissance period—particularly those of the House of Medici, Leo X (1513-1521) and Clement VII (1523-1533). Enlightened beyond their time and tolerant to a degree, they regarded even Jewish scholarship as an integral part of that intellectual life of which they were such passionate devotees. The acme was reached in 1524, with the advent at Rome of a certain romantic adventurer named David Reubeni. He pretended to be the brother of Joseph, king of the tribe of Reuben, by whom he had been sent on a mission to the potentates of Europe to request their assistance against the Moslems. It may well be that this incredible story was the elaboration of a perfectly genuine errand on behalf of the indigenous Indian Jews of Cranganore,[1] then hard pressed by their neighbours. In any case his tale was believed implicitly. Accompanied by an exultant escort, he rode through the streets of Rome on a white horse, to present his requests at the Vatican: and Clement proved so gullible as to give him letters of introduction to various crowned heads. Thereafter he made his way to Portugal, where at the outset his success was no less pronounced, though eventually nothing materialised.

His advent caused great excitement amongst the Marranos; and one of them, named Diogo Pires, a promising young official, was so stirred that he escaped from the country and declared his allegiance to Judaism, under his ancestral Jewish name, Solomon Molcho. He studied the Cabbala at Salonica and Safed, aroused enthusiasm in the synagogues of Ancona by his eloquent preaching, and sat at the gates of Rome amongst the beggars and the maimed in order to fulfil in his own person the Rabbinical legends regarding the Messiah. Gaining access to the Pope, he communicated a prophecy concerning a flood which was to devastate the Eternal City not long after. The catastrophe punctually took place (8th October 1530). Clement, correspondingly impressed, extended the hospitality of his palace to the heretic, whom all the laws of the Church condemned to death by fire; and when the Inquisition finally became aroused, is said to have delivered up a malefactor of similar appearance to suffer in his place. It was only when the dreamer had the temerity to abandon his refuge and to go to Ratisbon with David Reubeni to persuade the Emperor to adopt their

[1] See above, p. 122.

views that his luck deserted him; and he was burned in Mantua as a renegade (March 1532). In the end, Reubeni himself met a similar fate at a Portuguese auto da fé.

IV

The Jew had been quick to realise the potentialities of the new art of printing. As early as 1444, an agreement for the cutting of a Hebrew fount was entered into at Avignon between a wandering German craftsman and a member of the local community, but unfortunately no specimens of the productions of this earliest Hebrew press have survived. However, at the beginning of the year 1475, two were at work in Italy—one in the far south, at Reggio di Calabria, and the other in the north, at Piove di Sacco, not far from Padua. It was the former which finished first, and was thus responsible for the first dated Hebrew book. This was an edition of the commentary of *Rashi* on the Pentateuch—a curious illustration of the hold which the writings of that simple French scholar had upon his people.

Before long, there were Hebrew printing-presses (generally directed by German immigrants) all over the country, especially in the north. Of the 113 Hebrew incunabula (*i.e.* books printed before 1500) known until recently, no fewer than ninety-three were produced in Italy. The most important family concerned in this activity was that of Soncino, who published nearly one-third of this number, and are remembered as the Gutenberg and Aldo combined of Hebrew printing. They continued their activity (in the course of which they produced also Latin and Italian works of rare perfection) well into the sixteenth century. In Spain, the history of Hebrew printing dates from 1482; but it was cut short by the expulsion of ten years later, and so did not attain great significance.[1] In Portugal, on the other hand, the Jews were the pioneers of the new art; and several Hebrew books were produced before any printing press with Latin characters was set up. Similarly, the first books printed both in Africa and in Asia (outside China, which led rather than followed Europe) were in the Hebrew tongue. A significant illustration of the zeal with which the Jews embraced this 'holy art' (as they termed it) is the fact that among the earliest Italian printers a woman figures—Estellina Conti, of Mantua.

---

[1] There have recently been brought to light, mainly in fragmentary condition, large numbers of formerly unknown incunabula printed in Spain: and the accepted views with regard to the early history of Hebrew printing may have to be revised.

Early in the following century, the supremacy in the printing art, as far as Hebrew books were concerned, passed to Venice. Here a Gentile enthusiast, Daniel Bomberg, founded a press which enjoyed a virtual monopoly in the Hebrew book-world for many years to come. It was he who produced the first complete editions of the Bible with its full complement of commentaries (1517) and of the Talmud (1519-1523). Study, among the Jews, had always been regarded as a sacred duty. The invention of printing gave it an additional impetus: for henceforth every man, however poor, could boast his modest library. On the other hand, the diffusion of printed works in ever-increasing numbers from one or two centres (such as Venice in the sixteenth century), tended to foster an increasing uniformity in Jewish life and to establish fixed standards of creed and practice, which had hitherto been lacking.

North of the Alps, Hebrew literature owed its rehabilitation to a curious episode. A certain unscrupulous German apostate named Johann Pfefferkorn, who had secured his release from imprisonment for common theft by embracing Christianity, shewed his gratitude by attacking his old faith in a series of peculiarly scurrilous pamphlets. Notwithstanding, or perhaps by reason of, his ignorance of the subject, he concentrated his venom upon the Talmud and Rabbinic literature. His attacks were assiduously taken up by the Dominicans of Cologne, headed by their prior, Jacob van Hoogstraten. Thanks to their exertions, Pfefferkorn was supplied with letters of introduction and despatched to Vienna (1509). Here he obtained from the Emperor Maximilian an edict for the destruction of all Hebrew books which contained assertions hostile to the Bible or to Christian teaching. Thus armed, he proceeded to Frankfort-on-Main, by far the most important German Jewish community, where he immediately set to work so ruthlessly that even his clerical co-adjutors were dismayed.

The Jews, on their side, made every exertion to defend themselves and to vindicate their literature from the aspersions cast on it. After much difficulty they succeeded in having the question referred to expert opinion for decision. The cudgels were now taken up on their behalf by Johann von Reuchlin, one of the most famous German scholars of his day. During the course of a visit to Italy, he had encountered Pico della Mirandola, who had impressed upon him the importance of the Jewish Cabbala as the key to the great verities of life, and even as proof of the truth of Christianity. Thus stimulated, Reuchlin had begun to study Hebrew under the direction of Jacob

Loans, physician to the Emperor Frederick III. He knew, indeed, little about the Talmud, which he suspected to contain much superstitious material. But he was deeply stirred by this indiscriminate attack, which threatened to suppress even his beloved Cabbala. Accordingly, he joined issue eagerly. A Battle of Books started, which lasted for many years. Reuchlin, worsted before the ecclesiastical court at Mayence, appealed to the Papal *curia* at Rome, where in 1516 a favourable decision was elicited. Hebrew literature thus received official recognition as a mental discipline of independent importance. From this period dates the beginning of the long series of Christian Hebraists, who studied Hebrew literature for its own sake and not simply as a weapon for proselytisation. Reuchlin's argument in favour of the Jews, as 'members of the Holy Empire and Imperial Burghers', was in itself a refreshing innovation, even though it did not obtain immediate recognition.

The reverberations of the dispute continued to re-echo in Germany for some years. On the one side, behind Pfefferkorn, were ranged the obscurantists, bent on maintaining at all cost the perpetuation of the existing state of affairs. With Reuchlin were the more enlightened scholars, profoundly influenced by the new intellectual currents, and determined to seek truth wherever it might be found. Eventually the original motive was almost forgotten, and the dispute became merged in a movement wider and more significant by far, which was in the end to change the face of Europe and to make a final breach in the fabric of the Catholic Church.

V

The Reformation, in its early stages, seemed likely to bring about some amelioration in the hard lot of the Jew. Luther, at the outset of his attack on the Papacy, had asserted that hitherto the Jews had been treated as though they were dogs rather than men, so that good Christians might well have desired to become converted to this much-persecuted faith. There was little wonder, in his eyes, that the unbelievers had seen nothing to attract them in a system in the name of which they were made to suffer so greatly. Now that the Gospel was put before them in its purified, primitive form, he was convinced that their attitude would change; and he had high hopes that one of the most glorious results of his activity would be to secure the conversion of the house of Israel to the true faith.

He was deeply disappointed when he discovered that this was not the case; and gradually his attitude towards the Jews changed into one of profound hatred. His pen, when he wrote of them, seemed dipped in vitriol. He admonished his followers to burn their synagogues and to treat them without mercy; and in a sermon preached shortly before his death, he urged the princes of Christendom to put up with them no longer, but to expel them from their territories. While his injunctions were not implicitly obeyed, it remains a fact that, long after his death, there was little to choose between Protestant and Catholic Europe so far as their treatment of the Jews was concerned.

The Catholic world, on the other hand, had little hesitation in ascribing to the Jews a considerable degree of responsibility for the Reformation. This was true only inasmuch as the movement was based upon a return to the Bible, and that several of the Reformers, with this in view, studied Hebrew at the feet of prominent Rabbis of the day. Under the stress of the attack, the Church resumed the offensive; and once again (as at the time of the Albigensian movement in the twelfth century, and the Hussite movement in the fifteenth) the Jews bore the brunt. If it had been their influence which had brought about the disruption, it was plainly advisable to segregate them from Christian society and to keep them more strictly subjected and isolated than had hitherto been the case. There was little need, indeed, for fresh legislation—that passed at the Lateran Councils of 1179 and 1215, long neglected, provided a code sufficiently comprehensive. Accordingly, with the Counter-Reformation, there began a darker age for the Jews of the Catholic world. Gone was the contemptuous tolerance which had distinguished the Popes of the Renaissance. Its place was taken by a stern policy of repression, based upon the sombrest traditions of the Dark and Middle Ages.

On this occasion the enforcement was not temporary but perpetual, continuing almost without modification until, two and a half centuries later, a hurricane swept over Europe and levelled the old institutions to the ground. This period, as it happens, coincided with the birth of a new order of things and of ideas, when the conception of liberty of conscience was slowly beginning to make headway, and when, in many respects, the dead-weight of obscurantism was being sloughed off. We thus have the paradox that medieval conceptions with regard to the Jews were consistently put into execution in the Catholic world only when the Middle Ages had passed away. The Papacy, which had shewn more broadmindedness than any other power in its relations with the Jews ever since the period of the Barbarian invasions stained the last years of its temporal rule by reaction; and precisely those states which had hitherto been by comparison the most liberal in their policy, left behind by the march of ideas, were henceforth the most retrograde.

The turn in the tide came with the middle of the sixteenth century, when Cardinal Caraffa, in whom the most fanatical aspects of the Counter-Reformation were personified, became all-powerful at the Papal court. A couple of the inevitable apostates (one of them, Vittorio Eliano, was a grandson of no less a scholar than Elias Levita) followed precedent by denouncing the Talmud as pernicious and blasphemous. After a very summary enquiry, the work was condemned; and, in spite of the fact that it had been published under the patronage of so recent a pontiff as Leo X, it was consigned to the flames. In the autumn of 1553, on the Jewish New Year, all copies discoverable were burned publicly in the Campo dei Fiori in Rome. The example was followed all over Italy with a ridiculous lack of discrimination, no exception sometimes being made in favour even of Hebrew texts of the Bible itself. Ultimately, greater moderation began to be shewn, but only after the institution of a fantastically rigorous censorship.

Not much later, Cardinal Caraffa himself ascended the Papal throne as Paul IV (1555-1559). Reaction now became triumphant. One of the first actions of the new Pope was to reverse the policy of his predecessors, who had permitted Marrano refugees from Portugal to settle at Ancona under their protection. Without notice, he withdrew their letters of protection, and ordered immediate steps to be taken against them. Twenty-four men and one woman, steadfast to the end, were burned at the stake, while others who were not so stubborn were punished less drastically. It was in vain that the Jewish communities of the Levant endeavoured to organise a punitive commercial boycott of the Papal States and especially of Ancona itself—a gallant attempt, not to be emulated for nearly four hundred years. The suffering would have been greater still but for the intervention of the Sultan of Turkey, who addressed a haughty letter to the Pope, insisting on the release of those of the accused who happened to be his subjects—a strange reversal of the nineteenth century rôles of Protector and Persecutor.

Even before these proceedings had been instituted, the new Pope had initiated his policy with regard to the Jews. On 12th July 1555 he issued the notorious Bull which began with the phrase *cum nimis absurdum*. In this he stressed the 'absurdity' of allowing the present state of affairs to continue and renewed, down to its last detail, all the oppressive medieval legislation with regard to the Jews. They were henceforth to be strictly segregated in their own quarter (subsequently to be known as the Ghetto, in imitation of the existing Jewish quarter at Venice), which was to be surrounded by a high wall and provided with gates, closed at night. They were forbidden to practise medicine amongst Christians, to employ Christian servants or workmen, or to be called *signor*. They were excluded from the professions. Their commercial activity was restricted on all sides, none but the meanest occupations remaining open to them. They were forced to wear their distinctive badge, in the form of a yellow hat. They were forbidden to own real estate, having to dispose of that in their possession at whatever sacrifice.

This all-embracing code was henceforth enforced with the utmost strictness. With the death of Paul IV in 1559, there was a momentary respite, and the Roman mob delighted itself by crowning the statue of the late Pontiff with one of the yellow hats which he had imposed on the Jews. Thereafter, down to the end of the century, the Papal policy varied: a peculiarly promising interlude occurring under Pope Sixtus V (1585-1590), under whom the traditions of his Renaissance predecessors seemed to be renewed. But, with his death, there was a return to the obscurantism of the Counter-Reformation; and a series of regulations issued by Clement VIII from 1592 onwards finally ushered in the period of unrelieved darkness which was to last until the nineteenth century. Simultaneously (as once before, at the height of the former reaction, in 1569) the Jews were expelled from all the minor centres of the Papal states, where communities had previously existed in approximately one hundred places. Henceforth they were allowed to remain only in cities where they could be subjected to strictest surveillance—Rome and Ancona in Italy, Avignon and Carpentras (with a couple of minor centres) in France.

The Papal policy was more or less implicitly followed in the rest of the Catholic world—more particularly in the various Italian states, which continued to provide a model for half Christendom. Throughout the Peninsula, Ghettos came into being, and the Ghetto system was enforced down to its last petty detail. The only regions in which it did not apply were those under Spanish rule (including ultimately the Duchy of Milan, whence a general expulsion took place in 1597), in which Jews were not allowed to live at all. Moreover, the gradual extension of the temporal dominion of the Papacy—comprising from 1597 the Duchy of Ferrara, and from 1631 the Duchy of Urbino— brought under its rule further communities, at one time cultured and wealthy, the importance of which rapidly diminished henceforth. Thus from the middle of the sixteenth century, Italy, the ancient paradise of Jewish life in Europe, began for the first time to set the example of intolerance; and the Ghetto, in all its narrowness and all its degradation, became a feature of European Jewish life.

95. JEWISH HOMAGE TO THE POPE AT THE ARCH OF TITUS
From the engraving by Bernard Picart, 1723

Chapter XXIII

THE LEVANTINE REFUGE

———————•———————

I

The nineteenth century conveniently divided the world into two sections—the Enlightened and the Unenlightened. The former category, on examination, turns out to comprise exclusively the western European powers, with the more advanced of their offshoots beyond the seas, all wearing what is known as European dress and professing one form or another of the Christian faith. It was here that civilisation had made most progress. Culture was on a higher level. Literature was more flourishing. The fanaticism of a former age had passed away in favour of a general, though perhaps supercilious, tolerance. Supremacy in the arts of war had set the seal on Nature's choice. The Unenlightened portion of the earth's surface, not blessed with these manifest advantages, began, where the other left off, with the Moslem powers clustered round the basin of the Mediterranean.

It is not desired here to controvert this conventional grouping. In Jewish history, however, it is necessary to realise that, up to the seventeenth century at least, this differentiation did not apply. The Arabic culture of the Middle Ages was no less advanced than the Latin. The seats of learning at Cairo or Bagdad were as enlightened as those of Padua or Oxford. If political importance were taken as criterion, the Grand Turk was long the greatest military power in Europe. Above all (and it is here that the significance for Jewish history lies) the territories subject to the Crescent displayed a wise tolerance, testifying to a civilisation essentially higher than that of those which professed Christianity.

For when Christian Spain rid itself of the Jews, and they lost their last foothold in western Europe, it was under the Crescent that they found a breathing-space. From the Straits of Gibraltar to the Isthmus of Suez, and from the Atlas Mountains to the Balkans, fresh communities sprang up, or the old ones were quickened into a new life. Notwithstanding the vicissitudes through which they had passed, and the bewildering change in their environment, the refugees remained pathetically true in their new homes to the traditions of the country which had spewed them out. All along the Mediterranean coast there was a series of islands of Iberian culture, maintained by the Jewish exiles in the midst of a strange land. This state of affairs, not unnatural at the outset, perpetuated itself with memorable tenacity generation after generation. The culture of fifteenth-century Spain, in a fossilised form, continued to be preserved with utmost fidelity among the descendants of the exiles hundreds of years afterwards. On the Sabbath they brought out their ancestral finery, based on the fashions of Toledo or of Cordova before their ancestors were driven forth. In their houses they cooked Spanish dishes which were already old-fashioned in the time of Cervantes. Above all, they preserved their language. It was written in Hebrew characters, intermingled with Hebrew, Arabic, and other elements, and called 'Ladino'. But it remained fundamentally the old Castilian which the fathers of the majority had spoken—the same in which Isaac Abrabanel pleaded with the Catholic sovereigns for the withdrawal of the edict of expulsion. In it the mothers sang their children to sleep with old-world lullabies forgotten in the country where they were composed; while even the popular ballads, some dealing with the exploits of the Cid Campeador and his knights, recalled Spain of the age before Don Quixote. Generations after the expulsion, Spanish travellers were amazed to meet in the Levant little Jewish children who had never seen Spain, but who spoke a purer Castilian than they did themselves. Christopher Columbus, could he have been resuscitated four centuries after his death, would perhaps have found himself more at home in the Jewish quarter of some trading centre of northern Africa or the Near East than along the quays of Seville.

Already, at the close of the fourteenth century, the refugees from the outbreaks in Spain, fortified by *conversos* who escaped in order to revert to the faith of their fathers, had awakened the communities of northern Africa anew. The former residents had no choice but to defer, however unwillingly at the outset, to the superior number, learning, and initiative of the immigrants; and the authority of the Spanish Rabbis soon became generally acknowledged amongst them. After the expulsion of 1492, their number was immensely recruited. Along the northern coast of Africa, from Tangiers to Alexandria, and inland to Mequinez and Fez, the refugees settled by tens of thousands. For centuries after, most of the communities of Morocco continued to be governed by the Ordinances drawn up by the sages of Castile. The earliest book printed on the African continent was the product of a Hebrew press set up at Fez with types brought from Lisbon.

The sufferings of the exiles in the course of their readjustment were terrible. Many were despoiled at sea. Others were cast away on the coast, assaulted and murdered by the inhabitants, or sold into slavery. Their steps were consistently dogged by pestilence, famine, and fire. Even when they were at last permitted to settle down, they had to pay heavily for the privilege.

Thereafter, conditions still left a very great deal to be desired. The benevolence of the government was sporadic. It officially approved of degradation, and sometimes indulged in systematic persecution in the orthodox fashion. The Jews were fleeced frequently, arbitrarily, and unmercifully by the Moslem rulers—in this, at least, true counterparts of the monarchs of civilised Europe. Occasionally there were ghastly mob outbreaks. From certain cities, considered of especial sanctity, they were utterly excluded. In other places they had to live in a special quarter, known as the *Mellah*, which could conveniently be sacked at any interlude of popular unrest. They were forbidden to wear white or coloured clothing, ultimately developing as their characteristic garb the long black gown and round skull-cap still worn by their descendants. They had to remove their shoes when they passed in front of a Mosque or a school where the Koran was being recited. If they met one of the faithful in the street, they had to give him the right of way. The use of the horse, as a noble beast, was forbidden to them, so that they could only ride mules or asses. When the leaders of the community went to pay tribute, they had to assume a suppliant attitude, and to offer their cheek to the blow, real or feigned, of the official who received their homage. As in medieval Europe[1] it was they who had to act as executioners, so as to save true believers from the sin of putting a fellow-being to death. Moslem contempt reached its culminating point when women were permitted to unveil their faces to Jews and to slaves, as hardly being in the category of men.

Their position was hence hardly enviable. But, in practice, the Moslem governments shewed that they believed at least in tolerance, and—like the Popes at Rome—they seldom or never resorted to the

[1] Above, p. 212.

s

last extremity of expulsion. So long as the Jews could find a temporary resting-place, where they might live without disturbance, little else mattered to them; and they utilised to the full whatever opportunities they found. They were famous as artisans. They piled up fortunes at trade. Some (as in a former age) attained great influence in the state, as financial agents, diplomats, physicians, interpreters, and (particularly in Egypt) mint-masters. They often acted as consuls for foreign powers. Thanks to their personal address and linguistic ability, they were sometimes appointed Ambassadors and Ministers-Extraordinary to stolid Holland, aloof England, and even fanatical Spain.

Thus, for many generations, the benighted Barbary States compared very favourably indeed, when tested by the touch-stone of toleration, with the vast majority of the countries of Europe. It was significant that, when a European power obtained a foothold at one of the African ports, its advent implied disaster for the local community—as, for example, when the Spaniards captured Oran in 1509, Tunis in 1535, or Bougie in 1541. On the other hand, when Sebastian of Portugal fell in battle in Morocco in 1578, it is on record that his nobles felt themselves fortunate if they became the slaves of the Jews whose forefathers had been chased out of the Peninsula, rather than fall to the questionable mercies of the Moslem population.

II

By far the greatest number of the exiles of 1492 directed their steps further east, towards the central provinces of the Turkish Empire. Byzantium, during its protracted death-throes, had not maintained the gross fanaticism which had stained its earlier days. Its Jewish communities had continued to drag on a degraded and undistinguished existence, unenlivened over a period of many centuries by a single important event, or a single outstanding name. The fall of Constantinople in 1453, which seemed to the Jews of the west one of those supernatural visitations which were to herald the coming of the Messiah, gave those of the east a new lease of life. Excepting for the payment of the poll-tax which was obligatory on all non-Moslems, they were subjected to few disabilities, and almost all walks of life were open to them.

The Turks were essentially a military and agricultural people, despising a sedentary existence; and the trade of the empire was thus left almost entirely to Jews, Armenians, and Greeks. The various communities were organised on a new basis, and the Chief Rabbi, resident at Constantinople, was given a seat at the Divan next to the Mufti himself. Immigrants arrived from all over Europe, to take advantage of the new conditions. The exiles from Spain found a warm welcome, the local communities selling the ornaments from the Scrolls of the Law in order to succour those who were in need. 'What! Call ye this Ferdinand "wise"'—he who depopulates his own dominions in order to enrich mine?' the Sultan Bajazet is reported to have said, and he encouraged the immigration by every means which lay in his power.

Fresh communities were established, or the old ones revitalised, throughout the Ottoman Empire—at Sofia, Adrianople, Gallipoli, and Nicopolis, on the one side of the Bosphorus, and at Brusa, Magnesia, Smyrna, and Angora on the other, to mention only a very few places. Many cities contained more than one congregation, which faithfully preserved the minutiae of the religious tradition of the Spanish province, or even city, from which its founders had come. With them the immigrants brought their language, their acumen, their fortunes, their knowledge. Jewish physicians, trained in the school of Salamanca, were generally sought after. The earliest books printed at Constantinople and at many another place in the empire were in Hebrew—sometimes from types actually brought from Spain. International trade, throughout the eastern portion of the Mediterranean basin, lay very largely in Jewish hands. The expert Jewish artisans rapidly made a name for themselves, introducing to the Levant the methods and trade secrets of Toledo or Saragossa. The troops and vessels of the Crescent, when they made their forays along the Italian coast or sailed to encounter the Spanish fleet, were equipped with gunpowder and armaments manufactured by Jewish hands; and an increase of activity in the Jewish quarters of Adrianople or Brusa was assumed by foreign observers to presage an approaching sally of the Grand Signior.

From 1497, a stream of immigrants began to arrive from Portugal —either prudent individuals who had anticipated the General Conversion, or else devoted Judaisers who fled secretly afterwards. Exiles from Sicily and Provence, merchants from Italy, fugitives from Germany, all added to the number. But the preponderance and superior culture of their Spanish forerunners ultimately absorbed them all. Henceforth Spanish was the *lingua franca* of the Jews throughout the

Near East, being adopted even by the indigenous elements, in place of the Greek which they had previously used. The Sephardic rite of prayers similarly predominated, the primitive Byzantine ritual surviving only in a couple of out-of-the-way places—the island of Corfu, and Kaffa in the Crimea.

The first, and most obvious, place of settlement was Constantinople. In a short time the community of this city grew to be the largest in Europe, comprising as many as thirty thousand souls. But it was soon rivalled, and ultimately outstripped, by Salonica, which became through Jewish enterprise the greatest mercantile emporium of the eastern Mediterranean. More Jewish settlers, and still more, flowed thither from every part of the Jewish world. In the end it became a preponderantly Jewish city, as it was to remain for some four centuries. The non-Jewish population was in a distinct minority. Jews controlled its trade, its handicrafts, its industries, even its manual labour. A flourishing textile industry provided the Turkish armies with its uniforms. Jewish fishermen supplied the city with much of its food; and Jewish porters discharged the vessels which arrived in the harbour with every tide. The number of separate congregations soon rose to thirty-six. Each group had its own synagogue and organisation, based upon geographical origin and ancestral rite; and memories of Provence, Sicily or Andalusia: Lisbon, Evora or Otranto: were kept alive for long generations in their religious life.

III

The Spanish immigrants in Turkey comprised not only a valuable mercantile and urban element, but also the only section of the population which had thorough experience of European conditions and knowledge of European languages. In consequence, they became active once again in politics and diplomacy, as was so frequently the case under Moslem rule. The state concerned was in this case indubitably the most powerful in Europe. Hence, for the first time since the days of Hasdai ibn Shabrut, in tenth-century Cordova, individual Jews began to play an important, and in some cases even a crucial, part in international politics. It was seldom that the Sublime Porte did not have in its employment some Jewish physician—such as Joseph Hamon (d. 1518), an exile from Granada, or his son, Moses (d. 1565)—whose opinion was frequently consulted in affairs of state, and who was sometimes able to render great services to his co-religionists. In the second half of the century, a Jewish woman, Esther Chiera (assassinated in 1592), stood high in the favour of the Imperial harem, and was considered by foreign diplomatic observers to be one of the most influential persons in the capital.

No case was more striking than that of Joseph Nasi, whose career reads like a page out of some exotic recension of the Arabian Nights. Originally known as João Miguez, he was descended from a family which had fled from Spain to Portugal at the time of the Expulsion, and there had been victims of the Forced Conversion of 1497. As a titular Christian, his father had become body-physician of the Portuguese sovereign; while his aunt, Beatrice de Luna, had married the head of the firm of Mendes, who had built up out of a business in precious stones a banking establishment of international fame, with a branch at Antwerp which overshadowed the main establishment in importance. On his death, the widow had gone with other members of her family, including her nephew, to the Low Countries. It is reported that the Queen Regent of the Netherlands solicited the hand of her beautiful daughter, Reyna, for one of the court favourites. The mother replied, without mincing words, that she would rather see the maiden dead.

This incredible refusal made it advisable for the family to betake itself to a safer environment. After wellnigh incredible adventures they made their way, through Lyons and Venice, to Constantinople. Here they threw off the disguise of Catholicism. Beatrice de Luna became known as Gracia Nasi, the most benevolent and the most adored Jewish woman of her day. João Miguez married his cousin, the lovely Reyna, and was henceforth called by his ancestral Hebraic name, Joseph Nasi.

For many years to come, his career knew no check. He rose to high position at court, so that for a time he was one of the most influential persons in the Turkish Empire. He attempted to recoup himself for the confiscation of his property in France by the seizure of one-third of every cargo despatched from that country to Egypt. His interest was solicited by every power in Europe. He avenged himself on Spain by encouraging the revolt of the Netherlands. He patronised Hebrew letters, and did not hesitate to use diplomatic means to protect his co-religionists abroad. He repaid Venice for the indignities that his family had suffered at her hands by bringing about a declaration of war, in the course of which the republic lost the island of Cyprus. He was created Duke of Naxos and the Cyclades. At his palace of Belvedere, outside Constantinople, he displayed an almost royal state. No professing Jew in recent history had attained such power.

For a few years before Nasi's death, which took place in 1579, his political influence was on the wane, and he failed to become King of Cyprus, as had once seemed probable. Yet there was no reaction against the Jews as a whole. The former favourite was left in enjoyment of his dignities; and the Vizier's physician became a power in the state in his stead. This was a certain Italian Jew of German origin named Solomon Ashkenazi, born at Udine and educated in medicine at Padua, who had previously been in the service of the King of Poland. His ability, his linguistic attainments, and his tact had won him golden opinions at Constantinople, where he had come to exercise an influence comparable to that of Nasi, though less obvious: so much so that the election of Henry of Valois to the Polish Crown in 1573 was partly due to his exertions, and that his influence had secured the withdrawal of an edict of expulsion issued against the Jews of Venice shortly after the outbreak of war. It was now determined to take advantage of the qualifications of this much-travelled physician by delegating him, in 1574, Envoy Extraordinary to the Venetian Republic—a mission which he performed to the utmost satisfaction of his principals. He was employed, too, in the negotiations for peace between Turkey and Spain, and in various other diplomatic tasks.

Another famous Turkish Jewish statesman, whose career was closely parallel to that of Joseph Nasi, was Solomon Aben-Ayish (1520-1603). Similarly a Marrano by birth (under the name of Alvaro Mendes), he had made himself a name in Portugal, but ultimately settled as a professing Jew in Constantinople. He likewise became a power at the Sublime Porte, and was a highly important figure in international diplomacy. As one of the principal movers in the alliance between England and Turkey against Spain, he was in close touch with the great Lord Burleigh, and sent agents almost like an independent potentate to treat with Queen Elizabeth. It was a token of his standing that the Sultan created him Duke of Mytilene.

With the close of the sixteenth century, the golden age of the Jews in Turkey began to wane. The Ottoman Empire was shewing signs of decay. A succession of weak, and sometimes fanatical, rulers took the place of the brilliant military leaders and far-seeing statesmen of a former age. The more the power of the Sultan was usurped by the janissaries and the harem, the greater were the extortions and cruelties of the pashas who governed the provinces. The Jews themselves lost something of that international breadth they had manifested in the generation which succeeded the expulsion from Spain, and no longer produced representatives of outstanding genius. On the other hand, fresh centres of tolerance had by now begun to spring up in northern Europe, so that Turkish sufferance no longer stood out as anything exceptional. We begin to read, indeed, at increasingly frequent intervals of lapses from the old standards; of sumptuary laws, intended to mark out the Jews for contumely from true believers; of persecutions at the whim of various pashas; of terrorisation at the hands of the janissaries. There was, nevertheless, no radical change in the policy of the government, and no disaster on a larger scale. The Jewish people must always recall the Turkish Empire with gratitude because, at one of the darkest hours of their history, when no alternative place of refuge was open and there seemed no chance of succour, it flung open its doors widely and generously for the reception of the fugitives, and kept them open.

IV

The names of the Jewish statesmen in the Turkish court in the sixteenth century will always be remembered in connection with the gallant attempt they made to restore the Jewish centre in Palestine. The original settlement, in full decay after the abolition of the Patriarchate in 425, had been brought to an end by the devastations of the Crusades and of the Tartar invasion, which had succeeded them in the middle of the thirteenth century. True, the country never lost its place in Jewish sentiment. Throughout the centuries pilgrims had made their way thither, to pray at the tombs of the Patriarchs—sometimes, to remain. Thus, for example, in 1211, three hundred English and French Rabbis set out for the Holy Land; and it was there that the learned Moses ben Nahman had sought refuge, after his tactless victory at the Disputation of Barcelona in 1263.

The father of the modern settlement was Obadiah di Bertinoro, a saintly Italian scholar famous for his commentary on the *Mishnah*. Having determined to end his days in Palestine, he set out late in 1486 from his home in north Italy. The journey, which could to-day be accomplished comfortably in one week, took him over one and a half years. In this leisurely progress, he had ample time to observe conditions in the places through which he passed; and his letters to his father describing his experiences are among the classics of Hebrew literature. On his arrival at Jerusalem he was bitterly disappointed. Instead of the earthly paradise which he expected, he found corruption and oppression rampant. Cultural and moral life were at a low ebb; and there was complete lack of communal organisation. The Italian Rabbi's strong personality, combined with his scholarship and his eloquence, led to his immediate acceptance as the spiritual head of the community. In this capacity he instituted regular courses of lessons, founded a *yeshiba*[1] for the study of the Law, brought charitable and benevolent institutions into existence, suppressed corruption, and improved relations with the Moslem authorities. The ground was thus prepared for the numerical increase which was to take place a few years later.

On the expulsion from Spain, it was natural that many of the refugees, wandering about without an objective, turned their steps to the land which had been associated with their hopes and their prayers for so many centuries. Its Jewish population accordingly grew by leaps and bounds. Scholars and Rabbis who had previously been reckoned amongst the greatest luminaries of Spain, Portugal, and Sicily, established themselves there in large numbers, accompanied by many members of their flocks. It was not long before they were reinforced by others from all countries, unable to resist any longer the mystical attraction of the Holy Land. Communities of real importance were established, not only in Jerusalem but also at Tiberias, Hebron, and above all Safed, constituting a sort of spiritual Hansa among themselves. So great was the influx of scholars that in 1538 a certain Jacob Berab (a Spanish exile who had added to his reputation while acting as Rabbi in Fez but had been driven thence also by the Spanish invasion) considered that the time had come to re-establish Palestine formally as the centre of Jewish spiritual life. This he proposed to effect by restoring the ancient institution of Rabbinical ordination, long in abeyance, and thereby resurrect the ancient Sanhedrin, as a visible expression of the supremacy of Palestine in Jewish life. This revolutionary suggestion aroused so great a wave of opposition from some neglected scholars (led by Levi ibn Habib, the principal Rabbi of Jerusalem, who in his youth had been implicated in the Forced Baptisms in Portugal in 1497) that it had to be abandoned. The reintegration of Jewish life was as yet premature.

The newly arrived settlers supported themselves in many cases by

---

[1] Talmudical academy.

96. KHASRAW AND SHIRIN

Miniature from a Persian Jewish manuscript of the 17th Century. Jewish Theological
Seminary, New York (Adler Collection)

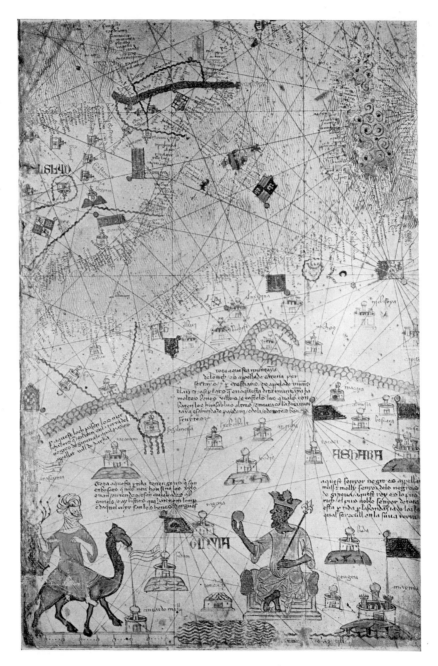

97. Spain and Northern Africa

From the Catalan Atlas by Abraham and Jahuda Crescas, Majorca, 1376-1377. Bibliothèque Nationale, Paris

98. JEWISH OATH BEFORE THE DOGE
Watercolour by Jan Grevembroeck (1731-1807). Museo Correr, Venice

99. Sabbatai Zevi (1626-1676)
Contemporary Engraving

100. Sabbatai Zevi receives a Deputation in Prison
Contemporary Engraving

manual labour or commerce. But a very high proportion, having
arrived at the country of their dreams, nearer to Heaven than any
other, considered it little less than an impiety to engage in any
occupation excepting that which was dearer to Heaven than any other
—the study of the *Torah*. For their livelihood they looked confidently
to the communities of the Diaspora, who by supporting them might
acquire a vicarious merit; and their confidence was not belied. Year
by year there sallied out to all the four corners of the earth the so-
called 'Emissaries of the Merciful', collecting funds on behalf of the
four Holy Cities of Palestine. The record of their vicissitudes and
trials, of the unlikely spots to which they penetrated and of the
unflinching courage which they shewed, constitutes a remarkable
page in the history of travel. Everywhere, from India to the New
World, these incongruous, sometimes uncouth figures were received
with deference, enjoying unlimited hospitality, preaching in the
synagogues, and going away burdened with the oblations of the faithful. They constituted over many centuries an important element in
the life of the Jewish people, bringing the latest currents of thought
and scholarship into the most remote communities, keeping alive the
memory of the Holy Land, and maintaining personal contact between
the far-flung offshoots of the Jewish world.

A less unworldly tendency was introduced into the Holy Land by
Joseph Nasi. He was, perhaps, the first person in recent times to
envisage the restoration of Jewish Palestine by practical as opposed
to supernatural means. Through his influence at the Sublime Porte,
he secured the grant of the city of Tiberias, which had long been in
ruins, and a tract of territory in the vicinity, with full seigniorial
rights. Here he proposed, it seems, to build up the nucleus of a semi-
autonomous Jewish state. With healthy common sense he realised
that something more than sentiment was necessary to make the land
flourish again as it had done in the past. Not content, therefore, with
rebuilding the city and its fortifications, he attempted to turn it into
a manufacturing centre by fostering the textile industry, in which the
Jews of the Near East had long enjoyed supremacy. Mulberry trees in
great numbers were planted for breeding silkworms; merino wool
was imported from Spain; invitations were despatched far and wide
for artisans and craftsmen to settle in the new colony; and arrangements were made for Jews of the Papal States to be transported from
the growing miseries of their daily existence in the Duke's own ships,
which were sent for the purpose to Venice and Ancona. His concep-

tions, unfortunately, proved to be in advance of their time. Innumerable difficulties sprang up which he was unable to surmount—
sentimental, political, economic. Nevertheless, interest in the scheme
was continued after his death by Don Solomon Aben-Ayish, Duke of
Mytilene, his successor at the Turkish Court, who secured the renewal
of the grant, and members of whose family set the example by settling
in the colony themselves. It was no more than a gallant experiment—
but an experiment which in the end served as the model for a decisive
attempt.

V

The most important of the new centres of Jewish life and scholarship was Safed, in Upper Galilee. At the time of the Expulsion it
contained a bare handful of Jews. A hundred years later it supported
no less than eighteen Talmudical colleges and twenty-one synagogues.
But the disciplines studied here were very different from those of
thirteen hundred years before, in the age of the Patriarchate. There
had always flourished, by the side of the Talmudic studies which discussed how a man should act, a mystical tendency which endeavoured
to ascertain how he had come into being and the nature of the unknown world. All of this lore was known as the *Cabbala*, or tradition,
being handed down from generation to generation by word of mouth.

The persecutions of the Middle Ages made the Jews turn their
minds more and more to the supernatural world, to counter-balance
and compensate the vicissitudes of ordinary existence. In the thirteenth century, there came to light in Spain a work known, from one
of its opening words, as the *Zohar*, or Book of Splendour. This was,
in form, a mystical commentary upon the Pentateuch in the Aramaic
language, replete with exotic speculations upon the origin of the
Universe, the nature of the Godhead, the allegories contained in the
Scriptures and the hidden sense of each episode and precept. The
fundamental conception was that the Law of God can contain nothing
trivial, and that every verse, line, word, even letter or stroke, has
some higher, mystical significance, which can reveal to the initiated
the very secret of the human being. Its quality varied, and every now
and again a semi-incomprehensible dissertation would be enlivened
by some sublime thought or magnificent prayer—'A man should so
live that at the close of every day he can repeat: "I have not wasted
my day" '; 'There are Halls in the Heavens above that open but to
the voice of song'.

The work purported to have been composed by the *Tanna*, Rabbi Simeon ben Jochai, in the second century of the Christian era. Its opponents, on the other hand, asserted that it was a fabrication by a certain Spanish mystic of the thirteenth century, Moses de Leo. Then truth lay in all probability between the two extremes; for the work, though a comparatively recent compilation, indubitably contained elements which went back to remote antiquity.

For the first few centuries after its divulgation the Zohar and the Cabbala in general did not exercise a very profound influence upon the life of the ordinary Jew, though it had passionate votaries in every land. With the expulsion from Spain, a new phase opened. It seemed obvious that this crowning disaster must be the darkest hour which presaged the dawn, heralding the final deliverance promised by the ancient Prophets of Israel. False Messiahs—such as Solomon Molcho —began to make their appearance here and there throughout the Jewish world, arousing the hopes of men to the highest pitch. It was inevitable that more and more attention should now be paid to the Zohar, in the hope that in its rhapsodies there might be some indication of the period when the Redeemer could be expected. Scholars of a mystical turn of mind directed their steps with one accord to Upper Galilee, where the action of the Book of Splendour was staged, where its saintly author had lived, and where his grave was still revered. Safed thus became what has been described as a revivalist camp in perpetual being. The traditional Jewish life was lived with an intensity rarely equalled, coupled with a mystical fervour which was all its own. The multitudinous precepts of the Law were carried out meticulously, but with especial regard to their hidden esoteric meaning. Study centred around the Zohar rather than the Talmud; and the anniversary of the death of Simeon ben Jochai was celebrated by a pilgrimage to his reputed sepulchre.

The tendencies were personified and given a new direction by the activities of one man. Isaac Luria was born in Jerusalem of a family of German extraction, in 1534, and was educated by a wealthy uncle in Egypt. Here, becoming engrossed in the study of the Zohar, he adopted the life of a hermit. For seven years he lived in isolated meditation in a hut on the banks of the Nile, visiting his family only on the Sabbath and speaking no language but Hebrew. The ascetic life had its natural result. He became a visionary, believing that he was in constant intercourse with the prophet Elijah and that his soul was privileged to ascend to Heaven, where it was initiated into sublime doctrines by Simeon ben Jochai and the other great teachers who had adorned his circle. In the end he removed to the 'Holy City' of Safed, where an elect band of disciples, comprising some of the choice spirits of the time, speedily gathered round him. Through them, he became known by the name of 'Ari' or Lion, being the initial letters of the words *Ashkenazi, Rabbi Isaac*. In this environment he lived until his death in 1572, at the early age of thirty-eight.

His personal fascination must have been extraordinary, to judge from the extent of his influence and the wealth of legend which gathered round his memory. Though he himself prepared nothing for publication, the notes of his discourses, collected by his disciples (particularly Hayim Vital, a refugee from Calabria) soon circulated throughout the Diaspora and had an enormous effect upon Jewish practice and the theory which inspired it. All the minutiae of religious observance, every letter of the liturgy, every action of daily life, became infused with an esoteric significance, frequently bordering on superstition, but often beautiful and sometimes profound. New prayers and meditations were composed, sometimes of remarkable charm, accentuating the spiritual significance of observances which had tended to become mechanical. The Zohar acquired a sanctity in Jewish life second only to that of the Bible. The dicta of the *Ari* were copied and studied more universally and with greater devotion than those of Maimonides. In distant Ghettos eager students attempted to determine, on the basis of the indications which he had left, precisely when the Messiah could be expected. The tendency is against the prevailing spirit of the twentieth century; but it is impossible to belittle the effect which it exercised three hundred years ago. It was the most vital movement in Judaism which had come forth from Palestine since the days of the Second Temple.

VI

One of the most eager of the intent circle which hung upon the mystical utterances of the Lion of the Cabbala in Safed was Joseph Caro (1488-1575). A child at the time of the Expulsion from Spain, he had been brought by his father to Turkey. At Adrianople, he had made himself a name as a scholar and a mystic. He was in close contact with the Cabbalistical circles of the Levant. He followed with eagerness the current Messianic movement, had a profound veneration for the unforgettable Molcho, and longed to be worthy like him of a martyr's death. He considered that he was always attended by a spiritual mentor, who admonished him at every turn and dictated every action of his life. In middle age he settled at Safed, attracted by the fame which that city was acquiring in esoteric doctrine. Yet he was destined to make his mark, not in mysticism, but another literary field.

Already, at the close of the twelfth century (as we have seen), the great Moses ben Maimon had codified the traditional law as expressed in the Talmud. A little more than a century after, Asher ben Jehiel (1250-1328), an outstanding German refugee-scholar, whom the community of Toledo had taken as its spiritual leader, made an abstract of the legal matter contained in each Talmudic tractate, as interpreted and supplemented by the later authorities. His son, Jacob ben Asher (d. 1340), had used this as the basis for a methodical code of the same type as that of Maimonides. This he called 'The Four Rows' (*Arbaa Turim*). Early in life, Joseph Caro had begun to write detailed annotations upon this work. Later on, he composed an abridgement, supplemented by additions from his own gigantic commentary. This he entitled 'The Prepared Table' (*Shulhan Arukh*)— indicating that the feast was spread, and that nothing remained for the guest but to help himself. It dealt clearly and methodically with the whole field of Jewish religious practice and jurisprudence in home, synagogue, counting-house, and law-court. It was essentially practical and prosaic; but occasionally there would be sudden flashes of poetical insight, or a mechanical precept would be given a new meaning through some shrewd ethical observation. The work, first published in 1567, attained an instantaneous reputation, being reprinted time after time, and spreading with the utmost rapidity to every corner of the Diaspora. It was accepted throughout the far-flung Jewish communities as the final standard of Jewish law and observance. Even scholars had recourse to it rather than take the trouble of poring over the authorities upon which it was based. Commentaries, and super-commentaries, were written about it. Abridgements were drawn up for the benefit of those who could not spare the time to consult the original. Finally, even translations of the abridgements were made for such as were ignorant of Hebrew.

Each trivial practice which the author had noted thus became sacrosanct. Every action of the Jew, from his rising in the morning to his lying down at night; from his home to the synagogue; from the synagogue to his shop, became regulated, stereotyped, and occasionally devitalised. With the decay of Jewish scholarship there were many communities (of the south of Europe and the Levant in particular) where the study of the Talmud and the allied literature now fell into rapid decline. All that was needed as a guide to Jewish observance was Caro's code, and upon it (together with the Zohar and the neo-mystical literature) their studies were now centred. Talmud and Midrash, Rashi and Tosaphoth, the medieval glosses and commentaries and codes—all this ripe literature was overlooked in an increasing degree: in Italy, the study was actually forbidden by the Church. In northern Europe, however, there was yet a sturdy body where traditional values still retained a stronghold: Poland, the second haven where, in the dark period which succeeded the close of the Middle Ages, Jewish life found a refuge and a breathing-space.

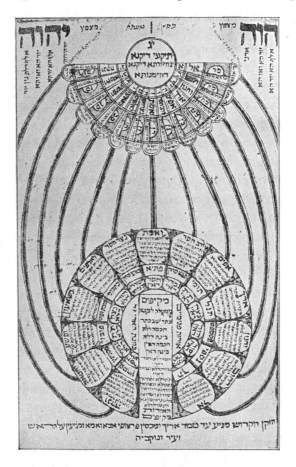

101. CABBALISTIC DESIGN
Jewish Theological Seminary, New York (Adler Collection)

Chapter XXIV

POLAND

————— • —————

I

Jews had been settled in eastern Europe, in the lands immemorially associated with the Slavonic peoples, from a very early date. Archaeological evidence shews that they were to be found as early as the first century of the Christian era in the Cimmerian Bosporus—now known as the Crimea. The Greek language which they spoke seems to indicate that these communities were off-shoots of those which had been established at an even remoter date in the Aegean Archipelago, though they were in all probability reinforced by fresh settlers who made their way northwards from Mesopotamia. Pious inscriptions demonstrate that, even in this remote spot, obedience to the traditional Jewish law was implicit. As the years passed, the area of Jewish settlement began to extend, notwithstanding the competition of Christianity, so that in the eighth century Phanagoria, a trading outpost to the north, was described as a Jewish town.

By slow degrees, the influence of Judaism impressed itself on some of the semi-barbaric tribes and kingdoms of the region. The most important of these were the Khazars—a mixed people, with a strong Mongolian strain, which occupied a territory comprised in what is now the Ukraine, between the Caucasus, the Volga, and the Don. For a period of two hundred years—perhaps longer still—they were one of the most important of the independent states which lay to the north of the Byzantine Empire. Early in the eighth century, Bulan, the ruling prince, recognised the merits of Judaism and formally adopted it as his religion. His example was followed by many of the aristocracy. One of Bulan's descendants, Obadiah, was especially memorable for the zeal with which he propagated the faith, constructing synagogues and inviting foreign scholars to settle in the country. The governing classes became thoroughly Judaised, their example being followed by many of the ordinary people: though, in accordance with the traditional Jewish principles of tolerance, followers of other religions were left unmolested. Throughout the golden period of the Khazar state—when even the intolerant Byzantines treated it with deference, when a Khazar princess became the consort of the Emperor and her son actually mounted the throne—it was considered essentially Jewish. Hasdai ibn Shabrut, in far-off Spain, heard of it with incredulous amazement, and opened up relations with the ruling Khan, Joseph.

It is a pleasing, but useless, occupation to speculate what might have happened had the Jewish statesman of the west been able to negotiate an alliance with the Jewish kingdom of the east. For it was by now too late. The neighbouring Russian tribes had already thrown off the Khazar yoke. In 965-969 the Prince of Kiev invaded the country and, in successive campaigns, overran the greater part of it. For half a century longer, independence continued to be maintained in the Crimean area, until in 1016 a short-lived alliance between the Russians and Byzantines conquered this last outpost.[1] Yet the memory of the episode did not die out in the Jewish consciousness. Descendants of the Khazars, men noteworthy for their learning and piety, were known long after in Toledo. Judah haLevi's famous philosophical work, *al-Khuzari*, was in the form of a series of hypothetical dialogues, in which a Jewish sage demonstrated to the ruler of the Khazars the superiority of Judaism over other religions. And, to the present day, the Mongoloid features common amongst the Jews of eastern Europe are, in all probability, a heritage from these 'proselytes of righteousness' of ten centuries ago.

II

The history of succeeding centuries in eastern Europe is obscure. We read of intolerant Greek abbots and bishops; of occasional riots and massacres; of Jewish merchants from the west—sometimes even from as far afield as Spain—pushing resolutely into the land of 'Canaan', as they termed it; of Rabbis of international reputation established at Novgorod and Kiev; of the gradual extension of the area of settlement northwards, into what is now Poland; of a wealthy community, as early as the eleventh century, in Gnesen, then the chief town of the region; of Jewish traders and tax-gatherers

[1] There is some evidence that the state survived for perhaps as long as another two centuries.

and even mint-masters, the coins struck by whom bear Hebrew lettering.

The incursion of the Tartars, in 1240-1241, was a turning-point in the history of eastern Europe generally. Russia itself was conquered by the barbarians, who subsequently accepted the religion of Islam. For centuries, the country was outside the bounds of civilised Europe, and our knowledge of the condition of its Jews at this period must depend in the main on conjecture. Poland was not conquered, but in 1241 there took place the first of a series of invasions, which devastated the whole country, and reduced the principal towns into heaps of smoking ruins. When the incursions ceased, conditions were desperate. Industry and commerce were non-existent. The middle class, never strong, had all but disappeared. No element intervened between the landed proprietors on the one side, and the serfs on the other. Accordingly the Polish sovereigns, from the middle of the thirteenth century, set about a considered policy of attracting merchants and craftsmen from Germany, under the protection of their native 'Magdeburg Law'. The invitation was responded to with alacrity. The Polish cities became repopulated largely by German elements, or else by those to whom German enterprise gave employment. The importance of Teutonic elements in Polish economic life is thus vast, its traces being discernible even at the present day.

Among the Germans, and after them, there came also large numbers of Jews, similarly attracted by the economic potentialities of the new field of enterprise. There had indeed been a tendency to migrate eastwards from the Rhineland ever since persecution had become endemic in Germany, from the beginning of the period of the Crusades; and this factor became increasingly strong as time went on. Economic considerations were even more potent: a fact which is shewn by the alacrity with which the Polish rulers, not generally memorable for broad-mindedness, welcomed the new arrivals. Boleslav the Pious, in 1264, issued a model charter of protection and liberties, based upon that which had been granted in Austria twenty years before, and securing them freedom of opportunity as well as security from molestation. Under the auspices of this, the settlement grew apace. Just as the Christian German immigrants introduced handicrafts and industry into the country, so the Jews opened up fresh avenues of commerce and provided the necessary finance. What proportion of the Jewish population of the country they actually constituted can never be ascertained. But in any case (in precisely the

T

same manner as the refugees from Spain in the Balkans after the expulsion of 1492) they were able to impose their superior culture upon their indigenous brethren. The latter adopted German costume, standards of culture, methods of study, and even language. In consequence, the vast majority of the Jews of Russia and Poland, whatever their immediate origin (as well as many of their descendants in other lands), still speak to-day the 'middle' High German which these immigrants brought with them. It is interspersed with Hebrew and Slavonic elements; it is written in Hebrew characters; it is familiarly known as *Yiddish*, or *Jüdisch-Deutsch*; but it is fundamentally the language which was spoken in the *Judengassen* of the Middle Rhine at the time when the great Cathedral of Cologne was being planned.

Though the rulers of the country were generally friendly to the Jews, confirming or developing Boleslav's policy, the population was not invariably so. Jealous merchants on the one hand, and fanatical ecclesiastics on the other, resented their privileges. The Christian immigrants from Germany had introduced with them (if there was need for introduction) their own intolerant standards. Clerical synods clamoured for the enforcement of the repressive legislation of the Lateran Councils. The massacres at the time of the Black Death were not stemmed at the frontier, an ancient chronicler recording that the Jews were exterminated at this period in almost the whole of Poland. Posen in 1399 and Cracow in 1407 knew Blood Accusations as frenzied and as deadly as any place in western Christendom could shew; and, in the middle of the fifteenth century, the fanatical John of Capistrano, embodying the reaction against the Hussites, was as successful in stirring up anti-Jewish feeling and excesses in Poland as he had been elsewhere upon his path.

Yet, by comparison with the neighbouring countries, conditions appeared attractive, while opportunity still abounded. Accordingly, the current of migration from western Europe continued. It reached its climax under Casimir the Great (1333-1370), the most energetic of all Polish sovereigns, under whom the country became to some extent a 'Western' Power. A determined opponent of the lawlessness of the nobility, his policy was such as to win him the spiteful sobriquet 'King of the serfs and the Jews'. In 1354 (under the influence, it was said, of his lovely Jewish mistress, Esther) he ratified and extended the provisions of the Charter of Boleslav the Pious of a century earlier. Every facility was given to the Jews for carrying on their business activities. They were allowed unrestricted domicile throughout the realm, as well as right of transit and (a curious commentary on the conceptions of the period!) access to the municipal bathing establishments. They were authorised to rent estates even from the nobility and the priesthood, or to hold them in mortgage. In order to secure impartiality, cognisance of disputes in which they were concerned was reserved to the Crown. In 1388 a similar charter of privileges was secured by the Jews of the neighbouring Grand Duchy of Lithuania, the history of the Jews in which (notwithstanding a temporary expulsion in 1495) remained very similar to that of their co-religionists in the larger country, with which, from 1501, it was united. The fact that the two states adhered to different forms of Christianity obviously made for a certain degree of tolerance.

Even when the age of terror in Germany had ended, Polish rulers continued to encourage the Jews. Sigismund I (1506-1548) in particular protected them, as he did other minorities; and his successors followed the same policy down to the debacle of the monarchy. Local excesses, on the other hand, recurred at not infrequent intervals. At some of the larger places—Cracow, Lublin, Posen—there were Jewish quarters, with their walls and gates and warders, in the full German or Italian style. Occasionally there would be some legislative enactment against the Jews, which might or might not be carried into effect. But, on the whole, they could count upon the royal protection: there was general, if not invariable, security for life, limb, and property; and economic life above all, left to flow in its own channels, was far wider and more ample than elsewhere.

For long generations, therefore, Poland continued to appear in the light of a land of promise for the Jews of northern Europe, and to receive a perpetual accession of new settlers—refugees escaping massacre, young men seeking opportunity, merchants from as far distant as Italy or the Balkans, hoping for gain. In 1500 the number of Jews in the country is estimated to have been only fifty thousand souls: a century and a half later, it had risen to half a million. Just as the expulsion from Spain concentrated the majority of Sephardi Jewry in Turkey and its dependencies, so, from the beginning of the sixteenth century, the main body of Ashkenazi Jewry—the remnants of the communities of medieval England and France and Germany, with others from farther afield—became concentrated in Poland and the surrounding Slavonic territories. It is from them that the overwhelming mass of the Jews in the world to-day are descended.

Polish Jewry was not by any means confined to the sordid occupations followed by its forefathers or by contemporaries in the adjacent countries. Some were indeed money-lenders, whose activities were regulated by the law; but these did not constitute a high proportion of the whole. There was a very large mercantile class, engaged in every branch of commercial activity. Many were interested in handicrafts and manufacture. The Gilds sometimes tried to limit their activities or to prevent them from opening shops in Christian neighbourhoods; but it was long before they met with success. Wealthy Jews are found as tax-farmers; they administered the excise and tolls; they were frequently employed as financial agents for the sovereign. Some leased and exploited the landed property of the nobility, or the Crown domains. They were universal all over the country as stewards and administrators of the great estates. They worked the salt-mines, purchased standing timber, traded in furs, exported surplus agricultural produce into Germany. The Jewish *Randar* (Arrendator), or innkeeper-taxgatherer, was familiar in the remotest villages. The poorer classes were itinerant pedlars, craftsmen, and sometimes even agricultural workers. Communities, or isolated individuals, were to be found in almost every hamlet, as well as in the great towns. The Jewish apothecaries (sometimes Italian in origin) enjoyed a high reputation; and more than one Polish sovereign had a Jew as his body-physician.

III

Nothing was more characteristic of Polish Jewish life than the remarkable degree of self-government which it attained. In 1551 Sigismund Augustus, the last king of the House of Jagello, issued an edict permitting the Jews of his realm to elect their Chief Rabbi and lawful judges, with authority to exercise jurisdiction in all matters concerning Jewish law, and answerable only to the Crown. All individuals were commanded to comply with their decisions and rulings, under extreme penalties. This measure has rightly been described as the Magna Carta of Jewish self-government in Poland; for it set the seal of the royal approval upon the natural urge of the Jew of the past to govern himself according to his traditional jurisprudence. From the governmental point of view, the system was useful. It was upon the Jewish community as a whole that there devolved the function of collecting the heavy taxes which constituted their *raison d'être*; and the function could not be performed efficiently if the communal authorities did not possess power to take proceedings against the recalcitrant.

The focus of Polish economic life was in the succession of great fairs held yearly in various centres. Hither streamed the Jewish merchants from every corner of the country. They comprised all classes, from the greatest scholars and communal leaders downwards. What more natural than that, on coming together, they discussed matters of common interest, or deliberated on matters in dispute between one community and another? Already in the first half of the sixteenth century, it had been customary for the scholars assembled at the fair of Lublin to adjudicate in accordance with Rabbinic law on civil cases which were brought before them. Gradually this became an institution. It was discovered, moreover, that these gatherings afforded the best opportunity for apportioning the amount which each *Kahal*, or local organisation, was to contribute towards the collective burden of taxation. As a matter of course, this convenient arrangement was backed up by the royal authority; and by slow degrees the *Vaad*, or Council, became omnipotent in Polish Jewish life. At the beginning, its authority extended over the whole of Poland and Lithuania. The Grand Duchy had a distinct fiscal administration of its own; and it was thus natural that its Jewish communities broke away and formed a separate organisation (1623). That of Poland ultimately became known as the Council of the Four Lands, or Provinces (comprising Great Poland, Little Poland, Podolia, and Volhynia), of which the kingdom was composed.

The Council, at its prime, was virtually the Parliament of Polish Jewry, with power nearly as absolute as that of any legislature. It was composed of thirty delegates, twenty-four of whom were laymen and the remainder outstanding Rabbis. All the more important congregations sent their representatives—an honour contested eagerly amongst themselves. Plenary meetings of the Council were held each year, not only at the Spring Fair at Lublin but also at that in the early summer at Jaroslaw, in Galicia. In cases of exceptional urgency, emergency assemblies would be held elsewhere. During the sessions of the Polish Diet at Warsaw, the Council would send an agent, or *shtadlan*[1]—generally *persona grata* at court—to watch over Jewish interests. Internally its authority was unquestioned. Besides apportioning taxation, it would assist in enforcing royal edicts; it passed sumptuary laws, to enforce moderation in dress and social life; it did

[1] Above, p. 256.

all that lay in its power to prevent undue competition: it supervised
the system of education; it acted as a court of appeal, and decided on
matters which were in dispute between one congregation and another;
it exercised a rigid control over Hebrew printing, prevented infringe-
ments of copyright, and on occasion protected local production by
forbidding the importation of one work or another from abroad. All
its regulations, however trivial, could be enforced if the necessity
arose, by the power of excommunication, backed up by the authority
of the state. A system similar in every detail prevailed (though on a
smaller scale) in the provinces adjacent to Poland proper. Nowhere,
ever since the decay of the Jewish centre in Palestine, had so complete
an approach to autonomy existed.[1]

IV

As has almost always been the case in Jewish life, learning followed
in the wake of numbers. The intellectual hegemony of German Jewry
had slowly passed eastwards together with its centre of gravity. In
the early part of the fifteenth century, Austria and the surrounding
territories boasted outstanding scholars, such as Israel Isserlein of
Neustadt; and there had been famous seats of learning at Erfurt,
Nuremberg, and Ratisbon. In the succeeding period, the pride of
place was occupied by Prague. Hence came, to be Rabbi in Cracow,
the famous Rabbi Jacob Pollak (*d.* 1541), the first important figure
amongst Polish Jewish scholars. His name is especially associated
with the curious method of Talmudic study which had originated in
South Germany, and goes by the name of *pilpul*—a species of mental
gymnastics centring upon the text of the Talmud. It was considered
the acme of intellectual achievement in this system to establish an
artificial analogy between different themes, to create elaborate distinctions between connected passages, to build up a syllogism between
texts which had nothing to do with one another, or to treat the end
of one tractate and the beginning of the next (relating to a different
subject) as though they constituted a continuous text. Notwithstanding some authoritative opposition, this extraordinary system
rapidly came to occupy a fundamental position in the Polish Jewish

---

[1] It should be noted that representative assemblies of the communities were not confined
to Poland. We find them all over the Jewish world—in Spain, France, Germany, Italy,
even England. It was nevertheless only in eastern Europe that they became a permanent
feature.

educational system. To study the plain text was considered elementary, and only a scholar who had proved his mettle in the intricacies of *pilpul* now counted for anything. The method was futile, wasteful, and from certain points of view even pernicious. But the minds of those trained in it became preternaturally sharpened; and, as the process went on, generation after generation, it produced in Polish Jewry a standard of intelligence, a mental adaptability, and a degree of acumen which has perhaps known no parallel.

The method was perfected by Shalom Shakhna (1500-1559) of Lublin, one of the Chief Rabbis appointed over the communities of Little Poland in 1541. His son-in-law, Moses Isserles of Cracow (1520-1572), was regarded as one of the outstanding Talmudists of his day, questions being addressed to him from every corner of the Jewish world. At the meetings of the Council of the Four Lands he was one of the most respected figures, while (unusual amongst Polish Jews of his generation, who regarded Rabbinic studies as the be-all and end-all of existence) he dabbled mildly in philosophical studies. It was his annotations upon Joseph Caro's *Shulhan Arukh* which adapted that compendium of Jewish practice for the use of northern Jewry.

An opposite tendency was represented by his contemporary and friend, Solomon Luria of Brest-Litovsk and subsequently of Ostrog (1510-1573). A descendant (according to legend) of Rashi, he desired to revive the intellectual standards and fashions which had prevailed in his great ancestor's day. No man opposed more vigorously the new-fangled systems of study: he sturdily objected to the codifications of Jewish law which had recently established themselves; and he reverted to the fountain-head of tradition, the Talmud, the obscurities of which he endeavoured to elucidate in his classical *Sea of Solomon*. In the subsequent generation, scholars like Mordecai Jaffe (d. 1612), Joshua Falk (d. 1614), Samuel Edels (d. 1631), and Joel Sirkes (d. 1640), continued to maintain the tradition of scholarship; and Poland became known as the home of the Talmud, just as Safed was that of the Zohar.

But the outstanding feature of Polish Jewish scholarship was not the ability of its foremost exponents, who perhaps fell below the standard of the French or of the Spanish schools, so much as the level of excellence attained by the average pupil. Nowhere else was higher education so widely diffused or brought to such a pitch of perfection. The words of a contemporary are more eloquent than any modern description can be:

'That which is notorious needs no proof: viz., that in all the far-flung settlements of Israel, there was nowhere so much *Torah* as in the land of Poland. In every congregation there were established *Yeshiboth* (Talmudical academies). The head of the *Yeshibah* was given an ample salary, so that he could maintain the institution without any forethought, and that his learning might be his solitary occupation. Throughout the year, the head of the *Yeshibah* did not leave his house, excepting to go from the house of study to the house of prayer. He sat continually, day and night, and studied the Law. Every congregation maintained young scholars, and made them a regular allowance week by week, that they might study with the head of the *Yeshibah*; and every young scholar had at least two boys who studied with him. Thus he had occasion to discourse by word of mouth upon the *Gemara*, with the commentaries of Rashi and the *Tosaphoth*, and he became accustomed to expound thereon. These boys similarly received their food either from the benevolent fund, or else from the food charity. If there were a congregation of fifty householders, they would support at least thirty young scholars with their boys: for every householder gave hospitality to one of the young scholars with his two boys. . . . In the whole of the kingdoms of Poland, there was hardly a single house in which they did not study the *Torah*. Either the householder himself was the scholar, or else his son, or his son-in-law studied perpetually; or, at least, he gave hospitality to some young student. Frequently, one would find all these in one house . . . .'[1]

This was the ideal in Polish Jewry in the sixteenth and seventeenth centuries; and it resulted in the training of an educated laity the like of which even the Jewish world had perhaps never before seen.

[1] Nathan Hanover, *Yeven Mezullah* (Venice, 1653), *ad fin.*

102. A Street in the Roman Ghetto

103. POLISH JEWISH TYPES

104. JEWISH ELEMENTARY SCHOOL
German woodcut. 16th Century

105. The Wooden Synagogue at Nasielsk (Poland), 1692
Drawing by M. Bersohn

ולשמח בשמחת תורה

106. Rejoicing in the Law
Painting on a Flag

107. MEDIEVAL SYNAGOGUES AT PRAGUE
Exterior. Engraving by Würbs

108. JEWISH CEMETERY AT PRAGUE

Chapter XXV

LIFE IN THE GHETTO

———————•———————

I

The canon of the Third Lateran Council of 1179, which forbade Jews and Christians to dwell together, was enforced at first only sporadically. In many cities the Jews continued to live where they pleased, and non-Jews had little compunction in having houses in the middle of the 'Jewry'. The places where there existed a formal Jewish quarter, enforced by law and rigidly shut off from the rest of the city, were in a minority. Least of all was the regulation obeyed in Italy, under the eye of the Popes, and with their actual example (so different from their precept) at hand for all to copy. In 1516, however, the Venetian Republic ordered the segregation of the Jews of the city in a special quarter, formerly known as the *Getto* [*Ghetto*] *Nuovo*, or New Foundry. A little later the *Getto Vecchio*, or Old Foundry, was added. Hence the term *Ghetto* spread throughout Italy, where the Jewish quarters compulsorily established after the middle of the sixteenth century became known officially by this name. In the south of France the parallel institution was known as the *carrière des juifs*; in Germany and the adjacent territories as the *Judengasse* or *Judenstadt*. Despite the difference in nomenclature, the system was everywhere similar; and it is worth the pains to examine, in greater detail, this typical setting of European Jewish life and the conditions to which it gave rise.[1]

It must not be imagined that the institution appeared to those who suffered from it in so harsh a light as it does to us. In most cases they fought fiercely against its establishment. But it soon became apparent that the Ghetto walls, though intended to keep the victims in, were no less useful in keeping their enemies out. It is significant that the

[1] In Poland, a regularly constituted Ghetto was to be found in only a few of the most important places; the forerunner being Cracow, where one was instituted, after a fire had destroyed much of the city, in 1494: it remained as late as 1868.

gates were furnished in many cases with bolts on the inner side for use in emergency. Moreover, with an insight rare in the oppressed, the Jew realised that segregation, however humiliating it might be, tended to be a powerful preservative of solidarity and culture. Thus we find the paradox that, at certain places in Italy, an annual feast-day was instituted, and long observed, to celebrate the establishment of the Ghetto.

The entrance would be through a low archway, provided with massive doors, and under the custody of Christian gate-keepers paid at the expense of their victims. In larger cities there was a second gateway, similarly guarded, at the far end; but (though this provision was occasionally neglected) it was expressly forbidden for there to be more than two. After nightfall it was considered a serious crime for any Jew to be found outside the Ghetto, or any Christian within it. The Ghetto gates were similarly kept closed, and its inhabitants utterly segregated on all major solemnities of the Christian year until the recital of Mass.

The hardship was not so great as might be imagined. True, in some places, the Jewish quarter consisted of no more than a single narrow lane or courtyard. In many cases, however,—in Rome, Venice, Lublin, or Prague—a whole labyrinth of streets and alleys was to be found, constituting a real town within a town. The street nomenclature within these ancient quarters still gives testimony to the nature of the life which once pulsated within them, as essentially Jewish as the inhabitants themselves. In Frankfort each house had its own sign, from which the families living in it often took their surnames; and the Rothschilds, the Adlers, and the Schiffs have made familiar, throughout western civilisation, patronymics derived from the sign of the Red Shield, and the Eagle, and the Ship, in that famous Judengasse.

One obvious difference would immediately strike the visitor—the great height of the houses. The extent of the Ghetto was rarely increased, and the only expedient to accommodate an expanding population was the same as that adopted centuries later, under the most modern circumstances, in America. Instead of the lateral expansion forbidden them, the Jews sought relief in a vertical direction, by the addition of storey upon storey to the already rickety buildings. From a distance, indeed, it seemed sometimes as though the Jewish quarter, towering high above the city, was actually constructed on rising ground. But the constructions were often more audacious than solid; and it not infrequently happened that they collapsed under some unusual strain, converting the celebration of a marriage or a betrothal into an occasion for general mourning. Similarly, outbreaks of fire were peculiarly dangerous in the Ghetto, the whole area being sometimes reduced to ashes before help could be brought from outside; and Frankfort, Nikolsburg, and Verona long remembered conflagrations which were in their way no less disastrous, though on a smaller scale, than the Great Fire of London itself.

The overcrowding led to another important development. The Jew, prohibited by law from owning real estate, was unable to purchase his house, even in the Ghetto, outright. There was thus no check upon the rapacity of the Gentile landlord, and no security for the tenant, who could be ejected summarily if a higher rental were offered. The solution of this difficulty was found in an adaptation of the ancient Jewish law of *Hazakah*, or proprietary right. This established, under the most severe social and religious sanctions, a sort of tenant-right in favour of the actual occupant, which secured him against overbidding on the one hand, and hence against exploitation on the other. Nobody was permitted, under any circumstances, to bring about the expropriation of the lessee, or to offer a higher rental than that actually paid. Occupation thus became almost equivalent to proprietorship. The property-right could be disposed of by gift or by purchase, devolved by heredity from father to son, and was frequently included in the dowry of a daughter; but, as long as the rent was paid, tenure was safe. This *jus gazaga* (as, in a curious hybrid form, it was termed in Italy) was recognised, in many cases, even by the civil authorities. It is a striking instance of the innate adaptability of the Jewish law to the most diverse circumstances, as well as a remarkable anticipation of the expedient resorted to in urban centres in our own day.

II

The Ghetto walls were not considered in themselves sufficient to prevent the contamination of the faithful by the leaven of Jewish unbelief. There was in addition the Jewish badge, first imposed by the Lateran Council of 1215, but consistently enforced only from the sixteenth century. In Italy, at this period, it generally took the form of a hat of distinctive colour. Originally, it was red, as it continued to be in some places to the end. But (so we are informed by Evelyn) one day a myopic Cardinal in Rome took a red-hatted Jew for a fellow-Prince of the Church, and greeted him as such. To prevent a repetition of this scandal, the distinctive hue was from that day changed, as far as the Papal States were concerned, to yellow.[1] In Germany, the badge retained the primitive form of a yellow circle, which had to be affixed to the outer garment above the heart. The heaviest penalties were enforced against those who dared to stir abroad from the Ghetto without their distinctive mark: sometimes, indeed, it had to be worn even within the gloomy precincts. Only in the case of those who were setting out on the perils of a long journey were the regulations relaxed. We know what a wave of lamentation and of protest was originally aroused by this supreme indignity, which put Jews on the same footing as prostitutes, and how sedulously individuals exerted themselves to be released from its provisions. But, ultimately, it appears to have become a point of pride; and the ultra-conservative continued to wear it, as the distinctive Jewish garb, even when its legal enforcement had fallen into desuetude.

Frequently, the badge of shame was the Jew's only touch of colour. Not that he was averse from gaudy and even extravagant clothing. He was prone, indeed, to err in the reverse direction, especially where his women-folk were concerned. Since this trait was considered a direct incentive to Gentile cupidity, if not enmity, there was enacted in almost every place a whole series of sumptuary laws, which regulated the costume of the Jews from headwear down to shoe-buckles, and limited above all the amount of jewellery which might be worn. Similar restrictions governed private festivities (such as those which took place in honour of a marriage, a circumcision, or a betrothal), stipulating even the sort of sweetmeats which might be handed round, the number of the guests, the nature of the various courses, and even the gifts which might be presented by the bridegroom to his bride.

There was hardly any limit to the tale of indignities to which the Jew was subjected in the Ghetto Age. Many famous communities—such as that of Venice—existed down to the eighteenth century on a precarious tenure under an agreement lasting for only a short period of years, continually modified and sometimes not renewed. Each year the representatives of the historic community of Rome had to pay homage to the Pope by the presentation of a Scroll of the Law, which the Vicar of God would return contemptuously over his left shoulder,

---

[1] It must be recorded, reluctantly, that this story definitely comes into the category of those which are *ben trovati* rather than *veri*, as the distinctive badge of the Jews in Rome was always yellow.

with a derogatory remark. Contributions were exacted for the up-keep of the House of Catechumens, to which their children might be snatched away for baptism at any moment, under the flimsiest pretext: the reported wish of a renegade relative, or a mock ceremony per-formed with ditch water by a superstitious nurse or a drunken ruffian, From the seventeenth century, outrages of this sort became more and more common, owing to the spread of the superstition that eternal felicity would be assured to any person who secured the baptism of a single Jew. Small wonder that Jews were forbidden under severest penalties from approaching the House, lest they should tamper with the newly imposed faith of the inmates. Sometimes, children yet un-born were 'claimed' for Christianity, and pregnant mothers dragged from their homes so that their offspring might emerge into an uncon-taminated environment; or else new-born babies would be seized from their arms and baptised forthwith.

To prevent any semblance of authority, the Jew was forbidden to ride in a carriage, or to employ a Christian servant, or even have some kindly neighbour perform for him the service of kindling a fire upon the Sabbath day. A love-affair (or more sordid connection) between a Jew and a Christian was regarded as a most serious offence, punishable by flogging, the galleys, or worse. The veriest urchin in the Imperial City of Frankfort or the Papal sub-capital of Avignon expected every Jew to get out of the way respectfully when he approached and bade him look to his manners.

Throughout Germany Jews, like cattle, had to pay a special toll, or *Leibzoll*, when they crossed the frontiers of the innumerable petty states, or entered any city. They could be forced to present a set of dice, or an equivalent monetary gift, at every customs-house in expia-tion of the casting of lots for Jesus' clothing at the time of the Passion. From place after place they were excluded, or admitted only during the day. When they appeared in the law-courts, the oath had to be taken *more judaico*, according to a special, degrading formula, and to the accompaniment of an obnoxious ceremonial. War was even waged upon their books, which were confiscated, censored, or burned with-out compunction. In a large part of Italy, indeed, the possession of the Talmud was a criminal offence; and early specimens of Hebrew printing are frequently disfigured by unsightly expurgations made by some friar better endowed with zeal than with a sense of proportion.

Throughout Eastertide, from Holy Thursday onwards, the gates of the Ghetto were kept rigorously closed, and no Jew dared to shew his face in the streets. Each year, at the Carnival season, gorged Jews, stripped almost naked, had to run a race down the Corso at Rome for the delight of the populace—a privilege shared with the women of the town. At the slightest pretext, the race was declared null, and had to be repeated on another day. This supreme indignity was abolished only in 1668, though a special tribute to compensate for it continued to be paid amid the jeers of the spectators for nearly two hundred years after. Worst of all, in accordance with Papal Bulls of 1279, 1577 and 1584, the Jews were forced at regular intervals to attend conversionist sermons, at which their ears were examined lest they should have been plugged with cotton-wool, and officials armed with canes effectively prevented the obvious expedient of slumber.

It was Germany which, combining ruthless logic with fiendish ingenuity, brought the repression implicit in the Ghetto system to its climax. Up to a certain point, Jews might be useful to the city or state; but, beyond this, their presence was superfluous, and hence resented. Official licence of residence was generally given for a specified number of households, which might not be exceeded. By the inevitable process of Nature, the population tended to grow. Births could not be controlled by any legal enactment. But weddings could, and the number of families kept down by this means. In consequence, rigorous control was established in many places over Jewish marriages. Only the eldest child of the family was allowed to take himself a wife and to build up his own home; or else marriage permits were issued in strict ratio to the number of deaths. In any case, no Jew was allowed to marry without official licence. Thus, the most sacred and fundamental human right was denied to that section of the human race which perhaps valued it most. South of the Alps, this infamous system never applied; but, to the north, it retained its force, in many parts, long after the Ghetto had been abolished.

The liberal professions were closed to the Jews (though, in the happy island of Corfu, they were permitted to engage in law). So was almost every other occupation and handicraft. They were not allowed to sell new commodities of any sort; though they were grudgingly permitted to deal in second-hand wares, this becoming a typical occupation down to our own days. To enter the textile or any other industry was to invite protest from rivals, generally followed by suppression by the government. It was only in tailoring that they were generally permitted to engage without interference, though they were not allowed to sell their wares direct to the consumer. It is not surprising, under the circumstances, that they had recourse to ingenious subterfuges—such as introducing an insignificant tear into a new article of clothing, so as to render it technically second-hand. Not being allowed to open shops outside their own quarter, they were driven into peddling, which, in time, they almost came to monopolise. The Jewish itinerant huckster, pack on back, was a feature in the rural scene, by the eighteenth century, all over Europe.

It was not possible to exclude the Jews, with their natural acumen and their widespread foreign connections, from trade in jewellery and precious stones. Money-lending and pawnbroking, like dealing in second-hand commodities, were imposed on them from above. In many Italian cities especially (Venice was an outstanding example), they were under the legal obligation to maintain establishments for this purpose, for the benefit of the poor of the city, as an essential condition of the tolerance which they received.

In those places where the restrictions were less strenuously enforced, economic life was organised much as it was amongst the Gentile population. From early times, for example, there were at Prague four Jewish gilds—those of the butchers, goldsmiths, tailors, and shoemakers. In the larger cities of Poland (as, indeed, had been the case in ancient Alexandria or Jerusalem) each gild or occupation had its own synagogue; and the visitor to Lublin could once inspect those formerly maintained by the coppersmiths, tailors, clerks, and porters.

Notwithstanding all restrictions, the profession of medicine continued to be followed, as in all former and subsequent ages, with especial enthusiasm. Frequently it was combined with the Rabbinate: indeed, it was customary for young men to combine their medical studies in the University of Padua with attendance at the famous Talmudical academy of that city. Thither flowed needy students, athirst for knowledge, from the *Yeshiboth* of Poland and elsewhere—to end, in some cases, as body-physician to the Grand Vizier at Constantinople. The Jewish doctor was still forbidden to practise his art on the person of true believers. Nevertheless, in time of emergency the eye of faith was sometimes dimmed. Crowned heads and prelates continued to consult their convenience, rather than canon law, when they appointed their medical attendants; and the yellow hat of the Hebrew practitioner was not too closely scanned as he entered the house of some dying patrician, or was hurriedly escorted over the threshold of the Vatican itself.

III

The Ghetto constituted in the fullest sense an *imperium in imperio*. It was only in his collective capacity that the Jew had any connection with the government, which barely recognised his existence as an individual. The community (*Judengemeinschaft, università degli ebrei*) represented the inhabitants of the Ghetto as a body; its duly appointed delegates (*massari, baylons,* or *Parnassim,* as they were variously called) being entitled to act for it juridically and politically. It must not be imagined that the organisation was democratic. At its head, by the side of the wardens, stood a small administrative council. This was generally elected by a larger body, comprising the major contributors to communal taxation, who formed a secondary council for the decision of important business. The proletariat, under this system, had no voice whatsoever in the internal regulation of communal affairs. In some conservative areas, such as the south of France, the community (other than paupers) was divided into three sections according to wealth, each having an equal voice in the administration: a system which obviously gave disproportionate influence to the moneyed classes.

Upon the communal government, as thus constituted, devolved the duty of raising the heavy taxation which was exacted by the government year by year from the whole body of the Jews. Added to this were the internal expenses of the community as a whole—the maintenance of the synagogue, the relief of the poor, the upkeep of the burial-ground, and the payment of the various officials. The latter included not merely the cantor, the beadle, and the Rabbi (at last become a salaried official), but also such functionaries as the secretary, the *Schulklopfer* who roused the faithful for service, the *shochet* or slaughterer, the postman, and the scavenger. In addition, there had to be found the salary of the gate-keepers of the Ghetto, in whose appointment the Jews had no voice, and with whose services they could have dispensed.

The heavy sums necessary for all these expenses were raised by a graduated tax on capital or on income—sometimes on both. In a narrow circle, in which each man was not only the other's neighbour but also his business competitor, strict enquiry was an obvious impossibility; and, in the main, the assessment was left to the individual conscience. The conditions governing the system, which differed greatly from land to land and from city to city, were frequently printed (especially in Italy) for the better guidance of the contributors. A special sermon, stressing the needs of the community and the obloquy of evasion, was in some places prescribed as an additional encouragement. The final sanction in case of disobedience or fraudulence was excommunication. Under the circumstances of Ghetto life, this spiritual and social penalty held fears greater than any physical punishment could have done, and was seldom ineffective. Nevertheless it was sometimes found impossible to raise the disproportionately heavy sums imposed; and in the course of the eighteenth century more than one community, including that of Rome itself, was reduced to bankruptcy.

Largely in consequence of its fiscal autonomy, the governing body of the community became omnipotent within the walls of the Ghetto. To it all edicts were entrusted for execution; on it devolved the maintenance of order and responsibility for the good conduct of individuals. On the other hand, it was empowered to adjudicate in matters of dispute; and it was in a position to suppress opposition, to appeal to the government to get its wishes carried out, or to secure the exclusion of unwelcome strangers. It regulated, in short, the whole of Ghetto life, occasionally overriding the Rabbi himself. In Prague the Jewish court, known as the *Meisterschaftsgericht*, was especially well organised, enjoying the fullest authority; and it even had its own prison to enforce its sentences and punish the recalcitrant. Prague, too, had its own Jewish town-hall, or *Rathaus*, erected by the famous philanthropist, Mordecai Meisel, at the beginning of the seventeenth century; with its clock-tower and the famous clock, the dial of which bore Hebrew instead of Roman lettering. In this, the Bohemian capital was exceptional. But most large Ghettos had their communal offices, their bathing establishments, their hospitals, and their inns— all, in fact, that a self-contained township could require.

IV

The centre of the Ghetto life was, of course, the synagogue. Externally, this was necessarily plain and unpretentious to a degree. Not only was there the constant fear of exciting Gentile cupidity, but even as late as the eighteenth century interference could be expected if the Jewish place of worship were enlarged beyond its earlier limits, or exceeded neighbouring churches in height. In the Papal States it

u

was forbidden to have more than one synagogue in each town—a provision which the community of Rome ingeniously evaded by constructing five under one roof to accommodate its various traditional 'rites'—Roman, Sicilian, Castilian, and the rest. Universally the synagogue was known as the 'school'—*schul* in Germany, *scuola* in Italy, *escolo* in the south of France. As a matter of fact, this was originally applied to the Jewish *community* (much as we speak of a 'school' of porpoises, or of the 'Saxon School' at Rome in the Dark Ages), being used in reference to the *building* only at a later date. The application is nevertheless symptomatic of the rôle of the synagogue in Jewish life as a centre, not only of worship, but also of study.

Though the religious tradition was everywhere fundamentally the same, each community in the course of time developed its own peculiarities. Many a place had its special fast, in commemoration of some local disaster; or its special *Purim* (with its record, sometimes, written in imitation of the Biblical book of Esther) to record the deliverance of the community from a modern Haman. Thus, at Frankfort, they celebrated year by year the anniversary of the fall of the demagogue, Vincent Fettmilch, who drove them out of the town after a brutal attack in 1616; and at Padua they kept up till recently the *Purim del Fuoco* in thankfulness at their escape from a conflagration in 1795.

By the side of the synagogue—before it, almost, in the consideration in which it was held—came the school itself. This was always given pride of place in the Jewish scheme of life; and, in this respect, the Jew of the Ghetto period did not fall short of the ideals of his ancestors. The smallest centre had its educational institutions, frequently under the charge of some pious association formed for the express purpose. A community of less than a thousand souls would maintain a Free School which might serve as a model for to-day. All expenses were defrayed by voluntary contributions, nothing being expected from the parents. The elements of the vernacular were taught, as well as of Hebrew. The number of teachers, and the size of the classes, were carefully regulated. Most remarkable of all, the poorer pupils received free meals, and there was a distribution of boots and clothing each year at the beginning of the winter. At some places there were special schools for girls. The universality of education is barely surpassed in any country of the Western World even at the present time.

Besides education, no conceivable species of well-doing escaped the scope of one or the other of the many pious fraternities which abounded in the Ghetto, for the Jewish conception of religion was broad enough to embrace almost every sphere of social life. There were numbers of associations with purely spiritual objects—fasting and confession and midnight prayer, in order to avert the Divine wrath and to hasten the coming of the Redeemer. Alongside these were others for study and adult education and charitable works. There was an association to help women in child-bed, and an association to admit male babies into the Covenant of Abraham. Brides were dowered by one fraternity, and prisoners solaced by another. In the great maritime ports, such as Venice, there were special bodies which saw to the ransoming of Jewish travellers captured and sold into slavery by the Knights of Malta or the Barbary Corsairs. At every stage of want or necessity the unfortunate could confidently expect succour from their neighbours, in one capacity or another. When a man fell ill, the fraternity for visiting the sick came to comfort him: when he died, one fraternity looked after the mourners, while another saw to his burial. Only in the Papal States were these activities curtailed, since there it was forbidden to escort the dead to their last resting-place with the customary dirges, or to erect any sort of memorial over their graves.

V

Yet these manifold religious and communal activities did not monopolise the Ghetto scene. Within that little world there was a Jewish society, with its own life, its own interests, its own diversions. There were the same petty enmities and the same jealousies to be found as in any other human circle: the same romances, the same comedies, the same tragedies of existence. Even a species of foreign intercourse was afforded by the hostelry which existed for the entertainment of strangers; though the general spirit of hospitality which was invariable, particularly when some wandering scholar appeared, must have jeopardised its prosperity.

In many ways the life was as characteristically Italian, or German, or French, as that of the great world outside. The artistic spirit of the country permeated the Ghetto to a marked degree. The synagogues were constructed by the most eminent architects of their day, and, notwithstanding their unpretentious exteriors, no pains were spared to make them places of aesthetic inspiration. Objects of ceremonial

use were elaborately chased—not always by Jewish artists. The bro-
cades hung before the ark and the mantles for the Scrolls of the Law,
embroidered by the matrons in the long winter evenings, were of the
finest. The most skilful silversmiths were employed to manufacture
the trappings for the scrolls and the lamps which swung from the roof.
The Sabbath lamp which was kindled in every home on Friday evening
was often of precious metal. The craft of the illuminator was kept
alive in the Ghetto long after it had begun to decay in the outside
world. The *Haggadah* liturgy for the eve of Passover was written and
illustrated by hand centuries after the invention of printing; and its
tradition was continued in woodcuts and copperplate engravings for
those who could not afford greater luxury. The scroll of Esther was
similarly favoured, and the artistic abilities of the Ghetto were
lavished upon representations of the ten sons of Haman strung up on
the gallows, in illustration of the enthralling story. In Italy, especially,
the marriage contract was richly illuminated—sometimes with an
excess of ornament.

It was characteristic of the innate Jewish conservatism that in
many countries (Poland and Turkey are outstanding examples) the
language spoken by the Jews amongst themselves was a foreign one,
introduced by the original refugees from Germany on the one hand,
or from Spain on the other. Even where the vernacular was in everyday use, the admixture of tongues inevitable among Jews naturally
resulted in borrowing occasional words in common parlance from one
language or another, especially from Hebrew. To this were added, in
consequence of close inbreeding, certain peculiarities of pronunciation and expression. The result was the creation of a number of characteristic Jewish dialects. In addition to the familiar Judaeo-German
and Judaeo-Spanish, there were also Judaeo-Italian, and, in the south
of France, Judaeo-Provençal. All these were frequently (in the first
two cases, almost invariably) written, and even printed, in Hebrew
characters. In the memoirs of an educated German Jewess of the
seventeenth century, one finds an admixture of nearly thirty per cent
pure Hebrew; and the proportion is not exceptionally high. The same
hybrid dialect would be employed, with an even higher smattering of
the holy tongue, in recording communal business and drawing up new
regulations. There was a vast popular literature—ballads, translations,
homilies, legal handbooks—for the women and others whose attainments were unequal to the full sublimities of traditional lore.

Social life was ample. The Purim season, each year, saw buffoonery and masquerades, and sometimes a fair. The Ghetto of Prague, on this occasion, would be thronged with girls in festive garb, who were entertained in whatever house they entered. Even the students allowed themselves some relaxation, and elected a Lord of Misrule, who flouted the Rabbi himself. The elaboration of the story of Esther and Mordecai gave rise to what was known in northern Europe as the *Purimspiel*, developing into a rudimentary drama. Itinerant play-actors went from place to place giving representations of this, or of scenes from the lives of the Patriarchs. Weddings and banquets were enlivened by professional jesters (*Schalksnarren*), the broadness of whose witticisms sometimes scandalised devout opinion. There were musical societies, which did not always concentrate their attention on synagogal harmony. Births, marriages, and other notable occasions would be saluted in a flood of verses. The pageants and processions which the Jews arranged in celebration of royal visits and similar events were famous. The wealthy ladies of the Ghetto had their salons, and the wealthy householders their private courses of study, to which they invited their friends. Dancing, though eyed askance by the more pious elements, was regarded on the more festive occasions of the religious year as a meritorious duty; and in Italy the teaching of that art was long regarded as one of the duties of a Hebrew tutor, and a Jewish speciality. Jewish instrumentalists, whose services were called upon more especially on the occasion of weddings, enjoyed no small fame in the outside world.

The Ghetto had its human side. It harboured sinners as well as saints—some of them sufficiently picturesque to arrest attention. Its members were always generous; but, if the truth be told, they were not invariably honest. Domestic life was pure, but the eternal triangle was not entirely absent from the human scene. Extravagance was sometimes excessive, and gambling so rife as to call for disciplinary intervention. The Jews, in fact, were men endowed with human passions as well as with superhuman endurance. Even the Rabbis were not always above criticism—as witness the ineffable, entrancing Leone da Modena of Venice (1571-1648)—that infant prodigy who developed into a hoary prodigal: jack of twenty-six trades, though master of none; polemist against his own convictions, and practiser against his own precept; a fortune-hunter, mildly addicted to alchemy, who lost more than one small competence at gambling, repeatedly condemned the vice, but was never able to tear himself away from it; withal a scholar of unusual breadth, who devoted himself to the interpretation of Judaism to the Christian world, wrote prolifically both in Hebrew and Italian, composed a handbook of Jewish practice for the information of James I of England, and preached so eloquently as to attract priests, patricians, and even princes of the blood, to hear his sermons.

VI

The Ghetto was thus a microcosm which faithfully reflected every aspect of the outside world, while giving it a pronounced Jewish tone. Recent observers have attempted to vindicate the institution, pointing to all that it achieved for the development and preservation of essential Jewish standards of life. Some inveterate lauders of that which is past profess even to look back on it with regret, as a lost bulwark against assimilation. To a certain extent this is true. Yet there is another side to the question. One tends to judge the Ghetto too much from its formative period, when the tradition of an ampler and freer life was still strong, and before the policy of exclusion had become absolutely effective. In its later stages, life was more restricted, more mono-tonous, and more dreary. Persons of the highest intellectual ability were condemned to pass the whole of their lives in self-contained communities, seldom numbering more than a couple of thousand souls all told, and cut off so far as was humanly possible from all inter-course with the outside world. One must imagine such communities, too, as living under the worst possible physical conditions—huddled up, indescribably overcrowded, in insalubrious quarters in the heart of great cities, egress from which (excepting between sunrise and sunset) was forbidden by law.

The results were what might have been imagined. The circle of human interests was intolerably confined. Life became indescribably petty. There was a superlative degree of inbreeding, physical, social, and intellectual. Keen intelligences were wasted by dealing with trivial themes. That which was meant for mankind was confined to a single narrow street. The intellectual fecundity which can result only from the constant fertilisation and cross-fertilisation of human intercourse became impossible. By the time that the Ghetto had been in existence for a couple of centuries, it was possible to see the result. Physically, the Jew had degenerated. He had lost inches off his stature; he had acquired a perpetual stoop; he had become timorous and in many cases neurotic. Degrading occupations, originally imposed by law—such as money-lending and dealing in old clothes—became a second nature, hard to throw off. His sense of solidarity with his fellow-Jews had become fantastically exaggerated, and was accompanied in many cases by a perpetual sense of grievance against the Gentiles responsible for his lot. As a counterpoise to the attempt of the authorities (and indeed of the whole world) to repress him, the Jew was driven to evasion; and sharp practices, at one time condonable, retained their hold in certain unhappy instances after their justification had passed.

The economic consequences were no less deplorable. Pauperisation rapidly increased, and the systematic blocking of opportunity made recovery almost impossible. The well-to-do emigrated to places where life was more ample, leaving behind them as a burden on their fellows those least qualified to fight the battle of existence. During the course of the eighteenth century, beggars became a social menace. In Germany they are reckoned to have numbered one-tenth of the whole population; while in certain places in Italy one person out of three was in receipt of public relief in one form or another.

Even from the more specifically Jewish point of view, the Jew was in a way degenerating. In the end he shewed signs of losing his sense of proportion. Every item in the traditional scheme of life was now sacrosanct, and had attained like importance in his eyes. The most trivial tradition was of equal weight with the most fundamental ethical teaching. Superstitions were on the increase, and in some cases acquired semi-religious sanction. Simultaneously, Hebrew scholarship was on the downward grade. The study of the ancient texts became more and more mechanical, so that the production of outstanding scholars even in the purely Rabbinic field was increasingly uncommon. After two centuries of Ghetto life, the institution appeared to be doing its work, and the repression of the Jew—physical, intellectual and moral—was far advanced.

109. LEONE DA MODENA (1571-1648)
From Riti Ebraici 1637

Chapter XXVI

THE DAWN OF LIBERTY

———————•———————

I

The heroic period of European history which was ushered in by the Renaissance saw the Jew, then, at a universal disadvantage. In western Europe he was systematically degraded, excluded from every honourable walk of life, and shut up in his Ghetto. In eastern Europe and Asia, under Polish and Turkish rule, his condition was somewhat happier. Here, conversely, he was a stranger in a strange land, representing an alien culture, speaking an alien language, and treated at the best as a privileged foreigner.

There was one part only of Europe (indeed, of the whole world, if we except the orphan colonies of India and China) where persons of Jewish stock were on a position of equality with the general population. This was the Iberian Peninsula. Since the close of the fifteenth century, the open practice of Judaism, in Spain and Portugal, had been an offence punishable by death. The Inquisition had been kept busy, endeavouring to root out this most unspeakable of crimes. It had become the wealthiest and most influential corporation in the whole country, capable of overriding the king himself. At frequent intervals it staged Acts of Faith, or *autos da fé*, which counted amongst the most magnificent spectacles which contemporary Spain could shew. In these, before the eyes of thousands who had streamed in from the surrounding countryside, condign punishment would be inflicted upon harmless individuals whose loyalty to the Holy Catholic Faith was suspect. Those who professed penitence would generally be stripped of their property and condemned to imprisonment, transportation, or the galleys. The minority who refused to confess their crime, or else gloried in it, would be burned alive. Nobles, princes, and ruling monarchs would frequently grace by their presence these spectacles, which, with an exaggeration of irony, were occasionally arranged in honour of a royal marriage, or in celebration of the birth of an heir to the throne.

110. WEDDING IN A GERMAN GHETTO

From J. C. G. Bodenschatz, Kirkliche Verfassung der heutigen Juden, 1748

OH. MENASSEH BEN ISRAEL.

A todos os Senhores de sua naçaõ Hebrea habitantes na Assia y Europa , principalmente ás Sinagogas Santas de Italia e Holsacia. S. P. D.

Ousa notoria hè , a todos os Senhores de nossa naçaõ, quanto de muytos dias a esta parte ey trabalhado, pretendendo se nos conceda na florentissima Republica de Inglaterra , publi- co exercicio de nossa religiaõ, movido naõ so do merito da causa, mas por varias cartas de pessoas virtuosissimas e prudentes. Iuntamente como avendo estado por duas vezes posto a caminho, fuy dos meus, por certas rezóns politicas, persua- dido dilatasse por entonces a jornada. Agora pois fasso saber a todos, como naõ bem convalecido aynda de diuturna doença , movido so de Zelo, e amor dos meus, despindome de todos os meus particulares inte- resses, como tenho significado, me parto oje a esta empreza, que seja para servico del Dio, e nossa vtilidade. E se bem alguns achandose afazenda- dos, e sobre tudo protegidos de clementissimos Principes, e Magistra- dos, naõ fazem muyta estimacaõ deste meu perpetuo cuydado , naõ de menos, conciderando eu o aplauso comum, o bem geral, a aslicaõ dos nossos oje espalhados tanto, q poderiaõ achar asylo e remedio na quella potentissima Republica, sem algũ... de ova; e juntamente ten- do atencaõ, a tantas almas, que dissimulando a religiaõ, viuem em tantas partes de Espanha , e Franca esquecid..., me pareceo naõ dejxar aynda que seja a custa de minhas faculdades, negoceo de tanto mereeimento E suposto que reconheco por cartas, e boas correspondencias, ser oje aquella naçaõ Ingreza, naõ a antiga enemiga nossa, mas mudada a Papistica religiaõ, muy bem affecta a ossa naçaõ como povo aslito, e de quem tem boa esperanca, naõ avendo neste mundo cousa certa, nem segura, suplico a todas as Kehilot Kedosot, q em suas publicas oracoens pessão affectuosamente al Dio, me dè sua graca nos olhos do benignissi- mo e volerosissimo Principe , sua Alteze Senhor PROTECTOR, e nos de seu Prudentissimo conselho, para que nos dem em suas terras liberdade, dónde possamos tambem orar ao Altissimo Senhor por sua prosperidade. Vale.

De Amsterdam a 1 de Setembro 5415

o H. Menasseh ben Israel

III. APPEAL OF MENASSEH BEN ISRAEL FOR PRAYERS FOR THE SUCCESS OF HIS ENGLISH MISSION, 1655
State Archives, Venice

112. MENASSEH BEN ISRAEL (1604-1657)
Etching by Rembrandt, 1636

113. RABBI JACOB SASPORTAS (1610-1698)
Engraving by P. van Gunst

114. BENEDICT DE SPINOZA (1632-1677)
Anonymous Portrait. About 1666. Rijksmuseum, The Hague

In the vast majority of cases the victims were the so-called Marranos—descendants of Jews who, in spite of all dangers, remained faithful in the secrecy of their homes to the tenets and (so far as was possible) to the practices of their old faith. They rested on the Sabbath, and they fasted on the Day of Atonement, and they celebrated the Passover, to the best of their ability. Many were the old customs, trivial perhaps in themselves, which they managed to keep alive, imbuing them in many cases with a disproportionate importance. If the more gloomy side of Jewish observance attained a greater importance in their eyes than the reverse, and they paid more attention to fasts than to feasts, the reason lay in the perils of their state, and in the constant necessity which they felt for contrition.

Possession of Hebrew books, and any knowledge of Hebrew, had become a manifest impossibility. Nevertheless the Marranos managed to retain cognisance of one or two disconnected words and phrases; and they addressed their prayers to 'the great God of Israel, Adonai'. Their prayers were composed in the vernacular—in many cases, in imitation of the traditional models; while, for guidance in practice, they had recourse to the Old Testament, in the current Vulgate version. Much restricted though their knowledge of Judaism was, they continued to adhere with whole-hearted devotion to its fundamental doctrines; and to their unshakable belief in the unity of God they added pathetic confidence in the unity and perpetuity of the Jewish people.

The Inquisition, on its side, continued to circulate lists of signs by which a Judaiser might be detected, and the whole population was enlisted to assist in its sacred work of hounding down the guilty. Thus, some mechanical household practice, or a regard for personal cleanliness, was often enough to cost a person of Jewish blood his life; and the offence of changing his linen on Friday night was sometimes the most important link in a chain of evidence which brought an exemplary householder to the stake. The lavish employment of torture was almost always sufficient to obtain details from any suspect. On the other hand, it must be realised that, according to its lights, the Inquisition was just. It seldom proceeded without good ground; and, once a case was opened, the ultimate objective was to obtain a full confession, coupled with an expression of penitence, which would save its victims from the horrors of eternal torment. The penalties which it imposed were considered more in the light of penance than of punishment: excepting in the case of the obdurate, who were safer removed from a scene where their example and influence might be fatal to others.

As time went on, the work of the Inquisition intensified rather than relaxed. There were ultimately some fifteen tribunals in Spain, and three in Portugal; and each organised *autos da fé*, with Marranos as their principal victims, at frequent intervals. In all, during the three centuries during which the Inquisition was active, it is reckoned to have condemned upwards of 375,000 persons, of whom one-tenth suffered at the stake. By the second half of the sixteenth century it had achieved a fair degree of success in the larger country. Except in the Balearic Islands (where they may still be traced even to-day in the contemned Chuetas) the native Judaisers—the descendants of those who had accepted baptism as a result of the terror of 1391 and the following years—had been all but stamped out. Their place was taken by immigrants and fugitives from Portugal, where conditions had been different and where, in consequence, crypto-Judaism had established itself more strongly. From time to time, the victims would include 'Old' Christians—persons in whose veins no drop of Jewish blood could be traced, who had become attracted to Judaism by reason of the ferocity with which it was persecuted and of the heroism shewn by its adherents. Down to the very last days of the Spanish and Portuguese Inquisitions, at the close of the eighteenth century, crypto-Jews provided a very high proportion of the victims. Thereafter the record becomes blurred and indistinct. However, in our own days, a traveller in the remote hill-country in the north of Portugal was amazed to discover a number of Marrano communities still paying lip-service to Christianity while faithful at heart to Judaism; and one of the most romantic episodes of recent history has been the movement which has sprung up amongst them for re-identification with the people and the creed from which they were so ruthlessly torn away four and a half centuries ago.

Judaism, then, however much it was proscribed, and whatever dangers were inherent in its practice, was a very real force in the Peninsula. It was notorious that a large proportion of those descended from Jews (all of them, without exception, according to some virulent contemporaries) adhered at heart to the faith of their fathers. One or two disabilities were indeed applied to the 'New Christians', as they continued to be called generation after generation. But, by the very nature of their situation, it was impossible to differentiate against them systematically. Accordingly, there was no economic activity, and no stratum of society, which they did not penetrate. They were to be found in every conceivable walk of life, from beggars to statesmen, from playwrights to revenue farmers, from cobblers to explorers. They almost controlled Portuguese commerce. They established banking establishments of European influence and reputation. The faculties of the Universities were crammed with persons of Jewish blood, who were vaunted as the greatest intellectual luminaries of Portugal until the time came to haul them to the stake. Half of the most illustrious physicians of the country were Marranos. Frequently (for security's sake, as it was believed) they entered the Church, in which some of them attained high rank. In the course of a period of only eight years there appeared at public *autos* in Portugal no fewer than forty-four nuns and six beneficed clergy, of whom some were canons.

Thus, while in all the rest of the world the Jew was considered an inferior being, conditions were fundamentally different in Spain and Portugal. No declared Jew was indeed admitted to the country. But there was a vast body of persons suspected to be Jewish at heart, but against whom no definite evidence was forthcoming, who were on terms of general equality with the rest of the population. They spoke the same language. They followed the same occupations. They lived in the same quarter. They dressed in the same fashion. Their way of life was outwardly identical, down to the least detail. They bore the high-sounding names which their ancestors had assumed at baptism. They were in the fullest sense Spaniards, or Portuguese, marked off from the rest of the population only by virtue of their descent and of their secret religious beliefs.

II

Ever since the close of the fifteenth century there had been a constant stream of emigration on the part of New Christians, eager to reach some spot where they might profess their ancestral religion in public. Their objects were notorious, and their expatriation was categorically forbidden by law. Yet evasion was always possible: either by flight, or on the plea of urgent business abroad, or (more characteristically still) on the pretext of pilgrimage to Rome. Accordingly, almost from the moment of the mass-baptisms in Spain, the Mediterranean ports were thronged with Marrano fugitives who had fled in order to return to Judaism. With the Forced Conversion in

Portugal, the tide became increasingly strong. Throughout Turkey and North Africa the existing congregations were reinforced by fresh refugees: often men of learning and deep piety, who had been involved despite themselves in the disaster of 1497. In some places, the Portuguese Marranos arrived in such numbers as to be able to found their own congregations by the side of those already in existence.

Not all left the European environment. Large numbers made their way to Italy, not a single city of which country (according to a contemporary report) was free of their presence. After the Marrano community of Ancona had fallen victim to the reactionary zeal of Pope Paul IV, in 1555,[1] the principal place of refuge was Ferrara, then under the tolerant rule of the Dukes of the House of Este. In 1581, however, the spirit of reaction penetrated hither also. A large number of persons who at one time of their lives had been titular Christians, were thrown into gaol, and three of them sent to Rome for execution. The main stream of migration was henceforth directed, as far as Italy was concerned, to Venice, where the 'Ponentine Nation' (as the newcomers were described, to distinguish them from the Germans and native Italians on the one hand, and the Levantines on the other), soon came to occupy a dominant position in the Ghetto, and in the commercial life of the city as a whole. Smaller colonies were established in Padua, Verona, and elsewhere.

A rôle of greater importance in history was played by that section of the Marranos who turned their steps in a completely different direction. Italian prosperity, as a matter of fact, was on the wane. America had been discovered. The tide of commerce, of navigation, of wealth, and of empire was transferred to the northern seas. The Mediterranean, from being the great highway of the world's trade, had become little more than a backwater. The place of Venice and of Genoa as the emporia of Europe was taken by the seaports of the North Atlantic. The position of Spain and Portugal in world commerce at this time was vital, in view of the fact that both the new continent in the west and the new routes to the treasure houses of the east had been discovered through their efforts—assisted, it may be added, by the enterprise and scientific skill of their Jewish subjects.

Every important mercantile centre of northern Europe contained, therefore, at this time a Spanish and Portuguese trading colony of greater or less importance. Among the commercial classes in the

[1] Above, pp. 268-9.

Peninsula, the New Christians occupied a commanding position. (So far was this the case that, throughout Europe, the terms 'Portuguese' and 'Jew' were at this time regarded as almost synonymous.) Hence it came about that the settlements dotted along the Atlantic seaboard, from the shadow of the Pyrenees to the Baltic, were composed in a very large degree of New Christians—that is, of secret Jews. The ultimate history of these varied. Some faded away or were absorbed in the surrounding population. Others maintained a dual existence for many generations. Others again, who had the good fortune to discover themselves in a more tolerant environment (generally under the rule of one of the vigorous Protestant powers of the North), were able to cut short the intervening period, and to organise themselves without loss of time into open and undisguised Jewish communities.

The most important of these colonies was that in the Low Countries. Since the early years of the sixteenth century, Marrano settlers had made their way in small numbers to Antwerp—the most important seaport in the north of Europe, at this time under Spanish rule. It was here that the House of Mendes had founded its great banking establishment. At intervals the secret community had suffered considerable disturbance on religious grounds, being temporarily broken up more than once. The revolt of the Netherlands put an end to the predominance of Antwerp, and its commercial supremacy was usurped by Amsterdam. This city became henceforth the principal Marrano place of refuge.

An ancient legend, which need not be discounted in all its details, gives a most romantic origin for the Amsterdam community. In the year 1593, we are told, a brother and sister, Manuel Lopez Pereira and Maria Nuñez (whose parents had suffered from the persecutions of the Inquisition), set sail from Portugal with a large party of Marranos, in the hope of finding some haven of security. The vessel was captured on its journey by an English ship, and brought into port. An English noble, fascinated by Maria's rare beauty, solicited her hand. Queen Elizabeth, hearing the story, expressed a desire to see the prisoner. Captivated, like everyone else, by her loveliness, she drove with her about London, and gave orders for the vessel and all its passengers to be set at liberty. In spite of this, Maria would not accept the tempting offer which she had received. 'Leaving all the pomp of England for the sake of Judaism' (as the old record puts it), she pursued her way to Amsterdam with her companions. Here, in 1598, they were joined by her mother and other members of the family.

Later in the same year she married one of her fellow-fugitives. This, as it appears, was the first wedding to take place in the Amsterdam community; and it was celebrated by a stately dance, in which twenty-four cousins of the bridal pair took part.

The activities of these recent arrivals from the Peninsula, titular Christians as they were, could not escape attention for long. It seemed obvious that they were holding Catholic services—at that time forbidden—and perhaps even conspiring against the newly established government. On the Day of Atonement, the size of the gathering compelled closer enquiry. The whole party was arrested and dragged off for examination. They were as yet ignorant of Dutch, and their difficulty in expressing themselves increased the suspicion against them. Fortunately, one of the leaders of the little group (Manuel Rodrigues Vega, *alias* Jacob Tirado, who had recently been circumcised notwithstanding his advanced age) happened to be familiar with Latin, and had the inspiration of explaining himself in that language. He made it clear that the assembly was not one of Papists, but of followers of a religion persecuted by the Inquisition even more ferociously than Protestantism; and he pointed out the great advantages which might accrue to the city if the New Christians of the Peninsula were encouraged to establish themselves in it. His appeal, whether to humanity or to interest, was convincing. The prisoners were released forthwith; the position of the refugees was regularised; and the colony grew with astonishing rapidity, throwing out offshoots to The Hague, Rotterdam, and elsewhere.

Meanwhile, a similar succession of events had been taking place in Hamburg, where Portuguese Marranos were to be found in small numbers from the closing years of the sixteenth century. They remained titular Catholics, and thus doubly aroused the ire of the Protestant population. A petition was accordingly presented to the Senate to expel these strangers from the city. The Lutheran academies at Frankfort and Jena, appealed to for their opinion, recommended that the Jews be received, under certain restrictions, in order that they might be won over to the love of the Gospel. In consequence, in 1612, the Senate formally authorised the Jewish settlement. Minor centres were established in the immediate neighbourhood at Glück-stadt, Altona, and Emden.

The third great centre of commerce in western Europe, and hence of Marrano settlement, was London. A colony of secret Jews which had established itself here under Henry VIII had been broken up with the re-establishment of Roman Catholicism by Mary. Another was formed on the accession of Elizabeth. It had been one of its members, Dr. Hector Nuñes, who gave Walsingham the first news of the arrival of the Great Armada at Lisbon. Another, Roderigo Lopez, was the Queen's physician, before he was involved in the intrigues of the Earl of Essex and hanged at Tyburn on a trumped-up charge of treason (1594). A tiny community existed for a short time also at Bristol. In 1609 the Portuguese merchants in London, who were suspected of Judaising, were expelled from the country, and the venture came to an end. New settlers soon began to arrive to take the place of the old. In 1648, on the fall of the monarchy, an attempt was made to secure universal toleration in the country, but the time was not ripe for it. Nevertheless, by the period of the establishment of the Protectorate, a little colony existed once more in the City, with one or two veritable merchant-princes at its head.

The popular attitude towards them had meanwhile begun to alter. The Puritan mind tended to regard the Jews with favour, as the ancient people of God. The more sanguine hoped, moreover, that the newly purified forms of Christianity would convince them of the truth of the Gospel, where the Church of Rome had so miserably failed. Cromwell himself, on the other hand, had the insight to realise the commercial importance of the Marrano merchants, whose information he had found invaluable in political matters, and whom he thought a useful instrument for fostering English trade.

There was living in Holland at this time a mystically minded Rabbi of Marrano birth, Menasseh ben Israel (1604-1657), whose fecund pen and voluble Latin had won him an unexampled reputation in the Christian world. Prolonged meditation had convinced him that the completion of the Diaspora, by the introduction of the Jews into England, was a necessary preliminary to the great Messianic deliverance to which all humanity looked forward. It was with him that Cromwell opened up conversations. After some time, Menasseh was invited to London to conduct negotiations personally, and a memorable conference of statesmen, lawyers, and theologians was convened at Whitehall at the end of 1655 to discuss the matter in all its aspects. The lawyers pronounced that there was no statute which excluded the Jews from the country. The theological and mercantile interests, on the other hand, were either opposed to their re-admission, or would countenance it only with such restrictions as to rob it of all attraction. By the close of the fifth session, Cromwell was convinced that the outcome would disappoint his expectations and be contrary to the best interests of the country. He therefore dissolved the conference, after a speech of extraordinary vigour, before it came to any definite conclusion.

Well-informed observers now expected that he would make use of his prerogative and assent to the application on his own authority. Month succeeded month, and it became evident that this was not to be the case. Instead of formally authorising the Resettlement of the Jews, he preferred to 'connive' at it: to allow those persons already in the country, or those who cared to follow them, to remain undisturbed, without making any official declaration on the subject. The little group of Marrano merchants in London gave up hope of anything more definite. In the following spring (24th March 1655/6) they presented a further petition to Cromwell, asking simply that they might 'meete at owr said private devotions in owr Particular houses without feere of Molestation', and to establish a cemetery 'in such place out of the cittye as wee shall thinck convenient'.

This was, it seems, granted, though tardily. Meanwhile the property of one of the group, which had been seized on the outbreak of war with Spain, was restored to him in consequence of his plea that he was not a Spaniard but a Jew—a member of the people which was undergoing such suffering at the hands of the Spanish Inquisition. Almost simultaneously, a house was rented for use as a synagogue, and a piece of ground acquired as a cemetery. The London Marranos had thrown off the mask. Their position was indeed still highly irregular. The Resettlement had not been authorised: it had been connived at. It was a typical English compromise—inconsistent, illogical, but unexpectedly satisfactory as a working arrangement. It was thus that the Jews regained their foothold in the land which had set the example in driving them out, three hundred and sixty-five years before.

At the same time, Marrano settlements had been formed in several of the French seaports, notably Bordeaux and Bayonne. The country was Catholic, and officially in sympathy with the policy followed in Spain and Portugal. Declared Jews were, therefore, unable to settle there. Marranos, on the other hand, might immigrate without interference, so long as they continued to call themselves Christians; and there was no over-meticulous supervision of their conduct. Now that the menace of the Inquisition was removed, they began to throw off precaution, and to revert more and more openly to their ancestral

faith and practices. Gradually a properly organised Jewish life began
to grow up, with its academies, its Rabbis, its oligarchic organisation,
its network of charitable and religious institutions. Synagogues were
built, thronged for worship three times each day, and frequently
visited by curious strangers. Scarcely any disguise was kept up. It was
obvious to all the world that these new-comers were Jews. They were
nevertheless not permitted to describe themselves as such. They were
officially designated as 'New Christians'—though it was notorious
what that appellation meant. They had their own Portuguese priests
and confessors (in some cases, perhaps, as little sincere as they were
themselves), who administered the Catholic sacraments to them as a
matter of form. They were married in church, in accordance with
Catholic rites, notwithstanding the fact that the Jewish wedding-
service was performed in all its detail at home. They took their children
to be baptised, though the rite of circumcision was performed upon
the boys by expert practitioners. It was only about 1730 that the transparent formality which had prevailed for two centuries was abandoned
and the New Christians of southern France were quasi-officially
recognised as Jews. The most important child of this strange settlement, in its earlier and more furtive days, was no less a person than
Michel de Montaigne, whose mother was descended from a Jewish
second-hand dealer of Calatayud in Aragon. Closely connected with
these colonies on the Atlantic sea-board were the Marrano communities encouraged by the Grand Dukes of Tuscany in the free ports of
Pisa and Leghorn—virtually the only places in Italy where the Ghetto
system was never introduced, and where the Jew was allowed to
attain the proper stature of a man. Similarly, in the overseas possessions of Holland and England—particularly in the West Indian islands
—a little nexus of smaller communities grew up.

III

It was to these places above all that the tide of Marrano migration
was directed from the beginning of the seventeenth century. Hardly
any rank or calling was left unrepresented. There were scholars, professors, authors, priests, friars, physicians, manufacturers, merchants,
soldiers, poets, statesmen. At one period the cosmographer, the
confessor, and the chronicler to the Crown of Spain, as well as more
than one royal physician, were Judaising simultaneously at one or
another of the Marrano centres abroad. A mere list of the names is

x

dazzling. Most prominent were the physicians like Elijah Montalto, medical attendant on the Queen of France and a doughty polemist for his faith; Zacutus Lusitanus, one of the outstanding authorities of his day; and Roderigo de Castro, creator of gynaecology. In addition, there were classical scholars like Thomas de Pinedo, ex-pupil of the Jesuits; historians like Roderigo Mendes da Silva; playwrights like Antonio Enriquez Gomez, Calderon's rival for the favours of the theatre-going public of Madrid; as well as merchant princes and financiers galore. A number of them were raised to the nobility; while the Spanish and Portuguese sovereigns did not scruple to have themselves represented in the Low Countries or at Hamburg by declared Jews, such as the Barons de Belmonte or successive members of the Nuñez da Costa family, who would have been burned without compunction had they set foot in the Peninsula. In the first native-born generation, there were produced intellectual giants of the calibre of Benedict de Spinoza, who was to have a profound influence on European thought. Little islands of Spanish and Portuguese culture, with their intellectual life hardly less brilliant and no less distinctively Iberian than that of Segovia or Braganza, were scattered all over northern Europe. Poetical academies were founded, at which elegant compositions which would not have disgraced the poetasters of the University of Salamanca were solemnly read and criticised; and a considerable literature—liturgical, polemic, poetic, philosophic, historic, dramatic—was produced, if not in the vernacular of the country, at least in a style and a language familiar to European circles. The members of the Marrano Diaspora were thus, in a very real sense, the first modern Jews.

The importance of these settlements, with their offshoots as far afield as India and America, was extraordinarily significant. In the economic sphere they played a vital part. From the beginning of the seventeenth century they formed a commercial nexus which has, perhaps, no parallel in history except the Hanseatic League of the Middle Ages. They controlled a good part of the commerce of western Europe. They almost monopolised the importation of precious stones from the East Indies and the West. The coral industry was a Jewish, or rather a Marrano, creation. Trade in sugar, tobacco, and similar colonial commodities rested largely in their hands. From the middle of the seventeenth century, Jews of Spanish and Portuguese origin were prominent figures in every important Exchange. They were partly instrumental in the establishment of the great national banks. The transference of the centre of the world's commerce during the course of the seventeenth century from southern to northern Europe is not the least important of the achievements which the Inquisition helped to bring about.

In Jewish life, similarly, the influence of the Marranos was very marked. Those who went to join existing settlements naturally became assimilated in all things to the condition of those whom they found there. They went to live among them in the Ghetto; they were compelled to wear the Jewish badge; they were subjected to every detail of the legislation which differentiated the Jew from the rest of mankind. But the pioneers who came to fresh countries, and founded their own communities, were in a very different position, and could be treated on their own merits. They had been accepted, in the first instance, as foreigners. They could not very well be excluded subsequently because they turned out to be not Papists, but Jews. It would have been preposterous to create a Ghetto in order to segregate persons whose society was sought and whose opinion was valued by the wisest and noblest in the land, or to distinguish by a badge of shame men who were admittedly the leaders of the intellectual and commercial world of their day. Not even fanatics could seriously propose the repression as an inferior being, merely because he had begun to attend synagogue openly, of a scholar who had been the ornament of academic circles at Coimbra or Madrid—especially if he displayed in addition (as many of them did) several quarterings of nobility. To admit him to full citizenship, indeed, was hardly to be thought of. But whereas hitherto such privileges as the Jews enjoyed merely qualified an utter inferiority, such restrictions as now persisted were the exceptions which proved the rule of complete liberty. Persecution was unknown; social disabilities were automatically removed; segregation, with its attendant humiliation, was no longer the main object of governmental policy; and for the first time since the age of Imperial Rome a healthy individualism was possible in Jewish life. The circumstance of the Marrano settlement thus provides the key to the remarkable paradox that those European lands, such as England and Holland, where conditions had hitherto been most adverse, and where exclusion was rigid, were now the first to treat the Jew with real tolerance.

Once the formation of a community of this nature was authorised, it was logically impossible to continue to exclude declared Jews, of less compromising antecedents, even though they might have been lacking in outward graces and general culture. Hence, on the heels of the Marranos, there came by degrees Jews from other countries, less attractive superficially, who automatically enjoyed the privileges which their polished forerunners had gained.

Almost immediately after the arrival of the Marranos at Amsterdam, a German influx began; and, before the middle of the seventeenth century, a congregation was organised. This rapidly established offshoots in the other important cities of the United Provinces, and attained supremacy in Dutch Jewry in point of numbers, if not of wealth. In almost identical fashion, 'Ashkenazi' Jews insinuated themselves by slow degrees into Hamburg under the cover of the Portuguese, setting up their independent organisation in 1671. Before long it was numerically the most important in Germany, as it was to remain until the middle of the nineteenth century. The garrulous *Memoirs* of Glückel von Hameln (1645-1724), the Pepys of German Jewry, have preserved for future generations a delightfully minute picture of the life of the local community, with its scholars and its rascals and its diamond-brokers and its hucksters, and its triumphs and its vicissitudes, when it was at the height of its importance. Similarly, in London, the establishment of an 'Ashkenazi' community dates from the last decade of the seventeenth century, from which time its increase was rapid. It was thus through the Marranos that western Europe was opened to Jewish migration, and that Jewish communities of a new type were established to serve as a nucleus and as a model in the new age which was about to dawn.

IV

Eastern European Jewry was meanwhile going through its hour of trial. Ever since the original period of settlement, conditions of Jewish life in Poland had compared on the whole favourably with those which prevailed elsewhere. The conditions of greater security and order which began to prevail in Germany after the beginning of the sixteenth century made the contrast less marked; but, notwithstanding recurrent attacks and petty persecutions here and there (Posen and Cracow being hotbeds of disturbance), the state of affairs, though by no means ideal, was still tolerable. In 1648, however, the Cossacks of the Ukraine, under their hetman Khmelnitsky, rose against the misgovernment of their Polish masters, whose political, religious, and economic oppression they deeply resented. In all of this, in their eyes, the Jews were implicated. Their religion was even more hateful to the Greek Church than the Roman Catholicism which the Poles professed, and endeavoured to impose: Jews, moreover, acted as stewards of the Polish nobles' estates or lessees of the forests and the inns and the mills. Accordingly the Cossack hatred against the Jews burned even more deeply than their detestation of their masters. Throughout the country massacres took place on a scale and of a ferocity which beggared anything which had been known in Europe since the time of the Black Death; and the horrors were accentuated by the refinement of ingenuity shewn in the tortures by which they were accompanied. In every captured city or township a wholesale extermination took place; the Poles betraying their Jewish neighbours in many instances in the mistaken hope of saving their own lives. Nemirov, Tulchin, Ostrog, and scores of other places perpetuated the glorious tradition of martyrdom 'for the sanctification of the name'.

This was the beginning of a series of waves of violence which completely broke the pride of Polish Jewry. Six years later, in 1654, the Czar of Russia took the Cossacks under his protection and invaded Poland; and, as the cities of White Russia and Lithuania fell before him, the Jewish residents were either exterminated or expelled. Simultaneously, Charles X of Sweden stormed into the country from the west, bringing fire and sword in his wake. The total toll of Jewish lives between 1648 and 1658 is estimated at no less than one hundred thousand. Still the period of tribulation was not at an end. There followed a protracted series of local disturbances, of petty persecutions, of ritual murder libels—the latter in such number as to lead to an appeal for protection to the Pope, who, after elaborate enquiry, once more declared the wretched story to be entirely without basis. Finally, lawless bands of 'Haidamacks' or rebels rose again in the Ukraine, and perpetrated atrocities rivalling those of one hundred and twenty years earlier, culminating in a shocking massacre at Uman in 1768.

The cumulative effect of all this was the ruin of Polish Jewry. The centre of Jewish life, such as it was, moved northwards, never re-establishing itself in Podolia and Volhynia as firmly as had been the case previous to 1648. The resolutions passed at successive sessions of the Council of the Four Lands reflect the straits in which the country found itself. Taxation progressively increased. Sumptuary laws restricted the outlay on family festivities, and even the number of weddings: an annual fast commemorated the anniversary of the massacre at Nemirov; and a score of regulations expressed public grief at the unforgettable recent tragedy.

Hardly less important were the repercussions outside Poland. All Europe now became acquainted with penniless refugees, fleeing from the Cossack terror. Even as far afield as Constantinople, the redemption of the captives who had fallen into the hands of the Tartars created a problem. Long-bearded, Yiddish-speaking Polish scholars became familiar figures in the Ghettos of Italy, collecting money to ransom their nearest kindred, or to re-establish themselves in life. Larger numbers made their way to Hungary, Austria, Germany, Holland, even England. With the recurrent disasters in Poland, and in face of the impossibility of economic recovery, what had been originally the merest trickle of emigration, and in 1648 became a sudden overflow, developed into a steady stream. The walls of the Polish reservoir were broken down. From the period of the First Crusade down to that of the Renaissance—from the close of the eleventh to the close of the fifteenth century—the tide of Jewish migration had been directed eastwards, from France and the Rhineland and Spain towards Turkey and Poland. The equilibrium remained fixed for approximately a century and a half. With the Khmelnitsky massacres the backward swing of the pendulum commenced; and a second wave, in a westerly direction, set in. This was to continue in varying intensity for three hundred years, and was not stemmed until it had completely recast the distribution of Jewish population in the Old World and the New.

The sequence of events was providential. The Marranos had succeeded in establishing themselves as pioneers in the various countries of north-western Europe. They were followed by German Jews, who consolidated the advantages which the former had won. On the heels of the latter, after an interval, poured the Poles, ultimately providing weight of numbers. In London, for example, there were settled in the middle of the seventeenth century no more than a score of Marrano families, who established a slowly increasing congregation. The earliest Ashkenazic community was formed about the year 1690. Within little more than half a century, there were four synagogues in London and at least as many in the provinces; and the total Jewish population of the country (throughout which the Jew was now a comparatively familiar figure) was at least six thousand, a good many of whom were of Polish origin. Thus, parts of Europe which had hitherto known nothing of the Jew began to be dotted with Jewish congregations, constantly increasing in numbers and in prosperity. The new settlements, moreover, were in many cases free from the insecurity, the fanaticism, the discrimination, and the social prejudice which even now continued to cast their shadow over the greater part of the Jewish world.

V

Meanwhile in Germany also (which contained more Jews than any other country of central or western Europe) a fresh type had been emerging. From the period of the Reformation, and particularly after the close of the Thirty Years War, there had begun to develop in that country a new variety of state: virtually independent (for the power of the Empire had dwindled almost to vanishing point), strongly centralised, maintaining an elaborate organisation, and looking to France as its model. The autocrats of these new absolutisms recruited their instruments wherever they could—even in the *Judengasse*. In time of war, a Jew was irreplaceable as Purveyor to the Forces; in time of peace, he was invaluable as Administrator of the Finances; at every turn, he might prove useful to provide a loan for the Exchequer, materials for a new enterprise, or jewels for the court favourites. Thus, almost every German state, whether it tolerated the Jews or no, admitted one or two (*Hofjuden*, or Court Jews, as they were termed) for the personal service of the monarch and his *entourage*. Naturally such persons had to possess considerable address as well as natural ability. They had to speak, to act, and to dress like normal members of society. They maintained splendid houses and magnificent establishments. It was out of the question to herd them up in the *Judengasse* or to force them to wear the Jewish badge. They were generally exempted from special taxation. Though not in all cases conspicuous for their Jewish devotion, or even for religious observance, they would as a rule be prepared to intervene on behalf of their co-religionists at any time of stress, and their fall was sometimes even more sudden and dramatic than their rise.

The history of German Jewry during the period under review is punctuated by such figures. There was Jacob Bassevi (1580-1634) of Prague, the first Central European Jew to be raised to the ranks of the nobility; Samson Wertheimer (1658-1724) of Vienna, Chief Factor to the courts of Vienna, Mayence, the Palatinate, and Trèves, who was responsible for the Austrian commissariat during the War of Spanish Succession; Samuel Oppenheimer (1635-1703), his colleague, who assisted his nephew, David Oppenheimer, to build up what was to be the nucleus of the Hebrew collection of the Bodleian Library at Oxford; and Joseph Süss Oppenheim (d. 1738), better remembered as 'Jew Süss', who for a short time before his catastrophic fall was omnipotent at the court of Württemberg.

In addition to these emancipated Court Jews, upon whom there was no restriction and who exercised in many instances an influence fully as great as any Christian of similar rank, there were now in Germany numerous so-called 'protected' and 'tolerated' Jews—jewellers, craftsmen, engravers—who were accorded special privileges for a limited period, and freed from the restrictions imposed upon the generality of their co-religionists. Below these was the proletariat, cooped up in its *Judengassen*, marked off by a distinctive badge, forced to pay special tolls, restricted to the most degrading occupations, and limited in the exercise of the most sacred and intimate human rights. A similar state of affairs prevailed in Alsace and Lorraine—German-speaking territories which, since the Peace of Westphalia, had come under the rule of France, but in which the old conditions still prevailed.

At intervals, reaction would momentarily triumph, in a manner more characteristic of the twelfth or thirteenth century than of the Age of Enlightenment. Thus, in 1670, the influence of an Empress of Spanish birth and Jesuit upbringing brought about the expulsion of the Jews from Lower and Upper Austria, including Vienna. This was as ineffectual as so many of its forerunners had been; and the beginning of the resettlement, destined to be more durable, dates from only five years later. The remoter results of the measure were, however, of considerable moment. The refugees became scattered throughout Germany and the adjacent lands. Some were admitted in the following year by Frederick William, 'The Great Elector', into Brandenburg, from which they had been excluded for the past century: and the community of Berlin was before long to be reckoned amongst the most important in Europe.

Similarly, in 1745, on the excuse of a charge of treason made against their co-religionists in Alsace, the Jews of Bohemia, and more particularly the famous community of Prague, were illogically condemned to banishment. At this stage an event unprecedented in European history took place. The semi-emancipated Jews of London

115. SYNAGOGUE IN HEIDEREUTEGASSE, BERLIN, 1712-14
Eighteenth-Century Drawing

116. WORMS SYNAGOGUE, BEGUN IN 1035
Lithograph

Phünderung der Iudengaffen zu Franckfurt am Main den 22 Augufti 1614. Nach Mittag nmb 5 uhr von den Handtwercks gefellen angefangen, vnd die gantze Nacht durch Continuirt, da dan ein Burger vnd 2 Iuden gar todt blieben, viel aber beiderfeits befchedigt worden

117. SACK OF THE JEWISH QUARTER AT FRANKFORT GHETTO DURING THE FETTMILCH
RIOTS, 1614
Engraving by G. Keller

118. Execution of Fettmilch. 1616
Contemporary Engraving

119. Expulsion of Jews from Vienna. 1670
Contemporary Engraving

120. EXECUTION OF JEW SÜSS. 1738
Engraving by G. Thelot

and of Amsterdam bestirred themselves in the matter. Thanks to
their efforts, the English and Dutch governments made diplomatic
representations to the Empress, begging her on humanitarian grounds
to reconsider her decision. In the end she revoked the decree as far as
the Jews of the provinces were concerned, though those of Prague
were allowed to re-establish themselves only some ten years later.
The episode indicated that the Jews, however much degraded and
treated as inferiors, were at least men, to whom the ordinary standards
of humanity should apply, and on whose behalf the civilised governments of the west were prepared, if the occasion demanded, to exert
mild pressure.

VI

Just as the new standards of life were beginning to emerge in
western Europe, a comet made a brief appearance which, by arousing
and then disappointing the Jew's most intimate dreams, all but
destroyed the romantic background of his life and thereby qualified
him all the more to face the new utilitarian conception of existence.
It had been a commonplace amongst the Rabbis since ancient times
that the Messiah was to come to redeem his people at the darkest
hour before the dawn, when conditions seemed to be at their worst.
Time after time, some unprecedented wave of disaster had seemed to
fulfil these conditions; and Messianic pretenders had never been lacking to fill the vacant rôle. This had been the case in the period of
Roman oppression, at the time of the rise of Islam, at the commence-
ment of the Crusades, and after the crowning tragedy of the Expulsion from Spain. No conditions seemed to correspond more closely to
all that was expected of 'the pangs of the Messiah' than the middle of
the seventeenth century.

Throughout the world, political conditions were peculiarly disturbed. Germany was still involved in the aftermath of the Thirty
Years War. The English had risen in revolt, and beheaded their king.
In Jewish life, the memory of the great expulsions of the Middle Ages
was still fresh. The fires of the Inquisition were defiling the pure
heavens of Spain and Portugal. Above all, the recent wave of massacres
at the hand of Khmelnitsky and his hordes in Poland and the Ukraine
—by far the greatest disaster of its sort in recent history—had filled
Europe with penniless refugees and brought home the magnitude of
the catastrophe. In addition, the Cabbalists of Safed, meditating day

and night upon the date and the nature of the final deliverance, had made this the principal preoccupation of every Jewish householder.

There was living at this time in Smyrna, in Asia Minor, a young man in his early twenties named Sabbatai Zevi (1626-1676). His father was agent to an English firm, and by this means he had, no doubt, become aware of the millennary dreams nurtured by the Fifth Monarchy men in England. He had come profoundly under the influence of the Cabbalistical school. His companions noted with respect how he mortified his body with repeated flagellations, and bathed constantly in the sea, both in summer and winter. Late into the night he could be heard chanting songs in Hebrew, Aramaic, or Ladino, in which the love of God for Israel was extolled in a manner and with a wealth of imagery easily susceptible of carnal interpretation. His appearance was unusually imposing, and his personal fascination strong; and gradually he came to be looked up to with a reverence which approached awe. Ultimately he became convinced that he, and no other, was the Messiah so long awaited.

In the course of a visit to Jerusalem he found his Prophet—a certain Nathan of Gaza, who was only too happy to assume the part of Elijah. Another adjunct was his wife, Sarah, a Polish girl who had lost her parents at the time of the recent massacres, and had been baptised into the Catholic Church. She had escaped from the convent in which she had been immured, with her reason shaken, and had come to the East convinced that she was the destined spouse of the Lord's Anointed.

Sabbatai's return home was in the nature of a triumphant progress. His reputation preceded him; and all along the route he was received with jubilation. Hardly a person doubted his pretensions, and the rare exceptions hesitated to voice their scepticism. Even in his own land the majority accepted him as a prophet. In a synagogue of his native Smyrna, one day in the autumn of 1665, he publicly proclaimed himself Messiah. Nor was he content to allow his claim to rest in the academic sphere. He divided Palestine and the adjacent lands into provinces, which he assigned with a generous hand to his more devoted adherents, who were to rule as subordinate kings when he came into his own.

Letters were broadcast throughout Europe, Asia, and Africa announcing the good tidings. Everywhere the approaching deliverance was hailed with jubilation. Prayers were offered up in all the synagogues on behalf of 'Our Lord, King, and Master, the holy and righteous Sabbatai Zevi, anointed of the God of Israel'. The frenzy of the masses knew no bounds. Chaste matrons fell into trances and prophesied the marvels which were soon to take place, in tongues of which they had previously had no knowledge. There was a wave of penitence and ascetic exercises. Special liturgies poured from the printing presses. Children of tender years were united in wedlock, so that they might beget bodies into which the few remaining unborn souls might enter, the last impediment to the Redemption being thereby removed. In some places business was at a standstill, men thinking of nothing but their approaching removal to the Holy Land. Sober merchants forwarded barrels of clothing and foodstuffs to the nearest port in preparation for the voyage. The merchant princes of the community of Amsterdam—men whose signatures would have been good for almost any amount on the Bourse—prepared a petition to forward to the pretender assuring him of their implicit faith. In Hamburg the elders of the community led jubilant dances in the synagogue. Almost the only prominent Jewish scholar in Europe to keep a level head was Jacob Sasportas, who had left London (where he had been Rabbi) because of the Great Plague of 1665, and endeavoured in vain to maintain a sense of proportion among his co-religionists.

Benedict de Spinoza was interrogated, and[1] saw no rational reason for doubting the possibility of a restoration of temporal rule by the Jews. A stir was created even amongst the Marranos of the Peninsula, some of whom attempted to smuggle themselves out of the country in order to participate in the Great Deliverance. In London, Samuel Pepys was informed 'of a Jew in town, that in the name of the rest do offer to give any man £10, to be paid £100 if a certain person now at Smyrna be within these two years owned by all the Princes of the East, and particular the Grand Segnor, as the King of the world'.

Thus encouraged, Sabbatai set out, on an indeterminate errand, for Constantinople. As he disembarked he was arrested by order of the Grand Vizier, and thrown into prison. This set-back made no difference in the eyes of his admirers: for was it not inevitable that the Messiah should suffer tribulations before his final triumph? They called the fortress of Abydos, where he was incarcerated, by the mystical title, 'The Tower of Strength', and they thronged to visit him, bearing rich gifts. In consequence, he maintained even now an

---

[1] As we know from an expression of his views on a different occasion, but unfortunately his reply to the enquiry (by Henry Oldenburg, Secretary of the Royal Society) has been lost.

almost royal state. He went from one extravagance to another: the climax being reached when he abrogated the fast of the ninth of Ab— anniversary of the Destruction of Jerusalem and of manifold other disasters in the history of the Jewish people—intimating that it was henceforth to be observed as a major feast, in commemoration of his birth.

At last the patience of the Turkish authorities was exhausted. Egged on by a rival prophet from Poland, who had failed to receive from Sabbatai that consideration which he expected, they summoned him to Adrianople. His adherents now imagined that the great day for which they had been hoping and praying had dawned. Further delay was impossible; and they speculated upon the precise method by which their hero would choose to assert himself. In the capital he was brought before the Sultan, who blandly placed before him the alternatives of apostasy or death. With a pusillanimity which is the most jarring feature in an otherwise harmonious career, the pretender chose the former. Donning the white turban of a true believer in place of his Jewish headgear, he publicly proclaimed his belief in Islam, and left the Sultanic presence as Mehemet Effendi, and a royal pensioner.

The most remarkable part of the whole episode was still to follow. Belief in the pseudo-Messiah's claims was not shaken even by this negation of all for which he had previously stood. The more devoted among his admirers maintained that the deliverer must have experience of every side of human life—even the lowest and most un-Jewish —before he could accomplish his mission; or else that it was only a phantom bearing his shape that had apostasised. Throughout the Jewish world, bands of devoted adherents continued to assert his claims. Their hero himself discreetly encouraged them, continuing to consort with his admirers and to practise strange rites in their company; until, surprised in the act, he was banished to Dulcigno. But his cult survived even his death at this place in 1676 (on the Day of Atonement, it was whispered). Many of his adherents, who had followed him into Islam, transferred their allegiance to his putative son. Down to the present day, their descendants, under the name of Donmeh, still maintain their identity in the Near East.[1] Outwardly,

---

[1] Up to the Balkan and Græco-Turkish wars, the main centre of the Donmeh was Salonica. Outwardly Turks, they were included in the subsequent exchanges of population: and the most important group at present is in Constantinople. The Young Turk movement of 1913 was led to a disproportionate extent by members of this sect.

they are strict Moslems: but, in the privacy of their homes, they perpetuate their own curious, mystical rites, recalling the strange episode
of three centuries ago. It is a distorted parallel to Christianity, with
the difference that it centres about the person of a Messiah who
apostatized instead of submitting to death.

Elsewhere the ferment continued in a different form. Wandering
prophets and mystics (such as Nathan of Gaza, or, in the early part of
the following century, Nehemiah Hayun) long continued to preach
belief in the Messiah who had renounced Judaism. Many Rabbis, of
the utmost erudition and piety, were suspected of cherishing a secret
allegiance to him. Nearly a century later, learned circles were con-
vulsed over a long period of years by a dispute between Rabbis Jacob
Emden (d. 1776) and Jonathan Eybeschütz (d. 1764), who was
accused by the former of having introduced allusions to Sabbatai Zevi
in certain mystical amulets which he had written. Others, stimulated
by the recent example, set themselves up as Messiahs on their own
account; such as Abraham Michael Cardoso (1630-1706), a Marrano
physician, who before his conversion to Judaism had been a favourite
of the ladies of Madrid; Mordecai Eisenstadt (1650-1729), a stirring
preacher, who fascinated the Jewish masses in northern Italy; or
Moses Hayim Luzzatto (1707-1747) of Padua, the most gifted Hebrew
writer of his day, whose genius introduced a fresh vitality into Hebrew
poetry. Even in Poland the infection was potent, and led to a curious
revivalist movement which culminated in the emigration of a large
band of pietists, dressed in white shrouds as a token of penitence, to
Jerusalem, where they confidently expected to witness the Redemption.

In the east of Europe especially there remained large numbers of
persons who maintained an implicit belief in these Messianic currents.
In the second half of the eighteenth century they found a rallying-
point in a certain Podolian adventurer named Jacob Leibovicz, (known
as Frank), who claimed to be the reincarnation of Sabbatai Zevi and
his successors. His adherents were soon to be numbered by thousands.
The alleged licentious manners of the new sect resulted in their
excommunication by a Rabbinical synod at Brody, which prohibited
until maturity the study of the Zohar (on which the Frankists depended
for their very existence). The innovators retorted by proclaiming
themselves Zoharists, at war with the Talmud and the Rabbis; and
they presented a semi-Trinitarian confession of faith to the local
ecclesiastical authorities. The result was a disputation in the fullest

medieval tradition, after which the Talmud was condemned and thousands of copies publicly burned. Ultimately the Frankists went over *en masse* to the dominant faith, proving as questionable Christians as they had been Jews. As late as the period of the French Revolution, one of the sights of the German town of Offenbach was Jacob Frank, self-styled Baron von Offenbach, living in great style on the offerings brought to him by his Polish and Moravian adherents. Shortly after his death in 1791 his designated successor, Moses Dobrushka (who went by the name of Junius Frey), was sent to the guillotine in Paris, with Danton. Frank's beautiful daughter, Eve, now became the 'Holy Mistress' of the sect, and kept the tradition alive well into the nineteenth century.

VII

A more remote effect of the Messianic stir was the birth of Hassidism. The revivalist movement in Poland permeated all sections of society, until it touched a simple Podolian lime-digger, Israel ben Eliezer (1700-1760). The cycle of legends which has gathered about the latter's personality has made it difficult to realise the exact import of his teaching. It is clear, nevertheless, that this man of the people revolted against the hegemony of intellect which had hitherto prevailed undisputed amongst the Polish Jewries, where learning had been considered fundamental to Judaism, and consideration was withheld from any person who was not a profound Talmudist. The new leader, a tender-hearted mystic of rare personal magnetism, taught that piety was superior to scholarship, and that it was the prerogative of any man, however ignorant and however poor, to attain communion with his God. The Deity, according to him, infused all creation, could be served in many manners and with every bodily function, so long as His worship was carried on with joy and gladness. Man could derive no advantage from the mortification of the flesh; it was by spiritual exaltation and complete abandonment of self that the gulf between earth and heaven could be bridged. On the other hand, there existed certain Righteous Ones (*Zadikim*) who were close to the Almighty, and whose intercession might sometimes sway His immutable will.

Gradually the little band of disciples who gathered round the Master of the Good Name (*Baal Shem Tob*: abbreviated as 'Besht'), as they termed him, in the little township of Miedzyboz, grew into many thousands, who adopted the name of *Hassidim* ('the Pious'). A

revivalist movement now swept through the Jewish masses of eastern
Europe. Prayer meetings were established at which feasting and
ecstasy and song were considered of greater importance than a mechanical recitation of the liturgy. After the founder's death, the conception arose of the presence in a few chosen families of special merit,
which passed down by hereditary right from one *Zadik*, or Righteous
One, to another, all designated to act as intermediaries between man
and God. Dov Baer of Meseritz (1710-1772), the earliest scholar
amongst the adherents of Hassidism, adapted the new doctrines to
the taste of the more learned elements, amongst whom it henceforth
began to make increasing headway. By 1772 the current had reached
Lithuania, and a secret Hassidic meeting-place was formed at Vilna.
This at last brought the traditional party (with the approval of Elijah
ben Solomon, the 'Vilna Gaon' [1720-1797], last of the Rabbinical
giants of the heroic age) to take formal steps, and issue an edict of
excommunication against all who followed the new movement.

It goes without saying that this measure proved ineffectual to stem
the tide. For some years to come, eastern European Jewry was divided
between *Hassidim* and *Mithnagdim*, or 'Opponents'. When the din of
battle died down, a new spirit had pervaded both sides. The *Hassidim*
now recognised the importance of the traditional order of things, and
counted Rabbis of outstanding learning and ability amongst their
numbers. The *Mithnagdim* had become tolerant, and their conceptions
were perceptibly influenced by the warm humanity of their erstwhile
opponents—a change symbolised in the next century in the ethical
teaching of the saintly Israel Salanter (1810-1883). Thus, *Hassidism*
was prevented from developing into a sect, and its adherents (once to
be numbered by the million) remained within the Jewish fold. Its
advent, nevertheless, had made an enduring difference to Judaism,
the poetical element in which it had reinforced: while its hold among
the lower, more impressionable classes, who felt the need for some
mystical constituent in daily life, was enduringly strengthened.

The pseudo-Messianic movement of the seventeenth century, with
its subsequent ramifications (notwithstanding the final debacle), thus
marked the close of an epoch. The Jews of the west were utterly
disillusioned. Their pride was touched; and it took them long to
recover from the blow. Never again was a pseudo-Messiah, relying on
supernatural powers, to obtain universal credence. The movement of
national redemption was ultimately rationalised. In the meantime,
the former dupes became severely practical, looking for Jerusalem in

their native land, scenting redemption in the public funds, and susceptible (sometimes over-susceptible) to the blandishments of Christian society—fit children of the century of Voltaire and of Rousseau.
The protracted Emden-Eybeschütz controversy undermined the
authority and credit of the Rabbinate. In eastern Europe, on the other
hand, while the giants of Talmudic scholarship were passing, a new
brand of Judaism was arising to which, for the first time, scholarship
was unnecessary, and the simpleton could consort on equal terms
with the Rabbi. Meanwhile, in the western countries a novel type of
Jew had emerged, speaking the vernacular, dressed like his neighbours,
mixing in general life, and socially emancipated. The Jewish Middle
Ages were clearly coming to a close.

121. Celebration of the New Year in Germany
From J. C. G. Bodenschatz, Kirkliche Verfassung, 1748

122. MOSES MENDELSOHN (1729-1786)
Contemporary Engraving

Chapter XXVII

THE FALL OF THE GHETTO

———————— • ————————

I

By the second half of the eighteenth century, the rifts in the Ghetto walls were becoming manifest. The western countries of Europe, as has been seen, had not introduced the institution after the Jews began to resettle in the seventeenth century. In Italy (except in the Papal states, where Pope Pius VI's *Editto sopra gli Ebrei* ['Edict concerning the Jews'] of 1775 recalled the worst aberrations of the Middle Ages) conditions were slowly ameliorating. In enlightened states like Tuscany, no great objection was raised if a few individuals lived outside the Ghetto, the gates of which were no longer closed with such punctuality as hitherto. Even in Venice, where the reactionary *ricondotta* of 1777 restricted commercial enterprise and accentuated the alien status of the Jew, the wearing of the Red Hat had fallen into complete desuetude. As far as Germany was concerned, the *Judengassen* no longer retained their predominance. Privileged persons were beginning to be admitted to the Universities and to mix in polite society; and the 'protected' Jews of cities like Berlin were more to the fore, and enjoyed greater influence than those who still lived, under the old obscurantist regime, in Frankfort and elsewhere.

The new position of the Jew in German society was typified by, and at the same time received a powerful impetus from, Moses, son of Mendel, or Moses Mendelssohn (1729-1786). Born at Dessau in a typically medieval environment, he had humped his back and sharpened his intellect by inordinate poring over the Rabbinical texts. In 1743 he had gone to Berlin in the wake of his teacher, Rabbi David Fränkel, having to pay the *Leibzoll* incumbent upon every Jew before being allowed to enter the gates. Here he picked up mathematics, Latin, and a smattering of modern languages; and he became successively tutor, bookkeeper, and finally manager, in the establishment of a wealthy Jewish manufacturer. In 1763, to the general surprise, he won a prize awarded by the Prussian Academy of Sciences for the best essay on a highly abstruse metaphysical subject. The achievement was all the more noteworthy in view of the fact that one of the two unsuccessful candidates was none other than Immanuel Kant, the only philosopher of his age.

Mendelssohn was henceforth famous. To the Germans, the pheno-menon of a Jew who was able to express himself in the vernacular with any degree of purity and elegance was as remarkable as that of a talking magpie. Exalted persons were curious to meet 'the young Hebrew who wrote in German'. The wealthy Jews of the Prussian capital took him to their bosom. He was advanced by the government to the rank of *Schutzjude*, or Protected Jew. Lessing took him as the model for the central character in his *Nathan the Wise*. All the com-munities of Germany looked up to him with adoration. His pen was placed unreservedly at their service; and a series of works in flawless style appeared in which, like another Philo, he endeavoured to recon-cile Judaism with all that was most fashionable in contemporary thought.

Emboldened by all this, the modern Socrates (as he was called, with reference to his appearance, as well as to his intellectual power) began a deliberate attempt to introduce current standards into the spiritual and literary life of the *Judengasse*. The new era was initiated by the publication of his famous edition of the Pentateuch, with a translation into excellent German and a collaborative modern com-mentary in pure Hebrew. By this achievement the Judaeo-German dialect, hitherto in almost universal use, was as it were split into its component parts. The translation initiated the vernacular literature of the German Jew, which in the course of the next century was to attain classical importance. The commentary broke through the Talmudic horizons, which had hitherto hemmed in German Jewish life, and thereby gave a powerful impetus to modern Hebrew letters. Mendelssohn's disciples, who collaborated with him in a pioneer literary periodical known as the *Measef* ('Gatherer'), and are known after it as the *Measefim*, further developed the tongue of their fathers as a literary vehicle, thereby initiating (so far as the northern countries were concerned) modern Hebrew prose, poetry, essay, and drama. The Jewish Free School, opened in Berlin in 1781, put Mendelssohn's educational ideals into practice; and his collaborator, Naphtali Hart-wig Wessely (1725-1805), the most talented of the neo-Hebrew poets, conducted a tireless propaganda in favour of their universal adoption.

The influence of Mendelssohn, decisive though it may have been in Germany and adjacent lands (in countries like Italy, it must be remembered, there was no need for a revival either of Hebrew letters or of the use of a pure vernacular), was not altogether good. He was a temporiser; and, though he was scrupulous in his adherence to ancestral practice, he was able to transmit to those who came after him more of the spirit of compromise than of loyalty. He broke down the social barrier which had hitherto existed between Jew and non-Jew. For a time the salons of wealthy and fashionable Jewesses (including more than one of his own daughters) dominated intellectual society in Berlin. The new generation could not preserve the balance between the old and the new. The wealthy David Friedländer, frankly concerned in the first instance with the entry of assimilated Jews like himself into Berlin society, cynically professed his willingness to adopt Christianity, if he were not expected to believe in the divinity of Jesus and might evade certain ceremonies. In the years following Mendelssohn's death, hundreds of his followers and admirers carried his principles to their logical conclusion by going over to the dominant religion, as he himself had gone over to the dominant culture. Among these were included several of his closest disciples and even (what is even more significant) his own children. His daughter, Dorothea, became the mistress, and then the wife, of Friedrich von Schlegel; his grandson, Felix, baptised in infancy, used his genius to enrich the music of the Church. These two instances are typical of the fate of the Mendelssohnian school as such.

In the political sphere the reactions of Mendelssohn's example were no less marked, but more favourable. The 'Enlightened Despots' of the age began to realise that the barriers between Jew and Gentile were not insuperable. Religious prejudice had ceased to weigh with the contemporaries and pupils of Voltaire; and they were convinced that, with a little judicious encouragement, every Jew would shew himself to be a Mendelssohn and in the end—who knows?—the age-long problem would be solved by wholesale assimilation.

It was Joseph II of Austria (influenced largely by the suggestions for the civil emancipation of the Jews by Moses Mendelssohn's Christian friend, Christian Wilhelm von Dohm) who led the way. In 1781, the year after his accession, he shewed the trend of his policy by abolishing the Poll Tax and the Jewish Badge. This was followed shortly after by his famous *Toleranzpatent* (2nd January 1782) in which his ideals received fullest expression. While there was as yet no question of placing Jews on civil parity with Christians, the principle was laid down that their disabilities were to be gradually removed and that they should be helped to mix in the life of the general population. The ecclesiastical restrictions upon them were abolished. They were encouraged (on paper, at least) to take up handicrafts and agriculture; they were allowed to engage in wholesale commerce and to establish factories; the public schools were expressly declared open to them; and the foundation of Jewish educational institutions, infused with a modern spirit, was fostered. Six years later an edict was issued ordering every Jew to adopt a proper, recognisable surname, instead of the Biblical patronymic which had hitherto sufficed in most cases. Special commissions were appointed to supervise the procedure. If any individual hesitated or demurred, some name was created for him and registered out of hand—often with intentionally ridiculous results, still perpetuated by their unfortunate descendants. These reforms were all the more important in view of the fact that the first Partition of Poland in 1772, which assigned Galicia to Austria, had enormously increased the number of the Emperor's Jewish subjects.

It cannot be said that this experiment was an outstanding success, as the Jews obstinately refused to become assimilated to the degree which was expected from them. In consequence, under Joseph II's successors, many of the new regulations became a dead letter. Nevertheless the example was followed elsewhere. In Alsace, in 1784, the *impôt du pied fourchu* (toll of the cloven foot), hitherto payable by Jews and cattle at every *douane*, was abolished, as far as the former were concerned, by Louis XVI, who, a few months later issued letters-patent which did away with some other major abuses. In Tuscany, too, the Grand Duke Leopold I (the Emperor's brother) included the Jews in the scope of his reforms, following the example already set in the Austrian possessions south of the Alps.

II

In the midst of these pious attitudes burst the bombshell of the French Revolution. The position of the Jews in France at this time was bewilderingly varied. The main body, comprising upwards of three-quarters of the whole, lived in the German-speaking provinces of Alsace and Lorraine, under conditions similar in almost every respect to those of their co-religionists of Germany. In the south-west—particularly at Bordeaux and Bayonne—there were the former Marrano settlements, still occasionally recruited from Spain and Portugal, but officially recognised as Jewish only since 1730. Avignon and the former Papal possessions of Provence (whose reunion with France was one of the earliest achievements of the Revolution) contained four ancient communities, whose ancestors had been living in the country perhaps since classical times, eking out their existence under the same medieval conditions as prevailed in Rome. Finally, a handful of immigrants from every quarter were living on sufferance in Paris.

The enjoyment by the Jews of the same privileges as other citizens was a natural corollary of the Declaration of the Rights of Man. Nevertheless, the Jew had so long been considered an outcast that many months elapsed before this elementary piece of logic could obtain general support, notwithstanding the impassioned pleas of demagogic idealists like the Abbé Grégoire. The Portuguese Jews of Bayonne and Bordeaux, followed by those of Provence, made out a case for themselves on the pretext that they were the *élite* of their people, and secured emancipation on 28th January 1790. This did not, of course, affect the vast majority in Alsace. At length some young Parisian Jews, fervid supporters of the principles of the Revolution, appealed for support to the Paris Commune; and fifty-three out of its sixty districts voted for a resolution in favour of the enfranchisement of all French Jews without exception. The Abbé Merlot presented an address to this effect to the National Assembly, but (largely on the grounds of the pressure of public business) the opposition again triumphed. At last, during one of the last sittings which preceded the dissolution, the deputy Duport suddenly forced the question. In the last few months, democratic ideas had been steadily gaining ground, and, to the general surprise, his motion was carried almost without opposition (September 27th 1791). Thus, for the first time in the history of modern Europe, the Jews were formally admitted equal citizens of the country of their birth.[1]

In the succeeding period, the Jews of France shared the lot of the remainder of the inhabitants of the country. During the Terror, one

[1] In the new-born United States of America, however, the principle had been accepted few years earlier—a fact which Continental historians tend to ignore (below, p. 395).

or two prominent individuals fell under the guillotine; and the synagogues throughout the country ceased to function during the supremacy of the Goddess of Reason. On the other hand, in every place to
which the armies of the young Republic penetrated they brought the
new gospel of the equality of all men, with its corollary of Jewish
emancipation. In Holland, full citizenship was accorded to them in a
constitutional manner by the National Assembly, under the pressure
of the French envoy, on 2nd September 1796; and in the following
year, for the first time probably in history, Jews were elected members of the legislature.

More dramatic by far was the change effected in Italy. Here, as the
French forces entered one sun-drenched city after the other, the
barriers of the Ghetto were broken down, and the Jews were summoned forth to the pure air of the outer world, to enjoy all the
privileges of other human beings. In Venice, the Ghetto gates were
removed and burned, amid great popular jubilation, on 10th July
1797. In Rome, the deliverance took place in February 1798. Everywhere the Jews formed part of the new municipal governments, and
were even granted commissions in the National Guard. It is true that
in the disorders which sometimes heralded the approach of the French
armies or followed their momentary discomfiture, attacks on the
Ghetto often occurred; and the peaceful record of Italian Jewry was
marred by massacres in a few places, particularly Sienna. Nevertheless,
in the end the French restored universal order, and under Napoleon
Bonaparte ('the Good Lot', as they punningly called him), the Jews
were on the whole able to enjoy their new-won privileges in tranquillity.

Much the same, though somewhat slower, was the progress of
events in Germany. In the Rhineland, as in Italy, the Jews were
emancipated in the first warm flush of enthusiasm which followed
the French irruption. A similar process ensued in those parts of the
country which came under French influence as the result of subsequent campaigns. In the kingdom of Westphalia, formed under the
titular sovereignty of Jerome Bonaparte in 1807, the Jews were soon
placed on the same footing of equality as in France.

In Frankfort (from 1806 the seat of government of the Federation
of the Rhine) Jewish disabilities were removed in 1811 after the payment of a very ample composition in lieu of the former Protection
Tax. Full equality was similarly granted in the Hanseatic towns after
their annexation to France. In the other German states under French

influence, limited emancipation was granted. Even in Prussia (the Jewish population of which had increased enormously in consequence of the second and third partitions of Poland, in 1793 and 1795 respectively) there was a perceptible amelioration after the French Revolution. This culminated in 1812, in the course of the national consolidation which preceded the War of Liberation, with a grant of complete emancipation, only governmental offices remaining closed. Though, the reforms introduced by Joseph II in Austria, had tended to become a dead letter under his successors, here also the new spirit was palpable.

III

With regard to the Jews of the French Empire proper, the organising genius of Napoleon Bonaparte led to an important series of experiments. Already at the outset of his career, in the course of his Egyptian campaign, his mind began to be filled with the glamorous potentialities of the age-old dreams of the Jewish people; and in a proclamation issued after the capture of Gaza he invited those resident in Asia and Africa to rally to the French arms and assist in wresting the Holy Land from the Turk. When the Empire was at its zenith, his mind turned to another aspect of the question. As he passed through Alsace in 1806, on his triumphant return from Austerlitz, he was assailed by the population with complaints against the Jews, upon whom they blamed all their misfortunes. Half of the estates of the province, including entire villages, were, they alleged, mortgaged to extortionate Jewish money-lenders, and a general massacre was to be feared. At the same time, certain Legitimist propagandists began to spread scandalous tales regarding the disproportionate Jewish influence in the Empire. From other quarters allegations were made that the Jews were evading conscription, despite the numbers decorated for gallantry in successive campaigns. No soldier, moreover, could fail to notice the trail of petty hucksters who followed incongruously in the wake of the armies to trade with the soldiers.

From this moment the question began to occupy the Emperor's mind. On 30th April it was discussed at a meeting of the Council of State, at which he expressed himself in a violently antagonistic sense. Before the next session, a week later, he had become more reasonable. It was now determined to summon a representative assembly, which should make an authoritative pronouncement as to the position of the

Jew in the modern state, and revitalise 'that civic morality lost during the long centuries of a degrading existence'. Only, where another ruler would have thought in terms of a Rabbinical Assembly, Napoleon's grandiose ideology could conceive nothing less than a revival of the ancient Sanhedrin, for fifteen centuries nothing but a memory.

It was in July 1806 that the preparatory body, the Assembly of Notables, met in Paris, under the presidency of Abraham Furtado—a Bordeaux Jew who had become prominent during the Revolution as a leader of the Girondins. Needless to say, this body gave satisfactory replies (erring only on the side of obsequiousness) to the twelve enquiries officially submitted to it. Immediately after the conclusion of its sessions, in the following February, the Sanhedrin was convoked to give its findings religious sanction. It was fastidiously modelled, so far as was possible, on its ancient Palestinian prototype. Among its seventy-one members (two-thirds of whom were Rabbis and one-third laymen) were representatives of all the provinces of the French Empire, including North Italy, Holland, and parts of Germany. David Sinzheim, Rabbi of Strassburg and the most noteworthy scholar of the country, was elected President, or *Nasi*.

After seven sessions, occupied in the main with formal business, the Sanhedrin voted without discussion upon the recommendations of the Assembly of Notables, and passed them as laws. The tenor of the whole was summed up in a clause to the effect that the Jew considered the land of his birth his Fatherland, and recognised the duty of defending it. To this succinct summary of the Imperial ideal those present replied in a truly Napoleonic fashion, rising as one man in assent, with the cry '*Jusqu'à la mort!*' Other clauses embodied a declaration against the practice of usury and a full recognition of the incumbency upon the Jew of the matrimonial laws of the state. There was no question of compromise; with Gallic suavity, any point of real difficulty was evaded.

The position as far as Jewish law was concerned was thus settled. The same genius which brought into being the Code Napoléon now set about reorganising with the same thoroughness the communities of the Empire. By an order promulgated from Madrid on 17th March 1808, every department containing two thousand Jews or more was to establish its 'consistory', comprising ecclesiastical and lay members. A central committee, consisting of three Grand Rabbis and two lay members, was established in Paris, with a general control over the local organisations. Thus French Jewry was organised in a hierarchy

123. SPANISH AND PORTUGUESE SYNAGOGUE OF AMSTERDAM
Exterior. 18th Century Engraving

124. FAMILY SCENE AT AMSTERDAM DURING THE FEAST OF TABERNACLES
Engraving by Bernard Picart, 1723

125. The Great Synagogue, London (Built 1722, enlarged 1790)
Engraving by Pugin and Rowlandson. From 'Microcosm of London', 1809

126. DEDICATION OF THE SPANISH AND PORTUGUESE SYNAGOGUE, AMSTERDAM, 1675

Contemporary Engraving

127. Opening Session of the Napoleonic Sanhedrin in Paris 9th February 1807. Contemporary Engraving

of mathematical symmetry, which still prevails. A number of less palatable additions were appended to the decree, reflecting current prejudices and justifying the title *Décret Infâme* by which it was subsequently known. For a period of ten years, no Jew was to be allowed to engage in trade without special permission; residence in a new department was denied to all but agriculturists; and no Jewish conscript was to be allowed to offer a substitute to serve in his place. Within the next few years, a large number of departments had been exempted from these last provisions, though they continued as far as the Jewish masses of Alsace were concerned. By this means, it was hoped that the over-concentration of the Jews in certain walks of life, and their social separatism, would at last be modified.

Whatever the merits or demerits of the Napoleonic Sanhedrin and the subsequent reorganisation (and it is frequently regarded, with good reason, as having set the footsteps of French Jewry upon the pathway of assimilation), there can be no doubt that it was a fine stroke of diplomacy and captured the imagination of the Jews far beyond the boundaries of the French Empire. On the invasion of Poland, Napoleon found himself greatly assisted by the gaberdined, ringleted local Jews, who rendered his forces every assistance which lay in their power. 'The Sanhedrin is at least useful to me', he is reported to have said. But sectional sympathy was powerless to avert the final cataclysm; and the fall of the First Empire, in the Armageddon which succeeded the retreat from Moscow, threw European Jewry into the melting-pot once again.

Foreign Office,
November 2nd, 1917.

Dear Lord Rothschild,

I have much pleasure in conveying to you, on behalf of His Majesty's Government, the following declaration of sympathy with Jewish Zionist aspirations which has been submitted to, and approved by, the Cabinet

His Majesty's Government view with favour the establishment in Palestine of a national home for the Jewish people, and will use their best endeavours to facilitate the achievement of this object, it being clearly understood that nothing shall be done which may prejudice the civil and religious rights of existing non-Jewish communities in Palestine, or the rights and political status enjoyed by Jews in any other country"

I should be grateful if you would bring this declaration to the knowledge of the Zionist Federation.

[signature: Arthur James Balfour]

128. THE BALFOUR DECLARATION
2nd November 1917

BOOK V

THE NEW AGE: 1815-1918

———•———

129. JEW PRAYING. Drawing by Max Liebermann (1847-1934)

Chapter XXVIII

REVOLUTION AND EMANCIPATION

———————— • ————————

I

The representatives of a score of European powers, assembled in Vienna in 1814 and 1815 (and solaced by the lavish entertainments of Fanny Itzig, the elegant Jewish hostess), spent long months attempting to patch together the political framework which had been shattered a generation before, on the outbreak of the French Revolution. Even Jews, for the first time in diplomatic history, sent their delegates to watch the negotiations; for it was obvious that their interests were likely to be profoundly affected. A proposal that they should be confirmed in the rights granted them during the period of French supremacy obtained powerful support—notably that of Hardenberg, the Prussian plenipotentiary. Accordingly, notwithstanding determined opposition from reactionary powers, led by Bavaria and Saxony, an attempt was made to establish in the new Germanic Confederation a uniform liberal policy, similar to that in force in Prussia since 1812. In the Act of Confederation adopted by the German governments, a clause was inserted to the effect that, pending legislation to regularise their position, the Jews should continue to enjoy all privileges granted to them in the various states. The reactionaries, however, secured the substitution of the innocuous word 'by' for 'in'. Thus the undertaking was rendered completely valueless, as any signatory could plead that the emancipation effected under foreign influence had not been granted 'by' the state itself.

The gate was thus left ajar, if not open, for reaction to enter. During the course of the next decade, the question of Jewish status in the newly organised Free Cities assumed international importance. Austria, Prussia, England, and even Russia, whatever their domestic policy, protested repeatedly against anti-Jewish measures. But, notwithstanding this, only Frankfort proved amenable, concluding a fairly equitable agreement with its Jewish community in 1824.

Bremen and Lübeck, on the other hand, went so far as to expel those settled there in recent years. In other states, there was no uniformity of status. Thus, Prussia had upwards of twenty different gradations in its various provinces. In the whole of Germany, the systems in force ranged from almost full emancipation to segregation in a semi-medieval sense. Large areas, comprising some of the most important cities of the country, resolutely refused to admit permanent settlers.

In Italy the reaction was even more pronounced, for there was a more or less complete return to the unenlightened system of the eighteenth century. In Lombardy and Venice, under Austrian rule, the semi-repression which obtained in the rest of the Hapsburg dominions was restored. Conditions in the kingdom of Sardinia, in Tuscany, and in most of the minor principalities were rather worse. In the States of the Church, the rulers of which had learned less and forgotten less even than the Valois, the Ghetto system was reintroduced down to the last detail, except for the wearing of a distinctive badge. In many places the gates of the Jewish quarter, destroyed and burned in the first flush of revolutionary enthusiasm in 1797, were again set up. Of all Europe, only Holland maintained the complete legal and constitutional equality recently won. In 1819, to the accompaniment of cries of 'Hep! Hep!' (the initials of *Hierosolyma est perdita*, and traditionally the anti-Jewish watchword of the period of the Crusades), sanguinary excesses against the Jews took place throughout Germany. Promising young men like Ludwig Börne and Heinrich Heine, despairing of ever being able to make their way in a hostile world as Jews, cynically accepted baptism, while continuing to preserve throughout life a nostalgia for the environment of their younger days.

Yet, however drastic the reaction, there was in most places a subtle difference between the old regime and the new. Before the close of the eighteenth century, the restrictions upon Jewish life had been universal, and opportunities were the exception. Now, opportunities were widespread, though they were still qualified by restrictions. The Jew was no longer an inferior, degraded being, marked off from his fellow-humans by dress, by language, by occupation, by interests. He had breathed the free air of the outside world. His horizons had been widened. He had known what it was to mix with the rest of mankind on an equal footing. From this point of view, it was impossible to set back the clock of progress, whatever legislative measures might be re-enacted. He had attained the status of a man at least. It remained for him to attain the status of a citizen.

In his exclusion from this he was not alone. The era in question was one of general reaction. Throughout Europe, in the preceding period, men had learned to know and to admire the forms of constitutional government; and the introduction of parliamentary institutions was regarded as the panacea for every ill and the goal of every liberal striving. The emancipation of the Jew would be incomplete without the extension to him of those constitutional rights which the rest of the population hoped to attain for themselves. The spread of universal conscription during the French Revolutionary wars, replacing everywhere (excepting in England) the old professional armies, had made no exception in favour, or to the disadvantage, of any creed. It thus proved a tremendous unifying force. The Jews drilled, fought, bled, by the side of their Gentile neighbours. They had been made to assume all the obligations of citizenship. To exclude them from its growing prerogatives was illogical to a degree, in an age when logic was treated with an almost superstitious reverence. Thus, whereas in the past the most optimistic could have aspired to nothing more than equality of economic and social opportunity under a benevolent despotism, men now thought in terms of those constitutional and political rights which were the inalienable right of every citizen. Hence the Jews of Central Europe flung themselves heart and soul into the revolutionary movements of the nineteenth century, which finally resulted in the destruction of absolutism and the establishment of constitutional governments from the Baltic to the Mediterranean, and from the Danube to the Pyrenees: and the triumph of constitutionalism, as they had hoped, was ultimately everywhere accompanied by emancipation.

II

After Holland, which never faltered in the policy followed since 1796, it was Restoration France which set the lead. Here, the new Constitution guaranteed religious freedom for all. Hence, when the restrictions imposed by Napoleon in his Madrid Decree expired in 1818, the constitutional position of the Jews was exactly the same as that of any other section of the French population. Almost the only differentiation left was that the former had to support their own ministers of religion, whereas those of the Catholic and even the

Protestant Churches were subsidised by the state. After the July Revolution of 1830, which converted France into a constitutional monarchy, parliament passed a motion to put Judaism on terms of equality in this respect with other officially recognised religious bodies. From now on, a state subvention was made to the Jewish cult—as had already been the rule in the Low Countries since 1815. In 1846 the degrading oath *more judaico*, which had hitherto been allowed to remain boldly, and was administered whenever a Jew appeared in the Courts of Law, was abolished. No further distinction or differentiation whatsoever between Jew and non-Jew now remained on the statute-book.

As far as Germany was concerned, the struggle for Jewish rights entered into a new phase in 1830 under the leadership of Gabriel Riesser, a magnificent orator and organiser, who though a Jew was one of the heads of the constitutional party in the country. Thanks to his advocacy, Jewish emancipation became a plank in the platform of German liberalism. The headway was very slow and there were frequent set-backs, but the direction was unmistakable. In 1833, full equality was accorded to the Jews of Hesse Cassel (who had already enjoyed it as subjects of the kingdom of Westphalia, but were now reduced to an inferior status). Brunswick followed suit in the following year, and Prussia, to a modified degree, in 1847. In the revolutionary wave of the *annus mirabilis*, 1848, Jews throughout Germany took a prominent part, confidently hoping that success would bring emancipation in its train. In Berlin alone, no fewer than twenty of them were killed in the street-fighting of 18th–19th March; and Gabriel Riesser himself was elected a vice-president of the *Vorparlament* at Frankfort. In the reforming fervour which followed, state after state granted a liberal constitution; and everywhere, except in Bavaria, the new code contained a clause removing Jewish disabilities. Almost simultaneously the Austrian and Hungarian Diets (in the latter case, mindful of the fact that a Jewish regiment had taken the field under Kossuth), carried motions in favour of full emancipation for the Jews of the Dual Monarchy.

A period of general reaction followed, in which the new constitutions were either withdrawn or else rendered nugatory. The new-won Jewish rights were seldom indeed cancelled; but, in actuality, they were drastically circumscribed. In Austria, the constitution of three years previous was formally withdrawn in 1851, on the understanding that religious liberty was to be respected. Nevertheless, by a legal

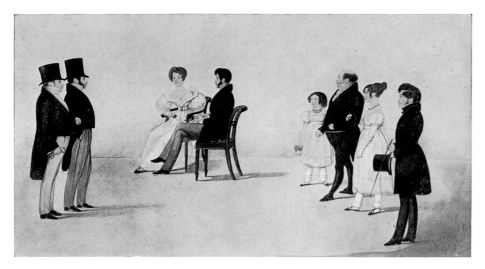

130. A Rothschild Wedding, 1826

Showing (right to left) Baron Lionel, his father Nathan Meyer of London and the latter's son-in-law and nephew Anselm Solomon of Vienna. Water Colour by Richard Dighton in the London Museum

Hepp! Hepp!

131. 'Hepp! Hepp!'

Anti-Jewish Riots in Germany, 1819. Contemporary print

132. INTERIOR OF TOURO SYNAGOGUE, NEWPORT, R.I., U.S.A. 1763

quibble, it was again made necessary for any Jew who desired to marry to obtain a special licence, the right to hold real estate was suspended, and the prohibitions against employing Christian servants or adopting Christian names were renewed. Elsewhere, conditions were much the same, even the oath *more judaico* remaining in force in many places until the second half of the nineteenth century was well advanced. Yet, in most cases, Jewish equality remained, on paper and in the hearts of the liberal leaders, as an integral part of the constitutional system; and, when the interlude of reaction was over, it automatically reappeared. There was full emancipation in Baden in 1862, in Saxony in 1868, in Austria and Hungary by the Ausgleich of 1867. When the North German Federation was formed in 1869, a clause was adopted abolishing all restrictions, of whatever nature, incurred by reason of religious opinion. The German Imperial Constitution of 1871 adopted the same principle, which thus became extended to the few states which had not yet fallen into line. Thus the emancipatory movement in Germany, begun when Moses Mendelssohn gained a foothold in Berlin society, was completed.

Elsewhere in Europe the process was closely paralleled. In Denmark the handful of Jews obtained extensive rights in 1814, were admitted to municipal office after 1837, and achieved full emancipation in 1849. The other Scandinavian countries followed suit somewhat more tardily; though the numerical importance of the persons involved was negligible. In Switzerland, as late as the middle of the century, intolerance was so extreme that most cantons refused to admit Jews even temporarily. This obscurantism resulted in a diplomatic struggle which lasted over a long period; for neither England, France, nor America was disposed to sign any arrangement with a country in a large part of which their Jewish subjects would not be permitted to settle or to trade. One by one, however, the various legislatures adopted a more liberal policy, the last falling into line in 1866. The last relics of discrimination were removed at the revision of the Federal Constitution in 1874, when full religious liberty was proclaimed.

In the various phases of the *Risorgimento* in Italy, the Jews were meanwhile playing an exceptionally important part. The Roman Republic under Mazzini, the Venetian Republic under Manin (himself of Jewish descent), the various enterprises of Garibaldi, owed more proportionately to the Jews than to any other section of the Italian people. The year 1830 brought, here as elsewhere, local and ephe-

z

meral attempts at Emancipation; and, in Rome, the mob tore down
the Ghetto gates. In the reaction which succeeded, the previous condition of affairs was restored. Even the barbaric institution of the
Forced Sermon was renewed. The kidnapping and forced baptism of
children, condemned by the earlier Popes, continued to haunt Roman
Jewish life; and almost incredible episodes recurred from time to time
to shock the conscience of Europe. The election to the Papal throne in
1846 of Pope Pius IX, in the warm flush of his reforming zeal, seemed
to herald a brighter day, and many abuses were removed. But it was a
false dawn: and the reactionary policy of the last days of the Temporal
Power obscured the long tradition of toleration which preceded it.

Liberal-minded Italians, however, were making the Jewish cause
their own, and found their mouthpiece in the man of letters, Massimo
d'Azeglio, author of the famous tract, *Della emancipazione civile degli
israeliti* (1847). In the year after the publication of this work, the
liberal government of the kingdom of Sardinia, which was assuming
the lead in the struggle for the unity of Italy, enfranchised its Jewish
subjects. This measure, elaborated and completed by successive legislation, was one of the few enduring fruits of the Year of Revolutions.
As, through the genius of Cavour (ably assisted by his Jewish secretary, Isaac Artom), the kingdom of Sardinia expanded into the kingdom of Italy, this remained one of its fundamental institutions.
Lombardy, Tuscany, Venice, the Patrimony of St. Peter, were all
added in turn to the dominions of the House of Savoy, and Jewish
disabilities automatically crumbled. At last, in 1870, during the
confusion caused by the Franco-Prussian war, Rome itself was seized,
to become the capital of United Italy. The Jews immediately became
accepted as free men and equals, emancipation being extended to
them formally by a decree issued less than a month later. Thus a
degradation which had lasted for three hundred and fifteen years came
to an end, and the oldest Jewish centre of the Western World was
enabled to look forward to a new phase.

If, in England, the progress of emancipation was somewhat slower,
the reason lay largely in the fact that the disadvantages from which the
the Jews suffered were inconsiderable. Their social emancipation
had been complete almost from the beginning. They were subjected
to no special regulations of great stringency, and the few disabilities
which proved the rule were shared by many of the general population
who belonged to dissenting forms of Christianity. The Jew lived
where he would, could enter almost any walk of life, and mixed

freely with Gentile society. Commercial restrictions were confined to a few galling limitations in the City of London, where no Jew could obtain the freedom and none but freemen were allowed to open shops for retail trade. Though, like the Catholic, he could not sit in Parliament, he at least enjoyed the franchise (though, indeed, this was hardly regular). It is true that popular prejudice was not altogether absent, and when in 1753 an innocuous measure was introduced to facilitate the naturalising of foreign Jews (the so-called 'Jew Bill'), the agitation against it rose to such dimensions that it was repealed immediately afterwards.[1]

In 1829, on the triumph of the movement for Catholic emancipation, an agitation was begun for similar legislation in favour of the Jews. It met with a good deal of support, both in the country and in Parliament. *The Times*, indeed, poured ridicule upon the idea, and contemporary caricaturists sneeringly depicted the deplorable spectacle of a Jewish old-clothes dealer taking his seat among the British legislators. In the main, the opposition was frankly religious, being based on the assumption that no Jew could logically be admitted to a share in the government of a Christian country. In view of the feeling aroused, the debate was postponed; and when at last a division was taken, the advocates of Emancipation were hopelessly outnumbered. Nevertheless, they did not despair.

When the Reformed Parliament met, in 1833, another bill along the same lines was introduced. It was championed in the Commons by Thomas Babington Macaulay, and in the Lords by the Duke of Sussex, sixth son of George III, a keen Hebraist and devoted friend of the Jews: and it passed the Lower House by a comfortable majority. The Upper, however, rejected it and its successors with monotonous regularity, in one session after another. Meanwhile the Jews were successively admitted to the Bar (1833), to the Shrievalty (1835), and to other municipal offices (1845). One or two outstanding individuals were raised to the dignity of knighthood or even baronetcy; while Benjamin Disraeli, a baptised Jew proud of his descent (to which he lost no opportunity of referring), attained a foremost position in the counsels of the Tory party. Minor disabilities were removed by the Religious Opinions Relief Bill of 1846, which left their exclusion from Parliament the only serious grievance of which English Jews could complain.

[1] The importance of this measure, merely giving a few foreign-born Jews the privileges enjoyed by their native-born children, is generally exaggerated.

Time after time, from 1847 onwards, Baron Lionel de Rothschild was sent to Westminster as their representative by the Liberal electors of the City of London; but the continued opposition of the Lords prevented the passage of legislation which would have enabled him to take the statutory oath. In 1851 Sir David Salomons, elected Member for Greenwich, endeavoured to force matters by occupying his seat without any preliminary formality; he was, however, forced to retire and submitted to a heavy fine for every occasion on which he had voted. Finally, in 1858, a compromise was reached, each House being allowed to settle its own form of oath; and, eleven years after his first election by the City, Baron Lionel took his seat. (Twenty-seven years later, his son was raised to the Peerage as Lord Rothschild, being the first professing Jew to receive that honour; and he was allowed to take his seat in the Upper House as a matter of course.) In 1871 the trivial religious restrictions which still prevailed were removed, and Jewish emancipation in England became complete.

III

In eastern Europe, ostensible progress was far slower. From the beginning of her history, Russia had been the least tolerant of European powers. During the embryo period of the Czardom, in the fifteenth and sixteenth centuries, a sporadic movement for conversion to Judaism, widely spread amongst certain elements in the population, was repressed with steel and fire. The rulers of the seventeenth century, such as Peter the Great, had been somewhat more favourably inclined, though far from benevolent; but the succession of Empresses who followed him were at one in their fanaticism, if in little else. Catherine I in 1727, Anne in 1739, and Elisabeth in 1742, all issued edicts expelling the Jews from Little Russia—the heart of the country. Successive partitions of Poland, however (1772, 1793, 1795), put the lion's share of that unfortunate land in Russian hands. Thus it came about that the European power which had hitherto shewn itself least disposed to welcome them ruled, in the nineteenth century, over the largest section of the Jewish people, equalling if not outnumbering all the others combined.

They were now living throughout the western provinces of the empire previously under Polish rule. Culturally they were hardly what an English or French Jew, familiar with the writings of the Jewish-born novelist, Disraeli, or the Jewish-born economist, Ricardo, would have considered enlightened, notwithstanding their passionate devotion to an older wisdom. Their intellectual interests were confined to the Talmud and allied literature; or, in the case of the *Hassidim*, to the prodigious attributes of one *Zadik* or another. They universally spoke Judaeo-German, or Yiddish, which they wrote in Hebrew characters. In dress, they clung with unnecessary conservatism to the fashions of a century or more earlier. Except for a very small minority of well-to-do merchants, their usual occupations were petty trading, innkeeping, and farming the various government monopolies; but a large proportion lived on the edge of destitution, with no means of sustenance whatsoever.

Their treatment at the hands of their Polish neighbours had progressively deteriorated since the close of the Middle Ages. It was only within the last quarter of the eighteenth century that they had been allowed to live in Warsaw. In the last years of the old regime, indeed, a more liberal spirit had dawned. A commission appointed by the famous 'Quadrennial Diet', in 1790, had gone so far as to advocate the civil and political emancipation of the Jews, but there was no time to do anything practical in this direction. During Kosciusko's revolt, a certain Berek Joselovitch had formed a regiment of light cavalry consisting entirely of Jews, which was almost wiped out in the defence of the suburb of Praga. In the Grand Duchy of Warsaw, formed under Napoleon's aegis in 1807, a little was done to ameliorate the Jewish status; but after the retreat from Moscow, the old order had been restored.

The policy of the Czars, from the outset, was to confine the Jews to the newly acquired western provinces (the so-called 'Pale of Settlement'), and to prevent them from spreading to other parts of the empire. In pursuance of this, between 1821 and 1824, more than twenty thousand souls were expelled from the villages in the governments of Moghilev and Vitebsk alone. The well-meaning Paul I (1796-1801) and Alexander I (1801-1825) seem, indeed, to have envisaged ultimate emancipation. They did their best to encourage handicrafts and agriculture; they admitted Jews, in a limited proportion, to municipal offices; and they encouraged the establishment of Jewish schools infused with a 'modern' spirit. Simultaneously, an attempt was made to establish strict governmental control over the *Kahal*, or Jewish communal organisation, which had acquired a close hold on every aspect of life. The object was confessedly to facilitate the absorption of the Jew in the general population: assimilation

being officially considered a prerequisite of emancipation. Enlightenment was not to develop—it was to be imposed. Under the circumstances, it is not surprising that the overwhelming majority of those
for whom the reforms were intended proved impervious to them.

In the last years of his reign, the liberalism of Alexander I had
given way to reactionary panic. This continued under his successor,
Nicholas I (1825-1855), whose malevolence towards the Jews was
enhanced by the prominent part which they played in the Polish
Revolution of 1830. Rendered nervous by recent developments in
neighbouring countries, he set himself to isolate his own from the
rest of the world, and to prevent any infiltration of western institutions, western ideals, and above all western liberalism. That the
Jews would be made to suffer more than any other section of his
subjects was inevitable. The treatment to which they were subjected,
and the special regulations devised to crush their spirit, had no parallel
in history, outdoing even the code enforced by the Catholic Church
at the period of the Counter-Reformation. Of some twelve hundred
legal enactments concerning the Jews, published in Russia from 1649
to 1881, no fewer than one half belong to this reign. An Imperial
ukase of 1827 extended conscription to them for the first time, with
the proviso that the normal period of service, instead of being twenty-
five years from the age of eighteen, should be in their case increased
by a further six years and begin in effect at the age of twelve (or, in
some cases, as early as eight!). This, it was hoped, would at least
break down the separatist spirit, for a child's continued fidelity to
Judaism under the knout of the drill-sergeant was unthinkable. Yet
even this ruthless measure failed in its object; and the steadfastness
shewn by many of these 'Cantonists' (as they were called) forms a
peculiarly touching chapter in the history of Jewish martyrdom.

By the Statute concerning the Jews, of 1835, the Pale of Settlement was yet further narrowed down. Jews were excluded from all
villages within fifty versts of the western frontier. Merchants who
desired to visit Russia proper could only do so after obtaining a
special passport, and provided that they abandoned the traditional
Jewish dress. The employment of Christian domestic servants was
prohibited. Synagogues were forbidden to be erected in the vicinity
of churches, and a strict censorship was established over all Hebrew
books printed in the country. Later, the Jews were expelled from the
towns as well as the villages of the frontier area. Special taxation was
imposed on meat killed according to the Jewish fashion, and even on

the candles kindled on Friday night. During the Crimean War, any Jew found without a passport was made liable to be drafted into the army. Only the intervention of 'Général Février', upon whom the Russians had relied to defeat their enemies in the Crimea, but who instead struck down the Czar himself, saved the victims from even worse sufferings.

With the accession of Alexander II (1855-1881), it seemed as though a new era was dawning. The young ruler, described by Disraeli in a moment of enthusiasm as 'the most benevolent Prince that ever ruled in Russia', was at least well-meaning, and set about a consistent policy of reform. The old ideal of excluding foreign conceptions and institutions was reversed, and an attempt made to secure the industrialisation, and with it the westernisation, of the country. The withdrawal, or at least mitigation, of the exceptional legislation against the Jews was an integral part of the process. The special regulations governing conscription were repealed forthwith, the infamous institution of the 'cantonists' coming automatically to an end. The whole empire was opened up, if not to all classes, at least to wealthy merchants, university graduates, and mechanics. Jews were admitted to the legal profession, and even to the magistracy. The concessions granted to the Polish provinces, in order to mitigate discontent, included the removal of sundry minor disabilities.

All this did not in fact amount to much. But the moral effect was important. Russian society as a whole began to manifest a more tolerant attitude. The process of Russification, no longer imposed so ostentatiously from above, began to make more rapid progress. If the Jews were far from enjoying the ideal status of their co-religionists in western Europe, it must be remembered that the idea of the constitutional monarchy and of parliamentary institutions had hardly begun to make progress in the Empire of the Czars. But, in those days of liberal enthusiasm, few persons doubted that this would ultimately be the case, and that the Russian Jews would then enjoy the same opportunities, the same rights, the same privileges, as their fellow-countrymen and as freemen all the world over.

IV

Russian conditions were paralleled only in certain of the Moslem states. Their communities had indeed lost by now much of their one-time significance. At the close of the Middle Ages, the Jewish world had been divided more or less evenly between the Northern and Mediterranean (or 'Ashkenazi' and 'Sephardi') elements. Since then, the former had attained an overwhelming preponderance, for the latter now represented only about one-tenth of the total; and the decline extended to the intellectual sphere as well, the communities founded by the Marrano fugitives in northern Europe having also lost their vigour. They were now living for the most part under the rule of the Crescent. In Turkey and the adjacent lands (such as Egypt) there was little to distinguish their lot from that of the native Christians, which, if sometimes unenviable, was generally endurable. (The principle at least of religious equality was indeed recognised by the Sultan in 1839 and 1856.) But elsewhere, the worst traditions of the Moslem Middle Ages were maintained, without a breath of liberalism or of hope to temper them. The *Mellahs* of the Barbary States perpetuated the misery of the Ghetto, frequently without its humanity. In the Yemen, where a tiny remnant of Arabian Jewry had remained in utter isolation from time immemorial, under circumstances not far different from those of their remote ancestors in Palestine, persecution became more severe as the nineteenth century advanced. In Persia, conditions were perhaps worst of all. Here, under the Shiah system of theology, which locally obtained, the Jews were considered ritually impure, not even being allowed to go out into the street when it rained lest they should pass on their uncleanliness to a believer. Physical maltreatment was distressingly common; and, as late as the nineteenth century (as had already happened in the seventeenth), mass conversion to Islam was secured by force, leaving behind large numbers of crypto-Jews very similar to the Marranos of Spain and Portugal.

The only sections of Asiatic Jewry whose condition gave no cause for misgivings were those of China[1] (now dwindling away rapidly in consequence of their isolation and privileged treatment) and of India,[2] where the native rulers never discriminated between one section of their subjects and another on the ground of religious belief. This condition of affairs, of course, continued under British rule; and less fortunate communities of backward states looked forward to nothing more avidly than the day when some western power, or at least the penetration of western ideas, would bring them relief. The process, here as in Russia, might be long and weary: but its completion was surely only a matter of time.

[1] Above, p. 202.   [2] Above, p. 122.

133. Rabbi Elijah ben Solomon
('The Vilna Gaon', 1720-1797)

134. Leopold Zunz (1794-1886)

135. Heinrich Heine (1797-1856)

136. Heinrich Graetz (1817-1891)

137. Sir Moses Montefiore (1784-1885)
From an engraving

138. 'Mendele Mocher Seforim' (Solomon
Abramovitch, 1835-1917)

139. 'Ahad Ha'am'
(Asher Ginzberg; 1856-1927)

140. Josef Israels (1829-1911)
Self-Portrait

V

One of the factors which had made Jewish Emancipation inevitable was the important part which individual Jews were playing in the new economic order. The Napoleonic wars had been succeeded by a period of unexampled expansion, in which the lessons of the Industrial Revolution which had centred in England were developed and spread to every country. Western Europe became, to an extent never previously equalled, the workshop of the world. Her merchandise, produced by newly invented machinery, was borne on vessels propelled by steam to the furthest ends of the earth. Her factories were busy; her soil was ransacked for minerals; her green fields were disfigured by long gashes as railroads were constructed between her chief cities, to reduce what had hitherto been a day's journey into one of less than an hour. All this was impossible without capital—the golden essence indispensable for the initial impetus of industry, and the lubricant without which its wheels must inevitably clog. The capitalist entered on a new era.

The influence of the wealthy Jew of a previous age had been strictly localised. He might amass a fortune—seldom, in fact, an enormous one. But he made it, and he spent it, within the walls of a single city. Civil disorders and governmental exactions generally prevented his substance from continuing unimpaired from one generation to another. In the activities of the great banking establishments of the period of the Renaissance, he took (contrary to what is generally believed) an insignificant share, if we except the activities of one or two Marrano houses, like that of Mendes,[1] which at one time seemed likely to rival the Fuggers. Stock-jobbers of the eighteenth century (like Samson Gideon [1699-1762], who helped to maintain public credit in England at the time of the Jacobite rebellion of 1745) sometimes piled up fortunes which at the time were considered enormous. But the new economic era which reached its climax in the nineteenth century gave opportunities hitherto unexampled. The field of activity now open overlooked national frontiers and was bounded only by the limits of the globe.

Finance became so important to the various governments that financiers began to treat with them like independent powers. Profits expanded in proportion to the scale of the enterprises; and the

[1] Above, p. 317.

adaptable Jewish mind, sharpened by centuries of Talmudic study, and invigorated by the fresh horizons which opened out as the Ghetto walls were destroyed, was there ready to take advantage of the new scheme of things. It was not that the Jews provided the capital—it had to be created first. But they made it mobile. They perfected the delicate machinery by which it was brought together and made available for industry, and they transferred it from country to country, as and when it was needed. Especially prominent were the Jews of Frankfort, who, occupying a strategic position both geographically and economically, established offshoots in almost every capital of Europe. Within the memory of persons who could still recall how the Frankfort *Judengasse* had to be closed every night, and how its inhabitants were distinguished from the rest of mankind by their yellow badge of shame, the cumulative influence exercised by their descendants in the world of finance was greater than that of almost any Power below the first rank.

The Jew of the new era was summed up, and almost personified, in the House of Rothschild. Meyer Amschel (1743-1812), the founder of the family (which, generations before, had lived at the sign of the Red Shield), had built up a lucrative brokerage business in Frankfort as agent for the Landgrave of Hesse Cassel. His third son, Nathan Meyer Rothschild (1777-1836), went over to England about 1796 and settled in Manchester, where he engaged in the cotton business. The delicate business of transmitting payment, in those troublous times, led him by slow degrees to interest himself mainly in matters of finance. He removed to London, where in a very short while he became one of the best-known figures in financial circles. He negotiated Treasury loans; his coups on 'Change were famous; he transmitted bullion to Spain for the payment of Wellington's troops during the Peninsular War; he organised an intelligence service so perfect that he was able to supply the Government itself with the first news of Waterloo.

When peace came, he extended his activities. His brothers, settled in Frankfort, Paris, Vienna, Naples, rendered possible an international organisation on a vast scale; and the House of Rothschild became, as has aptly been said, the sixth Great Power of Europe. No great enterprise was possible without their support. No important loan could be floated without their co-operation. Their word or warning often swayed the balance between war and peace. Ambassadors and ministers of state jostled one another on their stairs. They entertained magnificently in their homes; their benevolence was world-famous; they were lavish patrons of the Arts; and princes of the blood royal did not disdain their friendship. The acquisition of the control of the Suez Canal for England by Benjamin Disraeli in 1875 was rendered possible only by the fact that they were prepared to advance the ready money. The problem of whether the Jew should be allowed the parliamentary franchise or to exercise the profession of law, at a time when individual Jews could sway governments, was in fact trivial.

The Rothschilds were distinguished from other banking families of the same sort by their exceptionally widespread international ramifications, by their family cohesion (for a long period they intermarried to an alarming extent), and by an unmistakable hereditary financial genius, which was hardly less marked in 1914 than it had been a century before. They were, however, only one of many families which attained enormous influence in financial matters. In England, the House of Goldsmid was the greatest firm of loan contractors at the close of the eighteenth century and beginning of the nineteenth, breaking down finally the monopoly that had formerly cost the public so dear. The brothers Péreire in France (descended from a Marrano family settled at Bordeaux, one of whose members had perfected the first adequate method of teaching deaf-mutes) built up, and afterwards lost, an enormous fortune by subsidising the development of French and Russian railways. Achille Fould was Minister of Finance to Napoleon III. The Bischoffsheims of Mayence, with branches in London, Amsterdam, and Brussels, were nearly as widely ramified as the Rothschilds; and they were rivalled by the Sterns, the Oppenheims, the Goldschmidts, the Wertheims, the Seligmans and many another clan. David Sassoon of Bagdad established a banking dynasty at Bombay, which, within a generation, was the most powerful in the whole of the Orient: and his descendants rapidly established their position in the British moneyed aristocracy, in politics, and in literature. At a slightly later period, Baron Moritz de Hirsch built up an enormous fortune by financing the construction of the Turkish railroad system. When, in 1871, Bismarck demanded from a broken France an indemnity of hitherto unparalleled dimensions, the French President protested that, even had a beginning been made at the birth of Christ, such a sum could never have been brought together. 'That', replied the Iron Chancellor, who was accompanied by the Berlin banker, Gerson Bleichröder, 'is why I have brought with me as adviser one who begins to reckons his years with the creation of the world.'

Banking was not, of course, the only branch of activity in which the Jews distinguished themselves.[1] The earlier stages of the Industrial Revolution, indeed, when coal, cotton, and engineering were first exploited on a large scale, had found them at a disadvantage. Subsequently they made good. They became prominent as industrialists, manufacturers, inventors, above all as *entrepreneurs*. Pedlars developed into merchants with international connections; petty gold- and silver-smiths into bullion-brokers; working tailors into manufacturing wholesalers; dealers in scrap-iron and second-hand household utensils into metal-brokers. The Jewish stockbroker became a well-known figure upon every Bourse in Europe. German Jewish merchants, settled in Great Britain, exported her textiles and other manufactures to every part of the Continent. The Jewish old-clothes man, long the butt of caricaturists, who had hitherto been resorted to for the clothing of the lower classes, was displaced by the Jewish cheap tailor, who introduced (largely through the medium of Jewish labour) the methods of mass-production into the clothing industry. Thereby the luxury of a new suit was placed for the first time within the occasional reach of the poorest mechanic, while his wife and daughter were enabled to clothe themselves in a manner which, not long before, was considered the exclusive prerogative of the well-to-do.

With the progress of time, the field of enterprise widened. The Jews shewed an extraordinary aptitude for realising the implications of any new movement, in industry or in science, in literature or in art; and they were always to be found among its most enthusiastic followers when they were not numbered among its pioneers. Jewish genius for organisation and eye for detail were largely responsible for the development in all western countries, as well as beyond the Atlantic, of the waste-product business, of cheap catering, of the general store; while in the twentieth century they took a prominent

---

[1] The account which follows, in which an attempt is made to summarise into a few pages the economic process of a century and a half, is applicable to western Europe only. In Russia and Poland, semi-medieval conditions (above, pp.356-7) were protracted down to our own day; though in a few industrial centres, such as Lodz, 'the Manchester of Poland', the Jewish proletariat became wage-slaves in the worst sense.

As regards banking, the importance of the Jew diminished with the decay of the private houses and the growth of joint-stock institutions, from the beginning of the twentieth century; but by this time his position in economic life generally had lost its former distinctiveness.

share in the movement for the rationalisation of industry, the elimination of cut-throat competition, and the establishment of the multiple
and one-price stores: the lead thus being transferred from the private
bankers, whose influence was now on the wane, to the distributive
trades. The entertainment industry in all its branches (and, later on,
the new art of the cinematograph) seemed to have special attractions
for them; and they were prominent as actors on the one hand and
producers or distributors on the other. Innate taste and quickness of
perception were responsible for the reputation which they established
as antique dealers (another development of the second-hand dealer,
money-changer, or goldsmith). Throughout Europe they became
recognised as art experts, critics, and historians. In many countries
they were very prominently identified with the field of journalism—
another new opening. The artificially important community of Fürth,
outside Nuremberg (to which they were driven since, until the
eighteen-fifties, no Jew was allowed to remain in that city after sun-
down), rivalled Frankfort in the influence which its children were to
exercise in the world; and from it issued simultaneously, in 1848,
the founder of the Ullstein family, which was to be such a power in
the German press and publishing world; and the father of Adolph
Ochs, who was to found an organisation no less powerful, grouped
about the *New York Times*, in the United States of America. Baron von
Reuter (1816-1899) introduced a new standard for the transmission
of current news; Albert Ballin (1857-1918), founder of the Hamburg-
America Line, was responsible more than any other person for the
development of Germany's mercantile marine; Emil Rathenau (1838-
1915), with two other Jews, for the organisation of her electrical
supply; and Ludwig Mond (1839-1909), the immigrant father of the
first Lord Melchett,[1] for the establishment of the chemical industry
in England.

In professional activity and public life, the position was similar;
and there was no sphere to which the Jew did not penetrate, and in
which he did not distinguish himself. Ferdinand Lassalle created the
Social Democratic movement in Germany, and Eduard Lasker was
one of the few liberal leaders who dared to stand up to Bismarck.
Adolphe Crémieux, one of the most brilliant French advocates and
orators, was Minister of Justice in the Provisional Government of
1848, in which capacity he abolished slavery in the French colonies,
and capital punishment for political offences. In England, no lawyer

[1] Below, p. 417.

of his day was considered superior to Sir George Jessel. Heinrich Heine (a Jew at heart, notwithstanding his baptism) was the greatest of German lyric poets, just as Georg Brandes was the most distinguished Danish critic, and Graziadio Isaiah Ascoli the most eminent Italian philologist. Sarah Bernhardt and Rachel were figures of the first importance on the French stage. Science has always offered special attraction to the Jewish mind; and by 1945, upwards of twenty were awarded the Nobel Prize for outstanding eminence in this sphere. It is significant that a high proportion of the other Jews similarly honoured owed their recognition to their services in the cause of international peace.[1]

Names like those of Ehrlich (it is pointless to multiply examples) testify to brilliance in medicine. Haffkine was perhaps the world's greatest bacteriologist, and saved the lives of millions by his researches into the prevention of bubonic plague. Moritz Lazarus and his brother-in-law, Heyman Steinthal, founded the new science of racial psychology, and Cesare Lombroso that of criminology. Maurice Loewy was one of the foremost observational astronomers. It was the discoveries of Fritz Haber which enabled Germany to withstand a world in arms in 1914-1918; and his production of ammonia from the atmosphere made boundless supplies of fertiliser available, at a time when some agricultural experts were beginning to view the future with grave concern. The first navigable airship was constructed by David Schwartz, the first motor-boat by Moritz Jacobi, the first automobile by Siegfried Marcus: while the safety-match was the invention of Sansone Valobra, the microphone of Emile Berliner and colour photography of Gabriel Lippman. David Ricardo, the English economist, was of pure Jewish blood, though not a professing Jew. It was Zamenhof, a Polish Jew, who devised the international language, Esperanto. Hardly any publicist in Europe, in the early days of the twentieth century, was more influential than 'Maximilian Harden' (before his baptism, at the age of sixteen, Witkowski), the Jewish owner and editor of Die Zukunft. At this period, too, Sigmund Freud launched the new science of psycho-analysis, nearly all the most brilliant exponents of which continued to be Jews, while Max Reinhardt revolutionised the art of the theatre.

[1] The total number of Nobel Prize-winners of Jewish origin was exceeded numerically only by the French and German quotas, and relatively only by the Danes. But it should be borne in mind that the prizes are of Scandinavian foundation, and that a large number of those who are described as French or German (about one-third, in the latter case) were Jews. By 1967 the number of Jewish prize-winners exceeded 50.

Even art, in its more specific sense, came into its own, as the bare names of painters like Israels, Liebermann, Pissarro, Modigliani, and Chagall, and of sculptors like Antokolsky and Epstein, are sufficient to demonstrate. Henri Bergson was one of the most vital European thinkers—heir, in more than one sense, to Spinoza; and Luigi Luzzatti, one of the best-beloved contemporary figures, was Prime Minister of Italy. In the latter country, too, as well as in France, Jews (like General Giuseppe Ottolenghi, Minister of War in 1902-1903) rose to high rank in the military profession. Emin Pasha was one of the most intrepid explorers of his generation, and Rubino Ventura had a kaleidoscopic career as commander-in-chief of the forces of various potentates of the Far East. Sutro, Rice, Bernstein, and Schnitzler testified to brilliance in the dramatic sphere in various countries. While the Jew produced no musical composers of first eminence (unless we reckon Wagner, whose Jewish paternity is widely believed), the names of Meyerbeer, Mendelssohn, and Halévy nearly qualify for admission into this category: and their supremacy as interpreters and instrumentalists was unchallenged. Jewish philan-thropic enterprise was, of course, everywhere prominent. The organisation of the humane treatment of animals, indeed, owes its origin to Lewis Gompertz, who in 1824 began the movement which resulted in the foundation of the English R.S.P.C.A.—a Jew, working in the Biblical tradition. Noteworthy, too, is the fact that the Inter-national Agricultural Institute at Rome was founded by David Lubin. An Italian statistician calculated that the proportion of persons of distinction in the Jewish community outnumbered those in the general world by fifteen to one, holding a clear lead in every field excepting the hereditary nobility and the Church.

In colonial development, Jews were equally important. Congrega-tions were established and synagogues built in the early days of the development of South Africa, Australia, and New Zealand. Ten years before the English reached Natal, one Nathaniel Isaacs (1804-1872) had been recognised as its 'Principal Chief' by virtue of an agreement with the Zulu king. A little group of Jews originated the mohair industry in Cape Colony. In the febrile period of development at the close of the century, when the gold-mining and diamond industries put the fortunes of the sub-continent on a new basis, the Joels, Barnatos, Albus, and Beits played a part of paramount importance. Sir Julius Vogel (1835-1899) was Prime Minister of New Zealand as early as 1873; while, at a subsequent period, Sir Isaac Isaacs (b. 1855) was the first Governor-General of Australia nominated by the government of that Dominion.

When the age of sport began, the infiltration was no less marked. There was a tradition of Jewish pugilists in England going back to the close of the eighteenth century, when Daniel Mendoza wedded science to fisticuffs, and, with a number of his professional confrères, did a good deal to lessen the prejudice against the Jews among the lower classes. There was an interruption in the middle of the following century; but, in the twentieth, prominence in the prize-ring was such that Gentiles of unquestioned antecedents sometimes considered it advisable to adopt a characteristically Jewish *nom de guerre*. The Rothschild family interested itself at an early date in the Turf; and Jewish race-horse owners, who backed their fancies like gentlemen and bore their losses like Spartans, were soon reckoned amongst the most popular figures at Newmarket or Auteuil. There were Jewish champions at fencing, diving, steeple-chasing, running, and tennis-playing. It was a Jew who set the fashion in Channel swimming, soon to become the ambition of every enthusiastic amateur. In the course of a couple of generations, the Jews made up, and made up handsomely, for the long centuries during which they had been excluded from opportunity.

VI

The more settled conditions of the nineteenth century saw a rapid increase in Jewish population—due not so much to a higher birth-rate, as is generally believed (for, in fact, fecundity among the Jews was rather less than among their neighbours), but to a more hygienic manner of life, resulting in a lower death-rate. The number of Jews living in the world in earlier periods is by no means easy to determine by reason of the fact that our statistical knowledge is so limited and that vast numbers may have been resident in areas concerning which no evidence survives. Hence the current conjectures of 4,500,000 Jews at the beginning of the dispersion, dwindling by the twelfth century to 1,500,000, can hardly be accepted implicitly. From the twelfth century to the close of the seventeenth century the figures appear to have been almost static, wavering between 1,500,000 and 2,000,000. By 1800 the total had risen to some 2,500,000. Then, in the course of the nineteenth century, there was an unprecedented expansion. By 1900 the number of Jews in the world had risen to

10,500,000, and a generation later the total exceeded 16,000,000. The significance of the increase becomes apparent when one remembers that it was proportionately higher by nearly 50 per cent than that of England and Wales in the same period, and nearly five times as great as that of France. On the other hand, with the twentieth century the birth-rate of the assimilated Jewish bourgeoisie of the western countries declined catastrophically, so that without an influx from abroad (which rapidly succumbed to the same influence in its turn) the level of population could not have been maintained.

With equality of rights and opportunities, the vocational differences between Jew and Gentile began to disappear, or at least to be transferred to other spheres. True, there were certain industries from which he had been excluded in a former age, with which (as we have seen) the Jew began to be very prominently associated. On the other hand, the Jewish pedlar, who had once been so characteristic a figure, and had numbered at least one-third of the total male population in Germany and England at the close of the eighteenth century, now became almost unknown. Even agricultural life, notwithstanding the long period of urban residence and the difficulties which still obtained, began to hold out attractions. In central and eastern Europe, as well as in the New World and in Palestine, many farming colonies were established: and the number of Jews settled on the soil had risen by 1900 to 2 per cent of the whole, and by 1939 to over 6 per cent. On the other hand, the sturdy individualism inbred by past history could not be eradicated. The Jew universally displayed a disinclination to work in a subordinate capacity. As soon as he could possibly do so, the employee set up on his own account; and Jewish shopkeepers and small manufacturers stood out manfully against the advance of the trusts and multiple stores—even though the latter, as has already been pointed out, owed much of their impetus to Jewish enterprise. The break-up of the Ghetto was succeeded with amazing rapidity by the rectification of its untoward influences upon the Jewish physique. Within a very few decades, the former stoop was lost, the sallow complexion became less common, open-air life obtained an increasing hold, and inches were added to the average stature.

Meanwhile a profound sociological change was beginning. Hitherto, in almost every country of Europe, the Jews had lived a scattered existence. Communities were to be found in a large number of rural centres and townships. It is significant that the characteristic Jewish

surnames throughout the world, from Germany or Italy to India, are
to a large extent derived from little places the Jewish connection
with which has long since ended. This was the case, even in England,
where in the pre-expulsion period Jews were to be found in rural
centres such as Wallingford and Devizes, and after the Resettlement
at Penzance or King's Lynn. In Alsace, similarly, hardly a township
lacked its Jews. With the improvement in communications which
characterised the early nineteenth century, the intensity of local life
diminished; and the Jews tended therefore to drift towards the larger
cities. One after the other, the smaller places were abandoned; and
derelict synagogues or burial-grounds became characteristic features
of sleepy provincial centres all over western Europe. For a time
Jewish life shewed a predilection for the manufacturing towns which
had grown up as a result of the Industrial Revolution. Ultimately,
these, too, tended to be vacated in favour of the capital and a handful
of great cities. Thus, in 1816, the seven largest communities of the
country accounted for only 20,000 (or 7.7 per cent) out of the
257,048 German Jews: Hamburg, the most numerous of all, containing some 7,000. A century later the total Jewish population had
grown to 600,000, of whom approximately one-half were to be found
in the seven greatest cities. Berlin, by this time, comprised nearly
175,000, or a little less than a third of the whole. London is hardly a
faithful parallel, owing to its favoured position as port of arrival for a
large number of the successive immigrants and its overwhelming
importance in the national life; and it can never have held in modern
times a smaller proportion than two-thirds of Anglo-Jewry. In the
second quarter of the twentieth century, nearly half of the Jewish
people lived in great cities, and nearly a quarter in the handful with
a population of one million or more.

At the same time, attachment to Judaism in western Europe was
dwindling. Synagogues formerly filled to overflowing thrice each day
received their full complement of worshippers only on the most
important solemnities. The punctilios of orthodoxy were increasingly
abandoned. Home observances began to be relinquished. The closing
of business houses on the Sabbath became almost exceptional. Knowledge of Hebrew and of Jewish lore was reduced to a minimum;
and descendants of famous Rabbis considered it an achievement if
they could stumble through a single familiar page of the liturgy without committing a gross blunder. There grew up a vast number of
persons whose Judaism consisted of little other than an unquenchable

charitableness, annual attendance at synagogue, and an almost superstitious craving to be buried in a Jewish 'House of Life'. A degree of
assimilation even more complete was not unknown. It is computed
that no less than 200,000 Jews were baptised in the course of the
nineteenth century, and it was possible to meet persons, Jewish in
name, in appearance, and in characteristics, who indignantly repudiated all connection with the community.

Under such circumstances, it was inevitable that intermarriage
should have set in on an increasing scale. The proudest nobility often
recuperated its fortunes by a match with some Jewish heiress. Hardly
a single family of the English or Hungarian nobility—to take only
two examples—was free from some such admixture or alliance. In
some outlying centres, where the Jewish community was small and
the degree of assimilation complete, mixed marriages were sometimes
more numerous than the reverse. Within a couple of generations,
Jewish blood had begun to permeate the remotest strata of society,
fertilising genius as diverse as that of Marcel Proust, the novelist;
Alexandre Millerand, the French statesman; Sir Henry Newbolt, the
English poet; and Sven Hedin, the Swedish explorer.[1]

VII

In tending their own vineyard, the Jews were now somewhat re-
miss. The age when Jewish scholarship was confined to the study and
elaboration of the standard Rabbinic texts was now obviously past.
Knowledge of Hebrew had, indeed, so far degenerated as to be insufficient for any such study in a vast majority of cases. Moreover, a
general desire was felt to habilitate, or rehabilitate, Jewish scholarship in the eyes of the Gentile. Just as the Jew himself had come out
of the Ghetto, had shed his distinctive dress and his distinctive language, and had widened his field of interest until it embraced everything human, so (it was felt) Jewish scholarship must come out of its
isolation and be reinterpreted in modern terms, comprehensible both
in manner and in language to persons steeped in the intellectual
currents of the day.

Moses Mendelssohn, in his translation of the Bible half a century
before, had pointed the way: and the tradition remained centred

[1] One or two of the persons mentioned above on pp. 365-8 were similarly of mixed
blood—e.g. Sarah Bernhardt: while several more (e.g. Emin Pasha) were not professing
Jews.

above all in the country in which he had lived and worked. A simple scholar named Leopold Zunz (1794-1886), stirred by an attempt of the Prussian government to suppress the 'innovation' of a vernacular sermon in the synagogues, published in 1832 a work, *Die gottesdienstlichen Vorträge der Juden*, in which he shewed that the homiletical address in the language of the country was in fact an institution of immemorial antiquity, and the basis of much of the older Rabbinic literature. The volume still remains to-day a vast store-house of Jewish lore, to an extent rarely paralleled in a pioneer work. But it was more significant as the first attempt (unless we except the abortive experiment of Azariah de' Rossi, three centuries before) to apply modern critical methods and standards to the study of the problems of Hebrew literature. It was to this, later supplemented by a series of publications on the Jewish liturgy and synagogal poetry, that the study of the Science of Judaism or *Jüdische Wissenschaft* (as it is generally termed) owed its origin.

Zunz found worthy coadjutors. Moritz Steinschneider (1816-1907), the prince of Hebrew bibliographers, explored the treasures of the libraries of Europe, made them accessible to the learned world by his catalogues and articles, and demonstrated the immeasurable debt which western culture owes to the Jewish translators of the Middle Ages. The first history of the Jews since Josephus (with the exception of one or two medieval chronicles and elementary Protestant experiments) was that of Isaac Marcus Jost (1793-1860), published in the eighteen-twenties; but it was soon superseded by the monumental work (1853-1870) of Heinrich Graetz, based upon original sources in a bewildering variety of languages, which retains its fundamental importance even at the present day. (Later on, Simon Dubnow [1860-1941] achieved in Russian a work on a similar scale, emphasising the eastern European scene and the social-economic aspects, which Graetz had tended to overlook.)

In the outlying provinces of the Austrian Empire, Hebrew continued to serve as the medium of scholarship, though its method was modernised. The Galician Nahman Krochmal (1785-1840) formulated in his *Modern Guide of the Perplexed* a philosophy of Jewish history, which he envisaged as a series of Hegelian waves of rise and decline, faithfully reflecting every world tendency; while, in a series of penetrating essays, Solomon Judah Rapoport (1790-1867) recreated from scattered material personalities and movements of the Talmudic and especially post-Talmudic epoch, this providing the basis for much subsequent historiography—for example, the writings of Isaac Hirsch Weiss (1815-1905), the foremost historian of the *Halakha*. In northern Italy, Samuel David Luzzatto of Padua (1800-1865: an omniscient scholar and collector, who would perhaps be better remembered had he confined his work to a single field) together with Isaac Samuel Reggio of Gorizia (1784-1855), combined the immemorial traditions of Italian Jewish culture with the new conceptions which had come to the fore in Germany. German-born or German-trained scholars (such as Salomon Munk [1803-1867], who lost his sight in consequence of his assiduous labours in the field of Judaeo-Arabic studies) carried the seeds of *Jüdische Wissenschaft* to Paris, London, and elsewhere; though it was long before they struck root beyond the bounds of the German-speaking world. Scientific reviews were published all over Europe to act as the vehicles for the transmission and diffusion of the new science; supplementing the more commonplace vernacular periodicals which, from the close of the first quarter of the nineteenth century, had appeared in English, French, German, and Italian.

The laboratories for the new science were the various theological seminaries which began to be set up at this period. The old-time Rabbi, who owed his appointment to Talmudic learning and nothing else, was obviously an anachronism in an age when the Talmud had ceased to carry so much weight as hitherto, and when the position of the sermon in synagogal worship was becoming increasingly important. Moreover, the Jewish pastor was frequently expected to act as intermediary between the civil government and his community. He was regarded as the sample and the touchstone by which his flock were estimated. The latter, therefore, set themselves to produce a new type of spiritual leader, qualified not only to retain the respect of an enlightened community, but also to hold his own when associating with confrères of other faiths. It was confessedly with this object in view that the communities of the Austrian possessions in northern Italy established the first modern Rabbinical seminary, at Padua, in 1829, Samuel David Luzzatto being the foremost member of its staff. The example was speedily followed in France, Germany, Austria, and other countries of western Europe. In these institutions Jewish history, philosophy, apologetics, exegesis, and homiletics were taught, in addition to the Talmud. The Hebraic disciplines were generally supplemented by a parallel course in a University. Thus, the old-time Rabbi was displaced, and the modern Minister of Religion (frequently perpetuating the old title, though not the former qualifications) established his position.

Even in Russia the intellectual revival, or rather readjustment, was paralleled. There, to be sure, its nature was radically different. Whereas among the enlightened groups of the west it took the form of the presentation of a modernised Jewish scholarship to European circles through the medium of the vernacular, among the masses of the east it lay in the introduction of secular literature to Jewish circles through the medium of Hebrew. As the century advanced, there began to emerge in Russian Jewry an intelligentsia similar to that produced by the Mendelssohnian school in Prussia a generation or more before (though with significant differences), and owing a great deal to its example. The activities of the German *Meassefim* had, indeed, aroused a sympathetic echo in eastern Europe, and the periodical from which they took their name had a long series of imitators. A few devoted littérateurs, more noteworthy perhaps for their courage and industry than for their genius, began to produce a succession of works through which they hoped to introduce the fine flower of European culture to their Hebrew-reading co-religionists. Essays, poems, brochures, scientific works, finally even novels, began to be published in comparative profusion, in the tongue hitherto regarded as exclusively 'holy'. The movement was called the *Haskalah*, or enlightenment.

Unlike the parallel German tendency, that which had its birth in Russia gained rather than lost in strength with the passage of time: for it was afforded no opportunity of becoming diverted into vernacular channels, and thus developing into an abstract *Jüdische Wissenschaft*. Hebrew, thus rendered malleable once more, was allowed to wander beyond the purely scholastic sphere and the stilted Rabbinic phraseology; and the foundations were laid for a cultural revival which was ultimately to attain imposing dimensions. Four names only need be mentioned in illustration: Isaac Baer Levinsohn (1788-1860), essayist and philosopher in a mild fashion, the father of the movement; Judah Loeb Gordon (1831-1892), the first truly modern Hebrew poet; Abraham Mapu (1808-1867), the founder of the Hebrew novel; and Perez Smolenskin (1842-1885), who led an abortive revolt against what he regarded as religious obscurantism.

Parallel, but slightly posterior, to the Hebrew revival was a Yiddish one, producing a few poets and novelists of real genius who took as their subject-matter the life of the Jewish masses of the Russian pale.

This, perhaps, reached its culminating point in Solomon Abramovitch (1836-1917), better known as Mendele Mocher Seforim ('Mendele the Bookseller': also known for his Hebrew writings), who depicted small-town life with the genius of a Dickens, and Shalom Rabinovitz (1859-1916: 'Shalom Aleikhem'), the Yiddish Mark Twain. Abraham Goldfaden (1840-1908), a Roumanian, developed the burlesque plays traditionally associated with *Purim* into a drama on the Parisian or Viennese model; and, by the time of his death, the Yiddish theatre had attained real importance. The general progress, in the course of the century, was remarkable.

VIII

It was not to be imagined that the modernising tendency could fail to affect spiritual life. The traditional Jewish religious practices, evolved in Asia twenty centuries before, had easily been reconciled with the spirit of the Ghetto; but they appeared somewhat incongruous to a generation which was doing its best to steep itself in modern European life. To some extent, moreover, they had been consciously inspired by the wish to perpetuate Jewish separatism— the last thing which the rising generation desired. Prayers in Hebrew had become unintelligible to bankers whose education in Jewish lore was fragmentary. The noisy, intimate manifestations of traditional piety seemed supremely indecorous to those in whom piety had begun to wane: while persons familiarised with the stately ceremonial, careful organisation, and frigid decorum of a Church service could hardly conceive the beauty of holiness under any other form, and blushed at the thought of the comparison which a Christian onlooker might draw in synagogue.

Accordingly, *pari passu* with Jewish emancipation there had been a movement for religious reform. Israel Jacobson (1768-1828), financial agent for Jerome Bonaparte as King of Westphalia, and president of the Consistorial organisation established by him, was the pioneer. Filled with zeal for religious equality, he had established at Seesen, in 1801, a boarding-school where Jewish and Christian boys might be brought up in mutual toleration and amity. In 1810 he opened a synagogue for this institution. Here, for the first time in the history of modern Jewish worship (except in Prague and North Italy, under Renaissance influence), an organ was introduced; German prayers were heard as well as Hebrew, and the confirmation of adolescents of both sexes in the Christian manner was practised. These innovations were subsequently enforced by Consistorial decree: the sympathy of the government being so markedly on the side of the reformers that complaints were silenced by royal authority.

On the fall of the kingdom of Westphalia, when these innovations were automatically swept away, Jacobson removed to Berlin. Here, he and Jacob Herz Beer (father of the composer, Meyerbeer) installed in their homes services according to the new style. The reactionary Prussian government, objecting in principle to anything in the way of novelty in whatever sphere, had these private conventicles closed. Shortly after, Israel (Eduard) Kley, an enthusiastic pedagogue who had preached at the services, became headmaster at a Jewish school in Hamburg, where he gathered round him a small group of persons with views similar to his own. Thus, the first Reform synagogue was founded (1818); and a new prayer-book, comprising a number of haphazard alterations, was published for use in its worship. Advanced circles, throughout Germany, watched the experiment with eager expectation.

Thus far the rift between the two elements was not of primary importance. But it was obviously only a beginning. Zealous advocates of emancipation, from whose number the earliest sympathisers of Reform were recruited, were at pains to depict themselves as being simply Germans of the Jewish persuasion—not members of a body in whom race and religion and ethnic culture were inextricably intermingled. An integral part of Jewish ideology had hitherto been the national restoration to Palestine. To the new species of Jew this was superfluous: it was unnecessary: it was undesirable. 'This land is our Palestine, this city our Jerusalem, this House of God our Temple' became a platitude in assimilated circles; where the corollary might well have been added that the Parliamentary Franchise was their Messiah. There were numerous other points of difference—allusions to the former sacrificial worship, and the observance of supplementary days of the festivals (introduced at an early date by Mesopotamian Jewry in order to counterbalance any possible error in computation, and afterwards retained though the original cause no longer applied).

By slow degrees the Reforming element began to take up a more extreme attitude on all these matters. What had begun as a movement for superficial reform in synagogal worship developed into a general revolt against traditional forms and against Talmudic Judaism as a whole. The old ceremonial was discarded. The whole of the Rabbinical structure was repudiated. The Bible alone was taken as authoritative. In place of the Messianic idea in the old sense, there sprang up a new conception—that of the 'Mission of Israel', which could be accomplished only in dispersion. Reform found vigorous apologists in scholars like the radical Samuel Holdheim (1806-1860), who preached a conception of Judaism entirely divorced from nationality, and officiated at a Berlin synagogue in which the Sabbath was transferred from Saturday to Sunday. He found a whole-hearted collaborator in the encyclopaedic Abraham Geiger (1810-1874), the philosopher of Reform, who elaborated a theory of an evolutionary Judaism, constantly changing and perpetually renewing itself in accordance with the conditions of each succeeding generation. The movement was not, of course, confined to Germany. As early as 1836 its influence began to be felt in London, where a Reformed Congregation was organised in 1840, and a more extreme movement, under the name of 'Liberal Judaism', sprang up a couple of generations later under the inspiration of C. G. Montefiore (1858-1939). German immigrants brought the new ideas to America, where, by the middle of the century, Reform Judaism in a radical sense had established a strong hold.[1]

The evolution of Reform naturally drove the other wing to reconsider its position. Samson Raphael Hirsch (1808-1888), Rabbi at Frankfort, formulated a philosophy of strictly traditional Judaism which, without surrendering one whit to modernity, purported to satisfy the modern mind no less that that of Holdheim or of Geiger, yet did not render itself susceptible to periodical antiquation by subservience to the fashionable conceptions of the day. Between the two extremes a 'conservative' element was able to modernise synagogal worship externally and to accommodate itself to prevailing standards, without fundamental alteration of the liturgy or the official abandonment of any practice. Significant of the change of mentality was the fact that in France, in Germany, in Italy—everywhere, in fact, excepting in England—the very term 'Jew', with its opprobrious Ghetto connotation, was abandoned to a great extent in favour of 'Israelite' or 'Hebrew': while, with an unfortunate retrogression in ideas, the title 'Synagogue' gave way in many countries to 'Temple'.

In the long run, neither extreme triumphed. The incursions of Higher Criticism undermined the prestige of the Bible, on which the adherents of reform had at first implicitly relied. They were hence compelled, in spite of themselves, to recognise the importance of

[1] Below, pp. 397-8.

Rabbinic tradition if only as one of the stages in the evolution of Judaism. There was in the twentieth century a noticeable movement back towards ceremonial; and the Talmud once more took its place as a Jewish classic—not authoritative, indeed, but nevertheless important as a monument of national culture. On the other hand, 'Orthodox' Judaism itself, in western European countries, moved insensibly with the times. The more dignified methods of public worship and the hortatory sermon as opposed to the Talmudic discourse, which had been the original points of contention, obtained full sanction even in the strongholds of the old school; and more than one practice, which hardly seemed consonant with the age, dropped into almost universal desuetude. In time, moreover, occasional prayers in the vernacular, unimportant omissions, and trained choirs (sometimes even with musical accompaniment) obtained a foothold in synagogues which would have indignantly repudiated the suggestion that they had any leaning toward Reform.

IX

With the new era, a deep cleavage began to manifest itself between the Occident and the Orient. The western countries—especially England, France, and Germany, with the new-born United States of America beyond the ocean—now led mankind in science, in art, in literature, and in all else that made for human advancement. They were become the workshop of the world. They had invented the steam-engine and the spinning-jenny; they had evolved the only rational type of human dress; they had received (or were receiving) the supreme boon of parliamentary institutions. Countries were admitted or excluded from the charmed circle of civilised nations in proportion as they imitated them in these respects or no.

It was in these lands that the Jews had entered most intimately into general life, and in which their emancipation first became a reality. They had achieved (or were achieving) the benefits of parliamentary franchise, of elaborate communal institutions, of periodicals in the vernacular, of theological seminaries in a modern sense, and of communal leaders of unimpeachable elegance and address. Other countries of Europe—Russia, the Balkan States and, for the moment, Italy—were backward in this as in every other respect. The day would surely come, however, when the benefits of civilisation, and of parliamentary institutions, would be extended to them also; and Jewish emancipation, physical and intellectual, would automatically follow. In the background there loomed the Moslem world, straddling across Asia and North Africa, where the process might ultimately be repeated, though at a very much slower rate.

In the meantime it fell to the lot of the emancipated Jews of western Europe to assume the tutelage of their brethren—to obtain diplomatic intervention on their behalf in case of persecution, and to fit them for emancipation by means of education. Similar work, of course, had to be done among the immigrants from these less happy parts established in London or in Paris, who still needed assistance in order to relieve them from penury and to qualify them for citizenship. An admirable network of charitable organisations—such as the Jewish Board of Guardians in London, founded in 1859—was established for the purpose of alleviating their distress and supplying their spiritual requirements; and it was a recognised point of pride that though the community contributed its full quota to ordinary taxation, no Jew was ever allowed to become dependent upon public relief. It was generally acknowledged that the objects of succour, whether at home or abroad, were better versed in Jewish lore, and more meticulous in Jewish observance, than those who doled it out. The latter recognised the fact, but felt that their more advanced status in the scale of civilisation exempted them, to some extent, from the shackles incumbent upon their brethren. The indigent practised, as it were, a vicarious Judaism on their behalf.

It was the Damascus Affair of 1840 which initiated the eleemosynary era in foreign affairs, and confirmed Occidental Jewry in its position of patronising leadership. On 5th February of that year, Father Thomas, Superior of the Franciscan convent at Damascus, mysteriously disappeared, together with his servant. The Governor of the city was persuaded to institute an investigation in the Jewish quarter. By means of the bastinado, a sort of confession was extorted from a poor barber to the effect that a ritual murder had been meditated. In consequence, seven of the most notable members of the community were arrested and put to the torture. One died under his suffering, and one apostatised. The Governor, taking the words which had escaped from the others in their agony as an admission of guilt, applied for permission to execute them. In the meantime several other persons were thrown into prison, including sixty children, who were kept without food in the hope that their sufferings would induce their parents to confess. A general massacre seemed imminent.

When the news reached Europe and America, public opinion was deeply stirred. A meeting of protest, attended by Christians as well as Jews, was held at the Mansion House in London. Sir Moses Montefiore (who had been Sheriff for the City of London on the accession of Queen Victoria, when he had been knighted) proceeded to the east together with Adolphe Crémieux, the famous French lawyer, and Salomon Munk, the well-known Orientalist. This powerful delegation, authorised to speak in the name of the Jews of England and of France, was backed up by the diplomatic authority of the former power at least. On 4th August they reached Alexandria, and secured an order from Mehemet Ali, Governor of Egypt, for the release of the nine survivors. In Constantinople the delegates were received in audience by the Sultan, from whom they elicited a *firman* unconditionally acquitting the accused persons, pronouncing the ritual murder a gross libel, and confirming the inviolability of the persons and property of Jews throughout the Ottoman Empire.

The return journey of the delegation was like a triumphant progress. Never before had Jews achieved a success on behalf of their people so outstanding, so public, or so far-reaching. Everywhere prayers, deputations, public addresses, greeted the returning heroes, who remained until their deaths the idols of the Jewish world. The Board of Deputies of British Jews (a development of a joint inter-synagogal committee formed after the accession of George III in 1760), which had taken the mission under its patronage, was henceforth considered little less than an Anglo-Jewish parliament. Its growth was rapid, and it was at once the cynosure and the envy of all Europe. Montefiore and Crémieux were continually called upon whenever persecution threatened in any quarter of the globe. The former, especially, never turned a deaf ear; and the figure of the stately patriarch (who remained active almost to the end of his exceptionally long life) became no less familiar in the courts of Russia and Roumania than in the Jewish quarters of Palestine and Morocco.

In 1858 another wave of indignation swept through Europe by reason of the kidnapping at Bologna (still under Papal rule) of a seven-year-old Jewish child, Edgardo Mortara, on the pretext that he had been submitted to some sort of baptismal ceremony by a servant-girl six years previous—the most notorious of a long series of outrages which had terrorised Jewish life in Italy since the seventeenth century. Francis Joseph II of Austria, and Napoleon III of France advised the Pope to yield; a mass meeting of protest was held once again at the Mansion House in London, and the indefatigable Monte-fiore went in person to Rome to obtain the rectification of the out-rage. 'Pio Nono', however, remained adamant, and Edgardo Mortara was brought up in the dominant faith, ultimately attaining distinction in the Church. This fresh *cause célèbre* resulted in the organisation in Paris, under the auspices of Crémieux (who, notwithstanding his zeal for his persecuted brethren, had his own children brought up as Catholics), of the *Alliance Israélite Universelle*. This organisation had as its object the defence of Jewish rights whenever they were attacked and the diffusion of Occidental education and ideals—as the event shewed, of a notably Gallic tinge—among the less advanced Jewish communities of the world.

The Franco-Prussian War of 1870 naturally diminished the univer-sality of the appeal of this body. Accordingly, an organisation with identical objects, the Anglo-Jewish Association, was formed in England in 1871, to be imitated by the *Hilfsverein der deutschen Juden* in Germany some time later. East was east, and west was west, in the Jewish as in the political world (except that in the former case the dividing-line perhaps fell somewhere nearer the meridian of Greenwich). But mankind was confident that the benefits of education and of a liberal constitution would bridge the two, in God's good time. When that consummation took place, the millennium of peace, good-will, and toleration would dawn. It was under the cheering influence of this conviction that Jewry entered the last decades of the century.

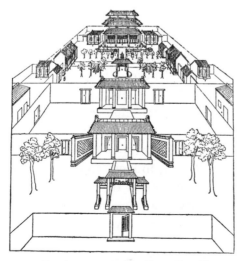

141. SYNAGOGUE AT KAI-FENG-FU, CHINA
(After Domenge and Bruker)

Chapter XXIX

ANTI-SEMITISM AND THE NEW DIASPORA

————————————•————————————

I

The halcyon days of interdenominational Liberty, Equality, and Fraternity, *in esse* or *in posse*, lasted as far as the Jews were concerned for little more than a decade. It was in or about the magic year 1870, with the establishment of religious liberty in Germany, Austria, Hungary, Switzerland, Sweden, and Rome, that the principles of Jewish Emancipation seemed to achieve their definite triumph. Its extension by the French in that year to their colony of Algeria formally carried the conception for the first time to the Moslem world. As far as Europe was concerned, the only parts now outstanding were Spain and Portugal, where the sparse Jewish re-settlement was not yet officially authorised; Norway, where causes for grievance were gradually disappearing; and (outside the charmed circle of the Christian powers) Turkey, where such disabilities as the Jews suffered were shared by the rest of the non-Moslem population. In the Balkan States, which attained independence from Turkish suzerainty as a result of the Berlin Conference of 1878 (overshadowed by the enigmatic figure of 'the old Jew', as Bismarck dubbed Benjamin Disraeli, Earl of Beaconsfield, a dominant figure in contemporary British politics) the principle of religious equality was imposed as a condition of autonomy. Finally, and regrettably, there was Russia, in which the vast majority of the Jewish people, was to be found. They were subjected, indeed, to numbers of disabilities, and deprived of political rights: yet at this time hardly more so than the other inhabitants of that vast autocracy, which at last appeared to be making slow progress towards western ideals of constitutional monarchy.

There had been in all countries reactionary elements which opposed Jewish emancipation tooth and nail, and acquiesced in it even now only reluctantly. In the last decades of the nineteenth century it was impossible to base such feelings, as hitherto, upon religious prejudice: for a new era of tolerance had titularly dawned, in which all creeds were respected and in which discrimination on denominational grounds was hardly conceivable. The opposition, therefore, took on a new aspect. With regard to Judaism it was sneeringly tolerant; but it transferred the basis of its prejudices from essentially religious to essentially national grounds.

Ernest Renan, the illustrious French student of Oriental antiquities, and one of the most brilliant thinkers in contemporary Europe, had first popularised the conception of 'Semitic' and 'Aryan', originally used to distinguish two groups of languages from one another, as racial terms—a highly questionable differentiation. Renan himself, indeed, denied that the Jews were Semitic, and doubted whether they constituted a distinct 'race'. (In point of fact, though the Jews may not have belonged in origin to one single stock, there had been no considerable foreign intermixture amongst them, except in eastern Europe, since the beginning of the Christian era.) Nevertheless, a reactionary coterie in Germany began to use the new terminology as a cover for the old prejudice.

The Anti-Semites (as they were named in 1879 by Wilhelm Marr, a highly jaundiced pamphleteer), insisted not only that the 'race' to which the Jews belonged was distinct, but also that it was inferior— which, in view of Jewish eminence in art, literature, science, business, politics, and general life, was demonstrably absurd. Over-looking the fact that most of the important nations of the Western World were comparative newcomers, and that the Jews had been established there for two thousand years, they purported to regard the latter as alien excrescences upon European life. They were scientifically distinguishable, it was asserted, by a lower cranial capacity; and they were inferior physically, intellectually, and morally to their fellow-citizens of the Aryan, and more specifically of the Teutonic or Nordic, stock, 'the fairest blossom on the human tree'. Their religion was not false in the old sense, but it was the expression of a lower moral conception, and thus inculcated a perverted moral sense. The Talmud was again attacked, with a resuscitation of all the medieval exaggerations, suppressions, and perversions; but this time on ostensibly ethical, rather than theological, grounds. The Jews were held to be responsible for every trouble or misfortune. If they had made their way to the fore in the business world, it had been only because of their unscrupulous methods. Their importance in contemporary life was regarded as the outcome of an organised attempt to secure domination. Even leaders of thought joined in the craze, led by the historian Treitschke, who spoke of the Jews as Germany's misfortune. Ultimately, there even developed a movement of opposition to Christianity, as being essentially Jewish and non-Aryan in origin, while some theologians who would not go so far found ingenious reasons for questioning whether Jesus of Nazareth could have been a Jew.

The movement, in its new form, owed its inception to the year 1873, when the wave of over-speculation, which had followed in the wake of the Franco-Prussian War, resulted in the inevitable crash. Popular resentment found its scapegoat in the only section of the speculating minority easily distinguishable from the rest. A number of publicists—Marr, Glogau, Dühring—fanned the flames, inveighing against what they termed the Jewish 'supremacy' in German life, and clamouring for corrective measures. No great importance was attached to the agitation till 1879, when Bismarck, the German Chancellor, who had climbed to power with Liberal support, made a political *volte-face*. Allying himself with the reactionaries, he now set about a ruthless attempt to stem the tide of democracy. The Jews, indebted to Liberalism for their emancipation, had been vocal upon that side in politics, and had provided it with more than one prominent leader (it is sufficient to mention Eduard Lasker). This in itself was sufficient to win the Iron Chancellor's resentment, and he had no scruples in reverting to the immemorial policy of making the Jews serve as whipping-boy, in the hope of discrediting the Liberal movement as such. His influence was now thrown into the scales behind the scenes. In support of his new policy, the Court Preacher, Adolf Stöcker, formed what he called the Christian Socialist Workingmen's Union— in reality bourgeois, reactionary, and diametrically opposed to the best teachings of Christianity. In the forefront of its programme was the restriction of Jewish 'domination' in business, society, and politics. The movement was eagerly joined by unprogressive middle-class traders, who resented the commercial competition of enterprising Jews; by aristocrats, who regarded them as intruders; and even by scholars, who vigorously championed the superiority of the Aryan, and especially the 'Teutonic', race.

Thus, the Anti-Semitic Movement was born. For a few years it gathered force. Books reviling the Jews poured out in an unending stream from the printing presses, and were answered by Jewish publicists with a volubility which served only to enhance the prominence of the question in the public eye. Deputies delivered inflammatory speeches in the Reichstag. On 25th April 1881 the Chancellor received from the newly organised Anti-Semitic League a petition demanding, among other things, the disenfranchisement of the Jews and the prohibition of further immigration into Germany. This document bore the signatures of no fewer than 255,000 persons. To accede to such requests, at the close of the nineteenth century, seemed out of the question. Nevertheless, a number of the minor discriminations demanded were already being acted upon quietly by the authorities. It was all but impossible for any Jew to obtain a commission in the army, a chair in a University, or any important office under the Government, without submitting to the formality of baptism. Popular passions found their expression in rioting in many parts of the country and attacks upon persons of Jewish appearance in the streets of the capital itself. More than once, disenfranchisement was debated in the Prussian Diet.

The movement was not confined to Germany. It soon spread to the Dual Monarchy of Austria-Hungary, where it was fanned by a ritual murder trial, in full medieval style, at Tisza-Eszlar in 1882 (to be followed, not long after, by similar charges at Xanten in the Rhineland and Konitz in West Prussia). In the same year there was held at Dresden the first of a series of international Anti-Semitic Congresses, at which fantastic restrictions were demanded.

Even France, the home of Emancipation, was not immune. Certain Catholic financiers had induced members of the aristocracy to entrust their capital to a banking organisation known as the *Union Générale*, which was intended to put the Jewish bankers out of business. Unfortunately, the *Union* failed catastrophically, and the sufferers found the usual scapegoat. Edouard Drumont, in his venomous *La France Juive* of 1886 (one of the most widely-circulated books of the century) now attempted to demonstrate that every trouble which had overtaken that country was due to Jewish machinations: a point of view strangely different from that held on the other side of the Rhine, where it was asserted no less spitefully that the Jews were assisting France to prepare her *revanche*. When Baron de Rothschild, with typical warm-heartedness, set about providing the poor school children of Paris with clothing, his action was denounced as mere propaganda. Matters came to a head in 1894, when Alfred Dreyfus, an Alsatian captain attached to the French General Staff, was accused of betraying

2B

military secrets to the German government. The whole affair was patently the result of an intrigue against the Republic, in which the French Anti-Semites and the clerico-royalist faction were intimately concerned. Nevertheless, to the accompaniment of a wild anti-Jewish campaign in the press, in the streets, in the Chamber, their victim was tried before a court-martial and found guilty. On 5th January 1895, loudly proclaiming his innocence, he was publicly degraded in Paris, and sent to the Devil's Island to serve a sentence of life imprisonment.

Subsequently it was brought to light that the famous *bordereau* in Dreyfus' handwriting, upon which the case against him had depended, was a forgery by a certain Esterhazy, a dissipated major in German pay. The clamour against the condemnation increased, the tone being set by Emile Zola's famous appeal, *J'Accuse*. The whole of France was divided into two camps, Dreyfusard and anti-Dreyfusard. Colonel Henry, of the General Staff, committed fresh forgeries to bolster up the accusation, and took his life when his action was discovered. Nevertheless, it was only in 1899, after a Liberal ministry had entered into office, that Dreyfus was brought back to France for retrial. A Council of War sitting at Rennes condemned him once more; but so obviously unfairly that the President of the Republic granted a free pardon. Later, the Court of Appeal quashed the verdict, and the innocence of Dreyfus was proclaimed to the world. Meanwhile, in 1897 and the following years, there was an outbreak of anti-Jewish rioting in Algeria.

II

In western Europe, the new Anti-Semitic movement had been on the whole academic in character. It was not able to affect governmental action on any important issue; and, though the feelings aroused were sometimes ugly, they never obtained expression on a dangerous scale. In Russia, on the other hand, the niceties of distinction between theory and practice were unappreciated. A great part of the pseudo-intelligentsia looked to Germany for inspiration in all matters, and regarded the new doctrines as a modern scientific gospel. On 13th March 1881—on the eve, as it happened, of granting a shadowy constitution—the Emperor Alexander II was assassinated. This was ample to give the reactionaries the upper hand; and, within a few weeks, Hell was let loose against the unfortunate Russian Jews.

On Wednesday, 27th April 1881, a dispute about the Blood Accusation in a tavern at Elisavetgrad, in the government of Kherson, served as the pretext for the outbreak of a riot. Rumours of approaching disorders had already reached the community, which had appealed in vain for protection. All that day and the next the fury raged unabated. Deeds of incredible barbarity were perpetrated under the eyes of impassive officials, and in some cases even with the co-operation of the soldiers of the garrison. Many persons were killed; women were outraged; five hundred houses and one hundred shops were demolished, as well as a number of synagogues; and property to the value of upwards of two million roubles was stolen or destroyed. The example spread like wildfire, being followed on an especially large scale at Kiev (8th–9th May) and Odessa (15th–19th May). By the autumn, outbreaks had occurred at no fewer than one hundred and sixty places in South Russia. At Christmas, another series began at Warsaw, the capital of Poland—where, owing to the valiant share taken by the Jews in the successive Wars of Independence, the old prejudice was thought to be completely dead. When this second wave was brought to an end in the following summer, it was succeeded by an epidemic of incendiary outbreaks, in consequence of which many Jewish families were ruined.

The whole of Europe stood aghast at this amazing reversion to savagery. It had been imagined that the age of martyrdom was passed. The civilised world had not experienced anything of the sort for at least five centuries, while even in eastern Europe there had been nothing comparable since the Haidamack massacres a hundred years before. It came as a shock to realise that, over so large a proportion of the earth's surface, conditions of barbarism still prevailed, and that millions of unfortunate fellow-mortals, for no ostensible reason whatsoever other than their adherence to an unpopular faith, still stood perpetually upon the edge of cataclysm. What was worse, governmental complicity seemed certain. To suspect governmental organisation was perhaps excessive; but it was notorious that nothing was done to prevent the outbreaks even when they were expected, to check them once they were started, or to punish those responsible when they had taken place. An illustrious professor who attempted to organise a protest was deprived of his chair. Pobiedonostzev, Procurator of the Holy Synod (who had formerly been tutor of the new Czar, Alexander III, and was now his principal adviser), cynically expressed his belief in solving the Jewish problem (it is said) by securing the conversion of one third, the emigration of another, and the extermination of the remainder. The word *pogrom* (the Russian term for 'devastation') entered into every European language, as a synonym for an unprovoked attack upon a defenceless minority.[1] Tens of thousands of homeless refugees were thrown destitute upon the charity of their more fortunately situated brethren. Public meetings of protest were held in London and Paris. Gladstone made a sympathetic allusion to the plight of the Russian Jews in the British House of Commons; and the United States minister at the court of St. Petersburg communicated a mildly phrased diplomatic protest in the name of his government.

Instead of taking steps to punish the culprits, the Russian government (without even the excuse of being able to point to self-defence in token of the ferocity of the hunted beast) attempted to solve the problem to which the attention of the world had been called by embarking upon a determined policy of repression against the victims. In May 1882 there were promulgated the infamous 'May Laws', by which the Jews were excluded from all villages and rural centres, even in the Pale of Settlement, outside Poland proper. The excuse for the new regulations was that the practice of keeping vodka shops and lending money at interest was demoralising the peasantry. Yet obviously only a small minority could possibly engage in these occupations; and even if the allegations had been true, there would have been no excuse for the ruthlessness with which the code was put into execution. In its subsequent interpretation, moreover, it became more and more severe, serving to restrict all movement and to cripple all trade. Even artisans, whom a previous law permitted specifically to live where they pleased, were affected. By an ignoble quibble, towns of as many as ten thousand inhabitants were classed as villages, and their Jewish population expelled. Ostensibly intended to be temporary, pending the revision of the general legal position of the Jews, the May Laws became in fact quasi-permanent, remaining in force almost until the downfall of the Russian monarchy.

With the passage of years, conditions shewed no signs of amelioration. That a Jewish problem existed in Russia (governed as it was by the medieval conception of one Autocracy, one Church, and one People) was arguable. The western provinces contained a vast mass of semi-alien population, with its own language, costume, appearance, religion, and occupations, amounting in some districts to over 15

[1] The earliest English use dates from 1905.

per cent of the total population and in a few towns to nearly 60 per cent. But, while ferociously resenting the fact that they refused to merge themselves into the national pattern, the government put all manner of obstacles in the way of their assimilation, on the plea that once they entered into Russian life they would dominate it. Hence fresh restrictions were continually devised by a succession of reactionary ministers, culminating in the notorious Von Plehve (assassinated in 1904). The Jews were excluded from the practice of law. The number of students admitted to the secondary schools and Universities was strictly limited. Jewish technical schools were closed. Meanwhile there was a constant series of expulsions from the rural districts, as well as from the interior of the country, in accordance with the interpretation of the May Laws. These reached their climax in 1891, when thousands of persons were deported in mid-winter from Moscow and other cities, and in 1898, when no fewer than seven thousand souls were ruthlessly uprooted from the government of Kiev alone. Jewish women were allowed to live in the great cities, and thus enjoy the benefits of a University education, only if they held the 'yellow ticket' of a prostitute.

The Russian example was followed (though generally without its most violent manifestations) in Roumania. From the seventeenth century there had been a more or less continuous stream of immigrants from the border districts of Poland to the Danubian provinces of Moldavia and Wallachia (at that time part of the Turkish Empire). The majority of them followed the same professions as their co-religionists to the north, earning their livelihood as petty traders and artisans scattered throughout the cities and villages. By the middle of the nineteenth century, when Roumania attained her independence, they numbered some two hundred thousand in all. The new state had come into existence under the Russian aegis, and the policy of its government was deeply coloured by the Russian example. After the accession of Prince Charles of Hohenzollern to the throne in 1866, Roumania was considered from this point of view the black spot of Europe. The Treaty of Berlin conferred full independence on the country, conditionally upon the concession of equal rights to all subjects irrespective of religious difference. This provision was ingeniously evaded by the plea that all Jews (though subject to military service and to every other civic duty) were in fact aliens, for however many generations their ancestors before them might have been settled in the country. Recurrent intervention on the part of the signatories to the Berlin Treaty was treated with contempt. As in Russia, the Jews were subjected to special legislation, deprived of equality of opportunity, and on occasion subjected even to physical violence: culminating in 1895, when an Anti-Semitic League was organised with the professed object of rendering their position intolerable. There was a widespread boycott after the failure of the harvests of 1899 and 1900, which added greatly to the stream of emigration. In Galicia (Austrian Poland) social and economic circumstances were hardly better, and there was a swelling tide of anti-Jewish feeling.

The Liberal movement of 1905 forced a shadowy constitution upon the Czars. By virtue of this, the Jews gained the franchise (a useless privilege, as matters turned out), though the other discriminations against them continued to be enforced. The reactionaries now organised themselves under the name 'Genuine Russians', with terrorist branches (popularly known as 'The Black Hundreds') in all provincial centres. Antagonism to the Jews became an integral part of their programme, for they hoped to discredit the constitutional movement by identifying it with this unpopular element. Their antagonism was, literally, to the knife. After the summer of 1882, the pogroms had remained a more or less distant menace for over twenty years, occurrences of the sort taking place only infrequently. But on 19th April 1903 (it was Easter Sunday, and the last day of the Jewish Feast of Passover) there was a fresh outbreak at Kishinev, which outdid in sheer savagery any of those which had preceded it, and obviously had semi-official encouragement, if not organisation. It was only after the conscience of Europe had been shocked by three days' continuous rioting, accompanied by much bloodshed, that orders arrived from St. Petersburg to restore order. Before long the example was followed elsewhere. In 1905 there was a further wholesale outbreak under the auspices of the Black Hundreds, which did not cease until fifty localities had been terrorised. Next year the example was repeated, atrocities on an especially large scale taking place at Bialystok. Within a period of four years, massacres were perpetrated in no less than 284 Russian towns, and the total number of casualties was estimated at fifty thousand. Throughout the country the Black Hundreds remained active, fomenting fresh outbursts; while the government not only failed to intervene, but even suppressed attempts on the part of the victims to organise themselves for self-defence.

In the summer of 1910, twelve hundred Jewish families were expelled from Kiev on the ground that they had no legal right of residence. In the following year a poor Jewish labourer, named Mendel Beilis, was arrested on the preposterous charge of having murdered a Christian child for ritual purposes. Although in the course of the investigations it became almost certain that a well-known criminal gang had been responsible for the crime, Beilis (and with him, in a sense, the whole of the Jewish people) was put on trial The case dragged on for two years, to the accompaniment of a wild Anti-Semitic campaign throughout the country; and when finally the unhappy prisoner was acquitted for lack of evidence, it was in terms which left discredit and suspicion on his co-religionists as a whole. Meanwhile, the astute Stolypin, Minister of the Interior, had succeeded in rendering the Constitution of 1905, and the partial emancipation which it had implied, completely nugatory; and the anti-Jewish laws continued to be applied with greater, rather than less, severity than before. The greatest agglomeration of the Jewish people, numbering over one-half of the Jewish population of the world, was reduced to a condition of misery, of rightlessness, of insecurity, of degradation, which recalled the traditions of the Middle Ages at their worst.

III

For the martyred Jews of eastern Europe, deprived of freedom of movement and of opportunity, and everywhere living in danger of an outbreak which might cost them their lives, existence in their native country had become a nightmare. Tens of thousands of them, moreover, uprooted by the May Laws from the homes where they had been established for generations, were now cooped up in vast Ghettos, on the verge of destitution. There seemed to be no prospect of amelioration, even of security, so long as they remained where they were. Their only hope lay in flight. With every fresh outburst of pogroms, a new wave of refugees made its way to the frontiers, fleeing for their lives. In 1881, within a few months of the bursting of the storm, ten thousand refugees arrived in a state of utter destitution at the single town of Brody in Galicia. Every road which led to the borders, every train bound westwards, every ship which sailed from the harbours, was choked with exiles. Some, anticipating attack, fled as a result of sheer nervousness; others, once the example had been set, from sheer imitativeness, or with no object other than making a livelihood. But, in every case, the constant menace of massacre, the displacement of population in the Pale of Settlement, and the restrictive influence of the anti-Jewish laws, was looming with greater or with less prominence in the background.

For the next thirty-three years, the new exodus continued without interruption. Before the end of the century, almost a million Jews in eastern Europe had left their homes: within the next few years, the number was perhaps doubled. The movement of population was greater in magnitude than any which had preceded it in Jewish history; and it was more important in its consequences than any event since the Jews first set foot in Europe, in the dark mists of antiquity.

In the neighbouring countries of Germany and Austria-Hungary, permeated with anti-Semitism, the strangers were eyed askance; so much so, that the proposal was recurrently made to forbid immigration from the east. In Roumania conditions were little more tolerable than in Russia; and that country, far from receiving the refugees, added perceptibly to their numbers. The vast mass pushed on westwards. They could be found in every capital from Stockholm to Lisbon. But, by some strange mass-suggestion, the overwhelming majority came to the Anglo-Saxon countries—the only parts of the world which were as yet free from dangerous manifestations of anti-Semitic feeling, and where, moreover, dazzling economic opportunity seemed open.

In England the whole face of communal life was altered by the immigration. At the period of the concession of Jewish emancipation, Anglo-Jewry had seemed to be finding its balance. A large proportion of the population was native-born, and in many cases could trace back its native ancestry for some generations. Of the remainder, most were probably of German origin, having immigrated to England in the period which succeeded the Napoleonic Wars, to which many of the provincial communities—notably in the new manufacturing and commercial centres of the Midlands—owed their growth. In the course of a very few years, conditions were completely altered. The Russian Jewish influx attained impressive proportions. In London, where the greater number settled (largely in the old centre in the East End) the Jewish population rose within twenty years from 47,000 to 150,000. Throughout the rest of the country, the old communities were reinforced and new ones were established. Most of the new arrivals were compelled by force of circumstances to enter the tailoring and allied industries. To the dismay of some backward

142. CONVERSIONIST SERMON TO JEWS OF ROME, 1829
Watercolour by H. Hess. Museum, Basle

143. KIDNAPPING OF EDGARDO MORTARA, 1858
Drawing by Moritz Oppenheim

144. Baron Lionel de Rothschild takes his Seat in the House of Commons, 26th July 1858

From *The Illustrated London News*

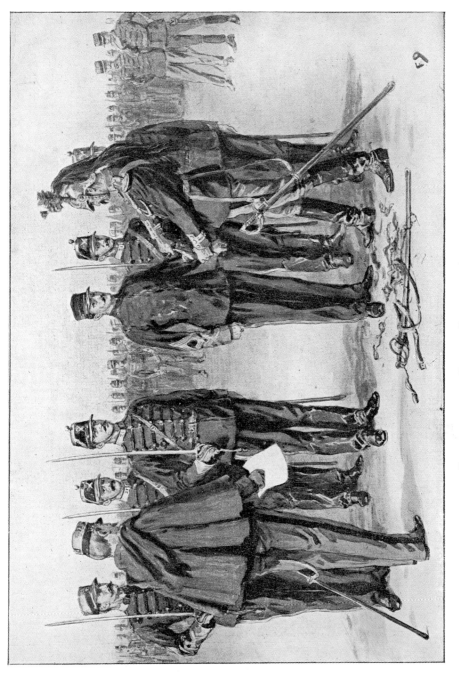

145. Degradation of Captain Dreyfus, 5th January 1895
From *The Graphic*, 14th September 1899

146. THE WESTERN ('WAILING') WALL ON THE TEMPLE SITE, JERUSALEM
Etching by E. M. Lilien

competitors, they began to utilise the sewing-machine, for the first time, as a scientific instrument of production. The general diffusion of cheap clothing, cheap boots, and cheap furniture, was given an enormous impetus as a result of their energy. They captured the cigarette-making industry, previously an American monopoly. A Yiddish press, a Yiddish trade union movement, a Yiddish theatre, followed on their heels; and, to the foreign quarters of London or of Manchester, were transplanted the language, the standards, the scholarship, the orthodoxy and heterodoxy, the methods, the institutions, and even the jealousies, of Pinsk or of Warsaw.

It was not long before the new arrivals began to make important contributions to English life—typified in the activities and writings of their forerunner and champion, Israel Zangwill (1864-1926), the first novelist of essentially Jewish interests who attained international reputation. But, at the same time, the influx was eyed not altogether sympathetically by some elements in the general population, who considered that Jewish competition lowered the general standard of livelihood and (confusing effect with cause) held the Jews responsible for the squalor of the cheap tenements in which they were forced to live. The agitation culminated in the Aliens Immigration Act of 1905, which stemmed, though it did not stop, the incoming tide. Conditions were very much the same in the overseas dependencies of Great Britain—Australia, South Africa, and especially Canada—where large numbers similarly found a home and galvanised the existing communities, established in the heyday of colonial expansion in the first three-quarters of the nineteenth century, into a new life.

IV

The English scene was imitated, on a scale larger by far, in the United States of America. '*And thus, having expelled all the Jews from all your kingdoms and dominions, in the same month. . . . Your Highnesses commanded me that, with a sufficient fleet, I should go to the said parts of India.*' With this significant passage, Christopher Columbus (perhaps himself of Jewish extraction) introduces his account of the expedition which led to the discovery of the New World. The connection between the Jews and the opening-up of America was not, however, merely a matter of fortuitous coincidence. The epoch-making enterprise of 1492 was very largely a Jewish, or rather a Marrano, undertaking. It was made possible by a loan which was advanced by the Marranos Luis de Santangel and Gabriel Sanchez, to whom the first reports of the discoveries were addressed. Among its patrons were several other persons of identical origin. The only high official concerned with the genesis of the expedition who was of 'Old Christian' stock had a 'New Christian' wife. Luis de Torres, the interpreter, who was baptised on the day before the expedition sailed, was the first European to set foot in the new land and to make use of tobacco.[1]

The Marranos of Spain and Portugal were quick to realise the potentialities of the New World and to transfer themselves thither. Soon they were to be found in every province. They were numbered amongst the *conquistadores* in Mexico, and subsequently controlled its trade with Europe, 'from brocade to sackcloth, and from diamonds to cumin-seed'. It was not long before they were followed by the Inquisition, which, after some little preliminary activity, became established in Mexico in 1571, and elsewhere in the Spanish dominions not long after. *Autos da fé* were staged which rivalled for magnificence, and for the number of their victims, the most resplendent that Toledo or Seville could boast. Nevertheless, the numbers of the secret Jews in the New World grew; and when, in the course of the first half of the seventeenth century, the Dutch conquered the Portuguese colony of Brazil, open communities (soon to be reinforced from Europe) were formed in its principal cities.

The Dutch rule was of short duration. In 1654 the capital, Pernambuco, was forced to capitulate and its community was dispersed. The refugees were scattered throughout the New World, where, in those places under English and Dutch rule, free from the fatal shadow of the Inquisition, they formed a network of little settlements. All through the West Indies—at Jamaica, Curação, Barbados, and elsewhere, as well as on the adjacent mainland—communities were now established which, for a couple of centuries to come, played a very important part in economic life.

Late in the same year (1654), a small party of refugees arrived in New Amsterdam (as New York, still under Dutch rule, was then called). Here, by the express order of the Dutch West India Company, they were allowed to remain, so long as 'the poor among them do not become a burden to the Company or the community, but be supported

---

[1] More sweeping assertions were formerly made, and there may have been other persons of Jewish extraction aboard.

by their own Nation'. Hence, this most distant outpost of the Marrano Diaspora, periodically reinforced from Europe or the West Indies, spread to the neighbouring regions. By the middle of the eighteenth century, communities, looking to London or to Amsterdam for spiritual guidance, were scattered throughout the American colonies—in New York, Newport, Philadelphia, Savannah, Charleston, and elsewhere. For the most part, their members were engaged in the import and export trade—in tobacco, sugar, wheat, sometimes slaves. Of Aaron Lopez, of Newport (d. 1782), it was said that for 'honour and extent of commerce, he was probably surpassed by no merchant of America'. Some of them were ship-owners; and it was a Portuguese Jew who first introduced the manufacture of spermaceti (then indispensable for the manufacture of candles) into North America.

In the War of Independence, the handful of two thousand Jews then to be found in the Colonies played an important part. Numbers of them adhered to the Non-Importation agreement. The names of Francis Salvador, 'scalped by the Indians'; Major Benjamin Nones, one of Lafayette's romantic Frenchmen; David Franks, Benedict Arnold's aide-de-camp before his treachery; and Hayyim Salomon, an immigrant Polish Jew who shewed remarkable gifts in the realm of finance; exemplify the sympathy of the Jews with the cause of liberty. On the other hand, the Hart and Pollock families of Newport, and Rebecca Franks, the toast of the royalist officers at Philadelphia, indicate that they were capable of appreciating the other point of view as well: while Abraham Wagg, a New York grocer, was sufficiently sanguine to attempt to negotiate a peace between the contending parties. As in England itself, the Jews of colonial America had been subjected to few disabilities; and the original constitution of the United States, with its stipulation that no religious test should be required as qualification for any public office or post of trust, virtually completed their Emancipation.[1]

Even before the War of Independence, the original Marrano stock of the Jewish community in the United States had been diluted to a considerable extent by new arrivals of German and Polish origin; and,

---

[1] It is noteworthy, however, that even in the United States full Emancipation unaccountably lagged, locally at least. It did not become a fact in Maryland until 1825, after a prolonged struggle: while the last remaining minor disabilities were not removed in North Carolina until 1868. In New Hampshire, the laws discriminating against the Jews and forbidding them to acquire legal residence were removed from the statute-book only in 1877.

as early as 1802, an 'Ashkenazi' community was organised by the side of the original 'Sephardi' one in Philadelphia. When peace was restored to Europe after the Napoleonic Wars, the tide of immigration increased enormously. New synagogues were opened in rapid succession in New York; and small communities sprang up all over the Middle West. England was well represented amongst the new-comers. But a majority were from central Europe—especially South Germany. The natural desire of the latter to better themselves economically was a factor less potent than the acute discomforts to which they were subjected through the re-enforcement of the anti-Jewish code—particularly the limitation of marriages which still prevailed in many places, which rendered emigration an inevitable course for almost every normally constituted young man. After the stirring events of 1830, and especially of 1848, the trickle developed into a stream, and a better class of immigrant began to join it. Men of culture and substance, who had participated in the revolutionary movement of those years, or who were disappointed at the wave of reaction which subsequently set in, turned their faces in increasing numbers to the new continent, where equal constitutional rights and economic opportunity were open to all. This period, it happens, coincided with the Gold Rush of 1849, when the sanguine of every nation imagined that fortunes lay awaiting all comers in the arid canyons of California, and set out thither with one accord from all parts of the world. Among the abiding results of the craze was the extension of the area of Jewish settlement to the Pacific coast.

At every incipient city and township, from New York to San Francisco, there was by now a little body of Jews—general merchants, or sometimes mere pedlars, who painstakingly covered every yard of the surrounding territory with their packs or carts. Slowly these became organised in rudimentary congregations. Hardly a town or village of Bavaria and Baden had failed to send some representative to the new land. It was generally in German that the sermon was delivered in their synagogues, and such periodicals as were published for circulation amongst them were often in the same language. By 1842 there were three German congregations in New York alone; and, in the following year, the German Jews established in America set up, as a common meeting-ground, the 'Independent Order B'nai B'rith' ('Sons of the Covenant'), which in the course of the next hundred years became an institution of inter-continental importance. Excepting in New York, the new arrivals submerged almost com-

pletely the Sephardi elements in the older congregations founded in
the previous century.

By the period of the Civil War, the immigrants were becoming
fully incorporated in American life. From the pulpits of every temple
(as the synagogues were now almost universally called) throughout
the land, sermons were delivered in English or in German, attacking
or defending the institution of slavery. Ten thousand Jews were en-
rolled with the armies in the field, on the one side or the other; and a
Jewish lawyer of rare ability, Judah Philip Benjamin (1811-1884),
served the Confederate government with distinction, successively
as Attorney-General, Secretary of War, and Secretary of State. Even
at this period there was more than a sprinkling of Polish and Russian
Jews, who had founded their own religious organisation in New York
in 1852, and who came over after the war at the rate of some four
thousand annually. Nevertheless, in culture, in wealth, in numbers,
and in influence, the German Jews exercised as yet an unquestioned
supremacy.

Under the circumstances, the new German spiritual tendencies
struck root rapidly in the country. As early as 1824, a small band of
enthusiasts in Charleston, fired by recent reports from Europe, had
seceded from the congregation and organised a short-lived 'Reformed
Society of Israelites'; while Major Mordecai Manuel Noah (1785-
1851), a swashbuckler playwright and politician who had attempted
to found a city of refuge near Buffalo for the persecuted Jews of the
whole world, had publicly advocated relief from 'burdensome' ceremonies at the dedication of a new synagogue in New York ten years
later. With later immigrants, some element of Reform came to be
taken as a matter of course. The new environment and new opportunities automatically loosened the trammels of tradition. Persons
who were exiled from their native land by reason of liberalism in
politics were not likely to remain conservative in matters of religion.
Enthusiastic Rabbis of the new school, who had found opposition at
home too strong, saw unrivalled opportunities for giving expression
to their views in the great Republic of the west, where everything
was in a state of flux and could be recrystallised almost at will by
any man of strong convictions and personality. And, in Isaac Mayer
Wise (1819-1900), Rabbi at Cincinnati from 1846, the progressives
found not only a vigorous spokesman, but also an organiser of great
genius. Largely through his influence, Reform Judaism of an extreme
type became deeply rooted in America; and radical innovations (such

as the supplementary Sunday service), which were exceptional in their land of origin, became comparatively frequent. Not only were synagogues expressly established for the purpose of following a revised ritual, but some which had been models of the most rigid orthodoxy at their foundation gradually drifted towards the Left. The last quarter of the nineteenth century saw Jews of German origin, and an interpretation of Judaism which harked back to Holdheim and to Geiger, dominating American Jewish life.

V

This was the state of affairs when the outbreak in the spring of 1881 initiated the Age of Pogroms in Russia. It was the period of the labour famine in America, when the continent absorbed each year hundreds of thousands of poor immigrants from every corner of Europe. The cutting of prices by rival shipping lines reduced the cost of the passage across the Atlantic, from Hamburg to New York, to a ludicrously low level. The measure of America's prosperity was estimated by the number of immigrants which she absorbed each month. With a dramatic suddenness, the infection spread to the crowded Ghettos of Russia, Galicia, and Roumania. The eyes of every Jew were turned to the new land beyond the Atlantic, where there was freedom from violence, where there was equal opportunity for all, where the very streets appeared to distant observers paved with gold. The earliest arrivals were actual refugees from the pogroms. But they were followed by others, who fled from the menace of a pogrom, or the possibility of a pogrom, or were frankly attracted by the prospects of economic advancement which America held out.

Every fresh wave of violence sent a new consignment of refugees beyond the frontiers, and gave the process fresh impetus. The mass-suggestion spread more and more widely. In the end, a majority of the Jewish people under the rule of the Czar were living either on remittances from America or else in the daily hope of being enabled to go thither themselves. The case was identical in the adjacent lands. Between 1881 and the close of the century, over 600,000 Jewish refugees from eastern Europe had landed in the American ports. The new series of pogroms which started at Kishinev in 1903 sent another half-million to join them in less than five years. In 1906, more than 150,000 Jewish immigrants landed, being nearly one-seventh of the total number of arrivals in that year. By 1929, the aggregate had risen to over 2,300,000, of whom 71 per cent came from Russia, 17 per cent from Roumania, and the majority of the rest from Austria-Hungary (especially Galicia). In the course of a single generation, one out of every three Jews of eastern Europe, it was computed, had crossed the ocean to settle in a new home. By 1904 the Jewish population of the United States, which thirty years before had barely exceeded 250,000, had risen to one and a half millions: a quarter of a century later, this figure was nearly trebled.

The new arrivals naturally tended to concentrate in New York— the principal port of disembarkation, as well as the greatest urban centre, and the most important hub of industry, in the whole country. Here, where up to 1825 one small synagogue could suffice the whole community, there were living a century later no fewer than 1,750,000 Jews, comprising nearly one-third of the whole population of the city. At no other time in the whole course of Jewish history had so many Jews, or anything remotely approaching that number, either absolutely or proportionately, been concentrated together at one spot. An attempt by some American Jewish leaders to divert the port of entry to Galveston, and thus extend the area of Jewish settlement, met with only a qualified success. Outside New York, communities which would in any other country have been considered of first importance, sprang up in Boston, Baltimore, Cleveland, Philadelphia, and elsewhere. An enormous settlement—second only to that of New York—established itself in Chicago. The American process was repeated, as was only natural, across the Canadian border, where very large agglomerations were to be found in Toronto and Montreal.

As in England, the new-comers, in an excessively high proportion, entered the tailoring and allied industries, in every branch of which they came in a short time to exercise a virtual monopoly. Through their means the industry was subjected to minute subdivisions, and its overhead charges hence greatly reduced (the so-called 'Boston System'). In cabinet-making, tobacco-working, the fur industry, and similar callings, Jews were equally prominent and efficient. Exploited mercilessly at the beginning by their employers—usually their own co-religionists—they evolved before long a very strong trade union organisation. The Amalgamated Clothing Workers of America, which was preponderantly Jewish, attained a membership of nearly two hundred thousand; and it was rivalled by the International Ladies' Garment Workers' Union. The two are memorable for the revolution effected through their means in the hygienic conditions in workshops, hitherto unspeakably foul and insanitary. This, however, was not achieved until general strikes in the so-called 'needle industries', in 1890 and 1892, had caused widespread misery.

But an agglomeration of millions of persons cannot be confined to one or two spheres of activity. Before long, the new-comers had entered almost every branch of industrial enterprise. They were farmers, mechanics, labourers, manufacturers, porters, builders, printers, glaziers. There were agricultural settlements, supported by philanthropic organisations in one or two states. Within the first generation, the sphere of activity was extended to cover the professions. The children of the original immigrants (sometimes themselves born beyond the ocean) became prominent as lawyers, physicians, journalists, authors, actors, painters, sculptors. The newly-established cinematographic industry gave ample scope for their enterprise and adaptability; and before it had been in existence for many years they were of the utmost importance in it, whether as producers, actors, managers, or distributors.

The East Side of New York, like the East End of London, became the seat of a curious, alien cultural world. There were whole streets, or even areas, in which nothing but Yiddish was heard—increasingly punctuated, it is true, by Anglo-Saxon idioms. Newspapers galore (modelled as closely as possible on the standards of American journalism), were published in the same language in steady profusion—dailies, weeklies, monthlies—to satisfy their intellectual needs. The Yiddish theatre attained a momentary importance in New York which it had never had in Warsaw. Yiddish poets, Yiddish novelists, Yiddish translations, found a ready, though not an affluent, market. It was in Yiddish that the vast literature connected with the Jewish trade union movement was published, and in Yiddish that the negotiations were carried on with the employers to improve the status of the labourers. The children received a rudimentary Hebrew education in hundreds of *Heders* and a smaller number of *Talmud Torahs*, the methods and general atmosphere of which were transplanted bodily from the Pale of Settlement. Old acquaintances, from any one province, or city, or township, would band themselves together to establish their own synagogue, or prayer-hall, or friendly society, with the result that within the New York Ghetto there was a host of minor divisions, according to their place of origin. There were synagogues of every degree of orthodoxy, reflecting the local atmosphere of every important community in Russia, Poland, and Roumania. To emphasise the contrast, there were Socialists of every shade of thought, some of whom accentuated their new-found liberty by flouting every religious tradition, and demonstrated as publicly as possible their contempt for the old order of things by holding their annual dances upon the Day of Atonement. Greybeards studied the Law, in the traditional sing-song, in innumerable stuffy Bethels; master tailors amassed fortunes and moved to fashionable districts; and, in the mire outside, the descendants of great Talmudists pushed barrows, endeavouring to earn a few coppers to keep body and soul together. It was a vast melting-pot into which all sorts and conditions of men were poured, and where they were merged and tried and moulded—no man yet knew into what.

147. LUIGI LUZZATTI (1841-1927)
Deathbed drawing by Enrico Glicenstein

2 C

Chapter XXX

A NEW WORLD

———————•———————

I

The European War, which broke out in the summer of 1914, and was ultimately to involve almost every nation in the world, proved a turning-point in the history of the Jewish people. The tide of emigration from eastern Europe, which had continued at such a remarkable rate since 1881, was automatically checked. At the outbreak of war, in order to impress the opinion of its western Allies, the government of the Czar struck a few benevolent gestures as though intending to ameliorate the condition of its down-trodden subjects; for example, the May Laws, issued as a 'temporary' measure thirty-three years before, were at last allowed to lapse. However, the tide of battle, as it swept backwards and forwards on the eastern front, overwhelmed time after time the old Polish provinces, on either side of the frontier, in which such vast masses of the Jewish people lived. What with the inevitable havoc of destruction and with ruthless deportations (often inspired by obvious anti-Semitic prejudice), many communities were completely destroyed, while thousands of families were reduced to destitution. Half the Jewish population of Galicia, recalling the atrocities of which the Cossacks were capable even in time of peace, sought refuge in the interior of Austria.

These sufferings were negligible by comparison with the aftermath. In Russia, the Czars paid at last the penalty of misrule, and in the spring of 1917 a revolution took place in St. Petersburg. One of the first actions of the new government was to proclaim the principle of equality for all, irrespective of race and of belief. A new—perhaps a golden—era seemed to have dawned for Russian Jewry. Yet, within a very short time, the movement took a new turn. On 7th November there occurred the momentous Bolshevik revolution, which dethroned the moderates and placed the destinies of the country in the hands of the Soviets. Before long, Russia was plunged into the throes of civil war. By the one side, the Jews were accused of being sub-versionists, and by the other of being counter-revolutionaries; and, whenever either temporarily triumphed (but especially the former), it was they who were treated as scapegoats.

Conditions were worst in the Ukraine, when an attempt was made to establish an independent republic under the hetman Petlura—a worthy successor to Khmelnitsky in more respects than one. The new state was invaded in turn by Bolsheviks and reactionaries, ill-armed, ill-disciplined, and generally unpaid. 'Whites', 'Reds', and Petlurists might all occupy a town within the space of a few days, each army bringing in its wake a new wave of massacre and destruction. When the disorder seemed to have died down, a fresh bid was made to over-throw the Bolshevik regime by a 'White' army under the Czarist General Denikin, whose name is associated with some of the worst atrocities in Jewish history since the Middle Ages. In almost every town and village, there took place a whole series of pogroms which made the outbreaks of pre-war days seem by comparison no more than displays of boisterous spirit. The dead perhaps reached a quarter of a million; while as many more fell victims to the deprivation and disease which followed in the wake of the armies. Those who re-mained alive were utterly destitute. The example of disorder proved infectious; and elsewhere in eastern Europe—in Hungary, Poland, Roumania—similar émeutes took place, though on a smaller scale, in the disturbed period which succeeded the conclusion of major hos-tilities in the autumn of 1918.

II

When the turmoil of battle had died away, it was obvious that the condition of the Jewish people had been fundamentally altered during the past ten years. In 1914 the great mass of the world's Jewry was living in the Russian Empire. This was now split up, so that, out of a total of nearly six millions in the territories formerly subject to the Czar, rather more than one-half were assigned to the new republic of Poland. Here, as in the other 'Succession' states which owed their birth to the recent upheaval, equality of rights and opportunity was ostensibly secured for all, without distinction of race or religion, by the 'Minority' clauses which—largely owing to the efforts of the Jewish delegations at the Conference of Paris, led by the historian-diplomat Lucien Wolf (1857-1930)—had been embodied in the successive Peace Treaties. The same was the case in Lithuania, Latvia, Estonia, Czecho-Slovakia, and above all, Roumania, which, through the annexation of a large part of Hungary, had now doubled its Jewish population.

For the lethargic Sephardi Jewries of the Near East (which had long ceased to produce great leaders and scholars, or to play an important part in general life), the War of 1914-1918 similarly constituted a landmark. They had not suffered to any great extent in the actual hostilities. Nevertheless, the tide of nationalism which followed the peace affected them most adversely. Turkey began re-organising itself as a national state, and could no longer tolerate gladly in its midst heterogeneous bodies, alien in culture, in religion, and in speech, as it had done throughout its former history. The dis-crimination which developed was felt especially by the Jews. An attempt was begun to abolish their separate institutions, to enforce the use of Turkish instead of the medieval Spanish which their fathers had brought with them from the Peninsula, and to oust them from the commanding position which they had previously held (together with Greeks and Armenians) in commercial and professional life.

Not dissimilar was the position in Greece, which had acquired the thriving port of Salonica after the Balkan War of 1912. At that time, the Jews of that city had constituted over 50 per cent out of a total population of a little less than 175,000. There was no place in Europe where they played a more prominent part in economic and general life; and a ship which arrived in the harbour upon Saturday had to defer unloading until the next day. After the restoration of peace in the Near East, the government methodically set about con-verting this important centre into a Greek city. A large number of the refugees brought over from Asia Minor were settled there. Simul-taneously, in consequence of the systematic blocking of opportunity, the Jewish population began to dwindle, absolutely as well as rela-tively: with the result that the Jewish majority which had existed for many centuries diminished into a definite, though not insignificant, minority. Thus the importance of the Sephardi communities of the Levant, which had been created in the aftermath of the expulsion from Spain in 1492, began to decline with increasing momentum; and well-informed observers imagined that they were in sight of final and definite decay.

The greatest body of Jews to be found in any one country of the world was now that settled in the United States of America. The tide of immigration which had been checked by the war was never allowed to resume its former scale, and ultimately became insignificant. Yet, as the result of natural growth, added to the unprecedented immigration of pre-war years, the total Jewish population here now exceeded four millions, as against some three millions in Poland and a couple of hundred thousand fewer in Russia. They were not important only in a numerical sense. They had prospered, with the rest of the country, while America was still neutral; the new generation had entered into every conceivable branch of economic and social activity; and they were now by far the most wealthy, as well as the most numerous, of all sections of the Jewish people throughout the world. But for the support which they so lavishly poured out from 1914 onwards, the measure of the disaster which overtook their kinsmen in eastern Europe would inevitably have been greater still. Synagogues of unprecedented magnificence, splendidly equipped hospitals and sanatoria, model orphanages, social centres, charitable institutions, sprang up throughout the country. Hebrew learning was patronised, when times were good, more lavishly if not more discriminatingly than had ever previously been known. From now on, it was mainly to America that Jewry throughout the world looked when any new enterprise was on foot, if not for leadership, at least for finance.

As the nineteenth century drew to its close, Jews (mainly belonging to the earlier waves of immigration) had begun to play a part of real importance in the economic and public life of the country. The house of Kuhn, Loeb & Company was one of the world's most important private banks. For several decades, Jacob Schiff (1847-1920), one of the partners in the firm, was the dominating figure in American Jewish life. Nathan Straus (1848-1931), who arrived in the country almost penniless, devoted his life and the fortune which he amassed to philanthropic objects, and derived his greatest satisfaction from the enormous reduction in infantile mortality which came about after he had established his chain of centres for the distribution of pasteurised milk. His brother, Oscar Straus (1845-1926), was first Minister, and then Ambassador, to Turkey; being one of the most noteworthy of a long series of Jews who represented the United States abroad in a diplomatic capacity. Louis Brandeis (1856-1941) and Benjamin Cardozo (1870-1938), jurists of the first distinction, sat simultaneously on the Supreme Court of the United States, being followed a little later by Felix Frankfurter (b. 1882). Julius Rosenwald (1862-1932) built up a colossal fortune through the mail-order business. His charitable donations were incredibly vast; and no man, after Lincoln, did more to improve the status of the American negro. At the other end of the social scale, Morris Hillquit (1869-1933) was one of the organisers of American Socialism; while Samuel Gompers (1847-1921), the creator of the American Federation of Labour, was for nearly half a century the dominant and moderating influence in the working-class movement.

Yet, notwithstanding these outstanding characters, and others like them, whom every year brought forward in increasing numbers, American Jewry inexplicably delayed the full justification of its supremacy. The younger generation tended to slough off the forms of traditional observance to which it had been brought up, without, in many cases, being attracted to the Reformed system, which had struck such deep roots in the country. Jewish education was at a lamentably low level. It was estimated that no less than 60 per cent of the Jewish youth of the country received no grounding whatsoever in their own hereditary culture; and, when money was poured out in profusion for every other conceivable object, this was largely neglected. In the circumstances, it is not surprising that, for the first time in Jewish history, learning failed to accompany numerical ascendancy; and, fifty years after the beginning of the great migration, it was impossible to count more than a handful at the most of native-born scholars who had achieved a reputation in the Jewish field. Indications seemed almost to point to the evolution of a denationalised, deculturalised, and dereligionised type of Jew, who would lose all touch with his past except for a cordial recognition of his origin, and a warm-hearted readiness to contribute to any eleemosynary object. Whether any positive contribution to Jewish life would ultimately emerge, commensurate with the importance of this new centre, time alone could shew.

With the cessation of immigration to the United States, for so many years the Land of Promise for all the ambitious and the persecuted of the whole world, the area of Jewish settlement began to spread: though (owing to legislative restrictions) the post-war movements of population were on a smaller scale. The temporary prosperity of France during the post-war period of monetary inflation attracted large numbers of new settlers to that country. The community of Paris more than doubled in a single decade. Large numbers of Russian refugees established themselves here, as well as very numerous Levantines from Turkey and from Greece. Similarly, the

Jewish population of the smaller countries of western Europe—
Norway, Sweden, Portugal, even Spain—greatly increased; while
fugitives from Russia settled in some numbers even in the Far East,
forming a chain of fresh communities as far afield as China and even
Japan.

A larger number turned their eyes to Central and South America.
From Mexico almost to the Straits of Magellan, Jews penetrated,
setting up in due course their synagogues and characteristic institutions all over the continent. Most were attracted by the Argentine,
where they reinforced the somewhat anaemic agricultural colonies
established by the charitable Baron de Hirsch, at immense cost, a
generation before as a place of refuge for his persecuted co-religionists
in Russia.[1] By 1945 the number of Jews in the country, which thirty
years before was less than 10,000, had approached 350,000. It was as
yet too early to see how far this process would go, or what permanent
results it was likely to have. In any case it pointed the way to a
revival of Judaism where it was least expected. Levantine Jews, who
had brought their native Ladino with them from Smyrna or Salonica
to Buenos Aires, found themselves, from the linguistic point of view,
completely at home; while Poles and eastern Europeans slowly discarded their Yiddish in favour of the vernacular. A possibility began
to show itself that the glories of Spanish-speaking Jewry, in full
eclipse for many centuries past, might be revived in the New World.

III

The most spectacular and the most important result of the war,
as far as the Jews were concerned, was the renewal of their political
connection with that little strip of land on the eastern littoral of the
Mediterranean, which had been the cradle of their people. Ever since
Jerusalem had been destroyed by Titus, they had prayed, with never-
flagging optimism, for its restoration. For many generations they sent
their contributions, from every quarter of the Diaspora, for the
upkeep of the Patriarchate and the Schools. The repeated Messianic
movements had been, from one point of view, nothing more than an
expression of the undying national hope. Pilgrims from every part of
the Jewish world regularly visited the country, and kept its memory

[1] For Baron de Hirsch (1831-1896), see above, p. 363. He had devoted almost the
whole of his immense fortune, of some £10,000,000, to the foundation of the Jewish
Colonisation Association (ICA), with the object of establishing refugees from eastern
Europe in agricultural life in America and elsewhere.

fresh by their reports. No opportunity was lost, in ritual or practice, to preserve the recollection of Palestine in the heart and the mind of its dispossessed children.

After the abortive experiment made by the Duke of Naxos, in the middle of the sixteenth century, for the restoration of a Jewish settlement around Tiberias,[1] nothing practical was attempted for many generations. Pious immigrants continued, nevertheless, to direct their steps towards Jerusalem, so that they might have the privilege of studying, or at least of dying, on the holy soil. By the middle of the nineteenth century there were some tens of thousands of Jews in Palestine, mainly living on the *Chalukah* (charitable distribution) sent by their co-religionists in Europe, and treated with contempt, occasionally variegated by maltreatment, by the Arab inhabitants. Meanwhile visionaries of various climes, as unlike as Napoleon Bonaparte and Mordecai Manuel Noah,[2] had vague dreams of being the instrument whereby the exiled people might be settled again in their ancient land.

The Victorian era witnessed a rationalisation of the old Messianic conception. The efflorescence of the national idea throughout Europe could not but colour the outlook of Jewish theorists, some of whom (as they watched contemporary developments in Flanders, Italy, and the Balkan States) began to think vaguely of the revival of an autonomous Jewish nationality. Moreover, the growing security of the Near East, and especially the benevolent interest which the European powers were taking in Palestinian affairs, rendered possible the development of a more systematic and self-dependent settlement. Philanthropists, Jewish and Gentile (like the munificent Englishman, Sir Moses Montefiore, his American counterpart, Judah Touro [1775-1854], and the Christian enthusiast, Laurence Oliphant [1829-1888]) elaborated schemes for diverting the pauper Jewish population of Jerusalem and other towns into productive work on the soil; and the *Alliance Israélite Universelle* opened an agricultural school near Jaffa. Rabbis of undisputed orthodoxy began to teach that the Messianic deliverance was not to be the prelude to the rebirth of a Jewish Palestine, but must be preceded by it.

The new conception found its first prophet in a German thinker, Moses Hess (1812-1875), who had been through the whole gamut of assimilation, only to find disillusion in the end. Returning in a premature old age to his own people, he pointed out in his *Rome and*

---

[1] Above, pp. 281-2.   [2] Above, pp. 343 and 397.

148. THEODOR HERZL (1860-1904)
Painting 1899

149. BEFORE RECLAMATION: THE SWAMPS NEAR LAKE HULEH, PALESTINE

150. AFTER RECLAMATION: THE BALFOUR FOREST

151. JEWISH COLONISTS PLOUGHING IN THE VALLEY OF ESDRAELON

152. HAYYIM NAHMAN BIALIK (1872-1934)

153. MEMORIAL TO PALESTINIAN JEWISH VOLUNTEERS FALLEN IN LIBYA, 1939-1945

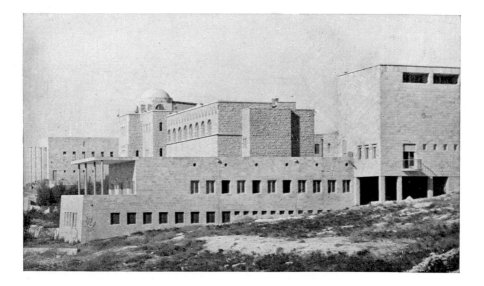

154. THE HEBREW UNIVERSITY, JERUSALEM

Jerusalem (1862) the insubstantiality of the ideal of emancipation as an end in itself. In trenchant language he criticised the attitude of modern Rabbis of every school, who, by regarding Judaism solely as a religious system, had sacrificed the national idea; and he affirmed that the reconstitution of a political nationality in Palestine was the only solution to the indubitable problem of the Jew. His appeal was of course disregarded, as that of an unpractical visionary: in just the same way as George Eliot's eloquent pleadings, in her novel, *Daniel Deronda* (1876), were hailed as nothing more than a welcome philo-Jewish gesture on the part of a distinguished Gentile. Still less attention was paid in western Europe to Russian-Jewish writers of the 'seventies such as Perez Smolenskin and others who, in a reaction against the assimilationist ideals of the contemporary *Haskalah*, began to preach a vague nationalism.

The Russian reaction of 1881 made a radical change in the attitude of many leaders of Russian Jewish thought, who now despaired utterly of the solution of the Jewish problem along the lines hitherto followed. In the following year, Leo Pinsker (1821-1891), a physician of Odessa, published a brochure, *Auto-Emancipation*, in which he demonstrated that the Jews (the Russian Jews at least) were nourishing an illusion in hoping ever to identify themselves completely with the peoples amongst whom they lived. Accordingly, he suggested the creation of a national homeland, preferably in Palestine, as the only expedient which could restore their dignity even in the Diaspora. He was not alone in his views, and a number of societies called *Hovevei Zion* (Lovers of Zion) were established (principally in eastern Europe), to carry them into effect.

Meanwhile, a trickle of the stream of migration from Russia, which had been opened up in that fateful year, had reached Palestine. While *Auto-Emancipation* was in the press, a number of young University students and others had formed an association under the name BILU (the initials of the Hebrew verse, '*O House of Jacob, come ye and let us go*': Isaiah ii, 5), and set out for Jaffa. Subsequently, under the auspices of the *Hovevei Zion*, a few agricultural colonies were founded in the coastal plain of Judaea. The work was embarked upon hastily, and was inadequately supported; but (thanks to the constant and munificent assistance of Baron Edmond de Rothschild of Paris [1845-1934]) the settlements managed to establish themselves on a firm basis. Thus, after three centuries, practical experiment in the colonisation of Palestine was renewed.

Hardly aware of all this, a strikingly handsome Viennese writer, named Theodor Herzl (1860-1904), was attending the court-martial on Alfred Dreyfus in Paris, in 1894, as correspondent of the *Neue Freie Presse*. He had been brought up in an assimilated environment—so much so that at one time he had advocated wholesale baptism of the children (adults could hardly be expected to change their beliefs) as the obvious solution to the Jewish question. But the Dreyfus Case convinced him that he had been wrong. Anti-Jewish prejudice, as it was manifesting itself in Russia, in Germany, and now even in France, the home of equality and fraternity, was not merely religious in origin. It was racial, as far as it was anything. But a people cannot submerge itself, even though it may desire to do so. The only key to the endless problem was therefore for the Jews to reorganise themselves as a nation, with an autonomous centre of their own. Only by this means could their dignity be restored and such scandals as that which the world was then witnessing be avoided: only thus, more-over, could those persecuted in eastern Europe find a secure refuge, where they would not introduce the germs of a fresh Anti-Semitic outbreak. Carried away by his enthusiasm, Herzl wrote at high pressure his famous *Judenstaat*, in which he elaborated these ideas and outlined a scheme in which mystical fervour and severe attention to practical detail were curiously intermingled.

This was the first step in the launching of the Zionist movement, with its object (as it was ultimately defined) of 'securing for the Jewish people a home in Palestine guaranteed by public law'.[1] Into this, Herzl threw himself with all the fervour and self-devotion of one of the ancient prophets (or, as his detractors sneeringly suggested, of one of the medieval false Messiahs). His magnetic personality gained him many adherents all over the world—particularly in eastern Europe, where the traditional devotion to Palestine was still over-whelmingly strong. He became the idol of the Jewish masses, as no other man had been since the days of Sabbatai Zevi. Among the upper and more assimilated classes his progress was disappointingly slow. Business men condemned him as being too visionary, and visionaries as being too sordid. Reform Jews had officially discarded the national idea and the hope for a return to Palestine, while their antithesis, the ultra-orthodox, considered that the Almighty would act in His good time, and that His hand should not be forced. Those who worshipped at the shrine of Emancipation feared that the revival of a Jewish

[1] The wording formulated officially at the Zionist Congress held at Basle in 1897.

nationality with its own centre would endanger their position in the Diaspora. The adherence of a few commanding figures, such as Max Nordau (1849-1923), the physician, critic and publicist, and Israel Zangwill the novelist (1864-1926), made up only in part for the general lukewarmness. Yet some, who did not see eye to eye with Herzl on political questions, were nevertheless in favour of the re-establishment of a Jewish territorial centre, where Hebrew culture might have its focus, and where the Hebrew religion, long atrophied, might develop naturally once more.

In 1897 there was held at Basle the first of a series of Zionist Congresses, to discuss how the new presentation of the eternally old striving of the Jewish people might be brought to fruition. Herzl thus felt himself authorised to enter into official negotiations in order to put his scheme into effect. With indomitable courage, backed by a mystical belief in his own mission, he obtained audiences with the various potentates of Europe, from the German Kaiser to the Pope, whom he endeavoured with varying success to interest. He had an official interview with the Sultan, with whom negotiations were car-ried on in 1901-1902, with the object of obtaining a charter for Palestine. Once this was secured, he was sublimely confident that it would be easy to obtain the necessary financial support. It is said that he might have succeeded had he consented to use his influence to silence the outcry in Europe and America against the Armenian atrocities. Whether this was the case or no, the negotiations broke down. The British Government, on the other hand, was so impressed that it offered Herzl for colonisation purposes, first a tract of land in the Peninsula of Sinai, between Palestine and Egypt; and then, when difficulties arose, a stretch of territory in British East Africa.[1] How-ever, it soon became patent that no land could possibly have the same appeal in the eyes of the Jewish masses as that of their fathers, and that they were not likely to make the necessary sacrifices on behalf of any other. Accordingly, after long and acrimonious discussions, the offer was declined. It had nevertheless served its purpose, by demon-strating to the world that, in the opinion of responsible European statesmen, Zionism was a factor to be reckoned with.

Not long after, Herzl died, worn out by his labours, at the early age of forty-four (1904). The importance of his achievement should not be mistaken. The Zionist ideal—the inspiration, the devotion, the psychological basis—had already been active among the Jewish masses

[1] Actually in Kenya, though this is generally termed the 'Uganda Scheme'.

of eastern Europe long before his interest became aroused. What he did was to make the movement a universal one; to provide it with leadership in the western European sense; and to introduce it to the knowledge of the outside world. With his death, its unity was shaken. Many of those who clung to his original idea, of founding a Jewish state no matter where, seceded under Israel Zangwill, to form the Jewish Territorial Organisation (ITO), which did some useful work in the subsequent decade in investigating the possibilities of Jewish settlement in Africa and America. Those who remained continued to work in the old tradition of the *Hovevei Zion*, along the slow road of petty colonisation and education. But whereas before Herzl's advent the movement had been small and chaotic, now it was world-wide, well-organised, and endowed with the potentiality at least of becoming a factor in international politics.

One of the first positive achievements of Zionism had been the creation of two financial institutions—the Jewish Colonial Trust and the Jewish National Fund—for carrying on its work: the former a joint-stock company supported by a large number of small share-holders, and the latter a non-profit-making organisation, maintained by voluntary contributions, for land purchase in Palestine. Neither, indeed, obtained more than a fraction of the money needed for the purpose as Herzl had conceived it. Nevertheless, through their medium and under the inspiration of the new ideal, the settlement of the Jews on the soil of Palestine quietly progressed. The whole country became dotted with agricultural colonies, where the labour and technical skill of Jewish workers was once more making the land of their fathers, desolate and neglected for many centuries, to flow with milk and honey. Among the sand-dunes near Jaffa a Jewish town-ship sprang up, named (with obvious Biblical reminiscence[1]) Tel Aviv, or the Mound of Spring; and a Jewish school of arts and crafts was established at Jerusalem. Thanks largely to the exertions and idealism of one man, Eliezer Ben Yehudah (1858-1922), the language spoken by the colonists was Hebrew—Biblical Hebrew, as it had been spoken by David and Isaiah and enriched by the medieval poets and philosophers, adapted to the needs of the day. Simultaneously, in Russia, the Hebrew cultural revival (which for many years past had contented itself mainly with somewhat vapid adaptations from Euro-pean languages) threw up a small number of writers of outstanding genius. Noteworthy among these was Asher Ginzberg (1856-1927:

[1] Above, p. 51.

better known by his pen-name of *Ahad haAm*—'One of the People'): a forceful essayist, the apostle of 'cultural' as opposed to 'political' Zionism even before the days of Herzl, and the man who was responsible more than any other for the inclusion of Palestine in the official Zionist programme as formulated at Basle. The latter's cold logic stood in sharp contrast to the fire of Hayyim Nahman Bialik (1872-1934), the greatest Hebrew poet since Judah haLevi, who was stimulated to his most poignant work by the Kishinev pogrom of 1903. Yet, all told, not more than a few thousand persons were directly affected by the revival. With its founder's death, moreover, Zionism lost its vitality, and in the course of the following decade much of its vigour was wasted in internal disputes. In the severely practical world which came to an end in 1914, the movement was considered the pastime of a few visionaries, and even in the Jewish world its positive achievements were on the whole ignored.

IV

The War of 1914-1918 divided up the Zionist organisation into two opposing camps. In the third year of hostilities, the desirability of conciliating the important and influential body of Jewish opinion in America elevated the movement into a political pawn of the first importance—especially to the Franco-British *bloc*, who desired to counteract the bad impression which their alliance with the arch-tyrant, Russia, had created in Jewish circles. Providentially, one of the English Zionist leaders, Chaim Weizmann (*b.* 1873), a gifted chemist of Russian birth, had made a discovery which proved of considerable importance for the manufacture of high explosive. Thanks to this, he got into close touch with official circles; and he did not fail to make full use of his opportunities.

Late in 1914, Turkey had entered the war on the side of the Central Powers. War-time gestures in which unoccupied territory is in question are notoriously cheap; and on 2nd November 1917 (only a few days before the Bolshevik Revolution, which was to have so profound an effect upon Jewish life in eastern Europe) Arthur James (subsequently Lord) Balfour, then British Foreign Secretary, issued a declaration which intimated that the British Government viewed with favour the establishment in Palestine of a national home for the Jewish people, and would use their best endeavours to facilitate the achievement of this object.

The effect of this pronouncement (soon to be confirmed by all the other Allied governments) was electrical. The German government attempted to counteract it not long after by an anaemic statement to a similar effect; but, since the territory of an allied, and not an enemy, power was concerned, its hands were tied. Already the Palestinian refugees in Egypt had recruited what was known as the Zion Mule Corps, which shared in the hazards of the ill-starred Gallipoli campaign; while the colonists in Palestine, at the risk of their lives, were doing everything in their power to pave the way for the British advance, notwithstanding the miniature reign of terror which now began. A series of Jewish battalions (one of them composed entirely of American volunteers) was raised and trained in England, and despatched to the Palestinian front. By the time of their arrival, however, the brunt of the campaign was over. At the time when the Balfour Declaration was prepared, it could hardly have been realised how speedily the Turkish defence in the south of Palestine would crumple. Only five days later, Gaza, which had long held up the British advance, was captured. Within six weeks, the Crescent ceased to wave over Jerusalem for the first time since the period of the Crusades. The realisation of the Zionist ideal, which two months before had seemed a distant dream, now appeared on the verge of realisation.

For nearly a year the Palestinian front was quiet. In the autumn of 1918 (with the participation of the Jewish battalions) the final operations took place which swept the Turkish armies northward in a disordered mob, and started the panic which led to the final debacle of the Central Powers in November. At the Peace Conference which assembled in Paris, no opportunity was given to the Allies to forget the pledges which they had made in the heat of the struggle. Moreover, though none of the victors felt inclined to relinquish its hold on any territory which it had conquered, the era of naked annexation was over. Instead, the system was evolved of 'mandates' under the League of Nations, assigned to some interested power to be administered, not in its own interest, but in that of humanity. Great Britain, in any case, would not have been disposed to tolerate any other state in control of the country which, no less than restive Egypt, commanded the Suez Canal and the path to India. Accordingly, by the San Remo Conference of April 1920, the 'Mandate' for Palestine was assigned to her to be administered according to the terms of the Balfour Declaration. This arrangement was formally confirmed there years later, by the Council of the newly-born League of Nations; and arrangements were made for the establishment of a 'Jewish Agency for Palestine' (which ultimately came into being in 1929, comprising non-Zionist as well as Zionist elements) to represent world Jewry in its relations with the Palestinian government.

Thus, for the first time since the abolition of the Patriarchate in 425, if not since the fall of Jerusalem three and a half centuries earlier, the political connection of the Jewish people with the land of their fathers—the land for which they had longed and dreamed and prayed throughout the long centuries of exile—was formally recognised. Hebrew was admitted as one of the official languages of the country. A prominent English Jew—Sir Herbert (afterwards Lord) Samuel (b. 1870), who had held a number of important political offices, culminating in that of Home Secretary—was sent out as first High Commissioner. A Jew was once more ruling the Holy Land— and supposed to rule it, too, in the interests of his brethren! It seemed as though the Messianic days had dawned; and throughout the world, pious Jews began to make preparations for spending the next year, literally, in Jerusalem.

The high hopes of this early period were not destined to last for long. Zionism had not, perhaps, taken full account of the Arab population in Palestine. They were not numerous; they were for the most part on a very low grade of civilisation; they had shamefully neglected the country, allowing large parts of it to degenerate into an uncultivated waste. But their sense of local patriotism became immensely stimulated when they found other persons interested in the land. The *effendis* of the towns resented the intrusion of a new element which would dispute their supremacy. Ultra-conservatives objected to the invasion of Occidental ideas. Religious passions, never more than dormant, were re-awakened. Unscrupulous agitators informed the peasantry, without the slightest basis in fact, that the newcomers would dispossess them of their lands, making no compensation. Just before the San Remo Conference, anti-Jewish riots had taken place in Jerusalem, resulting in the loss of a number of lives; and, in 1921, there was a recurrence in Jaffa, with even more deplorable results. Sir Herbert Samuel, unimaginative as he was upright, demonstrated his impartiality by neglecting the section which he might have been expected to favour. The clause of the Balfour Declaration which safeguarded the rights of the existing inhabitants was observed more meticulously by far than the main proviso; and severe restrictions

were placed upon Jewish immigration. The tradition set in this formative period could not easily be reversed; and in 1929, in consequence
of an absurd rumour that a plan was on foot to dispossess the Moslems
of the Mosque of Omar, on the ancient Temple site, another series of
anti-Jewish riots took place, with devastating effect, throughout the
country.

Notwithstanding all this, the positive achievements were far from
negligible. In spite of the vexatious limitations imposed, immigrants
arrived in a steady trickle from every corner of the Jewish world,
from New York to Bokhara. The Jewish population increased four-
fold in little more than a single decade. Fresh Jewish suburbs sprang
up outside the walls of Jerusalem. Tel Aviv, the first Jewish city,
developed with amazing rapidity. Considerable tracts of land were
acquired, especially in the Valley of Jezreel, by the Jewish National
Fund, with the aid of contributions from every continent, and prepared for settlement. New colonies were established here and there
throughout the country. Bands of *Halutzim*, or pioneers, were recruited in the Diaspora to perform the manual labour—tilling the
fields, building, road-making; and visitors used to European valuations
were amazed to meet among them many University men and women,
who had graduated brilliantly in various abstruse subjects, and were
masters of half a dozen languages. Modern methods of agriculture
were introduced. Hills were once more rendered fertile by the construction of terraces. The orange-growing industry attained impressive
proportions. Throughout the country, work of afforestation was
executed, swamps were drained, and malaria stamped out. A great
scheme was initiated for utilising the superabundant waters of the
Jordan, that most paradoxical of rivers, for the purposes of irrigation
and electrical supply; while the mineral deposits of the Dead Sea
began to be exploited by modern methods. The ignorant Arab *fellahin*
were informed that it was their duty to resent the intrusion; but they
could not fail to realise that their standard of living, the amenities of
their existence, and above all their physical health, benefited immensely as a result of it.

It was on the spiritual side, however, that the positive effects of the
experiment were most marked. The earliest enterprise of importance
carried out after the British occupation was the establishment in Jerusalem of a University, the foundation stone of which was laid before
the cannon had ceased to mutter, and which was formally opened in
1925. Here, scholars of the highest reputation, recruited from all the

great seats of learning of Europe and America, taught an increasing body of students of international provenance. A great library was built up, and a University press established which produced a series of works which enriched, not only Jewish, but also general culture. The medium of instruction was, of course, Hebrew, which had obtained general currency for all purposes throughout the new settlement, and which now entered upon a fresh period of productivity. Novels, plays, poems, translations, works of erudition, poured out in a steady stream from a dozen different presses. Rival newspapers and reviews (some of them enjoying a wide circulation) introduced the spirit of modern journalism. A Hebrew theatre was established, which attained international significance. Littérateurs of the highest reputation, such as Bialik and Ahad haAm, joined the settlement, where at last they found their proper spiritual environment. It was a literary and practical revival of a dormant language, unique in history. The traditional religious forms were, perhaps, somewhat neglected by the eager idealists of the younger generation. Many observances, however, which had long been disregarded, or had become fossilised, acquired a new meaning; and Palestinian Jewry, though sometimes characterised as irreligious, was certainly not unspiritual.

In the Diaspora, too, the effect of the incredible experiment was of paramount importance. It was assumed that only a fraction of the world's fifteen million Jews could find a home in Palestine. For the rest, it was hoped that the country would serve as an inspiration. This pious aspiration soon proved justified, though not, perhaps, in the degree which was hoped. A distinct Jewish renaissance was discernible, particularly amongst the youth. Those to whom the religious appeal meant little found something to take its place. Cases became comparatively common where members of completely assimilated families (like Alfred Mond, Lord Melchett [1868-1930], an important figure in English industrial and political life) re-identified themselves with their people. Modern Hebrew, previous to 1914 familiar only to a few idealists, slowly began to displace Yiddish and Ladino as the lingua franca of the Diaspora. Palestine resumed its place in the scheme of Jewish life.

BOOK VI

CATASTROPHE AND RESURRECTION

1918-1967

Chapter XXXI

CATASTROPHE

———————— • ————————

I

The overthrow of the old order in central and eastern Europe, the final completion of Jewish emancipation in every important country of the world,[1] the creation of the League of Nations with its solemn function of safeguarding the rights of minorities, led to a universal hope that the upheaval of 1914-1918, notwithstanding the sacrifices which it had involved and the disorders by which it had been followed, would usher in a millennial era, of true freedom and equality, for Jewry as a whole.

The events of the ensuing decades belied this. During the war, Jews had fought with equal bravery on all fronts; and statisticians in every country delighted to shew that they had actually contributed more than their normal proportion to the various armies. Some, indeed, had risen to high rank; and a professing Jew, Sir John Monash (1865-1931), had actually commanded the Australian forces in the field. More striking still were Jewish achievements in the period of reconstruction. Hugo Preuss (1860-1925), first Minister of the Interior in the German Republic, was responsible for the drafting of the Weimar Constitution; Kurt Eisner (1867-1919) was Prime Minister of Bavaria; Victor Adler (1852-1918), Foreign Minister of Austria[2]; several persons of the same stock were among the delegates at the Peace Conference held in Paris, and signed the subsequent treaties on behalf of their governments; while Rufus Isaacs, Marquess of Reading (1860-1935), after a kaleidoscopic legal and political

---

[1] After the establishment of republican government in Spain in 1931, the only parts of the world where the Jews remained legally unemancipated (other than technically 'uncivilised' countries such as Afghanistan or the Yemen), were, paradoxically enough, the French colonies of Morocco and Tunis.

[2] It should be added that Eisner was not a professing Jew, while Adler had nominally apostatised.

career which had apparently culminated in the dignities of Lord Chief Justice of England and Special Ambassador to the United States of America, was sent to India in 1921 as Viceroy, and for five years ruled with conspicuous success over three hundred million souls.

Russia, on the other hand, still constituted a perpetual problem. It is true that the Revolution had emancipated the Jews, fully and without reservations. They were officially recognised as constituting a separate nationality, with its own language and institutions. Persons of Jewish birth (though in no case Jewish by conviction or in practice) were beginning to play a part of importance in Russian life; and one, Leon Trotsky (1872-1940), was for a time among the outstanding figures in the new regime. Under the Soviets, ambitious schemes were started, with lavish help from anti-Zionist circles in America, for creating Jewish agricultural colonies in the Ukraine, the Crimea, and elsewhere, on a scale which rivalled, if it did not exceed, contemporary experiments in Palestine. It was hoped that the autonomous Jewish region of Biro-Bidjan, in Siberia, would ultimately be admitted to the Soviet Union as a constituent republic.

Yet, in practice, the Soviet system was in some ways even more disastrous to Jewish life than its Czarist precursor had been. The intensely individualistic Jewish nature was alien to the new scheme of things; while even the Jewish Socialist organisation, the *Bund* (which had been established towards the close of the last century), was suppressed as being too moderate for Bolshevik ideology, continuing to exist only in Poland. The vast majority of Russian Jewry had been middlemen and small traders—an integral, though humble, part of that bourgeoisie against which the Bolshevik revolution had been directed. In a republic of workmen and peasants it was, at the beginning, as difficult for them to find a place as it had been ten centuries previous under the feudal regime. A number were taken into the government service (now opened to them for the first time), absorbed in the factories, or settled on the soil—a process necessarily slow, difficult, and expensive. A very large proportion remained for a long while absolutely destitute, as unassimilable economically under the new form of government as they had been politically under the old.

Similarly, on the spiritual side Judaism suffered, with all other faiths, in the campaign against religion. Synagogues were closed down or converted into clubs, public religious teaching was prohibited, obstacles were placed in the way even of the fundamental rite of circumcision. Zionism was condemned as a bourgeois movement, its adherents being subjected to a merciless persecution and sent to Siberia. Hebrew was similarly frowned upon as a bourgeois tongue, every encouragement being given on the other hand to Yiddish, which was regarded as truly proletarian. There was, of course, no bar from either side against intermarriage, which went on at an alarming pace; and, with no logical tie remaining in Judaism, assimilation in the completest sense became rampant. Were Jewry to survive under such conditions—an unlikely hypothesis—it could be only as a purely secular body, lacking every spiritual bond, and deprived of that sense of communion with the past which forms the justification and the inspiration of nationhood.

Though the effects of Bolshevism on Judaism in Russia were fatal, abroad the Jew was stigmatised as though he were responsible for the new scheme of things. The fact that the Soviet government, deserted by or mistrusting the tools of the old regime, at first recruited a large proportion of its civil service and of its diplomatic corps from persons of Jewish origin, gave the latter a disproportionate prominence. Moreover, Karl Marx, the prophet of Communism, happened to be of Jewish blood, though he was baptised in childhood, brought up as a Christian, and attacked both Jews and Judaism fiercely in his writings. Hence there was another excuse for identifying the Jew, already un-popular, with the dreaded system which threatened to undermine the foundations of the established order.

Largely in consequence of this, or at least using it as pretext, a wave of anti-Semitism swept throughout the western world, staining the new heavens and the new earth which had been so painstakingly built up at the conference-tables in Paris. The prevalence of national-ist passions—whether stimulated by defeat or by victory, or by a feeling that the fruits of success had been withheld, according to the circumstances of the various countries—prepared the ground; and war-time hysteria, still prevalent, made it possible to believe any story or theory, however far-fetched. The fact that some Jews had profited in the wave of artificial prosperity which war-time conditions had provoked (though many more had been reduced to beggary), was taken as convincing proof that they had precipitated, or even planned, the cataclysm. Everywhere, Jew and Bolshevik were taken to be synonymous terms. Pseudo-scientific works were written to prove that the Jews were the 'revolutionary leaven', responsible for every upheaval that had taken place during the past century and a half, whether they were to be found in the country in question or no. It was seriously alleged that there was a universal understanding between Zionism, Bolshevism, and High Finance (all of them aspects of a hypothetical 'Jewish International'!) to secure the domination of the world; and a ridiculous farrago of nonsense, *The Protocols of the Learned Elders of Zion*, which purported to give the proceedings of a Congress held in order to bring about this object, ran through edition after edition in every language. Even the discovery that this egregious production was in the main an adaptation of a work written to satirise Napoleon III, three-quarters of a century before, did not shake credence in it.

Throughout the world—not excepting even England—there were signs of reaction. In America the superlative 'Ku Klux Klan' purported to champion the cause of the Nordic elements against Catholics, Negroes, and Jews; while Henry Ford (a well-meaning idealist, who had, nevertheless, amassed one of the largest fortunes in the world) implicitly believed every charge made against the Jew, and even went so far as to subsidise Anti-Semitic publications. That he afterwards retracted by no means compensated for all the harm that he had done. Social discrimination, too, was widespread; and, notwithstanding the growing acclimatisation of the Jew, he continued to be excluded systematically from many clubs, college fraternities, and even certain hotels.

More serious by far was the condition of affairs in central and eastern Europe. The Minority Treaties, in the framing of which the astutest legal minds in Europe had spent weary months, were flouted whenever it suited the turn of the government concerned. Though the wave of pogroms had been checked, actions of violence (sometimes with fatal outcome) were perpetrated almost daily. The Roumanian Government remained profoundly anti-Jewish, notwithstanding its solemn pledges. In Poland the Jews were excluded methodically from government employment, and squeezed out of the state monopolies. By adroit manipulation the thirty-five representatives whom they had triumphantly sent to the first Sjem were reduced, sixteen years later, to four. All over eastern Europe an attempt was made, and sometimes (as in Hungary) enforced by governmental action, to restrict the number of Jewish students in the Universities in strict proportion to the ratio of the Jewish population—the so-called *numerus clausus*—and student riots became the order of the day. More than one country, in defiance of the Minority Treaties, reduced

Jewish traders to the verge of ruin by enforcing Sunday closing even in the case of those who had already lost one day's business activity on Saturday. From 1924 there was a momentary diminution of actual violence; but there were still occasional outbursts, and the Jewish problem remained acute. The crisis which began to paralyse economic life throughout the world in 1930 disproportionately affected the Jewish middle-man; and in eastern Europe pauperisation set in on an alarming scale.

II

Most amazing of all was the course of events in Germany. Though at last German Jewry was fully emancipated, in fact as well as in theory, Anti-Semitism was attaining wilder extremities than ever before. Jewish pre-eminence, in one field or another of national life, was spoken of, resented, and attacked, as Jewish 'predominance.' The fact that some individuals had been able to accommodate themselves to changing economic conditions was resented by those who were less fortunate. It was alleged that they had established a stranglehold on German life, from industry on the one hand to art on the other. The new currents they had introduced in thought, literature, and drama, which had made Berlin the hub of European cultural life, were stigmatised as poisonous and deleterious. Even Albert Einstein (1879–1955), one of the most eminent contemporary scientists and author of the Theory of Relativity, drew upon himself a continual stream of obloquy by reason of his race. The anti-Semitic outcry against Walter Rathenau (1867-1922), the Minister for Reconstruction, who more than any other person was responsible for the rehabilitation of the country after the war, culminated in 1922 in his assassination.

With the momentary amelioration of general conditions, the anti-Jewish outcry was muffled. The recurrence of the economic crisis, however, gave it new force and a new outlet. The National Socialist movement, founded by Adolf Hitler in 1925, made up for its lack of a constructive programme by laying the responsibility for every ill which was besetting the country on the Jews, whom it professed to regard as an excrescence upon the body politic. Once they were driven out, or deprived of power, all would be well; and one of the cardinal points of the programme of the new party was their reduction to impotence.

For some years this was derided as the raving of a madman. Yet, in the end, the plight of the German people made them turn in any direction for help; and in 1933 Adolf Hitler became Chancellor of the German Empire. A reign of terror immediately set in for the Jews, reduced to a position worse than that of their co-religionists in Russia in the dark days of the past generation. They were thrust out, with no compunction, from government and municipal offices, from the Universities, from the professions, even from private employment. Physicians and lawyers were permitted to practise only in proportion to the numbers of the Jewish population, and later, only among Jews. Their businesses were boycotted, with official sanction and encouragement. They were forced to relinquish their association with the great economic organisations which they had created; with the museums that they had established; with the Academies that they had made famous. A journalistic campaign of unheard-of virulence was let loose against them, even in those organs of opinion which they had formerly controlled. Scholars, writers, and scientists of international fame who had built up Germany's reputation, whose discoveries had enabled her to withstand a world in arms, and whose prestige had assisted in rehabilitating her in the eyes of Europe, were reduced to beggary or driven into exile. For the first time in history, the persecution extended not merely to those who professed the Jewish religion, but to all, however devout in their Christianity, in whose veins any Jewish blood was to be traced, for three or four generations. Scenes reminiscent of the Middle Ages were enacted throughout the country; and the frontiers of barbarism were thrust forward at a stroke from the Vistula to the Rhine.

It was generally anticipated that once the initial period of extravagance was over, the country would settle down again more or less normally, and that Jewish life would be able to resume its even tenor, though perhaps with diminished intensity. These hopes were disappointed. Anti-Semitism was almost the only part of the magniloquent policy of the new regime which could be carried into effect by legislative enactment. For many of its supporters, moreover, the new racialism was a creed which justified any severity and every sacrifice. Thus, with the passage of months and years, the condition of German Jewry progressively deteriorated. Only, the spontaneous outburst of personal feeling which had characterised the first phase gave way to a cold, calculated code, deliberately excogitated by a government which thought of its difficulties mainly in terms of 'the Jewish problem', and in any case found this policy remarkably useful for filling its coffers and conciliating office-hungry followers. The medieval anti-Jewish codes were studied for precedents, which were imitated with ridiculous fidelity—including even exclusion from municipal bathing establishments. Buying from, and selling to, Jews was stigmatised as an act of treachery to the Fatherland. The new generation was brought up to consider the principles of anti-Semitism as inviolable, and the foundation of Germany's future greatness. Special benches for Jews and half-Jews were set up in the schools (until in the end they were excluded from them altogether), thus carrying back the persecutory system, in the name of racial purity, to children fresh from the nursery. In 1935, at the rally of the Nazi party at Nuremberg (once more become a hotbed of anti-Jewish feeling), a law was announced excluding the Jews in perpetuity from German citizenship. At the same time, they were forbidden to have Christian maidservants (of active years, at least) in their employment, and intermarriage or extra-marital intercourse with persons of 'Aryan' blood was made a penal offence. Local extremists carried matters even further, some places excluding the Jews entirely, as their fathers had done in the Middle Ages.

A community of over half a million souls, comprising one of the most vital sections of civilised humanity, suddenly found the ground cut from under their feet, with no prospect of security and diminishing hopes of earning a livelihood in the land where their ancestors had been settled for centuries.

The new Diaspora was in its way more striking than anything of the sort which had preceded it in human history. During the first year of the persecution, some seventy thousand German Jews left the country. The majority were not artisans or merchants, as might normally have been expected, but professional men—University professors, physicians, surgeons, lawyers, art-experts, architects, writers, journalists: in many instances men of international reputation, who had given up their best years and devotion to Germany's service. Within a short while, there can have been no country in the world where some famous German scientist or scholar was not at work. But it was, unhappily, a period of the most intense economic depression in recent history, when every nation was putting up barriers against those who might compete in the labour market with native-born citizens. The process of readjustment was, therefore, peculiarly painful. But, with every month that passed, the need for finding a new home became more and more grimly urgent.

III

At this stage a remarkable phenomenon became apparent. The development of a Jewish Palestine had been regarded by emancipated western Jewry, as a quixotic, semi-charitable undertaking, which might perhaps contribute towards the re-establishment of Jewish self-respect and the restoration of a Jewish culture, but could never play a really important part in solving the physical problems of the Jewish people. Nowhere was this view held more vocally than in Germany, the home of the Reform Movement and the classical land of assimilation. But, in its hour of trial, it was precisely to Palestine that German Jewry turned for succour—Palestine, the only country of the world which had escaped the economic crisis, and where, on the contrary (thanks to the impetus given by Jewish practical idealism) there was actually a wave of prosperity. So far was this the case that the Government opened the gates to immigration—somewhat grudgingly indeed, yet more amply than ever before. Accordingly, it was to Palestine that many dispossessed German Jews now went— including even large numbers who had previously been sternly anti-Zionistic in their views. It was the only country which was able to absorb them, or their hardly more fortunate Polish and eastern European co-religionists, on a large scale. In 1934 the Jewish immigration into the country was about 42,000, and in 1935 reached the record figure of 62,000. Within three years, over 35,000 German refugees had landed; and the figures did not shew any sign of diminishing. By the close of 1939, the total Jewish population of the country, which at the time of the Balfour Declaration had been some 60,000, approached 500,000; and Tel Aviv was one of the most modern cities in the Middle East, with nearly 150,000 inhabitants. Of the Palestinian Jewish population, some 15 per cent, distributed in 270 rural centres with a total population of 143,000, were engaged in agriculture, 40,000 of them living in workers' colonies. The wild chimaera which twenty years before had been ridiculed by hard-headed business men and experienced philanthropists was now the one bright spot on the Jewish horizon. No longer was it possible to talk of the Zionist experiment: it had become a reality. Palestine was not, indeed, Jewish; but, for the first time for fifteen centuries and more, there was a Jewish Palestine again.[1]

Though these mighty achievements could not be annulled, the

[1] The text of the original edition of this work, 1936, ended at this point.

promise of this period was not destined to be sustained to the full. In April 1936 there was a new Arab outbreak, differing from those which had preceded it in its duration, its cohesion, and the fact that it was in great measure due to foreign intrigue—particularly on the part of Fascist Italy, anxious to pose as the protector of Islam and to embarrass England in the Near East. A General Strike was proclaimed, to be intensified by non-cooperation with the Government and a boycott of the Jews. For many months organised gangster warfare was waged on Palestinian Jewry, with armed attacks against colonies, highway ambushes in the country and bomb outrages in the towns, and wholesale murder even of Arabs of more moderate opinions. Notwithstanding the overwhelming temptation to reciprocate violence for violence, the Jewish leaders managed to impress on their followers, with rare exceptions, a policy of non-reprisal; and the pent-up feelings of the *Yishuv* found characteristic expression in the establishment during this period of new colonies in the most dangerous areas and the creation of a port at Tel Aviv to remedy the dislocation caused by the inactivity at Jaffa. The active disturbances lasted until the autumn, being succeeded by a prolonged period of brigandage directed in an increasing degree against Arab moderates.

As soon as order was superficially re-established, a Royal Commission was sent to Palestine to enquire into the cause of the unrest. It reported that it was unable to see how the problems involved could be solved on the basis of the Mandate, and suggested that the difficulty should be met by dividing the country into two sovereign states, Arab and Jewish. The latter, however, was to extend to only some 2,000 square miles (less than one-fifth of the total area of the country, already truncated by the loss of the wide expanses of Transjordan in 1923); it was to be confined to Galilee and sprawling tentacles in the already highly-colonised plains; and it was not to include Jerusalem, which with its 75,000 Jews and great Jewish institutions was to remain with some other places under a perpetual British mandate. The idea of a sovereign state, however small, into which immigration would be untrammelled and which, therefore, might contribute solidly to the solution of the appalling refugee problem, had some obvious attractions, notwithstanding the fact that the fantastic frontier implied a Zionism without Zion. Accordingly, at their meetings at Zurich in August 1937 (though only after long and bitter criticism), the Zionist Congress and subsequently the Jewish Agency authorised negotiations with the British Government along the lines of the proposed compromise, in the hope that details might be drastically modified. Partition was, however, unanimously rejected by the leaders of the Arab malcontents; further disturbances broke out, and were only suppressed after a systematic military effort; and in the end the idea of partition was abandoned and an entirely new policy announced in a White Paper issued in London in May 1939. This set a maximum of 75,000 for future Jewish immigration into Palestine, to be spread over a period of five years, and intimated that, if possible, the British administration would be withdrawn in 1949 and the country left independent (though bound to Great Britain by treaty), with its Jews a perpetual minority. It was thus that matters stood when, that summer, the Holy Land came under a grimmer menace. However much Imperial policy or local difficulties may have made this decision seem necessary, it was a far, far cry from the golden promise of the Balfour Declaration.

IV

When the Nazis first came into power, they had insisted that their anti-Semitic doctrine was a matter of internal concern and application only. But, as he proceeded from one success of diplomacy or bluster to the other, Hitler discovered that, by fostering or playing on local anti-Jewish prejudices and posing as the champion of Europe against a mythical entity which he termed International Jewry (identified simultaneously, by an extraordinary feat of intellectual acrobatics, with Bolshevism on the one hand and Capitalism on the other), it was possible to create a pro-German party in other states which espoused totalitarian doctrines and, though otherwise hyper-nationalist, was inclined to look sympathetically on German aspirations. Prejudice was naturally intensified by the influx of refugees, domestic persecution thus indirectly serving a diplomatic end. Official and semi-official organisations of the Reich now began to carry on an unceasing propaganda against the Jews abroad as well as at home; and under the stimulus not only of German example but also (as afterwards became plain) of German subsidies, the peril spread with alarming rapidity to other countries. Even in the traditional homes of liberalism in western Europe and beyond the Atlantic there was a menacing growth of anti-Semitism, using the new vocabulary and a new technique, and organised in parties such as the Cagoulards in France (where the premiership of the Jew, Léon Blum, in 1936-1937 and again in 1938 exacerbated the parties of the Right), the British Union of Fascists in England, the Rexists in Belgium, the Silver Shirts and similar bodies in America—all at one in exploiting elementary anti-Jewish prejudice for remoter political objects, and ultimately in a lack of loyalty to their country.

In central and eastern Europe the reaction went beyond the realm of theory. To states less developed mechanically and economically, the fact that the new doctrine had been embraced by 'enlightened' Germany, and her political triumphs since the change, stamped it with something more than respectability. In Roumania, where the Minority Treaty had been flouted from the outset, violence became more and more usual and restrictions more and more galling, until at the end of 1936 Octavian Goga formed a professedly anti-Semitic government which set about emulating the German example forthwith; and although it remained in office for only seven weeks (December 1936—February 1937) and a momentary alleviation followed, the new doctrines were by now solidly established, as subsequent events were to shew. Reactionary Hungary, immediately Nazi-Magyar collaboration began in 1938, saw the introduction of restrictive racial legislation on the lines of the Nuremberg Laws, and the extension of the principle of the scholastic 'numerus clausus' so as to restrict participation of the Jews in every profession and calling to a maximum ratio of 20 per cent (ultimately to be reduced, by stages, until the proportion became derisory); and not even the discovery that the Prime Minister at the time was of Jewish extraction secured a reprieve. In Poland, though intense anti-German feeling prevailed, the Endek party introduced Nazi methods and ideology into public life; economic distress was increased by administrative discrimination; and the idea that the Jews, however long established, did not constitute part of the Polish people made such headway that the Government began to discuss mass-emigration—if only an outlet could be found—in terms not far removed from deportation. But most deplorable were developments in Italy, which since 1870 had become the classical land of Jewish Emancipation, and where Jewish equality had been more of a political and social reality than anywhere else in the world. Fascism had originally shewn no trace of anti-Semitism, except inasmuch as it is implicit in any hyper-nationalist state; Jews had, in fact, played an important part in the movement from the beginning, and Benito Mussolini had condemned Jew-baiting and racialism in biting terms. But, immediately the military alliance with Germany was concluded in 1938, the handful of 50,000 Italian Jews was offered up on the totalitarian altar. Anti-Jewish legislation on the German model was suddenly introduced, full-fledged; 'non-Aryans' were driven out of the public and intellectual life which they had adorned; and wholesale emigration started from the one land of Europe where the Jewish settlement had been uninterrupted, and on the whole tranquil, since remote antiquity.

More tragic still, of necessity, was the lot of the Jews in those countries which actually came under Nazi rule. In March 1938 Hitler's legions marched into Austria, and the greed, fanaticism, and ebullience of his followers were turned against that country's 200,000 Jews, mostly concentrated in the highly-cultured community of Vienna; the cloak of legalism was now abandoned, and there were no gradations to soften the blow. The Nuremberg Laws and the rest of the new German anti-Jewish code were enforced overnight. Prominent Jews, beginning with the head of the House of Rothschild, were arrested wholesale for no reason other than that they were Jews, brutally maltreated and thrust into concentration camps from which many never returned. Jewish businesses were looted, closed, or confiscated. Synagogues were turned into offices for the Nazi armed guards, whose principal occupation was Jew-baiting of the most elementary and degrading character. The consulates of those few countries the gates of which were not entirely closed to Jews were beset by long lines of pitiful refugees. To the east, thousands were driven over the frontiers of states unwilling to receive them, and many met their death as they wandered hopelessly in no-man's-land or drifted down the Danube in over-crowded boats which were not allowed to put to shore. Suicides rose to an appalling level. The Nazi leaders openly declared their intention to make Vienna *judenrein* —that is, clear of Jews; and, when asked where they should go, significantly replied that the river was still open.

In Germany itself, conditions had progressively deteriorated during the 'Cold Pogrom', which had lasted without interruption since 1933. Nevertheless, the Jews had somehow managed to re-establish an impoverished group-life, isolated economically as well as socially, and ultimately dependent on the few businesses that had managed to survive the perpetual boycott and the capital of the handful who were still well-to-do. Something of a spiritual and intellectual revival had resulted from persecution; and the educational system organised for children who were not admitted to ordinary schools, the self-contained cultural life which had now grown up to meet the requirements of men and women now excluded from a normal expression, the orchestras and dramatic performances in which artists dismissed from their employment served the needs of a public forbidden access to concert-halls and theatres, had demonstrated an amazing power of adaptation and resilience. Though elaborate new humiliations were introduced from time to time, though the more virile elements continued to emigrate, though what was left of the community was increasingly impoverished and increasingly aged, it seemed that something firm, durable, and admirable had been established amid the ruins. But for this very reason the new German-Jewish life was doomed to destruction, with tragic and brutal suddenness.

In October 1938 the German Government suddenly deported over the eastern frontier some 12,000 Jews of Polish origin. Nearly 5,000 of them were trapped in a no-man's-land near Zbonszyn, where they were herded under sickening conditions while diplomatic conversations dragged on concerning their fate. Among the sufferers were an elderly couple named Grynszpan, who had lived in Hanover for more than thirty years. Their seventeen-year-old son Herschel, who was in Paris, was half demented by what he heard, and as a reprisal shot and fatally wounded one of the Secretaries of the German Embassy, Ernst vom Rath. This provided the Nazi propaganda machine with a superb pretext to carry a long-premeditated scheme into effect. On the night of 9th November, when the news of the young diplomat's death became known, there was throughout Germany an appalling anti-Jewish outbreak led by Storm Troopers, so uniform and so universal in its nature that its subsequent official characterisation as 'spontaneous' was obvious mockery. (The responsibility was subsequently ascribed to the Chief of the Gestapo.) With hardly a single exception, all of the 600 synagogues in the country—including ancient buildings which had formerly been regarded as national monuments—were gutted. Almost every Jewish business house was sacked. A billion marks' worth of Jewish property was wantonly destroyed. Thousands of Jewish homes were raided, and some 30,000 individuals—not excepting Rabbis, however aged—were flung into concentration camps, where they were treated with incredible barbarity. There were hundreds—perhaps thousands—of deaths. The authorities looked on these scenes of violence, which outdid in scale any Russian pogrom or any medieval massacre, not merely impassive, but approving; and, as a legal punishment for the deed of their unbalanced co-religionist in Paris, a fine of 1,000,000,000 marks (one-fifth of their property, at a lavish estimate) was imposed on the Jews of the Reich. It was, moreover, ordered that all Jewish businesses should be transferred forthwith into 'Aryan' hands, the Jews, however, first making good at their own expense the damage to their property. German Jewry was wantonly, deliberately, and irrevocably smashed. A shudder of horror went through the civilised world. The pogrom was condemned by the British Prime Minister in the House of Commons, and the American Ambassador was recalled from Berlin.

Henceforth there was obviously no conceivability of a future for Jews in Germany. Prisoners were released from the concentration camps only on condition that they emigrated forthwith; threats, violence, and pressure were exerted on others; in no case was there any ultimate possibility of remaining. Conditions for the *émigrés* had by now become worse than ever by reason of the fact that, what with exchange manipulation, special 'flight' taxation, and so on, they were now able to take with them in currency value only some 5 per cent of the property they had saved from the debacle, so that even the well-to-do could look forward to nothing but a life of penury. But necessity overwhelmed all normal conditions. The tragic scenes of the past few years were multiplied and intensified. Few countries would now open their gates. Refugee-laden vessels, seeking a port where they might discharge their cargo of misery, became familiar on the maritime highways of the world; and tens of thousands went to places (such as Shanghai) where for the moment a visa was unnecessary or there was no immigration control, simply because they were admitted. Wild schemes were launched for the establishment of colonies in all manner of insalubrious tropical areas, in some cases on terms clearly designed to fill empty treasures; but even so the local populations generally offered an implacable opposition. On the initiative of the American Government, an international conference on refugees had met at Evian in the summer of 1938, but there was little practical outcome other than the clarification of what was already so tragically clear, that no country welcomed these enforced wanderers. Very few governments made any constructive contribution to the solution of the problem. Thanks indeed to the practical idealism and organising ability of Henrietta Szold (1860-1945: creator of the American women's Zionist organisation, 'Hadatsah', which had done so much splendid welfare work), arrangements were made for transferring many children from central Europe to a new life on the soil of

Palestine; and the country continued to absorb a limited number of adults, not all of whom, however, entered legally. The United States on its side adopted a somewhat more liberal policy than hitherto, enabling many immigrants to anticipate the normal date of entry; while Great Britain allowed herself to be used as a half-way house for refugees whose ultimate destination was assured.

By the summer of 1939, one-half of the former Jewish population of the Greater Reich had left the country. Yet, no sooner was some progress made towards a solution of the problem than it was intensified by fresh complications. The 5,000 Jews of Memel shared the lot of those of Germany when it was summarily annexed in the autumn of 1938. In Danzig the Nazi administration made existence impossible for 10,000 more, notwithstanding the nominal authority of the League of Nations. Czechoslovakia had been almost the only 'Succession State' where the rights of minorities had been respected and Jewish equality existed in fact as well as theory. In 1938-1939, with the disintegration of the country, the erection of Slovakia into a Nazi puppet-state, the annexation of large areas by Hungary and the absorption of the former Bohemia into the Reich, another 350,000 Jews—including some of the oldest and proudest communities of the Diaspora—were thrown into the vortex. By the autumn of 1939, areas which had formerly housed upwards of 2,500,000 Jews—more than one-quarter of the entire Jewish population of Europe—were under the rule or the direct influence of Nazi anti-Semitism.

So anguish was added to anguish, until in September 1939 Europe was once more plunged into war; into a war which was ultimately to engulf entirely the great reservoirs of Jewish population in eastern Europe, to overwhelm even the classical lands of Jewish emancipation in the rest of the Continent, to throw its shadow athwart the new Palestine, to see the revival of the Ghetto and the Jewish badge over vast areas, to result in massacres on a scale and of a ferocity which former history could not parallel, and in deportations which made the great Expulsions of the Middle Ages pale into insignificance. Never, since the dawn of their history, had the menace to the Jewish people been greater. Never could there have been more comfort in the prophetic teaching, which is the essential teaching of Judaism— that, however dark the future may seem and however long tribulation may endure, in the end unrighteousness cannot prevail.[1]

[1] End of the second edition, 1943.

V

On September 1st 1939 the German forces invaded Poland, and the second World War in a generation began. Within a few weeks, the country had been overrun, save for the zone occupied by the Russians, in which (as shortly after in the Baltic States of Lithuania, Latvia, and Estonia) the Soviet order was introduced. The German-occupied area contained upwards of 2,000,000 Jews—in the main poverty-stricken but imbued with unbounded vitality and deep loyalty to Jewish tradition and values. They were exposed forthwith to a systematic campaign of oppression. It was simple in a country under martial law to impose crushing fines, to carry out wholesale executions, to institute compulsory labour service, or to demand a supply of Jewish girls for the military brothels. But all this was incidental. There was hardly a town or village throughout the country in which Jews were not butchered at this period by the German soldiery, sometimes in fantastic numbers. The food ration allotted to Jews later on was barely sufficient to maintain life, being only one-half of what was allowed to Polish Christians, and a quarter of that enjoyed by Teutons. Shortly after the conquest of the country, the wearing of a Badge of Shame to distinguish Jew from non-Jew was instituted (November 1939), as prescribed in the Middle Ages but never enforced in Europe since the period of the French Revolution. In the following year, the Ghetto, too, was reintroduced as a formal institution legally enforced. The largest, holding even at the outset upwards of 350,000 souls, was that of Warsaw, inaugurated in the autumn of 1940. This was surrounded by an eight-foot wall of concrete with several massive gates —a gloomy city within the city: there was a similar walled enclosure at Lodz, while in a dozen other cities there were segregated areas, cut off by electrically charged wire fences. In the Middle Ages, egress from the Jewish quarter was allowed except at night; now, it was entirely forbidden without special permission, under pain of death for a second offence. The institution was, however, only a temporary expedient.

In order to make room for Teutons brought back from the Baltic States, Jews had been forced to give up their houses in certain places, and sometimes excluded from them entirely, thus leaving the 'Aryan' population uncontaminated. By degrees, this principle was extended, until expulsions had been effected from most of the cities with which Polish Jewish history had hitherto been most closely associated—

155. A Berlin Synagogue on Fire

156. Refugees from Germany boarding a Boat to England, December 1938

157. Jews being deported from Holland

158. In the Warsaw Ghetto

159. Open Grave in the Bergen-Belsen Concentration Camp

THIS IS THE SITE OF
THE INFAMOUS BELSEN CONCENTRATION CAMP
Liberated by the British on 15 April 1945.

10,000 UNBURIED DEAD WERE FOUND HERE,
ANOTHER 13,000 HAVE SINCE DIED,
ALL OF THEM VICTIMS OF THE
GERMAN NEW ORDER IN EUROPE,
AND AN EXAMPLE OF NAZI KULTUR.

160.   PLAQUE SET UP IN MEMORY OF SOME OF THE VICTIMS

from Lodz, the great textile centre, where the Jews had formerly numbered nearly 200,000, to Cracow, the ancient capital of the country, one of the oldest surviving settlements in Europe. The only community of first importance allowed for the moment to remain undisturbed was that of Warsaw, where the newly-established Ghetto became unbelievably overcrowded, its population rising to half a million. On the other hand, a Jewish reservation was now established in the region of Lublin to accommodate those who had been uprooted. To this restricted area, Jews began to be transported from all parts. But, in the end, yet darker counsels prevailed.

The astounding German military triumphs in the course of 1940-1941 made the Nazi Government completely indifferent to what was left of neutral opinion. The outrages now became more and more callous, spreading from Poland throughout Europe. In all the occupied countries, the leaders of Anti-Semitic propaganda in recent years were seen, after the German invasion, in their true colours, as traitors who did their utmost to weaken the armies in the field and to undermine public confidence. They then became omnipotent in the countries which they had betrayed. Forthwith, nineteenth century Emancipation was reversed, the Nuremberg Laws or their equivalents were introduced, collective fines were imposed, Jewish businesses and fortunes were sequestered, racial teaching was introduced into the schools, and the efficacy of the work of Anti-Semitism was taken as an index of loyalty to the New Order in Europe. The ground was thus prepared for the reign of terror, under immediate Nazi direction. Much the same pattern was followed everywhere. The sporadic violence at the time of the invasion was succeeded by a period of restrained oppression, during which, though restrictive legislation was put into force, there seemed some prospect of the re-establishment of an ordered existence. Then, by degrees sufficiently gradual to prevent an explosion of public opinion, the thumbscrew was tightened. The wearing of the Jewish Badge of Shame, now generally in the form of an armlet or a patch of the traditional yellow hue bearing the Shield of David and the word 'Jew', became universal throughout occupied Europe, being extended to Germany and Bohemia (with Moravia) in September 1941, and even into France and other western lands in the summer of the following year. (Later, this mark of degradation was applied to other 'inferior' races.) As in eastern Europe, Jews were assigned special ration cards, implying an allowance far below subsistence level. Deadlier still, they were deported from certain cities or areas, raids were made on their homes and institutions, and concentration camps were established, so that life became a perpetual nightmare. Generally, the native Jews were lulled into a false security while their fate was prepared, the refugees from Germany being the earliest victims, to be followed by other foreigners. At the beginning, the Jewish communal organisations were left in being as instruments for the nefarious work; when their utility had ended, they, too, were 'liquidated'. Monuments of Hebrew culture were, of course, not spared. Synagogues, however ancient, were often destroyed, their ritual appurtenances looted, and their libraries sent to swell the great Anti-Semitic collections now established in Germany. The destruction of its cultural patrimony was not the least negligible aspect of the tragedy of European Jewry.

The idea of concentrating the Jews in a special reservation in eastern Europe had meanwhile grown upon the German Government, who now regarded it as a zone whither those of all countries could be despatched, regardless of their antecedents or of their fate. In October 1941 the deportations from Germany began, the example being imitated elsewhere shortly afterwards: in the following March, orders were issued for the rate to be forced up to the level of 100,000 monthly. Thus, the 'Jewish Problem' would be solved within a very short time, once for all. Wherever the German authority prevailed, Jews were ruthlessly rounded up for despatch, being allowed to take with them at the most nothing but a handful of personal necessities. From every direction, trains of sealed cattle-trucks, densely packed with miserable humanity, rumbled over the railroads towards eastern Europe, in the stifling heat of summer or the deadly frosts of winter. In an appallingly high number of cases, to be sent on the journey was itself equivalent to a death-warrant. Yet those who died thus were more fortunate than those who survived to meet the terrible fate that awaited them at the end.

For before long, the conception of a Jewish reservation was abandoned in favour of a new idea, of indescribable cruelty. In the course of 1942, reports began to penetrate to the outside world of the horrors of the death-camps at Majdanek, Belzec, Treblinka, Oswiecim (Auschwitz), and elsewhere, in which Jewish deportees, first from Poland and then from all over Europe, were being exterminated by the thousand and score of thousand—by shooting, by injections, and above all by poison gas. It is hardly possible for the human mind to grasp the scale or the heartless deliberation of the atrocities which

took place, in the twentieth century, at the hands of ostensibly civilised human beings; nor can any written account, however conservatively phrased, appear even remotely plausible. It was computed that
at Oswiecim and the adjacent camp of Brzezinka (Birkenau) alone,
more than 1,750,000 Jews from various countries were murdered in
the two years ending in April 1944, and at Majdanek nearly
1,500,000. 31,000, including 13,000 brought from Hungary, were
shot in the Kamienitcz-Podolski region. Non-Jewish Poles, too, were
annihilated in vast numbers, but on nothing like this incredible scale.
It sometimes happened that the travelling gas-wagons, by which
thousands of persons were put to death every week, broke down from
overwork. In some places, according to the reports which subsequently circulated, pious Jews of the old school perplexed their
butchers by dancing to meet their death, in token of their perfect
submission to the Divine will. When the Nazis were driven out of
Poland, the scene of horror was transferred to the concentration
camps on German soil, especially Dachau, Bergen-Belsen, and Buch-
enwald, which attained ghastly notoriety throughout the civilised
world. Here, appalling numbers of Jews and non-Jews alike were
herded together in circumstances that made death by hunger or in
the gas-chamber a happy release. Large numbers, moreover, both
men and women, were used as specimens for carrying out ruthless
medical experiments; others were brutally sterilised. Of the hundreds
of thousands of human beings who perished in these camps in the early
months of 1945, a disproportionate number were Jews.

At Terezin (Theresienstadt), a medieval fortress-town in central
Bohemia, a vast Ghetto (mainly for the aged) was established, holding
at its peak as many as 65,000 individuals. Here, notwithstanding the
ravages of disease, conditions were somewhat less agonising than
elsewhere, though the area was emptied from time to time to make
room for new arrivals, the surplus being sent eastwards—never to
return. The young men, who could be used for slave labour, and the
women designated as prostitutes, were the most unfortunate of all,
for prolonged martyrdom preceded their butchery: only a minority
survived.

In Germany itself, before long, barely a single known Jew was left
alive; all those who were traceable had been deported, save for a
handful of the aged, and survivors in the concentration camps. This
was the ideal which the Nazis endeavoured to attain in all of occupied
Europe. On May 15th 1942, a law was passed by the Slovak 'parlia-

ment' providing for the expatriation of all Jews; and by December 75,000 of them had been conveyed to Poland to meet their fate. On the night of July 12th of the same year, a great round-up began in France, 28,000 men, women and children from Paris alone being herded in concentration camps near the capital in readiness for deportation. The handful of highly-assimilated Jews of Norway, who could not by any stretch of the imagination be considered a 'problem' or even an irritant, were attacked by the traitor Vidkun Quisling, with an energy which would have been ludicrous had its consequences not been so tragic; for all remaining in the country were arrested and deported—many for work in the Silesian coal-mines—their property, of course, being confiscated.

The centuries-long tranquillity of the Jews in Holland and the general sympathy of the Dutch population proved no safeguard: for all Jews who could be traced were ultimately rounded up to meet their fate, a handful only surviving. In no western land were their sufferings less justifiable, or so intense. In Amsterdam, the Portuguese synagogue only was left standing, but despite their different historic background its members suffered with their co-religionists. From Belgium, liberated somewhat earlier, at least 30,000 Jews out of 80,000 were deported: no organised Jewish life was left in Antwerp, formerly the largest community in the country, and only a skeleton organisation in Brussels. Hungary, so long as it remained an independent associated power, retained a modicum of humanity. But with the German occupation in March 1944 wholesale deportations began throughout the country, involving within a few months almost the entire population outside the capital. When, after an attempt to conclude a separate peace, the puppet Arrow Cross Government was set up in October 1944, that country, too, was drawn into the vortex; a pogrom on a major scale was staged in Budapest, and the deportees in the next two months numbered scores of thousands. (Fortunately, deliverance arrived before disaster in the capital became comprehensive.) After Roumania was converted into a totalitarian state and allied herself with Germany (June 1940), a determined onslaught was made on her Jews. Not only were restrictive laws put into force, on the Nuremberg model, but there was in addition an outburst of unbridled physical violence of fantastic horror. Even this was outdone when the Roumanian forces occupied Bessarabia and Bukovina; here, something like one-third of the entire population was exterminated. All told, in the autumn of 1941, it is believed that the Roumanians were responsible for the massacre of 100,000 Russian and native Jews: subsequently, some 130,000 were deported, under the conditions that had become commonplace, to the newly-annexed territories beyond the River Dniester. A single officer was alleged to have brought about the death of 50,000 individuals.

It was Jews of a different type and with a different background who were encountered by the Nazi forces when they broke through to the Mediterranean, but this did not affect their fate: indeed, they were among the worst sufferers. The Jugoslav Jews were almost exterminated, in circumstances of exceptional barbarity, the Croatian Fascists (Ustachi) vying with the Moslems of Bosnia in their bloodlust, and a reward being given for every fugitive handed over to the authorities. There was barely a single survivor of the very ancient Jewish community of the island of Crete, and only a handful from that of Rhodes. The same was the case in Salonica, once the greatest Jewish centre of the Mediterranean world, almost all of whose members were deported to an appalling fate. Even Bulgaria, with its relatively lengthy philo-Semitic tradition, was compelled to follow the Nazi lead, though not with quite the same intensity.

In Italy—still to some extent a free ally—it was impossible for the essentially kindly population to imitate Nazi bestialities, however painfully they adopted the Anti-Semitic code. Hence, even though the restrictive legislation became more and more harsh, it was an oasis of relative humanity in a hate-filled world. But, after the abortive attempt to overthrow Fascism in July 1943, Italy from Rome northwards became in effect a German-occupied country, and repression began in full force as everywhere else in Europe. The only areas (other than Russia) which were not overwhelmed by the disaster were indomitable England; the neutral havens of Switzerland, Sweden, European Turkey, and Portugal; and Finland, which remained democratic even though a German satellite.

The contagion spread to northern Africa. Into Morocco and the neighbouring regions, the Vichy Government introduced the same discriminatory code as in France, though economic and social conditions were so completely different; and Jews were sent by the thousand to forced labour in equatorial heat on the railways, or shut up in concentration camps which enjoyed an unenviable notoriety. When a German expeditionary force crossed the Mediterranean to assist the broken and unenthusiastic Italians, even greater bitterness was introduced; and there was bloodshed in many places, from

Tripoli westwards, before the Wehrmacht was driven out. Even in the Far East, in Rangoon, Singapore and Shanghai, the Japanese clumsily imitated the Anti-Semitic policy of the Herrenvolk, disregarding the fact that it implied the subordination of Asiatics to the supreme Nordic race. This was, however, a mere detail in comparison with the awful suffering in Europe. On 17th December 1942, the British House of Commons rose to its feet in homage to Jewish suffering. It was an unprecedented but barren gesture.

Only in one land was popular opposition in any way effective. When in the spring of 1940 Denmark was occupied, the people resolutely refused to enforce any discriminatory regulations; and it is said that the king threatened to wear the Badge of Shame himself if it were imposed on his Jewish subjects. Three years later, when the Germans took over the administration of the country, an anti-Jewish campaign was immediately opened. The Danish patriots were already prepared; and almost the whole of the inconsiderable community were ferried in all manner of flimsy craft over to Sweden, where they were hospitably received. For once, the Nazi beast had the prey snatched from his jaws. No country, indeed, lacked courageous citizens who shewed active sympathy—only thus was a Jewish remnant able to survive clandestinely in some of the occupied areas. Occasionally, there were demonstrations against the deportations; and to flaunt the Jewish Badge was a recognised patriotic gesture in France, Belgium, and Holland. In the last-named country, moreover, a general strike took place in February 1941 in an attempt, temporarily successful, to prevent the mass deportations. Even in Germany, collusion or craft made it possible for a handful to survive in some places. There were some who risked their own lives to help the hunted to escape, or took charge of the children when the parents were deported to an unknown fate. Frequently, the lead was taken by priests and nuns, following the example set by the Vatican itself. Yet even in such circumstances some persons were unable to suppress their proselytising zeal, or considered it their duty to bring up their charges in the religion with which they were themselves familiar. The losses to the Jewish people by infant conversion in this period, throughout Europe, were comparable only to those at the time of the Forced Conversions of the fifteenth century in the Iberian Peninsula.

In June 1941 Germany had attacked Russia. The initial arena of struggle included most of the former Pale of Settlement, where Jews were thickly established, comprising great aggregations such as those of Odessa and Kiev. All told, this area had contained some two-thirds of the 3,000,000 Jews of the Soviet Republics, in addition to something like 1,500,000 in the part of Poland occupied by the Russians two years earlier and in the Baltic States. The tenacity of the Russian resistance, the Nazis' fanatical hatred of the Bolshevik system, and the activities of the partisan forces, gave the excuse for terrific devastation in these areas, even when the line of battle was hundreds of miles away. As far as the Jews were concerned, this was intensified by the action of the Ukrainian levies who joined the Germans and now gave vent to their traditional hatreds. The onslaught developed into a campaign of extermination. A number of Jews were transferred eastwards in time, and some 250,000 former Polish subjects had found refuge in the interior of the country. Of the rest, only a minority survived, cowering in the ruins or fighting in the partisan ranks. Among the episodes of horror were the shooting of 60,000 Jews in an island in the Dvina near Riga, of 20,000 at Lutsk, 32,000 at Sarny, and 60,000 at Kiev and Dniepropetrovsk. In Odessa, as a reprisal, the Roumanians mowed down 25,000 Jews in a barrack building by machine gun fire. Simon Dubnow, the octogenarian historian of Jewish martyrdom, was among a group who met a brutal fate at Riga immediately after the German capture of the city.

Meanwhile, the tragedy of Polish Jewry was moving to its climax. Conditions in the congested Warsaw Ghetto, the only centre of real importance now surviving in the country, became worse and worse with every week that passed. A certain economic cohesion continued as the result of tailoring contracts for the German military command; but over one-half of the population had no visible means of sustenance whatsoever, depending for their existence on the charity of their poverty-stricken fellows. Typhus stalked at the heels of famine; and it was computed that the death-rate among the Jews was sixteen times higher than among their compatriots. Yet still, Hebraic values were able to reassert themselves. Cultural life flourished as before. An educational system was set up. A theatre continued to function. What was most remarkable, secret Zionist activities continued; and under the eyes of the German authorities, Jews made collections for work in Palestine, and young men and women prepared themselves as best they could in the hope of emigration.

This spirit of resilience was itself provocative. On July 22nd 1942, orders were issued for the deportation towards the death-camps of all the Warsaw Jews, without distinction of age or sex, save for certain potentially useful categories who were given a reprieve. They were to be allowed to take with them fifteen kilograms only of personal effects: resistance was punishable by death. The round-up began forthwith, and continued at the rate of some 4,500 daily. By September, the official number of those deported was some 250,000, few of whom now probably survived; and in the following October, only 40,000 ration cards were issued for distribution in the Ghetto. In April, when orders were given for a large contingent of the survivors to report, they refused to obey. There followed one of the most tragic, most amazing episodes of the entire war. On the night of April 18th–19th (it happened to be Passover Eve) German police and S.S. detachments attacked the Ghetto with the support of artillery. The surviving population, inspired by the underground Jewish fighting organisation, fought desperately in its defence with weapons smuggled in from outside. It was no haphazard episode. There was a co-ordinated command, and an organised medical service; contact was maintained with the Polish underground movement; women and girls operated machine-guns, and suicide squads broke through the German lines or blew up tanks with improvised grenades. More than once in the early stages the German troops were driven back, but fire was ultimately used to achieve what rifles and artillery could not. When the central region was at last overwhelmed, resistance continued in the outlying streets; when this was at last suppressed, a few stalwarts held out in the cellars and sewers. It was only at the end of May that the last embers of revolt were stamped out. The survivors— some 20,000—were rounded up and sent to the death camps, Warsaw being now *judenrein*. The three thousand years of Jewish history know of no episode more heroic.

With the need for a place of refuge more acute than ever before, and no alternative haven possible, Palestine assumed a greater importance than ever in the eyes of oppressed Jewry, given moral strength to face the future only by the hope of Zion. Yet the British Government adhered pedantically even now to the policy of the White Paper of 1939. Those who had escaped from the hell of central Europe, and made their way over the mountains and across the deserts, found themselves refused permission to enter the land of their hopes. Unscrupulous ship-owners and captains, sailing under the improbable flags of Central or South American republics, preyed upon the misery of the fugitives, promising to convey them to the Holy Land if they were extravagantly reimbursed. Sometimes a profit of £10,000 or £20,000 was made from a single voyage of a leaking ship, bought at auction for a few pounds. In such circumstances, disaster became a commonplace. A case which became notorious was that of the S.S. *Struma*, which lay off Constantinople for three months with nearly 800 Roumanian refugees crammed aboard—the Roumanian Government callously alleging that they had lost all rights by leaving illegally, the British refusing to admit them to Palestine, the Turks not allowing them to land. On February 23rd 1942, the ramshackle vessel put to sea with its cargo of human misery. On the following night it sank, with only a single survivor. Another disaster of the sort, in Haifa harbour, involved over 250 out of 1,900 'illegal' immigrants who had been transferred to the S.S. *Patria* to be deported.

Yet Palestinian Jewry at this time proved its value to England's effort. Not only were its factories and its technicians kept working at full speed, its scientists' ingenuity brilliantly employed, its superb medical service succouring the Allied sick and wounded, but the blood and courage of its young men were also lavished in profusion. When, in July 1941, it was necessary to occupy Syria to prevent it from being used as a German base, the Jews seasoned in the fighting under similar conditions against the Arabs in Galilee were irreplaceable as scouts, pioneers and irregulars, and served without stint, some even being released from internment for the purpose.

From the beginning, the Zionist representatives had clamoured to be allowed to recruit a Jewish army, so that the flag of Judah could be unfurled in the field against Israel's enemies. This elementary concession was not granted for fear of arousing Arab resentment. Nevertheless, Jews fought in exceptionally great numbers in the Allied ranks. It was the only war in modern history in which Jews were to be found only on one side, the total number of those under arms rising ultimately to well over 1,000,000. Moreover, in occupied Europe, the patriotic movements which continued resistance to the Germans in the dark years from 1940 onwards were composed to a disproportionate extent of Jews, both in the partisan groups and in the ranks of the 'free' forces overseas. (In Poland and France at least, there were specific Jewish divisions of the underground movement and the partisans.) Meanwhile, a Palestinian contingent—in fact overwhelmingly Jewish in composition—was raised in the Holy Land; at first only for para-military duties, though this was not the case afterwards. Jewish assault troops as well as Jewish transport and pioneers did good work in the British campaigns in Abyssinia, northern Africa, Greece and Italy, and redemption was brought to many ancient communities by these muscular kinsmen in khaki, wearing the Shield of David on their shoulders and obeying Hebrew words of command. It was, nevertheless, only towards the end of the war in Europe that the formation of a Jewish Brigade group was at last authorised, just in time for it to participate in the blows which brought on the final German debacle in northern Italy.

From the winter of 1942-1943, the tide of battle began to recede along the Eastern Front. During the course of the next two years, the Russians reoccupied the zone of former dense Jewish settlement, with the centres which had contributed so greatly to Jewish cultural life during the past century. Among the inhabitants who greeted the entering columns there were hardly any Jews. A few survived, lurking in the cellars, concealed by their neighbours, or fighting with the irregulars; a few more returned from the surrounding country-side when the German menace had definitely passed. But they were a mere handful all told. The cities where as many as one-tenth of the former Jewish population had survived were in a minority. Indeed, as the Germans retreated before the victorious armies, they exterminated the remaining Jews wherever they could, rather than allow them to be liberated. The same was the case elsewhere—in the Balkans and in central Europe, and in the zones liberated by the Anglo-American forces. Only in some of the occupied countries had the Allied advance been sufficiently rapid to save a relatively considerable nucleus. One of Adolf Hitler's promises, if only one, had been punctually kept before his death.

When the roar of the cannon had ceased, in the spring of 1945, it was possible for stricken Jewry to assess the extent of its disaster. The forebodings of the past five years were outdone by the reality. Of Poland's former 3,350,000 Jews, it was estimated that fewer than 55,000 were left in the country; another quarter of a million had been able to find refuge in Russia; the rest (save for a few thousands scattered through the world) were dead. Czechoslovakia had before the war some 360,000 Jews; only 40,000 were left. Of Roumania's million, there were now no more than 320,000; and Roumania had fared relatively well, owing to the speed of the Russian advance. Jugoslavia's 75,000 were reduced by almost nine-tenths; the 75,000 formerly in Greece in about the same ratio; Holland's 150,000 by at least four-fifths. Happy were lands such as France, where as many as one-half, or Hungary, where one-quarter of the Jewish population was left. In the whole of Bohemia and Moravia, only two Rabbis remained. Many ancient Jewish centres were obliterated. At Frankfort, only 160 Jews could now be found among the ruins. Of the 56,000 Jews of Salonica, once a preponderantly Jewish city, barely 2,000 could be mustered. The throbbing Jewish life of Vilna, with 54,000 souls in 1931, was represented on its liberation by only 600 survivors. If in due course others ventured out from their hiding-places, it was not in numbers such as to qualify the general picture. Since 1939, more than 6,000,000 Jews had perished out of the 9,000,000 who once lived in the lands through which the Nazi fury had swept—more than one-third of the entire Jewish population of the world, and half of that of Europe.

It was incomparably the greatest disaster in Jewish life; the greatest disaster, perhaps, in the life of any people since the dawn of history. The great catastrophes of the Dark Ages had embraced one or two countries only at a time; this raged simultaneously from the Arctic Ocean to the southern shores of the Mediterranean, from the Atlantic to the Volga. Nearly one-half of the world's Jews were simultaneously affected; at least twenty times as many persons had perished as in any other comparable period in their people's history. It is difficult for the mind to grasp, or pen to convey, the magnitude of the catastrophe.

Thus in 1945 Jewry prepared to face the future. It was a future utterly unlike the past. The total Jewish population of the world had tragically diminished during the last five years. Of those left, a high proportion were beggared and hopeless. The Anti-Semitism aroused by ceaseless and extravagant propaganda during this generation was still malevolently alive, using the demoralisation for which it was responsible as one of its justifications. A great majority of the survivors were now living under the aegis of the Soviet system, which held no promise for the future of Judaism. In Europe, only one Jewish community (other than the handfuls in Sweden and Switzerland) still held some potentialities for the immediate future—that of England. Excepting here, there was little left but penury and bitter memories. The European phase, which had prevailed in Jewish history for the past thousand years, had come to a violent end. The future lay preponderantly with the newest and the oldest havens of Jewish life—with the five million Jews of America, and the half-million Jews of Palestine. The Providence that guides the process of history had ensured that the Jewish future was safe.[1]

[1] End of the third (first illustrated) edition 1948.

Chapter XXXII

RESURRECTION

———————— • ————————

I

The scale and range of the disaster that overtook the Jewish people in this hideous decade left only one solution to its agonising problem: of this fact, those who remained were now almost unanimously convinced. If such things could happen in the classical centres of emancipation, it was clear that henceforth no land could be considered wholly safe; moreover, it was tragically obvious that any future resurgence of Nazism anywhere would begin where Adolf Hitler left off—not with anti-Jewish legislation, but with the gas-chamber. Only in an independent Jewish state could there be the assurance of security in this sense. There was a grim reminder of this, long after the war had ended, in the thousands of fear-haunted survivors from the death chambers, their prison-camp numbers indelibly tattooed on their wrists and ghastly memories searing their souls, who were scattered throughout Central Europe in barrack-like centres for 'Displaced Persons' or D.P.s—an abbreviation which in this period was to assume an overwhelming insistence in Jewish life. Morally incapable of return to the ruined homes where their kindred had been slaughtered, even if they were not faced with the hostility of their neighbours; physically unable to enter countries of greater opportunity because of stringent immigration laws; they could see no conceivable future except in Palestine; and the Palestinian *Yishuv*[1] was able and eager to succour them.

But, even now, the administration kept the gates of the country stubbornly closed to all but a mere trickle. The Labour party, which came into power in England immediately after the capitulation of Germany, had expressed in the most categorical fashion its sympathy with the policy of establishing an independent Jewish state in Palestine, thus raising Zionist hopes everywhere to a very high pitch.

[1] The term now applied generally to the Jewish settlement in Palestine: see page 429.

But routine proved tougher than promises, and power-politics stronger than idealism. The previous Palestine Policy was in fact continued, with an added insensibility which in the circumstances (for the Arabs in the country had done little in the years of danger to aid the British war-effort, and those elsewhere much to impede it) seemed ungrateful as well as callous. The great armies, still stationed in the country as an aftermath of the war, were now employed with the assistance of ludicrously strong naval forces in the despicable task of preventing the arrival of the 'illegal' immigrants, who now began to be smuggled through from Europe in increasing numbers. This policy, however, defeated its own object, for it made the establishment of a wholly autonomous Jewish area seem absolutely necessary, even in the eyes of many who were not Zionists in the full sense —not as a political or philosophical gesture, but for the fundamental purpose of saving life and maintaining hope.

II

Palestinian Jewry for its part could not admit that any earthly power could overrule their right and duty to give refuge in the land— their special relation to which, constantly reiterated in the Bible, had been recognised by the concert of nations—to their broken kinsmen who had survived miraculously from the crematoria. That horrible climax to the traditional quietism had drastically affected the Jewish mentality, and now led to an unprecedented revulsion of feeling. Armed clashes between the British forces and the Jewish population, now in great part trained for battle, became more and more frequent. Some of the latter, in their wrought-up state, began to find difficulty in differentiating between the Germans who had killed the Jews and the British who prevented them from being saved. Extremist groups —the National Military Organisation (*Irgun Zevai Leumi*) and the more radical Fighters for the Freedom of Israel (*Lohamei Heruth Israel*, sometimes known after their founder as the Stern Group) were strengthened by these happenings and embarked on a systematic terrorist campaign (not restricted to Palestine) reminiscent of the Sinn Feiners in Ireland twenty years before, or of their own ancestors, the *sicarii*, in Judaea in Roman times. The official leaders of Palestinian Jewry dissociated themselves from these outrages, some of which, however much they were in the classical revolutionary tradition, clouded the high idealism that had hitherto marked the national revival. But it was a moral impossibility for them to demonstrate their sincerity (as was demanded of them) by condoning passively the brutal policy of exclusion which was ultimately responsible for this deplorable state of affairs. Accordingly, in July 1946, thousands of persons throughout the country (including the leaders of the Jewish Agency) were arrested—by a foolish coincidence, on the Sabbath—and interned. The partnership which was once so close and had promised so well had degenerated into a state of overt hostility.

Ernest Bevin, the inexperienced Foreign Secretary in the Labour government, was meanwhile pursuing a blundering policy, which seemed consistent only in its determination to thwart, at the risk of any contradictions, the realisation even of moderate Zionist hopes. Shortly after the conclusion of the war, the President of the United States had asked the British Government to alleviate Jewish suffering among the 'D.P.s' on the continent of Europe by the issue of 100,000 immigration certificates to Palestine forthwith. Rather than comply, Bevin suggested the appointment of a joint Anglo-American commission of enquiry to investigate the whole question anew (November 1945). Although a majority of its members did not favour Zionist claims to the full, this body recommended the removal of the restrictions on land-purchase in Palestine imposed by the unfortunate White Paper of 1939 (still in force, notwithstanding its condemnation at the League of Nations) and the immediate admission of the 100,000 Jewish immigrants, as President Truman had proposed. The outright acceptance of the recommendations, as was naturally to be anticipated, would have ended the tension; instead, the British government made acquiescence conditional on a series of impossible stipulations—including the complete disarming of Palestinian Jewry, which would have left it powerless in the face of the dangers which might become imminent at any moment, and subject it irrevocably to Arab mercies should the Mandatory Power withdraw. Under the stress of the disappointment, the Palestinian disorders became worse. So did the policy of repression. Concentration camps, unhappily reminiscent of those in Europe from which they had escaped, were set up in Cyprus for housing would-be immigrants whom the might of the glorious British navy had intercepted at sea; and on one occasion the world's conscience was even more profoundly shocked, when those aboard one intercepted vessel, the *Exodus*, were actually shipped back to blood-soaked Germany.

In the succeeding months, the British cabinet advanced more than one ill-digested plan for a settlement of the problem which had begun to command universal attention and to attract almost universal obloquy or derision. In accordance with what was now become an obsession at Whitehall, all retained as a fundamental condition the drastic restriction of immigration. Hence, even if they had been acceptable to the Arabs (in fact stubbornly and irreconcilably opposed to any scheme which recognised the special status of Jews in Palestine) they could in no circumstances have been agreed to by any responsible Jewish leader. At length, Ernest Bevin, who had staked his reputation (as he stated) on finding a solution to the Palestine problem and was plainly humiliated by his failure, announced the British Government's intention of submitting the issue to the United Nations, it being naturally understood that the decision would be binding. Yet another commission of investigation was appointed, this time international. Once more impartial enquiry proved on the whole favourable to the basic Zionist claims; for (like the Royal Commission of 1937), this body recommended by a majority, not indeed the constitution of Palestine into a Jewish state, but the constitution of a Jewish state in the country, which was to be divided into two autonomous areas, one Jewish and one Arab; there was to be a two-year transitional period, during which the British government was to remain in control and in the course of which 150,000 Jews were to be admitted. The area assigned to the Jewish state, under this scheme, was to include the Valley of Jezreel, Eastern Galilee, most of the coastal plain (including Haifa as well as Tel-Aviv) and the desolate (but in the view of Jewish agricultural experts recoverable) district in the south of the country, the Negev, where several new colonies had been established in recent years and which was now assuming great importance in Jewish eyes. Jerusalem on the other hand, notwithstanding its long-standing Jewish majority, was to continue to be administered by an international agency; and the rest of the country, including Western Galilee and the whole of the central area, was, like Transjordan, to be Arab. (This was the original project; the expanse was to be greatly increased as a result of the victorious war which was to be waged, the New City of Jerusalem, above all, being retained in the Jewish region.)

Such a solution was diametrically opposed to the tendency of the administration during the past years and to England's fancied political interests in the Middle East; for these were now based on close collaboration with the League of Arab countries, recently formed under her auspices and stubbornly opposed—though it was logically no concern of theirs—to a Jewish state. It seemed nevertheless to be out of pique as much as policy that His Majesty's Government now refused to have anything to do with the implementation of any plan which did not command (as at this stage no plan could conceivably do) the agreement of both Jews and Arabs. Rather than this, it proposed to dissociate itself from the problem which it persisted in regarding as insoluble and withdraw from Palestine, petulantly excluding from the country meanwhile the commission appointed for the transitional period by the United Nations.

Notwithstanding this extraordinary and obstructive attitude, the General Assembly of the United Nations endorsed the partition scheme, with certain unimportant modifications, by more than the two-thirds majority which was requisite (November 29th 1947). The Arab States menaced direct action; and murderous attacks took place on defenceless Jews in many parts of the Moslem world. Palestine began to lapse into a state of civil war, the British forces very often actually failing to intervene to stop attacks on Jewish colonies and convoys, though they permitted the British-officered Arab Legion recruited in Transjordan to take a bloody hand. The *Yishuv* on its side organised its defence, frequently even passing over to the counter-offensive. Meanwhile, wholly confident (and, as events were to show, rightly confident) in its new-found strength, it gladly prepared to shoulder the greater task that was now seen to be imminent. Sullenly, the British prepared for withdrawal. By May 15th, as they announced, the Mandate which had been received twenty-eight years before from the now defunct League of Nations would be formally relinquished.

That day was a Sabbath. On the previous afternoon, therefore, a proclamation was read publicly in Tel Aviv by the outstanding personality of the *Yishuv*, David Ben-Gurion, Chairman of the Executive of the Jewish Agency, Prime Minister designate, and architect of the impending victory, that at midnight a sovereign Jewish state (later given the name ISRAEL) would come into existence in those parts of the country assigned to the Jews by the decision of the United Nations. In due course, Chaim Weizmann was to be elected its first President.

It was obvious that a period of stress and trial lay ahead. The armies of five Arab states were already poised menacingly on the borders. A nation unused to arms for nearly twenty centuries was to be submitted forthwith to the ordeal of battle. But the *Yishuv* had no doubts or hesitations. The age-old yearnings of a people had resulted, by devious and unexpected ways, in an achievement without parallel in human history. The promise of the prophets had been fulfilled. The Jewish State had been reborn.[1]

III

Hostilities had already begun between the Arab armies and the Jewish forces. The events that followed were among the most remarkable of Jewish history. The spirit of the Maccabees lived again, after more than two thousand years and under conditions still more difficult.

This epic sequel was dominated and inspired by the vibrant personality of David Ben-Gurion, who had played a prominent part in the life of the *Yishuv* ever since his arrival from Russia forty years earlier, and who was now at the head of the Provisional Government. The kernel of the Jewish forces was constituted by the former *Haganah* (literally, 'defence'). This body, organised long since for the protection of the Jewish colonies against Arab attacks, had been declared illegal by the British authorities in recent years, but notwithstanding this had been reorganised and expanded in secret. Its select troops, known as the *Palmach* (abbreviation of *Pelugoth Machaz*, or Assault Squadrons) distinguished themselves particularly in combat, while the extremist groups continued to fight, under their own leaders, with a ferocity which sometimes proved an embarrassment. The Arabs seemed to have everything on their side—numbers, equipment, position, and training. The Jews had little beyond their spirit of sacrifice, confidence in their leadership, and the realisation that there was no alternative to victory other than annihilation.

Already in April, the vaunted Arab 'Army of Liberation', composed of Palestinian recruits reinforced by 'volunteers' from the neighbouring countries, had attempted to cut off the colonies in Galilee from the rest of Jewish Palestine, but were routed near Mishmar haEmek by vastly inferior numbers of the Haganah forces. This —perhaps the first victory gained by Jewish forces in the field since the days of Bar Kocheba—proved the prelude to many other local successes. Tiberias fell into Jewish hands on April 18th. A few days later a firm hold was established on the great sea-port of Haifa, not-

[1] End of the fourth (second illustrated) edition, 1953.

withstanding its large Arab population. On May 10th, Safed, the ancient city of the Cabbalists, was conquered, the terror-stricken defenders imagining that they were being attacked by a mighty army. Two days later, Jaffa was surrendered to the forces operating from Tel-Aviv, so that the Jewish metropolis was liberated from the threat which had so long hung over it. Thus, on the day when the State was proclaimed, the Jewish forces were already in control of almost all of the area which had been assigned to the Jewish State by the United Nations.

However, simultaneously with the British evacuation, the regular armies of the five Arab states, confident in speedy victory over an enemy whom they knew to be ill-equipped and imagined to be without warlike spirit, launched a concerted attack on the new State, which they refused to recognise. To the south, the Egyptians occupied Gaza and advanced to within less than twenty-five miles of Tel-Aviv. In the centre of the country, the Arab Legion, composed of Transjordanians but with British officers, besieged and bombarded the modern Jewish quarters of Jerusalem and severed communications between this area and Tel-Aviv. Simultaneously, the enemy attempted to cut off the provisional capital from the north of the country, where the Iraqui forces claimed to have entered the coastal town of Nataniah. In Galilee, the Syrians and Lebanese threatened to overwhelm the Jewish colonies by sheer weight of numbers. Almost everywhere, however, the Jewish forces were able to hold their positions, and on most fronts to improve them. In the north, a brilliant counter-offensive even drove the enemy back beyond the historic frontiers of Palestine. It was by now abundantly clear that the new State could not be overwhelmed as easily as its enemies had hoped, and some even of its friends had feared.

The representatives of the United Nations, in the hope of establishing peace, negotiated a series of temporary truces from the month of June onwards. These did not however prove permanent, and each time hostilities were renewed the Jewish forces gained new victories. A navy and air-force had by now been organised and sent into action; enemy capitals were bombarded from the air; the flag-ship of the Egyptian fleet was sunk; the Arab cities of Lydda, Ramleh and Beer-Sheba were captured; Egyptian territory was invaded and, but for menaces from England (an action destined to prove fatal to her own interests) the Nile Delta might well have been occupied by the Israeli forces. In March 1949 a mobile column occupied Elath, on the

Gulf of Akabah, thus ensuring for the Jewish State an outlet to the Indian Ocean, for the first time since the days of the Hebrew monarchy.

Meanwhile however the Jewish quarters of Jerusalem, in the new city outside the walls (for the historic Jewish quarter of the Old City had been occupied and destroyed by the Arabs, after fierce fighting) had been subjected to siege and incessant bombardment. The entire area was now cut off from Tel-Aviv and the coast, and the sparse convoys with provisions and reinforcements could only force their way through at the cost of terrifying losses in dead and wounded. During the summer of 1948 however a new road, audaciously constructed across the mountains of Judah, relieved the enemy pressure on the ancient capital which, although still exposed to attack, was henceforth at least no longer cut off from the rest of Jewish Palestine. There now seemed to be the prospect that the new State would not only be able to maintain itself, but that it would be able to overwhelm its enemies on every front. However, before this could happen, thanks to the efforts of the representatives of the United Nations, a series of armistice agreements with the Arab States (except Iraq, which had no common frontier with Israel) was signed at Rhodes in the first half of 1949: that with Syria, on July 20th, marking the triumphant end of the War of Liberation. These agreements were intended to be followed by permanent peace-treaties, which however in the sequel the Arab governments refused to contemplate. The new State thus formed hence comprised effectively, not only the territories assigned to the Jews by the decision of the United Nations, but also the Jewish suburbs of Jerusalem (in effect, the whole of the new city outside the walls) and considerable areas originally assigned to the Arab State contemplated at the outset.

From the beginning, the Arab governments had proclaimed that any individual who remained in the Jewish-controlled area would be regarded as approving the new political arrangements and would share the lot of the Jewish inhabitants. Hence, on the outbreak of hostilities, a wholesale evacuation of the Arab population had taken place, in the hope of a triumphant and lucrative return. Moreover, the Arab population of other regions was seized with panic and took to flight. After the armistice, it was obviously impossible to welcome back to the Jewish State indiscriminately this potential Fifth Column, so long as the enemy countries refused to negotiate a permanent peace and might reopen hostilities at any time. This had a result of the utmost importance. Instead of being embarrassed by a numerous alien minority, as would have been the case had the Arabs accepted the decision of the United Nations, the Jewish State was composed of an almost homogeneous population. In some cities such as Haifa and Jaffa there were more or less significant Moslem minorities; there were Bedouin tribes living their primitive desert lives in the Negev, in the south of the country; there was a compact group, mainly Christian, in Galilee, especially around Nazareth: there were several thousand Druze, who had fought in the Israel ranks, on Mount Carmell All of these accepted—in the latter case, with enthusiasm—Israel citizenship. But the overwhelming majority of the population of the new state was Jewish.

It was a natural sequel both to the Biblical conceptions and to the tendencies of Jewish life in the Diaspora that the State was organised from the beginning on democratic lines. While hostilities were still raging (January 1949) a legislative assembly had been elected by universal suffrage, called by the ancient Hebrew name *Keneset*: Chaim Weizmann crowned his career by becoming first President and Ben-Gurion was appointed Prime Minister. On May 11th of that year, the State of Israel was admitted to the United Nations, after having been recognised by most of the world's governments, though not by any Arab or Moslem State. In the following year, the capital was transferred from Tel-Aviv to Jerusalem, almost in the shade of the Arab-controlled Old City: clearly, the capital of the Jewish state could not be elsewhere than in the place that had been for three thousand years the centre of Jewish spiritual hopes and strivings.

161. THE PROCLAMATION OF THE STATE OF ISRAEL read by David Ben-Gurion at the first meeting of the Provisional Council in the Tel-Aviv Museum, May 14, 1948

162. Independence Day Parade in Jerusalem, May 15, 1948

163. DR. WEIZMANN TAKING THE OATH AS PRESIDENT OF ISRAEL, January 27, 1949

164. THE MENORAH PRESENTED BY THE BRITISH HOUSES OF PARLIAMENT arriving outside the Knesset building in Jerusalem

Chapter XXXIII

THE STATE OF ISRAEL

———————— • ————————

I

It was the necessity of providing the 'Displaced Persons' with a place of refuge, where they would be able to rebuild their shattered lives, that had made the creation of a Jewish State imperative: and the State therefore had the moral duty of opening its gates to all who wished to enter. On July 5th 1950, the Keneset passed unanimously the Law of Return, whereby any Jew wherever born was given the right to settle in Israel. But, in fact, the immigration had long since begun. Throughout the difficult days of the War of Liberation, large numbers of the survivors of the Nazi death-camps had been enthusiastically welcomed. Within a short while the 'Displaced Persons' camps in Europe had been relieved of their burden of human misery. Later, the Jews of Iraq, whose life had been rendered impossible by a shamefully-defeated government, immigrated almost *en masse*, leaving only a few thousand behind. The ancient arabised communities of the Yemen, seized with a messianic ferment, were transferred to the country by a magnificently-organised air-lift, picturesquely called 'Operation Magic Carpet'. The isolated community of Cochin, in south India, followed this example in great part, as did many of the Jews of the Moslem countries of North Africa and a majority of the community of Bulgaria, devoted to Zionism since its earliest days. From San Nicandro, a village of south Italy, there arrived a group of peasants and artisans who had been led to embrace Judaism as the result of a profound study of the Bible. There were immigrants from every other country of the world, especially those in which the Jewish position was uncertain—above all, at this time, the Moslem countries, but later on even from those of Central Europe, behind the so-called 'Iron Curtain'. In 1958, the population of Israel, which had numbered about 655,000 at the time of the Declaration of Independence ten years before, had risen to nearly 2,000,000, of whom all

2G   (457)

but 200,000 were Jews. It was the largest Jewish community of the world, after that of the United States of America, with its 5,000,000 Jews, and of Soviet Russia, with approximately 2,500,000. The Jewish agglomeration of Tel-Aviv and its environs, now nearing 400,000, outnumbered probably any other in the Old World, being exceeded only by that of New York.

Obviously, the burden assumed by the new State in welcoming this disproportionate immigration, was a crushing one. It was not however acting in its own interest alone, but was shouldering on behalf of Jewry at large the burden of offering a shelter to the victims of persecution: and Jews abroad enjoying peace and liberty found themselves morally obliged to collaborate financially in the noble work of *Kibbutz Goliyot*, the Reassembling of the Diaspora.[1]

There was one unhappy exception. At one period of the epic struggle against the German invader, Russian Jewry had been encouraged to renew its relations with the communities of the western countries. It might have been hoped that the tragic isolation, which had lasted for twenty years, was now ended. But before long isolation was again strictly imposed, accompanied by an attempt to suppress radically what were elsewhere considered the normal manifestations of Jewish life: and in the end there were even signs of antisemitic reaction, in a fuller sense. Conditions were little better in other countries behind the Iron Curtain, in particular Roumania and Hungary, still comprising communities of considerable numerical importance. These once famous centres of Jewish life and intellectual achievement found themselves for the moment unable to participate in the greatest of Jewish adventures and achievements of modern times.

II

The peaceful development of the new State was however made more difficult by the continued intransigeance of its Arab neighbours. Smarting under the disgrace of their overwhelming defeat at the hands of this despised and pacifist people, they obstinately refused to enter into peace negotiations and maintained a state of perpetual tension along the frontiers, sending detachments across the armistice lines to raid the colonies, sabotage lines of communication, and

---

[1] Much financial and material assistance was derived also from the vast sums which the West German government now agreed to pay to Israel in compensation for the damage inflicted on European Jewry.

murder peaceful civilians. Reluctantly, the Israel authorities began to organise intermittent reprisals against some of the centres, in Jordan and particularly in the so-called Gaza strip occupied by Egypt, from which in particular these attacks were launched. But it was in vain. The Arab governments, encouraged now by some foreign States which were disappointed in Israel's political attitude, not only refused to recognise the new State or to open negotiations for a permanent peace, but openly threatened to wipe it out and end its existence once they had the opportunity. And that these were not empty threats was proved by the manner in which Egypt in particular, now under a nominally republican regime, was systematically building up her armaments, mainly with Russian help. The danger increased from day to day: and in November 1956 Israel was forced to take action.

In one of the most brilliant campaigns in military history, the Israel forces attacked the Egyptian positions and captured Gaza—the principal town in the Egyptian-occupied enclave in Palestine and main base of the raids made on Israel territory. The whole Peninsula of Sinai—the cradle of Jewish spiritual life three thousand years before—was overrun, nearly as far as the Suez Canal. The Gulf of Akabah was opened to shipping by the occupation of the Straits of Tirana, which had blocked the outlet to the Indian Ocean for the past ten years. Enormous quantities of munitions of war—mainly of Russian manufacture—were captured.

Israel was robbed of the fruits of victory, however. Great Britain and France had seen in the outbreak of hostilities the opportunity to reestablish their control over the Suez Canal, and invaded the area, ostensibly to maintain free navigation. This apparent attempt to revive the old imperialism gave the pretext for an almost universal display of self-righteousness at the United Nations: the errant Great Powers were called upon to withdraw: and in the aftermath Israel too had to give up her conquests. The campaign nevertheless had not been in vain. The Gulf of Akabah was henceforth open to her shipping, the port of Elath now developing greatly as the outlet for the products of the Negev and Israel's window upon the East. United Nations forces were stationed in the Gaza Strip and brought peace to that long-troubled frontier. And—perhaps more important—it was now obvious to the world that the people that had been reestablished in its ancient homeland did not exist on sufferance, but was worthy of the heroism of its forebears.

III

The ostensible triumph thus achieved over the two western powers much enhanced the prestige of the Egyptian dictator Abd-el-Nasser, now able to present his humiliating defeat as a victory. He thus was enabled to assume the leadership of the Afro-Asiatic countries that were now reasserting themselves, effected a short-lived political union with Syria which threatened Israel on two flanks, and increased rather than diminished his threats against that country, which he constantly continued to menace with destruction. Even the Suez Canal remained closed to Israel shipping, notwithstanding international treaties and the specific promises and undertakings given to her. Yet despite all this, conditions were now improved in some important respects. The brilliant success of the Sinai campaign proved a sharp lesson to the Arab states and made them cautious of provoking further military action: with the result that conditions temporarily became far quieter on the frontiers. Moreover, the presence of United Nations forces along the armistice lines to the south brought to an end the brutal raids that had been largely responsible for the outbreak of hostilities: henceforth, the farmers in the border settlements here could do their work of reclaiming and tilling the soil in relative security.

More far-reaching, though at the outset hardly to be anticipated, were the remoter consequences of the opening to Israel navigation of the Gulf of Akabah, the outlet to which at Sharm-el-Sheikh was also now occupied by United Nations forces. This resulted in a noteworthy change in the perspective and even in the geographical balance of the state of Israel. Henceforth in fact it could look effectively south and east as well as west. In consequence, the arid tracts of the Negev, hitherto considered almost unsuitable for permanent settlement, received an enormous impetus. New colonies were established, new industries developed, new towns created. Water was brought from the north for purposes of irrigation in an ambitious scheme. Those who were formerly familiar with the ancient Beer-Sheba as a small Bedouin centre in the midst of desolation now saw there an important city, one of the largest in the country, smiling in the midst of its gardens. The port of Elath was developed and with the improvement of the road-system and railway projects became potentially one of the most important centres of the communications of the country. A Jewish navy and Jewish merchant marine began to ply in the Gulf of Akabah and the seas beyond it. As a result, trading as well as diplomatic relations were opened up with the countries bordering on and beyond the Indian Ocean. Among some of the new African states Israel became a relatively important force, her experience in conquering an intractable soil and developing industries where none had existed before being of supreme value to them.

The country had at last the opportunity to take real advantage of its geographical position, constituting as it does a land-bridge between the three continents of the Old World. Not only, to be sure, in a material sense. Israel was capable also of acting as a spiritual bridge. Not being historically associated with any tradition of colonial exploitation, it could serve as the channel whereby the best of the culture of the West, of which it was naturally part, could be transmitted to those countries with which it now maintained closer and closer connexions. Young men and women of colour could now be met constantly on the benches of the Hebrew University or in the Kibbutzim, where they familiarised themselves with the methods, standards and ideals of this young-old country from which they could learn so much. In this sense, the importance and influence of the new Israel far exceeded its dimensions and its population.

IV

To be sure, dangers persisted. The neighbouring Arab powers, steadfast in their hostility, managed to secure the general adherence to their policies of the other reemerging Moslem states of the Mediterranean world, and even of some further afield, in which the lot of the old-established native Jews rapidly deteriorated. It is probable however that this would have occurred in any case before long, as a result of the rising tide of nationalism and anti-European-ism: the new factor was that there was now a land of refuge in which the fugitives could find a home. The reluctant withdrawal of the Western powers from the eastern and southern Mediterranean left Israel to some extent isolated in a political and military sense. The consequent necessity for perpetual military vigilance made it necessary for a disproportionate amount of the state's resources to be spent on armaments. But to this too there was another side. The perpetual need to stand on the *qui vive* indubitably toughened the fibre of the people. Its youth developed a spirit of unshakeable confidence. In the long nightmare of the Diaspora, a legendary characteristic of the Jews as a people had been timidity: it was remarked that among the Israel youth fear was almost unknown as a physical fact. The constant dangers that threatened the new state made it impossible for the Jewish communities of the world to abandon the practical solidarity which they had so effectively shewn when it had come into being. As a result, Israel helped the Jewish people at large to retain its sense of cohesion even in an age of dwindling religious loyalty: and where this was now in any measure revived, it was bound up with a strong sense of identification with the great Jewish enterprise in the ancient Land of Israel.

In 1961, Adolf Eichmann, the Nazi functionary who had principally organised Hitler's attempt to apply the 'Final Solution' to the Jews of Europe, and was thus directly responsible for the deaths of hundreds of thousands if not millions of persons, was traced in the Argentine, audaciously arrested, and brought to Israel. Here he was given by Jewish judges in a Jewish court, in proceedings carried out in the Hebrew language, an impeccably fair trial, such as none of his countless victims had known, for his indescribable record of illdoing. IIe was condemned to death and executed. The whole world had its attention riveted to the revelation, under conditions of strictest justice, of the horrors of which the Nazi regime had been responsible, and of the tenacity of the resuscitated Jewish state.

V

In the ensuing years it became more and more evident that the creation of the State of Israel had been in the fullest sense of the term providential. In the course of the 19th century, the area of Jewish settlement in the world had increased, this being accompanied generally by an improvement in their economic and political position: and they had won legal equality with their fellow-citizens at least in the countries of western Europe and their overseas extensions. It was under these circumstances that they had become established to some extent in the Far East and had created fresh communities in Central Africa, and that the Jews of the Moslem countries had emerged from their condition of medieval degradation. For the world of the 19th century had been a liberal world, which under the influence of western Europe had set the ideal of establishing nations on a basis of social uniformity rather than religious conformity.

As the twentieth century advanced, there was a general regression from these conceptions. As we have seen, the new ideologies had cut off a great part of the fecund Jewish communities of Eastern Europe from their coreligionists elsewhere at the time of the rise of communism at the close of the First World War: now, almost the totality of the exhausted survivors of the central European communities seemed destined to follow the same path, of spiritual suicide. In other regions of the world, in proportion as the European influences and the old traditions of colonialism receded, the Jewish communities—whether semi-autochthonous and long established, or created by recently arrived immigrants from Europe—became weakened, sometimes to the verge of extinction. The new negro states of Central Africa had no place in their economies and future prospects for the settlers who had formerly prospered there: in the revived Moslem states of the Mediterranean litoral the new nationalism reinforced by religion, quite apart from the tension created in the Middle East by the Israel–Arab confrontation, made the lot of the Jews more and more precarious. In Algeria for example, where a century before the native Jews had been the first to become French citizens by virtue of the Loi Crémieux, this privileged position now turned to their disadvantage.

In communist China, the once-prosperous modern Jewish communities were now eliminated: while in the other lands of the Far East the withdrawal of English and French rule generally proved a mortal blow to the Jews. With the exodus from Iraq, Yemen and other lands of Moslem Asia, both before and after the establishment of the State and the accompanying hostilities, there seemed to be the prospect that the Jews would be eliminated from the entire Asiatic continent, apart from Israel. (In this new age of continental strategy, Jewish history too was beginning to be staged on a continental scale, not as hitherto in terms of provinces or countries.) The same was true of a great part—according to some pessimists, all—the continent of Africa. As for America, the dissolution of the community of Cuba after the triumph of a new Leftist regime in 1959, gave a grim warning of what might happen elsewhere in the region in similar circumstances: while some observers thought that they could discern in some areas of Latin America, especially those where refugee Nazi leaders had been allowed to establish themselves, the precursory signs of the development of an antisemitic movement of the new German type.

Chapter XXXIV

THE SIX-DAY WAR

———————— • ————————

I

In the middle decades of the twentieth century, the communities
of free Europe gradually regained a measure of cohesion and
solidity, not however to be compared with the state of affairs that
had existed before the great disaster. On the other hand, the changed
conditions of the Moslem world, both as regards the Jews and as
regards Western influences generally, resulted in the virtual completion of the liquidation of the ancient Jewish communities of
North Africa and significant parts of Asia. The emigrants, if they did
not go to Israel with its ever-open door, tended to gravitate to
France, where in these years the new Sephardi influx resuscitated
Jewish life in many ancient centres and not only doubled, but to
some extent changed the character of, French Jewry. The whole
Jewish world was however affected to some extent by this new migration, fresh Sephardi centres now being established not in European
lands alone but throughout the English speaking world and in South
America. Even in Spain, there seemed to be signs of a change of
atmosphere and a limited Jewish revival.

On the other hand, the Russian enigma continued. While in
communist Hungary and Roumania the Jews were still able to
maintain a certain degree of independent communal and religious
life, in the U.S.S.R. itself the prejudices against Jewish religious
training or observance, coupled with an increasing opposition to
any manifestations of Zionist sentiment, became progressively more
marked. Whether this was effective in stifling Jewish feeling was
problematical: in the 1960's, the outside world heard with amazement that thousands or tens of thousands of young Jews gathered on
the occasion of the traditional feast of the Rejoicing of the Law outside the Moscow synagogue to dance and sing Hebrew songs, the
police being unable or unwilling to intervene. The enigma thus

165. STUDENTS OUTSIDE THE HEBREW UNIVERSITY IN JERUSALEM

166. RALLY IN MADISON SQUARE GARDENS, NEW YORK, in support of Israel
during the Six-Day War, June 11, 1967

167. ARMOURED ISRAEL PATROL ON THE BORDER WITH JORDAN, June 1967

168. Thanksgiving at the Wailing Wall, June 14, 1967

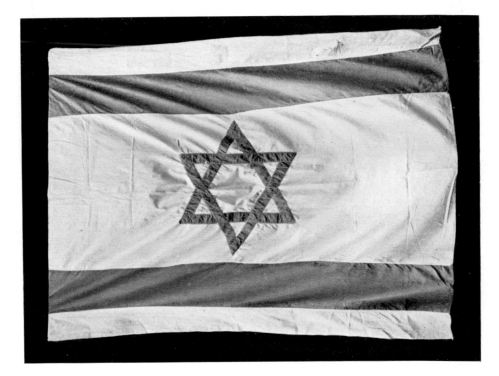

169. The Flag of the State of Israel

remained. The former Muscovite Empire had changed its constitution and its economy since the days before the Revolution of 1917, but its essential nature was not much altered.

II

This continued to be manifested in its policy in the Middle East, where it was now strenuously continuing its efforts to establish a foothold by encouraging the spread of communism and by the lavish supply of arms to the Arab states. For these there was only one obvious use—the cancellation of the humiliation undergone in the past and the annihilation (no less) of the state of Israel, whose existence they still refused to recognise and whose obliteration from the map was one of their main ambitions, as they incessantly proclaimed to the world. The principal enemy in this was the adroit Dictator of Egypt, Abd-el-Nasser, who attempted to justify his claims as leader and mouthpiece of the Arab world by being the instrument for the destruction of Israel. For some time his offensive was confined to words, owing to the salutary presence of the United Nations force in the Gaza strip and at the entrance to the Gulf of Akabah, as has been recounted: though he still illegally barred goods or shipping destined for Israel from passage through the Suez Canal, supposed by law to be open to the goods and shipping of all nations in peace and war. Meanwhile to the north terrorist raids were periodically made on Israel territory over the Syrian border, there were frequent attacks in the supposedly demilitarised zone on Jewish farmworkers, and occasionally even bombardment of Israel villages from the higher ground in Syrian hands—this provoking now and again organised retaliatory raids by the Jewish defence forces.

III

Confident in Russian support, in May 1967 Nasser suddenly demanded the withdrawal of the United Nations observers stationed not only in the Gaza strip, where they had ensured tranquillity for the past eleven years, but also from Sharm-el-Sheikh at the head of the Gulf of Akabah, where they had secured freedom of shipping. For some reason which must remain inexplicable, this insolent demand was immediately and tamely complied with by the United Nations Secretary General, hoping no doubt that no serious results would ensue. This however was followed within less than a week

2H

by the announcement that no Israel shipping would henceforth be permitted passage through the Straits: a menace clearly contrary to international law, like the blockade of the Suez Canal, and in effect an act of warfare. Meanwhile, there were more and more menacing concentrations of troops on the Israel borders, and King Hussein of Jordan, backed by other Arab states, made a military pact with Egypt. The die was cast. The Arab leaders not only gloried in the prospect of a war, but made it clear that it would be a war of annihilation, in which the Jewish state would be wiped out and its inhabitants butchered.

Israel prepared for the inevitable conflict. Levi Eshkol, the Israel Prime Minister since 1963 in succession to the veteran David Ben-Gurion, formed a Coalition Government. Not only Ben-Gurion himself but also Menahem Beigin, the former underground leader, joined the government, while the victor of Sinai, Moshe Dayan, became Minister of Defence.

On June 5th hostilities began. The Egyptians, the major enemy, moved armoured columns northwards in the hope of slicing the country in two and linking up with Jordan, and there was heavy shelling and bombing of Israel towns and villages. On the Israeli side however, the reaction was incredibly swift and extraordinarily efficient. Forthwith all the major Arab airports within radius were massively and scientifically bombed, and within a matter of hours the Egyptian airforce had been to all intents and purposes wiped out, even before it left the ground: the same took place on a smaller scale in the other neighbouring Arab lands. The Israel land-forces could now advance without interference from the air, which they did with model efficiency. In the Sinai desert, where the Jewish people had seen its birth, there took place the greatest tank battle as yet known in history, resulting in an overwhelming victory. Within a couple of days, the Egyptian army in the field had been virtually wiped out, and Israel troops had established themselves all along the Suez Canal. Simultaneously, a task force had reached and occupied Sharm-el-Sheikh, and the Gulf of Akabah was again freely open to all shipping. On the night of June 8th, the new-born Israeli naval forces struck simultaneously at enemy vessels in the harbours of Alexandria and Port Said.

At the outset of the fighting, King Hussein of Jordan had been informally promised immunity by the Israel authorities except in self-defence. Nevertheless, almost simultaneously with the opening of hostilities to the south, the New City of Jerusalem was heavily attacked by the Jordanians with artillery and machine-gun fire, nearly 1,000 private homes being hit and a large number of civilian casualties inflicted. The Israel reply was as decisive as it was short. Within less than three days, the entire Arab-occupied territory of the historic Palestine on the west bank of the Jordan had been occupied. The greatest triumph of the whole campaign was when on Wednesday June 7th the old walled city of Jerusalem—the true Jerusalem, from which Jews had been utterly excluded for nearly twenty years, and in which they had been subject to insult and humiliation for a hundred times as long—was captured by Israel parachute troops. It was almost the greatest military victory of all time in Jewish history: not since the Roman triumph nearly two thousand years before had Jews controlled the city which Judaism had made sacred and famous. That day, amid scenes of indescribable emotion and elation, the conquerors went to pray each in his own fashion before the Western Wall, the solitary relic still standing of the ancient Temple.

Now attention was turned towards Syria, and after particularly bitter fighting the northern enemy was ejected from the strong positions constructed along the frontier, from which the Israel border settlements had been harrassed for so long. Perhaps the campaign would have finished with the occupation of the enemy capitals —an achievement perfectly within the ability of the tough and now confident Israel troops—had not the Security Council of the United Nations demanded a cease-fire. But the hostilities ended with the Israel forces everywhere triumphant, and in control not only of the entire Palestinian territory west of Jordan, including both the Gaza Strip and the former legendary capital of their people, but of territory well beyond this both south and north, whatever was to be its future destiny. The Six Days War had been perhaps the most brilliant campaign in military history, even outdoing the Sinai campaign of 1956: the Israel army had shewn itself the best fighting force in the region—and the more so since it was a citizen army intent not on conquest but on self-protection.

IV

While all this had been happening, an unprecedented wave of expression of solidarity had spread throughout the Jews of the free world. All elements—Zionist and non-Zionists, young and old, religious and irreligious—demonstrated their sympathy with their brethren in the Land of Israel in body and soul, in moral support and in material contributions. The shattered unity of the Jewish people seemed to be reconstituted in this spontaneous expression of feeling, which shewed in a positive fashion the place that Israel had come to play in their lives: the realisation that if the State was now over-whelmed (and at one time this seemed probable enough) every Jew everywhere would be affected, Judaism itself would suffer as a religion a blow that might be mortal, the heritage of Jewish history would become meaningless.

Yet more amazing was what had become manifest in Israel itself in these critical days. Here was a people that within a generation had become a balanced state, had restored its nationhood, its language, its unity, had brought into being out of the raw material of pedlars and shopkeepers and students a martial youth perhaps superior to any in the entire world. This indomitable people had risen from its greatest disaster to snatch from the jaws of destiny its supreme victory. Our generation is too near to appreciate even now the scale of the achievement or the miracle of the rebirth.

BIBLIOGRAPHICAL NOTE

(The list which follows is not intended as a complete Bibliography of
Jewish History, nor yet as a list of the works used in the preparation
of the present volume. It gives only a small selection of the more read-
able works on the subject which are available *in English*, and which can
be recommended to the general reader who may wish to follow up the
subject. The very full Bibliography appended to the chapter on 'The
Jews in the Middle Ages', in the *Cambridge Medieval History*, vol. vii,
provides adequate guidance for the serious student.)

———————————●———————————

I. GENERAL

S. BARON, *A Social and Religious History of the Jews*. 3 vols., 1937.
[2nd ed., 1952 ——]. *The Jewish Community: Its History and Structure to the American Revolution*. 3 vols., 1942.

H. GRAETZ, *History of the Jews*. (The English translation by Bella Löwy
and others [1891–1892, 5 vols.] is based upon the earlier, un-
revised editions, is somewhat abbreviated, and lacks the foot-
notes and appendices, for which recourse must still be had to
the German original.)

M. L. MARGOLIS and A. MARX, *A History of the Jewish People*. 1927.
The Jewish Encyclopaedia.

L. FINKELSTEIN (ed.), *The Jews: their History, Culture and Religion*.
2-4 vols., 1949.

II. BIBLICAL AND CLASSICAL PERIODS

N. BENTWICH, *Hellenism*. 1919. *Philo-Judaeus of Alexandria*. 1910.

J. BRIGHT, *A History of Israel*. 1960.

E. BEVAN, *Jerusalem under the High Priests*. 1904.

Cambridge Ancient History.

J. GARSTANG, *The Heritage of Solomon*. 1934.

R. TRAVERS HERFORD, *The Pharisees*. 1924.

J. KLAUSNER, *Jesus of Nazareth*. 1925. *From Jesus to Paul*. 1943.

A. LODS, *Israel, from its Beginnings to the Middle of the Eighth Century*.
1932. *The Prophets and the Rise of Judaism*. 1937.

G. F. Moore, *Judaism in the First Centuries of the Christian Era.* 3 vols., 1927–1930.

A. T. Olmstead, *History of Palestine and Syria.* 1931.

W. O. E. Oesterley, *The Jews and Judaism during the Greek Period.* 1941.

T. H. Robinson and W. O. E. Oesterley, *A History of Israel.* 2 vols., 1932.

V. Tcherikover, *Hellenistic Civilisation and the Jews.* 1959.

III. Medieval and Modern Periods

I. Abrahams, *Jewish Life in the Middle Ages.* 2nd ed., 1932.

E. N. Adler, *Jewish Travellers.* 1930.

I. Cohen, *The Zionist Movement.* 1945.

Corti, Count, *The Rise of the House of Rothschild.* 1928. *The Reign of the House of Rothschild.* 1928.

I. Elbogen, *A Century of Jewish Life.* 1944.

P. Goodman, *Life of Moses Montefiore.* 1925.

J. de Haas, *Life of Theodor Herzl.* 2 vols., 1927.

The Memoirs of Ber of Bolochow. Translated by M. Wischnitzer. 1922.

The Memoirs of Glückel von Hameln. Translated by M. Lowenthal. 1932.

J. R. Marcus, *The Jew in the Medieval World: A Source-Book, 315–1791.* 1938.

J. Parkes, *The Conflict of the Church and the Synagogue: A Study in the Origins of Antisemitism.* 1934; *The Jew in the Medieval Community.* 1938. *The Emergence of the Jewish Problem.* 1946.

D. Philipson, *The Reform Movement in Judaism.* 2nd ed., 1931.

S. Posener, *Adolphe Crémieux: A Biography.* 1940.

G. R. Reitlinger, *The Final Solution.* 1953.

C. Roth, *A History of the Marranos.* 1932; *The Jews in the Renaissance.* 1960.

A. Ruppin, *The Jewish Fate and Future.* 1940.

N. Sokolow, *A History of Zionism.* 2 vols., 1919.

A. L. Sachar, *Sufferance is the Badge* (The Jew in the contemporary world). 1939.

H. L. Sachar, *The Course of Modern Jewish History.* 1959.

W. Sombart, *The Jews and Modern Capitalism.* English translation. 1913.

L. Wolf, *Essays in Jewish History.* 1934.

IV. LOCAL HISTORIES

Y. BAER, *The Jews of Christian Spain*, 1960, 1966.

S. DUBNOW, *History of the Jews in Russia and Poland*. Translated by I. Friedlander, 3 vols., 1916–1920.

W. J. FISCHEL, *Jews in the Life of Medieval Islam*. London, 1937.

A. L. ISAACS, *The Jews of Majorca*. 1936.

Jewish Community Series (I. Cohen, *Vilna*, 1943; A. Freimann and F. Kracauer, *Frankfort*, 1929; A. Kober, *Cologne*, 1940; M. Grunwald, *Vienna*, 1936; H. Vogelstein, *Rome*, 1940; etc.)

S. KATZ, *The Jews in the Visigothic and Frankish Kingdoms of Spain and Gaul*. 1937.

H. C. LEA, *History of the Inquisition in Spain*. 4 vols., 1906–1907.

M. LOWENTHAL, *The Jews of Germany*. 1936.

J. MANN, *The Jews of Palestine and Egypt under the Fatimid Caliphs*. 2 vols., 1920–1922.

P. MASSERMAN and M. BAKER, *The Jews come to America*. 1933.

A. A. NEUMAN, *The Jews in Spain: their Social, Political and Cultural Life during the Middle Ages*. 2 vols., 1942.

C. ROTH, *History of the Jews in England*, 1941; *History of the Jews in Italy*, 1946.

J. STARR, *The Jews in the Byzantine Empire*. 1939. *Romania*. 1949.

W. C. WHITE, *Chinese Jews*. 3 vols., 1942.

V. INTELLECTUAL HISTORY AND INFLUENCE

I. ABRAHAMS, E. BEVAN and C. SINGER, *The Legacy of Israel*. 1927.

J. JACOBS, *Jewish Contributions to Civilisation: an estimate*. 1919.

M. LIEBER, *Rashi*. 1906.

L. I. NEWMAN, *Jewish Influence on Christian Reform Movements*. 1925.

W. O. E. OESTERLEY and G. H. BOX, *A Short Survey of the Literature of Rabbinical and Medieval Judaism*. 1920.

J. S. RAISIN, *The Haskalah Movement in Russia*. 1913.

C. ROTH, *Jewish Contribution to Civilisation*. New ed., 1945.

S. SCHECHTER, *Studies in Judaism*. 3 vols., 1896–1923.

G. SCHOLEM, *Major Trends in Jewish Mysticism*. 1941.

N. SLOUSCHZ, *The Renascence of Hebrew Literature*. 1908.

S. SPIEGEL, *Hebrew Reborn*. 1931.

M. WAXMAN, *A History of Jewish Literature*. 4 vols., 1930–1941.

D. YELLIN and I. ABRAHAMS, *Maimonides*. 1908.

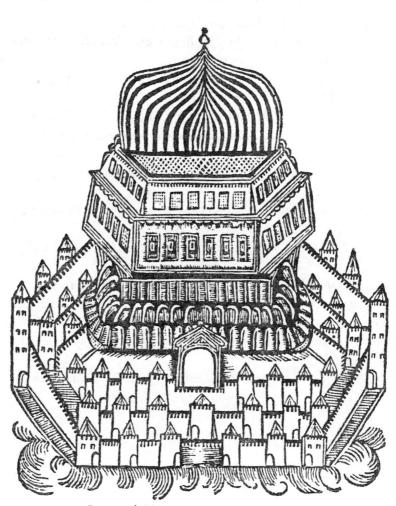

170. PRINTERS' MARK OF THE BROTHERS ASHKENAZI,
Constantinople, 1750

INDEX